Heliotrope

French Heritage Women Create

Edited by
Rhea Côté Robbins

Brewer, Maine

ISBN-13: 978-0-9668536-5-0

This book is dedicated to the French heritage women
whose lives represent the garden of thought that keeps the heritage strong

Heliotrope—French Heritage Women Create

Table of Contents/*Table des matières*

Family/Testimony—*Famille/Témoignage*

Foremothers/Heroines—*Aïeules/Héroïnes*

History/*Histoire*

Border/*La frontière*

Nature/Seasons/*Saisons*

Acadians/*Acadiennes*/Cajuns

Spirituality/*Spiritualité*

Heal/Healing/War—*Guérir/Guérison/Guerre*

Creativity/*La Créativité*

Cover-Artist Statement

'Keeping Your Arts About You'

La Fierté, a modern-day patron sainte' superheroine goddette. Her habiliments, a quilt as cape and cloak. She wields her implements, pen, needle, brush, book; as tightly as treasure. Her familiar, the butterfly, Légèreté, implies metamorphosis and the eternity of the Cycle. Stylized after Renée Falconcetti (*La Passion de Jeanne d'Arc*, 1928) and Rosie the Riveter, La Fierté is resourceful, creative and passionate about her heritage and her craft. Also moderne, with her fleur-de-lis tattoo and Zentangle quilted cape. She holds onto simple tools; in perpetuity creates a nexus of art, literature, and textile. –**Bridget Robbins**

Testimony given for the Franco-American Women's Institute

Why is this anthology vital and fundamental to our Franco-American heritage and birthright?

We, the modern Franco-Americans, carry within our transgenerational traditions and genetics a mixed legacy of profound spirituality and family bonds, mixed with cultural amnesia, racism and oppression. There are not many that care to "see" the big picture of the Franco-American culture and why acknowledging it matters. I have been inspired by books about other indigenous cultures and historical critiques of colonialism, and am amazed that so little has been written about Franco-American culture. My own intuition is that the redemption of the world will come from what we will be able to salvage from indigenous cultures. By "indigenous" I mean cultures that are deeply rooted in their values and sensitive to their natural environments. The Franco-American culture is that for me. My own involvement with my Franco-American family has given my life depth and a tangible connection to those things that are natural and real. It has made me more human. It has also increased my capacity for compassion and empathy. But empathy, a beautiful though endangered thing, is not necessarily a comforting experience.

I've talked to Franco-Americans who don't "get it" and belittle the tragedy of our decline. To them, it is but an insignificant blip of the suffering in the world. Of course, if we look merely numerically, it is a small number in comparison, for example, to the number of Jews killed during the Holocaust. However, just as every human being is a miracle of divinity and an expression of that divine spark, so is every human culture the creative gift of generations of imagination and experience rooted in the real world. Sharing the story (his-story and her-story) allows us to remember and recognize the unique value of our culture and traditions.

Our need and desire to assimilate into the grand narrative of the great American melting pot denigrated our culture and heritage. We were encouraged to feel threatened and "less than" the white anglocentric folks, while at the same time it was impressed upon us to "fit in," to not stand out. We could never successfully achieve without balancing and walking this tightrope, but many Franco-Americans have. Education has elicited a change. It is the right time to stand up and acknowledge our roots, our ancestors who came to this side of the Atlantic to follow their dreams of freedom and renaissance. This anthology allows the Franco-American legacy the opportunity for expression and validation in terms of its own traditional values, stories, poetry and art.

—Carolyna Saint Germain

Supporters and Donations—Fundraising, Crowdsourcing and more!

Heliotrope—French Heritage Women Create, under the working title for fundraising named as "Inspired, Inspiring, Inspire—French Heritage Women Create!" began a crowdsourcing, fundraising campaign on Hatchfund* and with your ***generous*** donations this project was successfully funded on June 6, 2015. Thank you/merci for your generous donations to underwrite this anthology project! Your support of this project helps to make the publication of creative works of the French heritage women a success! Without your support, this project would not have been possible. *Merci mille fois!*

*At AIM Hatchfund we are committed to developing and sustaining the careers of artists, allowing you the ongoing freedom to create and inspire. Our goal is to help artists successfully navigate the challenging world of online fundraising for their projects. Hatchfund is powered by AIM a 501(c)3 not-for-profit organization.

***Soeur*—Sister/*Frère*—Brother, $25 and under**

Ann Armstrong Scarboro, Ph.D., President of Mosaic Media Arts, Colorado
Anonymous, New Hampshire
Barbara Ouellette Ouellette, Maine
Anonymous, Louisiana
Cecile Poulin, Maine
Charles A. Scontras, Historian and Research Assistant, Bureau of Labor Education, University of Maine, Orono, Maine
Debbie Roberge, Maine
Denise R. Larson, Maine
Jim Sharkey, Virginia
Kat Johnson, Maine
Louise Tanguay-Ricker, Maine
Norbert Nathanson, Maine
Doris Provencher Faucher, author of the *Quebecois Series*, and husband, Norman Faucher, Maine
Paula Currie Raymond, Maine
Rina Soucy, Maine
Susan Gagnon, Maine

***Une Cousine*—Cousin/*Un Cousin*—Cousin, $25+**

Ann G. Forcier, LMHC, Massachusetts
Anonymous, Maine
Bridget Robbins, New Hampshire
Celeste Roberge, Maine
Christine Holden, Ph.D., Maine
Christine Théberge Rafal, Ph.D., Massachusetts
Clark A. Pomerleau, Ph.D., Texas
Darlene Kritzman, Maine
Dean Louder, Ph.D., Québec
Doris Belisle-Bonneau, Maine
Jacquie Giasson Fuller, Maine
Jesse Robbins, Maine
Josée Vachon, Massachusetts
Josephine Donovan, Ph.D., New Hampshire
Juliana L'Heureux, Maine
Lisa Côté Day, Lisa C. Day Photography, Belgrade, Maine
Lisa Desjardins Michaud, Editor, *Le FORUM,* Maine
Mary Rice DeFosse, Ph.D., Maine
Maureen "Mo" Perry, Maine

Mazie Hough, Ph.D., Women's, Gender and Sexuality Studies Program, University of Maine, Orono, Maine
Melissa MacCrae, Brewer, Maine
Michael J. Guignard, Ph.D., Virginia
Norman R. Beaupré, Ph.D., Maine
Steven Riel, Massachusetts
Susan Landry, Maine
Susan Pinette, Ph.D., Maine
Susan Poulin, Maine
Trudy Chambers Price, Maine
Ware-Butler, Inc., Waterville, Maine

Tante—Aunt/*Oncle*—Uncle, $50 +

Anonymous, New Hampshire
Anonymous, New York
Caroline LeBlanc, New Mexico
Florence Rose Martin, Maine
Jeanne M. Douillard, Massachusetts
Jeri Theriault, Maine
Leslie P. Choquette, Ph.D., Assumption College, History, Massachusetts
Marian "Mimi" desCognets, New Mexico
Pamela Morneault Gemme, Massachusetts
Polly Welts Kaufman, Ph.D., University of Southern Maine, Maine
Ray and Rachael (Giguère) Côté, Waterville Custom Kitchens, Waterville, Maine
Sabrina Côté Kelley, Michigan
Speaking Place, Maine
Susann Pelletier, Maine
Sylvie Charron, Ph.D., Maine
Tom and Lynda Côté, New Hampshire

Maman—Mother/*Papa*—Father, $100 +

Anonymous, Maine
Anonymous, New York
Bouchard Family Farms, Maine
Carl Côté, New Hampshire
Carolyna Saint Germain, Washington
Françoise Lionnet, Ph.D., Harvard University, Massachusetts
Kathryn J. Olmstead, Maine
Kristin Langellier, Ph.D., Maine
The Museum in the Streets©, Patrick Cardon, Cushing, Maine

Marraine—Godmother/*Parrain*—Godfather, $200+

Benjamin J. and Jana Robbins, Seattle, Washington
Catherine Daniélou, Ph.D. / University of Alabama at Birmingham, Alabama
Charles and Donna Côté, New Hampshire
Cynthia Berenson in memory of her mother, Elise Lambert, Massachusetts
David M. Robbins, Maine
Margaret Langford, Ph.D., New Hampshire

Other Support or Matching Donations

Michael Parent, Maine, who did not wish to be in a category
—Hatchfund, The Match 25 Challenge Fund, Nebraska
—Maine Arts Commission, Maine
—Maine Humanities Council, University of Maine, Orono, Maine

...more testimony for the Franco-American Women's Institute

What if the Franco-American Women's Institute, FAWI, hadn't been there?

What if FAWI hadn't been there? What if eighteen years ago my first wild search for project ideas hadn't brought up FAWI? What if I'd never found my capstone project and what if I'd had nothing to document for my mad non-traditional degree in French? What if FAWI hadn't led me to translate a Rhode Island novel with my university grammar? What if FAWI hadn't connected my new fancy French with my old heart French?

Would I have found the zeal to be a missionary of French among Franco-American kids? Would I have dared to begin teaching French at my age? Would I have thought it necessary that a few hundred teenagers should sing along with Jacques Brel, or understand some lyrics in La Bonne Chanson? Would they have known from where their names came? Or who had worked in those huge, gentrified mills downtown? Or why they still call her mémère? What if FAWI hadn't merged my plain people with glossy 21st century French high school curricula? Would a few hundred teenagers have ever known?

What if FAWI hadn't provided *moé pi toé*?* Would I have been fired up to write my people's stories? Would my aunts still be just faces in a box of old photos? Would I have known how much I needed to hear the terrific stuff others had to say? What if FAWI hadn't been there to cyber seal our stories in time, to help us grow, to keep us thinking, to let us smile and weep? Would we feel snuffed?

What if I had to start all over without FAWI or *moé pi toé*? I'd still be a successful American citizen but exploding with memories and no USB port. I'd still have my fancy French and my fancy grammar and my stories that nobody would ever know because they'd be disconnected and I'd assume nobody cared.

—Ann Marie Staples

** moé pi toé, FAWI's 'ezine, online since 1996 @http://www.fawi.net/*

Acknowledgements

I write this with great appreciation for all of the support that this anthology celebrating the Franco-American Women's Institute's 20th Anniversary has received. It is with deep gratitude that I recognize the community effort that demonstrates the understanding this work has received. To all who have made the publication of this anthology possible I am humbled and thankful for your participation in this process.

I wish to recognize and thank Kristin Langellier, Ph.D., Eric Peterson, Ph.D., Sylvie Charron, Ph.D., and Christine Holden, Ph.D., for their incredible assistance with the editing and proofing of the manuscript. Also, for your helpful suggestions at how to fine tune the work. The long and arduous task of reviewing submissions for publication is one which often goes unnoticed, but without which any book would be incomplete if not for the exceptional diligence in the editing and proofing stages. I thank you all for your time and effort in making this anthology the best that it could possibly be. With your dedication and assistance, this anthology is a reality.

I wish to thank Bridget Robbins for her beautiful cover design which she donated to the anthology project.

I would like to thank all the donors to the fundraising, crowdsourcing campaign that happened on Hatchfund. The donations are extremely important to a project such as the anthology because with the community's help in underwriting the work, the book becomes a team effort and something that creates community capital. So, for all of your contributions, financial, and in spirit, the creative voices of the French heritage women live in publication!

I wish to thank Hatchfund for the opportunity to work through their organization to crowdfund this artistic endeavor of publishing the French heritage women's creativities. For the help from Stephany Campos who helped with the entire process and was enthusiastic about the work of fundraising. Hatchfund contacted me and we both thought that Hatchfund's focus on artists and their creativity fit the anthology project and its goals. With Hatchfund the work of fundraising became a well-directed and professional event. Their support is responsible for much of the success for the underwriting of this anthology. Also, their Match 25 Challenge Fund was another aspect of support from Hatchfund as they matched donations up to a certain amount on the 25th of the month. The anthology fundraising was successful in attaining that match.

I also wish to thank the Maine Arts Commission for their Match Fund that was awarded through their partnering with Hatchfund. Again, recognition of this work in the anthology enriches all of us.

I would also like to recognize the Maine Humanities Council, University of Maine, Orono, Maine for their Sponsorship Grant that supports public humanities and innovative teaching programs on-or-off campus. Hopefully, this anthology will be taught in classrooms as well as part of public presentations as a result of the support from the Maine Humanities Council.

I wish to thank those who gave permission to reprint their work, either as quotes or as full length publication. The materials are varied and enhance the larger telling of the stories of the women's lives. The research that people conduct on the French heritage culture validates the importance of the contributions of the women of the culture. I wish to thank Annie Proulx for her generous support of this anthology and for setting the example of the writer's life and the inspiration she shares through her work.

For all who have help spread the word about the anthology project, your presence is so noted and I am grateful for the active work you contributed in letting others know of the call for works and for the fundraising efforts.

I wish to especially thank the contributors for your submissions to this anthology because with your voices, we are proven to be a strong, modern, future-focused community of creative people. That you have taken the time and effort to submit your creative works gives testament to our presence and future creative possibilities for others to experience and enjoy. We are a force to be reckoned with! Stay tuned everyone.

Most of all I also wish to thank my family for their support of this work. My husband, David who is the unending supply of constant belief in my efforts and I am always aware of how his presence enriches my life. Thank you to my children for their support and encouragment and to my grandsons, Xerxes, Lucien, and Ian who are a joy forever. Plus, don't forget, the office companion, Myla, the faithful dog.

I count myself as blessed to have the opportunity to be a part of the creation of this work to present a snapshot of the French heritage women's lives and to celebrate the existence of the Franco-American Women's Institute's 20th Anniversary and our work of making known the women's contributions. Merci mille fois!

Heliotrope—French Heritage Women Create

"Let me take the example of communication between settlers and natives in a colonial and postcolonial context. ... where it is the dominated who is obliged to adopt the language of the dominant ... the dominated speaks a *broken language*, ... and the linguistic capital is more or less completely devalued, be it in school, at work, or in social encounters with the dominant ... the form taken by linguistic interaction will hinge substantially upon this structure, which is unconscious and works almost wholly "behind the backs" of locutors. In short, if a French person speaks ... to a WASP, it is not two persons who speak to each other but, through them, the colonial history in its entirety, or the whole history of the economic, political, and cultural subjugation of blacks (or women, workers, minorities, etc.) in the United States."
—Pierre Bourdieu in *An Invitation to Reflexive Sociology*, "The Purpose of Reflexive Sociology (The Chicago Workshop)"

'they say, "you're lucky to be so bilingual." You wonder: "what's luck got to do with it?"'
—Susanne de Lotbinière-Harwood in *Re-Belle et Infidèle/The Body Bilingual*, "I write *Le Body Bilingual* a love affair-e in nomad's land"

Foreword and Forward

Kristin Langellier, Ph.D.

The only place to start is in the middle. The middle of a conversation about and among Franco American women. The middle of something we might call, for the moment, a Franco American narrative. For what else is an identity but a story folding, unfolding, enfolding in time, layered and wrinkled, worn thin in some places, thick and like new in others? Or what else is a cultural identity than a conversation we strain to overhear—almost inaudible or too many speaking at once, so far away or too close to sort out? The sounds of our own voices carried out by so many, sometimes in chorus, other times in contradiction or conflict, often in questions of "who is it that we are?" and "what is our story?" Voices spin from story to conversation to story to conversation to story, like drawing and twisting threads from a skein of many colors and different yarns, both tangled and smooth—a travail, yes, but well worth the effort to do, to make do, to make and do more with Franco American women's stories.

This anthology gestures to "the more" of the stories that spin from and within the conversations of Franco American women. Franco American women may be more a caravan crossing borders—once-immigrants, twice-immigrants, *voyageurs*—who move along an unmarked path than anything so complete as denoted by terms like "history" or "family narrative" or "life story." Yet the markings of all kinds of writings are there already and still always on the move and making more: more stories, and more of the story that we are coming to know. Notably, Franco American women in this anthology are not mere characters in others' stories, nor, worse perhaps, absences that echo back cultural invisibility. Here Franco American women author their own experiences and lives, memories and dreams, joys and sadness and angers and desires, achievements and losses. In doing so and in embracing so many voices and stories and moments, this collection insists that a Franco American narrative lives in the present of its doing, which is to say that it is about telling and hearing and changing as the caravan moves on and as the conversations continue to spiral and twine, turning themselves inside and out. In doing so, this anthology illustrates three hard-won truths about storytelling as Franco American women.[1]

A story is not a story until it is told. In these pages, a Franco American woman tells a story, that is, she takes something from her experience, her own or someone else's, and makes it into the experience of the reader, the listener, the viewer. The story, then, may take any number of creative forms. Encounter here and enjoy all of these and more: poems that take your breath away, music and artwork and handwork that embody cultural lives, eulogies and genealogies that link generations, texts and textiles that make Franco American women's experience sing and stand forth. Some stories come as whispers from the edges, some are shout-outs from a center, some are callings from and to others. They tell of cultural experiences that are muted and mundane as well as vocal and visible. As this anthology shows, story is always a plural *stories*, never less than *les*. There is no single, solid story of "the Franco American woman" which could fix and hold her still, contain and hold forth, exhaust once and for all and ever what "the story" *is*, not alone because these women and stories are still becoming, coming into being. The stories told here enchant, and they also disenchant. To say a story is not a story until it is told means that story and storyteller are clearing their voices (in English and in French) to clear some space and to get clearer on their cultural experiences in its variations. As they tell these variations, we appreciate the kaleidoscopic beauty of the questions: *which* story of Franco American women, and *which* Franco American woman?

A story is not told until it is heard. Enjoying the pleasures of diverse, dispersed, and persistent voices of Franco American women depends on the listener. In a word, storytelling begins with the *ear*. Hearing a story completes its telling just as reading completes writing and just as seeing completes showing. This is to say that these Franco American women writers *hear* something that may be missing or misunderstood, and they *listen it out loud* for others to hear. So hear in the pages here women who identify as Franco American from France, from Québec and Acadia, from New England and other American states: Francos by birth, by marriage, by proximity, or by preceding, as Native Americans, the first French in North America. Listen on the margins for sexual desire and diversity; women going solo and childless by choice; ambivalences, anxieties and assurances, unanswered challenges; everyday and extraordinary accomplishments; early and enduring activity in politics and public life;

mémère stories and *tante* stories and Franco *filles* growing up stories that complicate mothering and womanhood and heritage. Who is able to hear shards of storytelling is not given by bloodline but by fine tuning the ear to different registers, harmonies, melodies, and even noises, joyful or jarring: from the charms of the tropes of Franco American storytelling—family, food, and faith—to the surprise of the unanticipated sound which is simultaneously fresh and somehow familiar. To hear a story that is told is both hard work and big fun, painful and playful. A story is not a story until it is told, and a story is not told until it is heard because cultural survival is a shared labor of voicing *and* listening. To tell and to hear are creative and courageous acts of remembering, interpreting, and innovating meanings for Franco American women's lives.

And once a story is heard, it changes. If storytelling begins with the ear, we tell Franco American women's stories differently and we hear them differently, depending on context and circumstance. Once told and once heard, a story *changes* because it is protean: its meanings can shift and multiply, slip away and elude capture as well as shine through to show emerging truths about Franco American women. A story itself can change, and it can likewise *change us* because it lives in the potent moment of its telling. If these are stories about the legacies of Franco American women, they tell us as much about the *present* context of telling and listening, and they anticipate the future, too. As stories of change and changing stories, they re-member by putting the story together in a new or nuanced way in its telling or its hearing; they re-interpret a personal or familial or cultural event from the present, not just document and describe it; indeed, they re-invent identities for the future, not just recapitulate "what happened." The storytelling in this collection is for Franco American women of the 21st century. It is storytelling somewhat like when my father told us a story from our family canon *again*—like the one about how I got run over by the rotary hoe when I was three—which was not so much about our family's past as it was about how our family was changing in the present as each of us ten kids, in turn and including me, left home to make our way into the world. His storytelling gathered us, formed us as family, regrouped us—not to foreclose further change but to anchor and equip us to meet it with grace and the strength of all our stories.

And, in a way, this anthology also gathers us to listen to stories that we are privileged to hear into being and becoming for our future as Franco American women. Our reading and responses are indebted to the enormous ear and generous heart of Rhea Cote Robbins whose passionate labor has gathered all these voices here. May there be more and more Franco American women's stories to tell and hear.

(Endnote)

1. This description of storytelling is from Della Pollock's "Memory, Remembering, and the Histories of Change," D.S. Madison & J. Hamera, eds., *The Sage Handbook of Performance Studies* (Thousand Oaks, CA: Sage, 2006.) 87-105.

Introduction

Rhea Côté Robbins

How to pinpoint the one or many factors that address the situation at hand about the current climate of the Franco-American, French heritage women's lives? That is my task as I see it. And why is there a need for an anthology at this time of the French heritage women's voices?

I choose to use French heritage as a way to define the women of the culture given the vast diversity of what the group encompasses. I will interchangeably use the terms Franco-American, Acadian or French heritage, meaning women who have French ancestry—no matter where they are located. The work naturally borders on trans-national.

Who are the modern-day, voiced French heritage women and how do they choose to represent themselves if given the privilege and opportunity to do so?

As an observation, equally important to note are those who choose not to give voice to the chorus—silenced or self-silencing for whatever reasons, letting the silences remain for themselves. So noted.

Those who choose to participate in this anthology project to increase the knowledge about the lives of the French heritage women in terms of their stories told offer the reader an opportunity to better understand the complexities of their inherent legacies. Pasha Malla states in the *Globe and Mail*, "And then I read [stories] which are as varied in plot, style, structure, character and content and as taxonomically diverse, as any national literature ought to be …."

As a coherent group of complex voices speaking for themselves, these women help define the entire whole of being in a climate or atmosphere, and as a result, all, most, some are explained.

This anthology builds a sound, voiced against the silences, silencing, and silenced. The void is filled with the sound and visuals of the multiple women in this volume.

That is what the Franco-American Women's Institute has been about for the past twenty years—giving voice—a space to be heard, seen and read in the in the unknown or unknowing. Taking one's rightful place to be heard (unmolested). Not as the figment of someone's imagination or bad loop, but as full-bodied, real, true-to-self women/femmes.

On my journey; on your journey; on our journey and then what can be said about each of us on our way to our destination of choice. Depending on the so many factors of the three unities: time/place/action and the start of the beginnings to arrive at always or forever. My understanding and the proofs of my journey is the transnational borders or boundaries crossed as a citizen of my/our inherent identity/ies. Not to erase, but enhance or increase the understanding of my French heritage.

Multiple layers of inclusion to begin to understand the way I can cross borders and arrive at myself even better understood.

Women Crossing Borders is the evolution of the continued journey to the deeper understood self or selves. I've recreated the point of view in a brand new website by the same name:
www.womencrossingborders.com

The journey is individual and private while at the same time happening in the larger milieu of living on the surface of ordinary time/place/action.

Crossing borders, seen and unseen, inner-self and on the geography. As seen and defined by where or how far one has been on the journey. There is always more to see, hear, feel, taste, smell, and sense on this curve of learning. At any given moment the truth, a truth, but other more truths are there to learn the further one remains on their journey. It is important to begin the journey, and even more important to continue. We, of the first, second, third and fourth migration, in the United States are not Canada and we are not France, but we are a new iteration of what those entities mean because we carry them with us and we also define them as well. Often denied, the journey requires deep work to regain the elements that are our education. A catalog of explanation and meaning taken from the elements of daily life that went on in our absence from the self/selves. But not only of our pasts, but of our own creative, formulated present and future.

Who we are as we stand in our present selves—some having been on the journey longer, some who have gone to places of understanding and some who have not chosen to go further than necessary. As a woman and an artist, writer, I have chosen to go beyond the stereotypes or dominant ideologies because I am the one who believes there is more to be known in the beyond.

I believe in furthering the conversation by exploring the topics as comparison/contrast or more than the conservative point of view. I do not subscribe to the dominant ideology of closing down conversations before they even begin, but that happens too often and to the detriment and loss of furthering the knowledge or presence.

Writing is a form of artistic problem solving and I do not believe that the power of the sentimental goes deep enough to solve the artistic problem. Some would prefer to stay on the surface of the story; the truth is located deeper and more work is necessary to achieve the outcomes of addressing the truths. Respect is key. Some have been on the journey longer than others and a gendered point of view is necessary to gain the nuances of the truths. Men cannot speak for the woman. Despite the dominant ideology maintaining the status quo, the truth often is not expressed by the powers that be—but only a piece or part of the truth is told.

This is the reason why such a volume or body of work is necessary to examine an encompassing truth and to go beyond the reigning dominant ideologies. This is not a stance against, but more a push, thrust or focus towards the new and the possible so not to stagnate or lose momentum in attaining voice for the French heritage women; not to reject the traditional, but to build upon in a refashioned creativity.

What became obvious to me as I made my journey to the self—the French heritage woman, was that a safe space was necessary to get at the depths of the meanings of what does a Franco-American, French heritage woman look like? Feel? Think?

While encased in the general APB, all-points-bulletin, cultural work, there is not the space needed that is necessary to get at the depths of the meanings and depths of definitions. The need for the allowance of space to explore the creativity of identity is not a fact that is understood by many.

Women's lives are already overcrowded with caretaking and what is needed is an outlet for inquiry not dictated or overrun by the usual suspects of everyday living or concerns, nor driven by the controls automatically built into the cultures from both outside and inside the group.

Inside and outside the culture, the women are expected to do the caretaking of the public visage, image, the male ego, the classicism, language—access or not, "elites" accustomed to their needs being met at any or all costs, the dominant culture's premises of false superiority/ies, culminating in a secret, agreed-upon, silencing.

To address the silencing takes courage. To not name the issues perpetuates the silencing; to address the issues allows for a full-bodied, mature woman to emerge. Not an identity that is given or handed or fashioned by whatever controlling forces that exist in the women's lives, but identity freely chosen for the self, by the self and articulated through one's art.

Subject not dictated. Subject accessed through an artistic expression that gives depth to the multiple meanings of being a French heritage woman. Unfettered. Not against anyone or anything, but simply pro-being voiced. A gift of expressions.

Subject that goes beyond the dozen or so allowed, recycled topics: Tourtière, poutine, pea soup/chicken stew, ployes, crêpes, mills, French language—lost/found, Evangeline/Longfellow, Jack Kerouac, sainted mamans, old churches. Subjects—beyond the stereotypes, as the voice of tomorrow; or stop driving towards the future looking in the rearview mirror thinking that is the place to find our creative selves. Do not leave the traditions behind, but do not allow the past alone to dictate the future. The proof of all of our efforts succeeding does not remain in our looking to the past for guidance, but in the hands of the future generations and what they will do to define their heritage selves.

Personally, I do not know any young Franco-Americans of French heritage who have low aspirations; I refuse to accept that definition of the group. I think that is a description of a hijacked identity that belongs in someone else's dystopian playbook, not the Franco-American outlook towards the future. Play it where it lays ... where they are found and thriving as they are—a modern people of French heritage—those are the ones to receive and carry forward the culture. They do not even have to get up out of their chairs nor join a language table, club or group—do not need some country club membership to purchase, but are recognized as themselves—where they stand. Those are the French heritage owners-in-the-store of the culture of the present and future—they bake the bread *AND* own the bakery. I've seen it with my own eyes.

Believe in the power of being voiced; face the fears that silence, diminish and take the power of having a public identity. Let there be bilingual signs and menus; immersion chez-nous—visible to the outside of who we are on the inside.

No amount of carping can reduce the fact of the combined strength of the women being voiced through their creativities who create change beyond the festival-only, once-a-year celebrations. The everyday lives give testimony/témoinage to the fact of our presence on the geography.

The French heritage women's voices and all its variants—echoes of the times past vibrating the present and future. The Franco-American Women's Institute, FAWI, was begun for many reasons, but primarily to find a space where the voices of the women were open and free to speak or say their unique sounds. Despite the challenges or interferences coming from the usual, predictable suspects or situations, the FAWI place of being voiced stands for the carved-out-spaces, unmolested, almost free. Battle scars mean that as a woman-focused organization, FAWI was tested and won the continued right and example to be in its twentieth year of existence.

No small feat.

Still there are some who hesitate to be present to their own woman-ness in the face of this lop-sided gendered world—still fear their ownership of their womanhood. More importantly, there are one hundred women willing to be present to their woman-self featured in this book. The work remains as proof, and continues to be present, both to the self and the French heritage.

Historically, FAWI, and its predecessors, who can only be known almost sub-consciously, carries forward a tradition of other such women-focused institutions, works, from the late 1800s to the more recent past. Little did we know that we were acting on a long-held tradition of women coming together under the rubric of women-centered institutions and publication.

FAWI began in 1996 as a response to a gap in the work and knowledge being built about Franco-Americans. An idea occurred to me to build a place of making spaces for women to gather and speak without the bonds of expectations levied on their voices.

In the beginning of FAWI, the women met to form a body, a consciousness of their actual, physical presence. The meetings of the women helped to forge a public identity through many avenues of thought and discussions. There are many, many ways for a woman to be herself and of the French heritage culture. Some wished to focus on their pasts of language, food, song and shared identities—so they formed their own focus group. Some did not have the elements passed on to them from their pasts as deeply as others, but they did have a part—a knowledge of their mothers/mamans, mémères, ma tantes, to be present to their unique shared identities. Some reminded us that they had a mixed cultural background and they were pulling identity from more than just the French heritage.

Some perform. Sing. Present on panels. Draw. Paint. Photograph. Write. Take part in cultural events. And all believe in the work of promoting the unique voices of the women of the culture. Some edit, some write, some publish in the 'ezine *moé pi toé,* online since 1996, helping to express the modern-day French heritage women's voices. Other cultural organizations and institutions noticed and recognized the value of the work and cross-listed the website. FAWI has grown an online presence over the years and many international institutions list FAWI as a resource.

FAWI has promoted women's voices and contributions since its very start and has given to many writers publication credits or a platform to launch their writing career as well as the courage and knowledge to write.

FAWI represents a presence that was not subsumed in the general culture which often overlooks or leaves out the women and their contributions. One example is Jeanne Castille who worked diligently in Louisiana for CODOFIL, Council for the Development of French in Louisiana, and whose contributions have been erased. (Giacoppe, 176). While not ignoring the past of the women of the culture, but honoring the foremothers, FAWI represents the modern-day women's voices of what does it mean to be of the French heritage today.

Represented in this volume are the multiple, varied voices of the women of the French heritage. Here at the juncture of twenty years of existence for FAWI, we take the time to mark the anniversary with a mindfulness to the future of making known the voices through the creativity of the women.

This volume is a gift to the present and the future generation of the combined strengths of the French, heritage women. The submissions are the essence of what this anthology represents and how all this material showed up in my mailbox gives testimony to the alive, present and future-dwelling Franco-American, French heritage women ... all their writings were like a gift of all the possibilities I have imagined ... and they showed up ... like the two-by-twos for the ark. Like entertaining angels unawares.

The creativity in this volume is the legacy, the only legacy of the beyond-the-expected, and beyond-the-stereotypes as well.

Also, who are the members of the culture? Who is a member of the French heritage community? Does a book accomplish that when the "bigger" picture ignores the voice(s)? How to say who are the members or non-members? By birth, by blood, by association, by time-in, by legacy, by knowledge, by understanding, by isolationism, by rituals, by owning the identity, by living the culture, by ancestors, by relatives, by geographies, by sections of geographies, by access to language, or not—by which definition can you tell who belongs? Was it easier to tell who was of French heritage in the past than it is today? And then add to that the layer of creativities created in a particular place inside of a larger particular place.

And what of the becoming a part of the recognized voices of the larger place? According to David Mazel, "a national literature is often simply the literature of a dominant region elevated ... into that of the whole; writing rooted in outlying perspectives [is] demoted to the status of regional rather than national." (Mazel)

I wish to emphasize that pieces of all the stories or artworks carry a piece of the message—no one story or artwork says everything about the entire group, but together, their voices are a chorus. All the bravery is on the table. "As with most false dichotomies, 'we' understand 'them' through a singular narrative...." (Malla) does not apply when addressing the vast diversity of the French heritage women.

The cohesion of (survivance) for the future? Faith, language, and institutions as representations of the holy trinity of the saviors of the culture: one remains strong—the institution. The Franco-American Women's Institute is a part of the thriving lived lives of the French heritage culture. I can envision a retriangulation of the three pillars of survivance. Of the two remaining, there are certainly possibilities, but also the reappointment of other facets of proof of life for the French heritage culture. Creativity being a strong candidate as one of the new pillars of the culture. There can be many other factors that help sustain and support the living, lived culture.

If I were to devise a wish list for the future sound health of the French heritage, Franco-American, Acadian culture/group, my first item on the list would be a strong, vibrant producing artists' community—of all mediums of creation. Supported—financially/spiritually, published, modeled, exhibited, celebrated, fostered and more. I believe strongly that the arts are the perfect medium for the translation, transformation, trans-correspondence to the community-at-large as well as across the generations. Life-giving creativity is a value-added entity that travels through time and offers access, point of entry, entitlement, engagement, acquisition, return-on-investment, expression of modernity as well as self, among just a few of the benefits of fostering an arts community in the culture. The act of creating takes down the barriers and builds bridges to the world. Lord Durham in the Durham Report spoke incorrectly of the French being a people "without history and without literature." We have an opportunity to offer to ourselves and to the future, our creativities.

Many have generously contributed funds to help underwrite this project and for that I am heartily grateful. It is with deep gratitude that I recognize these women who have contributed their creativity—their words, artworks, photographs as proof of our creative, collective existences. I hope you will consume the work, as I have, with the marvel of how exquisitely the work represents the French heritage culture today.

References

Freitag, Florian. "Regionalism in American and Canadian Literature." In *The Palgrave Handbook of Comparative North American Literature*, edited by Reingard M. Nischik, 199-218. Palgrave Macmillan US, 2014.

Giacoppe, Monika. "North America's Francophone Borderlands." *The Palgrave Handbook of Comparative North American Literature*, edited by Reingard M. Nischik, 165-81. Palgrave Macmillan US, 2014.

Malla, Pasha. "Review: What Do These Works of Francophone Fiction Reveal to the Anglophone Reader? Thankfully, Nothing Cohesive." *The Globe and Mail*. N.p., 16 Oct. 2015. Web. 26 Jan. 2016.

Mazel, David. "Regionalism and Ecology." In *A Companion to the Regional Literatures of America*, edited by Charles L. Crow, 129-36. Malden, MA: Blackwell Pub., 2003.

Pacini, Peggy. "Re-constructing and Voicing Franco-American Culture: FAWI (Franco-American Women's Institute), when Franco-American Women Reclaim their Invisible Ethnic Heritage." American Council for Québec Studies, Burlington, Vermont. November 6, 2010. Panel presentation on Franco-American Literature.

Heliotrope

A word about the title and chapter epigraphs

As the title of the book, heliotrope, the word, came to me in my journaling and then the awareness of the breadth of that particular word, first, as a flower; then as a gem; next as an instrument; and finally as a color. And one more, as a day on the calendar. Oh, and don't forget as a perfume. Like a dream, a suggestion, a possibility, an essence of who and what we represent, the word heliotrope captures the imagination of all of that and more. If one were to choose which of the above possibilities of meaning to apply to the title of the book, I would say all of them.

Also, each of the chapters are noted with the language of plants and flowers, both in French and in English. I have been fascinated with the meanings of flowers and while thinking of the purpose of this volume, the idea came to me of the anthology resembling a thought garden. A place that grows all kinds of new and wonderful beginnings. The flowers and their meanings chosen for each chapter are sometimes expected, but also some are unexpected as are the stories or art work represented in this anthology and the meanings that they carry. Some are chosen for whimsy only.

The heliotrope flower follows the sun. The root of the word heliotrope is helio meaning "sun" and trope which means "one turned toward." In the context of the anthology, keeping one's face toward the sun—as in towards the horizon, the future, and the next event. "A heliotrope glance." In the language of flowers, Heliotrope represents devotion and in French, Héliotrope signifies "Je vous aime." Two qualities to admire when thinking of how one relates to their heritage and self in that heritage.

Heliotrope, also known as Bloodstone, is considered to be the most beautiful of the Jaspers, a deep, earthy green gem with spots of bright red. A gem that is both healing and magical. Bloodstone is used as a talisman of good fortune, with healing properties, and life-giving. Bloodstone is the traditional birthstone of the month of March. My mother was born in March and this is my way of honoring her with the title.

As an instrument, the heliotrope is a device that is used as a mirror to reflect sunlight over great distances to mark the positions of participants in a land survey. It was employed during large triangulation surveys. For me, the triangulation survey is an opportunity in this anthology to retriangulate the tenets of *la survivance*, *Notre foi, notre langue, nos institutions* (our faith, our language, [and] our institutions) into something new and reflective of our modern times. Something which speaks to the members of the French heritage group that tells the story of who we are today and not just of the past. We can measure our distances of where we are, where we have been and where we are going. I propose creativity as one of the new pillars of our going *beyond* survivance.

As a color, heliotrope fits the festive nature of the creative works published in this anthology. Purple is the color that was reserved for royalty. Purple is the color most often associated with royalty, magic, mystery and piety. Today, purple belongs to everyone. Purple is also the color that represents the Franco-American Women's Institute as well as the color of the women's movement.

Heliotrope as a perfume. Such an essence of freshness. Luxurious. Some outrageously expensive. Not unlike the perfume of the legacy of a heritage; notes and hints of fragrances—in our memory—smells are the remembrances that last the longest and touch the unseen spirits. Perfume is a gift from the gods and the Magi. Heliotrope is unique unto itself as is our French heritage-ness.

Heliotrope was also represented on the French Revolutionary Calendar in the Brumaire (22 October ~ 20 November) for the 27th of October was named Héliotrope. Heliotrope can mark our days as well.

As a word or a concept, the multiple facets of heliotrope offer a way to re-envision the creative lives of the present and future French heritage women. This anthology is given as a snapshot of our present definition of who we are and offers our creative work to the future. We honor our ancestral heritage and continue on our journey towards whom and what we will become.—**Rhea Côté Robbins**

Heliotrope

French Heritage Women Create

Family/Testimony—*Famille/Témoignage*

Giroflée—Fidélité à la famille
Gillyflower—Bonds of affection
Stock—Contentment
Wallflower—Fidelity in adversity

Quintefeuille—Amour de la famille
Cinquefoil—Maternal affection, beloved daughter

Rhubarbe—Gardez courage
Rhubarb—Advice

Asphodèle—Regret du passé
Asphode—My regrets follow you to the grave

Cactus—Chaleur. Amour maternel
Cactus—Endurance

"A Yard of Cloth"

By Annie Proulx

In the late 1980s on the day after Thanksgiving my younger sister Roberta and I went to visit our mother in her little apartment complex of housing for the elderly in Bristol, New Hampshire. At the time we both lived in Vermont on the west side of the Connecticut River. The day was mild for late November, heavy overcast, light rain and fog, one of those dark days that New England breeds in autumn. There were deer hunters on the road driving at twenty miles per hour, craning their necks to see into the scraggy woods.

Roberta and I are close in the sense that we often think and feel in similar ways. At the time we tried to visit our mother, Lois Gill Proulx, once a month. She had been ill for years with bronchiectasis, an uncommon degenerative lung disease which she fought with exercises, diet, medication, and willpower. Frequent bouts of pneumonia and colitis attacks lurked as accompanists. Her closest sister, Gloriana (beloved Hikee), had the same miserable disease, and in the summer of 2008 my cousin Eleanor Goodenough Milner and I, going through some of my mother's papers, came upon a poignant and upsetting correspondence between the two sick sisters. The sense of the hopelessly brave front, the running jokes, the closest sisterly bond, a hatred for stupid and condescending doctors—of all the things two people suffering the same illness can say to each other that no one else could understand—overwhelmed us. I can now barely open the box that holds those letters because all the disappointed dreams of these two hungry-for-love women fly in my face.

On the post-Thanksgiving day Roberta and I drove into the gathering gloom of Bristol. On the corner, a block from our mother's building, there had once been a wonderful rock shop full of minerals, geodes, bits of agate, amethyst crystals, odd mudstone shapes, slabs of malachite. But the sign was gone and in its place was a drooping banner in the window: DECORATOR FABRICS LOWER THAN WHOLESALE. Roberta and I both like beads, cloth, yarn, needles.

"Let's look on the way back if they're still open."

"Yes."

The dinner was pork loin, creamed onions that tasted exactly the same as they had when we were children, sweet potato, applesauce Roberta had made from a neighbor's apples, swapping him a chicken. Our mother was tired, but in fairly good health and spirits. She had exhausted herself for two days making the dinner. (Guilt! Guilt!) My mother and I each drank a glass of wine.

Late in the afternoon we left her. The light was fading. A thin mist blurred the small branches of the trees. At the corner we remembered the fabric sale sign. The place was still open. I parked the truck and we went inside.

There was no one in the shop. No one. Piles of folded fabric were stacked on long tables, bolts of shimmering brocade leaned against the wall. The shop stank of old minerals, stale cigarette smoke, and the scent of wet leaves and rain we brought in with us.

The bolts of fabric were as awkward as loose walking sticks and slid and fell against each other when we tried to pull any one out. It was difficult to see the patterns without knocking down a dozen of them. As we wrestled with the slippery bolts the door opened and a man came in.

In some inexplicable way he was repellent. His face was creased and seamed, his black hair combed over a narrow skull. Slack stubbled cheeks, discolored teeth. The bolts of fabric seemed viciously animated. The man began to talk to us in an obsequious, intimate tone of voice. His comments were inane, stupid.

"I know ladies like to rummage around with cloth."

The damn bolts of designer fabrics, probably hijacked, I thought, refused to stay in place. The man asked us where we came from. We evaded, simply saying "Vermont" and "across the river."

"Where in Vermont? What town?" He would not give up.

"Oh, central Vermont, around Montpelier," I lied.

Now he insisted we take his business card. The cards were just across the street in his antique shop. No, no, we didn't want him to bother. We refused. I was suddenly wild to get away from this man. He began to wind clocks, set the hands. I hated him. The fabrics were rich and fine, the prices very low, but it was impossible to make a rational selection with the man talking on and on in his oily way. Snatching up a bolt of fabric without looking at it, I said I would take a yard of cloth, try it at home and see if the colors were right. Anything to get away.

He produced a grimy yardstick from under the counter and a pair of scissors with a broken point. My sister leaned silently over an empty birdcage still encrusted with droppings. With a little flourish, and promising "I'll give you more than a yard," the man measured, cut briefly with the scissors, then tore the fabric and folded it into a small square. In the exchange of money his hand—very graceful and long-fingered—touched mine. Fever hot.

Yet we still could not get away. A barrage of advice to drive carefully, to take care, warnings that it was a bad night, there was fog, the road was slippery followed us down the steps. I thought his persistence extraordinary. Finally, alone on the sidewalk, we told each other that we had had a singular encounter.

We drove west through the mist and damp. The light was a somber, northern grey, the road blurred with light rain. Fog hung over the Pemigewasset. On the outskirts of town the road widened. We were alone on the highway. My sister was reading a letter. We came into the broad, sweeping curve that follows the river's course. In front of us, skewed across the empty road, in the smoking-grey silence were two smashed grey cars, pillars of steam rising from each, the road a fine carpet of glass. We stopped. Silence, stillness, all as static as a stage scene. There seemed no one in the terribly smashed cars, all the vehicles' glass on the road, the metal torn and compressed. A broad red runner of radiator fluid glistened on the web road. We went to the cars. I could see a slumped figure.

Other vehicles began to come up behind us, most of them pulling around and continuing on their way. A pickup stopped. Two young men leapt out and began to pull at the farther crashed car's door.

"Don't move them," I called.

Their hands withdrew from something, someone. My sister and I were at the nearer car. We saw the humped man, the blood, we saw he was young with thick, light hair, the brilliant red soaking into a blond mustache, something on the seat beside him like a brace, some plastic soda bottles. He moaned. My sister touched his shoulder. His face was grey, his eyes closed. His clothes sparkled with glass. He made a twisting hunch. His legs rattled. My sister's hand lay lightly on his shoulder.

Now cars were coming from both directions, swerving and cutting around or pulling over, the people getting out to stare. No police.

"I'll go for help," I called to the young men.

"The police station!" they yelled back. "Half a mile down the road."

"Don't move, we'll get help, help is coming." I said to the injured man. I doubted he heard me. I ran to my truck, looked back. My sister was still with him, her hand on his shoulder. I called to her. She stepped toward me, turned back to the injured man, again stepped toward me, but reluctantly, still looking at him, her hand still outstretched even as she came away from him as though she couldn't bear to leave him. A few days later we learned he had died from his injuries.

At the station the dispatcher called for police, ambulances, the Jaws of Life, fire trucks, someone to control traffic. In minutes flashing lights and sirens went by. We did not go back to the scene but headed home by another, longer road, many miles out of our way and clogged with traffic crawling through the thickening fog. I drove slowly and carefully.

My sister and I both believed the man in the shop had saved our lives with his delaying talk, his cautions. A minute or two earlier and it could have been us wrecked on the curve of the river road. It was a singular and disturbing incident and we both felt its importance.

That night I telephoned my mother and told her about the accident and about the man in the shop who gave us the creeps but had perhaps saved us.

"Ah," she said. There was a note of contemptuous amusement in her voice. "You know what his name is, don't you, the man in the shop?"

"No. He wanted to give us his card but I didn't take it."

"His name is Proulx," she said. In her tone—or did I misinterpret?—was her family's careful Yankee neutrality toward my father which I had come to see as rejection. This disclosure had the effect of an electric shock. The private questions welled. My sister and I spoke intensely to each other. The silence of our childhood, adulthood, suddenly broken. Who was this man with our name? Who were we? Who were our people? We knew so little. The American experience, the focus on individual achievement, the acquisition of goods and money to prove one's social value, is built on this sense of loss, this alienation from the warmth of the home culture, isolation from genetic bonds. This separation from one's tribe creates an inner loneliness that increases as one ages. There is in many people, especially immigrants, a burning need to complete the puzzle, to find the missing pieces. And what did it do to us, growing up as outsiders, as part of no place—we had moved more than twenty times by the time I was fifteen—as part of no people except our mother's pale-eyed Yankee clan who subtly gave us the sense that we were different and somehow tainted? Now we regret not speaking with the man who shared our name.

I have moved countless times in my adult life, too. Part of this peripatetic behavior is because Americans are a mobile people, but I come from a Franco American background, rootless people who have no national identity, who really belong nowhere in the United States. The groups closest to fitting in I suppose are the French in Maine who have chipped out a place, and the French from the Canadian Maritimes who, after the 1755 expulsion from Acadia, went to France where they were not welcomed, then to Louisiana where they became Cajuns (a corruption of the word "Acadian"). The places and habitations where we live have histories, though we rarely know them.

We slide into houses and apartments others have built and rarely have a clue about what went on there, if the first owner grew an orchard of cherries and pears, how came that bizarre stairway with risers of varied heights, if that large piece of slate in the backyard was a wolf stone, if Indians knew the place and what they did there. I wondered about those things as my family moved and moved again around New England, leaving our hearts in Vermont, on to North Carolina, then again in Maine, but not belonging to any of those places. Jack Kerouac nailed it when he wrote of "that horrible homelessness of all French-Canadians abroad in America."[1] There was one year in my life when I lived in Montréal, and several when I commuted there from Vermont to graduate school, picked up a little *joual*, became familiar with the flat riverine landscape and the shapes of faces. Years later came a weekend in my life when I went to a gathering of Franco American writers on an island in Maine. As I walked into the room I was slammed with the shock of recognition. Here were non-Anglo people, people with familiar lineaments, with long fingers and slender bones, with dark eyes and hair and certain ways of moving and gesturing. Tears came to my eyes and for a little while I felt the curious but lovely sensation of being with the home herd and fantasized moving to Québec, Montréal or the Gaspé or Montmagny. But by then I had been too long in solitude, too anglicized for the joy to last.

In 1993, plagued by questions of family origins, I engaged Diane L. a genealogical researcher in Connecticut, to see what she could find out about my father's tangled family and whether or not the Indian connection was real and, if so, what tribe or group. Over the next few years she checked birth and death records, consulted voluminous tomes of records on immigration, baptism, marriages, births, federal census reports, sextons' reports, corresponded with genealogical societies. For the Canadian end of the research Richard De Gruchy, a Montréal genealogist, discovered relatives whose names I had never heard. I found it all confusing, a total overload of statistical information about too many people. It seemed such a shifting, murky compilation of hundreds of people, that I felt quite overwhelmed as though I had been dropped into Peter Matthiessen's *Lost Man's River* as one of the multitude of estranged, wandering but related characters.

The branches of my father's family seemed to boil down to my father's mother, Phoebe Brisson, daughter of Olivier (Levi) Brisson and Exilda (Maggie) LaBarge, and my father's father, Peter Ovila Proulx, born in 1886, son of Michel Preault [sic] and wife Melina. New England clerks mangled French names and struggled hopelessly with Québec place names and all of these had multiple variations of spelling. St.-Rémi south of Montréal became St Remal, or St Remic, Canada. It seemed all members of the various family clans married three or four times, all had nicknames as well as "dit" names, all used Americanized forms of their birth names. They had enormous families with many infant deaths, often renaming new babies after those who had died. But gradually some clarity emerged.

My grandmother, Phoebe Brisson, was also descended from the LaBarges. The LaBarge connection led back to Robert LaBarge of Normandy, "a native of Columbière in the diocese of Bayonne" born in 1633. He came to Québec and settled in Montmorency where he married in 1663. His great-great-grandson, Joseph Maria LaBarge, born in L'Assomption, Québec, in 1787, left home in 1808 at age twenty-one. Hiram Chittenden wrote:

> He traveled by the usual route, up the Ottawa River and through the intricate system of waterways in northern Ontario which leads to Georgian Bay and to Lake Huron. Thence he went

[1] Jack Kerouac, letter to Yvonne Le Maitre, a critic-journalist who wrote for Québec publications, September 8, 1950. I am indebted to David Plante for the quotation, and to Isaac Gewirtz of the New York Public Library, who tracked down the source.

by way of Mackinaw Strait and Lake Michigan to Green Bay, and along the Fox and Wisconsin rivers to the Mississippi, which he descended to St. Louis. He used a single birch-bark canoe all the way, with only eight miles of portaging.[2]

In St. Louis he married "a Creole descendant of both the Spanish and French elements in the settlement of the Mississippi Valley" in 1813.[3] Later he answered a newspaper advertisement calling for one hundred good men to trap fur in the American west. So he became a member of General William H. Ashley's fur expedition of 1828, and a western Wyoming stream, La Barge Creek, near the town named La Barge, now bears his name. His name was attached to the creek and the town because of reports that he was scalped there by an Arickaree camping with or near the trappers. Although James Clyman and that wild liar James Beckwourth said that LaBarge had been killed, he was not killed.[4] Hiram Chittenden, in his biography of the son, Captain Joseph LaBarge, reports that the father carried a tomahawk scar on his head—perhaps from the Wyoming attack, although he was in other Indian fights on the Missouri. On that first westering trip Ashley's notes refer to the bluff west of Pass Creek to the south of Elk Mountain. Although there is no way to be sure, if the trappers were following the North Platte, that bluff was probably Bird Cloud's cliff, a notable landmark.

Joseph Maria returned to St. Louis, took up charcoal making, ran a boardinghouse and recruited young men for Ashley's fur-trapping enterprises. He fathered seven children. Three sons, Joseph (b. 1815), Charles S. and John B., were all steamboat captains. Joseph at age seventeen bound himself for three years to Pierre Choteau's ruthless American Fur Company as a "voyageur, engagé, or clerk," advanced rapidly to steamboat captain with a deep knowledge of the great river's shifting channels.[5] He became celebrated as the premier Missouri pilot and is said to have influenced Mark Twain's knowledge of steamboat captains.[6] In his first year of employment he spent the winter of 1832-33 in a Pawnee village in the vicinity of Council Bluffs, learning the language and ways of the tribe.

In 1837 the American Fur Company's ill-starred steamboat *St. Peter's* brought smallpox to the Mandans on the upper Missouri and lit the disease fire that decimated the western tribes in the following decades. LaBarge was not involved in this horrific encounter—Bernard Pratte, Jr., captained the *St. Peter's* on that trip. But LaBarge had his own experiences of epidemics. In 1883, in his second year of employment with the American Fur Company, he was on board the *Yellowstone* captained by Andrew Bennett. On board as passengers were the German naturalist and early ethnographer, Prince Maximilian of Weid, and the Swiss painter Karl Bodmer. A cholera epidemic was roaring through the country and broke out aboard the *Yellowstone*. The crew was hard-hit and Bennett was forced to go back to St. Louis to find new men, leaving the *Yellowstone* in the hands of young LaBarge. Local residents came to the riverbank and shouted that if the boat did not leave the state of Missouri immediately they would set it on fire. Both the fireman and the engineer were dead. Eighteen-year-old LaBarge fired up the boiler alone and navigated the boat to the west shore above the Kansas River. His reputation was made.

He alternately worked for the American Fur Company or quit them to make his own way, suffering several financial disasters. During his career LaBarge knew many of the famous people of his time. As a young boy he met Lafayette. Audubon—whom he disliked—was once his passenger as were the Jesuit missionaries Fathers Christian Hoecken and Pierre-Jean De Smet.[7]

---

[2] Hiram Martin Chittenden, *History of Early Steamboat Navigation on the Missouri River: Life and Adventure of Joseph La Barge Pioneer Navigator and Indian Trader for Fifty Years Identified with the Commerce of the Missouri Valley* (New York: Francis P. Harper, 1903), 1:3

[3] Ibid., 1:2.

[4] Charles L. Camp, "James Clyman," in *The Mountain Men and the Fur Trade of the Far West*, ed. LeRoy, R. Hafen (Spokane: Arthur H. Clark Co., 2003), 1:244.

[5] Chittenden, History, 1:23.

[6] For the best information see Chittenden, History, vols. 1 and 2. Paul O'Neil, *The Rivermen* (Alexandria, VA.: Time-Life Books, 1975), confuses the father, Joseph Maria LaBarge, with his son, the steamboat captain Joseph LaBarge. The result is snappy adventure rather than carefully checked history.

[7] Father Hoecken, after ministering to stricken passengers, died in 1851 on board the *St. Ange* during a cholera outbreak. Father De Smet who was also on board and ill with "bilious fever" survived.

He knew Brigham Young. Although Captain LaBarge's brother Charles died in 1852 in a steamboat explosion and brother John collapsed and died while making a boat landing at Bismarck, North Dakota, thirty-three years later, Joseph LaBarge lived to be eighty-four, an illustrious St. Louis citizen, dying in 1899. When I sent my father this information he had no comment. It might have mattered to him when he was a child, but not when he was close to his nineties.

The Brisson connection was less glamorous. Three early Brissons came from France to New France. Only one of them settled in the Laprairie-St.-Constant-St.-Rémi area—Sebastien Brisson dit Laroche, and according to the genealogist Richard De Gruchy, who worked on our problem, all the Brissons of St.-Rémi were descended from Sebastien, born around 1671 in Bordeaux, Guyenne, France. He married Marie-Marguerite Larivière in June 1722 in Québec.

Although I give little credence to the family belief in an Indian connection, I can see how descendants thought the Brissons were the link. Olivier, or, as he called himself, "Levi" Brisson, my father's maternal grandfather, came from St.-Rémi, a rural Francophone village in Napierville County south of Montréal, to Connecticut in the 1860s. St.-Rémi is near Kahnawake, the northern New York State Mohawk reserve on the St. Lawrence River. Levi settled in East Killingly, Connecticut, on the Rhode Island border and gained considerable local fame claiming be the father of forty or more children with three wives, all scattered in a trail from Québec to Minnesota to Connecticut. Several interviewers took down his story (reproducing his broken English in the standard caricature of the little French Canadian). We hear his voice:

> "I know I have feefteen child leeveing, how many more in Minnesota, Canada, y'odder place, O do not know. One time a was a well off, but a have so much seekness, so many funeral, eet make me poor. Mon dieu, when a feller raise t'ree beeg fam' like a rasie, she don' save much eef she leeve on farm. In se factory eet ees differaint. A feller she can put hees boys and girls in ze mill an save money 'n bimeby she kin go back to Canada and leave on her fa'm. Zat leetle girl here's ze youngest one. Ma wife, he have one m'but she ain't leeve. She bo'n dead and she have no place in ze church."[8]

From a cousin in Florida I have a copy of a photograph that shows the hawk-faced little man, reported to weigh only 110 pounds, sitting on his doorstep with five of his children. Strings of dried apples, which my relative was pleased to call bear claws, hung on the side of the house. My grandmother, about five years old, sits in the front row. At the time of the interview Levi Brisson was reputedly between eighty and ninety years old. They were living rent-free in an old schoolhouse by agreement with the school district. The Brisson children would maintain the pupil population necessary to keep another school and teacher going in accordance with Rhode Island regulations.

> Monsieur Brisson and his family are not squatters, as they have been represented, or misrepresented. They are, it is true, living on a part of the public domain, occupying a public mansion, but they are giving an equivalent, which, instead of making them, as they have been made to appear, semi-paupers, makes them really public benefactors, inasmuch as their accession to the district population makes possible the continuation of a seat of learning within its borders.[9]

The articles provide most of what we know about this man. *The Providence Journal* reporter paraphrased him as saying, "he was born in the parish of St. Remick, [St.-Rémi], near Montréal, in 1820, but could not recall the day of the month. He had lived in the States more than 40 years, half of that time within a dozen miles or so of Danielson, Conn. He was married three times. His first wife, Clemence Benjamin bore him six children, including one pair of twins. His second spouse, Mary Cyr, was the mother of 21, including two pairs of twins, and his third wife and pregnant wife, Maggie LeBarge, has borne him 11, of which four are dead."[10] If he had lived today he could have his own television program.

---

[8] "Father of Forty, Monsieur Brisson, the French-Canadian Patriarch in Foster," *Providence Sunday Journal*, June 3, 1903.

[9] Ibid.

[10] Ibid.

Levi Brisson died five months after the interview, and the *Windham County Transcript* ran the following obituary:

> Levi Bresson [sic], whose familiar figure was so often seen on our streets, died at his home November [illegible]. He was a Canadian half-breed and his Indian blood was very conspicuous in his features and loping gait. He was born near Quebec between 80 and 90 years ago. He clung to his Indian habits of living and always seemed to prefer some little cabin for a home near the edge of a forest. Reporters have made him famous on account of the great number of his descendents [sic], he being the father of 42 children. He was quaint and original in his sayings, voluble and social in his manner. The burial was Friday.[11]

However, newspaper reports are poor evidence, and the researcher Richard De Gruchy did not turn up any Indian connection at all, though speculating that because St.-Rémi was very close to the Mohawk Kahnawake Reservation perhaps the Brisson family had friends there, and "because of this somehow the notion of an Indian connection arose."[12] Diane L. agreed that there was no solid proof of any Indian connection. Although several of his descendants, including my grandmother, my father, and his cousin, Richard Brisson (a collector of Indian artifacts), believed in an Indian ancestor, the idea that Levi Brisson was a "half-breed" is not substantiated. My sisters and other relatives still hold onto the Indian ancestor.

Despite genealogical work in Connecticut and in Québec, Peter Ovila Proulx, my father's father, has not been tracked to his end and probably never will be. It no longer matters. My own father, George, said that he knew the man was lame, that he had had infantile paralysis as a child, that he was a skilled silk weaver. He always believed his father's family had come down from Trois-Rivières. The 1900 Connecticut census says Peter Ovila Proulx was then fourteen years old, could read and write, spoke English and was employed as a cotton spinner. He limped badly and was called "Turkey" Proulx because of his lurching gait. His World War I draft registration notes that he was short, had brown hair and eyes, and was a "cripple." The divorce record says that Phoebe divorced him after three years of marriage "for habitual intemperance." From somewhere there came the unsubstantiated story that after the divorce he stole a locomotive and returned to Canada. No death records have turned up the name of this Ovila Proulx. There was a small flurry of excitement when a record of an Ovila Proulx from Woonsocket, Rhode Island, who fought in the First World War turned up, but the description did not fit. Peter Ovila simply disappeared, as so many men have done.

A child begins to think about his or her name and perhaps subconsciously reacts to it. Alan Lightman is a physicist-novelist; Raymond Seed became a biologist; there is a plantsman name Peabody and a rancher named Vaca. Jeffrey F. Brain chose psychotherapy as an occupation, and Sonny Grouper was the developer of shark repellent. Oakes Ames (George Plimpton's grandfather) became a Harvard botanist. I do not know what Proulx (or Prou in the original form or Preault) means. No doubt there is a descriptor in genealogical name lists—some flattering phrase such as Brave-in-Battle or Steadfast. I don't know.

Mr. De Gruchy backtracked Ovila to our original Jean Prou, the first ancestor to come to North America. "His name was Jean Proulx. He was the son of Jean Proulx and of Louise Vallee of the parish of Notre-Dame-de-Nantilly, in the City and Arrondissement of Saumur, in the Bishopric of Angers, Anjou (today in the department of Maine-et-Loire), France and he arrived here sometime before 1672 for he married at Québec City on the 5 June 1673 to Jacquette Fournier."[13]

Although Jean Prou's employment contract has never been found, the census lists him as "a domestic in the service of Louis Couillard, Sieur de L'Espinay, Squire and Seigneur of Montmagny. Louis Couillard lived in the lower town of Québec, on rue Notre Dame. The house was full of people: 5 children between the ages of 2 and 14, the queen of the hearth, Geneviéve [sic] Després and two domestics, both named Jean. The two domestics, both 22 years

[11] *Windham County Transcript*, November 19, 1903, 4.

[12] Richard De Gruchy to Annie Proulx, May 6, 1996.

[13] Richard De Gruchy to Annie Proulx, November 25, 1996, 1.

old, were working out their indenture for the Seigneur....Thus we may conclude that Jean Prou arrived in 1666, was 22 years old and worked as a household domestic."[14] After three years he was allowed to own less than three acres "comprised of high woods" on the river la Caille. For this he paid an annual homage to the seigneur of "1 sol in 'cens,' 3 live capons and 9 silver livres in 'rentes,' and 9 days of work on the seigneurie."[15] He also had to give one-tenth of all the fish he caught to the seigneur, altogether rather tough terms. The land had to be cleared by hand, and he was still at it two years later. When, in February of 1671, Guillaume Fournier offered him 150 livres for his property he sold it and went back to Québec City. In 1672 Noël Morin, the seigneur of St.-Luc at Montmagny, granted Jean Prou some land at St.-Luc and an easier contract. He could keep his fish, but had to fell and cut four arpents of trees (an arpent is 0.85 percent of an acre) over the next year and live on the place as well. In 1673 he married Jacquette, the fourteen-year-old daughter of Guillaume Fournier. So he became one of the early settlers in Montmagny on the St-Laurent. Jean Prou stayed in Montmagny.[16] The census of 1681 lists him as owning a rifle and twelve head of cattle and working six arpents of land. He and Jacquette increased the population of Montmagny with fourteen children. But something went wrong. The historian Thomas Laforest wrote:

> There is a twenty-year hiatus during which Jean Prou is never mentioned in official or civil documents. He surfaced on 14 October 1701, completely run down and out. Had he tried his hand in the fur trade? On his return to Québec, Marie Anne Fortin, widow of Jean Picard, a provisions merchant, was waiting for him. She demanded, before the notary Chambelon, that he pay his debt of 700 livres and 16 sous for provisions furnished, which he admitted owing her. This debt was settled only after his death, from the proceeds of his estate.[17]

He died at age fifty-nine, March 1, 1703, leaving his widow with many children and a debt. She sold half the farm, including the house and barn, and moved in with her twenty-four-year-old son Joseph. The remaining assets were few—some land, one horse, one cow, three sheep, twenty-five chickens, four rifles, three sickles. By the time my father, George Napoleon Proulx, was born 250-odd years after his ancestor's arrival in the New World, all memory of Jean Prou had vanished from the family consciousness.

Through all of the Proulx baptism, birth, marriage, death records runs a black thread—"imbecile," "mulatto," "habitual intemperance," "her mark"—words one doesn't want to see in a family history, but they are there. It was a poor, mostly illiterate, rural clan of laborers unable to break out of the loop of continuing poverty and misery until my father, George Napoleon Proulx, managed it. Maybe he was right to put behind him all blood ties, to forego the history, the Québec language, culture and religion, to make his own world as so many Americans have done. I don't think any of his children understood how he saw himself, his ambitions, his life.

The Chicano word "*rasquache*" comes to mind. It has two meanings. The negative meaning is of poor, low-class, uneducated, disorganized and dirty people. The other meaning has been adopted by art critics to describe a vigorous Chicano sensibility, expressing resistance, resourcefulness and adaptability, iron and defiant energy. My father came from roots characterized by the first meaning and reinvented himself as an upwardly mobile white-collar American. His perpetual toast—"here's to bigger and better jobs and more money"—was one man's version of the American Dream. My conjectures about our vague French Canadian connection and the immigrant experience in general led to research for the novel *Accordion Crimes*.

A year after our father died my sister Roberta found a report in a January 1889 issue of The New York Times headlined THEY LEFT HIM TO DIE. The event took place 117 years before my father's death in 2006.

> MONTREAL, Jan. 10—Last Sunday the body of George Proulx was found completely frozen in the woods near St. Maurice and was conveyed to Piles, where the Coroner has opened an inquest, but it was adjourned till Jan. 17 owning to the absence of important witnesses. The whole story is strange and melancholy, and recalls the adventures of early colonizing times. About the end of last

---

[14] Thomas J. Laforest, *Our French-Canadian Ancestors* (Palm Harbor, Florida: Quintin Publications), 3:216.

[15] Ibid., 217.

[16] Without knowing this I went for several summers to attend the famous Montmagny accordion festival while doing research for the novel *Accordion Crimes*.

[17] Leforest, *Our French Canadian Ancestors*, 20:219.

November the deceased went to work in a lumber shanty near the source of the St. Maurice River. He fell sick, and when it was found he could not recover, the overseer determined to send him to Three Rivers. Having no conveyance two men were sent to help the invalid.

They started at the time when the cold was the severest at the beginning of the Winter. A heavy fall of snow followed, and the trail became impassable, when the travelers were in the dreary district of Tuque, about 100 miles from their destination, with only a few scattered shanties on the way.

In the middle of the storm the two protectors abandoned their charge on the River Bauke and left him to die. The dying man made an attempt to follow, but he was overpowered by cold and buried in the snow.

When these two men arrived at Piles they said nothing of the incident, but suspicions arose and a searching party was organized. Sandy Adams and Hercule Deseletz of Rivière Aux Rats found the body and conveyed it on a litter to Piles.

The conduct of the two men has caused great indignation, and when inquiry was instituted they could not be found.[18]

This unknown George Proulx joins the man in the fabric shop as another family mystery.

Addendum

Recently I discovered from the results of a genealogical DNA test that the Proulx family belief in an Indian connection is a myth. In our searches to know who we were we had never turned up anything to substantiate the Indian on paper except my great-grandfather Olivier (Levi) Brisson's obituary ("He was a Canadian half-breed and his Indian blood was very conspicuous in his features and loping gait.") Apparently it was on this slender sentence by an imaginative reporter that the Brisson family constructed their belief in the connection. My father's cousin, Richard Brisson, collected Indian artifacts and was convinced of Mohawk heritage. The question remains why the Brisson-Proulx descendants so eagerly adopted the identification.

From mid-19th century to the Depression of the 1930s a rock-ribbed New England of Protestant fishermen, lumbermen and farmers found themselves knee-deep in 900,000 Catholic French-speaking Québécois who had left their impoverished farms and ill-paid forest work for the land to the south, the land of riches described by "*l'oncle des États*." The French-Canadians tended to cluster in urban "*petits Canadas*" near the textile mills. Although many of the Brissons went to work in the mills, Levi's choice to live in the rent-free but isolated rural schoolhouse in Foster, Rhode Island, condemned the family to jobless poverty. He was too old to work, his third family of children were too young and the mills too far away. While many Québec emigrants enjoyed a higher standard of living with electricity, piped-in water and a steadier and higher income than on their marginal northern farms, Levi's family had none of this. They did not have the comfort of a "Little Canada" support group with their language, culture and religion. They were seen by the local townspeople as squatters and a drain on the public purse. They were pariahs, scorned as low-class rabble rather than assimilated; they must have burned with shame, with loneliness and the keen smart of discrimination.

The idea of the American Indian as "noble savage" leaked slowly into the public consciousness, replacing the early English settler's blanket opinion of tribes of murderous painted fiends. By the turn of the 20th century in New England, Indians had become burnished with the reputation for wisdom, skillful woodcraft and lore, and imperiled survival. For the Brissons, a thread of Indian identity could salve their feelings of belonging nowhere and restore a little dignity. Small wonder then that Levi's descendants seized on an ignorant reporter's unfounded assertion of "Indian blood" and used it to elevate their understanding of themselves and their standing in Québec-New England social structures.

Although this imaginary connection was seldom-mentioned by my father in his life, the burning ambition to make something of himself may well have grown out of this history. My personal sense of isolation and need to construct the lives of invented characters may also be part of that inherited sense of worthlessness.

—Annie Proulx

---

[18] *New York Times*, January 11, 1889.

Mémère

By Carolyna Saint Germain

In my heart and through my eyes, my grandmother, Mémère was the most beautiful and most loving person in the world. She was love personified. She was like the holy mother of Christ, Mother Mary: gentle, kind, compassionate, thoughtful, endearing, giving, and generous, without fault, without sin. When she held me in her arms and I lay my head on her bosom, her gaze filled me with bliss and I floated to heaven. She was my safe-haven, my teacher, my friend, my guardian. And I wanted to be all that for her, too. From the moment she held me as an infant, I wanted to give to her, in the same way she gave to me, that mothering, nurturing love. We had a mutual admiration towards each other and a sweet intimate connection.

My memories of being with her begin at about three years old and for eight summers she was my guardian angel. I was the sponge-child at her side, absorbing her life's principles, values and family traditions. She was filling this empty vessel, with her wisdom and prowess. As my life unfolded, I experienced the same life patterns and followed in her footsteps without conscious awareness at the time. It is in hindsight and with the help of the memories of others that I have learned this truth. It is so amazingly wonderful for me to realize that I am my grandmother.

When she died, I was eleven years old. I was so very heartbroken. I knelt on the prie-dieu and gazed at her beautiful old face shrouded in the pristine white satin casket encircled with blood-red roses and silently wept and wept. Hot tears scalding my cheeks and falling over my clasped hands, a waterfall of grief and sadness, I was sure that I would never recover from this merciless loss. The funeral parlor was filled with the odiferous effigies of dozens and dozens of roses and carnations and lilies and cigarette smoke so thick it was like fog in the room. My Godfather came to the casket, rested his hands on my shoulders and whispered in my ear, "Viens, viens. Allons-nous-en dehors." He gently encouraged me to my feet and led me out into the warm, dark, moonless summer night as the litany began again: "Je vous salue, Marie, pleine de grâce: le Seigneur est avec vous; vous êtes bénie entre toutes les femmes, et Jésus, le fruit de vos entrailles, est béni. Sainte Marie, Mère de Dieu, priez pour nous, pauvres pécheurs, maintenant et à l'heure de notre mort. Amen." I was so dazed and angry. I didn't know why everyone thought we had to pray so much for her succession into heaven. I knew she was already there. She was my saint! My guardian angel! I sank to the grass and lay there listening to the murmuring of the rosary, one decade in French, and the next in English, all the mysteries represented and prayed: the Joyful, The Sorrowful, the Glorious. I became mesmerized and a great calm took me over. I kept thinking, and praying, I guess. "I want to be just like you Mémère. Make me just like you." I must have drifted off because the next thing I became aware of was my Godfather waking me up to go to mémère's to go to bed. The vigil was over and tomorrow would be the funeral.

Saint Joseph's Church was packed like sardines. Everyone from a fifty-mile radius loved my grandmother. She had been so many things to so many people and for a long time. She could read French and English, so during World War II and the Korean War, people would gather at the farm in her big kitchen and she would read them the war news from the newspapers and letters that they had received from their sons, their husbands, and their fathers. I used to sit on the wood box next to the back door that led to the big shed-mud-dairy-room that was attached to the back of the kitchen. Mémère would let me sit there if I was quiet and didn't interrupt. I didn't understand much but I loved watching the people's faces as their expressions shifted and changed, as endless and imitable as waves on a beach. When my cousin would sneak in and get me, we would slip off into the barn to swing on the rope swing or run the rafters.

My grandparents had a dairy farm. During the summer one of my jobs along with my cousin was to run the cows in and out of the barn for milking and grazing, morning and evening. I lived outside in nature in the summers, running and cavorting in the meadows, pastures and gardens helping out with everything I could. Mémère taught me through her example how to love and cherish helping and being a part of everything. My favorite job was working the big stand-up milk separator in the back shed. It was taller than me and I would have to stand on a milking stool to turn the handle as pépère poured the milk from the milking pails into the top stainless steel bowl-shaped container. I could see my warped reflection in the stainless steel container. I had to turn the handle slow and steady. I loved that job! Watching the milk separate into the fat crème fraîche and the pure white milk and then the watery-milk, it was like magic. There were three separate spouts each leading into separate bowls. Mémère would then use the liquids according to the needs of the day and week. That fresh milk was so good! She had glass jugs and jars that were used for the milk and cream that she always boiled clean. Mémère had two ice boxes in the shed; one was just for the dairy. People came every day to buy her milk and cheese and butter. She always gave so much of it away if there was no money for the folks to pay. She would say to me, "La Sainte Mère de Jésus va me prendre soin." She was never afraid to be without. The iceman came twice a week with the big blocks of ice, and she would pay him with dairy and produce from her garden. He did not speak any English and so he always had fun making me laugh with his nonsense English words. He was my grandmother's cousin and later when he became too sick to work, he came and lived with my grandmother and she took care of him until he passed. I learned how to speak Acadian (that nonsense English!) with him and called him "mon oncle" even though he wasn't.

Mémère and pépère planted a huge vegetable garden and gave half of the produce away to their big family, relatives and friends. They had those magical "green thumbs" that everyone talks about and were very generous with everyone. I learned how to garden from their tireless teachings. Herbs, produce, vines, trellises, what "weeds" to keep which were useful and what ones to pull and add to the compost pile. I made many errors in the beginning but mémère never scolded me about it. She simply showed me again and again, and eventually I knew. There was a black snake that lived in the garden in the summer. I thought it was huge and I was scared of it. Terrified really! One early morning, Mémère and I went to the garden to harvest pea pods and there was the big black snake coiled up at the foot of the pea trellis pole. My heart went into my stomach and I froze, unable to speak or move. Of course I was barefoot so I hadn't bothered the cold sleeping snake as I softly walked up, and therefore it hadn't moved. But now, *I* was totally incapable of movement and it was slowly waking up with its tongue flicking in and out like only a snake can do. Mémère was walking up to me with her rubber mud boots making lots of noise and the snake began to wiggle and slither a bit. It was only a foot away from me and I just knew that it was going to slither over my bare feet. I could have just fainted but I really didn't want that snake to slither over my body! That was just too much to even think about! As mémère came down the row, she realized that I was traumatized and so she started singing a little French ditty. Her melodic voice broke through my frozen trance. I looked up at her coming towards me. She smiled and waved as she continued to sing this nonsensical song and I pointed my finger towards the ground where the big snake was. As she reached me we both looked down and the snake was gone. I was so relieved. I didn't care where it had gone. It had gone! And not slithered over my bare feet! Even though she had taught me before that the snake played an important role in the garden, and I knew it wouldn't hurt me, I just couldn't convince my fearful heart to chill out. So, mémère taught me the song she had been singing and told me it was a magic song; and that whenever I came in to the garden I should just start singing it as I entered the gate. Monsieur Snake would stay hidden from me because he knew that I was not afraid. He would never hurt me. He was mémère's friend and helped her keep the rodents and other critters out of her garden. That was why she had such great plants and why the squirrels and mice and other creatures didn't eat her plants. As we harvested the peas, I learned that song by repeating it a million times and I never came into the garden again without singing it at the top of my lungs. I did see the snake a few times but it would always wiggle and squiggle away from me.

Gentil Coquelicot

"J'ai descendu dans mon jardin
J'ai descendu dans mon jardin
Pour y cueillir du romarin.
Gentil coqu'licot mesdames
Gentil coqu'licot nouveau
Gentil coqu'licot mesdames
Gentil coqu'licot nouveau."

I was quite astounded to find the words to mémère's song on the internet and laughed quite heartily at myself because I had never, ever sung the words correctly nor had their correct meaning. (Can be seen/heard at

Mama Lisa's World online.) For me it was always about "I am coming into the garden now so you'd better go hide, Mr. Snake."

Mémère was a midwife. I know that she delivered my three older siblings and probably many of my cousins and others, too. Her dispensary was over the kitchen, the door on the left of the stairs. It was always locked and I was not allowed to go in, but I did peek in a few times when she would go in. There were three holes in the floor with metal grates covering them. The grates readily opened allowing the heat from the kitchen stoves to rise and warm the room. I saw those holes in the kitchen ceiling, and my oldest sister told me what they were and why they were there. She loved knowing more than me, so I was always able to get her to tell me things. Three small beds were lined up on one wall and two shelves and tables on another wall. After I became a midwife, I understood how perfect that room was for delivering babies. Even though I didn't get to experience that part of her life, I definitely learned it subconsciously through her knowledge. This transgenerational experience allowed me to receive the compliment that I was a "natural born" midwife during my training for midwifery. I credit this ability to my mémère. It saddens me a bit that I didn't get to see her midwifery talent but I do know that she must have been kind, knowledgeable and courageous.

The magic upstairs room was also the store room for her Blair products. I don't remember her delivering babies but I do know about her Blair sales. Blair sold home remedies, pudding and pie mixes, spices and seasonings. Mémère was a successful entrepreneur and helped pépère earn money in the summertime when he stayed home to run the farm. In the winter pépère went into the woods as a lumberjack. This was not his favorite thing to do, but everyone had to earn a living, especially in the winter. Twice a week, mémère and I would load up her wagon with her Blair products and we would set out shortly after noon to sell her goods. One day we would walk south for five to ten miles, stopping by all the rural homes and farms on one side of the street and on the way back stopping at the farms on the other side of the street. Everyone knew her routine so we never crossed the street until we were ready to turn around and come back and then we would do the other side. The next time we went out we would head north doing the same thing. I don't know how much she really sold but she would spend time visiting with everyone, and I would play with the other kids if there were any or just sit around under an apple tree waiting to move on. My job was to pull the wagon. The wagon was always lighter on the return trip. One of Blair's products were these coconut cookies that were about the size of an iPhone today. They were ridged and I just loved to dunk them in some cold milk. After supper on the days that we sold Blair, mémère would give me four of those cookies and I would sit on the front porch with her and pépère and the folks that dropped by and "dunk and eat" to my heart's content!

I was privileged with my own room at mémère's. When you went up the stairs to the second story, the landing was wide and had six doors emptying into the wide center vestibule. The one on the immediate left was the dispensary; the one a little to the right with a window next to it was the door to the third floor dormitory in the attic. The boys had five beds up there; it was quite cozy and had windows on each end and foot lockers at the foot of each bed. I liked it up there but girls were not allowed. My cousin would take me up if no one else was around. The next door to the right of the stairwell was mémère and pépère's room. I used to go in at night with mémère while she got ready for bed. I would sit on her cedar chest at the foot of her bed while she stepped behind her screen and took off her day dress and put on her night dress. Then she would come out and sit in her rocking chair. I would help her remove her socks and shoes. She'd unpin her hair from the bun on the top of her head, brush it and make one long braid to sleep in. When I got a little older, and could handle the hairbrush without tangling her hair, she let me brush it and braid it. She had a special cloth rag (un chiffon) that she braided into the lower portion of the braid in order to be able to tie it closed. It took me so many times to learn to get it right. She was so patient, showing me many nights in a row until finally, one night she said, "Ah! T'as bien fait!" I had done it well and correctly.

The door next to mémère's room was my little room. It was in the eaves of the house and had one little window with the bed under it. There was just enough room for one little dresser and a little wooden chair. I slept the very best in that bed in the window overlooking the apple orchard. All the roofs were tin, and the rainy days, with the drumming of the rain on the roof, became my favorite time to snuggle into my bed with a good book. I was like mémère and would read out loud to my cousins, *The Hardy Boys* and *Nancy Drew Mysteries*.

There were two more doors in the landing both big rooms with two big beds and chiffoniers and chairs. They were used for company and later for the sick relatives that mémère nursed and watched over. Mémère had twelve of her own children that she raised and some nieces and nephews, too. When the farm was built with the help of her and pépère's fathers and brothers, it was filled with children and family and relatives from the beginning until the end of her days.

The front parlor was filled with overstuffed burgundy colored velvet sofas and chairs and had a pedal organ that was played during holidays and funerals. Otherwise the room was closed off except for the yearly visit of the parish priest. Mémère would allow me to go in and play the organ, but I always felt like the room was haunted because I had seen three uncles have their funeral vigils in there and it creeped me out. But it was a gorgeous room as I look back on it. Christmas was celebrated in the parlour and it was the best place to hide when we played hide and seek because everyone was also a bit squeamish about hiding alone in there. It usually had to be two of us together or not at all.

Mémère had many women friends and they would come for tea in the late afternoon before supper. They chatted passionately in French, enjoying each other's company, drinking black tea with cream and sugar and sometimes a little whiskey if there was a need to encourage stamina and bravery for unrelenting circumstances. They gathered around the big kitchen table and giggled and laughed and cried raucously and wept silently and bitterly. It all depended on the circumstances and the company. Mémère always read the tea leaves for her friends if they asked. If they forgot she wouldn't bring it up, but when she was asked, she never said no. The tea leaves foretold many a calamity or a blessing without any undue prejudice. Her friends would come and tell her when she had predicted correctly and incorrectly. There may have some disparaging moments with all the gypsy-like forecasting but mémère never said no. The last summer that I was with her, I asked her to teach me this tea-leaf-reading business. At first she was not inclined to entertain me in such a fashion but I pestered and begged and she finally relented. As it turned out, I had the knack for it and she genuinely praised me albeit she was slightly fearful of what could come of it. She insisted that I never read tea leaves for anyone unless they requested it. I asked her how anyone will ever know that I read the tea leaves then? She giggled in her sweet little way and said, "Oh, ils vont savoir! Ne t'inquiéte pas." She was correct. People have always known.

Mémère's big farm house was a home offering solace and comfort to many, including me. After the funeral mass, everyone trooped into the cemetery and there was much weeping. Then everyone got into their cars and came to the house. I had never seen so many people at one time at the house. The parlour, the tea room, the big kitchen, the front porch, the circular driveway, the back of the house, all filled with men and women and children. Two big tables of foodstuffs, stories being shared, and music—fiddles, harmonicas, guitars and the organ. Mémère's Franco-American family celebrated her life and her passing into heaven. The voices and the music carried me to sleep in my little bedroom upstairs. And I think that maybe I dreamed of her, but maybe not. It could be just wishful thinking that she visited me that night in my dreams. But I do know that I choose only to continue to emulate her. I am my grandmother. I am my mémère.

French Canadian Pride

By Christine Cunningham

Mémère

In September 1911, a gaggle of young children were picking cranberries in Smart's Bog, near South Carver, Massachusetts, when photographer Lewis Wickes Hine approached them. We don't know exactly what Hine said, but my family knows that he talked to our Mémère, Bella Roy of Fall River, Massachusetts, then eleven years old, who wasn't a bit shy in sharing a little history with Hine.

"Been comin' here seven years," Mémère Bella told Hines, a school teacher-turned photographer and documentarian, "Been pickin' since I was five years old," she said in English, spoken with a noticeable French accent. (To view photo one information, see below)

Hine's now renowned black and white photographs of young children are recognized as a pivotal force in strengthening child labor laws in the United States.

At the time, few Yankees were accepting agricultural jobs in New England, so members of the American-French-Canadian community supplied cheap labor to Fall River's agricultural and textile industries, and they routinely straddled between seasonal work in the cranberry bogs and their jobs in cotton mills.

My arrière-grandmère (great-grandmother) Malvina, forty-five years old at the time, had brought Mémère Bella, six-year-old daughter Jeanette, who was just learning to pick, and seven-year-old cousin Anita, who began picking the previous year, to Smart's Bog. The Federal Census of 1910 indicates that Malvina was working as a spinner in a cotton mill. So it's possible she too worked in both the bog and at the mill during the year Hine took their photos. (To view photos information, see endnotes.)

The three girls likely missed out on early childhood play and school once they began to work in the bogs, where the tart, red berries ripen in the months of August and September. We know that Mémère Bella completed only a few grades of school. But children were considered a premium source of labor: historical accounts describe how a twelve-year-old child was capable of picking as many cranberries in a day as a forty-year-old adult, having such slender, nimble fingers.

No matter the age, working in the bogs was hard. Pickers had to kneel on soft, unstable turf, grasping into cloudy water for the small vines. Before 1900, berries were individually picked, but my Mémère Bella used a newer invention, the wooden cranberry scoop. While considered an efficient "ergonomic wonder" at the time, the scoop was far from perfect as a harvesting method because many cranberries remained on the vine to be picked later or left to rot.

Malvina may very well have brought the girls along rather than leave them under someone else's care. But the family struggled on the low wages my arrière-grand-père (great-grandfather) Thomas Roy earned as a weaver in Fall River's cotton mills, and the children's income likely helped support the family.

Thomas had moved from St. Albans, Vermont in 1878, leaving home at age 15 in order to seek employment in a cotton mill in Fall River—then called "Spindle City" because the region produced most of the print cloth in the United States. At its peak, Fall River had more than 120 cotton mills. Like most laborers who arrived in Fall River to work in the mills, Thomas probably rented a room in one of the thousands of wood, triple-decker tenements within walking distance of the mills, and earned an hourly wage somewhere between 60 cents and one dollar per day.

By the time Thomas married Malvina in 1890, he was a seasoned weaver, and she was proficient as a spinner. The city of Fall River was developing its infrastructure—laying sidewalks in the residential areas, oiling the main streets to reduce street dust, running trolley cars to transport residents, and using electric lights to illuminate the streets—accouterments that improved the quality of life for many citizens, depending on the area of town.

Malvina—whose parents were born and raised in Sorel, Quebec—and Thomas—whose parents came to New England from Brome, Quebec—and their children lived on Bowler Street in Fall River, in a neighborhood that the Associated Charities Housing Committee began investigating for poor sanitation and safety concerns. Bowler Street posed a problem, because a city dump at the foot of the street was found to be in poor condition, with garbage and decayed matter sometimes strewn under the windows of the tenement houses. Neighborhood occupants complained as well about the smoke and dust that wafted from the dump.

Fall River's Petit Canada Settlements

The number of French-speaking people in Fall River had increased from 100 families in 1868 to 600 families in 1891. In 1900, the year my Mémère Bella was born, Fall River touted a population of 100,000, of whom 40,000 claimed French Canadian ancestry. The mass migration of French Canadians from Quebec between 1840 and 1930 ensured the development of Petits Canadas settlements in Fall River—which soon boasted a newspaper in the native tongue, Francophone parish churches such as St. Anne's, which Mémère attended, and parish schools such as the all-girls Dominican Academy, where my mother Lorraine Durette attended high school.

These settlements meant, of course, that the Roy family would live in self-segregated neighborhoods over the years on Bowler Street, Orchard Street, Redye Street, Whipple Street, Cottage Street, and Ridge Street, mainly living among others of French Canadian heritage.

Lewis Wickes Hine

In 1904, a group of Progressive Reformers founded the National Child Labor Committee, NCLC, a private advocacy organization that aimed to abolish child labor. The thirty-seven-year-old Hine had left his job as a schoolteacher of botany and nature studies at the Ethical Culture School in New York City, on behalf of NCLC, to take photos of children toiling under adverse conditions in bogs, mills and factories across the country, between the years 1908 and 1924.

Historical documents describe how Hine feared he would raise suspicions among management and therefore used false pretenses to take photos of Mémère Bella and her cousin and sister, and other young workers. With a smile and a few kind words, he quickly established rapport with his subjects and interviewed them on some pretext while carefully scribbling verbatim comments—his hand inside his pocket. Using full frontal poses, Hine's intent was not to produce sentimental propaganda, but to depict the childrens' genuine vulnerability and innocence, and their need for protection. A methodical man, Hine was able to supply documentation of quotes, facts and figures to accompany his photos, which the NCLC eventually presented in public exhibits as well as in a published book called *The Survey.*

"There are two things I wanted to do," Hines explained later. "I wanted to show the things that had to be corrected. [And,] I wanted to show the things that had to be appreciated." When a company tried to treat the children well, Hine would say so. He described his work as "photo interpretation" because he understood that his photos were subjective. He was one of the first photographers in the United States to use photographs as a documentary tool.

Generally, Hine's work provided the Reformers with visual evidence of abuses at the turn of the 20th century. While NCLC was successful in reforming some state labor laws that banned children under the age of fourteen from work and established maximum work hours, effective legislation didn't become law until the New Deal in 1933. In Massachusetts, child labor in the bogs continued until the Fair Labor Standards Act in 1938. And even then, daytime employment of young children went unquestioned for some time after.

Despite the abuses and deplorable conditions for many children who were agricultural workers, Mémère told my cousin Ron that she liked picking cranberries, for it provided a chance to be useful and opportunities to inhale fresh bay air.

The Cotton Mills

Between 1905 and 1921, the cotton mills of Fall River employed 30,000 people in more than one-hundred mills.

We don't know how long Mémère continued seasonal work in the bogs, but census information from the years she was in her late teens indicates that she worked as a speeder tender in a cotton mill, replacing empty fiber bobbins with full bobbins—a position best suited for women because of their smaller, dexterous fingers. She and her female cohorts averaged $7.67 per week.

In 1919, at the age of twenty, Mémère Bella married Joachim Durette, a French Canadian born in St. Gabriel, Quebec, in 1893 or 1894. My pépère also arrived in Fall River at age fifteen to work as a weaver in a cotton mill. One census report listed King Phillips Mill in Fall River as his employer. Although Pépère barely completed a couple of grades in school, he eventually advanced to the position of machinist in the cotton mill and often was called upon to repair malfunctioning looms and other mill equipment, according to my uncles. While never well off, he and Mémère Bella managed to pay their bills and stay clear of debt, which was a source of immense pride for both of them.

Culturally Prideful

Mémère had told her daughter, my mother, the story about Hine's visit to Smart's Bog. My mother, who was born in Fall River in 1922 and is now deceased, passed the story on to my sister Melissa. Mother, who had enlisted in the WAVES during World War II and later attended three years of college on the GI Bill, was proud of the historic photos of her mother and her grandmother Malvina when she first saw them in the book, *Spinner People and Culture in Southeastern Massachusetts*, published in 1984—a gift from Melissa, who has taken considerable time to unfold our family genealogy.

Over the years, conversations with my mother, and my siblings, uncles and cousins have consistently referred to Mémère Bella's pride in her own French Canadian background and Roman Catholic faith. In fact, her excessive self-righteous behavior is central to our family lore.

Bella was twenty-nine years old, with four children, when the Great Depression hit in 1929. Like others, she and Pépère counted pennies, shopped carefully and simply did without in order to get by. According to one of my uncles, the family never relied on "handouts." Although Mémère and Pépère never bought a house of their own, they helped one son buy his home in New Jersey, and another purchase a small cabin on Cape Cod.

Mémère and Pépère had two daughters and three sons. The youngest daughter was born in 1924 but died at the age of two of diphtheria, a highly contagious disease spread person-to-person by coughing, breathing, direct contact or contaminated food. Following baby Therese's death, Mémère Bella experienced what my uncles have called a nervous breakdown and became fearful of germs and obsessive about cleanliness. "She was never the same," my Uncle Pete said.

Mémère had better command of English than my Pépère, and evidently ridiculed his less polished pronunciation of English. Yet French remained her primary language, and she and my mother, who was living on the West Coast by the late 1940s, always spoke in French on the phone and wrote in French in their correspondence with each other. At the same time, Mémère Bella frequently wrote nature poems—many in English—perhaps sensing the poetic form was forgiving of her own rough grammar.

While she evidently was impatient and demanding with easygoing Pépère, she calmly took care of her own father Thomas, who lived with the family for more than a decade after Malvina died in 1938. Mémère Bella made sure she fed the aging man well, supplied him with a daily shot of whiskey, replenished his pipe tobacco, and walked him to his chair on the balcony overlooking Mount Hope Bay, until the end of his life in 1957 at the age of 93, when she lay his body to rest in wake in the parlor.

Healthy pride turned to arrogance during holidays, when she liked to give extended family members the impression that she and Pépère were better off than they actually were. One Christmas, with relatives gathered round, she presented my mother, seven years old at the time, with a beautiful doll that Mom clearly adored. Imagine how crushed my mother was when Mémère Bella took the doll away from her the next day and returned it to the store because the family could ill afford the fancy doll.

Fourteen years later, when my mother stated her intention to marry her Jewish boyfriend, Mémère Bella was angry and embarrassed. With Pépère at her side, they visited the young suitor's home and beseeched his parents to forbid the marriage, and they agreed. To be a French Canadian meant to be a strict Catholic, and that required marrying a Catholic. Mémère never missed Mass. She attended St. Anne Church for novenas. She prayed the Rosary regularly. She sprinkled the house with Holy Water when a storm was looming or sorrow visited the family.

When my mother became engaged to my father, an Irish Catholic, Mémère Bella didn't shy away from expressing her disappointment about the new suitor's ancestral background. As my siblings and I grew older, my mother told us that she felt she could never please her mother. So while the lure of post-World War II opportunity on the West Coast may have been a big draw for my parents, we began to understand that the schism between my mother and grandmother likely prompted her to leave home without regrets.

Mémère Bella would have been pleased that she was the subject of Hine's photos—although she would certainly be astonished that they now are part of the National Child Labor Committee collection on the Library of Congress website and elsewhere across the Internet. But she also would be embarrassed that photos showed her working next to other immigrant groups, such as the Cape Verdeans, who were of Portuguese descent. Sometime in her childhood or early adulthood she developed deep prejudices for most other immigrant groups and people of color. She was known to warn her grandchildren not to walk home from school with children of other nationalities. And sadly, Mémère Bella usually omitted any reference to her own mother Malvina having Iroquois blood.

Throughout most of her eighty-six years of life Mémère Bella was a vain woman who dressed to make an impression, and to camouflage her lower socioeconomic status. Her fashionable hat, gloves, and shoes always complemented her dress. Naturally, she spent an inordinate amount of time getting ready to go anywhere—even the butcher shop or vegetable market. Yes, she loved clothes—both shopping for them and sewing them—and a cousin remembers her taking an hour to try on dozens of hats in the millinery shop.

She was a staunch Democrat. And she also had a lovely alto voice. The family cherished an album recording of Mémère singing the "Star Spangled Banner" on one side, and on the other, "Happy Days Are Here Again," the campaign song for Franklin Delano Roosevelt's successful presidential campaign in 1932. Written in 1929, the song remained for years the Democratic theme song. Despondent in 1952 because Democratic nominee Adlai Stevenson lost the presidential election to Dwight Eisenhower, Mémère was deeply offended when one of her adult sons named his son Dwight. And she phoned everyone in the family to let them know.

Despite her lingering depression and lifelong obsession with germs that followed her youngest daughter's death, Mémère apparently found solace when she visited Cape Cod. Once the sons signed the papers to purchase the cabin on the Cape, Mémère insisted that my then middle-aged Pépère learn how to drive (which also required that Pépère learned how to read and write in English!). Cousins remember their sometime precarious motor trips to the shore, and described Mémère's backseat driving. But they also remember that she would roll down the window as soon as my grandfather's car neared the sea, luxuriating in the fragrance of the salt air and scrub pines. As the bay came into view, she would offer a prayer of gratitude for "the good Earth."

For me, Mémère Bella remains the French Canadian matriarch who engaged her grandchildren in endless rounds of Fish, Old Maid and Crazy Eights, and awarded the winners with pennies or dried fruit or her homemade brownies. Just for us, she would prepare savory pork tourtière and crêpes with a sprinkle of sugar. One time, she and I sat down at the kitchen table to compose a poem about pussy willows, for a class assignment. Evenings, I remember her swaying to Maurice Chevalier songs on our stereo system. And, she and Pépère taught us a bit of French while we all sang Frère Jacques.

I certainly felt that she cared about us, even though she lived across the country. She wrote letters often, in her rough-hewn English, sprinkled with ain'ts and don'cha knows, and youz, and containing photos of her in a new hat or a poem she had composed about the pine trees and beach grasses at the Cape.

Sometimes her sensitivity surprised us. During one visit west, after Pépère died in 1964, she confided that she had apologized to my grandfather on his deathbed for being a less than loving spouse. "Please forgive me," she asked him. She had swallowed her pride in this instance.

Writing about Mémère Bella has shed a brighter light on her persona, which in turn could be generous, creative, fun-loving, prideful, self-centered, and petulant. Some of these characteristics probably were present in the young girl picking berries in the cranberry bogs of Southwestern Massachusetts and likely helped her survive difficult times.

As I look into the framed photograph of eleven-year-old Mémère Bella smiling from my bookshelf, I smile back and conclude that if we descendants are honest, we'll acknowledge that we too have inherited at least a few of her traits, especially her pride, for better or worse. **(See references next page)**

References

Huse, Donna. *Spinner,* Volume III: *People and Culture in Southeastern Massachusetts*. New Bedford, Mass.: Spinner, 1984. Print.

Photographs of the people in this piece can be viewed online, search for by ID number:
from: Albin O. Kuhn Library & Gallery Digital Collections
Id: cdm16629
from: Lewis Hine Collection
To view photo:
1. Bella Roy, said 11 years old. Been comin' here 7 years, been pickin' since I was 5 years old. Lives 44 Bowler St., Fall River. Sister Jeanette said 6 years old beginning to pick now. Also their cousin Anita (on right hand) 7 years old regular picker. Began last year.
Id: hinecoll/id/2639

and from
Library of Congress, Prints & Photographs Reading Room, Prints & Photographs Online Catalog
To view photos:
Annette Roy, the youngest worker. Said 7 years old. Picked last year. Lives 171 Orange Street, Fall River, Mass. Also Napoleon Ruel, 53 Hopkins Street, Fall River, Mass. Said 9 years old. Location: South Carver [vicinity] - Smart's Bog, Massachusetts.
Bella fifth from right, Malvina to her left.
Reproduction Number: LC-DIG-nclc-00128

Group of workers on Smart's Bog. Location: South Carver [vicinity], Massachusetts. Bella 10th from left, smiling into camera.
Reproduction Number: LC-DIG-nclc-00124

Group of Workers on Smart's Bog. Location: South Carver [vicinity], Massachusetts. Malvina in middle, daughter Jeanette on left.
Reproduction Number: LC-DIG-nclc-00125

Mémère

By Lucille (Lucie) Therrien

(Franco-American) This tender little song came to me during an artist-in-residence in Maine, when students and I bridged the gap between three generations, realizing we all had "mémères" (the affectionate name given a Franco-American grandmother) with similar life stories.

French version

1)"Mémère, please tell me, your story again
The one where you worked as a child at the mill."

Mon enfant," she would say "viens t'asseoir près de moi
Laisse-moi te bercer dans mes bras
Et ne pleure surtout pas, quand je parle de la fois
Où j'étais un enfant, employée d'la factrie.
J'étais une fileuse au moulin de coton
Je travaillais toute la journée, au métier à tisser
Pendant de longues heures, partie de la main-d'oeuvre
Avec un foreman, qui guettait c'que je faisais.

2) "Mémère, tell, how you moved to New England,
The farm, that you left in Quebec."

Écoute, ma jolie, nous étions tout petits
Ebahis par la grande industrie
Bâtie dans les grandes villes, des Etats-Unis
Exhilés de la mère patrie.
Le bruit des machines, nous rendait sourds
Nos poumons engorgés, de poussière de laine
Mais on pouvait s'acheter, à la fin de la semaine
Du tissu fabriqué, par les mains de nos ouvriers.

3) "Mémère, tell me again, how you met with pépère
How you wed at at only fifteen."

Ma petite," she'd explain," je l'ai rencontré
A la danse, vers la fin d'la veillée
On nous a présentés à la communauté
De la ville située, autour d'la factrie.
Il était le meilleur des gigueux de la place
Il dansait librement, au son du violon
Après un bon set, il est venu me raconter
Sa vie à l'atelier, d'la factrie, comme lainier.

4) "Mémère, please explain why I talk in English
And you always answer in French"

Tu vois," answered she, "pour parler au patron
Au voisin, au commis voyageur
Il fallut, nous les étrangers, apprendre à communiquer
S'ajuster, être acceptés, dans la société.
Engagés pour notre labeur, on s'assimilait de peur,
De ressortir, par malheur, au milieu de la foule
Mais le soir, à la maison, on sortait le gros chaudron
Pour mijoter les bons mets de nos traditions.
"Mémère, mémère, mémère, tell me again...."

<u>Mémère please tell me that story again</u>
English version

1) Mémère, please tell me, that story again
The one where you worked as a child at the mill

"Mon enfant," she would say, "come and sit by my side
Let me rock you and hold you in my arms
Don't shed a tear, when I speak of the time
When I worked, as a child, at the factory in town.
At the cotton mill, spinning at the wheel
I labored long hours, producing on a line
I sat on a stool,weaving at a loom
With a foreman who watched me, for hours at a time."

2) Mémère, tell, how you moved to New England,
The farm, that, you left in Quebec.

"Écoute, ma jolie, we were all tout petit
Overwhelmed by the great industrie
Built in the large cities, of America
We packed all our bags, and left dear Canada.
The noise of machines, drove us deaf
Our lungs choked from the dust of the wool
We purchased our craft, with the pay we had left
Linen and cotton, hand woven with love."

3) " Mémère," tell me again, how you met with pépère
How you wed at at only fifteen.

"Ah!" she'd explain, "I met him one night
At a dance, toward the end of la veillée
We were introduced to la communauté
Of the town that surrounded the big factrie.
He was the best jigger in the hall
He danced very free, to the violin
After a set, to the voice of a call
He swung me round and I joined in."

4) Mémère, please explain why I talk in English
And you always answer in French.

"Tu vois," answered she, "to talk to the boss
Travelin' salesman, or the neighbors in town
We strangers had to learn, to blend, to adjust
To accept, to fit in, and flow with the crowd
Hired for our skills, assimilating from fear
To hold down our jobs, and feed those so dear
At night, once at home, we cooked and we prayed
We sang a chanson, 'til the supper was made."

Mémère, Mèmé, and Me: Storytelling Grandmothers

By Kristin M. Langellier, Ph.D.

Prelude: In October of 2013 I was invited to give a keynote for the Grand Opening of The Franco-American Collection at the University of Southern Maine, Lewiston-Auburn. I thank James Myall and Maureen Perry for that kind and fun invitation. I gave the talk again in November 2013 at the Franco-American Center of the University of Maine, for which I thank Lisa Michaud. I add heartfelt appreciation to Rhea Côté Robbins for the opportunity to extend its audience in this anthology. The oral presentation has been edited for the written version that follows.

I begin my talk with a quotation by Alain Bérubé, a wonderful historian of Franco-American working-class culture. He writes:

> It's difficult for me to say the word *mé-mère* in public. It was a private Franco-American family word spoken only at home . . . that we always translated as "grandmother" when speaking to outsiders. It was one of a small category of words so charged with power they had to be said in hushed tones, with shame or reverence, or never at all. (1997, p. 50)

Bérubé writes that growing up Franco-American but ashamed to speak French gave him practice in not saying another word so often on the tip of his tongue: homosexuality. He likens the emotional power of these two words to trying to survive as a gay man in a fiercely Anglo and heterosexual world.

Happily, some things have changed to combat shame and discrimination for sexually diverse people. And, too, the word *mémère* can be seen and heard with pride in many public places. Searching Google Images, I found key chains (*Mémère* rules), T-shirts (Property of *Mémère,* Specializing in the Fine Art of Spoiling Grandchildren; got *mémère*?; I get my good looks from my *Mémère*; I Didn't Retire, I'm a Professional *Mémère*); poster art (Don't make me call *Mémère*!); *Mémère* tote bags and tattoos; and selfies with *Mémère* – and many more images.

What I will do in my talk today is to embody the tensive intimacy of being in public with mémère. I am a new *mémère* – our son has a son. My grandson is nine months old and lives with his parents in Biddeford. I am calling myself *Mèmé* (that's how we say it) and I hope that's what he will call me. He doesn't talk yet but he does chortle and shriek.

[Figure 1 My Grandson]

My questions today are: Where will my grandson hear the word *mémère*? What will he understand and feel when he hears "*Mèmé*"? How do we Franco-Americans tell *mémère* stories today? How can I tell mine? And might my grandson tell his? I am not going to be able to offer pat answers to those questions, but I will think through a few things about grandmothers storytelling. And along the way I will be telling a few *mémère* stories, too.

The First Story: Phoebe

So what is a *mémère* story? "A Tribute to Phoebe" by Kimberly J. Cook in 1987 in *Le Forum*, the bilingual publication of the University of Maine, is a good example. It starts this way:

> In 1917, Phoebe Ouellette married Thomas Marin. By 1937, she had carried and delivered eighteen children. After her first child was born the doctor told her she would never be able to have any more children because she nearly bled to death. Two of her eighteen children died shortly after they were born. One son died before he was old enough to marry and have children. Being a devout Catholic she could not practice birth control. One of my aunts asked her one time why she had so many children. Her reply was "Because I didn't want anyone to take my place." Phoebe, my maternal grandmother, was buried on the day before Mother's Day in 1986 and [was] 89 years old. At the time of her death, she had eleven surviving children, 104 grandchildren, 150 great-grandchildren, and several great-great-grandchildren. (Robbins et al., 1995, p. 66)

If my mother were here, she would be saying her signature "oh, my . . ." The sheer numbers — 18, 102, 150, the still-counting great-great-children — the first time and every time I read Phoebe's story I am overwhelmed by the numbers. Phoebe is all the more valiant when the reader finds out next that her husband Thomas died in 1937, leaving her a widow to raise 16 children alone. Talk about a "survivor story"!

I'll say a little more about Phoebe's story, but let me pause to parse what can be called the 'master narrative' of the *mémère*. In the first migration from France, she is the heroic mother who speaks the mother tongue of French and produces children for the motherland (Canada) to champion *la survivance*. In the second migration to the United States, the *mémère* story chronicles a Franco-American woman's birth, usually in Canada; childhood; moves to the United States and sometimes back home; work at home and in mills, factories, and farms; courting, marriage, and children; widowhood and old age, like Phoebe at 89.

In my research on the *mémère* stories published in *Le Forum* from 1977 - 1994 I identified five predictable motifs of the storytelling (Langellier, 2002) that tell us about the Franco-American world: (1) **heroic fecundity:** very large families that show the spectacular success of "the revenge of the cradles" (*la revanche des berceaux*) that doubled the population of French in North America every two decades from the 18th to the 20th century; (2) **chez nous:** making home and homeplaces as French cultural identity; kitchens and porches as symbols of *mémères*; (3) **family times and foods:** *dimanches chez mémère; visites* and house parties; *galettes, crêpes* and *ploys; tourtières* and *soupe aux pois*; (4) **hard work**: kinwork to raise children; food work and housework; farm work and work for wages in mills and factories (*on travaillait dur ce monde la*). (5) **language and religion**: social life centered around family, church, and parochial schools to bind French with Catholicism (*qui perd la langue perd la foi,* even as Anglicisms creep in and crowd out French).

Through these motifs, the *mémère* becomes a centralizing and compelling figure of Franco-American identity. She communicates pride, perseverance, courage, suffering, and sacrifice. *Mémères* in these stories 'do' and 'make do' – they do what has to be done to keep the family and culture going. *Mémère* stories like Phoebe's are indeed a genre of tribute. They not only *embody* Franco-American values but also *enchant* the Franco-American family as *Mémère* comes to symbolize the most French of the French, the most folk of the folk, and the most mythologized of the mothers. In this public story, mothers held the key to the survival of culture, religion, morality, language, and family, and "if they stopped behaving in the prescribed manner, if they ceased to embody all the ideal characterizations not only of French Canada but of humanity itself, they would bring down the social order in ruin about their heads" (Bouliane in Robbins et al, 1995, p. 10)

When I read this quotation, I always want to whisper "wow" and also "ow." Stories like Phoebe's show the enormous cultural power of *mémère* storytelling to anchor family and identity through difficult times. That's the "wow" whisper. At the same time, *mémère* stories ask them to carry a heavy load to be 'good' *mémères*, and that's the "ow" whisper. For there is a cost to perform the hard life of this ideal. Phoebe's granddaughter writes, "As I grew up, especially after I became a mother, I realized how terribly difficult life must have been for Phoebe. Life is hard enough now in the 1980s as a single parent with one or two children" (p. 66). There is also a price to those who do not conform to the gendered norms that underlie this iconic image. I think of Bérubé not being able to utter in public his gay identity (Michael Michaud is the more current example) and of all the women who for whatever reason are childless (but may become *mémères* nonetheless). Myths can lop off the existence of all the other *mémères*, including 'bad' *mémères*. And myths can also miss the *ordinary mémères:* like those who "made [their] way through joy and loss and prayer and pain not as an icon but as a *human*" (Edelman, 1999, p. 253).

I note, finally, that published, public stories about *mémères* circulate outside the family and are rarely written in *mémères*' own voices. We hear Phoebe speak a single line in the story above, "because I did not want anyone to take my place." What depths of meaning lie within this single phrase, in what it says and does not say? Equally important, we hear the granddaughter's voice, poignant and probing, constantly in touch with being the youngest daughter of the youngest daughter of Phoebe's eighteen children. Cook writes, "as my feminist consciousness grew, so did my realization that if these strong women had not suffered the oppression of the Catholic patriarchy I would not exist today" and "I wonder how much of 'me' has been based on my desire to make it all 'worthwhile' for them: my mother, and both my grandmothers, as well as the others in between." In honoring Phoebe and in herself becoming a mother, the granddaughter attunes emotionally to the weight of the *mémère* model as well as asking how it shapes and fits her experiences today.

The Second Story: *Maman*/Mom and Me

How am I, a daughter and granddaughter, telling a *mémère* story? I wrote this next story in 2002, about the same time I was studying *mémère* stories in *Le Forum*.

> *I was thirteen when my mother was pregnant – again – with the baby who would unsettle the symmetry of my profound place in the middle: I had three older brothers and three younger brothers, one older sister and one younger sister. But then two younger sisters – and baby makes ten: the Langellier*

tribe, clan, family. Someone at school, in one of those clusters of kids, a boy, said, "geez, Kris, don't your parents know about birth control." It got a laugh and I got red-faced, fell silent, felt the embarrassments of adolescence. More than by anything else, I have felt defined by my big family, a family size I interpreted in terms of our Roman Catholicism. But not yet in terms of my ethnicity, of being a French *Catholic family in an area of French Canadian immigrants, the towns in Illinois like Bourbonnais, Kankakee, and St. Anne that formed the Little Canadas (*Les Petits Canadas*) of the Midwest for families like mine.*

[Figure 2: Mother and Me]

After my father died I decided to get some of my mother's stories on tape, something I regretfully did not do enough of with my dad. In asking her to tell some family stories, she narrated scenes from her childhood, stories of her parents, fragments of French, Depression stories, grade school, work at 13, marriage, children, and, in her 50s, a GED and degree to work as a licensed practical nurse. My mother said, "We were all one thing," – meaning Catholic. And about her ten children she said, "you know I loved babies and it never bothered me to have another. We always made room." (In our little farmhouse it was one bedroom for the boys, one bedroom for the girls). When others began what she calls "limiting their families," she said: "I just didn't do that. I tried it, and I always felt guilty." Then a little laugh. "It didn't take with me." And I thought, is that it? Is that all? Two or three short sentences about all ten of us? About her life as mother of ten? I was searching for more and maybe also for myself among the multitude, the magnitude of this family. (Langellier, 2002, p. 56)

I ended my storytelling there, and now I can reflect on it from here. I notice that in my story my mother speaks just a few short sentences, something I never noticed before. I also observe some *mémère* motifs but with a difference from those in Maine: language and religion were not so tightly coupled in the Midwest. I think of this as how we got the Roman Catholic part of identity but not so much the French part. In fact there was actually no word *Mémère/Mèmé* in my family — just Grandma Provost (maternal side) and Grandma Langellier (paternal side). And so I always say 'I never knew I was I was French until I came to Maine" and starting getting 'it' – the Franco thing (Langellier, 2004). I reflect, too, that I'm the one who's added the French words and expressions to this talk, language I heard very little of in my family but language I've edged towards in Maine.

I am also noticing how these two stories about my mother are inflected with my desires and concerns, things like adolescent embarrassment, feminist questions about my mother's "heroic fecundity," and my own search for identity. We heard this in Phoebe's granddaughter's storytelling, too. Bruce Jackson writes that stories we retell for family celebrations like reunions and weddings and funerals, whether they are in embellished or brief form, "are true stories, all right, but they're at least as much our regard for the family now as they are a report of what happened then" (Jackson, 2007, p. 36). So, in the motherline, we make and tell our *mémère* stories about the past from the present, and they may be more a story of how we are now than of how we were then. I tell my mother's and my *mémère's* stories and my own. My mother tells me her mother's stories and her own.

The Third Story: Grandma (*Mémère*) and Mom (*Maman*)

The next stories I call the "canning stories," and they were told to me by my mother when I asked for her stories in 1997. She was 77 and I was 47. By contrast to the written stories you've heard so far here, these are oral stories from audio tapes. I transcribed them here to suggest the sound and rhythms as my mother told her stories, how she grouped phrases and paused and paced the telling, as well as how I listened with empathy, laughter, and questions. And so the canning stories are in my mother's own words as we talked one day in rural Illinois under the shade of the maple tree in the yard.

The first canning story is my mother's story about her mother, and it begins with her signature saying "oh, my . . . "

Oh, my.
And we had-

we always said we had some meager years,
but we were never hungry or anything like that.
We had a garden.
Now people in those Depression years,
many people were suffering.
And the people down South,
they didn't have anything, you know.
Remember when Roosevelt came in and saved them.
What a president.
And Mrs. Roosevelt, she went to visit them personally.

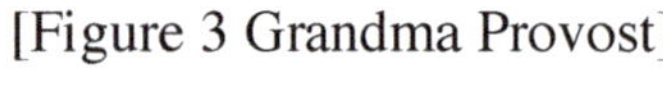

[Figure 3 Grandma Provost]

I pause the story to notice how my mother is telling it. She is talking from and describing a particular historical moment in the United States, the Great Depression, to situate this story about her mother, adding details of those times. Like my stories above, Mom is telling it from her perspective as a daughter and young child at the time. And it's always good to remember that she is telling the story to me, her daughter. Before I continue with the story, I want to show you Grandma Provost. Provost was her married name, and her birth name was Bouchard.

My mother calls her mother Momma, as you'll hear, and I always imagine this as the French Maman and so that's how I've written it here. Grandma and Grandpa Provost both spoke French although not to us grandchildren. My mother told me that they learned their prayers in French but otherwise her parents spoke it at home only when they didn't want the children to know what they were saying.

And so during those years, of course, Maman always canned everything.
And one day I remember she was especially tired
and she was canning tomatoes.
And she had one leg with bad varicose veins,
and she was sitting down
sealing her jars.
And one broke open,
and her leg got all burned.
Fell right in her lap,
all that hot tomatoes.
Uh huh.

I'm taking another pause to notice how my mother is telling this story about her mother. Her *mémère* story includes Franco-American motifs I outlined above: there's a mother with a big family, there's the hard work to feed them all in hard times, and there's the homeplace with the garden. As my mother tells this story, you might also notice that she positions her mother as a hero of sorts: her "*Maman* [who] always canned everything" is juxtaposed to Roosevelt and to Mrs. Roosevelt who saved the people suffering down South during the Depression years. She implies that by gardening and "canning everything," our family was saved, too, because they "never were hungry or anything like that."

The first brief event about canning tomatoes appeals to my empathy and emotions, and now to yours as you read. My mother's telling draws out these italicized words: "she was especially *tired*," she had "*bad* varicose veins," and "her leg got *all burned*" to create a sense of the difficulties Grandma experienced. To me, my mother's simple, evaluative "uh huh" at the end operates like the French-Canadian ethic to be tough, along with the Midwest farm ethic where stoicism in the face of physical labor and pain is ordinary. So this little story about daily life remembers my mother's mother to herself and to me; and in her own way my mother makes her mother heroic. In sparse and understated details, she renders Grandma Provost's world.

And, as happens in storytelling in daily life, telling this story leads my mother to remember another story about canning tomatoes. In this next one you'll also hear about Dorene, the closest of my mother's three sisters. And it may also be helpful to know that in Illinois we used corn cobs in our stoves for heating and cooking.

Another time she was canning tomatoes
and we had a little shed with a cobshed,
you know, on the place.
And she had us take the basket
and go out so her stuff would continue cooking.
And so we decided we'd count the cobs in that basket
Aunt Dorene and I. (Mother laughs)
So, of course, it took us way longer than it should have! (I join in her laughing here)
She came out to see what was happening.
Her tomatoes weren't cooking! (we both continue laughing)
That was funny.

I pause the storytelling again to notice that this second canning story is my mother's own story as a daughter—it's about my mother as little girl. Again it is a domestic scene of women's work, and Grandma Provost asks my mother and Dorene to replenish the cobs. As you see, they get distracted from their task – and I can just see those little girls counting all the cobs in the basket until Grandma Provost comes out check on them because her canning has come to a standstill. I have heard this story before, and I join my mother's laughter through the rest of it. I think about the few other stories my mother tells about herself as a daughter, and I realize that this episode – counting cobs in the cob shed — is as bad as her childhood behavior gets! I recall a passage in Nancy Miller's memoir about her parents: "I'm keeping myself alive as a child. I'm still asking myself the questions I can't answer, and especially one that haunts me: Was I a good-enough daughter?" (1996, p. 171). I wonder, does my mother ask this question. Do I?

I've been reminding you that my mother is telling me stories about her mother as I am telling you stories about my mother. And so this second canning story ends with what so often happens in storytelling: the listener asks a question: I ask, "how old were you, Mom?" She says:

Oh, pretty little, eight, nine, I suppose.
Oh, dear what you don't remember.

My mother's closing coda to this story, "Oh, dear, what you don't remember" – I love its ambiguity. She may be saying what you *do* remember as you tell *mémère* stories — but there's that negative in there, too. (It could be French, *n'est-ce pas*?) Her telling embodies this delicate question—what mothers do and do not remember—as they narrate to their daughters; and what daughters do and do not remember as they narrate their mothers' lives. And as all of us in the motherline tell *mémère* stories.

Hope Edelman (1999) captures this tension about telling stories in her book *Mother of My Mother* when she writes:

> [My daughter] will grow up knowing my grandmother only through stories she hears, which is just another way of saying she'll know her mostly through the stories I tell. Choose to tell. Already I feel the impulse to censor myself in her presence, to share with her only the narratives that portray the women in my family as heroines, as anchors, as champions of the fold. (p. 12).

So I think again of the mythic *mémères*. And as I think about storytelling in the motherline of *mémère, maman*, and me, I wonder, too, how we embody different generations at the same time in storytelling. Think about a photograph of your mother and yourself as you read this next quotation, imagining each variation: "she is a child and I am her mother; she is me and I am my mother; she is my mother and I am my grandmother" (Edelman, 1999, p. 254). And now I ask, when my mother tells her mother's story of the broken canning jar with understated emotion but enormous empathy, is she Grandma Provost? Is she my mother? Is she herself as a child? When she tells the story of counting the cobs, is she daughter or mother or grandmother? All three generations? When storytelling in the motherline, who is speaking and who is listening?

The Fourth Story: *Mèmé* and Me

Who are we as tell *mémère* stories? How do I tell my stories as one of ten children, mother of one, and *Mèmé* to one (at least so far)? When I tell my grandmothers, my mothers, and my own stories, who am I? How are we speaking for our *mémères*, for our mothers, and for ourselves? How do I be a *Mèmé* today, in this historical moment? Is there a 'me' in *Mèmé*? As my mother would say – and I say now, too – "oh, my."

The legacy of *mémère* stories are both public and intimate, cultural and emotional. *Mémère* stories appear to be nostalgic for a more traditional past, one we might imagine as more family-centered, with more clearly demarked roles for women and men, in a more religious and less materialistic society, and with a less assimilated French identity. But at the same time they embody an emotionally complex negotiation between generations about the changing histories of gender roles and cultural identities. How *does* a feminist daughter tell her mother's and *mémère's* story alongside her own? As I hope I have suggested above, telling *mémère* stories about intertwined but different lives is a delicate project. The cultural work that *mémère* stories do has a different goal and a different audience than telling stories within the motherline has; and yet they profoundly form and inform each other, depend on and define one another. As the terms of telling shift and as the conditions of the story change, *mémère* stories move and they move us in more than one way.

Right now I am remembering when I was in my 30s and pregnant with my son. I was pleased but also confused by the attention and approval that was showered upon me. And I came to understood that this affirmation had been withheld from me until then. This experience has been called "the mirroring of maternal approval that leads a daughter to want to reproduce" (Shulman, 1999, p. 86). And now I am a *mémère* and I think it's showering approval again.

I recall this quotation: "I used to think the world was divided between those who have children and those who don't; now I think it divides between those who have lost a parent and those whose parents are still alive" (Blake Morrison, quoted in Miller, 1996, p. 18). This reminds me of another story about my mother. As I tell it at this moment, I'd like you to know that my mother is 93 years old now. Memory loss keeps her from telling stories about her mother and childhood; but she asks for our daily stories, over and over. She's still living at home with full-time care by one or the other of us children or grandchildren — the payoff, finally, of having ten kids! And she's still going pretty strong, "I'm a tough old bird," she often tells us. My telling here expands a written version (Langellier, 2002):

> *It was one of those times I was home from Maine for Christmas. My brother Kevin is in this story, too, because Mom had asked us to go with her to the Martinton cemetery. Our brother Craig is buried there, and she and Dad had gotten a family headstone and that's what she wanted to show us. I can't say I was looking forward to this, but we said we'd go because she asked us to.*
>
> *I took two photos that day (the stamp date shows as December 29, 1995). The first photo has Mom in it, walking in the cemetery. You can see white patches of snow around the frozen grass. The fields behind the cemetery are bare and flat and wide in that Illinois way, and there are no leaves on the bleak, black trees. Mom is wearing a warm coat and gloves but no hat. And I can't say this for sure, but it looks like she's been picking up sticks from the cemetery grass, just like she tidies the lawn on every walk in the yard.*
>
> *The family headstone I was seeing for the first time is ordinary enough, a low rectangular gray granite with LANGELLIER carved in the center, Dad's and her names and birth dates below. I think that day I may have murmured, a little miserably, something like, "It's very nice, Mom."*
>
> *And then Mom is beckoning me to come around the back of it, with that little queenly wave she sometimes gives, and then she is pointing. Inscribed on the back of the headstone were all our first names, the ten children, two columns, five names in each: Lawrence, Dennis, Joan, Craig, Kristin, Celeste, Kevin, Keith, Darryl, Colette. That's what's in the second photo.*
>
> *I don't tell this as just a sad story because of what Mom said next, because she rushes to say, "You don't have to be buried here. But I just wanted your names there."*
>
> *And then there's this pause, it's pretty long, and she adds, "One dollar for each letter. Sixty dollars. Not bad."*

[Figure 4 The Family Headstone]

As I think about this story, I wonder: what do family stories of the past give us for the future when we must live without our mothers as we are living now without our grandmothers? How can we tell our Franco-American grandmothers' stories without turning them into myths or martyrs? How are our *mémères* human and diverse? I understand that as we make our *mémère* stories we are making each other. I recall the French feminist writer Annie Ernaux here: "I believe I am writing about my mother because it is my turn to bring her into the world" (1990, p. 32). And I consider again that when I as a daughter tell my *mémère* stories and make my own *Mèmé* stories I am keeping myself alive as a child and still asking myself the questions I can't answer. For storytelling grandmothers, I take guidance from Della Pollock, who writes:

> A story is not a story until it's told, and it's not told until it's heard. And once it's heard it changes and is open to the beauty and frailty of more change. Indeed, until *it* changes or until it changes *someone else*, until it becomes part of the vital histories of change it recounts. (2006, p. 93)

The Fifth Story: *Mèmé* and My Grandson

Mémère stories have to survive histories of change; and they have to change to survive. We imagine and re-imagine *mémères* in every generation. My last little story is itself imaginary – at least it hasn't happened yet. You may already have heard a version of it (Langellier, 2004). It's a scene in an elementary school classroom in Maine. The teacher says to the children, "Raise your hand if you are Franco-American." No one raises a hand. She tries again: "Who has French names in their family?" Still nothing or perhaps a hand or two. And once more she tries: "How many in here have a *mémère* or *Mèmé*?" And the hands go up. I see my grandson's hand go up, too.

Coda: Since I gave this presentation in 2013, my grandson has begun to talk, chatter, and generally carry on conversations with the world. He calls me *Mèmé* and my husband *Pèpé* with persistence and joy. My beloved mother Lenore passed away on August 22, 2014, at age 94. I told some of these *mémère* stories at her funeral Mass.

[Figure 5 My Grandson]

References

Bérubé, A. (1997). "Intellectual desire." In S. Raffo (Ed.), *Queerly classed* (pp. 43 – 66). Boston, MA: South End Press.

Bouliane, G. R. (1995). "Variations on a theme: The image of the mother in traditional French Canadian history." In R.C. Robbins, et al. (pp. 10 – 12).

Edelman, H. (1999). *Mother of My Mother: The Intricate Bond Between Generations*. New York: Delta.

Cook, K. J. (1995). "A tribute to Phoebe." In R.C. Robbins, et al. (p. 66).

Ernaux, A. (1990). *A woman's story*. Trans. T. Leslie. London & New York: Quartet Books.

Jackson, B. (2007). *The Story Is True: The Art and Meaning of Telling Stories*. Philadelphia, PA: Temple University Press.

Langellier, K. M. (2002). "Performing family stories, performing cultural identity: Franco-American mémère stories." *Communication Studies* 53(1), 56 – 73.

Langellier, K. M. (2004). "Where I come from is where I want to be": Communicating Franco-American ethnicity. In M. Fong & R. Chuang (Eds.), *Communicating Ethnicitiy and Cultural Identitiy* (pp. 297-312). Lanham, MD: Rowman and Littlefield.

Miller, N. K. (1996). *Bequest and betrayal: Memoirs of a parent's death*. New York: Oxford.

Pollock, D. (2006). "Memory, remembering, and histories of change." In D.S. Madison & J. Hamera (Eds.,), *The Sage Handbook of Performance Studies* (pp. 87 – 105). Thousand Oaks, CA: Sage.

Robbins, R. C., Petrie, L. L., Langellier, K. M., & Slott, K. (Eds.), *I am Franco-American and proud of it/je suis franco-américaine et fiére de l'être*. Unpublished manuscript, University of Maine, Orono.

Shulman, A.K. (1999). *A Good Enough Daughter: A Memoir*. New York: Schocken.

Colors

Mother taught her to be the glitter pink of rescued princesses,
the aquas of mermaid waters and magical seas.

She added the white of divine brilliance and unstained souls.
Then, subdued blue, because
as the song goes,
when you cry,
you cry alone
because
as the world goes,
crying in public is dangerous for a woman.

Mother wanted her to be steel –
hard, cold, sturdy,
because she wouldn't always be there
to protect her.

But not red.

Red in the Anglo world,
what mother sometimes called 'society,'
that world
did not like bigshots or angry girls
or ones
who showed their shame
at being
girls.

She listened well and glowed
pastels of rose and green
and white

but steel eluded her

Mother had forgotten:
steel must be tempered.

By Ann G. Forcier

Ora's Birthday

On this remnant of a summer day
as rain falls
as rain fell
on you
passing,
I am reminded of words you did etch in stone:

"I do not sleep."
"I am not here."
"I am the gentle autumn rain."

I still miss the good parts,
still want the untold stories,
still wish this thinning veil
between our worlds
thinned to nothing

so that I could come
again to your kitchen table,
watch the steam of a morning coffee fill your face
as you, in morning prayer,
watch your birds eat the crusts
you've saved them.

By Ann G. Forcier

Salvations

In a time of contemplation
in the time of Equinox and asters,
before the maple layer,
branches too burdened by the fruition of spring,
shed the weight of future lives.

Like surf clams dashed against beach rocks by hungry gulls,
the shells of white and black and pin oak seeds
lay whole, split, and shattered on
shore and grass
while
a silence of sparkles beneath the Acorn moon
remembered sunlight.

Perhaps it was on such a day that
Druids worshipped these woodland mothers,
these Thanksgivings of chipmunks,
these givers of sturdy board and shade.

Perhaps.

But on this day of contemplation,
in this time of long nights and hard cider
after the maple layer
after the acorns are gathered and buried,
your words are the cache
that saves our lives in the barrens
between remembering and renewal.

By Ann G. Forcier

Mill Song

My mother was a shuttle girl
pulling threads back and forth,
up and down,
creating cloth for others' profit.

Day after day, she worked
weaving threads for men to sell,
threads of cotton picked by sold men's sons.

She yearned for schooling missed,
calling it 'education.'

She prayed for strong daughters
while her fingers made bolts.

Down the loom she traveled,
a drop-wire girl
waiting
for threads to break

holding

tight the fray
while others wove the patterns.

By Ann G. Forcier

E

By Ann Marie Staples

Elle avait fait une liste quelconque sur laquelle j'avais vu ce matin-là pour la centième fois mon nom mal épelé. J'expliquais mon impolitesse.

- Y en a pas. On épelle ça A majuscule, N, N. Y a pas d'E. Y a pas d'E, pas de tiret non plus entre Ann et Marie. C'est juste A majuscule, N, N, espace, M majuscule, A, R, I, E. C'est tout. Ann Marie, un prénom en deux mots.

- Mais, Anne a toujours un E à la fin.

- Pas l'mien. Y en a pas. J'suis américaine. Y a pas d'E.

- Bien, si tu le prononces < Anne-Marie >, il ne faut pas corriger ceux qui l'épellent comme tu le prononces. C'est pas gentil. Ça donne une mauvaise impression aux gens de les corriger comme ça.

- Ça, je m'excuse. Mais tout de même, y a pas d'E. Pi' y'a pas de Z dans le nom de ma petite soeur. On épelle ça S majuscule, U, S, A, N. Pas de Z, pas d'E non plus. On est américaines.

- Vous comprenez pourquoi les gens épellent vos noms en français?

- Ben, oui. On les prononce en français quand on parle français, mais on est américaines. Y a pas d'E extra.

- Je vais téléphoner à ta mère ce soir. Il faut régler ce problème de corriger les gens tout le temps.

- Oui, ma Soeur, mais c'était son idée de nous donner ces noms-là. 'A voulait qu'on puisse bien se débrouiller partout dans l'monde. J'vais lui dire que vous allez l'appeler.

- Vas donc retrouver tes amies dans la cour avant la cloche.

- Oui, merci, ma Soeur.

Then :

- What took you so long?

- I got in trouble, again, for telling her how to spell my name right.

- They're adding E's and hyphens, again? Did you get to the part where Marie isn't your middle name?

- Nah, I'll let my mother explain that. I don't really care how they spell it. It just bugs my mother 'cause she knocked herself out figuring out names that fit in any language. She wanted all our relatives to be able say them in French.

Plus tard :

- Ma-a-a! I'm home!

- I'm upstairs putting clothes away. You'll have to come up.

- Ma, Sister Virgili's gonna call you up tonight 'cause I told her my name was Ann without E.

- J'comprends pas pourquoi on peut pas laisser tomber les E. She's just stuck in the old ways, I guess. Okay, I'll talk to her.

- Can I go over to Aunt Blandine's to play my Chubby Checker record?

- Ôké, mais juste une demi-heure parce que le souper est presque fini pi' ton père arrive bientôt.

Enfin :

- Matante Blandine, j'peux jouer mon record?

- Ô, la p'tite Henne-Meurrie! T'as passé une bonne journée à l'école? Où est Sou-Zenne?

Anyway, we let Ma have an E for Effort.

Franco-American Mother-Daughter Relationships

By Barbara Ouellette Ouellette

My mother, Meledore Ouellette, passed away July 3, 2014 at the age of ninety-nine. She always said she was one-hundred, but when reminded she was ninety-five or ninety-six, whatever she happened to be at the time, she would reply, "I'm almost one-hundred." We couldn't argue that fact with her.

My mother and I had a tumultuous relationship, but in the last years of her life we seemed to be happy with each other. My mother taught me many life lessons. I cherish those lessons and skills. One of the skills she passed on to me, which her mother passed on to her, was the love of sewing; any kind of sewing, whether it was embroidery, quilting, or even braiding rugs. My mother and I took a rug braiding course together, she was so good at it. I was not sure if I liked it or not, but went because it was time well spent together. The best time I spent with her was when I decided I needed to make a quilt. The quilt pattern was a favorite of all the Franco-American women on French Island, Sunbonnet Sue. My Mémè died when I was five and my older sister, Theresa, was sixteen. Mémè had a Sunbonnet Sue quilt that wasn't quite finished (I get that from her too), and my Pépè took it to the "ladies" on French Island and they finished it. My sister, Theresa, inherited it because she was older, and at five I certainly wouldn't have appreciated it. But, as I got older, I coveted that quilt. I wanted it!!!! So, I asked my mother if she would make the quilt with me. First thing I needed to do was ask my sister if we could borrow the quilt so I could make a pattern from it. Fortunately, she agreed, and I had the original quilt in my possession for many months.

We spent many winter nights, me cutting out the blocks, and the piece of Sunbonnet Sue. My mother called the quilt Bonne Femme. Most of the quilt is made of scrap material that both my mother and I had, just like Mémè had done. We looked for fabrics that were the same colors as the original quilt. At one point we were going through the fabrics, and I looked at my mother. She was just sitting there, probably lost in thoughts of her mother. I said, "What are you doing?" She giggled just like a little girl and said "nothing." We both laughed, and continued with our work. Once the fabrics were selected, we began the process of cutting out each of the little Bonne Femme dresses, hat, shoes, laid out the pieces on the quilt blocks, and my mother embroidered around each of the pieces.

I do cherish those times with her, and even more so since she has passed on to her next life. I have the quilt now, and my sister has hers. My Mémè's name was Demerise, and I have a niece and a great niece who has been given that name as their middle names. I'm planning on passing my quilt down to my niece Jessica Demerise, and I'm hoping against all hope that my sister will pass the original Bonne Femme quilt to my great niece, her granddaughter, Alexa Demerise. How fitting for those two women to have the ownership of those quilts.

I kept a journal as we were making this quilt. Here is an excerpt from the journal that summarizes the time I spent with my mother, and also my Mémè (in spirit):

"It amazes me how many pieces of our lives are going into this quilt, it is thrilling. I will treasure this quilt always. I am already treasuring the time spent with Mama making it. I'm treasuring the things I'm learning about myself, Mémè and Mama. How we are more alike than I ever thought."

Theresa, Mama, me and Deborah (sisters) with the quilt that was made to replicate my Mémè's.

Mama doing the embroidery.

Block in progress.

En Dedans De Mon Sang, C'est Toi

"Maman, who do you come from?"
She glanced down at me, over the side
of her ironing board. "Comment?"
"Papa, he told me you and your ten brothers
came to Maine from Montmagny, Québec
by train, and he said your grandpapa was a
Scottish bootleg who swore he would marry
a pug-nosed aristicrit the moment he spotted her
walking up the gangplank of his tall ship.

Was your grandmaman the pug-nosed aristicrit?"
Maman kept her iron moving, the corners
of her lips dimpling. She chuckled, then said,
"Aristocrat, ma belle—oui, c'était elle.
But I would not mention your Papa's tale
of bootlegging in front of the curé, tonight."
I nodded, wondering why monsieur le curé
would not enjoy hearing about her Grandpapa's
boot leg, which must be better than a wooden leg,
I thought. I eyed her apron, spying smudges
of the tourtières she'd baked for tonight's réveillon.

"So, is that who you come from, Maman?" I asked, then
quickly added, "Were you raised on pea soup, salt pork
and crêpes, a pinch of the belt and a heaping fear
of le bon Dieu?" Maman shook her head. "Hein, Papa
and his stories." She carried her iron to our kerosene stove,
and laid it on its heating plate, as I yanked a comb over
my rag doll's yarn hair. More questions brewing in my head.

"Did your papa have only a few coins jingling in his pockets,
when he herded you, your maman, and your ten brothers here,
Maman?—that's what Papa told me." I paused to lay my doll
beside me on the linoleum. "He said your papa came looking
for streets of gold but there was only cotton dust when he set foot
on Lewiston's cobblestones," I absentmindedly continued, mumbling,
"I never saw no gold or cotton dust on the streets." Maman snorted.
She tested her iron's heat, then walked back to the ironing board
where she picked one of Papa's shirts from the basket and sprinkled
water and starch all over it, rolled it up and grabbed another, and another,
before saying, "My parents came with nothing, hoping for
a life without dried fields and back-breaking farming.
My mother, that beautiful aristocrat, found that dream
for all of us. She found a way to set up a small dress shop
that grew and grew, because of her talent and flair, to
what feeds us all today. And my father, the poor
farmer, managed it with skills he'd never realized he had."

(Continued on next page)

I crossed my seven year old arms, and said, "Now I know who and where I come from, Maman." She smiled down at me, and said, "Tien, c'est bien, ma belle … and from where is that?" Feeling grownup, I said, "I come from bootleggers and aristicrits who came here with no money and worked hard so I could eat good food and get Christmas presents from le bonhomme Santa Clause." I took a breath, then continued. "And I come from the weave room of the Continental Mill."

Maman stopped ironing. And I added, "Papa said he fell in love with you, when you dropped your snuff box and he scooped it up and handed it to you. He said that's when I was born." Maman's iron slid across Papa's white Sunday shirt. She chuckled, then said, "Hein, ton Papa est dans toi sûrement … Be sure, ma 'tite, to add our marriage, the year before you were born, to this tale you whisper, in secret, to monsieur le curé, tonight."

By Cecile Poulin

Three Generations of Franco-American Women

Three Generations of Franco-American Women; Seated: My daughter Celine Day, my mom Rachael Giguere Cote and my daughter Rebecca Day. Standing in the back; myself, Lisa Cote Day and my daughter Rita Daniels.

In the background: my way of keeping the heritage and pride alive. Portraits of parents, grandparents, great-grandparents and great aunts and uncles of days gone by and the present.

—Lisa Cote Day

"Maddie Finds the Magic"

From "The Blue Dress" unpublished novel by Donna Hébert

At three, Simone's landlady Antoinette climbed the stairs and knocked, inviting them to meet her nephews. *"Et amener nos* instruments."

Leaving a note for the still-napping men, the women walked two flights down, entering a kitchen bursting with people and noise. Maddie met two young couples, one with a baby girl about Robert's age, the other with two of the most adorable dogs she'd ever seen, little foxy golden things with fluffy tails. They were making most of the racket, one turning cartwheels in the air like a circus dog. Both yapped constantly, but they settled down as everyone was greeted and found a place to stand or sit.

Simone and Nana ran back up and returned with four folding card chairs. "We'll ask the men to bring the rest down later," Nana said, slightly out of breath, as the dogs gave her the full greeting a second time.

Antoinette fed her nephews, Paul and Emil, while Emil's new wife, mother to the dogs, took them for a walk. Paul's wife brought the baby upstairs to the second floor and the house fell silent for a moment.

Yappy as they were, Antoinette liked the dogs. She'd never allowed her sons to have pets when they were children and she wished now that she'd given them a dog or a cat or even a fast car, anything that would have made their short lives more colorful, given them more joy.

She and Simone talked about the war one night while Simone's clothes dried and they waged their continuing battle over the cribbage board. They were frank with each other, like women of the same generation, though thirty years separated their ages. Simone shared things with Antoinette that she omitted from her weekly letter to her mother.

Simone and her mother still danced around the topic of marital status, but Antoinette knew why Simone remained single and never prodded her toward marriage. Like her sons, many good young men never came home The choices left to a woman in her thirties were the odd bachelor (and some were very odd, indeed!), the heartbroken widower with equally heartbroken and/or unspeakable children, or the rake. Slim pickings.

Even her brother came home different, Simone said. "Such a sweet boy growing up, outgoing, always looking after me at school, constantly cracking jokes. Since the war, he doesn't talk or joke much and seems happiest with his buddies at the Legion. A lot of boys didn't come home at all, like yours, God rest them both, but even the ones who did, well, they don't talk about it. You don't just pick up where you left off."

Antoinette had agreed, taking more cards. The war was long over, her grief a familiar companion. While it never disappeared, the sting lessened enough to allow her to philosophize.

"La guerre is the closest we come to *l'enfer ici*. It's the biggest sin there is, hurting the most people at one time. 'Thou shalt not kill' is a commandment and I don't think *le Bon Dieu* takes sides," she added, looking over eyeglasses. "Whoever wins, we all lose."

She'd picked up another card, checked her hand and counted out, slapping her cards on the table. *"Et malheureusement pour toi, cherie,* you just lost this game. Now *qu'est-ce-que* this *blague* about a handicap? I am immune from your nonsense!"

At the party, Paul and Emil emptied their plates twice and Antoinette parked coffee mugs in front of them. They turned their chairs around to face away from the table into the room and Paul reached down for his fiddle case. Emil gave him a note from the *accordéon* and they were off! Wives, babies, dinner, dogs, distractions were forgotten. Paul's bow flew across the strings, while his twin's hands danced over the *accordéon*.

Maddie was swept away on a sea of notes and phrases, punctuated by the most exciting rhythms she'd ever heard! Both men pounded the floor with their feet while they played, multiplying the urgency of their music. Maddie wanted to get up and dance - or maybe even fly - around the room! What she couldn't do was sit still, so she stood behind her chair and tried to tap her feet as she saw the men do. Antoinette caught Simone's eye. Her feet were tapping, too!

For the next half hour, the brothers played continuously, only stopping to slurp coffee and take off their suit jackets. Soon vests and ties were flung off too, shirt sleeves rolled up. They took large hankies out to mop their brows. Maddie giggled. Nana told her once that "horses sweat, men perspire, and ladies glow." Well, these two *had* been stomping like racehorses!

The door opened and two more men came in with a young woman who greeted Antoinette as *"Tante,"* and kissed her on both cheeks. Introduced as Colette, "a fine pianist," the woman sat down at the piano. When she played with Paul and Emil the new musicians, it was more than fine, Maddie thought. It was *glorious*. Colette's rhythms were clean and crisp and she kept her movements to a minimum, but Maddie heard a great circle of harmony pour out of the piano. There was no music, no written chords, in front of them, yet an electricity passed among them that could have burned, so intense was their linkage!

When they stopped for a break almost an hour later, everyone in the room cheered and stamped their feet. Maddie couldn't play a note with them. It went by too fast, but she filled two facing pages of her notebook with penciled images of the musicians, their faces shining like hers. And as glorious as the music was, Maddie thought they weren't just great players. They had real *stamina!*

Descending on Antoinette's buffet table "like bears in March," she teased, the musicians piled their plates high with a feast of Friday comfort food. Simone's dainty salmon pie competed with the large, cast-iron *'pot-en-pot aux fruits de mer,'* a fish pie with shrimp, scallops and lobster, layered with potatoes and carrots and onions.

The boys worked at the fish plant in Gloucester and were saving to buy their own boat. They'd manhandled the large cast-iron pot onto the table together. Inside the heavy cover, a thick crust sealed the top. The pie steamed in their outdoor oven that morning and stayed warm from Gloucester to Salem.

It would "feed a small army, or these boys and maybe one or two of their friends," Antoinette kidded them.

Maddie avoided the salmon pie, took what Nana called a "no-thank-you portion" of the *pot-en-pot,* and filled her plate with Nana's macaroni and cheese, her favorite Friday dinner. Nana scattered her canned tomatoes lightly over the noodles and didn't put the cheese into the sauce, where you wouldn't taste it, she said. The cheese and cooked elbow noodles went in together into the buttered Pyrex dish, then the tomatoes over the top, with a velvety cream sauce poured over it all and more cheese on top. If she were a condemned prisoner, Maddie thought, it would be hard to choose between this and Nana's pot roast as her last meal. The macaroni might win.

Twenty minutes later, the instruments were out again. Two more fiddlers joined the party and the room filled up. Paul played a tune for their upstairs guests and Emil joined him on *"Reel LeBlanc."* Maddie watched the fiddler's fingers and his bow, trying to remember the tune, which went by so quickly!

Antoinette advised those with plates on the floor to watch out for the dogs, which patrolled the room, sitting beseechingly in front of one guest, then another, until someone popped food in their mouths. Every time the door opened, their frenzied barking competed with the music.

Simone went down the street two blocks, returning with a sitter for the two babies. Then she came downstairs with Daddy and Papa, who joined the party. Antoinette and Simone moved the food onto the kitchen counters, while the men pushed the furniture back to make room for dancing in Antoinette's living room.

"Domino, les dames sont chaud!" boomed Emil, calling the dancers together. There were two squares, with another crowded into the kitchen and more dancers sitting on the stairs, waiting their turn. And so many musicians! Simone brought Maddie's fiddle and Mathilde's banjo downstairs and put them next to the piano. After an hour of dancing, they broke for more food and drink.

One of the men sang out with, "*Un p'tit coup, madame, un p'tit coup*!" When his wife brought him another beer, he laughed and kissed her, saying, "See, it works!"

Antoinette asked if Maddie wanted to play.

"Mama?" she asked, expecting to have to coax her, but her mother already cradled the banjo in her lap. Maddie took her fiddle out and Mama strummed a D minor chord. "Daddy's Jig" started a little ragged, but by the second half, they were in sync. Twice through and the tune started to pick up speed. People's feet were tapping and everyone was smiling, so they kept playing.

"Brava!" Simone and Antoinette clapped their loud approval when they finished. *"Encore! Encore!"* Simone put two fingers to her mouth and whistled, stamping her feet.

Of course the two women were pleased! Their "Thanksgiving in Salem" plan was a raging success! Yes, the tune was nicely played by both of them, but the music was a medium. Maddie and her mother were smiling at each other. *That's* what mattered! Maddie and Mathilde would remember this moment for a long time.

But there was even more as Paul and Emil joined mother and daughter, one on either side. *"Si tu veux. Jouer encore.* Again, please. *C'est une belle pièce.* Nice tune." Colette sat at the piano. The others waited, letting mother and daughter play it alone first, joining the second time around.

Maddie's heart raced. She'd watched them play before, the music driving her to her feet. But now she was not just in the middle of it: they were playing *her* tune, with the music spiraling up through her toes and out the top of her head, electrifying every cell of her body along the way. Barely touching the floor, her feet were still tapping. When she raised her eyes, Mama's brimmed with tears, but she was grinning and her feet were in perfect time with Maddie's.

"Now I really am flying!" Maddie laughed out loud in the middle of the tune. "If only Miss Teddy could see me now!"

Georges stayed for another hour, then went upstairs with Jules to relieve the babysitter. "Stay here, Mathilde. Play as long as you want," he reassured her. He hadn't seen his wife this happy in years and he wanted her to have a good time at the party. But for himself, he'd enjoyed about as much as he could stand. The noise of the music, not entirely unpleasant, was punctuated by piercing random yelps from the dogs, which were, their owner told him (to his astonishment) actually bred for that sound. He and Papa made one of their imaginary bets over how long one of those dogs would last at home before Nana swept it out the door!

Jules watched him try not to flinch at every bark. Loud noises had disturbed his son since the war. Loud music, a room full of people. Forget about fireworks. The factory where he worked must be as loud as the one that Jules himself clocked into every night, so that would be a trial, too. His son wouldn't attend a live ballgame even though he loved them. He'd sit next to the radio at home instead. He even refused to use one of the new power lawnmowers, saying he liked the hard work, liked knowing how to keep the blades sharp. "Those new mowers, they cut the grass too short anyway," he'd told his father.

Jules knew his son didn't return from the war the same man as when he left. But no one returned unscathed from war. It changed you. Some wore an empty sleeve; others wore their scars inside.

Georges checked his son and settled with a book on the couch. Jules paid the babysitter and walked her home, returning to Antoinette's. The party, in full swing since two, began to wind down. Some dancers left, but the musicians stayed, circling chairs together. Emil and Paul played Antoinette's favorite tune, one Lucien had written for her, *"Ne me quitte pas."*

Lucien and Antoinette had raised his nephews when their parents had perished in an accident with a log truck on Route 11. The twins, both a blessing and a keen remembrance of their own sons, filled the long-empty house with their youth and energy. Every Sunday, she'd cook up a big boiled dinner or a pot of spaghetti and meatballs. Everyone crowded around the table, first to eat, then to play music. Hours later, they'd get up and stretch. If only she could have bottled those Sundays. Lucien would have loved this party, too.

Papa stood next to Maddie, who closed her eyes as the waltz's plaintive movement from minor to major filled her senses. Papa tapped her on the shoulder. Looking up, she found him bowing to her, hand extended.

"S'il vous plait, mademoiselle, voulez-vous dansez?" Papa danced with Maddie when she was little. Back then, she stood on his feet and they marched around the room to the music of the Québec radio station. But now he was asking for real, so she curtsied and took his hand. Papa was a good dancer, much in demand in his youth as a partner. Nana told her once that she'd fallen in love with Papa while waltzing with him. "It was very *risqué* then, couples dancing together for a whole slow dance. People thought it was scandalous, but it was just fun, really. We wouldn't think it was naughty at all now."

Papa swept her around their little corner of the room. "Just follow me, *ma p'tite*. I promise I won't step on your feet and you're too big to ride on mine!" The lovely tune died away as he twirled her and made a deep bow, kissing her hand. *"Mademoiselle LeBlanc,* it was a great honor," he teased, but Maddie knew he meant it.

"Monsieur LeBlanc, c'est un plaisir! Enchantée!" Her French was coming along.

The tunes settled into songs, the singers taking turns. The twins offered another drinking song, then Colette countered her cousins with a song from her grandmother, Antoinette's younger sister. "You men all sing of drinking your next whiskey! You know what women sing about?" She challenged them. *"Les mal mariées!* Bad marriages! Sometimes I wonder if those two - the drinker and the unhappy wife - are married to each other!"

Colette taunted them with her *mémère's* version of *"Le petit mari,"* who was so small that his wife lost him in the mattress and the cat ate him up by mistake, thinking he was a mouse. That was if Maddie followed the French lyric right. Simone would know.

Antoinette called time on the party at midnight and asked for one last song, surprising everyone by asking Mama to sing it. "You know this one, Mathilde," Simone urged. "You sang it to Maddie over and over. I bet she knows it, too!

"Do you want to sing with me, Antoinette?" Mama asked, but she demurred.

"Tout la musique is in Lucien's *famille. Chantez-vous la!*

Colette played an introduction on the piano keyboard. Mathilde stood up and put her banjo on the chair. She coughed slightly and began to sing.

"Un canadien errant, banni de ses foyers." Everyone, Maddie included, sang the response line back. Then the second line, *"Parcourait en pleurant des pays étrangers."*

Banished from their home, they wandered in tears. Like Evangeline, Maddie thought. Mama'd sung this lovely lament over Maddie's cradle almost every night, playing along softly on mandolin. On the second verse, the girl chimed in an octave above her mother, moving to harmony notes on the responses. She reached for her mother's hand and held it.

Jules slipped his arms around his wife. *"Dansez?"*

Maddie and Mathilde finished the song together as one by one, the others dropped out, leaving her mother's rich alto and Maddie's clear soprano to fill the room, ending with the merest whisper of a chord from the piano. Jules waltzed Nana around in a tight circle, sneaking a kiss while everyone cheered. She was still his girl!

Eulogy for My Beloved Papa

Papa—you haven't left me—you are with me all day long.
The woman that I've grown into is **confident and strong**.
You showed me how to drive a car, to jitterbug, to swim—
You listened when my heart was hurt, and when I didn't win.

You might have taught me to defer to all authority
Instead, you let me **trust my self, my non-conformity.**
You gave advice or didn't—you let me **tell you what I need**
To **learn from my mistakes** is how you taught me to succeed.

From you I learned a l**ove of words**, the shades of what they mean;
To **talk it out, to compromise, to sometimes intervene.**
From you I learned the simple joy of planning for a trip
We've seen the world by train, by car, by bus and by cruise ship.

As an English teacher, and I didn't know this at the time
I reinforced the love we shared for books and plays and rhyme.
Because of you I **stand up straight, have faith in my decisions**
And know that if I make mistakes, I'll always be forgiven.

You'll be with me in formal gardens with their splendid color splash,
a visit to a history museum for a glimpse into the past,
or hollering out the question in a Jeopardy Daily Double.
If I question right and wrong, I know you'll keep me out of trouble.

Dad—rest in peace and know you've left the best of you behind
I'll carry on your legacy, with laughter, love and pride.

I love you, Dad.

By Cori Modisette
October 12, 2011

Lace, Story, and Doughnuts

By Elizabeth Fuller

There was a barn, and one of my uncles jumped from the loft into the hay and took a pitchfork in the ass. But which uncle? Was it Cliff, or Ray? And where was the barn? It wasn't at the house on Chapman Street, because my grandfather was a mechanic and not a farmer.

I can't remember and I can't ask and the story unravels a little bit more each time I think of it.

There were so many stories, and they were so good. Eight kids and their adventures in a time when TV was magical and there were stories on the radio. *The Shadow*, which I'd heard of, and another show called *Boston Blackie*, which I hadn't. They listened to it on Sunday nights gathered together around the radio. Sometimes my grandfather would make all eight of them line up in front of the fireplace to ingest some kind of nasty substance called Father John's, which I think was a brand of cod-liver oil.

I can hear my mother's voice, the way she dragged out the "a" in "Father:" "Faaaaaather John's." The sound is loud and clear, but the words—the words are slipping away.

Preserving those stories was important to me and they agreed with that. I wanted to write it all down, and once when I was in high school, I actually tried. But they all clammed up when I brought out the notebook and the pencil. Were they self-conscious? Were they ashamed? Or was I an interloper of sorts? Were the stories their stories and not mine to share? They are fading, regardless, and that pains me.

A generation's worth of separation. It might as well be ten generations' worth. My mother never learned to use a computer or a cell phone, let alone a smart phone or a tablet. My grandmother died when I was three. I don't know if she ever even heard of the things I take for granted. Things have changed, so much, so quickly.

Mom has been gone two years now, going on three. I remember when she taught me to knit. I was adamant that I MUST learn; a friend of mine was learning. She was the pretty one; I was the clever one, and I was not about to be outdone in the clever department. There was cursing and weeping and frustration and I threw the needles across the floor more than once, but eventually the movements made sense. The multiple thumbs I'd grown disappeared.

And there was the fabric, misshapen and awkward, but it was there. Loops woven in and out of each other. Mine. My mom's.

My mother's fabric. I hold it up to the light, and the more time passes, the lacier it gets, and I can't stop it.

Elizabeth, daughter of Cecile, daughter of Yvonne, daughter of ... was it Geraldine? Grammy Guerette, the one who smoked unfiltered Lucky Strikes and rocked in front of the picture window and swore in French when young women walked down the street in shorts? She passed long before I was born. I don't think I've even seen a picture of her. She is the stuff of myth now. She existed in my mother's memory. Now that my mother is gone, she exists only in my imagination.

I think it was her whom my aunt babysat. My aunt heard a thud and went upstairs to check on her and Grammy was lying facedown on the floor. My aunt, maybe eight years old—what did she do? Did she run to the phone? Was anyone else in the house? She was certain she'd found her grandmother dead. What she didn't know was that the doctor said a small glass of wine before bedtime would be good for Grammy and help her sleep. Grammy drank the whole bottle.

Three big yarn-over holes in that story—and I can't fill them in. Solid fabric turns to lace turns to threads. Generations pass. Our culture changes. The edges blur. Memory turns to story turns to myth.

Story is important. Story holds us together. It's necessary. It makes—and keeps—us human in an age when increases in technology drive people further and further apart. Real ceases to exist in a haze of light and sound and spin, except in the stories we carry in our hearts and pass down. The stories are the fabric we create, the stitches that hold us together. It may not be important to anyone but me that my aunt would pee every time someone said "mud puddle," or that one of my uncles took a pitchfork in the ass, or that my nana made homemade doughnuts with a cutter my grandfather made from a coffee can.

I may not be able to mend the holes in the stories my mother and family loved to tell. I can't tell them the way she did. But I can carry them the best I can for as long as I can. I knit the way my mother taught me, I can teach others, and she will live on in the space between the stitches. I have her doughnut recipe. And I have the cutter my uncle made for her from a tuna can. And someday, when I'm feeling brave, I will make doughnuts for my stepsons. And who knows? Maybe those doughnuts will become the stuff of story for their children. And she will live on in the hole in the doughnut.

"Ray," my grandfather would say. "Don't eat the hole in the doughnut." And he never did. He ate all around the hole, but never the hole itself.

But that's another, different story.

The Context for Une Âme Franco-Américaine à la France

By Kim Chase, daughter of Claire Bouffard Chase

When I was growing up, we spoke French at home and English in school. I greatly admired my mother's ability to move so effortlessly between her two languages. Until she was nine years old, she spoke only French. She heard English occasionally, being raised, as she was, in Winooski, Vermont, but she resisted learning English at first.

"Why should I learn English?" she asked her bilingual father. "It's an ugly language. And French is my mother tongue." Her father agreed, but added, "French is your mother tongue but English is the language of your country." She was fortunate to attend school at the convent where the school day was divided neatly in two, with French instruction for one half and English for the other. As a language teacher, I can tell you that no one has ever improved upon that model.

My mother always maintained her French and English; she was literate and read and wrote in both languages regularly. She was eloquent yet succinct in both. I can recall many times when it seemed to me that my mother wielded her two languages like superpowers.

When I was around twelve years old, I had some friends over who noticed that some of the books on our shelves were not in English. "What language is this?" they asked. I told them it was French. "Why do you have French books?" they asked. I will never forget the remorse I felt when I answered them by saying, ridiculously, "I don't know."

At some point soon after that, I remember coming to the realization that I was attempting to lead a sort of double life, French at home, English or "American," at school. I recall realizing that I wanted what my mother had, the ability to conduct my life, hopefully as gracefully as she appeared to do, between two cultures, two languages and, in many ways, two ways of life. In later years, my mother often told the story of how I came to her one day and said, "I have decided to reclaim my French heritage." Although I don't recall that event, I know that I made a conscious decision to acknowledge the French part of my identity as actively and conscientiously as the American part. I knew that in order to do that, I would have to be literate as well as conversant.

After graduating from the University of Vermont, I landed a job as a teacher in a short-lived Bilingual Education program in Franklin Country, Vermont, on the Canadian (Quebec) border. My supervisor was the indomitable Sister Cecile Brassard, or C.B., as we called her. My cultural awareness crystallized under her tutelage. She was a member of an organization called ActFANE, the acronym for "Action for Franco-Americans in the North East." I told my mother about it and said that she should join. She did, and became fast friends with C.B. as well as with Martha Pellerin and Rhéa Côté Robbins. These were friendships that she treasured to the end of her life and for which I am equally grateful.

Through her membership in ActFANE, my mother went to France. It was the first time she had ever been on an airplane, and I doubt she would have made the trip if the destination had been other than France. It is my understanding that the cost of her trip was provided by ActFANE and that she was, as "La Doyenne," an ambassador of Franco-America to France. She told me that in one conversation she had, a woman asked from what part of France she came. My mother said she was from the United States. The woman asked how she came to speak French so fluently and my mother explained. The woman said, "Mais comme ça, ça donne des frissonnes!"

I believe it was sometime after that trip that my mother wrote the following essay. I apologize for the clumsy translation. My mother was always more eloquent in her two languages than I can hope to be in one, but I believe the spirit of her expression nonetheless comes through. **(Continued on next page)**

A Franco-American Soul in France (On the Occasion of a Brief Stay in the Country of Her Ancestors)

By Claire Bouffard Chase
Translated by Kim Chase

I am in France. And I cannot believe it. This seems like a dream to me. I am at the foot of the Castle of Angers, in Anjou country, there where my ancestors populated the land. I raise my eyes to the top of the massive towers of this fortress and I wonder if my ancestors had, with the skill of an artisan, carefully placed one stone upon the other. Or else, had they bent their backs and buckled their knees under the crushing weight of these stones? I ask the stones to tell me, to reveal the past to me. The stones do not respond.

My heart full, I look around me at this land which does not seem strange to me yet does not appear to recognize me. That is why, today, Mother France, I speak to you, heart to heart, because my soul, silenced for more than two centuries, has found its voice again beneath your blue skies.

You cradled me in the first days of my infancy, you guided my first steps. Despite a harsh existence, facing risks at every turn, subject to countless challenges, I believed myself, under your protection, sheltered from misfortune.

I had hardly taken my first steps when the ground collapsed beneath me: The lightning strike of the English! Wolfe!

With Montcalm, you fall.

Yielding to this devastating defeat, you furled your sails, put away your standard and, grievously wounded, you turned your attention to Europe. Fearing yourself mortally wounded, you clung ever more desperately to the sunny Antilles, abandoning me to the intemperate storms of the North and of the English.

It is clear to me that you had a choice to make and that it must have been a bitter choice. I do not hold this choice against you. Faced with the enemy, now my master, I clung to the only birthrights left to me: my language, my faith, and my name.

Upon your defeat, I became a hostage to an uncertain future. I resisted the efforts of the conqueror to bastardize our beautiful French names in order to

(Continued on next page)

Une Âme Franco-Américaine à la France (À l'occasion d'un bref séjour dans son ancienne patrie)

Par Claire Bouffard Chase

Je suis en France. Et je n'y crois pas. Cela me semble une rêve. Je suis au pied du château d'Angers, en pays d'Anjou, là où mes ancêtres ont foulé la terre. Je lève les yeux vers le sommet des tours massives de cette forteresse et je me demande si mes ancêtres avaient, avec le souci de l'artisan, soigneusement placé ces pierres l'une sur l'autre. Ou bien, avaient-ils courbé le dos et plié genoux sous le poids écrasant de ces pierres? Je demande aux pierres de me le dire, de me livrer le passé. Les pierres ne répondent pas.

Le cœur gonflé, je regarde autour de moi et constate ce paysage qui ne m'est pas, il me semble, étranger, mais qui, cependant, ne me reconnait pas. C'est pourquoi, aujourd'hui, mère France, je te parle, cœur à cœur, puisque ma voix éteinte depuis plus de deux siècles, reprend haleine sous ton ciel bleu.

Tu as bercé mes premiers jours, tu as guidé mes premiers pas. Malgré une rude existence, lourdes de conséquences, sujette à d'innombrables dangers, d'un côté à l'autre, sous ton égide, je me croyais à l'ombre à l'abri du mal.

Tenant à peines sur mes jambes, soudain la terre s'écroule. Le coup de foudre anglais frappe! Wolfe!

Tu tombes avec Montcalm.

Cédant à l'affront, tu as replié tes voiles, serré ton étendard et, meurtrie, tu as tourné ton regard sombre vers l'Europe.

Te croyant peut-être mortellement blessé, tu as resserré plus près de toi les îles ensoleillées des Antilles et tu m'as abandonné aux intempéries du nord et de l'anglais.

Je comprends très bien que tu avais à faire un choix et que ce choix a dû être amer pour toi. Pour ce choix je ne t'en veux pas. Face à l'ennemi, devenu mon maître, je tenais férocement à ce qui m'appartenait de droit, mon langage, ma foi et mon nom.

Ôtage, au hasard d'un destin incertain, j'ai refusé obstinément à l'effort de bâtardiser nos beaux noms français pour faciliter l'effacement de notre race, au bénéfice du conquérant, qui ne voulait pas de moi mais avait besoin de moi à la suite de ta défaite.

(Suite à la page suivante)

erase any signs of our presence as efficiently as possible. This conqueror who would be rid of me but who, despite himself, had need of me.

Already, to the south of the border, the American colonies loudly proclaimed their discontent. Their rage manifests itself more and more from day to day. Though your wound at the hands of the British had hardly healed, you welcomed the American Benjamin Franklin. You lent your ear to his thoughts; you had confidence in his ideas. When all was said and done, you promised him your military support.

And I was there.

Valiant as ever, you returned to this land of North America, but it was not to care for me that you came. I was forever lost to you. Beneath the banner of the unforgettable Lafayette, at the clarion call, at the beating of the drums, standard flying proudly, you came to avenge yourself against the British enemy who had cost you New France. And you did indeed have your revenge.

But I, I was New France.

Victory in hand, did you, remembering the recent past, turn your gaze to me? History does not recall.

As for me, I was still there.

Seeking a more promising future, I crossed the border of the American colonies – now the United States – which you had so efficiently supported. Faithful to your memory, wherever my wandering path led me, I dragged with me my cultural and emotional baggage—all that you had left me—and spread your name.

I did not expect to stay. However, within a climate more tolerant than welcoming, I took root a second time. I found a second mother. She accepted me without complaint. She needed me. While providing me with the means of subsistence, she profited from my labors without ever truly embracing me. She is a good mother, she provides for me. I love her dearly.

Why, then, do I feel disinherited once again? Because, you see, my dear mother, my new country, like you, does not recognize me. And as for me, I am still here.

Déjà au sud de la frontière, les colonies américaines grondaient de mécontentement. De jour en jour leur rage se manifestait de plus en plus. Ta blessure aux mains des anglais à peine cicatrisée, tu as reçu l'américaine Benjamin Franklin. Tu as prêté oreille à ses discours. Tu a fait confiance à ses idées. Enfin, quand tout fut dit, tu lui as promis l'appuie de tes armes.

Et moi, j'étais là.

Vaillante, comme toujours, tu es revenue sur cette terre de l'Amérique du Nord, mais ce n'était pas pour me secourir que tu venais. J'étais perdu à jamais pour toi. Sous la bannière de l'inoubliable Lafayette, au cri du clairon, tambours battants, étendard au vent, tu es venue pour te venger contre l'ennemi anglais qui t'avait coûté la nouvelle France. Et cette revanche, tu l'as eu.

Mais la nouvelle France, c'était moi.

Victoire en main, as-tu, en souvenir d'un passé peu éloigné, penché ton regard vers moi? L'histoire n'en dit rien.

Moi, j'étais toujours là.

En quête d'un avenir plus promettant, j'ai franchi la frontière des colonies américaines devenues les États-Unis— que tu avais si efficacement soutenus. Fidèle à ton souvenir, partout où mon regard errant a conduit mes pas, j'ai trainé avec moi mon bagage, culturel et émotif, qui était tout ce qui me restait de toi, et j'ai semé ton nom.

Je ne m'attendais pas d'y rester. Cependant, sous un climat tolérant plutôt qu'accueillant, j'ai pris racine une deuxième fois. J'ai trouvé une deuxième mère. Elle m'a reçue sans murmure. Elle avait besoin de moi. En m'accordant une subsistance, elle a su profiter de mes labeurs, sans jamais me prendre sur son cœur. Elle est bonne. Elle ne me refuse rien. Je l'aime tendrement.

Alors, pourquoi me sentais-je désherité une seconde fois? Parce que, vois-tu, mère chérie, comme toi, elle ne connait pas mon nom.

Et moi, je suis encore là.

Born to Knit: A Knitter's Genealogy

By Melissa MacCrae

MacCrae *Knitters Family Tree
*Lenora "Nanny" Butler (m. James C. "Pa" MacCrae)
*Shirley Lamont (Daddy; Gramp) – *Pearle (m. Andrews)
*(m. Dorothy "Diddy" Beatrice Avery)
*(b. Joyce Elaine (m. Howe)
*(b. Melissa Ann Howe MacCrae—legal name change)
*(b. Martha Louise (m. Stepp)

For my dear mother, Joyce Elaine MacCrae Howe, October 28, 1934-January, 12, 2014

On a recent morning, a fifty-something woman glided into my yarn shop with bright eyes, arms outstretched. Her fingers connected with the nearest skein. She smiled. "Touching this yarn reminds me of my mother, who was a champion sock knitter," she said. "I don't knit, but I really miss watching her."

I have missed watching my Mum knit, too, since she died January 12, 2014. Fact is, I've always considered mine to be close-knit family, members of which knit when they are happy, even angry or sad. When I am feeling out of sorts, I need only follow my family tree, which boasts branches broad enough to span several successive generations of MacCraes who knit.

Remembering Mum motivated me to mine her knitter's wisdom, show up at Spin a Yarn most days, and for spinning this yarn. For her part, Mum relished the chance to let folks know that "we have a yarn shop in the family." The little-yarn-shop-that-could, then, gives substance to my legacy and this true story about knitting and the MacCraes.

At only eighteen, Joyce Elaine MacCrae followed her lifelong dream: she took her first trip outside the state and her first step toward her fifty-year-long career as a registered nurse, RN. Intense training came first via train from Maine to Boston, where she and her sister trainees used rare quiet time to create fancy, warm Argyle socks. Such intricate plying of traditional colors of black, red, green and yellow yarn flowed from bobbins linked to the knitted fabric suspended from needles bearing man-size socks, also may have filled occasional lonely moments.

Mum's own link to yarn and knitting had flowed naturally from father-to-daughter, when her Daddy, Shirley MacCrae, taught her to knit. That mode of sharing the knitting bug was gentler than the six MacCrae kids' initiation.

Their mother conscripted them into a home-based sock-knitting industry. She organized them age-wise, so each boy knit socks for his younger brother. Pearle was the baby, and only girl, so she may have been excused. That ingenious plan accomplished two goals: to keep the budding brood busy and to fill the constant need to produce stockings to clothe their feet.

Later, as a fifty-something man, middle child, Shirley put his early education to use after he suffered a severe work injury. He knit as therapy during his long convalescence. To fill the hours, he sat in his burgundy leather recliner and knit a traditional Ripple Afghan for each of his two daughters. Then, for each of his three grandchildren. Mine, in shades of green, and my brother's brown, are at home at the end of my bed.

Concerned that her Daddy might become bored, Mum spread the word about his knitting prowess among some hospital coworkers, and soon she was bringing bags full of others' yarn, with which Gramp knit them untold numbers of afghans, too.

Once each strip was knit, Gramp rolled and packed it in a plastic Glad Bag. Though she was working and raising a family, Mum also took on the chore of sewing strips together and attaching fringe to each afghan he had knit. Working on the afghans together enabled Mum to check on her dad's condition. She also may have felt it was her duty, since as a beloved granddaughter, curly-haired Joyce saw the only softer side of her father's knitting overseer, whom she called Nanny.

The child cherished the freedom of summertime, while she stayed with Nanny and Pa in an upstairs bedroom at their Seal Harbor homestead. That house, dressed in weathered shingles, still stands about a mile from

Seal Harbor Beach, and just around the corner from Martha Stewart's summer home, which she occasionally mentions on her TV show.

Still, long before Ms. Stewart became rich and famous, and did jail time for insider trading, Mum was cuddling with and getting knitting tips from Auntie Pearle, as often as possible at her home away from home. Decades later, I also knitted and purled with Great Auntie Pearle when Mum's Mum, Diddy, toted me along with her to the coast during her summer-long school vacations.

One of those visits earned a mention on the *Bar Harbor Times* society page when I was a little girl:

SEAL HARBOR – "Miss Melissa Howe, daughter of Robert and Joyce Howe, of Brewer, was the guest of Mrs. Pearle Andrews. ..."

When Mum, herself, was younger, a visit to Auntie Pearle was similarly reported on a *Bar Harbor Times* page, dated a generation earlier. Simply substitute Joyce MacCrae for my name, and you would swear you were seeing double on viewing both columns about my own and Mum's visits to the Seal Harbor House.

As she matured, Mum contributed toward her nursing-school tuition by working as a chambermaid at the Seaside Inn across the road from Seal Harbor Beach. She saved money and was doted on while staying with her grandparents. After a fire erased any evidence of the Seaside, the puny parcel on which it had stood, became a parking lot that still is used by residents and beachgoers alike.

Summer times on the coast faded into memory and, according to her plan, Mum worked for more than fifty years as a registered nurse. Meanwhile, she earned a reputation as a consummate–generous–knitter of all sizes and styles of socks, taming even the toughest patterns with ease. She also survived both breast and colon cancers. But the death of her only son, my brother Michael "Mike" Robert Howe, left a hole in her heart that neither pill nor potion could heal.

Though I am not a RN like Mum was, I am honing the art of caring that she exemplified and shared with me. I held her soft hands the day she died at home, and Dad urged me to put her rings on my fingers. The gold and diamonds glitter with every movement of my hands. The sparkling bands catch my eyes, while I teach a knit or crochet technique. When I miss her most, I stare at them, moving my hand side-to-side to catch the light.

Mum = Caring ... Spin-a-Yarn = Caring

So in her memory, my little yarn shop will endure as long as it can. Good thing knitters generally are caring folks, with whom I choose to spend my days. Her memory urges me to maintain Spin-a-Yarn into its fourth year and beyond.

Bikini

By Sally Bellerose

Mom was a housewife and a factory worker who wore a bikini in broad daylight in our back yard. This was 1962. Working-class western Massachusetts had a dress code. Skimpy bathing suits fell outside of that code. Perhaps my maternal grandparents, who were Québecois, failed to impart full knowledge of American mores.

Maybe it's because both *his* parents were Québecois that my jealous father never seemed to mind that his wife would occasionally step into her tiger-striped suit and out into the yard where she was surrounded by the picket fence he had built with his own hands.

In 1962, Canadian men's and women's swimwear featured less fabric and more skin than suits in the United States. But, despite his heritage, Dad never wore one of those skimpy bathing suits, not at the beach and not in the yard. The family sometimes spent vacations in a tent on the Maine shore. There, we learned the term "banana hammock." In Maine, we girls were always on the lookout for a Canadian man in a skimpy suit. No man in a Speedo was exempt from being exposed to a giggling fit, followed by "Bonjour" or an obscure "Dormez vous?" Anyway, Dad wore bathing trunks like everyone else's Dad from Chicopee.

Neither of my parents was hysterical about nudity the way some of our friends' parents were. If one of us kids, say, opened the bathroom door as Mom or Dad happened to be stepping out of the tub, it was no big deal, rating only an irritated, "How many times do I have to tell you to knock?"

This reaction was nothing compared to the overwrought embarrassment I witnessed when Mrs. Gilmartin's boob fell out of her sensible one piece bathing suit while she was hoisting herself out of the public pool. There was downright drama when Mrs. Kallowitz found out that Suzie Kallowitz and I had witnessed drunken Mr. Kallowitz peeing on a rhododendron. His wife berated him up one side and down the other. This didn't seem fair. How was he to know we had snuck out of the house at ten o'clock at night? All three of us would have gotten away without a word of reprimand if Suzie and I had been able to contain our eight-year-old glee. Until his wife started yelling, I thought peeing on a bush was funnier than a banana hammock.

Anyway, one day, Mom was working second shift at National Blank Book, a paper mill by the Holyoke canals that was known to turn a nice girl into a rough woman if she didn't watch out. Mom had the morning off. She only swore in extreme circumstances, certainly never the "F" word, *and* she raised poodles, the big standard kind not the dainty little miniatures, but still a refined breed, so I don't think she was a rough woman. Like every woman in the neighborhood, Mom didn't aspire to be any rougher than she already was. She wanted to be middle class, which meant a bigger house, better clothes, saying "not" instead of "ain't" and behaving like a lady.

So why did she wear a bikini? A Hollywood star like Brigette Bardot could get away with it. But Brigette Bardot had exaggerated womanhood, fame, wealth, and an agent to protect her. She could flaunt her body, not with immunity exactly, but she didn't need to be a lady the way regular women did. How Mom got up the nerve in the summer of 1962 to carry a glass of Tab with such nonchalance across the yard while wearing that two-piece, is to this day a mystery to me. We lived in a neighborhood of two-story houses with small back yards. Anyone who happened to be looking out a second-story window in any of the four houses adjacent to ours could peer down and see every inch of her skin except the part covered by that tiger-stripe bra and panties as she plopped herself down on the chaise lounge.

We girls were thirteen, eleven, and eight. We were all home for summer vacation and never knew when we might walk out into our back yard to find Mom unveiled. Any one of our neighbors could gain access to a one dollar pair of opera glasses at Mercier's corner store and peer luridly down at her. We knew because we had three pairs ourselves and kept vigil from our own second-story windows. When one sister was posted in the bedroom, one in the hall, and one in the bathroom, we had the immediate neighborhood covered. The view, we figured, was roughly the same from any of the neighbors' second floors.

We worried a lot more about men than women. Mr. Lesperance, young Mr. Kallowitz, or Mr. Gilmartin might be out of work with the flu or on vacation, never mind the myriad male offspring hanging around in the mostly Catholic neighborhood. Our brother didn't count. He was family. He was sixteen. If he had been paying attention maybe he would have been scandalized by Mom's display, but he was off working in the tobacco fields and much too interested in himself to get caught up in the mundane lives of his sisters and parents. Mom never seemed to be in her bikini when he was around.

The sister surveillance was not 100% of the time of course. It was a summer of grasshopper funerals (the corpses in match boxes) for Janie, my younger sister. She seemed to find a lot of dead grasshoppers. I suspected foul play. My older sister spent a fair amount of time walking back and forth to the library because the seventeen year old boy she had vowed to die for lived on the route. Then, of course, Mom was not the only show on the bill. Every kid in the neighborhood found a spot between the hedges when word got out that Old Lady Kallowitz was about to take a hammer to a snapper for turtle soup. You knew it was about to happen because Old Man Kallowitz would shoo his own grandchildren out of his yard and bring out the stained army blanket that the poor turtle got wrapped in before the deed was done. Where did that old lady and that old man get the turtles and where they really snappers like the Kallowitz kids claimed? The old man held the turtle. The old woman held the hammer. Who needed the distraction of Xbox, smart phone, or even television?

Even with all these distractions, more than once that summer, one of us caught our mother walking serenely out the back door, cleavage, belly button and all. We caught her, but we didn't know what to do with her. She and Dad were the people you told if you wanted to snitch on someone, and neither of them seemed to think Mom's bikini was a snitch worthy offense.

All any of us could do was to alert the other sisters and gather to kneel with our chins on the window sill and gaze down at her. Sunbathing she called it.

My older sister, Kathy stressed the bathing part. "Why doesn't she just take a bath on the back lawn?"

"The men are all at work," I cautiously defended Mom.

Kathy was thirteen and too outraged to suffer any justification of Mom's behavior. She made a face to indicate what a dolt I was. "Old Man Kallowitz is always home. You think men don't take days off? How about Old Lady Kallowitz? Wouldn't she love to get a load of Mom *sunbathing*."

It was true Old Lady Kallowitz, the turtle killer, roamed the neighborhood with bad intent. It wasn't scandalous for women to see each other's skin. Still the fact of Mom out there *like that* put her reputation in peril, no matter who saw her. And our mother was in extra jeopardy because even though she was only five feet tall, inch-for-inch, she was the prettiest woman in the neighborhood.

On this particular hot morning, all the stars aligned and the payoff for our surveillance arrived. It was too early for spying, but I happened to be seated in the upstairs bathroom. More out of habit than curiosity, I peeked under the shade. There she was, cleavage greatly exaggerated from this angle, cup of Sanka and the morning paper in hand. My brother had already boarded the van for the tobacco fields. My sisters hadn't even rolled out of bed yet. I pulled up my baby doll pajama bottoms and flew back to our shared bedroom. My sisters refused to get up. I took up my post at the bedroom window. Soon, I saw a mailman who was not *our* mailman coming down the street carrying an oversized sack.

"A man," I said into Kathy's ear, not loud enough to be heard through the open windows. "Mom's out in the bikini."

She gave me a filthy look and sat up in bed. All three of us peered at the man through our opera glasses as he took a big book out of his sack and stuffed it in the Lesperence's mailbox.

"Phone books," Kathy said knowingly.

"How's he going to get that big book in our mailbox?" Janie asked. It was a good question. The Lesperence's had a mailbox big enough to accommodate Mr. Lesperence's mailorder model airplane hobby. We had a normal mailbox. The fat phone book would never fit.

My older sister dropped her opera glasses. "Stay put," she commanded. "Don't take your eyes off him." She bounded down the stairs.

I didn't want to stay put. I left Janie with the same order Kathy had just barked at us and ran to the hall window to watch Kathy warn Mom that a strange man with a phone book was on the loose. I could see from way up there that Mom was not impressed with this information.

Kathy's mouth tightened and her hands went to her hips. Mom laughed. More than anything Kathy hated to be laughed at. I laughed, too. Mom turned toward the window. "Quit spying and come out here," she said.

Since I'd been caught red-handed, I waved at them. Mom waved back. Kathy stared at Mom's bust line and scowled.

Mom rolled her eyes. "I am in my own back yard." She pointed to the towel draped over the back of the chaise. "I have a towel." It was true she always had a towel with her even though she never got wet. "How did you girls get this way?" But what if she wasn't quick enough with the towel?

I thought I heard a faint knock at the front door. I definitely heard the back door slam. It was Janie running out into the yard, gesturing toward the front of the house. I bolted down the stairs. There was no one at the front door. I grabbed the afghan off Dad's Lazy Boy as I ran through the living room on my way to the back yard.

I almost crossed paths with the guy as he came through the side gate saying, "Good morning. Glad I didn't wake you folks." The disgrace of it, the danger, the adrenaline!! I rushed to join my two sisters who were already standing at her side. We created a screen of daughters to block his view. He was looking down at his bag, pulling out the phone book, saying, "Got your new telephone directory."

Mom had already twisted around and was smiling. Thankfully, she stayed seated in the chaise lounge. "Oh, thank you," Mom said. "Would you just leave it there on the picnic table?"

We held our breath. Was the threat avoided or did he see? Would he tell the tale all up and down the street? He left the book and turned away without making eye contact with any of us. I collapsed cross-legged to the ground next to Mom who was now frowning with her arms crossed, still firmly seated.

Mom stared at his back as the gate squeaked shut. Finally, she looked embarrassed.

Kathy glared at her.

Mom didn't notice. She was still staring at the gate. "Oh, shit," she said. Mom, who never said, "shit."

Janie sat tentatively on the end of the chaise. When she was not shooed off, my little sister put her head on Mom's thigh. Mom stroked her hair absentmindedly. "I hope he didn't realize I recognized him."

Kathy's mouth relaxed a bit. She squinted as if this would help her hear what Mom was about to say.

Janie lifted her head off Mom's thigh. "Who is he, Mom?"

"He used to work with your father." She seemed so sad. "He got let go."

"Fired!" Kathy corrected.

Mom shook her head in sympathy. "Poor man. Two kids in diapers. How much can he be making delivering phone books? He must be so embarrassed." She looked seriously from daughter to daughter to daughter. "Don't marry heavy drinkers, girls. No matter how charming or good looking, do not marry a man who drinks too much." Her eyes landed on Janie, who sat up and looked back at her earnestly. Mom stroked Janie's hair one more time. Then shook off thoughts of the poor phone guy with a forced smile. "You girls are up early."

Kathy's eyes drifted to the afghan on the ground next to me. I pulled the blanket to my lap so that Mom wouldn't notice that it had been touching the dirt. Kathy locked eyes with me and nodded at the afghan. I knew what she wanted. I wanted it too. I never would have had the guts to do it without my older sister's silent instruction.

Suddenly, with great dexterity, Kathy grabbed the afghan and threw it over Mom. Then with perfect timing, like a female tag team on World Wide Wrestling, we were on her. We wrapped the blanket around and under her. We would have stopped if Mom had ordered us to, but she squealed, laughing like a teenager getting thrown in a pool.

"What are you doing?" She could hardly get it out, she was laughing so hard. When it was absolutely clear that Mom was not angry, Janie joined in. The three of us carried our mother, who was fighting like a banshee and screaming with laughter, into the house.

I can't exaggerate how much fun this was; Mom allowing us to pretend we are saving her from herself. Mom laughing at us and herself and her own flesh, laughing wrapped in an afghan crocheted by our Mémère before she died, laughing as if some things that are usually not allowed, are sometimes allowed to be laughed at. It was maybe the most fun I'd had in my career as a kid up to that point. Between orders of "Watch her head," and "Open the door," even thirteen year-old Kathy was laughing.

Songs for my parents

After finishing graduate school and accepting a teaching position at Hollins University in Virginia, I woke up one day inspired to thank my parents. They had both spent endless hours reading my dissertation, endless pages analyzing the poetry of Francis Ponge. These words, while stylistically inspired by my study of Ponge's work, flowed freely out of my fountain pen as if they had been waiting patiently to embroider the page.

— Annette Sampon-Nicolas, Ph.D.

Pour Victor Sampon, mon père
Petite leçon reçue magistralement de Ponge et de Littré

Prononcé vitoire au XVIe siècle. Vis toi! Le son est juste ; Sans le c, sans le pont qui rattache vitoire à victor. Victor le vainqueur. Victorieux, avantage remporté sur les ennemis dans une bataille, dans un combat, dans un … assaut. Maître d'armes, l'escrime règne dans ta vie. Vainqueur, Victor, victorius. Toi, mon père, as su vaincre, as su remporter des batailles toute ta vie. As su me conquérir. Par tes paroles et ton esprit.

"Averum nus la victorie del champ?" (Chanson de Roland) Bien entendu la victoire des champs! La conquête de la vigne et des arbres fruitiers. Maître jardinier qui a donné plus de neuf mille heures à cette passion. Vainqueur des délicatesses des orchidées, des vignes, des rosiers. Victoria, très belle plante de la famille des nymphéacées qui croît dans les lacs de l'Amérique méridionale. (Quelle importance où elle croît ; elle peut être transplantée et peut fleurir grâce aux bons soins de tes mains.)

Sampon. Oui, sampont, sans pont nous dit-on en Belgique du petit patelin qui porte ton nom. Non. Quelle importance que ce village ait un pont pourvu qu'il produise des sampons! Le manque, la marque de l'exclusion. Et comme cela est juste que *sans* vienne du Wallon, de sai. Sampon, sans t, certes, mais jamais sans thé, mon père qui jamais ne se déplace sans sa nourriture céleste, son thé. Et notre pont n'existe peut-être pas en Belgique mais bien dans la Sapinière d'Argonne. Pont qui traverse notre rivière, celle des castors. Ne faut-il pas renommer la Peshtigo à Castor? Cela s'impose! Pont se rattache au sanscrit patha: chemin, mais aussi à pontus, la mer, nom ancien de la mer noire. Ne sens-tu pas l'air de la mer?

Sampon. Sans pont. Sent bon. Mais dorénavant jamais sans Ponge!

—Annette Sampon-Nicolas, mercredi 10 juin 1987 Roanoke, Virginie

Anne-Marie Jardon Sampon de la Sapinière d'Argonne

Anne-Marie pleine de grâce, d'art et de dons. Jardon. C'est inscrit dans ton nom. Jardon, jardin, jargon. Elle a des dons. Mais refuse de parler, de lire ou d'apprécier le jargon (surtout de critique littéraire). Puriste de la langue. Douée pour tous les idiomes. Son jardin est bien rempli.

Jardin de "gards," "maison," mais certainement elle tient bien sa maison. Jardon, jardin, à la place de l'o, j'aurais préféré le i, c'est plus juste. Et pourtant elle a tant de dons, cette Jarre D'On. Comme une jarre qui déborde, la nôtre, Anne-Marie, est bien remplie, de dons évidemment. Décidément, son nom lui convient bien. Revenons à nos moutons, car eux aussi elle les a bien soignés. Revenons à notre jardin. Jardin anglais, à l'anglaise, boucles à l'anglaise, jardins des plantes, des rois, d'Epicure, du Luxembourg, des Tuileries. Elle les connaît tous. Et elle va bien avec l'autre jardinier, Victor, roc, philosophe, historien, politicien, derviche, prêtre, stable, sur qui elle peut compter. Elle aussi est jardinière, à sa manière. Jardin de roches, entouré de fleurs, comme Prométhée, elle creuse, bouge, soulève, remue les rochers et les pierres et non pas à sa taille, mais bien plus grands! Un jardin qui produit des fruits intellectuels aucun n'en douterait. "Il disait qu'il aimait à voir croître dans les jardins d'autrui des plantes dont il avait planté les graines" dit Fontenelle de Leibniz. Optimiste comme ma mère. Pays fertile dont la culture est très variée et riche. Elle ne lance jamais de pierre dans les jardins des autres, non, au contraire, elle les recueille, les replace, les dispose à sa manière. L'art de la sculpture des pierres, c'est elle qui l'a découvert.

Elle a la passion pour les fleurs, les arbres, les oiseaux. Pour la nature intime et minuscule. (Voire la photographie, nouvelle passion découverte, nouvel art auquel elle s'adonne, les paysages, les pierres, les fleurs, sans oublier la neige, le ciel et les nuages!) Elle les connaît les plantes et aussi les légumes. Avec sa folie de légumes, elle aurait mieux fait de s'appeler jardin!

Anne-Marie de Jardin, voilà ce qui conviendrait à ma princesse, ma reine, ma mère, chez qui coule le sang bleu. La royauté de la jardinière de la Sapinière d'Argonne. Don, dom, domaine royal au Moyen Age. Il n'y a rien à faire, on revient toujours au royal avec notre donna de jardon. **(Suite à la page suivante)**

Elle règne, elle domine, elle met de la noblesse dans tout ce qu'elle touche avec l'autre jardinier, le victorieux du jardin (le jardin victorieux). Ils vivent bien dans leur jardin loin du barrage des castors, et pourtant ... après l'avoir quitté, la voilà qui se prend une nouvelle passion pour les castors! Petites et pas si petites bêtes qu'elle va étudier. Débarrassé du mal de mer, elle part à l'aventure, se lance dans le bateau toute seule part à l'exploration de rives inconnues.

Cela dépend du temps qu'il fait! Certes, notre experte de la météo aurait dû naître météorologiste! Elle remplacerait savamment ces gens à la télé avec en plus une sensibilité, une poésie du temps. Ma mère la météo poète à sa façon. Jar don ah non ça don ça ton ça tonne! Pas encore! Pas encore des éclairs! Du tonnerre! Ah, mais une éclaircie se fait voir. Le jargon de la météo, celui-là elle ne refuserait pas. Jargon, terme de joaillerie, espèce de diamant jaune comme de véritables hyacinthes. Le jars jargonne, il crie, quand il tonne. "Il n'y a beste n'oyseau / qu'en son jargon ne chante et crie / le tems a laissié son manteau/ De vent, de froidure et de pluye" chante Charles d'Orléans, un autre jardinier noble. Les artisans ont aussi leur propre jargon, mais elle les sait tous! Elle sait tout faire quand elle se décide. Mais faut-il d'abord qu'elle se décide ... elle sait tout faire, et avec quel art.

Un don est également une action d'accorder à quelqu'un, la propriété ou la jouissance de quelque chose. "J'accepte tous les dons que vous me voulez faire." C'est aussi quelque faculté extraordinaire accordée par une fée à un enfant. Par ma mère à moi. Par notre jardinière à nous tous. Notre jardinière fée n'arrête jamais de faire des dons. Ce qui vient du dieu de la nature. Poétiquement les dons de Flore, de Bacchus, du printemps, des fleurs, du vin, de la verdure. Assurément ses dons sont aussi des qualités, des avantages naturels. Je l'avais déjà dit, sa jarre est remplie de dons. "La nature la combla de dons ... Et l'art et le pouvoir d'affermir des couronnes/ Sont des dons que le ciel a fait à peu de personnes." (*Horace* de Corneille)

Et encore écrit Madame de Sévigné (qui elle aussi avait une fille) : "Vous avez le don de vous faire aimer quand il vous plaît et quelques fois plus, beaucoup plus que vous ne le voudriez" Est-ce clair? Mais oui, dans son jardin, notre grâce réussit sans essayer à se faire aimer. J'oublie la musique, la peinture, la cuisine, le dessin, la couture, les conseils, la tendresse, la générosité, la patience, le courage, l'enthousiasme, j'en oublie, tellement. Il y a tant de fleurs dans son jardin. Comment voulez-vous que je les mentionne toutes?

Dans ton jardon, je te salue, Anne-Marie pleine de grâce.

(Pour Sampon, voir le Victorieux, qui t'a gagnée, mon autre jardinier à qui je dois tout)

—Annette Sampon, le 1 août, 1987 Roanoke, Virginie

Beau Père

By Sally Bellerose

My father's head swivels toward the sound of metal wheels on cracked linoleum. He sits on the side of the cranked up hospital bed, hands demurely in his lap.

"Dinner," I announce.

He smiles at me, the vacant, resigned smile he's adopted for rehab. The family calls this nursing home a rehab as if a euphemism can make him well. It's beatific, my father's rehab smile, his cherub, Zoloft, "look how good I'm behaving—get me the hell out of here," smile. His easy smile. I don't mean easy for him. These days I'm not a good judge of what is easy and what is hard for my father. I mean he's trying to make himself look easy, compliant, a person easy to live with and care for.

And it is easier to sit with him and listen to the stop and go rattle of the food cart as it makes its way toward room 220. Easier than his morphine and Haldol rants in the emergency room. Easier, but less interesting. What kind of daughter finds her father's pain and fury interesting? Well, break-your-heart interesting. Exhaustingly interesting. Terrifyingly interesting. And funny. Father's glorious, funny rage.

He rubs his hands together.

"Cold?" I ask.

(Continued on next page)

"Little bit." He smiles. I drape his gray wool cardigan over his shoulders. The slack softness of it, the warmth without friction, comforts me. Right now it seems to comfort him. I've seen the same sweater clutched at his chest, tight as a straight jacket.

My father rages in two categories. The first is the "Old Bastard" rage. The "Old Bastard" is what he calls his body, as if his body were someone else, someone he can yell at like a school kid to make behave. It surprises me that when he yells he often takes the Lord's name in vain, something he never did when he raised his voice to us as kids.

"Jesus Christ, give the Old Bastard something to stop the pain."

His cursing against his back, his heart, his kidneys, his coccyx, don't surprise me as much as his profanities against The Church. The man who taught me that the Pope is infallible and that a wafer on the tongue during Communion really does become the actual flesh and blood body of Christ during Communion rails like a condemned witch against Catholicism.

His most persistent complaint is The Church's "piss poor" job of dealing with pedophilia. He is most troubled by the litany of French Canadian names associated with the abuse.

"Levigne, Pelletier, Dupre, Jesus Christ."

It hurts him to spit out the names of his countrymen. It exhausts him to speak of "These God damn hypocrites." Before his illness, he was not a man who had much practice ranting, certainly not against his beloved Church.

The food truck stops outside the room. The tray is placed on Dad's bedside table by a sixteen year-old girl who doesn't seem to like her after-school job. I pour milk from a waxed container and am relieved beyond reason when he eats the whole meal.

He pushes the food tray away and lies back. As I crank down the bed he says, "I'm not going back to church until priests can marry." I don't argue the implied cause and effect of this statement. There is no church in rehab.

The next day is not an easy day. My father lies at a forty-five degree angle in a hospital bed in an open cubicle in the ICU. We are all there. My mother, myself, my three siblings. The morphine, and the rant, and his bitter complaints, that the doctor won't let him drink and the nurse has stolen his ginger ale, have knocked him out. His eyes are closed. He looks dead, mouth slack, lips slightly blue, tubes in his arms, tubes in his nose, oxygen, heart monitor, the whole shebang. I'm squeezed between the IV pole and the bed holding one of his hands. My mother is pinched between the heart monitor and the bed holding his other hand. My sisters and brother are at his feet.

The priest walks in. The priest, dressed in white collar, vestments, and prayer book, with his decanter of holy water swinging on a gold chain. It is time for Extreme Unction, the Last Rites, which, lately, we have been instructed to call the Sacrament of the Sick. But you can't fool my family with a turn of phrase. We are gathered for the Last Rites. Again.

Daddy has had Last Rites how many times since January? So many times that when I catch my brother's eye we grin and look away. It has become funny, this dying, this lack of dying. We're starting to believe "The Old Bastard" will never leave us. What kind of children experience their own father's Last Rites as a recurring punch line? We love him. There is no doubt we love him.

The priest is a very black man with a Jamaican accent, probably not French Canadian. A serious, but smiling man, whose large eyes easily take in the six other bodies in the small room. My father is looking deader by the moment. The priest hurries with his ministrations. The family of my youth hold hands around Daddy's deathbed and the black priest in his black suit with his white collar and sash mumbles in Latin.

And I do feel the spirit. We all feel the spirit. And my daddy lies so still. And the priest shakes the water over his head, his throat, his solar plexus, his thighs and feet.

And again, up to his head, swinging the holy vessel. And I swear by the God of my childhood, my Daddy's mouth pops open, like a newborn sparrow, and the holy water rains in and he grins and says,

"It's about time you gave me something to drink."

This is the forest primeval…

If my father was outside on a Saturday morning working in the yard, and spotted me through the kitchen window doing the chores I hated and which I had to do before I was allowed to run off to the woods, he'd make me giggle by singing loudly:

"Oh Susanna, don't you cry for me. I come from Alabama with a ***band-aid*** *on my knee."*

My father sang songs, unfurled the poems of Longfellow from memory, told goofy jokes, delighted in the music of Satchmo, played the piano in the style of Fats Waller, and admired the post-war discontents of *New Yorker* writers O'Hara and Salinger.

He praised the lopsided potted geranium I sketched with watercolors, and mailed off poetry I wrote about fishermen and the dark sea to the *Cape Cod Times*. When I was in high school and my boyfriend called me on the phone, my father made silly talk, saying I was hiding under the ironing board, or that I was in the bathtub and hadn't been seen in days. He always referred to Bogie's wife as Betty Bacall, and he'd speak of her in a tone of voice that made me think she might have been an old friend.

As a kid, I knew so few facts about my father and his family, where and whom he came from, and what his growing up was like that I could recite the short list like a litany or an incantation.

He was from Worcester, Massachusetts.
He was an only child.
His parents separated when he was a youngster, around age 12 or 13.
He went to college, and graduated from divinity school.
He was in a barbershop quartet.
He met my mother when he was assigned pastoral duties at the small-town church in the town where she grew up.
When the Second World War broke out, he married my mother.
He renounced the privilege extended to clergymen to decline active duty, and enlisted in the coast guard.
He received emergency medical training at Columbia University, and then headed to Greenland. He saw no battle, but survived years of ice-locked seas and grey skies, attended to the aches and pains of crewmates and Eskimos, and became a shipboard chess whiz.

Several years after the war ended, I was born.

Within a year of my birth, he was diagnosed with Hodgkin's disease, a virulent cancer of the lymphatic system. He received a grim prognosis: six months to live. He was thirty-two years old.

My father's mother appeared in a series of snapshots in the drugstore envelopes my mother kept in a jumble in the bottom drawer of her bedroom dresser. After a while—perhaps my third birthday—this round-faced, smiling grandmother was no longer at the dining table in the cake-and-candle photos. The grandfather, my father's father, was in none of the packets of spiral-bound photos taken with the Brownie camera.

Christmas cards came from Worcester, from the grandmother, from Great Aunts, Janet and Agnes and an Uncle Burt; Aunt Clara sent me a crisp $2 bill every December.

And there were annual checks from the grandfather, too, who lived in Fall River, alone.

But I never saw these people, nor understood who, exactly, they were. I sent off dutiful thank you notes, like dropping pebbles in a well, and listened for the echo to gauge the distance.

Once the grandfather wrote back to me; I had addressed the note to Grampy Landry. He told me to call him Ken.

I saw that grandfather, whom I never called Ken, only twice that I can recall. The first time was at my father's funeral. My father lived for sixteen years with cancer, most of those years in remission, but then the disease raced through him, a thief out of time, stealing him away from me.

When the grandfather came to the funeral, I saw him, standing at the door to the small church, off to the side, flanked by a row of pine trees. He looked so much like my father that I thought he was a ghost.

The second and last time I saw him was at my marriage party, four years later. The ghost stepped out of an old car and walked toward me.

And that's all I remember of my French-Canadian family. My French-Canadian grandfather, who outlived his only child, my father, the beautiful thread that wove me into a tapestry that I knew nothing about:

I knew nothing about Kenneth, Edward, Ulric Eric, Laurent Rene, Pierre, Celeste, Marie, Armand, Rene, Marie Madeleine, Antoine, Marie Blanche, and Rene le jeune, who was born in France, in 1634, and died in Nova Scotia.

I did not know until I was well into my adulthood that I was of French-Canadian heritage, a secret gift from my father, Raymond Edward Landry.—**By Susan T. Landry**

For my Father, Lionel Pelletier

Bending for sweet strawberries
You fall in the late morning heat
Onto your hands and knees.
No dew now on the straw.
Sun shed that hours ago…

This always was your sort of devotions—
The hard ground softened only a little
        By grass or hay.
Your prayers not talk or chant,
        But motion, getting going, moving
        Toward
        What is
Created, breathing, red, sweet
Of a season
Bending in this, your last week
Of summers
For strawberries.

By Susann Pelletier

Pastoral

I ignored my mother that Sunday morning,
She calling me home from the pasture across the road,
To go to mass.

This meadow had beckoned me early,
Acolyte of grass, rock wall and pond,
Of the pebbled brook.
That shimmering chain to everywhere, and
Every altar,
Binding me to this joy,
I ran with the stream, lifting water in my hands,
Throwing offerings to the breeze,
And onto the tongues of cows and dragonflies there,
Onto the rocks, under my bare feet, and cow pies,
That teemed with little maggots,
White life, like the roiling of creation itself,
Before the world was flat, before earth was the center
Of universes, before the planet orbited the sun, before we sailed
So many seas, like invincible gods at the mast,
Circumnavigating, yet failing to find
The mystery of prayer at the brink,
Like at the edge of nowhere that is this place.

And to the day I said, splaying water from the stream:
"I am the maker of rainbows!"

I ignored my mother that Sunday morning,
I was gone again, no "goodbye"
And no " I'm coming, Mom," when she called,
This silence, like a shunning.
I imagined her standing on the just-swept steps,
Looking for me,
Delicate hand, untanned, raised to her brow,
The sun, the summer, too much,
Terrifying with their bids to abandon,
Like little fires licking at her heels, her church dress, her hat,
My face flickering in the flames
Of this morning of being six,
Morning like an inhalation of a whole life's breath,
An exhalation of ecstasy, of falling, scraping knees, bleeding,
Of falling, and not caring as I ran, my eyes set on every horizon,
And there were so many of these,
Where the stream ran and almost sang, the cows lifted their eyes to blue sky,
And bowed to the grass.

By Susann Pelletier

Soliloquies Loosely Based on *Pépère*'s Fear of Falling Trees

I. *Pépère*

Cut it down! Cut it down!
Before it hits someone!
Me! You! Your mémère!

II. The Academic's Answer

Can a restless limb be trusted?
Split from the trunk into two
one branches out over the lawn
reaches across through the living room
window, catapults pépère from his easy
chair. He's flung into a forest
he fears will menace him.
Kindling crisscross his stocky body
until he's indistinguishable from the pillowy
needles on the bed-like floor,
But the woods forgive the injuries
he, his ancestors, wrought. The burned,
scarred bark, the metronome saws
that frightened their young and old.
They forgive the cutting of a limb gone awry,
knowing human beings do not understand
the perfection, asymmetrical, trees seek.
Pépère is cradled in the bough
that never breaks, in the tip top
embrace of the crookedest pine.

III. The Poet Herself

A woodcutting contest is in my blood.
Circles of trees chopped into
sawdust, spring up again,
so that the trees once there
and not there, appear,
disappear, a photo flip book
are never permanent, yet never gone.
These trees are the fiber of my bones,
ligaments, joints, the valve of my heart,
the mouth of one in flight.

IV. Nobody in Particular

As if it were the bleeding of angels,
he bled into coffers held
by knobby-kneed priests.
Or maybe not. At any rate,
the trees were particular.
They waited until the sun

was straight on so as to cast
no shadow, so as to print no snow bank
blue. The oldest dropped

a knot from its side.
Pépère never saw it coming
as he was contemplating a bee.

V. Heretic

A snow bank of bees? Murdering trees?
Yes. I have shaved words

sharper than mouse hairs
from the hide of time.

I have peeled wounds off lotus petals
more purple than a man's lies.

I have counted a frieze of spirals
into a melodious room.

I have succumbed my eyes
to no steady vision of prayer

to no knowable predilection of the divine.
I await I know not what

and cannot know my will
undone. And I am not always content

with the green bottles of air suspended
above my head. I want no containment

and yet I have no idea
of what the world unlisted is.

VI. Pagan

Plant randomly
with the incantation
eat this seed earth.
Await a plant, a tree, a
breath drawn from the silt
to your lips, to the maw and snuffle

(continued)

of every animal, the cold and warm
blooded, the bloodless. Ingest solace
to the very filament of bone
to the soul which knows no species.

VII. The Woodsman

I didn't start off seeing her
as a tree among brush, among the old,
sick, hollow. One night a star threaded
a pine needle, and there she stood.

I saw the moon fall off
a supper plate,
a woodcut heart
tremble on the wireless wind.

My love smells of resin.
The sticky perfume of hidden crevice
smack in the middle of rough
bark, silk's opposite, yet consistent

as my hand roves
over ridges, unsplintered, satisfied.

VIII. The Hedonist to the Ascetic

Alone in the pine
a wormwood leaf for lunch
you admonish yourself
for the taste of sumac.
For kissing milkweed tender
as labia bathed
in a bare trace of stream,
toweled by waning sun.
For hunting burrs to cling
playfully to your ankles
a thin calligraphy of scratch.
For you, the trees stand
sentinels against licentious thought.
Yet the trees fling seed
waltz in twos and threes
a tango of twirling needles
burn down the burning day.

By Angela Hebert

Lexicon:
pépère = grandfather
mémère = grandmother

CHILDREN

YOUNG – BEAUTIFUL – FUNNY

LIVING – BREATHING – ENERGY

NEEDY – NURTURING – CARING

CREATIVE – CURIOUS – QUESTIONING

MISCHIEVOUS – SNEAKY – IMPISH

LAUGHTER – HEARTFELT – JOY FILLED

HONEST – FRANK – DIRECT

LOVING – GIVING – OPEN

RISK TAKERS – FORGIVERS

BACK AND FORTH

IN AND OUT

OVER AND UNDER

WHATEVER PATH IS GIVEN

CHILDREN ARE WILLING TO FORGE THROUGH

WITH TENACITY – GRACE AND STYLE . . .

By Paula J. Currie-Raymond

When as a child you watch your parents roll pennies for groceries

you know being poor
is a woman with her hair caught in a lathe
her hair ripped out at the roots
her hair dipped in a dye bath of blood,
her scalp steaming in a metal bucket labeled medical waste.

When you watch your mother roll nickels for the rent
you know being poor
is a snowman migrating to Miami
a snowman picking grapefruit in twelve-hour shifts,
the scent of citrus and bug spray stinging his anthracite eyes.

You know life is not cyclical
is not equal parts good luck/bad luck,
it is a man descending into the anthracite shaft,
black air coating his larynx, his lungs, it is
red blood blown into a white handkerchief
and on Saturday nights
it is black air rasping against his lover's nape.

When your brother smashes his piggy bank to buy a catcher's mitt
(pig shards skittering across the oilcloth floor)
you know being poor
is a snowman with his head forced upwards to stare at the sun.

When you watch your father rolling pennies for the doctor
(migraines that drown his vision with torrents of light)
you know being poor
is a snowman sweltering in Florida heat,
his head melting into runnels of sweat.

You know being poor
is a grandmother wiping tables at four in the morning,
a grandmother stacking one more plate on the sturdy shelf of her breasts
(someone stubbed out a cigarette in his eggs)
is a grandmother with varicosed legs,
with hips as breakable as the saucer she drops.

My knees ache as I pick up the shards.

By Ellen LaFleche

Things to Remember, Things to Teach

Culture is having odds and ends for grandparents
Mémère, Pépère, Nana, Granddad,
a set of silver with mismatched handles.

Culture is the "caca" crusted to the bottom
of my Pépère's old ashtray
smelling of old moons and forest fires.

Culture is scones with a short "o"
rounded by a country across the sea,
knuckles kneading dough, bones churning flesh.

Heritage is a rusty washer in my palm
smelling of old logging chains
black half moon nails and
a backyard tilled by a forest of proud spines.

Heritage is a pair of lips reaching for brown glass
as loved ones are livers and givers
filtering poison with hands staining black.

Heritage is a stuttering engine
and left-shoulder ache taught to me like algebra
the same calculation error in my blueprints
.

Family is lip on withered cheek
hands laced with tumultuous rivers
valleys and folds, a trembling landscape.

Family is mother holding mother
while brothers are burrowed in foreign soil
roots splitting and separating
in preparation for spring peaches.

Family is chains cracking, links lost
chipped glasses and cuffs chafing and
cages opening for wings to spill out.

By Emily Cote

Tombé

By Jacquie Giasson Fuller

If Louise didn't leave everything until the last minute, she wouldn't have to run around *fou comme un balai* every morning!

Mémère Gagne rocked slowly in the glider beside her kitchen window, watching her granddaughter scurry through the rooms, snatching up keys, her iPhone, her purse....

The way the young did things these days! It wasn't only Louise; when her sons Larry and Joe-Joe visited from down South, they were the same way—chatting a mile a minute, playing on their phones, running back and forth to the stores for things they'd forgotten to bring with them. Couldn't anyone sit down anymore without popping right back up?

"Okay, Mém, see you tonight!" Louise rushed over, planted a *p'tit beck* on the top of Mémère's head, then was out the door for the day.

Mémère gazed out the window into the drizzle, watched Louise hurry to her car with the gigantic purse held over her head to keep off the rain. She flung herself behind the wheel and drove off.

Mémère resumed her slow rocking. *Fou comme un balai!*

The room was quiet now, start of another day. Tuesday… or Wednesday, maybe. Not Thursday for sure; that was Louise's day off. Work in her chair this morning, nap in the afternoon. Then *Ellen* and her crossword book. Then turn on the oven for whatever Louise would cook for supper.

She bent to the yarn basket on the floor beside the glider; time to start a set of *peeshoes* for that step-great-grandson in Arkansas, even if she wasn't sure kids would want to wear them anymore. Well, if they didn't, they should! They'd kept her three boys' feet toasty during the long Maine winters, plus they loved shining up the floor after she put down the Johnson Wax, zooming around the kitchen like Montreal Canadiens in those fuzzy wool slippers. She chose a lime green yarn for the base, a ball of brown for the pompoms—boys liked brown!—then dug out a crochet hook and settled back to start the chain base.

There were bangings and clangings from across the street; the city workers had started in early today, taking down the old River Mill in her section of Bateston's Gas Patch. She'd watched them for an hour from Guillome's old La-Z-Boy in the *salon* yesterday afternoon, until it made her so sad, she had to close the curtains. Eighty-six years living next-door to the place made it feel like losing a friend. The family albums upstairs were packed with pictures taken in the shadow of that mill: Papa and Maman resting on the porch steps, she and her sister Germaine in frilly First Communion dresses, Guillome kissing her cheek during their dating days, their boys showing off their Easter baskets—all with that enormous square of bricks and windows in the background.

What Guillome would make of it, if he was here to see!

She checked the kitchen clock—almost seven-thirty; her visitor would be arriving soon. She set down the crocheting, rose from the glider, and walked carefully in her own slippery *peeshoes* to open the kitchen's front door. There was Menou, her neighbor Marcel's *p'tit chat,* sitting as still as a plaster statue on the top porch step, waiting for her.

"Come on in, *toi-là!*" she greeted him cheerfully.

"*Meeeeeew*," he responded, shaking off the rain as he leapt past her into the kitchen.

She closed the door and made her way to the counter, Menou hovering beneath her duster and winding his slippery damp fur between her shins, back, forth, back again.

"Allo' Menou-Menou," she greeted him, bending to brush the top of his head with her fingertips.

She brought a can of Friskie's down from the *armoire*, pulled the tab and spooned the mush onto a dessert plate. Menou jumped onto the counter and pressed his face into the dish; Mémère watched the dangerous-looking little teeth working over the morsels.

She tossed the empty can into the waste bucket that overflowed with trash and smelled badly—what a mess her kitchen was! If she could do more to help Louise, but her sore hips meant she couldn't stand for very long anymore. That big pile of *vaisselles* at the sink… floors unwashed since last Christmas! Louise had a *belle coeur*, a beautiful heart—but this housekeeping, what Guillome would make of it! Not to mention Maman, who could work six days at the mill, come home to take care of her family, and still the rooms sparkled all year-round.

"We're the Orphan Twins now," Louise had said sadly, after her father, Mémère's oldest son Gerry, had crashed on a motorcycle road trip four years ago. She'd lost her mother to cancer a few years before that. "Just me and you. What would I do without my *Mém*?"

And what would she do without Louise? Someone to hold onto after Gerry's passing, an irreplaceable loss—she'd never say a word about the housekeeping. Thanks to Louise's *belle coeur,* she was still in her home, too, a blessing, as one by one she'd seen her *tantes,* her sister, friends and cousins, go into nursing places because no one could take care of them anymore.

She took the plate from Menou after allowing him a few last laps, then watched him *de-lish* his cheeks and whiskers, the little tongue wetting a paw, then toweling it over his face. A *propre p'tit chat,* that one, not like the dirty city cats who came to do their *toilette* in her yard. Now, his routine was to climb into Mémère's yarn basket and sleep until around noon, when he'd go back to stand by the door, ready to get home to Marcel.

They were making their way to the glider when the phone rang from its spot on a side table in the *salon,* so Mémère turned and slowly continued in that direction. She didn't get many calls anymore, with her boys Larry and Joe-Joe living out of state and Gerry in Heaven now with Guillome. It could be her old friend Lorraine from church—she knew to let the phone ring on long enough so she'd have time to get to it.

Menou followed close beside her.

"Attention, toi-là," she warned, stepping carefully as he began his figure-eight between her shins.

"*Meeeeww,*" he responded.

As she reached a hand out for the phone, she felt the pompom of her right *peeshoe* catch Minou's underbelly; he scooted to the right just as she too tried to move that way to avoid him. She waved the extended arm wildly in the air, but there was nothing to find there... so down she went.

"Meeeeeew."

Menou's wail drew her back into the room. She opened one eye. A swirling in the rug slowly resettled into the old floral pattern, and she gazed around to find everything in its place—the sofa there with its big lumpy cushions, the phone on the table, silent now. Poor *Jesu* looking down at her from His crucifix over the TV set.

There was some pain—throbbing in the right knee and her left ankle, which was twisted beneath her in an odd way. She lay, breathing quietly, taking time to come back.

Menou sat on the other side of the room, watching her; when she caught his eyes he gave a concerned "*meeeeew?*"

"Viens-t'en." She stretched a hand toward him and he hurried over, flopped down and began kneading his needle-claws into her breasts. "Oh, *Menou-Menou...*" she said, stroking him. "Look what you did to Mémay."

A powerful crash from outside; the floor beneath her vibrating. *Beep-beep* of backing trucks so close, it sounded like they were about to smash through the wall and run her over. She raised slowly onto an elbow and braced forward to slide her *fesses* back toward the La-Z-Boy's ottoman, trying to help by pushing with her left foot, but the slightest movement of the ankle made her cringe. A bad sprain, maybe even broken! She reached around to hug the ottoman, trying to lift onto her right knee, but that brought a terrible stabbing pain. She flopped back down again.

"Meeeeeew..." Menou whined in a tone that suggested he found her efforts annoying.

"I know," she said to him. "Mémay has a big problem."

She rested against the ottoman, listening to the clamor outside ... she'd need to get up somehow. She shouldn't have refused when Louise offered to buy one of those Help-Me-I-Fell bracelets they show on TV; that would be handy right now! Marcel would want Menou back in a while; plus, she needed to pee. But then... a deeper concern—when her cousin Fern broke her elbow last summer, she'd gone directly from the hospital into the Marcotte Manor. For "rehab" they told her, but she never left, and her nephew had just sold Fern's house. Louise had taken her to the Manor for a visit last month, and Fern only stared at the floor, lost and confused.

When you're old enough, a broken ankle could send you into a home.

One of the city trucks pulled up just outside the nearby window and stopped, releasing a *gshhhh* of exhaust and then idling there. Mémère heard a worker shout the F-word that everyone, even Louise who was *propre* in many ways, said too much. Mémère gazed up—the River Mill's roofline was now in pieces—jagged edges and empty window holes. Like those crooked Lego houses Louise would build when she was little, sprawled right here on the rug where Mémère lay now. The mill that had kept Maman and Papa, her and Guillome and most of the other families in the Gas Patch and *P'tit Canada* going… what Guillome would make of it! All being taken away!

The phone *brrriinggg'*ed; she looked to it, high over her head on the side table—no way to get over there! Six long rings before the answering machine beeped on: "Mémay, it's Louise! I forgot to say I'm stopping by Wal-Mart after work; won't be home until around four, okay? So don't you worry! Have a nice morning … maybe you're in the bathroom?"

Click.

Mémère straightened her upper back against the ottoman and leaned toward the window; this allowed her to just rest her chin on the sill. Balancing in this position brought painful spasming in her ankle, but she ignored it, lifting both hands to bang on the glass. Three workers in yellow rain suits stood at the back of the big idling truck. "*Hey guys*!" she shouted. "*Help! Help!*"

Menou jumped onto the sill beside Mémère's head, his long tail sweeping her nose as she pounded at the pane, calling to the workers again and again.

She guessed it was around noon.

The idling truck had left and another come to replace it. Mémère rested against the ottoman, Menou purring on her lap. She'd slapped wildly at the glass before the second truck came, and watched, dismayed, as the men moved to the mill's entrance archway farther down the street, where they now stood smoking and chit-chatting. Her *fesses* ached. A few more tries to lift onto one knee had brought the same terrible sharp pain; now the knee had turned a marbly purple.

"*Merde,*" she muttered. She was even tempted to say the F-word!—but couldn't do that with poor *Jesu* hanging right there on the wall.

She wouldn't cry. Why bother? Tears hadn't changed a single thing in her eighty-six years—you gritted your teeth and kept going, and then you kept going some more. It was only the middle of the day … a long wait for Louise. If Marcel worried enough about Menou, he might call someone to check on her, but he was no better than she was! Hooked to oxygen in his wheelchair; he couldn't even make it down his own porch ramp without help. She tightened the muscles in her thighs, the urge to pee pressing her badly now.

"*Jesu*," Mémère directed her words to the crucifix over the television set. "Help, *Jesu*." For good measure, she turned to the portrait of Guillome on the opposite wall. "Help me, Guillome! Help!"

Sometime later, she woke to the sound of rain *pit-pitting* the window pane. Menou lay sprawled across her chest, one paw stretched upward, pressing into her nose. Mémère moved him aside, shifted as she could to release the stiffness she felt everywhere.

Strangely quiet outside now, and one corner of the mill building gone. What Guillome would make of it, nothing but sky where the bricks had been! The *Bateston Sun-Journal* had run a story saying the property would be turned into a "city lot." In the Gas Patch, with its little crooked streets and rundown houses full of families, a mill had fit in just right. What good could a "city lot" be to anyone here?

She winced, unable to hold it a second longer. Covering her face with both hands, she allowed a circle of pee to seep into the rug beneath her.

Two-forty-seven p.m. said the voice on the answering machine, after a frantic message from Marcel. "Hey, Mémère—where's Menou*?* If he's at your place, send him home, okay?"

Menou had curled up on the rug just outside the circle of pee. He'd occasionally lift his head, give her a glance, then nestle down and go back to sleep.

Mémère brought her chin back to the sill and caught a glimpse of a bright blue umbrella moving in her direction—the Somali woman who'd moved into the house on the other side of Marcel's was passing by with her little boy. The woman was completely swaddled in orange cloth, only her hands and her dark round face peeping through. What Guillome would make of it! African people living in the Gas Patch!

She pounded at the window, calling to them, and the mother and boy looked in her direction. The boy raised a hand, waving happily; the woman frowned, pulled the child deeper beneath the blue umbrella, and scooted him away.

Mémère slumped back against the ottoman.

It wasn't surprising the Somali woman was afraid. One afternoon while letting Menou out, she'd heard someone driving by yell "*Get your Muslim ass out of my country!*" to the woman's husband, who was being nice, shoveling snow off the walk in front of Marcel's house. Louise said the Somalis she knew at work were good people, but she'd heard that some of them could be mean. One thing was, they seemed to do everything for their families, like Maman and Papa had done for her, like she and Guillome did for the boys until they grew up. Now Larry was off in Arkansas; Joe-Joe in North Carolina, and poor Gerry in Heaven… only she and Louise left. Except for housework, there wasn't much Louise needed help with. She was one of those *jeune filles* who could fix cars and dig holes; she'd even jacked up part of the porch last year when they found some of the floorboards rotting.

Then there was that step-great-grandson Mémère had never even met, who didn't send thank-you cards for Christmas gifts—what was his name anyway? Something weird, like *Ajax*. Once Larry put him on the phone, and the boy talked in that lanky way, like those Southern people you see on TV, said he was eating jelly on his *bray-ed*. He didn't sound like a kid who'd care about polishing floors in his *peeshoes*.

Three-fourteen p.m. Marcel had just left his fifth message while Menou *meeeeew'*-ed his demands to be let out, pacing between Mémère and the kitchen door.

Quiet outside now. The rain had stopped, trucks and workers gone home for the day. All the left side of the River Mill was gone. There was a time she might have been happy to know they'd tear it down one day—back when Papa lost two of his fingers in his carding machine, or when she'd get those splitting headaches from the banging of the weave looms, or a hot summer day made standing at a spinning machine feel like being at the mouth of Hell.

But … there were some good things to remember, too. There were almost always jobs for people. You made okay money; you had good friends who sang *Les Fraises et Les Framboises* with you in time to the pounding shuttles. You didn't run around *fou comme un balai* before work; you even took the time to make the bed while Guillome read the *Bateston Sun* in his La-Z-Boy. You had your coffee and *corton* toast, and then you crossed the street to the mill holding Guillome's hand until you could be together again at suppertime.

It was people in China working jobs that people in the Gas Patch used to do. So what could the people here do to earn money? Even Louise, smart enough to get As in college, could only find work subbing at the Catholic school up the hill. If you tore down a mill and put in something that gave people work, that could be worth it—there must be a way a "city lot" could help the families around here.

She sighed, *rendu au bout* with being on the floor. She was hungry and thirsty; her knee and ankle pulsing with pain. If she had the remote, she could at least turn on *Ellen*. If she had her yarn basket, she could work on that *peeshoe*. If she wasn't so *vieille femme*, she could vacuum up the *mousses* she saw now under all the furniture, or maybe scrub the filthy arms of the La-Z-Boy. Eighty-six years of staying busy meant that doing nothing felt like an act of sin.

How could she be home if she couldn't walk? How would she let Menou in and out? Or get back and forth to the *toilette?*

"Merde!" she said. And then had to let herself pee again.

Late-afternoon sunlight broke through the clouds; with the mill's left wall missing, its rays fingered toward her on the rug. The odd brightness it brought to the room highlighted a scum of dust everywhere, the TV screen filthy. Even poor *Jesu* looked like He needed a polish.

Mémère was fed up, and it was clear to her that Menou felt the same. He wouldn't come anymore when she called, but stood delivering his mournful *meeeeew*s from a spot by the kitchen door.

She gently rubbed her purply knee. It could be that it was not good. The barriers were everywhere—the long row of porch steps leading down to the yard. The low bathtub, almost impossible to get out of! The heavy cooking pans; doorknobs that turned hard. Shoes and stockings to pull on, although that ankle wouldn't be taking more than a *peeshoe* for awhile…

She didn't want to leave Louise. How could she leave Louise?

After a while longer ... *finally,* the familiar *whoosh* of Louise's car approaching and turning into its spot beside the house. Mémère felt the rush of relief, her heart lightening at the familiar thudding up the porch stairs, the opening of the kitchen door.

"*Menou*!" She heard the surprise in Louise's voice. "Why are you still here?"

"Meeeeeew..." he answered, and then the door closed behind him.

"*Help!*" Mémère called, hearing Louise begin the searching for her, going into Mémère's first-floor bedroom, into the bathroom, and finally, she was at the doorway of the *salon*, her eyes grown large.

"*Mém! What happened?!*"

Mémère soon felt enclosed in a jumble of arms and soothing words; she stiffened and drew within herself a bit—these young people and their hugs for everything! Being fussed over was something she'd never gotten used to in a family of *grit-your-teeth-and-keep-going* types.

"Are you hurt? *Oooooh,* look at that knee!"

"My ankle's sore," she explained. "Me and Menou were on the floor all day!"

"Oh, *Mémay*...." Despite her gentle touch, Mémère winced as Louise examined the swollen ankle and knee. After determining she was otherwise all right, she went to the kitchen to call 911 and pour her a glass of water.

Mémère heard her giving the address as "Yes, across from the River Mill ..." Directions she'd been giving others all her life—soon to be meaningless!

"You were right, Louise, I needed a Help-Me bracelet." Mémère took the glass of water, and after a few sips, added quietly, "I couldn't help but pee."

"Don't worry about *that,*" Louise said, settling behind her on the La-Z-Boy to watch for the ambulance. "That's not such a big deal; that's fixable. When I think of what could have happened!" She rested a hand on Mémère's shoulder, and her voice wobbled: *"What would I do without my Mém?"*

There was a splattering of sunlight against the far wall where Papa's piano had stood, its faint outline still visible on the old wallpaper. She'd given it away after Gerry—the only one of her boys who'd inherited Papa's talent—had died. The house so still now, of music and of many people she'd loved: *tantes* and *oncles,* Papa with his pipe, her sister Germaine, cousins and second cousins—all who'd sung and laughed together in this room ... gone now. Down to her, *vieille femme*, and this good grandgirl. And one day... Louise alone.

"When you're eighty-six, broken bones change things," she said.

"They'll give you pain pills and wrap up your *boo-boos,* and then we'll come home and eat and go to bed!" Louise said firmly.

She heard the ambulance siren approaching from deep within the city.

"If I can't walk," she said.

"We'll make it work! I'll take off a few days.... We'll have the emergency button for when I'm not here, and if we need to, we'll hire those women who come in to help. "

"If I'm too much for you?"

"Don't worry!" Patting her hand. "Me and you; you know the drill!"

The ambulance pulled in just outside the window, its red roof light spinning fast.

"If you meet a nice man?"

Louise made a face. "Who needs a man when you've got a *Mém*?"

They laughed. There was that *belle coeur* right there; how blessed Mémère felt! That long line... Papa, Maman, Guillome, Gerry and his poor wife Marlene ... their lives, their sufferings and dyings. To bring her this gift, the fruit of their days, their lovely Louise!

She saw the determination on her granddaughter's face as she stood and hurried into the kitchen.

The hope of the young! It wasn't always right ... but it wasn't wrong.

Heavy thumping like storm troopers on the porch steps, a pounding at the kitchen door.... Mémère gave a hurried last look around the room ... the comfortable old sofa! The shadowy stain of Papa's piano! Guillome's La-Z-Boy! The dusty *Jesu*!

Could she be there, in her glider in the morning, watching Louise running *fou comme un balai?* Menou would be wanting his visit. Even if that boy in Arkansas wouldn't wear them, *peeshoes* needed making! What would the Gas Patch look like when the River Mill was finally gone? Whatever could they do with a *city lot?*

Trouver Son Chemin

Feu? asks the young man,
pointing at his cigarette.
Here in the dark I'm not sure it's my stop –

Chaville, Rive Droit, toward *Versailles*
and *feu, feu,* my mind gropes
until I find matches in my bag.
Merci. He cups flame to his face
and slouches down the street
I finally recognize as mine.

I'm often a little confused here.
Running in the *Parc de Fausses Reposes*,
I stick to the paths, count my turns,
and still get hopelessly lost. *Perdu*
until I find *L'Eglise Sainte Bernadette*,

on the *parc's* periphery, so odd
in this land of cathedrals
and *les grands vitrails* –
small windows colored
like willow, sky, daffodil.

I think of Bernadette,
my aunt, not the saint.
Well, maybe the saint too,
a simple girl who felt unworthy,
though it was she

who saw the Virgin.
Aunt Bern, not one for visions,
escaped the convent. Sleek-haired,
Franco-American flapper, smart enough
for an office job, she raised five kids,
managed a hard husband,
and would have liked this squat
church where I sit for a long time
amid the tang of polished pew
and incense. Afterwards, I easily find
Rue des Bons Chances

and my borrowed condo—up the hill
from the train I hear each night
from Paris, from Versailles.

I sit on the balcony
with a last glass of *Muscadet*,
thinking of Bernadette,
her mother, and all her tough
sisters. *Bastille* Eve and

fireworks splash the stars.
On the terrace below,
neighbors' faces lit
by glowing cigarettes,
their language, liquid
and spirited, same
as my grandmother's,
same as my aunts'.

By Jeri Theriault

"Rosemary"

Artist Statement

While I've been making poems most of my life, I began making visual art in 2007. Though I love drawing, my favorite pieces result from the use of color and texture; usually this means collage like the piece, "Rosemary."

I have always been drawn to the textures and colors of fabric. My collages are inspired by the models I have taken in Continuing Education courses with Martha Miller at Maine College of Art. I build them using bits of brightly colored paper, most of these from magazines. This is a contemplative and forgiving process for me; it's important to me that I'm recycling as I create something new.

The creating of a collage is similar to the creation of a poem, bits and pieces considered and pieced together. Making collages is also similar to the patchwork quilts my memere made.

Like my poems, the collages are anchored in narrative. "Rosemary" is a good example of narrative. Since the model was knitting as she sat, looking down at her hands. I tried to capture her serenity in this piece.

Creating art—whether I'm drawing, making collage or painting—is fun and challenging. I also think it pushes my poetry; it's possible to entertain an idea both visually and literarily. **—Jeri Theriault**

Body Parts

Chapter Sixteen from unpublished book, working title, By Way of Canada

By Kim Chase

My mother's sister Luce was a wreck of a woman by the time I got around to looking at her with a critical eye. Almost all of her kids were grown, but her abdomen still swelled like a perpetual pregnancy or some other kind of growth.

"Prolapsed uterus," my mother explained. "I wish she'd get it fixed."

Ma tante Luce often said she could feel it slipping out between her legs. I don't know how she coaxed it back in.

She had a horror of doctors which extended to dentists and accounted for the state of her teeth. Many of them were gone or worse, and when she laughed we could all see the ruined remains. She waved her cigarette wildly when she laughed, scattering her ashes.

All of my aunt's physical defects came sharply into focus for me one day when my mother was talking about her legs.

"You've always had such beautiful legs, Luce." It probably wasn't the first time my mother had made the remark, nor was it the last. But it was the first time the incongruous observation impressed me enough to make me take a long hard look at ma tante Luce.

I'm looking at a hag, I thought on that day. I cannot tell my mother's sister from a hag.

Her hair was steely, stringy, straggling; she combed it tight against her scalp, hacking off a few random locks when it grew too long. She smoked constantly, her cigarette an expressive extension of her hand. How could my mother miss it? But no, it was only legs my mother mentioned if she talked about her sister's appearance. Beautiful, dancer's legs.

The people in my mother's family seemed to perceive one another as loose assemblies of body parts, most of which had been procured from their original owners: Pépère Tucker's forehead, St. Anthony's toes, a widow's peak, a dancer's legs.

"You have your uncle André's eyes," ma tante Luce said to me one day.

"So she does," said mon oncle André. "Give 'em back!"

I didn't mind having mon oncle André's eyes. He was one of my favorite uncles and the most handsome, especially for a priest. Having Pépère Tucker's forehead, on the other hand, was a different matter. I only knew him from the portrait hanging over the fireplace in my grandparents' living room.

"Your forehead is the spitting image of Pépère Tucker's," my mother used to say.

"Ma," I argued each time, "he's bald."

"Makes no difference, believe me. And his chin. You've got his chin if I ever saw it."

"Did you?" I asked. "Did you ever see it? Because he's got a beard in that picture, you know. Look."

"Never mind. It doesn't hide the jaw-line. I never understood why a man would want to hide a nice jaw-line beneath a beard."

"I promise, Ma, that if you stop telling me I look like Pépère Tucker, I will never, ever grow a beard."

My relatives were not content to trace healthy body parts to those of their forebears. They were also concerned with missing or maimed limbs or organs, such as my father's leg, held together by metal plates, or his bad eye from the time he got hit by a car.

"You can't even tell he's blind in that eye unless he's tired," my mother bragged. "*Et puis ça louche un peu*. It wanders a little."

There were problem parts that ran in the family such as heel spurs, which made it hard to buy shoes, or arches so high they stretched to another size when you stood up. There were the baby teeth, blamed on Mémère Goudreau, which locked around the jaw and refused to yield to incoming teeth. They were hard, small and bright white, and if my grandmother was in any way vain, it was about her teeth.

"Her permanent teeth never came in, just stayed where they were, up in her gums," my mother said. "She polished her teeth with baking soda and cleaned between with button-hole twist, long before anyone ever thought up dental floss."

Then there were the ear problems, mine included. I had chronic infections from infancy on. My mother would get up with me late at night when the pain was the worst. She heated sweet oil in a pan, testing it on the tender inside of her wrist to make sure it wasn't too hot. I braced myself for the burning drops—two or three was all it took before the abscess burst. The pain then was like a knife driven into my head, but afterward the discomfort subsided.

My mother stroked my head while I cried, apologizing for the genes responsible for my suffering.

"I'm sorry it had to be you, *chérie,* but it hasn't skipped a generation of this family yet. You know, the Blacks have their sickle cell anaemia, the Irish have their spina bifida. With us, it's ears."

Sometimes she told me stories to pass the slow-moving time of the night or to lull me back to sleep.

"You're lucky you can still hear anything at all. Two of my cousins went to live with a foster family when ma tante Madeleine died. They were treated very poorly there, but none of us in the family knew. The younger one, Alexis, had ear infections, like you, but they went untreated so, in the end, he was almost completely deaf. By the time I knew him, he had a horn he held up to his ear, and if you yelled into it, he could hear something, we never knew how much. He would rub his hand over his heart and smile to show how happy he was to have heard, how good it made him feel inside.

"Your cousin Julie put a bean up her nose when she was just about your age. Stuck it right up her nose where it sprouted and began to grow. Makes perfect sense when you think about it, a damp, dark place like that. Well, it festered and abscessed, caused her no end of pain. Finally, your aunt took her to old Doc LaMarche.

"'Tell me, Julie,' he said. 'Did you, by any chance, put a bean up your nose?' She had to admit it by then, of course. She was in too much pain. Doc LaMarche removed the bean and its sprouts and told Julie to stop putting things up her nose."

The tale of Julie was my favorite earache story. At least the pain I suffered wasn't due to my own stupidity and there had to be some virtue in that.

My ears continued to trouble me, so the doctor began removing body parts I didn't even know I had and didn't miss when they were gone: tonsils first and then adenoids. Truth be told, I couldn't even picture them when they were described to me in detail. The grown-ups spoiled me after each operation. My siblings and cousins didn't.

"Stupid baby," they hissed. "Think you're a big shot just because of your dumb ears."

Even after I ran out of removable parts, the earaches continued. My mother took me to a specialist.

"Chronic mastoiditis," he said. "We'll have to operate."

"What else can they take out?" I asked my mother.

"A small part of your ear," she said, "but they'll put it right back this time. Just as soon as they fix it." I could tell she was worried.

The surgery took a long time, longer than the specialist had told us. When I woke up, I had a thick bandage over my left ear and I couldn't sit up. I tried, but moving made me feel like the bed was tipping over backwards to dump me on the floor. My mother called me softly from nearby. I turned slowly until I could see her. She held my hand, the one that wasn't taped to a plastic tube. She looked sick to me, puffy and pale, the way she was when I saw her in the hospital after she had her gall bladder out.

"Now your ears will be fine," she said. "You're so lucky! My poor cousin, Alexis, I've told you about him before, haven't I?" I blinked, hoping she would take it for a nod, hoping she would tell me anyway.

"He wasn't always deaf, you know," she said. "He must've been able to hear when he was little because he spoke almost like a normal person when I knew him. They stayed with us briefly after the authorities took them away from those awful people. We all felt bad, of course, but how could we have known? They were still up in Canada and ma tante Madeleine never kept in touch.

"Alexis' older sister Giselle was made to do chores barefoot even in the bitter cold of winter. When she came to live with us, the soles of her feet were harder and thicker than leather. She had to have two toes removed because of frostbite."

I had never heard this part of the story.

"The nuns took them in, eventually," my mother said, looking past me. She had a way of departing when she told certain stories, as if she took leave of her body. "They lived out the rest of their lives working in the convent, just working as regular people. Giselle never joined the order, she just cooked for the nuns and Alexis took care of the grounds."

After the surgery, my left ear improved, but my right ear continued to plague me. My sisters and brothers told me it stunk like something was rotting inside my head. They were trying to be mean, but I knew they were right. Sometimes I could smell it myself.

When I was twelve years old, the specialist told us that my right ear drum was gone and that he could replace it with a small patch of skin from my right arm. My mother told him to go ahead.

For reasons I never understood, the little rectangular scar on my arm earned me the respect of all the kids in the family. They stopped teasing me about my ears and asked me to show the scar to their friends.

"See that?" they would say. "That's her eardrum."

That summer, our next-door neighbor Sherri came home with her face all black and blue, a thick bandage covering her nose. Her four-year-old son took one look at her and screamed.

I ran into the house.

"Ma," I said. "Sherri looks like someone beat her up!" My mother rolled her eyes.

"Nose job," she said. "Waste of money. And that poor little boy, seeing his mother like that." She told me what a nose job was and I spent a long time pondering the ramifications. If I could change my appearance, where would I start? More to the point, where would I stop? I was twelve years old and there was little about my looks that I didn't dislike.

Around that time my cousin Isabelle, Luce's youngest, was at the age when teenage girls play the same rock song over and over and over again. Isabelle had a different favorite each week and she rigged the stereo so it would play the same 45 incessantly until someone, usually ma tante Luce, made her stop.

I worshipped Isabelle. She was small, dark and exotic looking, where I was tall, blond and plain. Her hair was rich, brown and curly; mine was fine, limp and straight as straw.

Sometimes Isabelle let me come into her room and listen to music with her. I couldn't understand any of the songs; the words were clear, but they made no sense. Isabelle said I was too young to understand the symbolism.

The most mysterious song of all was called "In the Year 2525." It confused and frightened me, but Isabelle said it was a sign of the times to come.

"You can't change it, "she said ominously. "It's your future."

The strangest lines of the song were:

> "Pick your sons, pick your daughters, too
> From the bottom of a long glass tube."

Isabelle explained the concept of *in vitro* fertilization to me and I wondered if she was making it all up. It was Isabelle who had told me a short time before how human reproduction worked and I hadn't yet resolved whether or not it was a credible theory. It seemed ridiculous, appalling and, above all, unlikely.

But to choose your children from a tube? I pictured perfectly formed babies, only a fraction of an inch long, cooing engagingly from their tiny tubes, hoping to be picked by parents shopping for offspring. Most people would have trouble guessing what the babies would look like when they grew up, but for my mother and aunts it would be simple. Every time a new cousin was born into the family, it underwent the ritual cataloguing of features and body parts:

"She'll be tall, like her father."

"He has that little bump on his nose, just like mon oncle Sévérin."

"Look at those beautiful ears, so close to her head. No one has ears like that except Mémère. No question where *this* baby comes from!"

Cousins were born in abundance, then cousins of cousins and babies of cousins. To me, they were all shapeless, bleating bundles when they arrived. Their features were no more distinct to me than those of the rag dolls I used to make with my grandmother when I was small. Eyes, noses, ears, mouths. So what?

Listening to Isabelle's rock music provided a welcome respite from the French folk songs my mother and ma tante Luce played whenever they got together. There were no more fiddlers in the family except for the few who still lived in Québec, so they played their records in order to recreate the music of their youth.

"Soirée in a can," ma tante Luce called it. La Bolduc, La Famille Sansoucy, Armand Desrochers, La Famille Dion. The aunts played their music with almost as much enthusiasm as Isabelle played hers. It was old-fashioned and tacky in my opinion and when my friends were around, I begged my mother not to play it.

"Oh, I understand, believe me," she said. "Sometimes you just don't want to be French, eh?"

"Ma, we're not French, we're American, in case you hadn't noticed."

"French, by way of Canada, and American. That makes you Franco-American, if you want to get specific."

"Like Spaghettios?" I said. "Thanks, but I think I'll just be American."

At school it was possible to not be French. Although many of my·classmates were French and although they knew I was too, we never talked about it at school.

Eventually, I went to college away from home where no one knew me or my family, so no one could tell me whom I looked like, and any signs marking me as French had apparently disappeared. I was invisible. At first it felt like freedom, but the longer I was away from home, the more I missed being French. It wasn't the language or identity so much as the noise, everyone talking at once, the statements ending on the upswing, the chaos that passed for conversation in my family.

I went home as soon as I graduated. I fell in love with a "French boy," as my mother like to brag. My husband Gérard and I wound up buying a house three blocks from my parents. When I had my first child, I resigned myself to the fact that she would have to undergo the ritual analysis of her body parts.

"Look at that hairline!" my mother said to me when she first held my baby Lisette. "She's got that same clean hairline your sister has. You, on the other hand, had hair growing all down your back for the longest time." When she was done matching my baby's body parts to as many of her relatives as possible, she started in on my husband's side of the family.

"Well, there's no doubt in my mind who the father of *this* baby is."

"Ma," I said. "Stop."

"Take a look at her upper lip." I looked at my sleeping baby's face. In the middle of her upper lip was a tiny ridge.

"Where'd she get that little ridge?"

"Don't you ever look at your husband?" my mother asked.

"What?" Gérard said. We inspected his upper lip and sure enough, there was my daughter's upper-lip ridge, only bigger and partially obscured by a moustache. I sighed and took the loose collection of body parts I had produced away from my mother.

"Lisette," I said firmly, "looks just like herself."

Ma tante Luce died of lung cancer when I was pregnant with my fourth child. It seemed harder on my mother than the loss of any other sibling. I had always suspected that Luce was my mother's favorite.

I was, as I liked to say, twelve and a half months pregnant at my aunt's funeral. I did all the socializing I could and then sat in a quiet corner willing my baby to grab any last minute body parts and get born. My mother sat down next to me and pushed the hair back from my forehead the way she used to when I was very small.

"Not a spiritual experience any more, is it, *chérie*?" She patted the growth on my lap. "You carry just like Luce did."

Dear God, no, I thought. Anything, but that. I looked at my mother.

"It's true, believe me. From behind, you couldn't even tell she was pregnant. You're the same way, all in front. Too bad you don't have her legs."

After the funeral, some of us went back to Isabelle's house. We fed the kids and then had tea in the kitchen.

"Listen to that music," Isabelle said, waving her cigarette toward her daughter's room.

"What music?" I asked. "I can't hear anything.

"What's new?" Isabelle said. She picked up my arm and yelled at my eardrum scar. "Can you hear me now?" She went into the hall and bellowed at her daughter.

"Chantal! Chantal, come out here!"

"What?" Isabelle's oldest slouched out of her bedroom.

"Turn down the damn music! Are you playing that Céline Dion again? You know I can't stand her whiny voice."

"You and ma tante Luce used to love the Dion family, didn't you Ma?" I asked. I vaguely remembered an album cover featuring a dark-haired girl, a full face with a rounded, somewhat prominent nose.

"Back when she was still French," my mother said, rolling her eyes. "I'm with you Belle – now all she does is whine."

"I think it's what they did to her nose makes her sound like that. Chantal, go get the picture to show your aunt."

The CD cover Chantal produced showed a sharp nose in a pinched face.

"Are you sure that's the same one?" I said. "The one in La Famille Dion?"

"Look at the eyes," my mother said. "That's all that's left."

"Her nose is *razor sharp*," Chantal said. "Almost like Michael Jackson's. And when she had a baby, it was really a twin because they did fertilization and you know what? They froze the twin. *They froze it*. They're going to have it later."

I looked at Isabelle. She shrugged.

"I'd take her word for it," she said. "She reads up on all that stuff."

"*Oh, Seigneur.*" My mother rolled her eyes again. Isabelle lit another cigarette.

"Tell me you're not smoking again, *chérie,*" my mother said.

"What's it look like, ma tante? You can blame that on my mother."

"It's a little late for that," my mother sighed. Isabelle waved her cigarette dismissively.

"It's all right, ma tante. We all have to die sometime." She waved her cigarette again, casting ashes all around. For a moment, she was ma tante Luce, without the prolapsed uterus, without the ruined teeth. It was just her hand, holding her cigarette between the same two fingers, scattering her ashes.

"You have your mother's hands," I said.

"Took you long enough to figure that out," my mother said. "But she doesn't have her legs. No one had legs like my sister Luce."

My mother fished around in her purse until she found an old photo. It had been taken several years ago behind my grandmother's house. It was just my mother and Luce, standing beneath the willow tree. My mother was pretty and plump all over, as she had always been. My aunt looked exactly as I remembered her, except there, beneath the steely grey hair, the missing teeth and ballooning abdomen, were the elegant legs of a dancer.

In honor of my mother and grandmother:

I was three when my father died, leaving my mother with four small children. I was the youngest.

My mother had been raised by foster parents, Jenny and Oscar. Oscar had died and Jenny was at death's door. She knew nothing of her birth parents. She was alone; we were raised on welfare.
In my late 20s, I discovered my passion for dairy products. By 1980, I completed my study of dairy science and established Kendall Farms. By 1985, I was making Kendall Farms *Crème Fraîche*, the best *crème fraîche* in this country. The French say it is equal to that of Normandy.

Studies completed and business established, I had time to research my mother's birth family. My grandmother's name was Cloutier, her family from Normandy, the birth place of *crème fraîche*.

Grand-mere, your blood flows in my veins. Merci.

Follow your passion. You will be surprised where it leads.

Sadie Kendall, Kendall Farms *Crème Fraîche*

Pépère's People, Pépère's Place

By Lynn Plourde

The following is part of a chapter from an unpublished young adult novel **"Breathe"** *by Lynn Plourde. After Jaycee's beloved Pépère dies, she suffers panic attacks. In this chapter, Jaycee begins to "catch her breath" again when she attends her Pépère's family reunion and visits his family homestead in Aroostook County.*

"*Merci, ma fille*." Several older ladies thanked Jaycee for holding the door open for them. Then Jaycee, her mother, and grandmother entered the Knights of Columbus hall for the Cyr family reunion.

From the moment they stepped inside, they knew they were with family. No name tags to wear—*ma fille, mes amis, hon, sweetie,* and *dear* worked just fine. No introductions. Probably because handshakes had no place in this room—hugs, giant bear hugs for everyone. Energy—the energy should have been harnessed. Bangor Hydro Electric could have lit up the County for a month with the energy from all these Cyrs. The colors—pink, red, purple, chartreuse, lime, magenta—and that was only one woman's dress. The patterns—plaids, stripes, polka dots, checks—and that was only one man's outfit. The food—tourtière pie, creton, dynamites, baked beans, boudin, chicken stew. And that didn't include the desserts. There were twice as many desserts as all the other foods combined—potato candy, sucre à la crème, whoopie pies, peanut butter fudge, pets de soeurs. The sounds—French mixed with English, English mixed with French. And always hands flying faster than mouths were flapping. The laughter—the universal language of the hall. Jokes about how many Frenchman does it take to ... knee-slapper stories that grew bigger with each telling, pranks that would make the Three Stooges proud. Jaycee, her mother, and her grandmother didn't know a single person there, but it didn't matter. They belonged to Pépère, and so they belonged at this Cyr reunion. *They* were family.

The three of them had meant to stay together, but it didn't happen. They ricocheted around the hall as if it were a giant pinball machine and they were the balls.

At the food table, Jaycee tried a sliver of tourtière pie. A bit more cloves than Pépère used, but still good. So good, she followed the sliver with a wedge. And followed that with a giant whoopie pie, licking the creamy filling that oozed out between the two chocolate cakes.

Walking past the dance floor, Jaycee heard, "*Viens icitte, la fille*," and suddenly she found herself spinning and whirling and twirling with a middle-aged Frenchman. His feet shimmied in a blur across the floor. Jaycee couldn't keep up. She tried, but after stepping on his toes for a third time and too breathless to apologize, she saw her lifeline—Mémère. She grabbed her grandmother by the hand and pulled her into the dance, substituting older legs for younger legs, but the older ones were more experienced. Jaycee stepped back and watched as Mémère jitterbugged. Mémère hadn't lost any moves, swinging and swaying and dipping with the man, a synchronous masterpiece. Jaycee had always cherished her memories of watching Mémère and Pépère jitterbug. They could "cut a rug" better than anyone she knew. Mem and Pep had always teased Jaycee that the younger generation didn't know how to dance. And Jaycee believed them as she'd watched in awe all their jitterbugging through the years—at weddings, anniversaries, birthday parties. But not recently. After his strokes, Pépère couldn't dance anymore. But obviously Mémère still could. If Jaycee squinted enough to blur her vision, she could pretend that it was Mem and Pep still jitterbugging out there on this dance floor. She smiled at that fuzzy vision. But before she could rescue Mémère and make certain *she* wasn't going to have a stroke, Jaycee was whisked in a different direction.

The card tables—Canasta, Whist, Sixty-three, Charlemagne. Her mother pulled her over to a Charlemagne table with open seats. But as Jaycee and her mother started to sit opposite each other, someone asked, "You know each uhder? You come togeder?" Jaycee and her mother laughed and nodded. Of course, they did. There was no denying it. One of Jaycee's nicknames was Linda Junior. She'd been told she was a spitting image of her mother, the twenty-five-years-ago version of her mother. "Can't play togeder den. Dat's cheating." Jaycee and her mother juggled chairs until they sat opposite strangers. Jaycee was surprised to see she ended up with a young partner. He was probably a little older than her, but still Jaycee didn't know many people from her generation who knew how to play Charlemagne. And the average age of the people at this reunion was well over the half-century mark, maybe nearer the three-quarter century mark.

The cards were shuffled, the bidding started—four clubs, five hearts, six clubs, take the game. Didn't make the game. They all laughed. When her partner smiled, his brown eyes had a twinkle that looked familiar, strangely familiar. More bidding—no more taking the game though. It was close, but Jaycee and her partner won. The older Cyrs around the table teased them. Prince Charlemagne and Princess Charlemagne they called them. They were too young to win. Must be a fluke. So they played again, against new opponents, and won again. More twinkling in those brown eyes, more teasing by the elders.

Suddenly, someone stopped the music and squawked into the microphone. *"Attention"*—the French pronunciation. "Attention"—the English pronunciation. *"Temps pour le portrait.* Time for the photograph. *Dépechez-vous.* Hurry." Everyone scurried to the stage for a group photo—some standing on the stage, some sitting in chairs on the stage, some sitting on the floor at the edge of the stage, some standing on the floor in front of the stage. Two to a chair, some on knees, some in laps, squeezed in tight, then tighter still. There were too many Cyrs, coming out of the woodwork. But they jammed in, all of them. *"Un, deux, trois—souriez.* One, two, three—smile."

After the photo, Jaycee looked for her mother and grandmother in the sea of faces. She started to feel a tad claustrophobic. Too many people sandwiched in too tightly. So she headed for the door. She knew they'd find her. It was all right—all right to seek air, all right to get control before it slipped away, all right to follow Dr. Robichaud's advice. Jaycee stepped outside. It was cold. What she'd been told was true. Aroostook County was cold in November, but it was a pure cold. She exhaled and delighted in seeing her breath.

"I can see my breath." Jaycee giggled into the phone.

"What the heck are you talking about?" asked Dirk on the other end. "I call you up in Aroostook County and you tell me you can see your breath? What's in the air up there? Be careful you don't get arrested, Jaycee."

"Aw, shut up, Dirk. The only thing I'm under the influence of is fresh air. And, I'm loving it. I don't have to worry about panic attacks and that suffocating feeling if I can *see* my breath, if I can touch it." Jaycee waved her hand through the fog her breath made in front of her face.

"So no attacks since you left?" Dirk asked.

"Nope, in fact, I've felt better than I've felt in a long time."

"That's good, Jayc. Glad to hear it. Just make sure you don't stay there, no matter how fresh the air is. I want ya back here."

Jaycee smiled at his comment and rubbed her cheek gently with her index finger, the spot Dirk had kissed yesterday. Yesterday seemed a million years ago. Maybe she'd dreamed it. "Don't worry," she said. "You can't get rid of me that easily."

A pause, then Jaycee changed the subject. "I'm surprised the phone reception is so good."

"Yeah, you're coming in loud and clear. Where you standing? On the top floor of your high-rise hotel?"

"Ha ha! Not quite. I'm standing at the edge of an old potato field."

"A potato field?"

"Yup, my Pépère's potato field."

"You're jumping into the middle of a conversation again," said Dirk. "Care to back up so this conversation will make sense to *both* of us."

"I'd be happy to, but I only have a few minutes. My mother and Mémère are waiting for me. We just found Pépère's old homestead, and we're going in to explore it."

"Hope ya don't get busted for breaking and entering."

"We won't. It's deserted."

"Well then, I hope you don't find any ghosts."

"Dirk, I think maybe that's exactly what all three of us hope we *will* find. They're waiting for me. Gotta go. Bye!"

Jaycee wished she'd had time to tell Dirk everything, but it would have to wait until she got back. Then she'd share each and every detail of the trip—the prop plane ride and the free, floating feeling it gave her, the Cyr family reunion with its circus atmosphere, plus how they'd found Pépère's old homestead. After a couple of wrong turns and a trip down three dirt roads, Jaycee's mom drove while her Mémère rode shotgun, saying "Ooh, I think it's that road. Or maybe that one." At the same time Jaycee tried to keep track of where they actually were as she studied page sixty-five of the *Maine Atlas & Gazetteer.* As soon as Mem saw it, she gasped. It was an old, overgrown farmhouse, but to all three of them it was the palace of the man they all loved.

Jaycee's mother and grandmother were standing at the door to the homestead holding hands. "Are you ready?" they asked Jaycee.

She nodded and grabbed Mémère's free hand. "Here we go!" she said as all three of them burst through the door, stepping into the middle of Pépère's stories.

"The stove, the old cook stove," Mémère squealed in delight. None of them seemed to notice mice had made a nest inside. Instead they envisioned the stove burning in winter, in summer, in every season, with loaf after loaf of homemade bread.

"Remember the kitten story?" Jaycee's mother asked.

Jaycee and Mémère nodded. Jaycee's mother continued, knowing they wouldn't mind hearing it again here, especially here. "It was a Sunday morning. Time to get cooking. Sunday dinner was always a big deal. But when Pépère's mother, Mémère Cecile, got ready to lift the burner and stoke the fire, she heard a strange mewing. She popped off the burner and there was . . ." She paused as if trying to remember something.

"Mittens!" chimed in Jaycee and Mémère.

"Yes, Mittens. Thank you." Jaycee's mother laughed. "I could remember the kitten's names, but not the mother's. Well, anyway, Mémère Cecile lifted that burner and *MEOW*—there was Mittens all curled up with a batch of newborn kittens inside that toasty woodstove. No Sunday cooking that day—they had to eat day-old bread, cheese, and canned peaches for dinner. And they named Mitten's kittens . . ."

"Smudge, Smokey, and Biscuit!" All three of them exclaimed together, then laughed.

"Look—the hand pump." Jaycee pointed to the sink. "I don't think I've ever seen a kitchen with a hand pump."

"But you've *heard* about one?" asked Mémère.

"Oh, yeah," said Jaycee. "Friday night was bath night. Mémère Cecile got out the washtub, set it in the middle of the kitchen floor . . .

"There." Jaycee's mother pointed to a spot opposite the door.

"Or there." Mémère pointed to the space in front of the wood stove.

"Or there." Jaycee pointed to a third spot nearer the sink.

"Doesn't matter." They all agreed.

"Continue, Jaycee," said her mother.

And Jaycee did. "After the washtub was set, then it was Pépère's job to fill kettle after kettle with water from the hand pump, heat kettle after kettle on the woodstove, and pour kettle after kettle into the washtub for bath time. Nine thousand, nine hundred, and ninety-nine kettles—he said it took."

They all rolled their eyes at Pépère's exaggeration. He'd always exaggerated. Oh, how they missed it. "Roll up your pant legs" was his favorite expression when he was telling a story filled with a lot of bull—meaning if you didn't want to step in the bullshit of his story, then you'd better roll up your pant legs so you wouldn't get them all dirty. Jaycee smiled as she remembered his expression and rolled up her own pants to the delight of her mother and grandmother.

Jaycee continued the story. "The girls were first. They didn't work in the barn and fields so they didn't get as dirty as the boys. Pépère's sisters had the first turn in the washtub. After they were done, the bath water was the color of tea, a weak tea. Next were Mémère Cecile and her mother, Grand-Mémère Ouellette. They were too old to get too dirty. The bath water looked more like a strong tea when they finished. Then the little boys, Pépère's younger brothers, had a turn in the washtub. They were covered with grit and grime, but cleaner than Pépère—so they went next. The bath water changed to the color of coffee, black coffee. Then it was Pépère's turn. By the time he stepped into the washtub, the water was chilly and slimy—so he just did three quick dunks, skipped the soap, and jumped back out. Finally Pépère Joe, Pépère's father, took a turn in the washtub. He always swore up a storm at how dirty Pépère must have been to turn that bath water the color of mud and so thick with sludge that he had to use a sledge hammer to break open a hole to climb into the washtub. Pépère protested that it wasn't his fault, but he claimed no one believed him."

Mémère chuckled at Jaycee's story and then tried the hand pump in the sink. It creaked and groaned, then spurted air, not water. Might come in handy—an *air* pump, thought Jaycee.

They stepped into the front room—*le bord en avant*, as Pépère used to call it. The only remaining piece of furniture was a piano—a wobbly piano on three legs, too large to ever fit through a door. The homestead must have been built around it. Maybe so. After all, they'd all heard the stories about Mémère Cecile and her beautiful soprano voice and her prancing piano fingers and the time she'd performed with the popular songstress Kate Smith's show—the Cyr family's greatest claim to fame, to date.

Mémère wiped away some cobwebs and tried the keys. They barely budged—uneven, stiff, and swollen like a row of arthritic knuckles. She coaxed out a few sour notes, then slapped her hands over her ears. "Ouch! Music shouldn't be painful."

"What do you think it used to sound like?" Jaycee asked.

"Not a note out of place,' said Mémère. "Mémère Cecile wouldn't have had a note out of place, just like she never had a hair out of place."

"Can you imagine their Saturday night get-togethers in here?"

Mémère glanced around the room and answered, "Yes, I can, Jaycee. I really can."

"Me too," said Jaycee's mother.

"Me three," added Jaycee with a smile.

"Shall we?" asked Mémère.

Jaycee and her mother nodded. Mémère started them off—singing *Alouette* while miming playing the piano, as if it were in key, as if the parlor were filled with Pépère and his brothers and sisters, with Mémère Cecile, Pépère Joe, and Grand-Mémère Ouellette, with the cousins who lived a half mile up the road and the other cousins who lived a half mile down the road.

Alouette, gentille alouette
Alouette, je te plumerai
Je te plumerai la tête

Mémère laughed and pointed to her head.

Jaycee and her mother echoed and pointed to their heads. *Je te plumerai la tête*

Mémère's turn. *Et la tête*

Their turn. *Et la tête*

Mémère. *Alouette*

Theirs. *Alouette*

All together . . . *Ahhhhhhhhhhhhhhhhhhhhhhhhhhhhhhhhhhhh* . . .
as long as they could stretch the syllable, as long as they could hold their breaths.

Mémère held hers the longest. Maybe holding, controlling one's breath came with age, with practice.

Alouette, gentille alouette
Alouette, je te plumerai....

They continued singing *Alouette*, at the top of their lungs . . . *le nez, les yeux, le cou*. Each time pointing to their noses, eyes, and necks. Mémère continued pantomiming playing the piano while Jaycee and her mother took turns playing different imaginary instruments—the fiddle, spoons, harmonica, scrub board. When they finally ran out of body parts and instruments, they stopped, reluctantly.

Mémère smiled. "Oh, their Saturday nights must have been magic, pure magic. I'm just glad Pépère told us all about them and taught us some of his old songs."

"Yeah, we used to sing them for hours on long car rides when we were kids," said Jaycee's mother.

"He taught me, too," added Jaycee. "He would bounce me on his knee for hours, singing his French songs. I think I was only two or three years old when I learned them."

"I can't say I ever truly *learned* them," said her mother. "I don't know what they mean—just that they're fun to sing."

Mémère laughed. "I don't think I have a clue what they mean either."

"I didn't know until I took French in school. Wanna know?" Jaycee asked them.

They looked at each other and shook their heads.

Jaycee laughed. She'd let them stay ignorant if that's what they wanted. Probably their imaginations cooked up wilder and wackier images than plucking feathers off a bird.

Next they headed down cellar. Fortunately they'd brought a flashlight. The electricity wasn't working or as Pépère would have said, "Can't open dee light." They stepped gently onto the dirt floor, not sure what was buried there after all those years. They stared into decades-old canning jars scattered on shelves, trying to decipher if they were fat green beans or skinny pickles or perhaps another moldy vegetable.

"Hungry?" Jaycee asked, gesturing toward the jars.

"Yuck—those are decades and decades old," answered her mother.

"Yeah, but guess who would still eat them?" asked Jaycee.

"Pépère!" all three of them agreed.

"He'd eat anything that wasn't moving—and probably quite a few things that *were* moving!" added Mémère as she shook her head.

Jaycee laughed, knowing that her grandmother's statement was more truth than exaggeration. "Can I take one?" Jaycee picked up one of the jars.

"Are you crazy?" asked her mother. "You'll catch some strange disease from it."

"I'm not gonna eat it, Mom. I just want a souvenir of this place, of Pépère's place."

"But what if it breaks? It could be toxic." Her mother looked skeptical.

"Let her have it, Linda. She just wants a memory to hold onto. I want one, too." Mémère reached into her pocket and pulled out a piece of ivory from a piano key. "The piano wouldn't fit into my pocket, but this fits and it was loose," she explained.

"No explanation needed, Mémère." Jaycee hugged her grandmother as she clutched her own jar treasure.

Then they climbed back up to the main floor and continued up to the second floor, holding their breaths on the creaky staircase, hugging the wall side rather than the rickety banister, tiptoeing down the hall, ducking under a cobweb chandelier, into the back corner bedroom—the bedroom where Pépère was born. They each touched the brittle flowered wallpaper on the slant made by the eaves, where Pépère Joe was said to have hit his head after looking down at his first-born son for the very first time. Pépère used to love to tell that story about his father, how he'd leaned over and looked closely at wrinkly, newborn Pépère wrapped in a bundle in Mémère Cecile's arms as she laid in bed. "*Mon dieu*," he'd said. "*Ses yeux—brun!*" Grampie Joe jumped back up with a squeal of delight and bonked his head so hard on the eaves he passed out on the floor. Mémère Cecilee had to climb out of her birthing bed, get some water, and throw it at Pépère Joe to bring him back to. She ribbed him for the longest time—that giving birth was harder on him than her. But Pépère said his father didn't mind the teasing. It was worth it to see that his son had brown eyes from the moment he was born—the sign of a true little Frenchman.

Jaycee reached up and peeled off a strip of wallpaper, placed it in her mother's hand and said, "your souvenir, Mom." Her mother smiled.

As they turned to leave, grandmother, mother, and granddaughter fell silent. They walked back through each room one more time, savoring each place, each space—and the stories in between the spaces. Today the stories had been told for the umpteenth time. This time *they'd* told them for Pépère since he wasn't there to tell them himself. But then again, maybe he was. This house seemed to have its own breath. Maybe it was the stir of the wind through all the nooks and crannies. Maybe it was the echo of all the lives that had passed through these rooms. Maybe it was their own hearts beating, beating, beating in rhythm, as one heart, not three hearts. Today they were connected to each other in a way they'd never been connected before. Today they were connected to Pépère in a way they'd never been connected to him before. If it were possible to step inside a man's soul and grab hold, they'd done it.

They left the homestead the same way they'd entered, three generations hand-in-hand, hanging onto each other, into the early evening darkness.

"It's snowing!" Jaycee whispered.

She wasn't sure why she'd whispered—maybe because this moment seemed fragile, maybe because the snow-globe-style snowflakes seemed fragile, like bubbles, and she was afraid her breath might melt them.

Her whisper didn't melt the snow. Instead the flakes fell onto all three of their faces—only then melting and mingling with their tears.

Something You Have But Cannot Find

By Rhea Côté Robbins

Taken from unpublished manuscript, "If These Walls Could Talk"

Salvage—Sew and Save

A collection of sewing rummage should be part of your sewing equipment. Fabric scraps, buttons, old belts and trimmings should be systematically saved so that you don't waste time searching for them nor money replacing something you have but cannot find.
—*The Complete Book of Sewing: Dressmaking and Sewing for the Home Made Easy*, 1943, Constance Talbot

I do not have too many stories about maman when she was a girl. She would tell me she didn't remember too many things. "We were poor," she'd say "we'd make our own fun." That was a little vague to my inquisitiveness. To my question of "how many dolls did you have?" she would say, none. "None?" That was a highly unlikely thing to happen to a little girl in my mind. How could you not have a doll? No money for dolls, she'd say. Our brothers would carve us a doll at Christmas, but we never had a doll from the store. Oh, I had a great imagination, she would tell me. I had paper dolls. See, I knew you would have some dolls, I countered. I would make my paper dolls cutting them out of the Sears catalog or magazines. After we were through with cutting out of the Sears catalog, it was used as toilet paper in the outhouse when the new catalog came out. This would be the same outhouse I used when we would visit mémère, but for me, there was regular toilet paper, but I still could not figure that out. How did those glossy paper pages from the catalog manage to wipe your bottom? I can just imagine everything slippy-sliding all over the place. It did not look the same back then. It was more like a newspaper. Even worse, I thought. Wouldn't it leave a mess? Oh, she would laugh, we would sit there, read the catalog as we sat there, lose track of time because it was one of the places we could go to be alone It was all right.

To her, everything was all right. In fact, her answer to everything, up until the day she died was, "Things always work out in the end," coming from a woman whose situation did anything but work out, even in the end. But, then again, I'm not so sure that she isn't right.

Mémère Daigle thought I was the most spoiled little girl in the world because she, mémère Daigle, had worked, at age ten, in the factory in Fall River, Massachusetts. With the optimism of an eight-year-old, I thought I would impress her when she was visiting us one day. I thought I could do this because I was praised in the family for not breaking my toys, so I lined up all my dolls, even my baby girl doll I had when I was first born with her fingers completely chewed off and totally naked. I found her a dress for the show. I lined up all twenty-six dolls to my mémère's horror. She lamented to my maman on how could she spoil me like that? Maman said to her, "She has so many dolls because she does not break her toys." I was justified and cleared of all charges.

What stories I do have comes from one of maman's older sisters. One of the stories has to do with hats that mémère Daigle had bought for the twins, Rita, maman and Rhea, my aunt, out of a silvery, shiny material like cotton sateen and they were playing in the tall grass in front of the house. All that could be seen from the window in the house where the older sister was watching them were their hats bobbing in the tall grass. She writes me in a letter: "Anyway, I can still see both, your mom and her sister, playing in the long grass on the front lawn—all we could see was those two silver heads bobbing. Mom had bought them hats, shiny silver to protect them from the sun."

Another story goes like this: "As you know, your momma was always fatter than Rhea, she used to go to grandmother's through the little path we had that went behind the Ouellette's house and got two apples, one for herself and one for Rhea. On her way back, she had to climb a high-like rock we called Roché. Well, by the time she was up that, she had both apples eaten and turned back for more. Finally, she made it with one left for Rhea, she had three to her twin's one. Grandma thought she was cute, but told her make sure you get home with one for your sister."

I was the girl maman always wanted. When I was born, dad said, there, now you have your girl. Maman took off my diaper to make sure I was a girl and she said I peed on her pillow. That was my hello. Girls are prized in our family; boys too, but the girls were the long-awaited. Boys were the standard, those who would carry on the family line; girls came by special delivery. After a long line of boys, mémère had a girl, they called her Blanche at baptism, but at home she was called Queen because they had had a girl after a long succession of boys. Maman and her twin were numbers fifteen and sixteen in a family of seventeen. Those twins were as prized as the first. So, to have a girl was a joy and to be a girl was a joy. This was the way of the family.

What's your family story? Write it here:

What's your family story? Write it here:

Foremothers/Heroines—*Aïeules/Héroïnes*

Palmier—Victoire
Palm—Victory

Coquelicot—Consolation. Repos, tranquillité. Ardeur fragile
Poppy—Consolation

Lychnis fleur de coucou—Irrésistible sympathie
Ragged Robin—Wit

Renoncule—Reproches, raillerie, perfidie, méchanceté; surprise et joie malgré les reproches
Ranunculus—Radiancy, charm

Lewiston woman highly regarded by Franco-Americans

By Dawn Gagnon, of the *Bangor Daily News* Staff

Lewiston—In Maine's Franco-American circles, Madeleine Giguere is known as "la marraine," the godmother, a title indicative of the high regard in which Giguere, her work and her efforts on behalf of others are held.

A Lewiston native, Giguere is one of last year's recipients of a Maryann Hartman Award. The awards, sponsored by the University of Maine's Women In the Curriculum and Women's and Gender Studies programs, are presented each year to three Maine women who have inspired others through their work and community service.

While Giguere's work as an educator and researcher has earned her respect throughout the United States and Canada, many believe her effort to collect and report data on the state's Franco-American population is her most significant contribution. Tracking statistics about Mainers of French descent remains an area of study that few—if any—other Maine researchers have tackled.

"Nobody else has done it. It's really tedious work," Giguere acknowledged in a recent interview at her home on Germaine Street, not far from the home at the corner of Webster Street and Orange Street where she grew up the only child of a Lewiston doctor and a public school teacher.

Nevertheless, Giguere is responsible for identifying the large percentage of Maine people who are Franco-American, an estimated one out of three, and has extracted from otherwise lifeless United States Census figures meaningful information about the state's French heritage.

Her ground-breaking work with Maine's Franco demographics began in the early 1970s, a heady and exciting period of ethnic revival many say was sparked by the Vietnam War. With the nation's social structure turned on its ear, people of French, Irish, African, American Indian and virtually every other cultural extraction began reclaiming and reexamining their heritage and beliefs.

Giguere's findings helped shed light on the social and economic characteristics of Mainers of French descent.

"She believed in the power of numbers," said author Rhea Cote Robbins of Brewer, who nominated Giguere for the award. "Madeleine determined her course of work in tracking the French through the United States Census because she believed that numbers do open avenues for other kinds of change to take place.

"Having a visible and viable presence on the national level increases and enhances the possibilities for Franco-Americans to be seen as a political body."

In 1986, Robbins said, Giguere led an effort to include a question on ancestry in the 1990 United States Census to help determine the size of cultural groups. Without the ability to indicate ancestry, as well as language, Franco-Americans would have continued to be perceived as a much smaller portion of Maine's total population than they are now.

Though Giguere officially retired from her post as head of the University of Southern Maine's Sociology department in 1990, her extensive knowledge of Franco-American demographics remains in great demand.

"She's a walking library," says Senator Judy Paradis, D-Frenchville. "She's a wealth of information. I've been a fan of hers for years. She's one of our gurus."

Giguere's most recent effort involves her work as a member of the Commission to Study Development of Maine's Franco-American Resource, created by legislation presented by Paradis.

"She's a legend in the field," said Connie LaPointe-Brennan, commission chairman. "We've learned a good deal from her."

Among Giguere's contributions to the study, which looks at the potential of the Franco-American community regarding economic development opportunities, are demographic profiles, information on education levels and breakdowns on where people who speak French can be found.

A report to the Legislature on the findings of the study is in draft form. The final version is expected to be completed in about a month.

Giguere said keeping on top of changing Franco demographics has become more difficult since budget cuts closed the state's data center. As she was interviewed for this story in her home in a quiet Lewiston neighborhood, Giguere listened for the fax machine in her home office to deliver data from MISER, the Massachusetts Institute for Social and Economic Research at the University of Massachusetts, the closest source she was able to find for census information about Maine.

Though Giguere's academic career has taken her as far away as Jamaica, her heart has never strayed far from Lewiston's brick mills and canals.

"It's my home. I wouldn't want to move anyplace else," she said with characteristic frankness.

Giguere has surrounded herself with things most important to her, many illustrating the interconnected and recurring themes that have fueled her life's work: her French ancestry, the importance of family, the Roman Catholic Church and the mills of Lewiston.

The shelves in the living room are filled with photographs that span generations, including pictures of her paternal Giguere and maternal Cailler forebears, who, like many other French Canadians, migrated to New England in search of a better life.

"They came here for a job, and they believed in hard work," she said. "They pursued happiness through family, community and service."

On one wall of Giguere's bedroom hangs a painting by Marc Poirier, depicting a view of Lewiston from the Auburn side of the Androscoggin River, which once powered the textile mills for which Lewiston was known. The scene takes in, among other things, St. Peter's Roman Catholic Church. Founded in 1870, it was the first parish in Maine established to serve the French-speaking Canadians who came to work in the mills. Eight years later, the parish started the state's first bilingual parochial school.

On another wall is a copy of a 1709 map of the Côte-de-Beaupré—Île d'Orléans region in Quebec. The map shows where, on the northern bank of the St. Lawrence River, Giguere's forebears lived centuries ago.

On a table is a reliquary, yet another variation of the intertwining themes. The small shrine, which once belonged to her father, holds minute bone fragments of St. Gabriel Lalemant, St. Jean de Brebeuf and Charles Garnier, three of a group known as the North American Martyrs, six French Jesuits and two assistants killed by the Iroquois between 1642 and 1649, a period of fierce rivalry between Iroquois and Hurons who were allied with English and French colonists.

Though her educational pursuits kept her away from Lewiston for extended periods, she found herself settled in 1965.

"I started being a faculty activist in 1970-71 because the women were underpaid at the university, in spite of having the same credentials as their male counterparts," she said.

In her presentation at the Hartman Awards reception, Robbins noted Giguere and some of her colleagues organized the University of Southern Maine women to push for the adoption of affirmative action guidelines in the University of Maine System. Because of this work, then-Governor Ken Curtis appointed Giguere to the Governor's Advisory Council on Women, one of several leadership posts she held in the equal rights arena.

Giguere, however, does not see herself as political, a characteristic she believes holds true for Franco-Americans as a group.

"One of the characteristics of Franco-Americans is that they don't rock the boat," she said. "They are family oriented, kin oriented. They are interested in making a living, but not in being the richest or most successful."

But she points out that becoming involved in local politics enabled many French-Canadians in Lewiston to make the move from mill jobs to more desirable occupations. Such was the case with her own grandfathers. One became chief of police and the other landed a coveted post office job.

Since retiring from the University of Southern Maine in 1990, Giguere has served as volunteer director of the Franco-American Heritage Collection at the University of Southern Maine's Lewiston-Auburn campus, a post she held until a year ago. In that capacity, she screened some 2,000 books and entered them into the university library's URSUS computer data base, developing carpal tunnel syndrome in the process. She copied all the Franco-American papers onto acid-free papers and stored them in acid-free compartments to preserve them for future generations. She helped research a recently published history of St. Peter's and St. Paul's Parish in Lewiston.

Among her current projects is to research the life of Lewiston newspaperwoman Charlotte Michaud.

"That's this box right here," Giguere said, pointing to a cardboard box filled with documents about Michaud, who she admits intrigues her.

"She was a contemporary of my mother's and I saw her any number of times," Giguere said. "It's a bit of detective work. She did write a lot. She wrote Dorothy Parker-like verse. She fancied herself a dance critic."

Born in the late 1800s, Michaud was the daughter of a printer for *Le Messager*, a French-language newspaper published in Lewiston from 1880 through 1966. Giguere describes Michaud as a "young, perky woman" when she embarked on her writing career at the Lewiston paper, but she lost her job when a new boss arrived and became a free-lance writer for such publications as *La Presse* of Montreal and the *Portland Press Herald*.

Among the trends that Giguere has tracked over the decades is the continuing decline of the use of French in Maine. But how to reverse that trend–or even if it should be—is something that Giguere admits escapes her.

"I've never been an activist in that sense ... I never went out proselytizing," she said. "I've never felt responsible for doing something about [saving the language]. If there's a French event, I go to it. I'm part of the audience ... My feeling is that it's very difficult to maintain [French] in an English-speaking atmosphere.

"I can remember going to my aunt's as a child and they were listening to a French station from Montreal," she said. That Lewiston continues to have access to French television and radio stations might be a key to the use of the language in the future.

"We need to be fluent in all aspects of the language—not only the literature, but the recipes and sports and soap operas," Giguere said. "The context has to change. If you do have to speak French to your grandmother as I did, you continue to speak French."

The Archiving

We sort photographs,
    booklets, and clippings –
recollections,
    we come now to know.

To find a place…

Sheets from store ledgers,
    concert programs, wedding invitations,
    certificates of first communion.

We hold what they touched,
    saved
when others might have discarded.
    Papa peers over this newspaper,
    Maman sets down this parish bulletin.

To find a place for all...

The stories, theirs,
    now ours,
we listen.
Voices depending on us;
    faces, our vision.

The evidence before us,
    what is it to define,
to outlive,
    or stay behind?

To find a place for all we can…

We come to see their lives,
    ourselves,
recognized.

By Jan Hitchcock, Ph.D.

Madeleine Giguere

Poem in memory of Madeleine Giguere (1925-2004), distinguished Franco-American scholar and citizen, this poem is revised from a version written on the occasion of her retirement as Volunteer Director of the Franco-American Heritage Collection, Lewiston-Auburn College, University of Southern Maine, January 1997.

Do you want to know about Acadian culture? Just ask, Géraldine Chassé

Dick Harrison, former editor/publisher/interviewer
Originally published in *Aroostook Magazine*

AM: *Aroostook Magazine*
GC: Géraldine Chassé

AM: Were you born and raised in Aroostook County?
GC: In St. Francis, Maine up-river.
AM: In a French Acadian family?
GC: No. Pelletier is a nice French Canadian name, but I have a lot of Acadian grandmothers, my great-grandmother on the Pelletier side was a Daigle; I go way back to the original founders of the area.
AM: Explain briefly who the Acadians are, where they came from, and what's the relationship between them Acadians and the Cajuns in Louisiana.
GC: Okay. The Acadian came to North America—to New France—at St. Croix Island in 1604. They tried establishing a permanent colony because fisherman and trappers were coming back and forth between Europe and the New World. Ami I going too far back?
AM: St. Croix Island is where?
GC: It's in the St. Croix River between Calais, Maine and St. Stephen, New Brunswick [Canada]. But the colony started and stopped and started and stopped, finally, to make a long story short, these people we call Acadians lived and moved across the bay into Grand Pré and into Nova Scotia which was the original Acadia. They lived a beautiful, peaceful life, the original families came around 1632, the families and the children. These people are the basis for our Acadian culture. The French Canadian, on the other hand, came in 1607 and opened up Québec. Now you will find different names from the Acadians and the French Canadian. Now we take a great deal of pride in our Acadian culture up here [Aroostook County, St. John Valley], because we're a pocket, an isolated pocket of remnants of a 17th century culture. Our French shows you that and some of our customs; like the children used to say, their dad still had a foot in the medieval ages because he was old-fashioned. Now the—Cajuns, oh yes, I wanted to go back to the deportation, so anyway, whenever France and England sneeze at one another in Europe, naturally it was felt in New France or in the New World. So Acadia went from one country to another, but the Acadians were stubborn, they refused to be taken in by the British even though the British had conquered Acadia. What happens in 1755, the British owned Acadian after many wars, and we won't get into that. They wanted to get rid of the French people because they thought they were rabble-rousers, so they started deporting them from 1755 to, oh, a good 20 years. Some of these people were put in ships and, of course, deported. Some of them went through the woods. Our ancestors didn't get on the ships; they were refugees, they went up to the French territory in Canada and eventually found their way down there. Now the Cajuns, on the other hand, some of them were deported and sent back to Europe, some of them were sent down along the eastern seaboard by the British through deportation. A lot of these Acadians found their way to Louisiana, the West Indies, some of them even went down to the Falkland Island; they were scattered all over the place. An obstinate, determined ethnicity that did not want to be assimilated. So a lot of these Cajuns knew about Louisiana being a French territory, so they thought they would be received there. Those that were sent to Europe longed to return to New France because they had had such an idyllic life in Acadia, or they just hung around there and the French people who were there, they weren't any better to them than the British had been. But Spanish ships were hired and they brought some of these Acadians originally to Louisiana. And, of course, there's the corrupt pronunciation of "Acadian" for "Cajun." Now, I've been down there a couple of times and I'm going down there next month, I just want to do it at my own pace this time. I had been with the Park Service and I had been with the college.
AM: Acadians and Cajuns are originally from New France, from Acadia, which comprises parts of Nova Scotia and New Brunswick and parts of Maine.
GC: That's right. And you'll have pockets of Acadians and Cajuns in just about every state in the Union.

AM: So the people in Upper St. John Valley originally lived in New France, were driven out by the British, and traveled up to St. John Valley to what is now northern Maine.

GC: The Madawaska Territory. The St. John Valley was the Madawaska Territory.

AM: You've been involved for 30 or more years in preserving and rediscovering the local culture, the Acadian culture in Aroostook County. Where did your efforts begin?

GC: (laughter) I love this part! First of all, I had lived in New York City five years. I was a school teacher, my sister was a physiotherapist, my other sister was a nurse, and the three of us decided to see what it was like. We lived in New York and then we decided there were greener pastures beyond the Mississippi, so I've been in the southwestern states; I love the southwest I took a semester at the university in Albuquerque because it was a border town and wanted to live there and I didn't want to waste my time. And then we ended up in California. My two sisters stayed in California, but I had planted my roots in the Valley. I had taught school, a country school, and my mother used to say "Tu a planté des racines, you've planted roots." Well, my other two sisters, they went to school, they took off and never returned. But I was lonesome for the river and I was lonesome for the little churches on both sides of the river and I was just lonesome for the St. John Valley. So I came back and that's when I met my husband, Ernie. That's a long story. Well, anyway, when I met and married Ernie, I used to look out my kitchen window and I used to see this white wooden cross out on the flat and I would say, "Ernie," of course Ernie was only interested in potatoes. I would look out the window and I'd say, "Quoi, c'est ça, Ernie?" and he would say, Ah, c'est des français qui sont logé une première maison, les premières français." The first French people. So having traveled around the country and having always been curious about historical places, whether it was in Texas or in Albuquerque or in New York, I couldn't believe the people of the area had absolutely no desire to learn about themselves. They were a little embarrassed, so I can see where the Anglo influence was, a carry-over probably from the deportation. They were embarrassed about their French names; they were embarrassed about their French accents. When I married Ernie in '51 and I saw the cross there, nothing was ever mentioned about the Acadians or the first people. So I read up a little bit and I was involved with youth work and I used to take my 4-H-ers down there and we'd discuss what Acadia was all about and all this sort of thing. Well, in '69 Madawaska was getting ready for its centennial, and so single-handed I took out the old Underwood typewriter, which skipped letters and everything, and I looked around to organize a society; we needed some kind of a vehicle to work out of.

AM: To mark this 100th anniversary?

GC: Yes, because nobody was making an effort. I always have been interested in history no matter where I was, so I contacted the Maine State Library and they referred me to mainly the historical societies and all the people involved in the preservation of culture in the State of Maine. So one thing led to another. We organized the Madawaska Historical Society in '68. It was so funny. They recommended we get a competent attorney to incorporate. The "authorities" said, "incorporate right away" because you never meet so many contrary people who are interested in preserving culture—we all believe we're right, you know! So we organized in 1968. We're over thirty-one years old now, we're still going strong, and we've done a lot of work, a little museum. In '78, ten years later, we stared our family reunions, Acadian Festival.

AM: So you were involved in the establishment of the Madawaska Historical Society, you were involved in the establishing the tradition of the annual Acadian Festival and Family Reunion.

GC: I wrote columns to local papers for whatever family happened to be, and so one thing led to another and then I got involved in publications. There was very little available on publications. We had "L'Histoire de Madawaska" by Rev. Thomas Albert, which was fine. A lot of controversy surrounded it because it was not documented and all that, but little-by-little, I learned over the years. Now I handle publications through this area, local artists, local writers. And so when Ernie became sick, I had to discontinue all these things because he was in a wheel chair and I was not going to put him in a nursing home. And then in my great, big house, if I couldn't find a little corner for him, I'd have felt awfully guilty. So he had a good two years here at home, and the whole family was involved. I had five boys and one daughter. I wanted some children, but I didn't intend to populate the world by myself, but it looked pretty bad for awhile. Being an old school teacher, I had this grandiose fantasy that all my children would be Ph.D.s; I got two that graduated from college; the others all started and quit except my son, Jim. He was a hippy! He's still got his long hair. He has his garbage business in Arizona—he's done very well!

AM: Let's get back to your involvement with Acadian culture and history and bringing it back to the fore. Before we started, I asked you to list some of the things you've been involved with. You mentioned the University of Maine at Fort Kent Archives, every historical society in the St. John Valley, The Acadian Heritage Council, and the Acadian Cultural Exchange of Northern Maine.

GC: I was appointed by the Secretary of the Interior to serve on the Maine Acadian Preservation Commission.
AM: What does that involve?
GC: That was through the Park Service. Federally funded. I was one of the founding directors. [Senator George] Mitchell, [Senator Bill] Cohen and [Maine Speaker of the House] John Martin got the ball rolling that we have a unique culture up here that was worth preserving and we worked on that for three years. It did give us quite a shot in the arm. It made us known nationally. But like I said, the Park Service had its own agenda and it lacked the soul and the feeling that the local people had about their own culture. It became too academic. I may be wrong in saying this, but I imagine you have to go by priorities, I'm an old school teacher, I'm a college graduate, BUT I believe in the soul of anything, and this culture of ours definitely has a very strong living soul, a spirit. Now, I don't know if you were familiar with Blackie Cyr, Claude; he served on the Commission with me. The Park Service would have all these professionals out, archeologist, and anthropologists from all over to come over and tell us who we were. And, of course, the Acadian Party in Canada is political, now I want to emphasize that. Here, ours was strictly cultural. It was home-based, it was fireside, and it was kitchen table, our religion, and our language. It's up to us *dans le foyer* to preserve this. I serve as a consultant at the University of Maine at Fort Kent's Acadian Archives and I love the head of the Archives, Lisa Ornstein; Lisa's a dear friend of mine, so is Nick Hawes; nice young couple, but they are from away. Very capable.
AM: The UMFK Archives; can you explain what that is?
GC: They're doing the same thing only with monies, tax monies, through academia to preserve our culture, and they do!
AM: Are they overlapping, are they duplicating, are they each doing different things? It sounds like you're involved with all of them.
GC: Well, the Heritage Council is a spin-off from the Acadian Preservation Commission which was administered through the Park Service. We were in operation for three years and we got a million dollars and all of that, to pay outsiders to come and tell us who we were. After the Commission was let go, the Park Service stepped back, and we formed the Acadian Heritage Council. On that council, we have people from the community, it's not these specialists. I refer to academia, but that encompasses a lot of layers. The Council itself, the state, the communities are involved, all the towns in the Valley are involved, all the Chambers of Commerce are involved, all the historical societies are involved, people like me. I'm the Acadian Cultural Exchange.
AM: That's another.
GC: That's a private thing. I make publications available.
AM: You organized the Acadian Cultural Exchange of northern Maine; that's your project?
GC: That's my final one.
AM: For now.
GC: For now. Well, at my age I don't know if I'll be getting much into any more, but my children are interested. For a long time they kept referring to "mama's Hysterical Society."
AM: What is the Acadian Cultural Exchange?
GC: It's a consulting organization, really. I don't actually do the research, but if you want to do genealogy, I can tell you who to contact. I have people from all over that come see me. There's hardly a day I don't have a call or someone. This week, I've had somebody from West Paris, Maine. I had a place from upstate New York and I had someone from San Clemente, California come in. They come in. I work with the Archives. Now whenever Nick and Lisa need something, guess who they call? The old shoe. Yesterday, Nick called, wanted to know if I knew of any bus tours going to the Acadian World Congress?
AM: The Congress?
GC: Yeah, in Louisiana, next month. "*Le Congrès Mondial.*" The Acadian World Congress. They had one in New Brunswick, Canada in the past [1994].
AM: Is this the same as the World Francophone Congress? There was one in Moncton last year. Is that a broader-based conference?
GC: This is a continuation of that.
AM: And this is just for Acadians or is it for all French-speaking people?
GC: No, it's considered Acadian, but francophones go because somewhere up there we all have these Acadian grandmothers tucked away, you know. So, anyway, Nick called and he said somebody wanted to know if anybody was taking a tour to the Congress. Well, I had looked into it myself, but at my age, I don't want to be on a bus for

four days to go to Louisiana, so I'm flying out. So I told Nick, I gave him some tours out of New Brunswick and the prices and everything. It's little things like that. The Acadian Exchange does a little bit of everything.

AM: You're an information resource for anything to do with Acadian culture and heritage.

GC: In the Valley, yes.

AM: This sounds like a one-person operation. Are you the Acadian Cultural Exchange of Northern Maine?

GC: My daughter and my son are involved. We're not an organization; we're not tax exempt. You know I have this beautiful old house, which I don't know what I'm going to do with, and after you see my library and you'll see the volume of traffic I have here, I've been considering making a research center. Work with the Madawaska Historical Society and the Acadian Archives. I don't know what I'm going to do because this is one of the oldest houses in the area. We are on historical ground. We gave the property for the museum and the land down at the railroad track; the Society bought where the cross is and all that from Ernie and me. So we are a historical site even though we are semi-commercial now. Let's see what the future holds.

AM: So far we've been jumping around from the Acadian Archives, the Historical Society, the Heritage Council, and the Exchange. Let's focus on the Acadian Cultural Exchange of Northern Maine. You say it encompasses all these other projects and programs. What do you mean by encompassing the programs; they don't necessarily fall under the Exchange?

GC: They do not fall under the Exchange, but they come to me. These organizations come to me. Let's say it's a family reunion or the Acadian Festival or it it's a recipe for Acadian food, they come to me to check out. I even help adoptees find their biological parents; I've already found seven. I work with the police department, the town office, the Chamber of Commerce, they send them: "Go see Mme. Chassé." So, you see, this Exchange includes a lot of things.

AM: At first, calling this an "exchange" left me with the impression that it is similar to a student exchange program in schools, where someone from Aroostook County may spend a year at a school in Europe, for example, and a student from that European school spends that same year here in the County. But it seems that the Acadian Cultural Exchange serves as a resource for the exchange of information; if you don't have the answer, you can tell someone where to go to get the information they seek. [The Acadian Cultural Exchange—contact: Acadian Archives Building , University of Maine at Fort Kent, 23 University Drive, Fort Kent, ME 04743, Phone: 207-834-7552]

GC: Yes. I'm on the Internet. There was a lady who wanted to know something about her uncle who worked for the Bangor & Aroostook Railroad, whose name was Michaud, wanted to know about a funeral of a Michaud that had his legs accidentally removed in a Bangor & Aroostook accident. We sort of looked around, we found the material they wanted in some of my publications, so this is what I do. People don't know where to start.

AM: For the past 30 years, you've been deeply involved in researching, gathering information, and working to "revitalize" interest in Acadian culture. Where does this drive come from?

GC: I'm just an old country school teacher at heart. I love to learn. I like to share what I learn. I'm so pleased when a young person shows an interest. Like my daughter, who for a long time, kept thinking Mother was a little weird because she loved cemeteries and things like that. Well, now they're on the Internet and they see all these people that share the same interest I do. Now, the presentation of the cemetery slides I'll be giving next week, those photographs were taken 20 years ago, of every cemetery in the Madawaska Territory, both sides of the boundary. Twenty years later people come to me and want to see my slides, so it's kind of interesting, you know. I've been a member of the Maine Old Cemetery Association since its inception in '68, so when they come to the Valley, or to the County, they have somebody here.

AM: Do you have an ultimate goal, a dream of what you'd like to ultimately accomplish with all this effort that you've been devoting for the past 30 years?

GC: My primary goal is that the next generation is proud of who they are. They just wanted to forget their cultural heritage. Ah, that was not important. They anglicized their name and there were a lot old-fashioned theories and legends that were still intact, the way you brought up your family, and, you know, like a pregnant woman doesn't go to church on Sunday when she started to show, things like that. So, these were all little tidbits of information that sort of really got me involved, and not only that, but the bottom line is that the new generation, the young people are proud of being a Chassé, or being a Pelletier. They're proud of who you are because for a long time, the people up here were not. It was just like the people with their Native American heritage, they're just now coming out in the open and admitting that they had an Indian grandmother.

AM: To what do you attribute this low self-esteem among Acadians in Aroostook County, in the Valley; what's the source of this shame, this lack of pride?
GC: We were working to survive, we had our large families, and we were farming people. We had these large families so we could survive on the farm. *Les anglais* would come in and they got all the top jobs, the administrative jobs, and we had this feeling, well, if I even fight with the authorities we've got a lot of talent in this valley. Why do you go out and hire somebody from Ohio to head the Acadian Archives in Fort Kent? I was telling Dick Dumont when he was president of the University of Maine at Fort Kent, I was pounding him on the chest, you know. He mentioned the fact that this Lisa was a very well organized person, who she is, and she's done a beautiful job with the Archives. I don't always agree with her, and I tell her, and she appreciates that. And, so, it made the Frenchmen feel, well, maybe there's something wrong with me. I discovered this truly when I did youth work and I was responsible for organizing entertainment at the University of Maine with my kids from northern Aroostook. And so, of course, this had been a driving force behind me, behind the reunions, behind preserving of the culture. Be happy who you are, you know. I know to start with the Jewish people in New York. They were all refugees, well-educated Ph.D.s from Berlin, they were Jewish, and they were chased out. Some of my best friends had been on the 2,000-mile Hitler death marches. They were just beautiful people and I learned so much from them and the value of what life was. So this is what I've been trying to pass on here.
AM: It sounds like you've been the driving force behind the efforts to make people recognize that they need not be ashamed but should take pride in their culture and their background here in northern Aroostook. How would you rate your progress and your successes?
GC: We've come a long way. These reunions have done wonders. Now you take the Chassé reunion, for instance. Chassés were not Acadians, they came from eastern France, and our progenitor had been deported for dealing in black market salt. The only people who had access to salt were the tax collector and the king. Well, this 19-year old Jean Chassé was going to make a fast buck, so he and 98 others were deported. Now when we started delving into the Chassé history, "Oh no! We're not gonna tell that; that's embarrassing." See, right away that came to the surface; "we're not good enough." But the reunion committee turned it into our float centered on salt. We had salt presentation at the mass, salt played a big part of our family reunion, so of course Jean Chassé was not demonized and, like the University of Montréal says, these first people didn't come to American because they were angels! So we all ended up being proud of who we were, Chassés. We planted our tree, we put a monument down there, we wrote a book, we fought and argued and everything, but we had a beautiful reunion. But the bottom line was, they were proud to write their name. Now, these are all little steps taken in preserving our culture.
AM: Do you have an ultimate goal over the next few years, something you'd like to see happen, something that hasn't been established?
GC: It's happening now, with the younger generation taking over. Now the Dumont family reunion we had this year, oh, it was not a big one, but it was one of the best organized. The young people utilized modern technology. They had a beautiful reunion and it was all young people. So, like I say, it's happening now, the young people get at the wheel and they're continuing what we started.
AM: Are there people who are going to keep this work going when you've stopped?
GC: Well, the Heritage Council is doing a good job. But, on the other hand, when the buck stops, so does the interest. In my case, it's a private thing, it's a love affair.
AM: Are you suggesting that much of the effort by other groups is driven by money?
GC: I have a tendency to say yes. I'm not saying 100 percent now, don't quote me saying that, but as old timers, we have tendency to judge, right. So far I have seen that the only time there was an interest shown by a certain element was as long as there was a dollar attached to it. That's my way of putting the money was being funded. When we started the Madawaska Historical Society in '68, we started in with a federal program, the Bilingual Education Program, Title 7. They were duplicating what we were doing.
AM: They were duplicating the efforts that were already being made on a voluntary basis?
GC: That's right, and that's what is being done with the powers that be. That's why I became, why I distanced myself from the Park Service, because they have their own agenda, they take over, they promote the Park Service. I felt our heritage, culture took a back seat. They're doing the same thing in Calais, there, with St. Croix. I told Bob Reynolds, the superintendent of Acadia Park—this is all done out of Acadia Park now—What in the devil did they know about us people, how we felt? Bob Reynolds said, "Géraldine, what do you make of this?" I said, "Well, to tell the truth, Bob, we're spinning our wheels in the dust. You've got nothing concrete to show for these

three years of work being done." Maybe I was a little harsh. He just laughed; cantankerous old lady, you know. But that's exactly how I felt. And one other thing, I want to emphasize is that I'm building in interest in Acadian and French culture, but I'm also part Scotch and Irish. So I do not like to leave out the other ethnic groups.
AM: Let me ask one more thing about French in the schools and bringing back the language skills. For a long time, children whose first language was French were prohibited from speaking French on the school grounds, and now it's turned around 180 degrees. Why?
GC: Federal dollars. Federal dollars.
AM: There's money to support bilingual education programs; was there not money before?
GC: No. Because they forbade you from using French.
AM: Was this a local prohibition, was it state law, was it federal regulations that classes were taught only in English?
GC: You asked me why the French people had low self-esteem: they were forbidden to be who they were in their classrooms. I remember when I taught school up in St. Francis. See, I grew up on the French-Scottish-Irish neighborhood up in St. Francis. I don't know if you know about the moosetowners, and all that; we call 'em moosetowners, but there's this pocket of Scotch-Irish, Cathy Pelletier stuff, you know. So we never felt discriminated against even though we learned our prayers and catechism in English. Papa and mama always spoke French in the house.
AM: French was your first language?
GC: Yes, and then when I married Ernie, Ernie was strictly French with a thick accent, but I was not ashamed of his accent because Ernie was a self-made man; matter of fact, I did a book on him when he turned 80. So we never felt persecuted like some of the French kids here in St. David, or the back settlement of Ste-Agathe. My kids couldn't believe it. They'd say, "Mama, why do the teachers play favorites to the kids from town instead of the kids that travel on the bus?" Well, most of the French kids were farm kids, hard workers, and my kinds noticed it; they brought it to my attention, because I was not aware it was so prominent in the schools, because I came from St. Francis and there was none of that.
AM: I normally close the interviews by asking if there is something you'd like to say, some point we haven't touched upon.
GC: It's like I said a while ago, we've come a long way. More and more people are realizing how fortunate they are to be bilingual in this area. The rest of the country's finally waking up, The County, or the state, finally realizing that the dumb Frenchmen haven't been that dumb after all. So other than that, I hope the young generation continues to appreciate who they are, what their background is, and make the best of it. I have no grandiose plans or anything; it's just that we should continue. We're doing it through federal funds, bilingual program, immersion, they have 'em up at the school which is nice. Some of the parents, the young parents are pleased. Now whenever I give a talk in any of the schools, the parents always come and enjoy it as much as the children do. I have a whole little ritual that I use, and so all I hope is that they continue going the direction they're going, whether it's private or federally funded.

Camille Lessard-Bissonnette—Author of *Canuck*

By Janet L. Shideler, Ph.D.

As the daughter of an immigrant woman, an immigrant woman myself, and a voracious reader, I spent much of my adolescence and early adulthood hoping to discover a literary voice that articulated the experiences of immigrant women. I wanted to find someone who wrote about how we bridge two cultures, about how we identify home when we occupy two, and about how we reconcile our often divided loyalties even as we decide what matters most to us as individuals. When fate—and graduate studies—led me to Camille Lessard-Bissonnette, I knew at once that I had found that voice. Just as her writings resonated with me, I also knew that what she recounted was, more significantly, the tale of many *Franco-Américaines* whose story was largely untold. On this, the occasion of the 20th anniversary of the Franco-American Women's Institute, what could be more appropriate than to include "amie Camille" in the celebration?

Camille Lessard was born in 1883 in Sainte-Julie-de-Mégantic, a rural village in Québec's Mauricie-Bois-Francs region. She was the second of seven children born to Pierre and Marie Lessard. Early on, Camille displayed traits—intellect, ambition, passion, talent—that would help her to overcome various obstacles to success, including the grueling poverty endured by her family. At the age of 16, she became a rural schoolteacher, a position typically reserved for the brightest young woman in the community, no small feat when one considers that her parents, while hard-working, were both illiterate. In pursuing this career path she became, in a sense, an educator for the entire community and was responsible, along with the parish priest, for the intellectual development but also the moral growth and the overall well-being of all, not just of the children in her charge.

However much she might have enjoyed both the multiple duties and tremendous respect that came with that position, Camille left it behind to move with her family to Lewiston, Maine, in spring 1904 as her parents sought to better the family's financial situation. There she succeeded in securing employment at Continental Mills and thus joined the ranks of millworkers from the area and from around the globe. While others might have seen this as a humbling occasion, Camille Lessard was forever grateful for the opportunity to share the experiences of her working-class sisters and brothers. In that setting she further matured and became a keen observer of humanity. With that attribute, however, came an obvious dilemma: with whom and by what means would she share what she had seen and experienced? In 1906, Camille submitted her first article, entitled "Deux larmes," to Lewiston's French-language newspaper, *Le Messager*, accompanied by a letter in which she offered her services as an unpaid contributor. Indeed, so committed was she to her newfound "calling"—journalism—that she followed her daily labor at the mills with work at home every evening on articles, a routine that led her to coin the term "écrivailleur" (*Le Messager* 9 juin 1909: 1)—writing worker or working writer—to describe herself in her two occupations. Her persistence paid off when Editor Jean-Baptiste Couture invited her in 1908 to become a full-time member of the newspaper's editorial team.

Thus it was that Camille Lessard, writing under the pseudonym Liane, began directing *Le Messager*'s "pages féminines." Women's pages such as hers were by this time an established column in newspapers in French Canada and, it follows, in newspapers in French-language communities throughout the Northeastern United States. In Quebec, "Francoise," "Madeleine," and "Gaëtane de Montreuil," among many others, already had devoted female readers. No doubt influenced by her counterparts there, to whom she respectfully referred as "mes grandes soeurs du Canada" (*Le Messager* 26 avril 1911: 3), she initially took on many of the same topics that they addressed in their columns: love, marriage and motherhood chief among these. It wasn't long, however, before she began to distinguish herself from these "big sisters," sometimes in content, sometimes in tone, and most often in opinion.

One of the first and most obvious differences was the *directrice*'s insistence on adding the workplace to the discussion of women's realm. She was audacious in her praise of employment outside the home, thereby moving women beyond marriage and maternity. In fact, she was often vocal in her opposition to the societal expectation that women—French-Canadian women, in particular—would have only two choices, namely marriage and motherhood OR a religious vocation, and she used her column to argue that girls and young women must be educated for a life without marriage. In her view, anything other than instruction that prepares women for employment outside the home further disadvantages an already vulnerable segment of society. Clearly Camille Lessard's first-hand experience of the workplace, however arduous that experience undoubtedly was in the mills, provided her with a glimpse of other options for herself and for other women. More significantly, distance from the ideological grip of Quebec allowed the young journalist to develop a distinct and bold vision. Her courage in articulating a different future for Québécoises and Franco-Américaines alike cannot be overstated: even though the proletarization of women was increasingly as much a reality in Quebec as it was in its diasporic communities in the Northeast, the province's leadership persisted in denying the social change that was in front of them, rejecting, for example, incontrovertible evidence that increasingly married women and mothers were working outside the home.

That distance also encouraged Camille Lessard to go beyond supporting the presence of women in the workplace and beyond lobbying for educational reform so that she might bravely take on more contentious matters. For example, while still praising the beloved institution of the family, she urged young women to leave those households in which their sacrifice was rewarded by tyranny and abuse, especially directed at them by their fathers. And, troubled by the financial, physical, and emotional suffering that often resulted from the successive maternities that had been promoted by French-Canadian clergy in particular, the women's page director supported family planning.

However, it was in her plea for women's right to vote that Camille Lessard was most outspoken. As early as 1910, she ably argued in favor of women's suffrage in a public debate in Lewiston. In addition, she often devoted her column to defending suffragettes, including everything from their political goals to their dress and physical appearance. Yet, despite the clear differences between her position and that of her counterparts in French Canada who would take many more years before moving beyond their very cautious, somewhat timid domestic feminism to embrace the women's suffrage movement, the outspoken Franco-American journalist remained, nevertheless, respectful of other women's pages columnists. That said, reserve and respect were not always her style. To men who disputed women's right to vote, Camille was sarcastic in her responses and razor-sharp in her reasoning to counter their arguments. Perhaps surprisingly, though, she reserved her wrath for those women who had the greatest means to effect change but chose instead to oppose and obstruct the advancement of women's rights. To the wife of Canadian Prime Minister Wilfrid Laurier, for example, she writes: "Vivez dans le luxe, continuez à être heureuse, Lady Laurier, mais de grâce n'entravez pas la marche de celles qui sont moins fortunées que vous" (*Le Messager* 30 mars 1910: 1). The greatest hurdle to solidarity, as Camille saw it, was not age or occupation or even socio-economic class. Rather, it was indifference about the conditions in which other women lived. In her view, with good fortune such as Lady Laurier enjoyed, came great responsibility. Those who sought to shirk or deny that responsibility were guilty of betraying all women, an unpardonable offense.

Responsibility was always important to Camille. Indeed, it was a sense of responsibility, of duty to her readers that inspired her in her journalism. Certainly she was not alone among *directrices* in the conviction that women's columns could serve an important role in enlightening one's readers. What distinguished her efforts, however, was what she was able to share with them, in no small measure because hers was a perspective informed by her unique experiences and background. Whereas most women's columnists were urban, convent-educated middle-class and upper middle-class women who worked primarily from the confines of their homes, Camille was, of necessity, immersed in the public sphere from a young age. As a rural schoolteacher, she witnessed ignorance and illiteracy, but also ambition and hope. Later as a millworker, she observed—and demonstrated—determination and hard work in response to seemingly insurmountable poverty. She also saw and experienced the barriers to success that result from gender and/or socio-economic class, despite one's efforts and merit. For Camille, the former "éducatrice" committed to improving the lot of others, beginning with educating them, there was never any doubt about why she wanted to be a writer or for whom she wrote: "Je veux écrire pour les pauvres, les humbles, les ouvriers" (*Le Messager* 24 mai 1911: 3).

Just as her move to the United States had broadened the young woman's experiences, so too did it expand her view of what she should discuss with her readers. For example, she used her column to respond to Quebec's repatriation efforts. It would have been enough that she even broached the subject in the women's pages, overlooked as it was by her peers. However, the immigrant writer went further. She who had once nostalgically declared "Je n'aime que mon pays" (*Le Messager* 18 février 1908: 1) had come to appreciate the opportunity provided by the adopted home to her and others, and so she denounced detractors of the United States and critics of Franco-Americans as "vieux fanatiques" (*Le Messager* 9 juin 1909: 1).

Shortly after this bold attack, unparalleled by few French-Canadian or Franco-American journalists of the time regardless of gender, Camille's life was to take an unexpected turn. Despite her own plea to other women to become more independent and autonomous, it was familial duty and sacrifice that once again called Camille, this time insisting that the dutiful daughter return to Canada with her family in 1912. The Lessards participated in colonization efforts in western Canada, making their way to a settlement just outside Edmonton, Alberta. For her part, Camille secured a position as the Director of the French Department of the Edmonton Municipal Library. One might think that this move would forever silence the once vocal journalist. Instead, Camille's departure marked a new phase. If the early years were a time in which the young woman discovered what it meant to be Québécois(e) and Franco-Américain(e) in a rapidly changing society at the turn of the 20th century, the next years were what I would consider her exploration of North America, not unlike journeys made by the voyageurs and coureurs des bois. And like them, she saw no boundary that should not be crossed: "Pourquoi cette barrière entre mes deux pays?" (*Le Messager* 13 octobre 1933: 12).

From Edmonton she moved to Los Angeles, and then on to Saint Louis, Missouri. Still later she was hired to work as a colonization agent—the only woman to fill that position—for the Louisville and Nashville Railroad, headquartered in Louisville, Kentucky. Ever the écrivailleur, Camille once again combined work with writing, recording not only what she witnessed during her rail travel throughout the U.S. but also the lasting impressions that these scenes made on her. *Le Messager* published her contributions in the early 1930s, and in 1938 she briefly directed the women's pages of Montreal's *La Patrie* newspaper. What would a poor farmer's daughter from rural Quebec turned unskilled immigrant millworker have to share with readers? The same journalist who had astonished her readership with her bold stance on women's rights was determined to expose them to the injustices she witnessed. Camille told them about poverty endured by Southern share-croppers, about lung disease threatening the lives of miners, about racism that denied humans their God-given rights and restricted their full participation as citizens, about the depletion of the ozone layer [in 1933!], and so much more.

The 1930s were also significant as the period in which Camille Lessard tried her hand at fiction. *Le Messager* published *Canuck* first in a weekly serial format and then as a novel in its entirety in 1936. *Le Journal* newspaper of Lawrence, Massachusetts, also published the work the next year. Centered around a female protagonist who immigrates to Lowell, Massachusetts, from rural Quebec with her impoverished family, many of the themes that were predominant in Camille's women's pages became the rich plot of this novel. Among these were women's sacrifices for family alongside rebellion against patriarchal abuse of power, women's increased freedom as a result of the ability to engage in salaried labor alongside the wish to find love and companionship. Much of *Canuck*'s complexity lies in its exploration of the psychology of its female protagonist. Nonetheless, in the empathic approach that was writer Lessard's trademark, the joys and sorrows of other characters are also prominently featured. What tellingly is not prominent is religion, although the protagonist's brother does, thanks to the efforts of his mother and sister, become a priest. The role of France and French Canada in exploring and settling North America figures as an important theme as well, incarnate in the mysterious character of Père l'Allumette. Finally, the protagonist's marriage later in life at the end of the novel, while not discussed at length, does, nonetheless, foreshadow Camille's own nuptials.

Following her own advice to her readers, Camille Lessard decided to forego marriage for many years, marrying at the age of 60. At that time, she wed former Connecticut Senator Napoléon-P. Bissonnette. Most notable among his personal and political causes, Monsieur Bissonnette was a labor unionist and a respected supporter of the suffragette movement. While there is little that is known about the marriage, it would appear that Camille might finally have found both the intellectual companionship and the shared values that were, in her estimation, so essential to a happy marriage.

Camille Lessard-Bissonnette crossed and re-crossed the border, particularly following the death of her husband, until her own poor health urged her to settle again in southern California. She passed away in Long Beach in 1970 at the age of 87. In the end, time and distance separated her from her two homes—Quebec and New England—but her writings leave us little doubt that her attachment to both remained intact. What is most striking perhaps is the depth of her affection for the milltown where, despite all the barriers she faced—language, culture, class, and gender—she accomplished much on behalf of the people she loved and for whom she wrote with extraordinary passion and conviction. To Camille, then, is the last word:

La vie me mène et me ramène; je vais où le vent me pousse, la cage où je me débats est vaste comme l'univers, mais aux barres de cette cage j'y ai accroché une fleur toujour fraîche, toujours belle et je lui ai donné le nom de 'Lewiston' (*Le Messager* 20 janvier 1932: 4).

Woman Suffrage: Ally or Enemy for Maine's Franco-Americans, 1917-1920?

By Marian desCognets

A Thesis—Master of Arts, History, University of Maine, May, 1988, an excerpt

In September, 1917 Maine held a referendum on woman suffrage that was defeated by a more than two-to-one margin. The ideological hostility of the Catholic Church, more specifically the Quebec Catholic, and because Maine's large Franco-American Catholic population, may have been influential in the overwhelming defeat of the referendum.

Evidence from the two leading French language newspapers in Maine, Biddeford's *La Justice* and Lewiston's *Le Messager* however, showed that Franco-American intellectuals were ambivalent about women's suffrage. They showed a growing awareness of the American political system and recognized the potential benefits to survivance of female suffrage.

Introduction

On September 10, 1917, the State of Maine held a referendum asking voters, among other things,[1] whether to extend the franchise to women. Votes for women had been proposed since the middle of the 19th century. Since the beginning of the 20th century the legislature in Maine had been presented with either a bill or a petition supporting female suffrage almost yearly.[2] Soundly defeating the referendum, Maine showed a marked distaste for enfranchising women. Franco-Americans, whose numbers in Maine made them a potential political force, were encouraged by at least one of their defensive, conservative, and highly reactionary newspapers to reconsider their traditional anti-suffrage attitudes.[3] They do not appear to have responded favorably to these urgings. The referendum was defeated by a more than two-to-one margin statewide, and, in Lewiston which, out of a 1910 population of 26,247, had 10,841 residents who had either been born in Quebec or whose parents had been, the referendum vote was 654-1315 against female suffrage.

Study of Franco-American attitudes toward female suffrage reveal surprising information about this ethnic group in Maine. The difference among Franco-Americans on woman suffrage in 1917 can give us insight into their relations with each other, with other American Catholics, and with people living in the province of Quebec.

The aim of this paper is to show that Franco-American culture and ideology, largely shaped by strong and enduring ties to Quebec Province, conditioned the Franco-American response to the 1917 suffrage referendum. To demonstrate this, it will be necessary to describe Franco-American society, its similarities to Quebec, and how those similarities may have shaped Franco-American attitudes about women and their proper function in society. There was not a consensus, however, and the diverse attitudes of Franco-American society underscored the growing ambivalence of Franco secular leaders toward woman suffrage as their attitudes were revealed in the two leading Franco-American newspapers in Maine.[4] Outlining the suffrage movement will provide added background for interpreting the failure of Maine's referendum in 1917. Changing Franco-American ideology was not the result of concentrated suffrage activity, but rather was evidence of growing acceptance and understanding of political realities in the United States.

The movement to extend suffrage to Maine women was part of the larger movement happening throughout Europe and North America during most of the 19th and early 20th centuries. The characteristics of the movements in both the United States and its neighbor, Canada, were very similar. Pro-suffrage forces in the United States may have been more vocal and militant than those to the north, where suffragists prided themselves on the reasonable tone of their campaign,[5] but their messages were based on the same arguments. It was getting harder for anti-suffragists to justify the continued political exclusion of half the population in avowedly democratic nations. In the midst of a great war that was affording women unprecedented opportunities to enter what had been previously all-male domains, the old reasons for not allowing women to participate in the public sphere seemed transparently outdated. Clearly women were a permanent part of the work force despite those who argued that their place was in the domestic sphere.

> Suffragists further promised that granting women the right to vote would improve the political situation by offering better government, new interest in elections, a vital strengthening of government, increased influence of rural areas, ... tremendous strengthening of the good interests in cities strengthened, the spread of democracy at home, the introduction of the moral force of women, and, most important of all, the elimination of antagonism brought on by sex discrimination.[6]

One of the most potent anti-suffrage arguments was based on the teachings of St. Paul, who believed the subservient place of women in society was part of a divine plan. Women were to complement men, not be their equals. Suffragists responded, also using the Bible as their defense, and "the ethical teachings of Jesus became the principal religious argument for woman suffrage."[7]

Almost everywhere suffragists were white, middle-class, and Protestant. Their numbers were small and for years they lacked the broad-based support necessary for national victory. Any success was the product of hard and determined volunteer work over many years. Some of the early suffragists, like Susan B. Anthony and Elizabeth Cady Stanton, worked to gain suffrage for women their entire lives and died before final victory in 1920. The suffragists were often the subjects of bitter ridicule and suffered many more defeats than victories. Yet, in Canada, "all provinces from the Ottawa River to the Pacific had yielded to the pressure for woman suffrage" by 1917.[8] In the United States a similar situation existed. Eleven states had granted full suffrage, all west of the Mississippi River until New York state gave the vote to women in November, 1917. Thus, by 1917 in both countries, large areas had responded favorably to female suffrage. In the states where women were still being refused suffrage, however, opposing forces had solidified into organized and potent foes. In states with potentially decisive electoral votes the fight promised to be especially sharp as the opposition would concentrate all their strength to ensure no further extension of female suffrage.

In Maine, as elsewhere, the movement was white, middle-class, Protestant, and exceedingly small. In a largely rural state where communication was difficult in the best of times, Maine's suffrage association also suffered from a lack of funds and workers. There were not enough volunteers with the financial freedom to devote time and money to educating people about suffrage issues; and it was believed that there was "absolute ignorance on the subject"[9] of female suffrage. When the possibility of a state referendum was raised, there were conflicting opinions between the local and national levels as to its value. The professionals at the headquarters of the National American Woman Suffrage Association, NAWSA, in New York City had arrived at the conclusion that state referendums in general were no longer productive since the opposition had become entrenched in the remaining anti-suffrage states, all of which had had at least one unsuccessful referendum. In Maine where the chances for success were "slight," [10] a referendum might harm the movement by syphoning off precious funds and workers.

The energetic and talented president of the NAWSA, Carrie Chapman Catt, elected in 1915, had conceived a strategy that was called "Mrs. Catt's Winning Plan." Several decades without adding any new states to the full suffrage roster had shown Catt that the movement had lost its momentum and was floundering without direction. It was essential to organize at the national level to provide centralized leadership and concentrate efforts in key locations. The new strategy, developed secretly by the national leaders, was to exert pressure on Congress to pass the Susan B. Anthony Amendment, making it illegal to refuse a person the right to vote on the basis of sex anywhere in the United States.[11] After finally gaining the support of President Wilson for the proposed suffrage amendment, Mrs. Catt called for "a whole new approach to the work ahead, the election of national officers who would stick to their jobs until the end, and, above all, the adoption of a program which would enable lobbyists in Washington and campaigners in the field to feel a unified organization behind them." [12] In 1917, the eyes of the national headquarters were on the most important referendum to date, in New York State. Catt wanted to focus the full energy of the suffrage movement on New York and other large strategic states rather than waste precious time, workers, and funds on unimportant states where the chances of success were minimal. The main focus of the movement throughout the final years before victory was, therefore, on increasing centralization to stop the fragmentation that had been occuring,[13] and reversing the negative connotations that had arisen from constant defeat. It was believed that utilizing the power of the women who were already enfranchised in the full suffrage states was a more effective way of showing Congress the political potential of allowing women the vote.

Maine was just such an unimportant and risky state. The decision to place a women's suffrage question on the referendum had been debated, tabled, and delayed by the Maine state legislature, causing one member to protest that the fight over women's suffrage was being conducted "in the corriders"[14] not on the floor of the State

Legislature. Finally the legislature agreed to hold the referendum in February of 1917, leaving a mere six months to prepare for what appeared to be a futile effort. This time was further shortened by the impracticality and unpredictability of travel in Maine during the wet and muddy spring. The chances of educating an apparently uninterested population living in remote rural areas was thus very small. Maine had no organizational structure in place that could compensate for the liabilities of climate and demography.

Moreover, Maine had been a "dry" state since a prohibition law had been passed in the mid-19th century, and suffrage activity in both Canada and the United States was traditionally linked to temperance. Often the same workers were working simultaneously for both causes. Therefore, those people aligned with, or sympathetic to, the liquor interests were fearful that granting female suffrage would strengthen temperance forces and indefinitely continue prohibition.

Finally, Maine's large Catholic population, estimated to be 110,000 in 1905,[15] was believed to be both ideologically hostile to female suffrage and "unreachable" by the predominately Protestant suffragists.[16] The additional barrier of language made the large percentage of Maine Catholics who were of French-Canadian heritage even more inaccessible. Admonished by their religious and social leaders to remain loyal to their French-Canadian heritage, Franco-Americans consciously kept themselves separate from Protestant New England society.[17] There is no evidence of Franco-American participation in suffrage work. Franco women were not members of the state and local organizations neither were there efforts to include Franco-American audiences on suffrage speaking tours. In the debate that took place over female suffrage in Maine, Franco-American women made no public statements.

When this referendum was defeated by a more than two-to-one margin[18] it was a surprise to no one, except, perhaps, the disappointed Maine suffragists, who called it a "disaster."[19] There was evidence of voter apathy, or as a suffragist put it "of the supreme indifference of male voters."[20] The previous year's gubernatorial election had garnered 151,430 votes, yet fewer than 60,000 had gone to the polls for the referendum. However, it reflected more than apathy that 414 towns throughout the state were opposed to female suffrage with only ninety-one showing a favorable majority, or that few large towns or cities were pro-suffrage.

Although the defeat was predicted[21] and the opponents of suffrage were easily able to marshal disparate forces to defeat the question, a closer look at the facts surrounding the suffrage issue leads to some more probing questions. The following chapters of this thesis will explore some of the factors influencing the apparent decision of Franco-American voters to oppose the enfranchisement of women, and reveal views that separated Franco-Americans from their fellow American Catholics and from their own intellectual leaders in New England.

There has been the suggestion that the "ethno-religious factor ... was the most important single conditioner of their electoral behavior,"[22] overshadowing all other considerations. The evidence shows that Franco-Americans may have remained spiritually loyal to the ideology promulgated by the Québec Catholic Church leadership rather than that of either the American Catholic Church or their own secular leaders. On the subject of female suffrage, an issue that seemed to attack their most sacred institutions as defined by their "ethno-religious" outlook, Franco-Americans disregarded the urgings of their intellectuals in the Franco-American press. They also ignored the changing views within the American Catholic Church on female suffrage, preferring the traditional concepts of women in Franco-American society which were defined according to the teachings of the Québec Catholic Church. The Quebec church was able to effectively defuse any suffrage activity within the province's borders, remaining until 1940 the only province in both countries to refuse women the right to vote. While it is possible to blame the referendum's defeat on several factors, the hostility of the Quebec Church towards female suffrage influenced its adherents in Maine, where in many large towns Franco-American participation "largely determined the vote" on any given issue.[23]

ENDNOTES

Introduction

1. "Besides the suffrage amendment four other constitutional amendments, submitted at the last session of the legislature, will be acted on. They provide for the removal by the governor and council, of sheriffs who fail or neglect to enforce the prohibition liquor law, the division of towns into voting districts, amendment of the military law, and provision for the apportionment of representatives in the event of merger of towns and cities." *Bangor Daily News*, September 10, 1917. 1.

(Continued on next page)

(Continued)
2. Edward O. Schriver, "Deferred Victory: Maine Women Successfully Strive to Obtain the Vote, 1873-1974." Unpublished manuscript.
3. *Le Messager* (Lewiston, Maine 1916-1917).
4. *Le Messager*; *La Justice* (Biddeford, Maine, 1916-1917).
5. Catherine Cleverdon, *The Woman Suffrage Movement in Canada* (Toronto: University of Toronto Press, 1950; repr. 1974).
6. Schriver, 83.
7. Aileen S.Kraditor, *The Ideas of the Woman Suffrage Movement 1890-1920* (New York: Columbia University Press, 1965), 92.
8. Cleverdon, 105.
9. Ida Husted Harper, ed., *The History of Woman Suffrage*, (New York: J.J. Little and Ives Company, 1922), VI 1900¬1920, 240.
10. Harper, VI, 238.
11. Eleanor Flexner, *Century of Struggle: The Woman's Rights Movement in the United States* rev. ed. (Cambridge: Harvard University, 1975), 289.
12. Flexner, 290.
13. Schriver, 59.
14. Legislative Record of the 78th Legislature of the State of Maine, 1917 (Augusta: Kennebec Journal Print, 1917), 211.
15. William Lucey, *The Catholic Church in Maine* (Francestown, New Hampshire: H.M. Jones Co., 1959), 277.
16. Kraditor, 148.
17. Norman Sepanek, "A Profile of Franco-American Political Attitudes in New England," in *Franco-American Overview*, 3, 213-233.
18. The vote was 38,838 against female suffrage and 20,684 for. Harper, VI, 243.
19. Schriver, 88.
20. Isabel Greenwood in an unpublished speech given on September 10, 1917. Special Collections, Fogler Library, University of Maine, Orono.
21. Flexner, Chapter XIX; Schriver, 59. Both describe how opponents of the state-by-state approach had predicted defeat.
22. David B. Walker, "Politics and Ethnocentrism: The Case of the Franco-Americans" (Bowdoin College, Brunswick, *Maine: Bureau for Research in Municipal Government*, 1961).
23. D.B. Walker, "Presidential Politics of Franco-Americans" *Franco-American Overview,* 3, 201.

Margaret Chase Smith—Is She or Isn't She (Franco-American)?

Margaret Chase Smith was born in Skowhegan, Maine, on December 14, 1897. Her entry into politics came through the career of Clyde Smith, the man she married in 1930. Clyde was elected to the United States House of Representatives in 1936; Margaret served as his secretary. When Clyde died in 1940, Margaret succeeded her husband. After four terms in the House, she won election to the United States Senate in 1948. In so doing, she became the first woman elected to both houses of Congress.

Senator Smith came to national attention on June 1, 1950, when she became the first member of the Senate to denounce the tactics used by colleague Joseph McCarthy in his anticommunist crusade. Following her "Declaration of Conscience" speech, some pundits speculated that she might be the vice-presidential candidate on the 1952 Republican ticket. The opportunity, however, never materialized. In 1964, Senator Smith pursued her own political ambitions, running in several Republican presidential primaries. She took her candidacy all the way to the Republican National Convention in San Francisco, where she became the first woman to have her name placed in nomination for the presidency by either of the two major parties. In the final balloting, Smith refused to withdraw and so wound up coming in second to the Republican nominee, Senator Barry Goldwater.

After four terms in the Senate and thirty-two years in Congress, Senator Smith lost re-election in 1972. She retired to her home in Skowhegan and began planning for the establishment of a library. The Margaret Chase Smith Library opened in 1982 and for the next dozen years, she presided over the facility, meeting with admirers, former constituents, politicians, policymakers, researchers, and school children. Margaret Chase Smith died at her home on Memorial Day, May 29, 1995.

—Biography taken from the Margaret Chase Smith Library website.

The Debate: Margaret Chase Smith—Is She or Isn't She (Franco-American)?

Can you determine whether Margaret Chase Smith identified as a Franco-American, French heritage woman in her life and career? Why do you suppose she might not have done so or is there sufficient evidence that states that she did identify with her mother's French heritage? Do you identify with your heritage? Why/why not?

Patricia Wallace, W. *Politics of Conscience: A Biography of Margaret Chase Smith*. Westport, CT: Praeger, 1995. Print.

"On 14 December 1897 Dr. J.N. Merrill delivered a baby girl to twenty-one-year-old Carrie and twenty-two-year-old George Chase in their home on North Avenue. According to her certificate of baptism from Notre Dame de Lourdes in Skowhegan, Margaret Chase Smith was christened Marguerite Madeline Chase on 18 December 1897. While the certificate lists her father as George Chase, it lists her mother as Caroline Morin and sponsors as Lambert Morin and Adile Lessard. The rumor that Smith was French-Canadian, which carried stigma, haunted her entire political career, but the speculation was always that Chase had been anglicized from Chasse, not that *Murray* was originally *Morin* or that Margaret Madeline was Marguerite Madeline."

Endnotes:

Certificate of baptism, Notre Dame de Lourdes, Skowhegan, Maine; John Murray interview with author, 21 September 1988. When MCS learned that I had received the baptismal certificate, she wrote to say that she was sending a copy of her birth certificate giving "the correct names of myself and my mother and father." This certificate has the spellings used in the text. MCS to Wallace. 11 August 1989; Birth Certificate, State of Maine, Office of the Clerk of Skowhegan, 21 March 1952.

Maine Memory Network lists Margaret Chase Smith as a baby
Contributed by Margaret Chase Smith Library
Black and white photograph of Margaret Chase with her parents, George Emery Chase and Carrie Murray Chase, taken in 1898.

(Continued on next page)

Margaret Chase Smith genealogy compiled by Robert Chenard, Franco-American Women's Institute

1. Margaret Madeline Chase married Clyde H. Smith
2. George Emery Chase married
3. Caroline M. Morin 1896, Skowhegan, ME
4. John Wesley Chase married
5. Margaret Nolan
6. Jean Lambert Morin married
7. Marie Boulet 1866, Waterville, ME

Janann Sherman. *No Place for a Woman: A Life of Senator Margaret Chase Smith*. Brunswick, NJ: Rutgers UP, 1999. Print.

"At some point, Lambert Morin changed his name to John L. Murray. For much of his life, it was difficult to be a French-Canadian Catholic in Maine. Reluctant to assimilate, linguistically and religiously separate from their neighbors, French Canadians were objects of prejudice, hostility, and sometimes, violence. The mid-1850s were years of extreme nativist agitation throughout the Northeast. In Maine, xenophobia found expression in a series of ugly incidents involving the burning of Catholic homes and churches, and in one case at least, the stripping, tarring and feathering of a Catholic priest."

Patricia W. Wallace. *Politics of Conscience: A Biography of Margaret Chase Smith*. Westport, CT: Praeger, 1995. Print.

"By the end of April the campaign had turned ugly. Cora E. Edgerly of Portland put out an extensive mailing titled "Why I shall Not Vote For Margaret Chase Smith." Edgerly's fourteen reasons varied from the scurrilous to the malevolent, which was not to say to the inaccurate. She considered Smith "lacking in education," a Catholic, and out to get Joe Martin as a husband. Edgerly "didn't like the way Smith got her first husband" and believed that Smith "slipped into Congress on the coattails of her dead husband."

In addition to Edgerly, whom Lewis deemed "the primary smear tactician," Smith supporter Mildred Childs reported a "whispering campaign" that the congresswoman "was really French" and had changed her name to Chase from "Chasse." Another rumor held that Smith was supporting her late husband's illegitimate child, Rita Quinn. The person spreading the rumors, Childs maintained, was a paid employee of Governor Hildreth, and his "express purpose was to travel around and spread ugly rumors" about Smith."

Endnotes:

Smear Charges and Replies file, 1948 Election folder, MCS Papers.

Correspondence file, 1948 Elections folder, MCS Papers.

Frank Graham, Jr., Margaret Chase Smith: *Woman of Courage* (1964). May 2016.

"As mentioned, Margaret Chase Smith's 1948 primary campaign was marred by an organized effort to smear her. ... Soon, variations of the charges began to appear around the state with individuals issuing their own updated versions complete with gossip and personal attacks.... Her family heritage was attacked inaccurately by assertions that she had changed her maiden name from Chasse to Chase because she was ashamed of her Franco-American roots. Her mother's maiden name was Morin. She made no effort to conceal the fact."

Endnotes:

Correspondence file, 1948 Elections folder, MCS Papers.

Glen Adams. "Michaud makes mark in Maine history," *Bangor Daily News*, November 9, 2002. Web. May 2016.

"Margaret Chase Smith, who became one of Maine's towering elected leaders, had significant French-Canadian ties, but she never chose to bring them to public notice.

Smith was first elected to the Senate in 1948 and went on to become ranking Republican on the Armed Services Committee and submitted her name for nomination as president in 1964.

According to [Bob] Chenard's research, Smith's mother—whose maiden name was Morin—was 100 percent Franco-American and her family emigrated from Quebec.

'Margaret Chase Smith never admitted her Franco-American roots, mainly because the Franco-Americans back then ... were almost second-class citizens," said Chenard. "So if she were to have said anything about her Franco-American heritage ... she may not have won the elections.'"

Christian P. Potholm. "Margaret Chase Smith: The Persistence of a Political Archetype," *The New England Journal of Political Science* , Volume IV, Number 1, 2009. Web. May, 2016.

"While she was in office during an era when there was considerable prejudice against those of Franco American descent, according to Patricia Schmidt, one of her biographers, she never acknowledged the French ancestry of her mother

(Continued on next page)

(whose parents had anglicized Morin to Murray after coming to Maine from Canada in the 1860s), and probably did not know about it. According to Schmidt, it was not until Smith was 75 and out of office, that Smith travelled to Quebec to discover that her grandfather's dark secret was that he had been christened Lambert Morin (Schmidt 1996).

This analysis appears to be a significant mistake on Schmidt's part. According to both Paul Mills and Merton Henry, Margaret Chase Smith …knew full well that her grandfather Murray had been Franco American and while she did not trumpet that heritage, neither did she deny it. (Mills 2009) To prove his point, Paul Mills rightly cites Frank Graham, Jr.'s earlier biography, *Margaret Chase Smith, Woman of Courage* which clearly states her Franco American lineage. (Graham 1964). Since Graham had excellent access to Senator Smith in this authorized biography, and he clearly puts her French-Canadian blood in her hereditary makeup, this seems a fair assertion, regardless of much that has been said to the contrary (Graham Jr. 1964). Margaret Chase Smith's relationship to her Franco American heritage is complicated and to date somewhat clouded. …In researching this article, I also noted that whenever they touch on the question of her Franco American roots, Smith's biographers have tended to accent her Quebec ancestry and relations. But more recent scholarship and pedigree charts now track her lineage further back to the Pierre Morin dit Boucher family of Port Royal in Acadia, quite a different (or more multi-faceted) lineage than previously assumed (Morin 2008). Today we now know that Smith sits within both important lines of Franco American heritage, that of Quebec and of Acadia. In any case, all of this was not widely known during her career and it may well have been that on balance, it was as much through her championship of working men and women, rather than a *sub rosa* acknowledgment of her ancestry which gained her the support of many Franco Americans in Maine."

Endnotes:

Graham, Jr., Frank. 1964 *Margaret Chase Smith, Woman of Courage*. Omaha: John Day.

Mills, Paul. 2009. E-mail to the Author, July 31.

Morin, William F. 2008. *Presentation of Genealogical and Socio-Anthropology Materials Relating to Margaret Chase Smith Pedigree of the Morin Family of Arcadia (sic) and Accounts of Late 19th Century Francos of Brunswick Maine*. Brunswick, ME: privately printed.

Opinion Editorial. "Maine Voices: LePage could rewrite Franco-Maine's political history," *Portland Press Herald*, September 27, 2010. Web. May 2016.

"Numerous Franco-Americans have been defeated in primary races for statewide office. Curiously, Margaret Chase Smith, arguably Maine's most prominent politician of the last century (serving in Washington from 1940 to 1973), had French Canadian roots.

Her mother was a Morin, and that side of the family was 100 percent French, but the cautious Smith did not make her heritage known in an era where some Maine voters were anti-Catholic and perhaps anti-French as well.

(Maine had an active Ku Klux Klan for many years, and the Maine Historical Society has several chilling photos of Klan parades in rural Maine after World War I.)"

Ellen Fitzpatrick. "The Unfavored Daughter: When Margaret Chase Smith Ran in the New Hampshire Primary," *The New Yorker*, Page Turner, February 6, 2016. Web. May 2016.

"Her Senate campaign, in 1948, would largely rely on female voters, organizations, and members of the press. Estimates that sixty-four per cent of Maine's voters were women offered Smith an opportunity that could be exploited when her primary opponents questioned her qualifications on the grounds of her sex; she characterized any assertion that "the Senate was no place for a woman" as "a direct challenge to every woman in Maine." But she also insisted that as "proud" as she was of being female, she sought no votes "because I am a woman." An eleventh-hour smear operation, accusing her of Communist sympathies because of her support for labor, New Deal legislation, the United Nations, the Truman Doctrine and the Marshall Plan, among other positions she had taken, outraged the candidate. More personal accusations that she was actually French Canadian (a maligned ethnic group among some in Maine), or a woman of loose morals also circulated. In the end, the effort to denigrate her and tarnish her record gained little traction. When the primary votes were counted she had crushed the opposition. 'Mrs. Smith Victor Over Three Men,' the *New York Herald Tribune* announced. She won her Senate seat in a landslide in the general election."

Truth Telling/*Dire la vérité*

Sureau—Bonté
Elder—Zealousness

Coréopsis—Joie constante, coup de foudre
Coreopsis—Always cheerful

Ophrise-Arraignée—Dexterité
Spider Ophrys—Adroitness, Dexterity

La Douce-amère—Vérité
Nightshade, Bittersweet, (Woody)—Truth

Embers Come In All Sizes

By Judy Dow

I've had several wonderful elders and olders in my life to learn from. They protected, guided and educated me in very different ways. I love them all. Mali Keating helped me to learn about the land and its history. Mali was full of fire and she shared her burning passion with me. For many years we would travel throughout Canada learning about our family's history and the genealogy that accompanied their stories. I, in return, helped Mali to learn about basket making. We would sit at either my kitchen table or hers, cleaning spruce roots for days and then using the delicate roots to sew our birch baskets together, and always sharing history and stories. I miss Mali even though part of her still burns within me.

Sometime around the passing of Mali, Doris entered into my life. I know there is no such thing as coincidence so I'm convinced this was one of those things that was supposed to happen. Doris is a more methodical person than Mali, reasoning everything out before making a step. This was clearly something I needed to learn. The fires that burned deep down inside made me passionate about correcting history and protecting the land. It was clear that now was the time to learn how to control the fires that erupted from time to time in my life.

Doris Cota Seale, she was the co-founder of Oyate, a Native organization that reviews children's literature for historical accuracy, stereotypes and bias, a librarian for 45 years and a recognized poet and author. Doris moved back to Vermont, her place of birth, to retire. During this time we have become closer and closer. Doris's love for poetry is just beginning to rub off on me. I never cared much for poetry. I didn't really understand it. Doris has patiently tried to help me understand its power.

I have always continued to burn a fire deep down within me, taking on one cause after another. Doris quietly guided me about my travels through life these last twenty-plus years and then wrote poems to express her feelings. With a touch of time and patience I've begun to understand. This is a snippet of my stories and Doris's poems. Doris and her poems have showed me how to slow down, take a look at my life and reflect on what I see and do. It seems to me that someone had a plan all along for both Mali and Doris to be in my life and for that I am so thankful.

An Intervale is an old English word for a long narrow valley between two high points. It was used to explain the common pots[1] along the rivers of the northeast. When you get out of New England, you will be hard pressed to hear this word again. To the Wabanaki people that lived here before the arrival of Europeans, a Wolhana was a long narrow valley on a north/south river and a Pasahana was a long narrow valley on an east/west river. These places were special. They were the common pots, the places that provided fertile land along a river for the foods the indigenous people needed to survive. They were also the places where the animals commonly went to find their food. These animals provided the meat and clothing that the people needed. This was a shared spot, preserved and respected by all. This land today is often referred to as either a floodplain or floodway or both, and here in New England this land was never traded or sold off.

The Winooski Intervale is a Pasahana, a long narrow valley on an east/west river, running right through Burlington, Vermont. This particular Intervale is home to my family. My mother's family, LaCasse, was the last family to live at and farm the Ethan Allen Homestead positioned on a high point directly in the center of the Intervale. My great-grandparents had ten children; most of them went off to become farmers around the perimeter of the Intervale. My mother's parents had sixteen children. The land was important to them. The land was their survival. They respected the land.

My father's family, Fortin, lived on the perimeter of the Intervale. His family was not farmers but rather hunters and fisherman. My uncles made two-ended boats and oars—some say the best in town. They fished in the Winooski River that meandered through the Intervale just in sight of their backyard. They hunted in the Intervale and the open land around it. Fish were a main staple in our diets. I have to chuckle when I hear people say, "We must be Indian because we were taught to put fish in our gardens." Damn, we would have had our butts kicked if we put fish in the garden! We fished for the food, often shared the fish with those less fortunate, and gave thanks for it. We never put the fish in the garden; we put their skins, guts and heads in the garden to fertilize the land. I think I'll leave the story of "fish in the garden" for Squanto and the Pilgrims.

This beautiful, peaceful land was home to five large, French Indian families all of whom became targets of the Vermont Eugenics Survey. In the late 19th Century, there began to be an interest among scientists and sociologists in the possibility of improving the human race by controlled breeding programs. From 1925-1937, in an effort to "breed better Vermonters," the Vermont Eugenics Survey campaigned to shape public opinion and social policy. The Survey targeted people it referred to as "degenerates" or "the three D's: defectives, dependents, delinquents." The Survey's definitions were purely subjective and included poor people with large families, poor people who were dependent on public charity, poor people who were living off the land, poor people who may or may not have had certain physical or cognitive disabilities, poor people whose family relationships did not fit the social "norm" of the time, and poor people whose children were frequently absent from school. The Vermont Eugenics Survey played the race card, and the policies that resulted from it—including institutionalization, sterilization, and removing children from their families—devastated the Wabanaki communities. To this day, the wounds remain deep, cultural continuity has been disrupted, and there are now many Wabanaki families who continue to "hide in plain sight." This ember eventually became another fire within me that ignited and burned brightly.

As time went on, Burlington grew to be the largest city in the state. These five families began to intermarry and move to other, more rural, parts of the state. But the root families still remain here today. I grew up on the perimeter of the Intervale. I played in the Intervale, hiked in the Intervale and fished in the Intervale. In recent years I've been recording the stories of elders, their stories about growing up in the Intervale. Fascinating stories of survival, moonshine, rum running, prostitution rings, burning the Intervale, and hunting and fishing in the Intervale, I love their stories, not exactly as WASP history has recorded it.

In the spirit of being "green," the Intervale land was purchased and given to the Intervale Center, an organization of people hoping to live in a "green" way while preserving the land. Being "green" is a funny thing when it comes to preserving the land. If not done correctly it is really "green washing." The land will only be sustainable if it is used for what Mother Earth intended it for. The bigger picture must be considered when looking at whether something is "green" or not. Somebody once asked me what that means. I found it odd that they would ask. To me it's common sense, but then what is common sense? So, I'll try to explain it. If you build a house on the side of a hill that is constantly changing its shape during the wet season you are not using the land in a sustainable way and you are not using common sense because your house will probably slide off the side of the hill as it changes shape. Trying to relate that to the Intervale is much the same. The Intervale is like a bathtub: when you fill it up with stuff the water level rises. That is why Intervales are commonly both floodways and floodplains. Its intended purpose is to try to provide a place for the excess water from the river during peak times of flooding. If you build in the floodway, you raise the water level and the water has to go someplace else eventually. That other place might be harmful to others. Now, you might get away with this if you only build in the floodplain but the people from the Intervale Center built 100% in the floodway. The floodway is the stretch of land directly on either side of a meandering river. When a river swells, it quickly takes over this land to go along in a straight path. I learned very early on in life that the shortest route between two points is a straight line. That is what the floodway is—the straight line. The floodplain is everything else that floods.

You might be thinking, "Well, there have been people using the Intervale forever, so why is it a problem now?" When my great-grandparents, grandparents, and parents farmed, hunted and fished this land they never lived in the floodplains, just as the generations before them didn't. The Pasahana was a place to visit for food; it was the common pot, not a place to permanently set up a village. Would you live in the middle of your pot of food? Their farms and homes were not in the floodway or the floodplain. They kept all their farming equipment out of this land and brought it into the floodplain when appropriate. They didn't fill up the bathtub. To them, to the people that could read the land, this was common sense. To the current Intervale people, it is not.

The people from the Intervale Center have built buildings, placed gas tanks next to these buildings to heat them, and then discovered this was illegal because the tanks could float away. So, they attached huge cement block anchors to the tanks in an effort to keep them from floating away. They have built berms and stockade fences to divide the land into individual farms between a half-acre and 20 acres. They have placed the boxes from 18-wheeler trucks or built little sheds on almost all of the farms in an effort to provide storage areas. They have built many 100-foot greenhouses to extend the growing season. But the most egregious fact is that they built a 26-acre compost facility in the floodway and on a known burial site. They dug trenches down to the water tables around the compost in an effort to catch the more than one million gallons of leachate (run off from the piles). They've built all this and more within the floodway, less than a couple hundred feet from the river's edge. Slowly, they have been building and raising the water level in the bathtub over the last twenty-five years. Hence another ember ignited.

The Intervale Center's lack of knowledge about the land was unbelievable to me. It couldn't be that they were doing this on purpose, could it? They clearly didn't understand using the land in either a good way or a sustainable way. Just down river, less than five miles away, were the descendants of the Indian people that used this land for generations. What would happen to them if this area flooded? I knew the land would repair itself, but I wasn't sure about the people down river. I began a five-year journey of trying to educate the Intervale people about the history of the land they now occupied. I'm still traveling this path. I have successfully gone through legislation and had the compost facility closed and moved. But the city of Burlington seems only interested in receiving awards for being green and so they, too, fight reality. It's amazing the power and spin they can put on this story in the name of being "green." Of course, everyone wants to be green—it's the right thing to do. But only a few want to admit this is "green washing." And very few want to understand using the land in a mutually sustainable way.

I visit the Intervale often, usually after I've recorded stories from the elders. The Intervale brings me back to their time. I bring my camera almost every time I visit. My walks can go anywhere from a half-hour to five hours. Usually an eagle appears some place in the visit. She often moves along 100 feet ahead of me as if to say, "Follow me." I do follow and I have found the most horrific things at the end of her trail. This lack of understanding has been difficult to deal with. Doris has been there with every step. "Call me before you enter, call me when you leave," she often says. She listens to my stories, makes me think of what I should do next and helps me to navigate the entangled political system. The fire within me flares brightly when I see the abuse of this land; Mali often comes to me in dreams. The land abuse is sometimes too much to handle. My comfort is that the old ones, they understand that I am doing my best; the system is big, and they help when they can.

When things were the darkest, Doris came through with yet another poem. The lesson for me this time was persevere, help will be there eventually.

Judy

She walks the old, old roads,
This land her own
For ten thousand years,
Watching
In the places
Where the old ones sleep
She keeps
The compact to protect
The land does not forget
Sister to the Eagle,
Daughter to the earth.

By Doris Seale

My friend Nancy Gallagher and I met some fifteen years ago. Nancy used to be a high school biology teacher. She went back to college for her master's degree. Using her knowledge of biology and her history skills her final thesis paper became a book called *Breeding Better Vermonters*. This book is the story of the Vermont Eugenics Survey, VES, and a dark time in Vermont's history. I first met Nancy at a presentation I was doing at a local college. She had many questions, and her questions raised many questions within me. Finally we met sometime after the presentation and began a journey together that forever changed my life.

Nancy slowly introduced me to the eugenic records with all their mysteries and pain. She was worried about what I might read in the records, she did not want me to get hurt. She did not know my family or what connections might be hidden in these records, nor did I. As Nancy continued to educate me about what the VES was and the results of this survey on my family and friends, those stories that I had listened to for almost fifty years now took on a different meaning. "Listen," my father told me over and over again, "I tell you these stories because they are important to remember." I now sit here with huge tears flowing down my cheeks as I remember his words. I just never knew how important they would be. He has passed on now and I'm saddened that I can't tell him that I remember.

Just as slowly as Nancy introduced me to the eugenics records, I introduced her to family, friends and special places like the Intervale and the mouth of the river. We began to build a trust with each other. My father always said, "What is talked about in this house stays in this house." I never quite understood why then when he said it, but I do now. My father's message was pounded into me for years, and sharing with Nancy was difficult at first. There were hidden fears that I didn't understand. There were worries. But we continued to build trust and educate each other slowly.

Together Nancy and I interviewed people about their lives in the 1920s and 1930s. We did research in places I never knew existed. I often went to bed at night only to quickly sit up and find a bed full of ancestors explaining things to me. I kept a paper and pencil by my bed and made notes during the night. The mind is amazing in how it sorts out things. The next morning, I would be off investigating something else. One path after another gave me one answer after another. The answers were never what I wanted to find, but I followed the trail anyway.

My great-grandmother's death certificate stated that she died in the Waterbury State Hospital. "Family unknown" was written in big letters. Why were they unknown, I wondered? Family is everything. Why was she there? The Vermont eugenics records revealed a photo of my aunts and uncles as children with red circles around their heads. Why? What had they done? They were children! It became clear to me that this family line had been the largest family targeted by the Survey. Why? Was it "Who" they were? Was it "What" they did? Was it "How" they lived? Questions, questions everywhere, I didn't really want the answers, but somebody wanted me to know them. I couldn't sleep. So I just kept digging. Finally the painful story slowly unfolded.

This survey was created during a time of great social reform in the early 1900s to 1940s. I visualize it as a collection of records used by people of authority, legislators, police, teachers and medical people to research a particular family they were interested in. A library of sorts, located on Church Street in Burlington, complete with the old-fashioned index card catalog files. At this time, it was believed that people could be bred to produce a better person just as was being done with cattle, horses and sheep. There were good genes and bad genes, the scientists told the world. The bad genes were costing the taxpayers too much money, they continued. Laws were passed and this "library collection" was used to document which people should be institutionalized and/or sterilized, which people possessed the so-called bad genes, and which families needed to be broken up for the "benefit of the children." The collection of survey records was, of course, subjective and often incorrect, but it didn't matter. It was the latest science, so the world thought. If you don't believe me, just ask Hitler's scientists; they will tell you the truth. To them, this was indeed the latest science and they were proud of their work. The targets of these records most of the time didn't even know there was a bullseye on their head. They didn't know their way of life was not seen as appropriate for the WASP people of this state. They didn't know the stories they shared made family members the next target. Stories are important to their history. I remember dad saying, "what is talked about in this house stays in this house." I remember, and now I know why. They didn't know if they lied to protect their families, their stories were recorded as the truth. They didn't know that living around the Intervale or at the mouth of the river so that they could continue living off the land like generations had done before them was not an acceptable life way anymore. They just didn't know. They just didn't know.

The restless nights continued for what seemed forever. I began to realize if I told the story to others, a little weight might be lifted. I couldn't continue to hold the story within—it was too much. I was overwhelmed. I talked with my father about the story. He didn't understand it as a complete story, but he understood parts. He agreed it must be shared but we needed to protect others who didn't understand that these records were many times untruthful and subjective to the times. Knowing the information existed could be very hurtful. What was not okay back then was sometimes perfectly okay with society today, and this might not be understood. "Things change," my father told me, "we just need to adapt to these changes." So I told Doris.

Dead silence came from the other end of the phone. "Are you there? Doris?" "Yeah." Doris began to unfold her life's story. Oh, my God, I'd seen it one hundred times before in the records. I didn't know. I didn't know it was her story too. We both wondered about Doris's family. How many others were out there with similar stories and didn't know? I needed to know; this could not happen again. This must not happen again! It reminded me of the "invasive" plant. "Pick off their heads and they won't reproduce," a University of Vermont scientist once told me speaking of purple loosestrife that had been introduced to the Intervale.

Doris's mother died when she was very young. "She died of polio," Doris told me. Doris's father was placed in an institution and the girls, Doris and her two sisters, went to Kurn Hattin, one of the many institutions the eugenicists used to place the children of families they chose to break up. The Inbox came through again shortly after our conversation with yet another piece of what Doris calls "swamp gas."

"I have to admit it kind of spooks me, when I get one like this out of the blue, whole and complete. I wonder if I should use a pseudonym for Kurn Hattin," the email said. "Hell, no, Too much history has been hidden," I replied. This story must be told. I was beginning to feel that Doris might be sorry she came home to Vermont. This worried me.

Kurn Hattin

It is hard to understand such fear,
How they came to a land that was strange,
Unlike anything they had ever known,
How they saw us
Coming out of the forests
Out of the mountains
Through the tall grass that had no roads
Where they were lost.
They saw us,
And we were like nothing they had ever seen before.
With our dark skin
With our feathers
With our paints,
We were the embodiment of their fear,
And that was all.
It could have been no other way
They did not need to decide
They knew already
That we would have to die.

By Doris Seale

Nancy and I have tried as we might to explain the history of the VES. This was a "Survey"—a survey based on pseudo-science, a destructive survey that was indeed misused. This was a survey much like what had been done in other states. But the students, social workers, educators and scientists that worked to collect and document this research did not do the institutionalizing or the sterilizing of the people listed in the survey. That nasty deed was left to others, but still descendants of the people listed in the survey records insist on holding the VES as the organization directly responsible for actually sterilizing and institutionalizing their relatives.

Vermont was peppered during the 1920s with the KKK, vigilante groups as well as other "good well-meaning groups" like the Mother's Milk Club. The KKK targeted primarily French and Indian Catholics in Vermont. Other vigilante groups targeted the poor and the sick and those who suffered from tuberculosis; and, of course, many French Indian people in Vermont were also poor and sick. Indian people in Vermont have had stories passed down for what seems like forever of families being broken up, of families being institutionalized, and of family members being sterilized. These stories hurt, breed fears, and create misunderstanding. These stories in many cases continue to hide the real history of what happened to family members.

So our research continues. We continue to document geographically where the VES families lived, and where they live today. Slowly a pattern has emerged. The VES office was located in Burlington on Church Street, a bustling downtown business section of the city and close to the University of Vermont College where Professor Henry Perkins, the head of VES worked. We knew the first people that were targeted were those already in institutions; mental hospitals and jails provided the first part of the list. We decided to place the people targeted second, approximately 5,000 people, and the five largest families in the records on a map. This showed that they totally surrounded the Intervale and the waterways next to the Intervale. We noticed also that their descendants quietly moved away to more rural areas. This moving out of town eventually expanded the records to different places in the state.

The Intervale, the common pot, and the place that Indian people and their descendants still went to for survival, this beautiful land was also a target. The Vermont Children's Aid Society was a main tool that the Eugenicists used to find their targets. They followed the children and the children followed the land.[2] How disgusting that the two most vulnerable things were used as tools of destruction in the name of science.

My father's stories of survival are many, most taking him directly back to the Intervale. He hunted and fished for food there and hunted muskrat in his early twenties to sell for the ever-popular muskrat coats of the time. My cousins, who are older than me, helped my father to skin and tan the muskrats in their backyards on the perimeter of the Intervale. He, along with others, also burned the Intervale every fall in an effort to reduce the amount of old, dead plant growth the following spring. Specific plants then appeared in early spring that the muskrat were drawn to for food. The lack of tall, dried and matted grasses made it much easier to spot the muskrat, which ultimately led to a larger income and survival. And the act of tanning in one's backyard made them targets for the Eugenicist; this was a lifeway not suitable for WASPs of Burlington.

He also told me stories of the good times in the Intervale: the toboggan run, skating on long pond, delivering moonshine on his bicycle, and collecting the hot coals in a coal hod as the trains dropped their load of ash before entering city limits. This coal meant they would have some heat that would last for a long time. He showed me the trails that they used to collect firewood and the fields that were farmed when he worked as a hired hand on the farm his uncle was the foreman on. "This was hard work," Dad told me, "but this was the good times," he said.

I try and remember the good times when I visit the Intervale; I try to remember the beauty. Sometimes it's difficult, but I try. Seeing the bulldozers and machines reshaping the land, not using the land in a sustainable way makes me feel sick inside. Knowing what is on and in this land and watching it turned over and over is upsetting, at best. I've read the archeological reports, all twenty-three reports showing the history and the location of burials, and I often visit these locations to pray as I try and remember the good times. Usually I'm met by my friend, the eagle, or a gently breeze, my senses are alive here. I've listened to meeting after meeting where Native people and archeologists describe and discuss how sensitive the Intervale land is, "the most sensitive place in this state," one archaeologist said. Yet the bulldozers never stop—7 a.m. to 4 p.m. they roll on and on.

Nancy and I were asked to do a presentation at the University of Vermont library. It was for Women's History Month. We saw it as another opportunity to educate, but at this time we felt we needed to put faces to this story. We collected old photos of my father as a child and his mother and grandmother. We also collected a few photos from Doris. Finally we put a power point together and told the story. We told the story of family survival, the burials and the connection with the Intervale, and the role of a mother in all of this.

Nancy drove to my house and together we went to pick up Doris. It was a beautiful evening and the presentation went well. We stayed for a while, speaking with members of the audience. Finally, we all piled into the car. It seemed like a good time to ask, "Do you guys want to take a ride down to the Intervale?" I said. "Sure," everyone agreed. So we drove the mile downhill from the University of Vermont to the dirt road that meandered through the Intervale. The night was dark and the beginning of the road was well lit with streetlights, but as we continued down the road we could only make out the silhouettes of the huge mounds of compost that seemed to go on and on forever and faint outlines of the greenhouses and farm buildings. No eagle came to greet me tonight. Occasionally yellow glowing eyes scurried across the road but that was about all you could see. My emotions are all over the board. When I walk the Intervale trails, disgust, peace, pain, and worry usually pop into my being. Tonight was different, I had the shivers tonight; I turned the knob on the heat up. Early the next morning this popped into my email.

Archeological Sensitivity

These are my Great Grandmother's bones.
I know they are here
Somewhere.
They are here
Returned to Earth
From here she came
To lie in peace
Her journey done,
Come home.

I can't find it.
I cannot find the place.
Where is she?
What have they done to the land?
I do not recognize this place
I do not recognize a thing.
What have you done?
Please,
Give me back My Great Grandmother's bones.

By Doris Seale

"We're both too far into this to stop now… JUST. Do not push yourself on this. Too intense, goes too deep, be careful."

Oh, my God I just shivered. Doris's letter continued, "NOW. Be careful with this stuff. I have great misgivings about sending you this one, so I'm giving you another, because this is what we need to remember, now. THIS is for your dreams."

In Winter

We see the bones of our Mother
Stripped bare of all adornment
And they are beautiful
Beyond what I can say.

By Doris Seale

I will put this one up there with the good stories from my father. I will remember and carry them with me always. Thank you, Doris, thank you Mali, and thank you, dad, for the good stories.

I am a basket maker and I made the two installations below to show differences in the backyards and priorities of the time.

Footnotes

[1] A Common Pot is a bowl-like piece of land that runs alongside of a river. In this case it's 1,700 acres. The land is very fertile and usually floods regularly. For more information read *The Common Pot* by Lisa Brooks.

[2] The children were often targeted for missing school, playing in the roads, missing the 9:00 PM curfew and more. Usually they missed school because they were hunting, fishing or foraging for the family. It took a lot of people to feed such large families of twelve and more. They played in the roads because most of the people in their communities didn't have cars.

Childhood backyard of my father.

Childhood backyard of Henry Perkin, Executive Director of the Vermont Eugenics Survey.

NOT SO MUCH THE SAME PLACE

Prelude
In a time when neighborhoods had names,
a house in Brightwood was built
by *le grand-père* for *la grand-mère*,
and the extended family,
la ma tante and *le mon oncle*.
Their daughter [*la maman*] lived there too.
After she married, so too her husband [*le papa*]
and their children [*les enfants*].
I was their eldest child [*l'âinée*].
When *la grand-mère* died, the other grandparents,
mémère and *pépère*, parents of *le papa*, moved in.
This is the story of a family [*la famille*],
a Springfield, Massachusetts neighborhood,
and the tree that watched over them all.

NOT SO MUCH THE SAME PLACE

in an old city neighborhood,
across the street from the extended family home,
the maple tree stands tall and strong
rooted deep in a tiny space
between tar and cement

1922
In this "*p'tit Canada*"
Allo! Viens nous visiter!
[Hello, come visit!]
the front porch swings
at the extended family home even as
a branch of the KKK
moves in on Main Street.
Crosses burn in Agawam, South Hadley, Southwick, North Adams.
"The Klan is consecrated to keeping America Protestant." *
It's not so much about the blacks here,
it's those Catholics, yes, the Italians and Irish, too,
but especially the French hordes from the north
taking over northeast industrial cities. **
La famille does not know of such things.
They cannot read English newspapers.

All the while,
robins nest in the maple tree's branched embrace.
Below, on back porch steps,
cream-topped milk bottles clink in metal carriers,
brought by milkmen in horse-drawn carts.
Bread arrives. It's *M. Poulin* at the door:
Comment ça va, Madame? Vos enfants sont biens?
[How are you, Madame? Your children are well?]

The singing iceman plunks
a cold square in the icebox on the porch.
Drunken Ben hawks fruit and vegetables as
housewives tumble down stairs,
jostling for position behind the truck.
"*C'est une frotteuse*" is overheard,
as a neighbor speaks of her sister obsessed
with keeping a clean house.
Families take the trolley downtown.
The Great Depression hits.

in an old city neighborhood,
the maple tree stands tall and strong
rooted deep in a tiny space
between tar and cement

Cooled by the maple tree's expansive reach,
the "Cat Man," his long white hair wrapped in braids,
collects rags. Maple seeds fall,
children catch "helicopters" and make "soup"
for their tea parties.
Pigeons waddle on nearby roofs,
birds sit on telephone wires—like notes on music lines.
Children test their balance on wrought iron rails,
or crouch on walks to watch ants march.
Trucks rumble, back up in side yards
and coal flies down chutes to
blackened cribs, shoveled into winter's
roaring furnaces. Radiators hiss and moan.
Across the street, on the hill
in Lincoln School playground,
sleds, toboggans, and wood skis
fly on winter's snow,
happy cries echo in frozen air.

1938
The Great New England Hurricane roars in,
the Connecticut overflows its banks
and boats float on Main Street.
The lonely daughter [she's not yet "*la Maman*"]
watches from the porch
of the house her *Papa* built.
She prays the water will drown all memory of loss:
five baby brothers under six months old,
her three-year-old sister in the 1918 flu,
her loving *Papa*, from a fatal heart attack.
This last, her greatest loss; she was 12.
She and her *Maman* [not yet *la grand-mère*]
are the only two left.

in an old city neighborhood
the maple tree stands tall and strong
-the hurricane has not damaged it-
rooted deep in a tiny space
between tar and cement

1941
Long summer nights and radios blare:
"The Shadow Knows," "Tom Mix,"
another Red Sox loss.
FDR talks.
Boys travel farther than their dreams...but,
war is not the adventure they'd sought.
Families tend Victory Gardens
in small city plots.
Women work in factories,
sew baseballs at home.
Girls play baseball, form girls' clubs,
write letters to soldiers and sailors,
gather for parties and sightseeing trips.
In '43 two men in khaki
knock on tenement door.
Jeannette's screams—she's the mother at the door—
echo off apartment blocks.
Another Gold Star in a lonely window.
Le mon oncle drives a 1938 Packard.

1946
The maple trees' October leaves
put out their best for a gaggle of brides.
On the front porch, a beautiful bride,
sheer tulle veils her face as
she descends the front steps
of the house her *papa* [*le grand-père*] had built.
The bride: (not yet *la Maman*)
C'est l'jour de mes noces. [It's my wedding day.]
Je suis misérable. Maman est très fâchée!
[It is the most miserable day of my life. My mother is so angry with me!]
Her mother: (not yet *la grand-mère*)
Pourquoi tu m'fais ça? [Why are you doing this to me?]
J' t'ais tout donné! [I've given you everything!]
Si tu m' laisses, j' va mourir. [If you leave me, I will die.]
La Maman, le Papa and *les enfants*
will live with *la grand-mère*
in the extended family home.

1954
Children skip to schools.
In the public school—
"Only English spoken here!"
In the Catholic school—
A.M. English lessons, French in afternoons.

Friends walk to
Memorial Square Library
for books in which to lose themselves,
sneak off to Beal's for penny candy,
a five-cent candy bar.
Black and white TVs begin to appear.
La famille can't afford one yet.

Les enfants play hide'n'go seek,
peek behind the maple tree's wideness,
and grin when they can't be found.
Friends tie on skates and roll
on uneven brick walks, ride bikes
in the Lincoln School playground.
Garbage men pick up food waste
from metal cans buried in the ground.
Children ice skate in Calhoun Park.
Sundays—stores closed.
Families visit.

Weekday afternoons,
Le Papa walks home with a group of
workers from factories, blocks away.
Laughter moves on the breeze as
the men tease away the hard labors of the day.
One hears: *Lui, il a une crotte sur l' coeur.*
[There's an anger he can't let go of.]
as they talk about their boss at the factory.
Laundry fresh out of the wringer,
flies on lines strung off
backyard porches.
No one locks their doors.

The Catholic churches—
an important presence in Brightwood.
Latin, French, English words
spoken, whispered, sung
as incense hovers, sanctifies.
The French stucco, the Irish brick
—two blocks, miles distant—
The Irish don't like
the French very much. ***
And Pierre, what's going on
behind the rectory door?
Eleven years old: innocence fractured
by a priest's touch.
Who can you to go to, who trust?

in an old city neighborhood
the maple tree stands tall and strong
rooted deep in a tiny space
between tar and cement
its roots creep up to the surface.
i want to live!

The 1938 Packard is gone.
La famille walks everywhere—
to Flebottes for groceries
loaded in the Red Flyer,
to *l'Eglise S. Thomas d'Aquin,*
one block away.
They take the bus to Forest Park
for picnics, or
to ice skate on Porter Lake.
On summer nights, *la Maman* calls,
"Children come home! It's 7 o'clock;
time for rosary on the radio."
Les enfants—they make up stories
to pass the time away—
itch to return to jump rope songs,
swings in the park, marbles in the sand.

1959
A small inheritance from *la ma tante*.
A bold blue Chevy Impala station wagon.
Tailfins protrude outward, not upward.
A three-seater,
les enfants clamber to ride backwards.
Now, *la famille* drives for groceries,
a Sunday drive to anywhere, or
Allons visiter la famille—
visits to other family members.
Gas is 35 cents a gallon.
Excitement ripples in steamy August
les enfants pour out to watch
fire trucks scream in. (False Alarm!)
On the corner,
the red box has a broken glass.
No one saw who did it.

1961
In the extended family home,
la grand-mère is dead.
There is relief not grief.
The family moves upstairs,
the house is theirs.
Downstairs, *le papa*'s parents find a home.
Out back, *les enfants* climb
the telephone pole's metal rungs
to flat garage roof,
or play army men in a backyard sandbox.

One late afternoon winter
Mémère finds *Pépere*
in the cellar of the old house.
Anguished cries after next day's headlines:
"Local Barber Found Hanging From a Pipe"

This was not supposed to be published!
Les enfants cry as they leave for school.
Adults ask:
"Can there be a Catholic funeral?
He's the father of a priest, after all!"

in an old city neighborhood
the maple tree stands tall and strong
(is it over100 years old by now?)
rooted deep in a tiny space
between tar and cement

Terror runs down Cumberland Street,
Marie Anne, a twelve-year-old girl
is raped by two men on her paper route—
they wait for her in the dark hallway
of a neighbor's house.
Police sirens. Who called?
The child runs, she cannot contain her grief.
Her mother scolds: "How could you!"
and tries to wash out memory with a cloth.
No one must know of this shame.

Crisp leaves crinkle in October's breeze,
colors cry out their joy.
Squirrels with full cheeks, scurry.
A puppy chases flying leaves.
Rakes scrape cement.
Huge piles of maple leaves line curbs—
les enfants dare to jump in before
red fires make a smoky haze.
Inside, roaring furnaces are silent,
dirty coal dust gone;
clean, efficient oil makes
metal radiators rattle and clank.
Color televisions are becoming *de rigeur*.
Teens dream of owning transistor radios.

1966
La Maman, le Papa and
les enfants move away.
L'âinée is glad to leave;
too much death and sadness in this house!
She hopes that a life somewhere else
will bring peace.
She asks herself:
"Why is it so easy for my *Maman*
to leave her childhood home?"
There is so much she does not understand!

in an old city neighborhood
the maple tree stands tall and strong
[*someone has placed a new fence*
behind the tree to protect it]
rooted deep in a tiny space
between tar and cement

1970's
Tensions ride high.
Como esta? replaces *Comment ça va?*
In the Brightwood section of the City of Homes,
French carpenters are forgotten.
Le grand-père's first house is a parking lot.
An old, blind French couple is robbed
in their own home.
In the French Catholic Church, the pastor
rails against newcomers.
A people once not welcomed
now proclaim:
"YOU are not welcome here!"
One night, the French school burns.

Drug deals on the streets.
Riots and looting
after a Puerto Rican man
is killed by police.
Springfield Hospital, now BMC,
takes over the neighborhood.
At the French church
a new name, Spanish signs.
The Irish church is now
the North End Outreach and Youth Center.

Brightwood burns.
Across the street from the once French Church,
Nuestra Señora de Guadalupe
stands on the corner.
Her angels cannot stop flames
in this neighborhood
of burned-out shells.
Everyone locks their doors.
Old metal swings, gone—
safe, solid plastic
in the Brightwood School (once Lincoln School) playground.

New aromas on the breeze.
No *tourtières* on *le jour de l'An*,
[No meat pies on New Year's Eve.]
it's *arrozo con polo* [chicken with rice]
for dinner tonight.
New cadence on the street,
salsa, rap, reggaeton.
Main Street, a drag strip on hot summer nights.
Au revoir, Mme Bolduc! ****

in an old city neighborhood
the maple tree stands tall and strong
silent, seasonal witness noticed by only a few
roots rubbed smooth by blasts of wind, sand, rain,
but the leaves are dry, branches fall more easily.

2013
The tree is gone now,
cut across its rotted core, no rings tell its age
except its girth, six feet wide and huge,
gnarled roots extending out eight feet on either side.

A bare expanse of sky
  where once shade extended its wings
and birds nested
  and children played.

   O tree – where is our life?

By Jeanne Douillard

Notes:
*The Rev William J. Mahoney, principal lecturer of the KKK from Atlanta, GA, addressing a crowd in Boston. (*The Springfield Republican* newspaper, Springfield, Massachusetts, October 6, 1922).

** "'This is Not a Catholic Nation': The Ku Klux Klan Confronts Franco-Americans in Maine." *New England Quarterly*, 82:2 (June 2009), 285-303.

*** The Irish felt the French were taking their place, both in the workplace and the church. The early French workers refused to engage in strikes and the more vocal Irish blamed them for decreased wages and a tightening of the job market. A power struggle quickly unfolded within the Church as well. Such was the intensity of feelings on both sides that violence occasionally erupted.

**** Mary Rose-Anna Bolduc was a French Canadian singer and musician. She was known as *Madame Bolduc* or *La Bolduc*. She is often regarded as the first singer/songwriter of *Québec*.

The Alley

It is straight and narrow

It is the playground of my youth

No other children play here . . . just me

To entertain myself or not

The toys are the brick walls for me to write on with my chalk

Or to throw a ball up against it while I play "onesees"

No one there to see if I am cheating

It is the place I am told to go

It is a path that leads to nowhere

At each end there is a light yet I do not move

It is the dungeon where I am told I must stay

Centurions monitor my every move

They walk slowly by, peering in –
sharp glances

They stop to make sure I am where I should be

No words are spoken – body language says it all

They have no weapons to keep me at bay

Yet I stay

I have no backbone to stand up to their jeers

I decide I belong in the alley if I cannot stand up on my own

It becomes my solace – my place to cry alone – unheard – uncomforted

I make things up – I pretend a lot – I talk to Jesus

He becomes my friend –

I decide the alley is my cross to bear

I carry it well . . .

By Paula J. Currie-Raymond

TRANSITION

Cette année la ferme blanche est silencieuse
Et avec elle le rituel de son tintamarre
Que ramène le passage des saisons.
Elle vit mal la fin d'une tradition.
Son noir silence engloutit
Plus d'un siècle d'histoire édifiante
Consacrée à la survivance de la terre familiale
Défrichée, labourée,
Ensemencée, fertilisée,
Moissonnée.

D'une œuvre de longue haleine
Transmise en un geste ancestral
De père en fils
Elle métamorphose la personnalité
Cisèle le caractère des gens du pays
Façonne en profondeur leur âme
Courageux, déterminé
Résilient, tenace.

Où sont donc passés
Ces arpents de terre cultivés
Qui bordaient nos routes campagnardes
Et les terrains éventrés
D'où émergeaient les sillons vaporeux ?
Où sont donc passés
Les platins fleuris roses et blancs
Qui parfumaient le vent d'été
Et les lourdes corvées d'octobre
Suivies de festivités champêtres ?

Faut-il croire qu'une telle façon de vivre va disparaître
Qu'une nouvelle perspective alors va naître ?
Faut-il donc se résigner à l'oubli
Des rites tissés au passages des générations,
Des labeurs de cette minorité courageuse
Et de l'auto-suffisance des fiers habitants de mon pays?

Par Rina Boucher Soucy

LIGHT

Soft silent sleepy
Bitter batter butter
Sharp shiny shimmer
Big bold bright
Warm white wild
Fire flash fright
Big bold in the night . . .

By Paula J. Currie-Raymond

Square One Conversations

By Rhea Cote Robbins

—Having been treated less than because of my Franco-American background and heritage, do I as a Franco-American/French heritage woman have unstated privileges to address issues of social justice?
—Does the woman status alone qualify me to address the inequalities and issues?
—Do I wish to right the collective, heritage-bearing wrongs in regard to the neglect and silencing of the voices of a perceived "outsider" group?
—Do I continue to participate in Square One conversations, always having to explain from the beginning the reasons why this work belongs on the cultural/linguistic/etc. maps?
—Where does a person who has been deprived of their heritage, culture, langauge, etc. go to reconnect to their birthright?

Some simply do not address the issues.
Others take a crack at the opposition.
Some find the world comical at best.
Others issue statements to counteract the imbalance.
Still, some are aware and diverted elsewhere.
Others create conversations of import.
Some scurry at the first sign of trouble.
Others run into the burning building.
More, some, than others, watch the building burn.
Others have had no opportunity to speak—throughout the years.
Some believe they speak for the Others.
Others do not wish to be spoken for by Some.
Some, (un)used to being voiced, are unaware.
Others know, for both, the circumstances well.
Some do not need to know, for both, the circumstances.
Others complain of Some not hearing them.
Some speak to some, but not to Others.
Others explain Some to others.
Some play at being French in only some cases and not others.
Others possess the perfect language better than some.
Some speak fluent home to chez-nous.
Others attempt authenticity on the surface.
Some believe it necessary to step away from their heritage/culture/language to be with Others.

(Continued on next page)

Others ignore the subject of Some heritage/culture/language.
Some heritage/culture/language lies untouched.
Others' heritage/culture/language represents Some. Many. Most.
Some lose touch with their own self and their ancestors.
Others believe the loss of Some is for the good of the others.
Some know the pain of their losses while Others feast on appropriated cultures.
Others believe their false superiorities to be true.
Some reinforce their false premises.
Others bloat the truth to reflect the lies told in effigy.
Some, alone, cry silently within at a loss they barely know, understand or speak.
Others blandly, boldly continue with their privilege and opportunities to sound out all the same.
Some limp toward their contorted identities hidden in the closet still. Or, Forever.
Others insist on English Only, the last war's victors' language.
Some hide their bilingualism and there are no written proofs in the public spaces.
Others believe—To The Victor, The Spoils.
Some join that party and pretend to be traitors. To themselves mostly.
Others allow some to join their English Only Brigade.
Some climb to the top of the English Only mountain and plant a flag.
Others cram some into the cannon to shoot them across the bow as a warning shot to Some.
Some run and hide for cover.
Others claim all of Some are dead, or dying in the heritage/culture/language.
Some hide in plain sight and do not take on the issues.
Others believe that as long as Some are quiet and good. Silent. They are O.K.
Some, as long as they do not bring up any issues and are Silent, also believe they are O.K.
Others continue to pretend their innocence and superiority because they won the "war."
Some continue to belong to their heritage/culture/language in their heart of hearts—knowing there are no winners in any wars.
Now what?
Back to Square One of do I own the issues?
And do I want to do anything about them or it—the issues?
And since all are some or others:
Some like pretending to themselves their ignorance is their bliss.
Others are not so comfortable in the state of oblivion.
Do I want the burden of addressing the issues? Or pretend...

Home/House—*Chez-nous/Maison*

Joubarbe—Jaune ou rose, refroidissement
Houseleek (Hens and Chicks)—Vivacity, domestic industry

Chêne (feuilles)—Courage, force, solidité et prospérité
Oak Tree—Hospitality

Hysope—Pureté et humilité
Hyssop—Cleanliness

Houx—Prévoyance
Holly—Domestic happiness

Genêt—Jaune, humilité
Broom—Neatness

Lupin—Besoin de calme
Lupin—Voraciousness, imagination

Weaving French Heritage through Texts and Textiles

By Annette Sampon-Nicolas, Ph.D.

In a French fairy tale, a mother who has been turned into a mouse transforms old rags into new clothes for her children. When her children awaken to find the new clothes, they recognize their mother's fine stitches and are reassured that she is well. As I read this tale to my children when they were young, it stirred memories of my own mother's fairylike handling of needles and the magical apparition of new clothes on my chair when I was a child. She often stayed up late finishing a dress I needed for a special occasion.

One evening, as I put the finishing stitches on a pair of Capri pants for my daughter, I reflected on how all aspects of needlework, textiles, and texts have played a vital role in my family's daily life and history. I had never given much thought to how the touch of rich fabrics, the smell of freshly sheared wool, the weaving of hand-spun yarns, and the joyful colors of embroidery floss are as essential to our lives as the weaving of words into texts, of herbs and vegetables into aromatic dishes. The passionate world of words, texts, languages, sketching, painting, singing, vegetables, flowers, gardening, and cooking was simply the environment in which I have been immersed since birth.

French literature has been at the heart of my life ever since my father's voice called out "Mignonne" or "Cassandre," his voice singing through the house calling me names from beautiful Renaissance sonnets. My childhood was transformed into a magical kingdom where a giant was born from his mother's ear, and the rhythm of rain on the attic roof was echoed through the melodic rhymes of French poetry. Literature was not limited to reading books for a class. It meant going to the theatre to watch classical plays by Racine and Molière. It also meant spending an entire summer on a family literary and architectural tour of France visiting medieval cathedrals and Renaissance châteaux. At home, literature was life. It was quoting Cyrano de Bergerac: "Moi, c'est moralement que j'ai mes élégances" (My form of elegance is moral) when my mother forbade me to go downtown in my cutoffs, while I reassured her that my soul was as pure and elegant as Cyrano's. Leaving Belgium as a child to move to Wisconsin signified that my brothers and I spent every summer studying French grammar. High school was filled with formal French classes, and reciting poetry in a special category for speakers of French. My first literature teacher was my father and he instilled in me a passion for reading and literature. Both of my parents, through example, shared their passion for teaching. They taught me that nothing can surpass the mysteries and beauty of the written and spoken word. Nothing can replace the joy of an hour spent with a book or an hour teaching French language and culture. We had left Belgium when I was a child, but French continued to be the only language allowed in our home in Wisconsin. Wherever we went, all that was French heritage accompanied my family.

But where did this passion for needles, thread, yarns, and fabric originate? What inspires me and my children to return again and again to start a new project? No one in my close family has ever chosen a career in the field of fashion, textiles or design. Nothing would indicate that we would become a family inspired by the art of needlework. Could this passion have been passed down through the generations?

My great-grandmother in Belgium had been a professional seamstress and tailor. I remember my mother's stories of how the women in her family all perused the latest French fashion magazines and copied haute couture designs for their own wardrobes. During the war, they learned how to transform an old sweater into new pairs of socks, and how to take an outgrown coat and create a new skirt for a growing child. This passion for needlework passed down through the generations crossed the Atlantic on a ship with my mother. On this ship were her trunks filled with a large wooden loom on which she wove children's clothing, and her wedding trousseau of intricately embroidered hand-made sheets, pillowcases, and napkins lovingly monogrammed by my grandmother and aunts, with intertwined "J" for Jardon and "S" for Sampon. These trunks would cross the plains, and find their home in Wisconsin.

My own life has been woven with all forms of needlework. When I was six, my mother taught me to cross-stitch my first piece, a Delft tile design of bright shades of blues. Throughout my childhood, she created clothing for me and for my dolls. While I might have lost interest in needlework and sewing when I reached high school, the opposite proved to be true. It was the height of the mini-skirt and bell-bottoms era. And true to my family in Belgium, if I could not afford to buy fashionable designs, I would learn to make them. Thus, with the help of my mother, I made pale yellow bell-bottoms and flowered mini-dresses. Since we spent every summer inside the walls of beautiful old Québec city, my mother signed me up for sewing classes where I learned the fine art of sewing by hand and how to use a sewing machine. Needle work was often inspired by other cultures and after spending a year studying in Portugal, I fell in love with hand-knit knee socks with red and black designs, bright blue tablecloths embroidered with white flowers, and cheerful peasant blouses. As always, once I was home, my mother taught me the art of knitting socks on four needles, of embroidering flowers, and of crocheting delicate cuffs on blouses.

Meeting new friends from across the world inspired us to learn petit point and create wall hangings and pillows. Before moving into my first apartment, my mother and I sewed curtains, slip covers, and a quilt. As she taught me everything she knew about needlework, she continued knitting beautiful sweaters with matching scarves and mittens, for me.

There was a period during graduate school when I did not have time to dedicate to needlework. Instead, I devoted my time and energies to textual weavings. After all, the word text and textiles share the same Latin root, texere, or weaving. In many respects, I was never far from needlepoint, as my pen replaced the needle and my paper the canvas. Instead, I devoted my creative energies to textual weavings. As the French writer Colette so elegantly put it, I embroidered white paper with my words.

As I awaited our first child with my husband Alain, who also enjoyed the fine art of needlework, we crocheted baby blankets, cross-stitched children's samplers, and sewed bumper pads and quilts. Before the birth of our daughter Claire, my mother knit many treasured bonnets and sweaters, created a delicate christening gown, which are all in a trunk, along with my own baby clothes finely woven by my mother. Over the years, she knit matching sweaters and nightgowns for my daughter and her dolls, designed a delicate kimono for an Asian American Girl doll, and transformed our children's drawings into brightly embroidered wall hangings.

Even before they could hold a needle, our son and daughter rummaged through sewing chests searching for materials with which to create a costume. One summer, my daughter and I discovered my old, worn-out childhood sewing box. Made of straw, trimmed with blue ribbons, musty smelling, it still contained my treasured ribbons, lace, eyelet, long narrow glass tubes filed with tiny pink and blue beads, bits of tulle and satin which I had used to make my own doll clothes. Fairy-tales about sewing in the night and the discovery of my childhood sewing box led me to dream about fabric, embroidery floss, and balls of yarn in my life.

Costume design and sewing were always important to my mother. Photos show her dressed as a Greek goddess and a medieval queen, costumes she had made when she acted in plays in Belgium. In Wisconsin, she created costumes to wear to Mardi Gras balls held at the Cercle Français, where people of French heritage gathered to keep their culture and language alive. And each year, proudly wearing regional costumes, the French-speaking community shared their dances, songs, and cuisines at the Folk Festival with a multitude of other cultures. Many years later, in the early 1990s, my mother created new costumes so that we could participate in the Local Colors folk festival in Virginia. Recently, my mother's costumes were worn by our French assistant and my students, as she taught them French folk dances. The love of costumes was passed down to our children. At a young age, our son Julien became enamored with fabric and started making costumes for Anime, manga, and Cos-play conventions. Later on, he designed and sewed prom dresses for his friends. Our daughter Claire also made clothes for her dolls, created her own costumes, and now takes sewing classes. It is remarkable how talents and skills seem to pass down through the generations.

As I crocheted blankets for children for their college journeys, cross-stitched sundrenched Provençal scenes, I cherished the passion for needlework. Like my mother who stayed up late putting finishing touches on my clothes, my husband and I spent many nights finishing new clothes for a beloved bear or a Christmas stocking for a doll. I never made a conscious choice about handing down my love of needles and sewing. It came naturally through example. It traveled from Belgium with my mother and from France with my husband, whose family also proudly claimed tailors. It was handed down by generations of women who knew the necessity and the joy of needlework. It crossed the Atlantic, the cornfields of Wisconsin, and the Blue Ridge Mountains to find a home in Virginia.

The canvas of our lives will always be embroidered with needlework and with tales of fairies sewing in the night. Being exposed to sewing and needlework my entire life has given me a love for anything related to fabric and needles. After I lost my mother, I discovered countless boxes filled with yards and yards of multi-colored fabrics, dozens of skeins of wool, embroidery floss of every color, knitting needles and crochet hooks galore. Along with these, paper patterns from the 1950s, a harlequin Pierrot costume, an intricately made multi-string clown puppet. Also, unfinished projects. A trunk filled with remnants of all the fabrics from my mother's projects. Remnants filled with memories, which we always intended to make into an American quilt. One unfinished treasure, close to my heart, is a large quilt on which I work a little at a time, trying to match my mother's perfect, tiny, loving stitches.

My life, like that of my mother, of my grandmother before me, and of my children today, has been woven with a delicate yet complex blend of needlework, art, singing, music, gardening, gourmet cooking, language, literature, and everything French.

Chaise Gabion

Celeste Roberge

Title: Chaise Gabion
Medium: Waterjet cut stainless steel, 1,350 pounds of river rocks
Dimensions: 24" x 72" x 27"
#3 in edition of 10
Photo Credit: Celeste Roberge

Artist Statement

Chaise Gabion is a waterjet-cut, TIG (Tungsten Inert Gas) welded, fabricated stainless steel chaise lounge filled with river stones. It measures 24" x 72" x 27" and is fully functional. I designed the chaise lounge after years of working with antique Victorian chaises in the *STACKS* series of sculptures where I embedded furniture in thousands of pounds of stone. With *Chaise Gabion*, the stone fills the sculpture rather than surrounds it.

The word gabion comes from the Italian "*gambionne*" translating to mean "big cage." In civil engineering, a gabion is the metal netting that keeps stones on a steep slope from sliding onto the road. Also, in French, "*gabion*" is a two-handled basket used for carrying agricultural products or used in dredging rivers. I use the concept and structure of the gabion in both my *Cairn* series and in the designed stainless steel furniture series.

Chaise Gabion is designed to be the archetypal chaise lounge, however, it is modernized, using AutoCAD software, waterjet cut from full sheets of stainless steel, fabricated using TIG welding and metal screws, and then filled with small smooth stones, whether they are beach rocks, river rocks, or quarry rocks. Through the juxtaposition of its historical references, its design, and its materiality, *Chaise Gabion* has multiple meanings: it is a modernist sculpture in form, with postmodern overtones; it is a functional piece of furniture; it is a real engineered structure that acts as a gabion; and, of course, it is a poetic object.

Chaise Gabion has led me to the design and fabrication of other furniture forms that pay homage to historical figures and to the raw materials of metals and ores such as the series *Chairs for Mining*, where each chair refers to a specific metal ore in its title.

Meditation for weaving and spinning

Dream the ocean unrolling its bolts of lace.
The spume and hiss of it. Lace can hiss. Yes, it can hiss:
I remember my wedding veil seething against my scalp.

Eight hours a day my father spun fiberglass thread.
Dream him on his coffee break. How he crouched behind the loading dock,
his cigarette peering like a birdling from the nest of his hands.
Dream the warm smoke soothing the slivers of glass in his lung.

Dream the spindle resting on Beauty's thigh.
Flax can sing as it's spun into thread.
The flax sang to Sleeping Beauty, it sang.
But the spindle, that old serpent, leapt in her hand.
Dream the serpent's hiss,
the fatal drop of fingertip blood.

My grandfather stirred vats of boiling dye.
Green steam stained his cheekbones.
Dream the witchy stick that swirled the pigments.
My other grandfather dipped yards of fabric into the steaming hues.
Nights he wept blue water into my grandmother's lap.

Dream Snow White's mother drowsing over her needlework.
Snow's real mother, not the wicked image in the mirror.
Her embroidery needle dipping into the hoop,
dipping out, tender as coitus.
Dream it again: the fatal drop of fingertip blood.

My mother worked the weaving room.
Dream her dreaming after a twelve-hour shift.
Even asleep, my mother felt the shuddering:
how the looms rattled her backbone,
trembled her mouth like a tantruming child.

Dream the miller's daughter salting unspinnable straw with her tears.
Dream something witchy about that nameless gnome,
the spindle coming alive in his hands.
Spinning straw into gold,
the metallic thread slashing his fingertips.

Dream the miller's daughter marrying the king who would have murdered her,
the lace bridal veil hissing against her eyes.

By Ellen LaFleche

GRAND MÉNAGE

Quand revient le printemps
Les ménagères du rang
Empoignent vadrouilles, plumeaux et pinceaux,
Et s'acharnent à « netteyer » la maison.

De la cave au «/pti-grinier »
La « guenille » à la main
Elles frottent et décrottent sans fin.
Comme naguère
Au de temps de grand-mère
La bataille n'a pas changé
Mais l'artillerie s'est perfectionnée
M. Clean et Spic & Span.
Camarades, aux armes !

Ôte les châssis doubles
Lave les vitres
Sors les tapis
Aère les rideaux
Balaie les toiles d'araignées
Époussette les bibelots
Enjolive les murs
Polis les meubles
N'oublie pas les « garde-robes » !

Déplie, replie
Défais, refais
Déplace, replace
Mais dépêche-toi
Dépêche-toi, donc !
Vite ! Débarbouille-toi !
Mets tes habits neufs
Ne sais-tu pas
Que demain c'est l'été ?

Par Rina Boucher Soucy

Pica

potatoes taste of dirt
that's moldered from
rain and summer sun

diet staples
we grew up on
katahdins kennebecs
norlands russets
canadian shepodys
baked boiled
scalloped stewed
served first on our plate

in July we watch and wait
for new ones
under rigid green vines
dotted with blossoms

eagerly we dig them
with three-tined fork
or bare hands
until fingernails fill with dirt
and hurt

never mind

we pull up small knobs
brush hastily leaving
delicate traces of brown loam
bite one
white flesh cracks
satisfying our primal palate

betheny chambers anderson
trudy chambers price
1.11.15

Desperate for Donuts

By Laurie Meunier Graves

Every day, it seems, is national something or other day, but June 5 just happens to be National Donut Day. I am a donut lover from way, way back, when I worked at Dunkin' Donuts during those halcyon times when each store had honest-to-God bakers who made donuts fresh every six hours. I ate more donuts than I care to admit, but because I was biking to work—ten miles round trip—I was fit and lean.

In 2008, I wrote a longish essay called "Desperate for Donuts." In honor of National Donut Day, here are some excerpts, slightly edited, from that piece. The edited version was posted on my blog ***Notes from the Hinterland***.

The Good and the Bad

Ironically, they are the perfect shape—a circle, round like a mandala, the symbol of eternity—and this should make them the perfect food. But fried in oil, perhaps drenched in glaze, covered with sugar, frosted, or even plain, they are not good for you. Not even a little bit.

Then there is their status. Jill Lightner, a West Coast writer, has called them the "dumb blonde of the pastry world." Patric Kuh, another West Coast writer, described them as a "street thug ... strutting past Madeleine and Éclair." There are also all the donut/cop jokes that have become so ubiquitous they are now clichés.

But ... there is something about fried dough that transcends its lowly status, that crosses class lines, that worms its way into people's appetites, even though they might not like to admit it. Simply put, fried dough is delicious, and donuts are the epitome of fried dough. There is nothing more sublime, say, than a raised donut, newly fried, dipped in glaze, and eaten just as soon as that glaze has dried.

A Brief History of Donuts

"When it comes to donuts New England is a place apart." —John T. Edge, *Donuts, An American Passion*

New England can reasonably claim to be the epicenter of the American donut world, and its donut tradition stretches all the way back to the Pilgrims, who, after staying in Holland, brought fried dough, which the Dutch called olykoeks (oily cakes), to the New World. These ur-donuts had no holes, were yeasted, and had raisins, apples, and almonds in them. John T. Edge ... has described them as "deep fried fruitcake." A daunting thought, but I would certainly give them a try if the opportunity presented itself. Naturally, as the Dutch settled New York, they brought their olykoeks to this region as well, and fried dough had a firm foothold in what would become the thirteen colonies.

According to legend, Sea Captain Hanson Crockett Gregory, from Rockport, Maine, invented the hole in the donut sometime in the mid-1800s. Out at sea, with a holeless, olykoek-type donut in one hand and the ship's wheel in the other, he supposedly stuck the donut on the spoke of the wheel, thus inventing the donut hole. Is this true? Only Captain Gregory knew for sure, but he somehow managed to convince the *Boston Post* his story was true and was duly accorded fame for his "invention."

From there, donuts, complete with holes, went international, and they did so in a most unusual way—they went to France during World War I with the Salvation Army. Here again, we have the stuff of legend. In 1917, four Lassies (as the women in the Salvation Army were called) traveled to the camp of the 1st Ammunition Train in France. The soldiers wanted pie, but there were no bake ovens for the Lassies to use. However, they did have a kettle, oil, and the ingredients for donuts. From that first day, when two of the Lassies fried 150 donuts, word spread, and other Lassies soon began making donuts for the troops. Eventually, Lassies, often only two of them, would go on to make as many as 2,500 in one day for the grateful soldiers. Hence, the term "doughboy" was born. You might die miserably in the trench or be poisoned by mustard gas, but at least there were donuts to be had before the horrors of battle. It wasn't much, but it was something.

A Donut Tour

"We devalue the things that give us pleasure." —John T. Edge

I have a dream, a fantasy of sorts, that John T. Edge, a food writer who hails from the South, would come as far north as central Maine and that we would go on a donut tour together. We would start in Augusta, at Bolley's Famous Franks, early in the morning when their donuts ... are still warm. Taking time to savor Bolley's tender, old-fashioned cinnamon donuts, we would then hurry to Frosty's in Gardiner ... marveling at the oh-so-fresh honey-dipped donuts.

From there it would be off to Willow Bake Shoppe in Rockport, whose cake donuts are impossibly tender and whose chocolate donuts are satisfyingly rich. I would perhaps introduce "wicked good" into Edge's vocabulary. After all these donuts we would need a bit of a break, and Camden, on a sparkling day, would be the perfect place to rest. Finding a bench in the park overlooking the shimmering harbor, we would discuss the various donuts we had eaten, and I expect Edge would want to compare them to donuts he has eaten in other parts of the country. But in the end, Edge would return to a line from his own *Donuts: An American Passion*. That is, when it comes to donuts, New England is a place apart.

Wet Wool
from *A Very Ida Christmas*

Susan Poulin writing as Ida LeClair

I miss the smell of wet wool. In a world before polar fleece, that's what winters smelled like in Maine. Wet wool, wood smoke and beans slow cookin' all day Saturday. Beans cookin' still smell like love to me.

And wet wool! From the hats and mittens Nana made us, from the socks that Mémé knit. Mémé also made us "pichous" (knit slippers with pompoms). During the winter, you left your boots in the mud room and only wore pichous in the house. At Nana's and Mémé's there was a basket of pichous by the door to put on when you visited, just like at our house. These women were tidy and didn't want you trackin' snow all over their polished floors.

My sister Irene and me would play outside for hours with our friends, makin' snow forts and snow men, ridin' our flying saucers down the hill over to the Hughey's, skatin' on the pond behind Shirley's farm. All of this unsupervised, you understand, not like today. Back then, you were told to go play outside and your parents didn't want to see you 'til lunch or supper. It was pretty safe, too, 'cause we traveled in packs with our friends, brothers and sisters and their friends, all together in the great outdoors.

I remember when Irene and me were little, on Christmas day, after we finished unwrappin' our presents, our parents would take us up to the camp road. There we'd meet up with Aunt Denise (my father's sister), Uncle Dominic, and our cousins Mark, Maureen, Kathy and Scott. It was a dirt road with packed snow, and my father and Uncle Dom would tie a toboggan and a couple of sleds to the bumper of an old Ford pickup truck.

Then the girls would get on the toboggan in order of age: Irene in front, 'cause she was the youngest, then me, Kathy and Maureen. Scott and Mark were on sleds, one on either side of the toboggan, laying on their stomachs. Once we were all set, Dad got into the truck with our mother and Aunt Denise, and off we'd go! I still remember the jerk as the slack came out of the rope and the toboggan started to move, and laughing like crazy as the truck picked up speed. We probably weren't going all that fast, though, 'cause Uncle Dom could keep up, runnin' behind to make sure nothing happened. But it sure felt fast! I can still remember Kathy's arms around me and Maureen's boots by my elbows, my arms around Irene, feeling her shaking, she was gigglin' so. No helmets either, just good, ol' fashioned fun: wet wool, truck exhaust and all.

Then you grow up, and in some ways Christmas is the same. But it's also, well, different. And not always merry. There was the first one after my mother died. That was tough. Then there was the year Charlie and me got a great deal on a Caribbean cruise, and I spent Christmas day in Jamaica, sitting in the sun, drinkin' Piña Coladas and cryin' my eyes out, I was so lonesome.

Then, of course, there was the year pork pies killed my grandmother. I kid you not. See, it's a holiday tradition. The pork pies, not the dying. In our family, as a rule, we try not to die around the holidays. It kind of puts a damper on things. Pork pies, or tortières, are a French Canadian delicacy, a pie filled with ground pork, potatoes, onions and spices. You eat it during the holidays with homemade piccalilli. I like my pork pie with lots of catsup, though my husband, Charlie, prefers his plain.

Let's face it. Pork is the food of my people. It was always a staple at Réveillons, the big party traditionally held after Midnight Mass, with tons of food and drinking. Along with the pork pie, there'd be baked beans made with salt pork, homemade biscuits, and roast pork with homemade apple sauce. For desserts, we'd have pies, bread pudding with heavy cream poured on top, and Christmas pudding made with suet and served with a hard sauce. Then the music and dancin' kicked in. I don't know how my parents did it, staying up, partying 'til 3:00, 4:00 in the morning only to have Irene and me wake them up at 5:00 to open presents. It probably helped that they had still had a buzz on!

Now, Midnight Mass is at 7:00. Afterwards we eat lasagna, 'cause it's easier to digest, and we save the pork pie for breakfast, Christmas morning. Somehow, it just wouldn't seem like Christmas without pork pie, piccalilli, and heartburn.

Non-Contestant–or–Almost Unlucky in Love

New Year's Eve—our first meet-his-friends' date.
Like kids, we kicked the snow
by Ray and Barbara's.
Steve's ex, Franny, would be there,
but that was all right.
We'd stored our old loves away.

We entered with others crowding close—
then paused a moment.
Tugging off mufflers, scarves, and hats.
we piled them on the coat racks.
"Where's Franny?" we heard.
I turned; a guest fell silent.

Before us glittering by the tree
sat Franny.
With introductions made we talked.
Quickly I moved elsewhere.
I passed napkins, trays, and snacks
for bustling hostess Barbara.
Then, I sampled party games:
Charades, "What's my Name?" and poker.

And Steve? He went from friend to friend
telling jokes and stories.
Together, even when apart,
we partied that night as a couple.
Off by the tree, a laughing group
crowded close to Franny.

At twelve we all sang Auld Lang Syne
to cheer the New Year in
I'd come as Steve's friend; we left as a team.
The evening's dynamic had joined us.

Ray later confessed the friends' failed plot.
It hadn't worked as planned.
Steve and I married one fine June Day
—right there, at Ray and Barbara's.

By Margaret S. Langford

Ida

Ida reinvented her life at the Home.
When Steve and I went there, she beamed.
She told us she knew how lucky she was.
They'd found her some millwork nearby.
The boss had fired some lazy hands.
There was a second-shift job just for her.

At the Home, no one shared her vision.

Did she think she still partied Saturday nights,
when the long workweek had ended?
Did she sometimes return to life after the mill,
to the next scene in her drama?

For awhile, in years past, she'd been on the road
with Babe, her truck-driver husband.
Sometimes she spelled him; she drove a mean rig.
She kept up with the best of them, always.

Did Ida linger after her death?
Steve and I often wondered.
She'd have loved the wake, the funeral, the meal,
with all her friends and relatives.
We tried not to smile—but almost gave up—
it was so very hard not to.
Was she perhaps laughing with us? At us?
Why not?
She'd always done so.

By Margaret S. Langford

Judith Rose Lacadie Hill–Art Works

Artist's Statement

The interplay of knotted, wrapped, and woven linear elements and the translucency of colored glass are the basis for my woven baskets. These wire sculptures challenge the perception of basketry and its implied function. While some of my work suggests containment, other baskets are inverted and become a canvas ... a "fence" for glass and metal objects. Much of my work in the textile field has focused on basketry. The technology I use to weave wire baskets is based on my research done for my thesis "Survey of Materials and Construction Techniques of Maine Indian Splint Ash Baskets and Contemporary Interpretations." The Maine Indians used composite blocks to make baskets that became narrow at the top (pack basket). The composite block was made of many pieces of wood held together with string. When the basket was finished the middle block was released, allowing the side pieces to collapse inside the basket. I build my forms out of plywood held together with screws. As I weave up the outside of the mold I take out the screws and the mold is released on the inside of the basket. — **Judith Rose Lacadie Hill**

French Island
15.5" x 9" x 16"
French Island is a multilayered iron wrought wire basket filled with glass collected from the shores of French Island and is seated on a wooden beam.

Birch Bark Basket
10" diameter by 20" tall
Birch Bark Basket is a cylindrical woven basket with a solid piece of birch bark held together with two strips of birch bark interlocked in the plain weave of the basket.

New York, New York
7.5" x 7.5" x 20"
New York, New York, a basket inspired by the New York skyline, is woven with stainless steel wire and strips of aluminum.

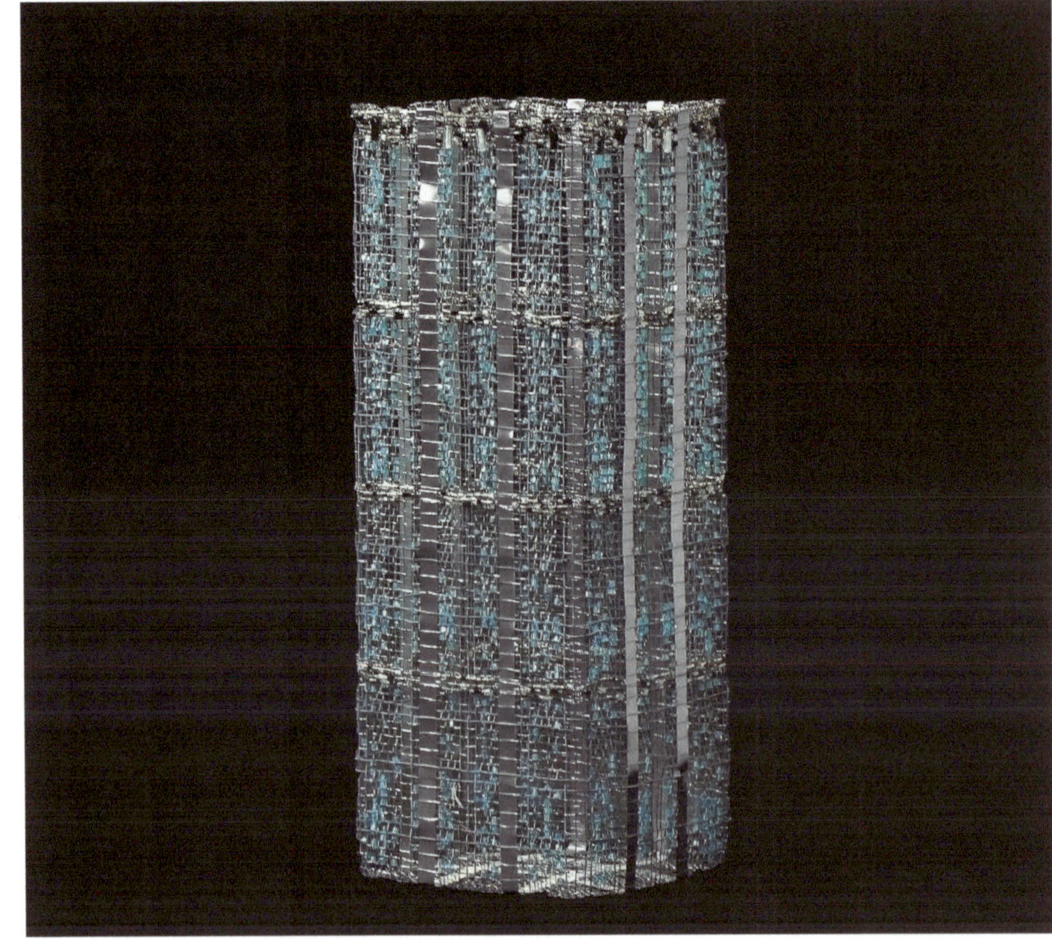

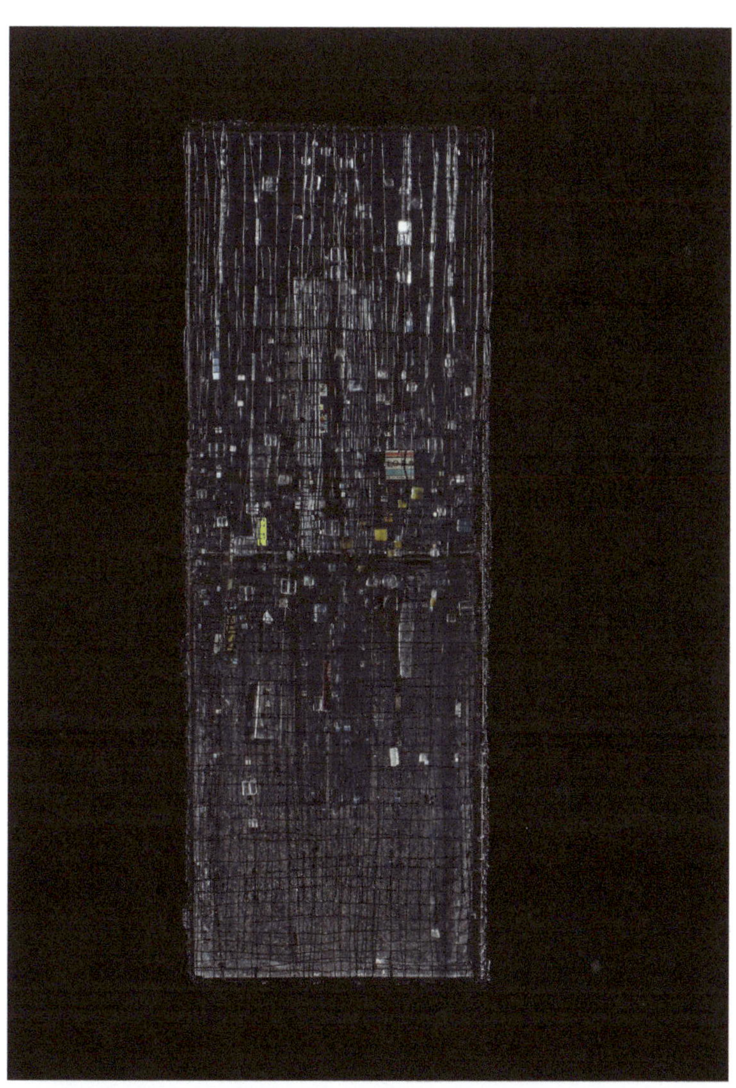

New York, New York II
8.5" x 1.5" x 24.25"
New York, New York II is a multilayered, inverted wire basket wall piece, which incorporates broken glass and mirrors, strips of old tins, glass beads, and semi-precious stones.

The King's Crown
8.25" x 8.25" x 11"
The King's Crown is a handwoven brass wire basket with semi-precious beads that interprets a king's crown.

Occupation/*Travail*

Rose trémière—beauté
Hollyhock—Ambition

Le laurier des montagnes ou laurier d'Amérique—Ambition
Mountain Laurel, Calico Bush—Ambition

Rose centfeuilles—beauté, grâce, volupté
Hundred-leaved rose—Dignity of mind

Lobélie—Bonnes pensées
Cardinal Flower—Energy

Bouton d'or—Ingratitude. Raillerie
Buttercup (Kingcup)—Desire for riches

Pensée, Viola tricolor—Nostalgie, souvenir
Pansy, Purple—You occupy my thoughts

Verveine—ravissement. Amour platonique. Enchantement pudique. Épouse-moi
Verbena (Vervain)—Enchantment, Sensibility

The Women Who Ran For Public Office

Georgette B. Bérubé

(1927-2005) from Lewiston served in both the Maine House and Senate from 1970 to 2000, Mme. Bérubé had more state legislative service than any other woman in Maine's history. In 1982, she was a candidate for Governor of Maine. For many years she hosted a French radio show in central Maine and served on the Finance Council of the Catholic Diocese of Maine. Mme. Bérubé was proud of her French heritage and her many contributions to her community and to her State made a difference in the lives of all of her constituents. We join her family and the citizens of this State in celebrating the life and accomplishments of this exceptional woman and we acknowledge the innumerable contributions that she made to the Franco-American community. She wrote *Thank You, Georgette* about her foray into politics.

Excerpt from *Thank You, Georgette*

"Saturday, 8:20 am, February 1970. I picked up the old ringing rotary phone and after the customary "Hello" a man's gruff voice said: "This is Louis." "Louis?" I asked. "Louis Jalbert," came the imperious reply. "I hear that you're thinking of running for the House. I can tell you right now that you're not going to win. Now, if you're interested in politics, you should start by joining the County Democratic Women's Club. They're getting ready for a card party as a fund-raiser. You can help them set up the tables. That's where you start." "How can you say this—you don't even know me nor what I am capable of in serving in the Legislature." "My dear, I know everything about you, including the size of your underwear."

So began Georgette Bérubé's foray into politics. At a time when few women served in statewide and national offices, women like Bérubé challenged local and state Party Machines. In her memoirs and speeches, Georgette Bérubé provides an insider's view of Maine politics. Serving in both the Maine House and Senate from 1970 to 2000, Georgette Bérubé has more state legislative service than another other woman in Maine's history. In 1982, she was a candidate for Governor of Maine. For many years she also hosted a weekly French radio program in central Maine.

Sarkela, Sandra J. "Lucia Cormier Vs. Margaret Chase Smith: Debate For The Maine Senate Seat, November 5, 1960." *Contemporary Argumentation & Debate* 26.(2005): 51-62. *Business Source Complete*. Web. 23 May 2016.

Lucia Cormier vs. Margaret Chase Smith: Debate For The Maine Senate Seat, November 5, 1960

By Sandra J. Sarkela, Ph.D., University of Memphis, Communication Studies

1960 is often remembered as the year Americans witnessed the first televised presidential campaign debate. There was another political campaign "first" that year, however, one that received national attention at the time, but that has been largely forgotten today. Each of the major political parties in the state of Maine nominated a woman to be its candidate for the U.S. Senate that year. This was the first time two women ran against each other for a U.S. Senate seat, a situation that did not occur again for twenty-six years, and has been repeated only four times. Democrats nominated Lucia Cormier, minority leader in the Maine House of Representatives, and Republicans continued their support of incumbent U.S. Senator Margaret Chase Smith. In addition to national publicity, the campaign culminated in a debate between the two candidates, which was broadcast on both radio and

television, Sunday, November 6, from 5:00-5:30 p.m., two days before the election.

The historical significance of this debate lies not only in the fact that it was a "first" for women, but also in the forgotten fact that it represented a culmination of forty years of growing political activism among women. *Time* magazine's September 5, 1960, cover story on the race began by asserting "Next Nov. 8 will very likely go down in history as Ladies' Day, with women voters outnumbering men for the first time in any peacetime presidential election" (p. 13). The article continued:

> In many areas, a feminine candidate is a required entry on any well-balanced ticket, and across the land more bonnets than ever before are in the political ring. Three women are running for the U.S. Senate, 26 for the House of Representatives, more than a hundred for legislatures and other statewide offices, thousands for county and local political jobs that range from board of education to justice of the peace. The nation's biggest, most eye-catching feminine contest is building up in Maine, where two women are matched, for the first time ever, in a race for the United States Senate (p. 13).

Buttons from 1960 Maine Senate race (Margaret Chase Smith vs. Lucia Cormier), first Senate campaign where both major party candidates were women.

This two-woman contest, therefore, reflects the significance of women's expanding activity in local and national politics throughout the period from 1920-1960, women who were not victimized by the "feminine mystique," but who established a foundation for the revived women's movement of the 1960s.

Reference

As Maine goes . . . . (September 5, 1960). *Time*, 13-16.

Also see TIME Magazine Biography: Margaret Chase Smith and Lucia Cormier, Grades: 4-8, ISBN: 9781480768161, https://www.teachercreatedmaterials.com/

Lucia Cormier as part of The Portland, Maine Women's History Trail

Taken from Maine Women's History Trail, Portland, Maine Website
The U.S. Custom House
312 Fore Street at Custom House Street

Lucia Cormier (1909-1993) was the only woman District Collector of Customs in Maine. President John F. Kennedy appointed her in 1961, and she held the position until her retirement in 1974. A former modern language teacher in Rumford, Cormier served six terms in the Maine House of Representatives. She was elected as the first woman minority floor leader in 1959. She ran for the U.S. Senate in 1960 as a Democratic candidate opposing incumbent Republican Senator Margaret Chase Smith. *Time Magazine* thought having two women running for the Senate from the same state was so unusual that it featured a picture of the two of them on its cover.

An article archived in news/google/newspapers, from *The Lewiston Daily Sun*, June 24, 1961, title states "Bids Customs Post For Miss Cormier." Portland (AP) —Senator Edmund S. Muskie, D-Maine has requested President Kennedy to appoint Miss Lucia Cormier of Rumford as collector of customs for the Maine-New Hampshire district, the *Portland Press Herald* reported Friday night. Miss Cormier made an unsuccessful bid to unseat Sen. Margaret Chase Smith, R-Maine last November. [Article was buried on the Wedding Announcement page.]

Maine Franco-American Hall of Fame, excerpt:

The House Calendar

The Advance Journal and Calendar of the House of Representatives

ONE HUNDRED AND TWENTY-SEVENTH MAINE LEGISLATURE
FIRST REGULAR SESSION

21st Legislative Day — Wednesday, March 18, 2015

RÉSOLUTION CONJOINTE HONORANT LES FRANCO-AMÉRICAINS
JOINT RESOLUTION HONORING FRANCO-AMERICAN DAY
MAINE SENATE
127TH LEGISLATURE

ORDERS

(4-1) On motion of Representative FREDETTE of Newport, the following Joint Resolution: (H.P. 667) (Cosponsored by President THIBODEAU of Waldo and Representative: MARTIN of Eagle Lake, Senators: CUSHING of Penobscot, MASON of Androscoggin)

RÉSOLUTION CONJOINTE HONORANT LES FRANCO-AMÉRICAINS

Considérant que, l'état du Maine est nommé après la province du Maine en France et que les villages de Paris et Calais portent les noms de la capitale de France et du port français de Calais, respectivement; et

Considérant que, plus d'un tiers de la population du Maine est de descendance française et canadienne, et les franco-américains du Maine ont contribué beaucoup à la beauté et la qualité de cet état; et

Considérant que, le français est la première langue de milliers de citoyens du Maine, et il y a eu une augmentation de l'utilisation de la langue française et une appréciation croissante de l'héritage franco-américain à travers l'état; et

Considérant que, des clubs et des associations pour promouvoir la culture et la langue française sont nés à travers l'état, y inclus le caucus francophone à la capitale; et

Considérant que, les gens qui parlent couramment le français et l'anglais sont une ressource économique et culturelle pour l'état du Maine; et

Considérant que, le tourisme culturel sera accru par les véritables centres franco-américains à travers l'état et la grande présence de franco-américains dans le Maine peut renforcir davantage nos relations avec le Canada, la France, et les autres pays francophones; et

Considérant que, le premier Jour Franco-Américain a été célébré mercredi, 6 mars, 2002, à la Capitale de l'État; maintenant, alors, qu'il soit

Résolu, que nous, les membres de la Cent-Vingt-septième Législature, assemblés dans la première session régulière, au nom des gens que nous représentons, proclamons que mercredi, 18 mars, 2015 est le Jour Franco-Américain, soit célébré à la Capitale de l'État; et qu'il soit aussi

Résolu, que le Jour Franco-Américain soit célébré pour commémorer la riche histoire du peuple français dans l'état du Maine et aux États-Unis d'Amérique.

JOINT RESOLUTION HONORING FRANCO-AMERICAN DAY

WHEREAS, the State of Maine is named after the Province of Maine in France, and the towns of Paris and Calais owe their names to the capital city of France and the French port city of Calais, respectively; and

WHEREAS, more than 1/3 of the population of Maine is of French and Canadian descent and Franco-Americans in Maine have contributed much to the beauty and quality of this State; and

WHEREAS, French is the primary language of thousands of Maine citizens and there has been a resurgence in the use of the French language and a heightened appreciation of the Franco-American heritage throughout the State; and

WHEREAS, clubs and organizations to promote French culture and language have sprung up throughout the State, including the Francophone Caucus at the Capitol; and

WHEREAS, fluent French-English bilingual people are a cultural and economic resource to the State; and

WHEREAS, cultural tourism can be greatly enhanced by the genuine Franco-American centers throughout the State, and the large Franco-American presence in Maine can further strengthen our relationships with Canada, France and the rest of the francophone world; and

WHEREAS, the first Franco-American Day was celebrated on Wednesday, March 6, 2002 at the State Capitol; now, therefore, be it

RESOLVED: That We, the Members of the One Hundred and Twenty-seventh Legislature now assembled in the First Regular Session, on behalf of the people we represent, proclaim that Wednesday, March 18, 2015 is Franco-American Day, to be celebrated at the State Capitol; and be it further

RESOLVED: That Franco-American Day be celebrated to commemorate the rich history of the French people in the State of Maine and the United States of America.

SPECIAL SENTIMENT CALENDAR

In accordance with House Rule 519 and Joint Rule 213, the following items:

Maine Franco American Hall of Fame

Proclamation- from the legislature

(5-14) Doris Belisle-Bonneau, of Auburn, on her induction into the Franco-American Hall of Fame. Ms. Belisle-Bonneau serves on the Board of Directors for the Franco American Collection at the University of Southern Maine's Lewiston/Auburn College, represents Franco American interests on the L/A Advisory Committee and co-chairs the Academic Affairs Committee. Since 2003 she has volunteered at D'Youville Pavilion in Lewiston with a focus on serving the French-speaking residents. She co-created and developed the Maine French Heritage Language Program under the auspices of the Franco Center and the University of Maine at Augusta. The program provides an after-school culture and language program for students from kindergarten to grade 6 and is currently active in Augusta and Lewiston. We acknowledge Ms. Belisle-Bonneau's service to her community and to the State, and we send her our congratulations on the occasion of her induction into the Franco-American Hall of Fame;

(HLS 134)
Presented by Representative MELARAGNO of Auburn.
Cosponsored by Representative BICKFORD of Auburn, Representative SAWICKI of Auburn, Senator BRAKEY of Androscoggin, Representative LAJOIE of Lewiston, Representative ROTUNDO of Lewiston, Representative GOLDEN of Lewiston, Representative BROOKS of Lewiston, Senator LIBBY of Androscoggin.

et aussi, Chevalier de l'order des palmes académiques
Proclamation République Française
Ministère de l'Éducation Nationale
De L'Enseignement Supérieur et de la Recherche
PALMES ACADÉMIQUES
Le Premier ministre, par décret en date du 1er janvier 2015
A nommé Chevalier de l'ordre des Palmes académiques
Madame Doris Belisle-Bonneau, Auburn
Pour Services Rendus à la Culture Française

Comments shared with the *Lewiston Sun Journal* and at the decoration for the Chevalier Award at the Franco Center on May 18th.

Monsieur Le Consul Fieschi, Canadian diplomats, State dignitaries, Members of the board at the Franco Center, Members of the Board at the Franco-American Collection at Lewiston Auburn College, my family, friends, and other distinguished guests.

I would like to speak about the privilege of receiving this award, thank you to all those whose support I feel here today and challenge this community. Given the nature of this distinction, I have chosen to address you in both French and English. How many of you speak French? Raise your hand. How many of you understand French? Raise your hand. Good. This will be fun.

C'est mon honneur d'accepter la distinction de chevalier de l'ordre des palmes académiques.

It is my honor to accept this distinguished award from the Society of the French Academic Palms and of inductee in the Franco-American Hall of Fame.

Ma mère Diane Castonguay qui était coiffeuse et mon père George Bélisle, tailleur de pierre seraient fiers de moi aujourd'hui.

My mother Diane Castonguay who was a hairdresser and father George Belisle who was a stone cutter would be proud of me today.

Je me décris souvent comme une petite fille Franco de Lewiston/Auburn qui a été bénie d'être élevée dans une famille bilingue; qui a travaillé pendant les étés dans le moulin et qui a été la première de sa famille à recevoir des diplômes de l'université.

I have described myself as a little French girl from Lewiston/Auburn who was blessed to be raised in a bilingual family, who worked summers in the mill and who was the first in my family to achieve several college degrees.

C'est la capacité de parler français qui m'a permis d'explorer des cultures francophones, d'apprécier le magique de notre héritage, et finalement de respecter mes traits de personnalité qui n'étaient pas toujours appréciés ici.

My ability to speak French set me free to explore different francophone cultures, to appreciate the magic of our Franco American heritage, and ultimately to respect personality traits that sometimes were not always valued here.

Je me souviens d'être critiquée de parler avec mes mains, de travailler trop fort, d'aller trop vite, pour être déterminée (boquer). Je ne savais pas comment travailler ou m'améliorer d'une autre façon.

I recall being criticized for talking with my hands, for working too hard, for going too fast, for being determined, even stubborn. But I just did not know how to work or grow or improve any other way.

J'accepte cet honneur au nom de tous les Franco-Américains dans le Maine qui ont travaillé fort et en particulier ceux qui habitent les villes de Lewiston/Auburn.

I accept this honor on behalf of all the hardworking Franco-Americans in Maine and especially those in these twin cities, Lewiston/Auburn.

Mois je suis fière d'être Franco et d'habiter à Lewiston-Auburn.

I am proud to be a Franco-American and to live in Lewiston-Auburn.

Maintenant vient le défi. Je vous laisse avec le défi de soutenir la résurgence du français dans le Maine et à Lewiston/Auburn.

Now comes the challenge. Support the resurgence of French in Maine and in Lewiston/Auburn.

Le printemps passé, Anne Murphy a fait un reportage sur la radio publique Our World.

Last spring Anne Murphy did a story that was broadcast on Public Radio-Our World.

L'histoire décrit le mouvement de résurgence du français dans le Maine en trois parties.

The story captured three essences of the resurgence of French in Maine.

Elle note l'ambiance des ainés à "la Rencontre" au Centre, l'énergie des enfants dans le programme de l'après-midi à Sherwood Heights et le désir des immigrés français pour communiquer avec ceux qui parlent Français à Lewiston/Auburn, Maine.

She highlighted the ambiance of seniors at "la Rencontre" at the Center, the energy of the children in the Maine French Heritage Program at Sherwood Heights, and the desire of French-speaking immigrants to connect with French speakers in Lewiston/Auburn, Maine.

Nos villes sont devenues multiculturelles et diverses.

The twin cities have become multicultural and diverse.

Soyons fiers ensemble.

Let us be proud together.

Il faut connecter la détermination de nos grands-parents à la synergie de nos enfants et les richesses culturelles des émigrés francophones.

Let's connect the strong will of our grandparents, to the synergy of our children and to the rich cultures of Francophone immigrants.

Maine Franco-American Hall of Fame

ONE HUNDRED AND TWENTY-FOURTH LEGISLATURE
FIRST REGULAR SESSION
21st Legislative Day
LEGISLATIVE RECORD - HOUSE, March 25, 2009

Recognizing:

the late **Viola Quirion**, of Waterville, on her posthumous induction into the Maine Franco-American Hall of Fame. Mlle. Quirion was a Francophone who worked for more than 40 years at the C. F. Hathaway Company shirt factory in Waterville where she was an outspoken leader in the local union. After her retirement and despite having cancer and other illnesses, she became active in a movement to make prescription drugs affordable for older people. Mlle. Quirion helped organize discount-drug bus trips to Canada, made an appearance on "60 Minutes" and appeared before congressional committees in Washington D.C. She was not an elected official or a political lobbyist but a hardworking, relentless woman who believed in pursuing a cause that she believed was right. United States Representative Thomas Allen said of Viola Quirion: "Maine is a better place because of the legacy left by this courageous woman." We join her family and her community in celebrating her remarkable life and her induction into the Maine Franco-American Hall of Fame;
(HLS 152)
Presented by Representative BECK of Waterville.
Cosponsored by Representative TRINWARD of Waterville, Representative TUTTLE of Sanford, Representative CAREY of Lewiston, Representative AYOTTE of Caswell, Representative BEAUDOIN of Biddeford, Representative BOLDUC of Auburn, Representative CROCKETT of Bethel.

Recognizing:

the late **Honorable Georgette B. Bérubé**, of Lewiston, on her posthumous induction into the Maine Franco-American Hall of Fame. Serving in both the Maine House and Senate from 1971 to 2000, Mme. Bérubé had more state legislative service than any other woman in Maine's history. In 1982, she was a candidate for Governor of Maine. For many years she hosted a French radio show in central Maine and served on the Finance Council of the Catholic Diocese of Maine. Mme. Bérubé was proud of her French heritage and her many contributions to her community and to her State made a difference in the lives of all of her constituents. We join her family and the citizens of this State in celebrating the life and accomplishments of this exceptional woman and we acknowledge the innumerable contributions that she made to the Franco-American community;
(HLS 151)
Presented by Representative ROTUNDO of Lewiston.
Cosponsored by Representative CAREY of Lewiston, Representative BICKFORD of Auburn, Representative BEAULIEU of Auburn, Representative TUTTLE of Sanford, Representative BEAUDOIN of Biddeford, Representative BECK of Waterville, Representative BOLDUC of Auburn, Representative CROCKETT of Bethel, Representative CROCKETT of Augusta, Representative GILBERT of Jay, Representative LAJOIE of Lewiston, Representative MARTIN of Eagle Lake, Representative PRATT of Eddington, Representative THERIAULT of Madawaska, Representative TRINWARD of Waterville, Representative WAGNER of Lewiston, Senator CRAVEN of Androscoggin, Senator JACKSON of Aroostook, Senator MARRACHÉ of Kennebec, Senator SIMPSON of Androscoggin, Senator SULLIVAN of York, Representative AYOTTE of Caswell.

READ and PASSED and sent for concurrence.

Other inductees—complete listing of sentiments at the Franco-American Collection, University of Southern Maine at Lewiston/Auburn:

Rachel Desgrosseilliers (Auburn)

Ms. Desgrosseilliers's family immigrated to Lewiston from St. Ludger, Canada. She grew up speaking French in the vibrant Francophone world of Lewiston, going to L'Eglise St. Famille and reading *Le Messager*. Preserving the history, telling the stories and honoring the memory of Franco-Americans have been a great part of Ms. Desgrosseilliers's professional life for the past decade. Ms. Desgrosseilliers has been the director of the Museum L-A for the past 3 years.

Anne L. Roy (Van Buren)

Mrs. Roy has been a remarkable force for the preservation of the French-Acadian heritage of the St. John Valley and the rest of Maine. For several years, she has been the director of the Acadian Village in Van Buren. She oversees the repairs and growth of the Village, which is a replica of Acadian life in northern Aroostook County in the early 1900s. Mrs. Roy was instrumental in planning and developing on-site the Levasseur-Dube Museum, the Martine Pelletier Book Nook and the Violette Industrial Building. Since 1982, she has also been the president of L'Héritage Vivant-Living Heritage Historical Society. She is the director of the Maine Acadian Heritage Council and vice-president of Le Club Français. A native of the St. John Valley, she has taught for 38 years, with 34 of those years at the former Loring Air Force Base in Limestone and in the town. Retired from full-time teaching in 2003, she now works part-time with special needs children in M.S.A.D. #24. She actively volunteers in the community as secretary of the Daughters of Isabella, is a member in good standing with the Friends of the Morneault Library in Van Buren, is chair of Mercy Meals for her church and is a member of the local American Legion Auxiliary. Mrs. Roy has a special place in her heart for her many elderly friends and is a familiar face at Borderview Nursing Home in Van Buren. In 2001, Mrs. Roy was the recipient of the Alumna of the Year Award from the University of Maine at Fort Kent. She is presently the coordinator for the Town of Van Buren's 125th Anniversary Celebration, as well as the Acadian Village's 30th Anniversary.

Rita Saucier Dubé (Lewiston)

She and her husband Paul owned and operated Dubé Travel Agency, where their bilingualism was a real asset, as it was when they traveled the globe. As a member of the board of St. Mary's Church, Rita has raised funds for the Franco-American Heritage Center. The Heritage Center, a former church in the heart of "Petit Canada," was built by the French-speaking immigrants in the early 1900s. It will now be a museum, performing arts center and education center to pay tribute to those immigrants who were a vital part of the industrialization of Maine. These individuals brought their language, culture, Catholic faith, work ethic, strong family values, patriotism and good citizenship to the building of a better society. Rita, a mother and grandmother of 3, is a very important part of the effort to preserve the French heritage, language and culture. Rita and the Franco-American Heritage Center pay tribute to her ancestors' efforts to build Maine.

Marie-Anne Gauvin (Madawaska)

After retiring as a French teacher in Connecticut, she returned to her native Madawaska and has been a relentless advocate for the preservation and active use of French in the St. John Valley. She became involved in the Save Our French movement in the 1990s and was one of the founding members of Le Club Français, a nonprofit advocacy group for the French language. She created the club's inspirational and meaningful newsletter, "Le Fanal," which she continues to write under her pen name, "la pie bavarde." She also chairs the organization's finance committee, which she steers with aplomb and common sense. She was instrumental in securing a trust fund from Marvin and Marie-Reine Mikesell from Chicago, Illinois, and is making sure that those and other funds will be dispensed wisely to help younger generations learn French.

also—(up to 2016)

Mona Lavertu (Madawaska)
Rhea Côté Robbins (Brewer)
Mary Rice-Defossé (Lewiston)
Cecile Dufour Pozzuto (Madawaska, posthumous)
Cindy Larock (Lewiston)
Lisa Marraché (Waterville)
Aliette Deland Couturier (Lewiston)
Claire Lafrance Auger (Sanford)
Sr. Solange Bernier (Lewiston, posthumous)
Theresa Marin Ouellette (St. Agatha)
Annette Lebel Daigle (Fort Kent)
Judy Ayotte Paradis (Frenchville)
Julie D. Albert (Madawaska)
Madeleine Giguère (Lewiston)
Alice LaChance (Waterville)
Constance D. Côté (Auburn)
Cleo Paradis Ouellette (Frenchville)
Cecile Vigue (Waterville)
Agnes (Daigle) Beaulieu (Madawaska)
Geraldine Chassé (St David)

Marble Steps to Maine

By Juliana L'Heureux

When being introduced as a Franco-American reporter, the host usually begins by saying something like this: "Juliana L'Heureux writes about Franco-Americans, but she's from Maryland." In other words, I'm not a Franco-American. Which, of course, begs the question of how I can write about a culture that's not my own?

Indeed, for the past thirty years I've had the privilege to write at least one, sometimes two, stories every week about Franco-Americans. These articles are published in newspapers, journals, blogs and anthologies. Writing about Franco-Americans is an interesting reporter's beat because the culture is as diverse as the East Baltimore neighborhood where I grew up.

When growing up, I learned the value of family stories. Writing about Franco-Americans helped me to bind these stories with the cultures of my roots. Except I've also learned how Franco-American stories are set apart from others. In fact, Franco-Americans haven't really melted into America's "melting pot." Instead, hard working French-Canadian immigrants were often more like itinerant laborers than immigrants. Yet, in other ways, I didn't see much difference between the cultural Franco-American stories and those I heard from a myriad of immigrant families who were my neighbors in East Baltimore.

Maryland's founder was Lord Baltimore. He requested the colony from the British Crown to serve as a haven for England's Roman Catholics, who were looking for religious freedom. Eventually, Baltimore City became a haven of hope for second- and third-generation European immigrant families. They settled in the growing city's eastern neighborhoods, a place where white marble steps were the pride of all the doorways.

There were no shortages of trees in Baltimore when I grew up there. In the 1940s and '50s, carefully planted trees were spaced with precision between row homes. They never seemed to grow much, but they were there to provide a splash of nature in an otherwise austere concrete landscape. In our tightly knit neighborhoods, Baltimore's famous white marble steps extended into the horizon, like an urban Apian Way, leading to places where the streetcars went.

Patterson Park was beautifully different. It was a recreational common, connecting the parallel lines of row houses, the architectural lineages that were lined up like soldiers at attention, in the East Baltimore neighborhoods. Patterson Park was a central refuge for our ethnically diverse neighbors.

As a matter of fact, a focal point of the park to this day is an unexpectedly lovely pagoda, just like the kind a tourist would expect to see in Japan. This oasis brought out the best in the multicultural neighbors, who often didn't even speak the same language.

When I grew up in East Baltimore, our neighbors included German, Polish, Italian, Sicilian (not to be confused with Italian), Russian, Ukrainian people and ethnic names I could hardly pronounce. Yet, almost everybody managed to get along! Perhaps Patterson Park was our green town hall. It was where children rolled down grassy hills and squirrels scrambled from tree to tree. As a matter of fact, Patterson Park, with its majestic pagoda, is still among Baltimore City's hidden treasures. It's literally located just across the concrete street from perfectly parallel rows of white marbled steps. Each set of sparkling white steps leads to the entry into a proud row home, usually a three-story masonry house, decorated with painted window screens depicting nature at its best, like waterfalls or stately swans swimming in clear ponds.

Built in 1890, the pagoda has endured through decades of use and abuse. Thanks to community support, it's been fully restored to its original beauty. Although a structural curiosity, for those of us who grew up in its shadow, the pagoda was symbolic of vision. Although we were never allowed to climb to the top, we could imagine what it was like if we were looking at the world from up there.

Living on the second floor of one of those East Baltimore row homes, my mother often let me sit at the kitchen table to play with a very old fashioned toy typewriter. It wasn't a real typewriter, but it did type. A small, central wheel pointed to a letter. Every letter was typed with great effort, as the typewriter ribbon was pressed by the corresponding key. "D-e-a-r N-o-n-a", my mother would say, as she then patiently waited for me to turn the little wheel to each letter she named. In fact, every week, I carefully typed a letter to mail to my Italian Nona in Monesson, Pennsylvania. She loved my letters. They almost always started with "I am fine. How are you?"

These formative childhood memories became my developmental stepping stones. Like the marble steps that led into my house and to those of all of my neighbors, these childhood memories also led to a realization about how writing could expand my horizons. Wow! I could communicate with Nona in Pennsylvania! Likewise, I could write to anybody, anywhere and at any time.

As a tribute to my mother, it should be evident to realize how the vision I anticipated, while rolling beneath the grassy shadows on the Patterson Park Pagoda was somehow infused into my little toy typewriter.

Writing about Franco-Americans is as gleeful an experience to me as typing a letter to Nona. Hopefully, my reports have contributed some sense of normalcy to Franco-Americans, who have only recently enjoyed the opportunity to take pride in their culture. While many history books hardly give French-Canadian immigrants any mention at all, the fact is, millions of patriotic Americans are Franco-Americans. Each person with Franco-American ancestry has a special story to tell to future generations. While reporting about thousands of these stories, I've valued the diversity, resourcefulness and creativity of Franco-Americans. Colorful language variations are probably the most evident example of Franco-American diversity. In my opinion, a colorful French-language one-act play might bring an awakening to the cultural diversity if the actors included portrayals of Acadians, with French-Canadians and the Métis in an animated conversation!

More often than not, the Franco-American family stories are ingrained in the threads of American history. Incredibly, most Americans are not aware of how the French saved George Washington's American Revolution from disaster, before the victory at the Battle of Yorktown, Virginia.

Obviously, the vision I yearned to see from the top of the Pagoda helped to open my mind to the possibilities of life outside of East Baltimore. Among the experiences I've enjoyed since leaving my home city has been a rewarding career as a professional registered nurse and a published writer.

My husband likes to say I've been a Franco-American for fifty years longer than I was the daughter in an Italian-Ukrainian immigrant family who lived in East Baltimore and then moved, even further east, to Dundalk, in Maryland.

Franco-Americans have allowed me to tell personal immigrant stories. Like a cultural translating machine, the stories I've written are nearly the same ones I heard when growing up, but reported from a distinctly Franco-American point of view.

Those white marble steps that stretched out to the Baltimore horizon became the stepping stones to the American dream for many who shared my upbringing. Franco-Americans didn't always have the opportunity to step away from their tightly knit French neighborhoods.

Metaphorically speaking, the white marble steps eventually led me and my family to Maine, where I've been honored to write about my husband's Franco-American heritage. Although Franco-American history has been under-reported and, as a result, undervalued, my decades of covering the many aspects of the group's identity has, hopefully, helped to instill pride in the culture that predates the founding of America.

Of course, I'm not a Franco-American, but a reporter who has observed the culture from the big picture level, and it has been my honor to report what I've seen.

My Genealogy Work

By Linda Côté Dubé

I started doing genealogy in 1976, and have never stopped. I have amassed a huge collection of information from newspapers, books, town records, obituary cards, etc. I have collected names A-to-Z of the people prevalent in the St. John Valley in northern Maine and Canada. All of this is done on index cards and they are held in five custom-built cabinets (total thirty-eight drawers mostly in three dividers each and one cabinet in four dividers).

The face of the card consists of a married couple, when and where married, birth date and place, death date and place, burial place, his parents and her parents (always spouse maiden name). It could also include multiple marriages, stories and tidbits of information. Some have baptismal dates and godparents. It also could include notes and pictures. On the back of the card are their children, with spouses, marriage date and place, birthdates and places, death dates and places, burial place. Any info that I can get on anyone is included on the card.

When doing a particular family, I start off by photocopying in all books available in the St. John Valley, that certain name. We have a huge collection of Marriage Repertoire books, now housed in Fort Kent, which was Leon Guimond's collection. Truly a "gem" for the St. John Valley!

Then I compile all that data, piecing every married couple with their children. I fill in the back of the card first. Then go through all those sheets again, and fill in the face of the card. Once accomplished, it's ready to type.

I am presently finishing up the "Parent" family. Since that family has four different common ancestors, one line is finished.

I can pretty much do anyone's genealogy.

Also, I have done both the "Dubé" and "Côté" families genealogy on bed sheets. I drew lines on the sheets. I start with the first generation, next line is second generation, third line is the third, etc. A total ten generations are shown. Every generation is written in a different colored permanent magic marker. The information is written in cursive writing. The same color at the top of the couple's name means that they are all brothers (only males are listed). Looking at the colored number at the bottom of the couple's name, you can find that colored number at the top in the next generation, and this will give you their children. The pattern is like that all the way through. So you can go forwards or backwards on those sheets. Also, I have a printed index with the couple's names accompanied with the different colored numbers for the top and the different colored numbers for the bottom. The Côté wall chart has 9,838 names written on it.

The *Côté Genealogy Books* are a five-volume set and contain 8,240 families along with their children and over 1200 pictures used. As the saying goes, "a picture is worth a thousand words." It is very easy to understand and there is an index in the back of each volume, so you can locate your family on that mentioned page number.

You'll notice around your relative, his or her brothers and sisters with their families, then first cousins, etc. The book is done by generations. This is truly The Cote Family Bible ... a must to own. Truly a masterpiece collection and a family heirloom. Total 2,006 pages.

Also other books available:

Dubé
1997 - 2 Volumes
1017 pages
"Dubé" books also cover; Duby, Dubey, Dubee, Dubie, and Dubay

Ouellette
1988 - 3 Volume Set
1310 pages

Bouchard
1990 - 3 Volume Set
1041 pages

Martin
2002 – 2 Volume Set
1188 pages

Theriault
1993 - 2 Volume Set
966 pages

Paradis
1989 - 2 Volume Set plus Supplement
1096 pages

—All of my books have around 490 pages, and include indexes. If you have any specific questions, please email me at cotedube@hotmail.com or call me in Madawaska, Maine.

Franco-American Woman as Author—The Girlfriend Book—How-to for Franco-American women.

La Jeune Franco-Américaine, The Young Franco-American

By Alberte Gastonguay (1906-1978), translated by Madeleine C. Paré Roy, is a study of the life of a young woman who is seeking her way in the world. She meets many suitors and comes to the conclusion of a satisfactory ending in the ways of traditional culture. In the English literary tradition there is the morality tale, but in the Franco-American literary tradition there is what I call the "Happy Husband Hunter's Handbook" which speaks to the way one seeks one's life in the Franco-American culture. Thoughtfully.

"A more specialized study of Franco-American novels of the 1930s found they were not devoid of interest, particularly as they shed light on contemporary attitudes and values. **Alberte Gastonguay-Sasseville (1906-1978)**, the daughter of a prosperous insurance agent in Lewiston, Maine, published *La Jeune Franco-Américaine* in 1933. The novel tells of a young woman's struggle to remain faithful to her Catholic and Franco-American upbringing despite the lures of modern life (e.g., the blandishments of a divorced man, the amorous advances of her employer, the bad example of a girlfriend who leads a life of debauchery)."—Comments from: *The French-Canadian Heritage in New England*, by Gerard J. Brault

La Jeune Franco-Américaine

Par Alberte Gastonguay

Un extrait—Le Debut

Depuis longtemps l'âme du père Carignan était pensive. La terre lui était chère, ses aïeux y avaient ensemencé leur travail et leur coeur. Dans les veillées passées au coin du feu, pendant que le vent secouait l'érable centenaire, en famille on jasait des États-Unis, de ce pays ruisselant d'or. Le fils de Pierre était déjà parti, et quand les lettres arrivaient, Pierre se disait heureux et satisfait. Carignan voulut tenter fortune. Après avoir longuement mûri le projet, un jour on fit les malles et la famille dirigea ses pas vers le Maine, dans la ville presque alors inhabitée de Lewiston. Il y avait déjà quelques familles américaines qui tenaient le haut du pavé, telles les Garcelon, les Gray, les McCarthy, fiers descendants des premiers colons. Près de la rivière Androscoggin qui aujourd'hui encore fertilise et féconde les filatures et qu'on nomme le canal, les Carignan bâtirent leur demeure, bien modeste. On ne jouissait pas de l'électricité alors, les chandelles et plus tard les lampes rendirent de grands services, mais le père et la mère avaient mis tout leur bonheur à voir pousser les bambins drus et nombreux. On travaillait la ferme en aimant le pays d'adoption. Quelques semaines passèrent quand d'autres familles originaires de la Beauce, vinrent rejoindre les Carignan. C'étaient des Casavant, des Marcotte, des Paradis, des Joncas. Ils formèrent alors le premier élément canadien-français à Lewiston. Ils parlaient leur langue maternelle et encore aujourd'hui, nombreux sont les plus âgés qui ne parlent pas encore un mot d'anglais. Ce petit noyau canadien s'est développé, a été fidèle à sa langue et à ses moeurs, si bien que cette terre foulée par leurs pieds porte depuis lors le nom devenu traditionnel: "le Petit Canada."

An Excerpt—The Beginning

For a long time now the very soul of Mr. Carignan had been preoccupied. The land that his ancestors had sown with their labor and their love was very dear to him. During those evenings spent gathered by the fire as the wind shook the hundred-year-old maple trees, the Carignans chatted about the United States, that country streaming with gold. Peter's son had already left, and when his letters arrived, Peter seemed happy and satisfied. Carignan wanted to tempt his own fate. After deliberating the possibility for a long time, the day came when they packed their belongings and the family made their way to the then nearly uninhabited town of Lewiston, Maine. There already were a few American families who held the high ground of the town, such as the Garcelons, the Grays, and the McCarthys, those proud descendants of the early colonists. The Carignans built their home near the Androscoggin River, whose waters even today flow into what is called the "canal" and are essential for the functioning and productivity of the mills. It was a very modest house. Since they had no electricity, candles and later on lamps provided a great service. The father and mother based their happiness not on material goods, but rather in watching their many children, who were close in age, grow up. They worked the farm and loved their adopted country. A few weeks went by when other families originating from "la Beauce" came to join the Carignans. They were the Casavants, the Marcottes, the Paradis and the Joncas. They formed the first nucleus of French-Canadians in Lewiston. They spoke their native tongue and even today, many members of the older generation don't speak a word of English. This small core of Canadians evolved, were faithful to their language and their principles, so much so that the land they trudged since their arrival has traditionally become known as "le Petit Canada," "Little Canada."

Language/*Langue*

Sabot de Vénus—Caprice
Lady's Slipper—Capricious beauty

Châtaignier—Justice
Chestnut Tree—Luxury

Jasmin commun— amour, volupté, tentation féminine
Jasmine, common white—You are cheerful and graceful

Clandestine—Amour caché
Motherwort—Concealed love

Ma Vie

By Lisa Desjardins Michaud

I am originally from the beautiful St. John Valley, a small town in Northern Maine called Van Buren. I was born there and lived there until the age of thirty. Born to French-speaking parents, in a French speaking community. I spoke mostly French until the age of five when I started school. From then on I spoke mostly English, we were told that the French we spoke was not the "correct" French. My mother always insisted that we speak French, and that it was important to retain our mother tongue. After all, my grandparents who lived two houses from us spoke mostly French and understood very little English. In our household we spoke a mixture of both, French and English. My parents spoke to us in French, we replied in English. Everyone living in our small community communicated in a mixture of both … it was not uncommon to hear someone say, "*On va prendre une ride au town*," or "*On mange de la cake*." And oh, how I love to hear that *mélange* of self expression when I return home, it just warms the heart!

We associated ourselves with being Acadian, when in fact we we're a mixture of Québécois as well as Acadian. My family lines of Desjardins, Berube are from Québec and then I have the Acadian side of Soucy and Thibodeau. But, for some reason we were content in associating ourselves with Acadian side as that is who we were.

I lived in this small close-knit community for thirty years, married, had a child, and later divorced. After discovering that the opportunities for employment would be greater if I left the Van Buren area I ventured to the Bangor, Maine. I have been gone from my hometown, but my heart remains there. When I return there is always a warm fuzzy feeling when I arrive in the beautiful St. John Valley ... my home where I am truly home! Where the people are warm and welcoming; where you are greeted with a "*Comment ca va*?" and a hug.

Being Franco-American is so much more than language. It is customs, traditions, it is the blood that flows within our veins, it is what and why we say and do and sometimes act and react differently from others. Being Franco-American is the chicken stew, ployes, réveillons, family, religion that makes you who you are. Unfortunately, there are many that no longer have the language portion of the culture, but that does not make them any less Franco-American; they are still part of the heritage and culture that has been handed down from generation to generation. The proud, hard-working, honest people that have come before us, who have shaped who we are today.

I began working at the University of Maine in Orono in January of 1996 as a pool person, working in different departments replacing people on vacation or doing special projects. My first placement was in the Sociology Department and once that position ended I began working at the Maine Center for the Arts as it was called before it was renamed the Collins Center. As this position came to an end, there was an opening at the Franco-American Centre. I applied and was hired in Sept. of 1996 as the secretary. In 1998, I was promoted to Communications Coordinator/Managing Editor of *Le Forum*. I have been assembling the Centre's bilingual cultural quarterly journal for seventeen years. My role in piecing the *Le Forum* together is also about finding those pieces. Encouraging writers to share their work, their voice, their creativeness with others. My motivation in compiling the issues of *Le Forum* is rooted in all these gifted and talented contributors who allow their voices and experiences to be shared. *Le Forum* can be viewed on-line at the Franco-American Center's website.
Other pertinent websites that may be of interest such as the library and information about Maine's French Communities are also available.

I must also mention our Oral History website. Several years ago I approached Dr. Marc Chassé regarding hour and hours of oral interviews he conducted over many years that had been recorded on VHS tapes. I shared with him the urgency of digitizing those tapes for preservation as soon as possible. With each passing day these tapes were deteriorating. He agreed. We digitized his collection, well over two-hundred, two-hour tapes onto DVDs, but we took it one step further. We wanted these voices to be accessible, shared and heard. It was not enough to simply digitize them, they would remain silenced by being stored on a shelf. We created a website where the interviews are available for viewing in their entirety.

Names Properly

My mother's maiden name rolls on the breath,
tongue soft against the teeth, the final *n*
all but lost — *Drouin.*

Her married name's tougher at the start,
tongue tip tight against the teeth: *Te*, *te*
like the tut of a flag

in stiff weather, like the clip of my pépère's
ax in the north woods. The *h, l* and final *t*
all bear my father's silent

weight, his *sais pas*, his melodic humming.
The *r* growls from the back of the throat,
glottal. Controlled.

I practice speaking both names properly —
Drouin et Theriault, the only French
I was given as a child.

I learned the English sound of things: *tenement*
and *church*. *Split shift* and *overtime*.
No *maison*. No *église*.

Ma mère smothered in the sea of otherness.
Mon Père sounding like something swollen
and still.

I retrieved my lost language from textbooks,
learned it as a visitor to my own life.
Drouin et Theriault —

an early song, I've kept all along — wind
in trees, thread unwinding from factory spools.
The feathery quilts

qui mes grands-mères ont toujours fait.

By Jeri Theriault

Just a Name

I hear your name

but I don't recognize it.

You repeat it once more but I can't make sense of it.

Then, I ask: "How do you spell it?" And that's when… I understand.

Another French name gone astray.

Why? I wonder.

How did the *o* turn into *wo*? When did *é* become *è*?

Why was *gné* transformed into *guené*? Who thought that the silent *s*, *t*, and *x* should step into the light?

Will you mind if I ask?

It might make you uneasy.

You might say to yourself "*I should know*." Or you might think "*Why bother?*"

How did your mémère say it?

Do you remember?

Did pépère disagree? Did he feel the need to assimilate

adapt, adjust, accept

and change the name?

Some language experts say that *French will disappear*!

Give it a hundred years!

More or less.
It happened once already:

Lapierre – Stone

Leblanc – White

Moulin – Miller

Boulanger – Baker

Yet, some names did survive… barely.

Franco-Americans!

Will your great grand children ever know

they are Francos?

How do you say

Gagné

Tétreault

Beaulieu

Desjardins

Laplante?

Do you know?

Do you want to know?

The truth is… I understand.

Because it takes effort energy

even courage…to explain, to be different,

to stand up

for the sake of heritage,

and say: This is how my name should be pronounced, uttered, spoken, told, SHOUTED,

said, murmured, muttered, whispered…

"Hello! Oh… actually,

it's okay.

You can say

Yvan.

Don't try

to say

Yvon.

I don't mind…"

Kind of.
Deep down, you know that it's more

than language.

It's memories.

Sometimes painful, sometimes magical, spiritual, even comical.

It's smells,
and landscape.

It's *Ben oueyons!*

It makes you smile, and it makes you cry too… sometimes.

It's your culture;

old traditions, a way of life; expressions,

habits,

mannerisms,

opinions,

reactions,

hopes and dreams; permission … to dream, permission … to remember to look ahead,

to feel.

It's not

… *just a name.*

By Louise Tanguay-Ricker

Trente ans Une Chose Speciale M'appartiens "TON NOM"

Tu doit être fier de moi!
C'étais pas dur
Ton esprit était pres de moi
Jamais je pensait autrement

Je sais que tu avais envoyer
Quelq'un pour prendre ta place
J'étais forte, pour tenir une chose qui
était si chere pour moi
"TON NOM"

Je crois j'ai faite quelque chose de bien
Je laisse quelqu'un libre
Et tu était toujours la
Croix moi je t'aimais, j'ai gardée
"'TON NOM"

Trente-ans est bien longtemps
Mais j'ai les faite, tu doit être heureux
Quand tu t'en allait loin.
Je sais que tu voulait t'en revenir

Tu nous a laissée seul
Mais c'était la Volonté de Dieu
Je savais où tu allait
J'ai gardez,
"TON NOM"

Ça doit avoir être dur
Pour toi nous dire un au revoir;
Les larmes coulait de nos yeux
Mais j'ai gardée
"TON NOM"

Cette poésie a été faite pour le trépasser de mon mari trente-ans passé. Cette poésie a été tribut pour lui.
Composée par
Ida Bourgoin Roy, (1921-2007)
De Van Buren, Maine
Le 19 de Novembre, 1999

Est-ce que le Bon Dieu parle français?

Par Brenda Mounier

Pas si le **Bon Dieu** parle français.....?
J'souhaite ça.
Parce qu'elle a été élevé en français.
Jamais appris à parler anglais.
Si non, comment **IL** va lui pardonner ces péchés?
Comment **IL** va comprendre ce qu'elle a passé?

Est-ce qu'**IL** a couru avec elle après des 'moiselles,
nu pied dans la poussière du vieux chemin de campagne?
Est-ce qu'**IL** l'a vue après tirer les vaches,
après fouiller des patates,
après ramasser du coton
dans les rangs des clos de...hier
les plis de misère entre ses yeux?
J'souhaite ça.

Est-ce que c'est **Lui** qui a guidé ses mains
qui brassait le couche-couche,
qui attelait le cheval,
coupait le maïs tendre,
qui tordait le linge, doigts rouges et gercés dans le vent d' nord froid?

Est-ce qu'**IL** a compris quand elle a dit,
"J'prends mari, j'prends pays"?
Est-ce qu'**IL** était là quand son ti bébé
a poussé son premier cris?
J'souhaite ça.

Est-ce que c'est **Lui** qui faisait aller ses pieds
dans la valse de la vie,
ou dans un 'ti' two-step si joli
au milieu de l'après-midi?

Je me demande s'**IL** est là asteur à son pied de lit....
après la consoler
après lui parler
lui tenir la main
après la rassurer que tout quelque chose sera o.k.
et tout ça .....en français?
J'souhaite ça.

Je me demande s'**IL** l'a juste entendue souffler ses dernières
"Marie, pleine de grâce". . . . .

Alors asteur.....est-ce qu'elle pourra aller à l'école, là où elle est?
Est-ce qu'on va la punir si elle parle français?
Elle voulait juste connaître comment écrire son nom, tu sais......

Est-ce que l' Bon Dieu parle français?
Est-ce qu' **IL** est peut-être même....Cadjin?
J'souhaite ça.
J'souhaite ça un tas.

New Voices, Lost and Found Stories
Nouvelles voix, Histoires perdus et trouvés

Marguerite des prés—Simplicité du cœur
Wild Daisy—I will think of it

Lin—simplicité, gratitude
Flax—Fate. I feel your kindness, benefactor

Wisteria, Glycine, bleue—Tendresse, amitié réciproque
Wisteria Glycine—Your friendship is agreeable and pleasing to me

Géranium Lierre—Relation stable
Ivy Geranium—Bridal favor, your hand for the next dance

Kennedia—Beauté mentale
Kennedia—Mental beauty

"You Don't Say"

By Cathy Plourde

The oil sizzled and splattered when Mémère dropped scoops of batter into the fryer. Old-fashioned potato donuts. *By de jeez* these were good. Her donuts were basically a ball but the batter dripped and spread before the grease sealed it into an egg-shape. I loved the crispy tips and edges, and the soft cake-y middle. It's hard to say if plain or sugar rolled or cinnamon-sugar rolled were the best.

I was probably six or seven and this is what Mémère was doing when I had the first conversation I can remember having with her, leaning over the counter of my Dad's childhood home to watch the donuts bob in the grease. I was telling her a story—it could have been about a mystery book I'd read or a TV show or something about school or the donuts with sprinkles that we got at the bakery at home in upstate New York. We didn't see each other much as their farm in Fort Kent was far and the infrequent trips were limited to Christmas or a summer vacation. I remember the donuts, and that several times she interjected my story with *"You don't say."*

What?

I was unfamiliar with her thick St. John Valley French accent and didn't know her well enough to recognize her conversational quirks. It took a few minutes but I figured out what she was saying and I didn't like it. And, she kept saying it. I was getting as hot as the oil.

"You don't say" is as innocuous as "Really?" or "Huh!" or "Cool" but all I knew then is that, yes, I did say, in fact I just said it, so why would she say I didn't say? I had a meltdown and got sent upstairs for some back talk, and my mother explained that Mémère was just chatting with me, that she wasn't trying to be mean. "You don't say" was just an expression..

Oh.

But I was still in trouble (again) for back talk and I was made to apologize. What I didn't yet know is that over her long life Mémère excelled at upsetting people, making it a finely honed skill. She could generously be labeled as ornery. Mémère and Pépère celebrated their 50th wedding anniversary in 1982. She lived to be ninety-four, widowed for the better part of twenty years. She was the kind of mother-in-law who cleaned the oven or emptied all of the wastebaskets in the house within the first five minutes of her arriving for a visit. Born a Dubois, she married just before her sixteenth birthday and Pépère was a woodsman. God, the Catholic Church, and the rhythm method gave them nine children, one who died as an infant and another who only lived to about the age of two. Seven was a fairly small clan in comparison to the ten or more children that were common in the French Catholic community. Mémère's eldest daughter, who had moved to Connecticut, was pregnant with her first child at the same time that Mémère was pregnant with her last and so my uncle was born a few months after his nephew. With that child-bearing trajectory, living on a small farm in view of the bridge crossing the St. John River into Clair, New Brunswick, Pépère gone most of each month in the woods, and winter arguably occupying six months of the year ... hell yeah, I'd probably be ornery too. Ornery may have been a way to survive.

I've often wondered what it was like for her, essentially a child bride. Was she ready? Was she scared? Catholicism has very specific doctrine and rules for living, many of which were cited in my ill-fated attempt to avoid Confirmation (e.g., no sex before marriage, no birth control, no gay). Did the religion's structure give her a feeling of safety and support? I think she had to be very brave. Did believing she was in God's plan help her meet the challenge of being a young mother and running a household? Or, was she just always ornery and that helped her manage whatever came her way? I never asked her, and she didn't say.

While, matrimonially speaking, some of the aunts and uncles had "lived in sin" or gotten divorced, Mémère didn't have to say what she thought. Subsequently, she neither approved of my living with my future ex-husband prior to marriage, nor when we divorced in 1996. Nothing was said to me but I doubt my aunts and uncles were that lucky. And there was a lot that could be said about my getting married at twenty-three, just a year out of college. In 1990, twenty-three was the new sixteen.

My fiancé was, as my other grandmother diplomatically said, "intense." My parents tried to dissuade me, but I didn't want to listen. I was afraid of being wrong. I didn't comprehend that love might not be enough to overcome the inherent problems that come from being married to an addict; and even though he was clean for the first half of our relationship, he still behaved like an addict. I thought, gee, what pretty red flags everywhere. I didn't wonder what they were for.

I stayed as long as I could, as I was determined, detrimentally so, to make it work. I was unsuspecting of classic mind games which addicts and/or abusive people can pull out: you see, *he* wasn't the one with a problem drinking; *I* was the one with the problem and maybe I should see a doctor for that. I believed him.

'You don't say.'

I will say I got out alive, and that outcome wasn't guaranteed. The internal scars still pull sometimes; he had said he wouldn't leave any marks and he didn't that you could see. I've had years of sweat dripping from palms and accelerated heart rate that came from spotting a red Ford 150 or a crew cut—and there are a lot of both in Maine. Classic PTSD—post-traumatic stress disorder. It happens less these days. I'm eternally grateful there were no children. The rest of my family agrees. I was pleasantly surprised when long after the divorce Mémère mentioned she was happy I had always kept my surname instead of taking his. Huh. "You don't say!"

But I don't think Mémère would have been happy to learn that I had fallen in love with a woman. When I fell in love two weeks before she died, I confess I felt lucky, relieved that I didn't have to deal with breaking the news to her.

One summer—after the divorce and long before I came out to myself—Mémère was at my parents' house for an early dinner as was typical of many Sunday afternoons. But this sunny afternoon on the back deck with the mosquitos and crudités, she had brought an anti-gay petition she had picked up at church that morning—as one does. I declined to sign it, but, unforgivably, she pushed it to my aunt who was also visiting. My aunt: mother of two of my cousins, one of which is unapologetically and uncloseted-ly gay.

I've no idea whether or not my aunt ever had an honest talk with Mémère about my cousin. A number of Dad's six siblings have children that are gay and perhaps unsurprisingly this fact never gets talked about openly, though I've heard things like, "How could they do that to their mother?" Or, "I think that's your cousin's 'special' friend." Or, just radio silence. You just don't say these things.

I'm sure these were just a few of many not-so-subtleties that put my coming out as bi—first to myself and then to friends and then to family—on a very slow train. And when I told my parents, they didn't talk to me for about five months.

The June weekend of Mémère's memorial service in Fort Kent, when they placed her ashes on the hill looking over the St. John River, next to Pépère, I was in North Carolina with the love of my life, Kara. We had scheduled a weekend getaway in the Blue Ridge Mountains before I knew the date of the burial—or I'd like to think that was the case, I can't quite remember if that's true or if I had decided not to make the trip to the County—Aroostook County. I lived less than an hour from my parents, and I tended to not spend a lot of time with them, and more so now that I had the Kara secret. While at this point I had been out with my sister for over a year, I hadn't had the conversation with my parents because, you see, I rationalized, it was "academic" and possibly even cruel to do so when I didn't have a woman in my life. "*You don't say.*" Yep. I said nothing. But when I met Kara—as storybook earthshaking profound, this feels four hundred percent right, and this is who I've been waiting for and to whom I hand-write daily love letters kind of falling in love—I still said nothing. Rationalizing skills deployed: it wasn't yet clear if or how we could manage a relationship because Kara lived in North Carolina and I was committed to being in Maine for the foreseeab le future...so what's to say? The need-to-know maxim applied nicely.

Okay, I had a bad case of the chicken shits. "*You don't say.*"

Mémère had a habit of taking turns with which of her offspring to be mad at. She'd complain to the other siblings but give the one silent treatment in response to their slight whether or not it was real, enhanced or imagined. She would show up for a family function and do a masterful job of portraying herself as hurt and victimized. It's amazing how much space an ornery French woman, who couldn't have been more than 4'10" in heels, can take up in a room.

Dad was the Bad Son more often than the other siblings combined, simply by virtue of proximity. My grandparents had moved to southern Maine in the late '80s as it was closer to medical services, closer to several of the children and fairly equidistant to the furthest four, with Mom and Dad at Ground Zero. In one of my favorite stories of Dad on the outs, Mémère befriended a young couple from church, leading them to believe she was a widow neglected by her children. The widow part was true. They invited her over to dinner several times doing what they likely thought was a Good Christian deed, supporting a member of their church community. I forget how Dad found out that this was the story she was telling, but it's a small town and while the surname Plourde is akin to Smith when up in the County, they were the only Plourdes in town. It was a matter of time before her duplicity was revealed. Dad can dish as good as he gets, especially when his mother pulled publically humiliating stunts. No one cares for you? "You don't say." And you don't say that when it's not true.

For myself, with my parents, I think the only times I was truly in the Bad Daughter category is when I moved in with my future ex-husband and then almost exactly twenty years later when I finally told my parents about Kara. To be fair, and to claim my part, I've never been good about keeping them in the loop with life developments. Instead, they usually get news presented as a *fait accompli*. And, *de nulle part*. I am going to Europe. I'm not attending graduation because I'm in Europe. I'm moving in with my boyfriend. I quit my job. I'm in grad school. I left my husband. I bought a house. This is my live-in boyfriend; uh, no, wait, actually I asked him to move out.

I've fallen in love with a woman and she's moving to Maine to live with me.

I had done nothing that would have prepared them for this news, though a part of me seriously thought my mother knew or suspected. She'd bring up gossip about an old field hockey teammate who had come out, or mention a cousin. A number of my friends were gay. I wasn't silent about my opinions about equality. I directed a play that was the subject of a documentary that was all about being gay. I had an ongoing theatre project in support of gay youth. It was obvious, I thought, right, if you were paying the least bit of attention? *"You don't say." You did not say.* No, I didn't say, until Kara and I sorted out how to manage the 800-mile distance: she would quit her job, move to Maine, live with me. At that point I couldn't put it off any longer. I had to say. Now.

I did wait until the weekend after my father's birthday. He wasn't super thrilled with having a birthday as it was, and this would have been the icing on the cake.

Having chosen the date to come clean, I arranged to see my folks. I sat waiting for them to get home, positioning myself in a rocking chair in the corner of the kitchen addition, the woods to my back, the small breakfast table a suitable buffer between us for when they got home and I asked them to sit down as I had something I wanted to tell them, I rehearsed. They were about a half hour late getting home. I was staked out in the chair where I rocked and rocked, my insides rocking with nausea, nerves, and dread. When they got in, and without any preamble, I announced I had someone in my life, someone I've known for a while but it took us a while to figure out what we felt for each other. This person was a woman, and her name was Kara, and she's moving to Maine in a few weeks. I explained my identity wasn't anything new—to me. I had just not shared this aspect of my life because I didn't think it was all that relevant and because I didn't know how they'd react. But, under the current circumstances I wanted to be honest with them and I needed them to know because the relationship with Kara was real. They were more than shocked and were getting more upset as time went on; so I left saying I'd wait to hear from them, as I guessed they would need a little time to think through this. I told them my sister knew, if they wanted to talk to her about this she was willing to do so.

It was a remarkably short conversation.

Driving away, I called Kara and told her it was done. I called my sister and told her it was done. This was mid-July.

I have no idea what happened after I left, or what my folks had to say to each other. We've never talked about it.

Kara's parents had been apprised of me and the upcoming move earlier that summer. Kara had first let them know about me by saying, "I've met the woman I'm going to marry." (She had also said that to me in our first five minutes. Which I ignored. Mostly because it gave me panic attacks.) They may have been surprised, but this was not a typical conversation with their daughter. They were quite supportive and planned a visit for October. They arrived on a Friday night and gamely slept on the odd bed in the guest room of the apartment we rented as furnished. Due to the damp conditions in the garage where I had been storing both of our belongings, I had placed the mattress on top of the full-sized bed in the guest room. It was as unstable as a sandwich with too much filling, but there was nowhere else to put it. They were too polite to mention it for a few years anyway.

On Saturday we drove them around in Freeport and Bath, and that evening they asked Kara if she would let them invite me to come with the family to Costa Rica for their 50th anniversary. Her parents, her brother and wife and their baby, and Kara had been planning all year for this trip. They said they saw how happy Kara was and considered that I was now in the family.

Kara's parents had about ten years on my parents and had had twenty-five years to adjust to knowing their daughter as a lesbian. Her parents treated us kindly, and they treated me as normal. Since I hadn't heard from my parents since July, it was a relief to have support and unconditional acceptance.

There is little hyperbole in reporting that Kara repeatedly insisted, "You know this means we have to get married." This is a remarkable declaration of intention as, since the late '90s when she got divorced, she had told anyone who asked that she would never get married again, and in the unlikely event of falling in love would assuredly maintain separate residences. Similarly, I had said that I wouldn't go so far as to use the word "never" having had bad experiences with using that word in the past, but I was quite, quite certain that I would not be getting married again. So when Kara would bring up the "M" word, my typical response was to stick my fingers in my ears, roll my eyes back into my head, and chant "La la la la la la ...." Mature. I know.

My sister and I generally coordinate Thanksgiving and Christmas plans and try to overlap a visit at my parents' house for one of the holidays. We had been in touch that year a fair amount more than usual, and a little more after I broke the news to Mom and Dad. The holidays were coming upon us and she was upset to hear they had not been in touch. She said she would handle it. I don't know what she said to them or whether it was via a phone call or an email, but it had an effect. I heard from Mom within a few weeks and I invited them to meet Kara. This was late November or early December.

The four of us met at Becky's Diner for lunch—a meal out provides a neutral setting, natural beginning, middle and ending, and the location gives everyone the safety of a public location. *There's Nothing Fine-ah than Becky's Dine-ah*. It was completely uncomfortable but we got through it, which is what we all needed. A first step. We were welcomed to come over for Christmas dinner.

Often the older people get the more entitled they feel to say whatever the hell they want. Mémère was very sensitive to the term French-Canadian. We were *Acadian*, she would correct snappily, not French-Canadian. You do not say French-Canadian and Plourde or Dubois in the same sentence when around Mémère. One Christmas dinner at my folks' house, my brother-in-law, who is fluent in French, and my uncle started talking in to each other—I don't remember what was being said but it was a light, jokey exchange in slightly exaggerated accents. Mémère cut in, in English, addressing my brother-in-law: why did he move his hands when he spoke in French? Didn't he realize that was rude, an unkind stereotype? Silence. The long awkward kind you drive in with a bus and parallel park it. Usually she saved this kind of attitude for her children and wasn't so public, but he had punched a button. More than stunned, he offered that he hadn't realized that he was moving his hands while speaking and—and she cut him off to inform him that actually he was moving his hands, she saw him, and that she didn't appreciate him making fun of French people. Making another start for an apology, he graciously said that nothing was meant by it, he would try to be aware of it. Okay then. And, more silence. I think I said something along the lines of "On that note, please pass the mashed potatoes," and the spell was broken. We all had more wine.

"Kara and I went to St. Johnsbury, Vermont and were married on our one-year anniversary by a Justice of the Peace in a strange museum memorializing a wealthy family's odd collections of taxidermy, war memorabilia, and bric-a-brac."

Looking back, we've decided that her behavior, while inexcusably rude and surpassing 'ornery' by a mile, might've had to do with her experience of the French being made fun of for speaking with their hands. To her, gesticulating was as big of a clunker as if my brother-in-law had asked "How many Frenchmen does it take to change a light bulb?" But that was Mémère. She would say what she wanted to, and not really concern herself with the details of whether or not she was rude or hurtful. "How do you get a Frenchman to stop talking? Cut off his hands." "You don't say." *She* was allowed to say, but, you—no, you don't get to.

I didn't get an actual say in whom I fell in love with, I just fell. I just knew. However, choosing to follow through on the desire to be with Kara is in some ways one of the bravest things I have done. We both took risks. But I think that bravery is what other people think when they look at you and try to imagine making the same choices but can't imagine it, and when at the same time you know you are only doing what you know you have to do, regardless of the risk, circumstance, or outcome. While we were in Costa Rica celebrating her parents' 50th anniversary over the Thanksgiving weekend, Kara asked me again to marry her. How romantic is that, complete with howler monkeys in the distance? I said yes. But I'd have to let her know when I was ready. And I'd be ready when I could think about getting married and still breathe normally, which was an actual problem.

Kara and I went to St. Johnsbury, Vermont and were married on our one-year anniversary by a Justice of the Peace in a strange museum memorializing a wealthy family's odd collections of taxidermy, war memorabilia, and bric-a-brac. We told no one, risking wrath and hurt feelings. I reasoned surely this was the best plan ... we both had had full-on weddings in the past ... we didn't want the expense ... who would come to Vermont in February on a five-week notice? And inevitably the wedding event becomes more about other people than it does about the two people getting married, right? Let's have a reception in August in Maine instead, that will be easier and lots more fun. Kara agreed to whatever I said because I had said yes.

In true Cathy-*fait accompli*-fashion, subtle as a brick, our families and friends got phone calls, emails and texts where the White Mountains allowed for cell tower reception as we drove home. I'm pretty sure this really made my mother angry, and I can understand that being excluded feels crappy because it is crappy. We tried to make it up to everyone by throwing a three-day series of events in August; and while the mini lobster rolls and massive blueberry crisp were out of this world, it didn't change the impact. I'm sorry for that, but so far I've only said that here.

I'll be ninety-three and Kara will be ninety-five on our 50th wedding anniversary, a year younger and a year older than Mémère when she died. By luck and by choice we don't have children to get mad at and/or to help take care of us in our old age. We started married life together in our '40s and I think we were both brave to do so because we both know firsthand how bad a marriage can be. I doubt Mémère, as a sixteen-year-old new bride, fully understood what she was in for when her life was set in a very specific direction, in equal parts as defined by the confines of the Catholic Church, the harsh climate, and options limited to her gender and era. But from a young age she had put one foot in front of the other, much as her Acadian ancestors had done while either resisting or surviving The Great Upheaval. She marched for sixty-one years with Pépère, and carried on for more than seventeen years without him. So she was ornery along the way. It happens.

Mémère had twenty grandchildren and even though statistically speaking some were bound to be lesbian, gay, or bisexual, or transgender, I think she'd find having gay grandchildren very disappointing, at best. I wonder if she would even acknowledge it. I wonder what she'd think of Pope Francis.

Sometimes you don't say. Sometimes you need to work on it.

Je suis

By Mary Ellms

It starts with a Canada Mint. At least I think that's what they're called. It's one of those thick and round white mints with the word "Canada" imprinted on it, though as soon as I pop it into my mouth, I remember that I always preferred the pink mints to the white ones. Where have I had these before? I bite through the mint, its texture the same reluctant chew that I remember.

But maybe it starts before that.

My coworker asks me if I am Franco-American. I'm not sure how to reply. There's French heritage on my mother's side of the family, but I'm not sure who or how far back. I tell my coworker that I think my grandmother is French. But then I wonder if she really is or if this is one of those stories that I've told myself so often that I can't remember whether or not it's true.

My life is full of those kinds of stories. They are snippets of all of the tales I've heard in my twenty-eight years, the fragments that get caught in the net of my selective memory. I piece together memories in ways that make sense to me, but may not be 100% accurate. Like the Canada mints: one of the elderly women in my family used to keep a bowl of them on her dining room table, but I can't remember who. My great-grandmother, maybe? Fish served every Friday at school: I think this is because of all of the Catholics in my hometown, but I don't know if that's true. Avoiding banks on Fridays because they were shoe shop pay days: this really happened, but I don't know why being stuck in Friday bank traffic is something I remember so clearly. Too-chay pies: a word I don't even know how to spell but I know how to say. These are the fragments I remember. Sometimes I have to infer or invent the stories to go with them.

Here's a true story: When I was a little girl, I heard the term "All-American" somewhere, probably during the sports segment on the news that my parents watched every night. I was certain that it applied to me. Being "All-American" meant you were from America and your parents were, too. It meant someone who was pure-blooded American and who didn't have ancestors from anywhere else, and I was one of those someones. [To this day, I'm not sure why I thought that was what "All-American" meant.] I was quite sad when my mother told me that I was, in fact, not "All-American," at least not according to my definition. I was a little English, a little French, a little German, and a little Cherokee Indian. I felt disappointed to be any of those things.

What does that even mean, to "be" something or to "be" from somewhere? As far as I knew, I was from a tiny town in Maine, and it didn't make a bit of difference where some relatives I had never met were from.

But then again, why is this something I don't know about? How can you not know your heritage? It's not like I was part of a closed adoption. I know my parents. I know my grandparents. But beyond them is a void.

Can Mainer be a heritage? If so, I would proudly claim that.

I've often fantasized about what it would be like to be part of a family with a rich cultural heritage. A family like the Portokaloses in *My Big Fat Greek Wedding* or like *The Sopranos*. A huge family that speaks English and another language, has cultural food on holidays, and has unique traditions that aren't common to the entire United States. Not only is that not like my family, I don't even know any families like that. I'm sure they exist, but my only experience with them is through TV and film.

This is my family. There are three of us. Mom, Dad, and me. The only foreign languages we speak are the little bits of French I remember from school and "French," otherwise known as profanity. We eat lasagna at Christmas, ham at Easter, and lobster and red hot dogs in the summer. Does that count as culture?

I think my hometown had a large Franco-American population. I say "think" because I don't know how much evidence remains of their French history. If you look at the surnames of the families in town—Gilbert and Clukey, for example – they don't look French. It's as though the town's written records have been Anglicized, many traces of French heritage removed. Even the French names that remain—Cote, LaRue, Fournier, Dube—are pronounced with an American accent: **coat**-ee, luh-**roo**, **four**-nee-ur, **do**-bee.

What is an American accent, anyway? I say that as if there's only one, but I don't talk like people from Texas or Wisconsin or New York. I guess when I say that these French names are pronounced with an American accent, what I really mean is that they're pronounced without any sort of French accent.

Anyway, in my hometown, somehow a Franco spirit remained. Grandmothers would speak French at home but not teach it to anyone. The Catholic Church had a towering presence (and when I say "towering," I mean it both figuratively because it was vital to so many townspeople and literally because the church was on top of a hill overlooking the whole town). Then there was the characterization of people as "French" as though that meant something other than "of French heritage." It was common to hear phrases like "she's an old French woman" and "he's a lousy old Frenchman" tossed about carelessly. Depending on the context, "French" could mean anything from stubborn to lazy, cranky to bossy. I don't think it ever meant anything good.

But the question still remains: am I Franco-American or not? I do some research. I spend a few hours digging through my hometown's on-line obituary archives looking for names, though I could have saved myself a lot of time by just calling my mother or grandmother on the telephone. No matter. After a lot of dead ends and name spelling variations, I find it. My mother's mother's mother, born in Québec. So it's there, a French connection. But what does it mean? Does this make me Franco-American, three generations later?

I ask my grandmother about her mother, the one who was born in Québec. Gram has little to say, other than that her mother and her mother's siblings all spoke French. I ask Gram if she speaks French. She shakes her head. "I used to. Not anymore." I ask her why she stopped. She doesn't have a reason, other than to say, "When you're not around it all the time, you lose it."

I think there's more to it than Gram's willing to share. You remember that old lady from the movie *Titanic*? She said, "A woman's heart is a deep ocean of secrets." That's my grandmother. Somewhere inside her are some answers to my Franco-American heritage, and I doubt I will ever get them all out. I'll be lucky if I get any more than she's already told me.

I did try to connect to Franco-American culture once. My high school required students to take at least two years of a foreign language. All of my friends wanted to study Spanish, and I couldn't understand it. "But we're all French," I remember saying to them. "Why wouldn't you want to learn French?" The consensus wasn't that the language was bad, but that the teacher was bad. I didn't care. I wanted to learn French. I tried to convince my classmates to join me, to no avail.

I took French I and II. I thought I was doing well and making good progress: I knew how to say and write numbers and colors, I knew the French alphabet, and I knew how to ask to go to the bathroom. Our French classes were always small, so there were a lot of opportunities to practice conversational skills. During one class, I was partnered with a girl named Sarah, and we were supposed to work on our vocabulary and phrases together. I can't remember what the particular word was that we were working on. I do remember, though, Sarah saying, "My grandmother doesn't use that word. She says _______ instead. I've never heard this word before." The teacher overheard Sarah and asked her to repeat the word she knew. Sarah did, and the teacher snapped: "No. We do not use the bastard French in my classroom." Sarah and I were dumbfounded. When the teacher saw our shocked faces, he laughed it off before he walked away.

During my junior year, I was the only student in my high school who wanted to take French III. The course was cancelled due to lack of interest.

My high school hired a new French teacher my senior year. I don't know what happened with the previous one, but Sarah's family probably filed complaints about him. But the new teacher was fresh out of college and fun. She only had to teach introductory French that year since there were no advanced students remaining. Except me. I still wanted to take French III. So she arranged for me to take French III as an independent study during one of her French I sections. She had me read and translate *Le Petit Nicolas*. I worked on that in class while she taught all of the basics to the French I students around me. I'd be lying if I said that I wasn't paying attention to her French I instruction. Hearing her teach made me realize that my first two years of French courses had been a joke and had omitted a great deal of material I needed to know. I received credit for French III, but it really felt like I was starting over.

In college I was required to demonstrate "intermediate proficiency" in a foreign language, so naturally I signed up for French. What I should have done was take French 101 and start at the beginning again to make sure I hadn't missed anything along the way and that I had all of the basic skills. What I did instead was start with French 102. My high school French courses enabled me to opt out of the introductory class and go right into the second level, and since it saved me time and money, I decided to skip French 101.

My first college French course had a young male teaching assistant who was from France. He was the one who graded all of our papers. He was always very friendly and polite to me, but deep down I believe he felt pity for me and got a good chuckle out of how horrible my French was. I believe this because of the way he laughed at me when I asked him to explain his corrections on my papers and when I tried to pronounce écureuil, the French word for squirrel. I'm still not sure how to say it. I don't even remember his name, but I can picture him laughing at me. Despite my struggles, I somehow managed to get a C+ in that class. Even though I passed, it was starting to feel like French was something that was just not meant to be part of my life.

It was around this point that I remembered another fragment from my childhood: my piano teacher's husband preparing for a trip to China. To help him conquer the language, he wrote the Chinese words for various household items on sticky notes and then placed them all over the house. When I went there for my lessons, there were sticky notes on the door, the chairs, the lamps, and even the piano. I tried this technique after my first college French class. I walked around my dorm room and challenged myself to remember different words. "That's la fenêtre," I said, pointing at the window. "I'm going to close la porte. I sleep on le lit. I have un chien noir waiting for me back home. But before I can go home for the weekend, I have to read le livre." If it worked for my piano teacher's husband, it could work for me, too, right?

I took French 201 the following semester. This class was much smaller and more serious about the language. I felt like I was learning something for the first time. I was starting to put together sentences. I was starting to notice grammatical errors in my writing. But our final exam was a twenty-minute conversation with the instructor in her office. I had never been able to speak French well. All I could picture was my high school teacher yelling at me about bastard French and the French teaching assistant laughing at me. I was terrified for the final and dreaded it the entire semester.

Now I can't remember that final exam that I dreaded so much, but I got an A- in the class.

That was the last French course I took, ten years ago. I only remember bits and pieces of the language. I had to look up some of those French words I just wrote. I guess now I understand what my grandmother meant when she said, "If you don't use it, you lose it."

Learning the language was my major attempt to connect to my Franco-American heritage, but I don't think I could remember enough of it today to last a day in Montreal or Paris. Without it, I don't feel like I have any connections to my Franco-American heritage. Most of the Francos in my home area are Catholic, but no one in my family is, at least not in practice. The only food we ever ate that was distinctly Franco was too-chay pie, which I said before I don't even know how to spell, and I didn't even like it. And besides my great-grandmother, I'm not sure if I have other Franco-American ancestors. I'm not sure if this part of my heritage outweighs all of the other parts, the English and the German and the Cherokee Indian that my mom said I have. I'm not sure what role it plays at all.

I guess what I'm trying to say is that I don't even know what it means to be Franco-American. When I Googled "Franco-American," the first result was the Franco-American Food Company, whose SpaghettiO's I ate obsessively as a child. Then I saw images of several Franco-American celebrities, none of whom are particularly vocal about their heritage. I see so many cultures and ethnic groups in the United States with their own distinct identities: Italian-American groups, Latin-American groups, Chinese-American groups, each with distinct languages, food, music, and ways of life. Franco-American seems less clear, more fuzzy to me. Maybe it's because I've been embedded within it my entire life? I don't know. I just wish there were more tangible things I could tie to this heritage to give it more weight in my life.

The state of Maine has a lot of festivals and events celebrating Franco-American culture. I hear about them on television and in the newspaper, but they make me feel conflicted. Part of me would love to go. Part of me is eager to see what exactly "Franco-American" means and how people enact it in their daily lives. The other part of me, the part that always wins, avoids the topic. I'm convinced that I don't belong there. I don't speak French. I don't know the music. I don't recognize the names of popular Franco-American people and characters. I'm certain that as soon as I walk in, I'll be labeled a fraud. So I don't go at all.

I tell you all of this in an attempt to answer my initial question: Am I Franco-American? The simple answer is yes, technically. But the real answer is more complex. I don't know if I'll ever know all of the ways this ancestry is affecting me in the present.

If it started with a Canada mint and a simple question, then it ends with more questions. Or maybe I should say it doesn't end at all. Now that I'm thinking about it, now that I'm paying attention and asking questions, it is just beginning.

Being Aunt Peg

By Nicole Ouellette

Weekend sleepovers at Aunt Peg's house were where I drank my first Coke float. And it kind of blew my mind.

We did lots of cool stuff at Aunt Peg's actually. It was better than having a sleepover with a friend my own age because Aunt Peg had a car and a fully stocked kitchen. It felt like those weekends, anything was possible.

Aunt Peg had her own apartment, the epitome of being a cool adult. She decorated it how she wanted and I couldn't think of anything it was lacking for comfort or style. But the best part of all weekend sleepovers was Aunt Peg herself, who wasn't some stuffy old lady or overly cautious guardian. She had an ironing board with a shirtless man on it. She wore big costume jewelry. She even had a boyfriend. Aunt Peg wasn't like most adults I knew, and I really liked that.

I couldn't wait to be like Aunt Peg when I grew up. She lived in Presque Isle which, an hour from my home, seemed very cosmopolitan. I could see myself grown up, living in some faraway place with an apartment, a job, a boyfriend.

Then, Aunt Peg got married. I was twelve but even then I knew it was the end of an era. It was selfish but I felt sad. I knew enough to act happy, of course. Everyone else seemed so happy Aunt Peg was getting married, but all I could think about was what was going to happen to her apartment? Our sleepovers? Her ironing board?

Aunt Peg moved out of her apartment into a big house. We would visit sometimes, but it was different; life had shifted.

Aunt Peg got married when she was in her forties so having kids wasn't expected, but I always wondered if she would have wanted them. Part of me thinks my sister and I were partly fun diversion and partly birth control, but that is all speculation.

I've never asked my Aunt Peg if she wanted kids because, honestly, I've never thought that was any of my business. You make decisions in your life, or don't, and end up where you are. You take the job in Boston or don't take the job in Boston. You go to graduate school or don't go to graduate school. You have kids or don't have kids.

In my early twenties, I broke up with my would-be fiancé because he wanted me to have a baby. At twenty-two, saying I wasn't ready to have a baby felt true. Saying I would never be ready is something that took me ten years longer to say.

"Someday, you'll have to grow up."

After that relationship ended, I manifested my own destiny as a young, single adult. I had several cute apartments, and several cute boyfriends. I went through a period of insomnia baking in my mid-twenties that gave me a small burn scar on my wrist in addition to a couple extra pounds. I had a powder pink bedroom. I went to London and Bosnia for three weeks. I started a blog from my laptop that turned into a full-time business. I saved for my retirement. I watched a lot of reality television. Some Saturday nights, I closed the bar, and others I didn't even get out of my pajamas. I played cribbage. I swam laps. I paid taxes and bills.

In short, I lived my life. It didn't feel any more or less significant to anyone else's life, but I liked it and it was mine.

Now don't get me wrong, I struggled like anyone starting out: finances were in short supply, careers seemed sporadic, friends and romances came in and out of my life. But I still felt like I was on some vacation. The fun was going to end at some point and I'd have to "settle down," which to me always meant getting married and having kids.

During this period, my sister and her husband bought a house and had a baby. I saw myself finally as my own version of Aunt Peg, getting my niece in a little harmless trouble but mostly having fun and biding my time until she got old enough for sleepovers. Biding my time hoping I wouldn't have to "grow up," which seemed like a sad, inevitable event.

"But you'd be a great mom."

Like many people who have found themselves in their early 30s without ever being married, I did have a few close calls. Legally binding myself to someone who definitely wanted kids felt like setting myself up for disaster. If their answer was "yes" or "maybe" to kids, I got out of there. But in truth, none of them really seemed like a good match for me long-term. And so I enjoyed not growing up a while longer through dating.

Some of these men really wanted me to be a mom. One boyfriend and I got into a heated argument on the subject one evening. His main points hit every point of insecurity and were also completely illogical to me. Who would take care of us when we are older? (Yeah, that's why there are so many people in nursing homes who don't get regular visits.) We'd be good parents. (I'd also be a good scientist, but I'm not doing that either.) We were going to regret not having kids. (Studies show more people regret kids than not having them.)

We never quite recovered from that fight. And how strong I stood my ground that night showed me how certain I really was. And at first, I felt quite guilty about not wanting to apply for the job of motherhood for which I seemed qualified. But since I didn't even have a partner, I actually wanted to commit to, worrying about my final answer to the motherhood question seemed a little premature.

"When you meet the right person, you'll want to have kids."

When I met the man who would become my husband, I knew it. He was smart, kind, funny, a better person than I am. I can feel the energy change when he walks into a room, even if I can't see him. I sleep better next to him than I do alone. All that and yet ... I did not want his babies. Our babies.

It was all going so well at the beginning that I dreaded the kid conversation, the one that turned into so many hurt feelings with other men. I felt myself wincing as I told him I didn't ever want kids, probably never. His expression did not even waver. "Nicole, I want to build a life with you. Kids don't matter to me."

The kid issue was the one thing that made me hesitant about marrying him. During our one and a half year engagement, I double, triple, quadruple checked with him. I brought it up in marriage counseling. All the while, he firmly held his position: that he could have gone either way, kidwise, and that in choosing me, he understood and was happy with choosing a life without children.

And so we got married. There was nothing else to do.

Like Aunt Peg, I had to make concessions when I got married, like giving up my pink bedroom to move into a bigger house. I now understand that what's called "settling" when you are with the wrong person is called "compromise" when you are with the right one. He probably would have asked me to give up my shirtless man ironing board, if I had one.

Despite compromise, I am thankful my husband has never tried to change fundamental traits about me. I still sometimes cook when I can't sleep. I can still close a bar if I've napped in the afternoon. I am still cool Aunt Nicole to my niece. People talk about "growing up" and "settling down," but what they don't talk about is how to be a hybrid of who you were and who you want to be.

The kid issue was the one thing that made me hesitant about marrying him. During our one and a half year engagement, I double, triple, quadruple checked with him. I brought it up in marriage counseling. All the while, he firmly held his position: that he could have gone either way, kidwise, and that in choosing me, he understood and was happy with choosing a life without children.

In my first year of marriage, I began charting a course. Because if you're not going to spend two decades of your life raising the next generation, you have to figure out what you are going to do with that time. The idea that I was choosing the no-kids path (versus having it chosen for me in a medical or circumstantial way) is something no one really talks about. The main female narrative is bearer of life and unconditional love for that life. If I wasn't going to do that thing that made women women, am I still one if I am opting out? What do people do when they are not raising kids? Why was I so abnormal? Or, am I normal?

Say what you want about Facebook but I will be forever grateful to it because it gave me the name for what I am: childfree.

Around this time, I became Facebook friends with my church's organist. She periodically posts articles, every two to three weeks, about the childfree lifestyle. I clicked on one that was certainly designed to make me click, something like "Eleven Reasons Why I'm Not Having Kids" or "Ten Things Never To Say To A Childfree Friend." (Why do these articles always have some kind of number in them?) I read and liked the articles. I even private messaged her, thanking her for posting them. She is a religious woman in a long marriage, and I can understand her view might not be the most popular among her peers. But posting these articles got me the information I needed, it named what group I belonged in, and so I could find others.

Childfree. That's what I am. It was nice to have a label. Comforting. Almost normal.

A few weeks after discovering my friend's childfree status, we had an Airbnb guest in our house. "Are you guys childfree?" she asked me. Ah ha! I knew what that was and I had been itching to talk about it. She was the first person I "came out" to, and she broke out into a huge smile.

"I am too! You have to check out Reddit's Childfree Community!"

In this on-line community with almost 100,000 members, the childfree spectrum is more diverse than I could have ever imagined. Sure there are the people referencing "crochfruit" that clearly disdain kids, but many people are also moderate, posting news in a "not for me, thanks" tone. It turns out that, like parents, non-parents are also diverse with varied lifestyles and reasons for their choices.

Between my friends and this on-line community, I got the courage to come out on Facebook recently. In one week, I had been asked eight times about my reproductive plans and International Childfree Day landed on August 1st, so it was perfect timing.

Some people asked me why I did it; I am not entirely sure, but I will say admitting out loud to this thing inside of me I've been afraid of for ten years felt great. I guess I don't want for people to wait until I am past childbearing age and speculate. I want them to know I have chosen this path with my eyes wide open and have given it a lot of thought. I want them to know it is ok to say it out loud.

"You'll never know unconditional love if you don't have children."

One of my very best friends is divorced with two high school-aged daughters. They occasionally have me over for Family Dinner Night. Another friend who lives down the street has a seven-year-old daughter who, upon finding out I was childfree, loves me even more because she is also childfree. Besides my nieces and nephew (I married into more family), I am grateful to have kids in my life and being a part of their growing up.

As my mom said when we were growing up, "Everyone needs an Aunt Peg." I like to think in a world of social media, and in the small community I live in, I can be Aunt Peg to a lot of people.

And as for not knowing love, I am not sure what to say to that. We could also say the poor don't know riches because they've never had a bank account, but we know that is a limited way of looking at the world. My family, my friends, my pets, and my husband have all taught me about love. And my Aunt Peg has taught me how love doesn't have to be from a parent to change the life of a child and sometimes all it takes are a few scoops of ice cream in some root beer.

Addendum:

My husband told me he was leaving me on a Friday night in spring. The whole thing took under fifteen minutes and left me breathless.

This event made me question everything I thought true in my life, including this essay right before its scheduled publication.

After a fair bit of reflection though, getting divorced doesn't change what I have to say. While I don't understand entirely why my husband left, I'm pretty sure it wasn't because he wanted children.

As much as you ever know about another person's reasons anyway.

Maybe kids would have kept our marriage together.

But more accurately, maybe they would have imploded it faster. Or made this whole thing a lot harder than it already is.

All I can say is what remains. My truth remains. My love remains. And I remain.

Title: Bonne nuit
Medium: oil on panel
Dimensions: 8" x 10"

Rachel Breckinridge

Life is chaotic and full of various aspects. We have many things that come together that form who we are as people. However, being a Franco-American is a constant in our lives. It is a permanent part of who we are, a comfort in our chaotic lives, which is what I hoped to show in this painting.

The way life should be

By Sylvie Charron

I was born in Bordeaux, France, educated in Paris, fell in love with a cute American, and immigrated to the United States with two suitcases in which I had packed a pressure cooker. I then had the good fortune of studying in Wisconsin for my Ph.D. The United States has been good to me.

Before I moved to Maine, I had no idea that that there was such a large Franco-American population of Québécois and Acadian origins in Maine. What a wonderful surprise!!! I also discovered the discrimination they had suffered BECAUSE they were French and usually destitute when they arrived. I had never imagined that someone could not feel pride in being French. Yet they worked hard and accomplished much. Now most are pretty successful. In Waterville, I discovered that many people indeed still spoke French or had parents and grandparents who did. I would listen to pink-haired ladies in department stores heartily engaged in conversations that I was delighted to comprehend. I also remember a funny story with the carpenter who built our house. He swore that he did not speak French, even though his name was French. His parents did, he said. But when I could not understand his lengthy explanation about a window, and after all else failed, he explained it in halting French, AND I UNDERSTOOD! I felt such a kinship with the French residents of Waterville. I always preferred doing business with them. They were funny, hardworking and trustworthy. Somehow this connection made them feel like family.

So, as a professor of French, it became my mission to become acquainted with Franco-Americans, to celebrate our culture and language, and to find out what has been retained from our shared heritage. It was such a privilege to encourage students to reconnect with the language, literature, poetry, music and art from the French speaking world, and to convince them that we are all trees from the same forest, with variegated foliage and colors. I love listening to 'local' French, to the sounds and expressions that I can recognize but that we have not necessarily retained in Bordeaux or Paris, but that I had often encountered in my readings.

When Rhea Côté Robins looked for translators for *Canuck*, it was such a joy to read the book and transcribe it into English so that Franco-Americans or Mainers who no longer speak French can reacquaint themselves with the history of mill workers at the turn of the 20th century, told from a Franco-American voice. It was also fun to co-teach Franco American Culture with Sharon Nadeau from Lewiston who had lived the culture firsthand, and with Margaret Farmer who had researched the Franco-American food ways of Jay, Maine. Through this class and others, I discovered with delight Québécois and Franco-American literature, and had the good fortune to become acquainted with artists and writers of the culture.

My hope is that the children of Maine will realize the value of these French roots and of the beauty of the language and culture in its diversity. I also hope that they reacquaint themselves with our Québécois neighbors. So many of my students, even after years of studying French, have not crossed the border! For the life of me, I cannot understand why.

I do remain optimistic that Mainers can reconnect with this rich heritage and with French Canada which is so close and so beautiful. I am so glad to live in Maine! It is, indeed, the way life should be, partly because of its Franco past, which is as beautiful and vibrant as the surrounding seas, lakes, mountains and hills. My father, when visiting a long time ago, exclaimed: "Mais c'est le petit paradis!" It says it all....

Coming of Age/*Passage*

Hamamélis, "noisetier des sorcières"—"Vous m'envoûtez"
Witch Hazel—A spell, reconciliation

Chêne (feuilles)—Courage
Oak Leaves—Bravery

Épilobe en épi—Unissons-nous. Peut signifier une demande en mariage
Fireweed—Celibacy, wounded love and pride, rejuvenation. growth, good ally
also known as French Willow—Bravery and humanity

Nénuphar—Cœur pur
Water Lily—Eloquence

Dirt Roads and Parentless Days

By Anne Marie Prudhomme

I was fifteen and it was 1983. He was an Irish boy and I can still remember the shape of his tapered fingers as they held my hand down by the river. He "asked me out" as we walked through the weeds on that early spring day. I said yes, yet I wasn't sure if I wanted him or if he wanted me. We never moved past a short sloppy kiss during the following fleeting weeks together. He didn't call much, he didn't want to talk a lot, he wanted a slow thing leading to a feeling of home neither of us had. I had met him and his rough and fun-loving coterie of older boys through my sister's boyfriend from school. My sister's boyfriend lived in the same neighborhood but wasn't quite one of them, choosing to pursue his academics over a multitude of bonfire parties and lost nights. Yet, that one spring day so long ago it had been determined by my sister and her boyfriend that the Irish kid would go after me. My sister had called earlier to tell me she was on the way. The raggedy apartment my family shared had no proper living room yet it was right across from the Reading train station and every time a Boston and Maine diesel engine would idle, our bedroom floor would rumble as if the trains were telling us to travel, go, do not stay. I waited, curling back my hair with an iron. I heard a car beep and my sister yelling to come out. To get to that river in the woodsy outskirts of suburban Boston, I had been picked up in an old Chevrolet with my sister and the others at least five across on a bench seat and three in the front. At the wheel, was a swarthy looking man of almost twenty, Bastian. He had cut most of the sleeves off of an old blue button-down shirt. He was unshaven and had a head of thick curly black hair and bright blue eyes. He was slightly sunburnt on his driving arm while the rest of him was a creamy color. He didn't look my way once that day, not even through the rear view mirror. I squeezed in. The car might bottom out on wide turns, but no one would stop us that day. The smiling boys in the car made happy introductions. I felt safe crawling in.

We cruised down Main Street then stopped for cigarettes and a case of beer, although Bastian had at least half a pack rolled up in his sleeve. Crumpled bills and silver coins were dug out of pockets. Someone they knew met us in the package store parking lot. What was left after the guy they knew got his due went into the car's tank; and then with radio blaring, it was on to the river. Afterward we all went to Bastian's house by the forest, where tarred roads became a dirt road, and we all left the car straight for the adjacent pine trees. On colder days, the party would be held in Slim's room, Bastian's freckle-faced brother. The day was warm. A mesmerizing fire roared. We sat on the surrounding felled trees and stumps waiting.

Teenagers began to steadily flow in carrying brown bags. A slightly older mustached man brought a keg. At first, everyone shuffled by with a solemn sense of maturity, as if it had already been contemplated and decided that all of our lives would be hard work with small rewards and that the only real wealth would be society with each other. Having fun would be our awkward ritual. Bastian sipped, smoked, poked at the fire, and soon looked my way in the darkness. People roared, laughing like the cackle of the fire; they were excited by cocksure hubris, work-related tales, hilarious exploits, and icy stories of northern places. A few girls flirted jokingly with Bastian. I was silent. My sister sat on her boyfriend's lap smoking something and telling her own stories; making everyone laugh, including Bastian. I kept quiet. I was grateful for the bounty offered me in a can or two, in a cup or two, and in a look or two, happy for the misery of a lonely apartment slipping away. I thought about the last year while everyone enjoyed the fete. I had just broken up with a blond-haired man of nineteen a month earlier. He had an old British last name. He was a car mechanic, breaking the hearts of his parents because he was running untamed with girls like me instead of being tethered by college and girls like them. I had timidly broken up with him when he had come by later the same day and had broken the front door window of the apartment in a rage. After he had paid my father later in that week to fix the damage, he had disappeared for good. I was relieved because I thought he might beat me next. We had dated for six months when his alcohol and drug use began to scare me away. Traveling together, there had been complicated and wild parties in Boston lofts, there had been a fogged-up car with his friend and my friend groping as we were parked in a state forest listening to Yes and George Carlin on cassette tapes, there had been a car crash by a local community college, with him at the wheel, where I could have died.

However, what really bothered me was that I had never met his family or had ever been in his house. His mother had asked him about his little friend's address and he had told her, and she had replied to him that I was from by the tracks, the shabby part of town. "A girl from there?" she had scolded him. He could have kept quiet, yet he had sheepishly told me this one rainy night while we talked in my kitchen. It had been one of the many nights he had been welcomed by my sister, my father, and my friends in my little home. Why did he ever tell me what his mother said? It was mean. During the same conversation he said that his mother had suggested that my French last name lined up with my sorry address. I actually shed a tear, but it wasn't for him and it wasn't for me. It was shed for ignorance I did not yet comprehend. Staring at the fire in front of me I thought about what I should do moving forward. I wanted to work on orderliness that spring and summer, to just be a kid before junior year. I stared at the fire and thought of the freedom of turning eighteen and how nice it would be to take a train from South Station to anywhere. The Irish boy came back to the heated circle from throwing an ax at stumps with the other boys in a game of wood darts. He put an arm around me and we stared at the fire.

There was another bonfire party a few weeks later and the bonfire grew as the crowd around it did. Bastian looked at me while poking the wood. Coaxing the fire, he looked at me with a slight, half-smile. He finally spoke to me. "Wat ess wid your hair Anne Marie, et ess orange!" His deep-voiced drawl had an accent. He chuckled and turned away. I turned red, embarrassed. I explained to him how my friend had said that hydrogen peroxide and a high-set blow dryer would give me blonde highlights in my auburn hair, and instead I had gotten frizzy clown-orange hair. Bastian chuckled and said, "you don' need tah be blonn." It was another fun night. The weather had turned warmer and the Irish boy only ever took me to Bastian's woods, never to his own house. I understood, and kindness insisted on not asking questions. His house had difficulties as did mine. Bastian's place felt like a home for many. Bastian's family didn't care about the bonfires as long as they were put out; to them, young people should enjoy nature's bounty. For me and the Irish boy however, parents weren't around. His mother was divorced and struggling, working the dayshift in the bars. My father was hardly home himself, at sea or on the job, and my mother, who called when she could, was half a country away in Louisiana.

It had been one of the many nights he had been welcomed by my sister, my father, and my friends in my little home. Why did he ever tell me what his mother said? It was mean.

We would get a ride in Bastian's car after Bastian's day of hanging drywall in Boston or his brother Slim would pick us up in his own Rambler; hence, the apartment became a satellite of the bonfire. Sometimes on a weekend afternoon, we would all cram into the kitchen of the tiny apartment and I would make jam sandwiches for every one of the brassy hooligans who were always hungry, sandwiches made from my grandmother Ann's own Maine blueberry crop. Every one of them said her jam was delicious. Then plans would be made. Sometimes, my sister and I would look for change for beer or gas behind cabinets and in the corners of bureaus, just in case. Most times Slim would get his hose and gas can and take a walk.

When Bastian saw me he would slightly chuckle and say "Anne Marie" as if I were a joke he was playing on himself. Bastian, the Irish boy, Slim, my sister and her boyfriend, our girlfriends, and at least three others would ride around local towns and visit people. We were without rules, yet constrained by the chains of something compulsory, willingly killing a futile desolation through a restless camaraderie. The boys were sometimes crude and bickering but they were always gentlemen, they were always low on money but never short of clever stories, and they took me and my sister just the way we came, never asking for anything. No one ever mentioned all that might be lacking, ever. No one noticed because we had each other.

The nights got hotter and the Irish boy's calls presented themselves almost nonexistent. Scenarios of romantic possibility floated around in my mind, but hardly the one that came. One evening, the phone rang and my sister answered. It was Bastian, tall, gorgeous, blue-eyed, black-haired Bastian. The flowering feeling in my stomach made little sense as all focus fell upon the phone call. My sister looked confused and slightly worried as she handed it to me. He wanted to pick me up with his buddy Mick, and maybe I could go to his house and we could have some beers with some other friends? His family was in Maine, and there was no party tonight but he would like to see me. The Irish boy was not mentioned. I felt like taking a chance and said yes. Bastian arrived and knocked on the front door, politely asking if my father was home. He wanted to meet him, and tell him that he would have me home early. "He's not home right now," I told Bastian, as my sister, curious and wide-eyed, shooed us off. "Next time" Bastian said. I sat next to him in the car with Mick by the window. We drove down Main Street, and as the orange summer sun hit the metal of the car, I wished that we could just drive away forever through forests, down highways, all through America. Bastian took my hand as he said “Hi, Anne Marie.” He lit a cigarette and cranked down the window to let the wind into the car. I did not care where the night went being with the scruffy man with the handsome face and a tough quietness and ever-present strength. I was an observer and participant in this new experience and that he held my hand and wouldn’t let go was all I needed to know. Our silence, this something French between us, this acceptance of all that is inevitable before it happens, it already was good enough for me to remember. Obliging Mick looked away and smiled as we pulled into the dirt road.

Bastian and Slim’s younger siblings, mother Bea, and their father, were in a small border town in St. John Valley where their Acadian-descended mother spoke only French. It was near the Acadia of my great-grandmother’s birth, a French woman who had come to North Adams, Massachusetts with her second-generation French husband. They had moved there to make shoes in a factory. Later, I would learn that both my great-grandmother and Bea’s maiden names were the same. Yet, on that night I only thought of Bastian. We were all sitting in the living room watching something on television while beers were passed around. The Irish boy came by and saw us together on the couch. He left with Mick to see some girls, while Slim went out on a date. Bastian offered that black couch uncomplicatedly, as if having me over to his home for a first date was the only way to ever court a girl. Alone on the couch we listened to a Johnny Cash record. “My mother loves this song,” he said. A song played, about a ring of fire. “Thees one reminds me of you,” and he moved my orange hair out of the way as he went in for the kiss.

That night made me feel less childlike and more of a woman. Our pain met without words. Bastian held his French on his tongue, with him I carried mine brighter. He knew my poverty and by offering me a space on the black couch he decimated my sadness to nothing more than a juvenile nuisance. This was the love he gave, beside the kisses and first “I love you” that night. I knew the chances taken on a keen love might eventually hurt as much as they healed—that I had learned from the British-named boy I did not love. However, that night, there was strictly love and no shame anymore, none in tiny apartments, missing parents, or orange hair. He was incredibly rich and generous to me, with his dirt road, intertwined family and humble home.

Bastian called every day. We talked for hours at a time about our dreams, our desires, and our disappointments. He trusted me with his accent and I trusted him with my every thought. We became protectors of each other’s secrets. I wondered what it was that he saw in me. The girls threw themselves on their knees for him, and that was not going to change for me. So, did he really love me? I hoped that he did, and in the meantime he became my best friend. I wanted to offer him everything he needed in this world, including confidence. That unique accent he was shy about, I was thrilled by it. He had a stilted, methodically slow speech in which words chosen carefully had to be precisely loaded with meaning. I knew he would lose a lot of his accent in time, and that made me distressed, but that would be supposed progress. I thought he kept quiet because people might accuse him of stupidity when he was anything but stupid, but there were a lot of unenlightened people who might judge him, like the mother of my British-named ex-boyfriend. I loved the sound of his voice, and I loved the way he spoke in lilting words learned from a French-speaking mother. It was pure narrative as modern destiny and I wanted to sound just like him. He didn’t have a distinct North of Boston inflection because his words were Acadian, decided, clear of form, solid and thought out. Sometimes he stopped himself from using French words with me, French that he spoke with his mother. I didn’t want him to stop himself, but he felt this was what had to be done. “I love your voice, Bastian, and the way you speak, the words that you say.” This is all I could say to him without making him self-conscious.

One of our shared secrets was that we both wanted to be artists. How could we possibly pull that off? The world would laugh at us. We were born for work, to fall into the cracks. We were tolerated in school using our quietness and resoluteness as a skill to avoid any notice. But in the harbor of Bastian’s small room, feeling the setting sun on the window, we became poet laureates and brilliant scholars. Bastian would draw for me in pen his nightmares and magical thoughts, and he would ask me to read out of the Edgar Allan Poe anthology he had permanently borrowed from the library. “Pleez rehd ta meh . . .” and I did gladly, shyly. We could not then name it, yet as we studied Poe’s words we both felt his addictions, the loss, the sadness, the impatience of a short life. We would lie still for hours in each other’s arms on his bed beckoning the love lost in Poe’s mythological writings. It was as if we were all the same person.

I felt that Bastian didn’t trust himself, and now, I see that he felt the same about me. I asked him one night if he would ever consider college, he laughed at the idea, “no college,” he said. It divided me into a million fragments of sorrow. Who else would hear past the silence beside us? I would always know how smart he was, how creative he was, how he spun words into many paper letters riveted with vulnerability. One said, "Anne Marie, I am so sorry, you did not even know this, I got scared that you wouldn't love me anymore and that I would lose you. I can't lose you. Please say that you love me always, please . . ." (As if it were ever in question, mon cheri.) He was patient and kind, and when quiet, his chuckles at something I said or did would give him away. We escaped together lost in a dream of what might be, lost in hope if only we had a chance.

Our relationship lingered one year into the next. We met almost each day after school and work. There were unhinged outings to the beach, to see his friend in jail, to visit his cousins in the city, to help a single father friend of his raising his baby alone. There was the time he stole a Christmas tree for me and my sister and the time he brought us both suede boots he had "found" on a friend's delivery truck. Many times, we took the Orange Line into Boston with our gaggle of friends and we wound up by the Charles River, drinking out of paper bags. On the Common, we would silently loathe the Yuppies listening to concerts on the ticket-paying side of a brown wood wall, hearing muted notes blindly, the young professionals enjoying sounds we could not hear. We would make our own noise laughing down the street, causing a slight commotion. Bastian always contentedly smiled at the ground when we finished the contents of the paper bag, amused at the rebellious girl hanging off of him, a surly girl in love. Though my hair color was changing from various colors to natural brown, he always looked at me as the orange-haired girl on the black couch who did not need to be blonde.

A girl turns toward womanhood at sixteen and I wanted Bastian as my family. My sister was as busy as his brother Slim was, and Bastian's dirt road and cluttered bedroom felt more like home to me than the parentless, empty apartment in Reading. We lived only for each other, connected without language. His friends said he was pussy-whipped but he was the one who had said to me let's get married soon, on one calm day in his bedroom. I hadn't wanted a boyfriend and now I wanted to be the French boy's wife. In the moments of that day I told him how beautiful his drawings were and that with his imagination and judiciousness he would be a great artist. He looked at me a minute. A pause on his face I have never seen again in my life, he looked shocked, gratified, and convinced all at once. He turned away and said, "Yeah, right." Then he looked at me again. I told him we could both go to college and beat the world at its own game. We could build a new life together. I felt like the life we lived was graffiti with heartbeats anyway. In any way, life could be art. We wouldn't always have to live on nothing. We could be artists together leaving the dirt road and parentless days behind. He laughed at me. That could never be. This was the life granted. We would be outcasts by walking away from all we had. My only chance to stay with him was to only stay, to have little French babies, to have mémère watch them, and to work. Dreams upon dreams filled my head. "I'm meant to work, no college." Bastian said.

It was agreed that our parents would meet and talk alone, and decide whether or not an elopement would happen. Maybe I could get my GED, and go straight to work? Maybe I could live with Bastian, get my diploma, and then we could go to the courthouse one June day? Maybe we could even get married in Saint Theresa's Church? Bastian and I waited at the kitchen table while my father and Bastian's parents talked. Bastian's father and my father talked of their years in the service. My father, the storyteller, talked for what seemed like hours. "Anne Marie has been a trouble to me, it is hard with no mother there, but she keeps the house, she is a hard worker. Your son has been good for her, Mrs., you are Acadian? I am Acadian on my grandmother's side. She was a tough woman who left Canada for Massachusetts, a strong woman, a good woman, the memories of a loving woman who took no nonsense, my grandmother Sadie . . . man, did she give my grandfather what for . . ." he felt at home with Bea. It was done. Our plans were quashed by all three. The plans were considered a risk on all counts. They included wasted opportunities, dropping out of high school for good or teenage motherhood. All involved found that my age of majority would arrive soon enough and then it wouldn't matter. Bastian and I were disheartened, and silently relieved. I was not shocked at the answer, only at the consideration.

In the tiny apartment I thought about what had happened. I knew the conversation happened because it was Bea looking out for me and protecting me like another mother. Her kitchen table was the orbit of the neighborhood, and it was there that we first met, only days after my first date with Bastian. "Allo Awnn Mehreh, seht down" she said. I loved her calm fortitude right away. Once, she insisted that her sons Bastian and Slim go to Mass. They jumped immediately. "Anne Marie, are you coming too?" she asked. "Yes, thank you" I replied. She invited everyone and they followed.

Sometimes, when she said oui instead of yes, I thought that it must be difficult to speak constrained English and to live far away from St. John Valley where French was spoken freely. It would make me rebellious and sad. In this vein, she would sing in a deep sweet voice at the table when she got time alone. At night, Bastian and I would slip in and she would be there singing under low light into a tape recorder, preserving songs in every clear and resounding utterance. I was so impressed with her courage to sing her French songs just for herself and her memories of a place where *joual*, patois, Franglish or whatever else it could be called made perfect sense. I was in awe of her. I treasured, like all who knew her, the time I had talking with her because her questions and answers were contemplative and sympathetic. One day she asked to talk with me alone. My nerves almost paralyzed me, but I sat at that table. She asked if I wanted to marry her son. I couldn't answer so I said yes with a big smile. Her words came out slowly. She said that if she didn't have two young children she would get a divorce. "It is not easy when you are young . . . perhaps in time . . ." she said. I didn't understand. She left it at that. I knew it was a warning of some kind.

Soon I knew her intent. After two years, Bastian and I fell apart. On the job with French Canadians drinking "un screwdriver" in their juice cartons stirred with tools, Bastian met with older women attracted to his good looks and unassuming personality. The Irish boy told me everything because he said that I deserved better and that he was still my friend. I thanked him with a hug. I asked Bastian and was hit by a wall of confession and tears, promises of retribution, begging, grabbing of hands. I pulled away but then fell into his arms. He was sensitive as always, contrite. He asked me through tears if I believed in ghosts. I said yes, I do. The ghosts are here he told me, and I believed him. We held each other and told ghost stories; he closed his eyes and I wiped his tears after mine had dried. Bastian was my first love and he was my closest friend, he would have beaten the crap out of anyone who had hurt me. Yet, he burned me and haunted me like a ghost. Maybe we pushed too hard much too young for far too much. Maybe he just wanted to be free and my love wasn't worth enough. One night a few months later, Bastian told me about his dalliance with a girl a grade or two below me at school, how she had mocked me asking him to leave me for her because wasn't she the better cherry? And there had been others. I pleaded with him through the last of that night's tears. Why was he unkind, turning me into a joke? Why? Why had I shown such devotion, eschewing several chances of my own to date interested boys by explaining my committed relationship with Bastian? We would never be together again but I would always feel loyalty to the man I had once wanted to marry. He didn't know why. The last time together as a couple we laid back on the bed in the room I shared with my sister, the diesel trains rumbling across the street. It was warm and we were sweaty. I was crying. We were silent. Bastian spoke. "This is me, I have to be free," he said. I sobbed. I did not want to possess him. I wanted us both to be free, free from want and regret, free to be something other than limited.

Weeks passed with endless calls. We talked for minutes this time, not hours. I forgave him and loved him, but he was no longer my protector and confidante. Mick knocked on the apartment door a few times asking me to give Bastian, who was waiting in the car, one more chance to talk in person because he needed me back in his life. I had to say no. Each time, I went to bed and cried because I needed him in my life too. I wanted to open that door, but I knew that if I did, I would hate myself. Eventually, he gave up on coming around, and although we talked on the phone occasionally, it would never be the same. My dreams of a beautiful singing mother-in-law, my dreams of little French babies, my dreams of sharing life with my best friend, an artist, were all over.

I have thought of Bastian, Bea, and his family many times. What would life have been like if we had married in 1986? I remember Bastian and Bea, and realize that history is made now. If we had been together in 1686, 1786, or even 1886, would we have met on an Acadian farm? Would we have wed right away in a little chapel by the sea? I picture the local priest, laughing a bit with a sly smile while looking down, insisting that we go forth and make many French babies. We would all sing, dance, and imbibe by a bonfire celebrating a rite of passage in a simpler life. I think of all the New Englanders with French in them scattered through each state, hidden away, like sprinkles all over a frappe. We do not always find each other, and do we share our heritage when we do? We should proudly celebrate by a big fire and sing loudly into a tape recorder. I am glad that I found Bastian and I am glad that he found me. What I learned from him and what he gave me, a self-definition, was well worth any pain.

Bastian reached me on-line a few years back. I told him I recall how smart he is and that it is always a good time to be an artist. He shared his memories of our relationship. I exalted in how he had actually seen our time together as a legitimate alliance because I had thought that I was long gone from his memory, a blank space unwritten and unspoken, yet now he was a ghost alive among what is departed. Similarly, our Acadian antecedents from Canada and Maine, somehow relegated to Massachusetts, are the ghosts of a romantic past and a maternal love that thrive unbroken.

Fall

"Today has been the worst day of my life. I'm bleeding."

By Betty-Ann Khoury-Burns

"Please sir, please let me go! I promise I won't ever do that again!" I remember pleading with the principal, looking up at him from that overstuffed wing back chair in his office, my feet barely touching the floor. Mr. McIntyre towered over me, arms folded across his chest and shook his head. His jowls jiggled like Jell-O. Slowly, beneath his moustache, his teeth appeared.

"Just why should I excuse you, my dear Eva, when finding you and Roger Greenleaf in the girls' bathroom is just about as bad as you can get? This is the third offense, isn't it, Eva?"

"Oh please, Mr. McIntyre. I really can't stay today. Not today. You see, I promised Father Daigle that I'd come by after school and arrange the altar. For Lenten Mass tonight. I do that every Wednesday during Lent. I can't miss. I just can't. Please. Please let me leave, just this once. I'll stay . . . tomorrow! Yes. Oh yes! I'll do it then. I'll stay tomorrow!"

As I trudged up Mayflower Hill on my way to Notre Dame Church, I did not feel pleased with myself. I had been caught after all, but I was fairly certain that Mr. McIntyre liked me, and that by tomorrow, he wouldn't be too hard on me. Just last week, hadn't he called me out of class to show the new girl, Pamela Knotts, around the school? Despite myself, I grinned, and pulled the belt to my wool jacket tighter around my waist. Hoisting the hood up about my neck and yanking the drawstring closer under my chin, I turned the corner and felt a gust of winter whip my face. When I left the schoolyard, it had been daylight and warmer, but moving east away from the setting sun, I felt the wind shift. Earlier, at noon, with the spring thaw, my footsteps mixed the mud and snow into brown sugar-like slush. Now, as darkness approached, the temperature plunged, and my rubber galoshes crushed the ice crystals forming at the puddles' edges. I had about another mile to go.

Turning left on Gilman Street, past the public library –my favorite haunt –I headed for Park Street and the old church, a Gothic style structure supposedly modeled after the original in Paris. But unlike the original, Notre Dame of Lancaster had only one tower. It wasn't just the tower, but the spire above it that loomed higher than any other building in town. Taller than the newly remodeled gold-steepled U.S. Post Office, where my uncle Everett worked as Postmaster, the tower could be seen from miles away in all directions. It was his postcard from Paris that made me want to learn all about Notre Dame, Gothic architecture and cupolas, those curious little houses for iron bells.

I climbed the icy brick steps leading to the platform of the church, taking extra precaution not to fall. Two nights ago, on the way home from school, I had fallen on a jagged piece of ice, snagged my cotton stockings, and made a nasty run from the knee to the ankle. Today I was wearing my last pair and Mum had warned me, "Eva, you gotta make 'em last till spring." We had sat together that night next to the kerosene stove, my grandmother's sewing basket between us, and I watched her slip my stocking over the darning egg, taking miniature stitches to catch the run.

As I approached the front of the church and its two vault-like wooden doors with massive wrought-iron hinges, I veered left. I headed toward the back to enter by a smaller door on the side of the building. Once inside the vestibule, I turned left again and walked slowly down the cold damp corridor, toward the entrance for the main altar. My boots squished and rubbed with every step, the sound echoing against the walls of that massive empty space. Pausing at the altar rail, I genuflected, made the sign of the cross, and bowed my head toward the tabernacle. Mr. McIntyre was still on my mind, so I whispered a quick thank you to the statue of Our Lady. I lit a candle and offered a daily Mass for the rest of Lent as my penance.

Turning away from the altar, I gazed down the long dark main aisle to the inside front door. I was completely alone in the church, not another soul to be found. I walked to the center of the aisle, and found myself surrounded by stained glass windows, depicting the fourteen Stations of the Cross. My eyes rested on the ninth station, where Jesus falls the third time, the weight of the heavy wooden cross crushing his back. I wasn't sure how long I stood there separated from time, but the words on the plaque kept repeating in my head: "O Jesus, let me never yield to despair. Let me come to You in hardship and spiritual distress."

The sound of the metal bolt unlatching the vestibule door shook me from my thoughts. I turned and proceeded back through the corridor to find Mrs. Getchell. A cold blast accompanied her as she entered. Overweight by thirty pounds and in her late sixties, she was still perky. She took it upon herself to launder the linen every week. The frizzy lock of hair that poked out from her green knit cap gave her an elfish look. She greeted me with her frosty breath, just before the door swung shut.

"Hello there, pet, see you beat me here this week. It's no wonder what with this arthritis slowin' me down an' all, or maybe it's just this awful cold. Can't seem to tolerate it the way I used to. The cold I mean." Wheezing to catch her breath, she motioned with her mittened hand, "Where would you like these, dearie?" and without waiting for a response, headed straight to the vestry. "We'll just place this basket next to one of these chairs."

"That'll be fine," I replied.

The two chairs were favorites of Father Daigle, heirlooms from Archbishop Flannery, prior vicar of Notre Dame, and before each mass, he'd sit in one or the other and inspect his vestments. Sometimes alone, I would run my fingers over the soft satin upholstery and trace the gold fleur-de-lis embossed in blue at the top of the headrest.

"How long you been helping out with the Monsignor's altar preparations, missy? What's it been, now, two years?"

"Almost four years, Mrs. Getchell. I started right after my First Communion, when I turned eight."

"My, my, time gets as slippery as ice when you get to be my age. Seems much shorter to me. Well, missy, I'll be on my way and leave you to your chores."

"Bye, Mrs. Getchell. See you next week. Remember, Sunday will be Palm Sunday, so there'll be extra." I returned to the laundry basket and sat in one of the chairs, to begin folding the altar linen. Glancing up, I looked over at the mahogany armoire and spotted a garment caught in the crack of the door. Recognizing it as one of Father Daigle's vestments, I stepped to the cupboard and opened it, freeing his alb. I closed the door carefully.

On my way back to the chair, I was suddenly rooted in my tracks. There on the seat, was a strange black spot. Where did that come from? I bent down and puzzled over it. Oh, of course, Father Daigle must have spilled some wine. But why hadn't I noticed it before? I stood there riveted. The size of a fifty-cent piece, it glistened for a moment, and then soaked directly into the fabric. I touched it. I rubbed my forefinger and thumb together, wet and sticky. I brought my fingers to my nose to smell them. There was an odor, but I couldn't identify it. I put my finger to my mouth. It didn't taste like wine. But then how would I know? I'd never had wine. It did remind me of metal though, like iron, rusty iron. I still couldn't understand why it would be wet. I'd have to clean it right away, so it wouldn't set, whatever it was.

I immediately thought of Clorox, but knew almost as soon as the word came to mind, there would be none of that here. Water, then, that would have to be the answer. Hot or cold? I didn't know. I'd have to try both. But which first? Cold? I'll try cold. That usually did the trick, got stains out. I rushed to a small alcove where there was a sink. Pulling a rag from the edge of the basin, I saturated it with cold water and sped back to the vestry.

I tried rubbing it just a little and waited. Nothing. Maybe if I rub faster, and try sponging and rubbing. Again, nothing. In a burst of desperation, I started scrubbing. The spot seemed a little lighter, fainter perhaps, but remained, stubborn, almost indignant. If only I had some Clorox, I'm sure that would do it. I returned to the washroom in search of some cleaning fluid. Under the sink, tucked away behind the faucet pipes was a can of Old Dutch Cleanser. I grabbed it, soaked the rag once more – this time with hot water, as hot as my hands could stand – and retraced my steps to the chair. If this didn't work, what was I going to tell Father Daigle? I sprinkled the cleanser directly onto the fabric. "Oh God, I shouldn't have done that," I said out loud, brushing the excess grit from the upholstery. Maybe I should have used cold water again, instead of hot. I was so confused. I rushed back to the washroom, soaked the rag again, and mid-stride, I crossed myself on my forehead with my right thumbnail saying, "in the name of the Father, the Son, and the Holy Ghost."

On my knees in front of the chair, I tackled that spot as if it were a monster I needed to destroy. By now the grains of cleanser had soaked into the tapestry, and as I scrubbed, a slimy lather began to form. I worked the foam into the spot and soon began to make progress. The spot was fading, and with a few more vigorous scrubs, it disappeared. My efforts, though, left a white ring tinged with blue. "My God, oh my God, how am I ever going to explain all this to Father Daigle?"

I placed the laundry basket over the spot but knew full well that covering it up was not the answer. Sooner or later, I'd have to come up with an explanation. But right now, I felt weary. I still needed to carry the altar cloths to the apse. Once more as I passed the tabernacle, I genuflected and made the sign of the cross. This time as I got up, I had to grab the altar rail. For some reason, I was just so tired. I steadied myself, paused and looked up at the crucifix hanging at the back of the apse. Even in my fatigue, I believed being in service for the Lord was good. I remembered when Father Daigle first asked me to take care of the altar.

I had been sitting in the second pew with the rest of the girls. The boys, including Roger Greenleaf, were in the front row. Sister Mary Margaret had just finished telling us all about the procedure for lining up to receive our first Holy Communion. By alternating, "boy-girl, boy-girl," each of us would have a partner as we approached the rail. I sat there, counting the numbers off from right to left until I reached the boy directly in front of me, trying to figure out who was going to be my partner. I was hoping it wouldn't be Jerry Upham, his yellow stringy hair looked like greasy hay, and his dirty fingernails reminded me of chicken claws.

According to Sister Mary Margaret, we were supposed to practice this procession before Father Daigle came in to watch and to instruct us, but he had arrived early and was speaking to Mother Superior at the podium. I could not take my eyes off her. She was a tiny woman, but she appeared much grander because of her stark ebony gown and the stiff white bib tucked under her chin. She spoke in soft whispers to Father, her gestures prompting her long sleeves to wave and the large silver crucifix, suspended from her neck, to swish back and forth. A shoulder-length black wimple framed her rosy face, pinched by the bleached calotte covering her forehead.

Earlier, Mother Superior had spoken to us about this most Blessed Sacrament, The Holy Communion Wafer. We must hold it gently on our tongue until it dissolved, "never under any circumstances let your teeth touch the wafer, and swallow it immediately." Sister Mary Margaret had introduced Mother Superior as an "Ursuline nun, of the teaching order, founded in Italy." She went on to tell us that unlike Italy, there were places in the world like Africa where Christ was not known and missionaries counted on contributions from children like me and my classmates to bring them "The Word of the Lord." Sister Mary Margaret had been pointing her finger at us, "Now you children save all your pennies for those poor pagans," when Father Daigle stepped down and approached her. She stopped abruptly, turned to him and smiled, "Boys and girls, remember I told you we would have a visitor today? Father Daigle is here to talk to you. Please give him your attention."

"Good morning, new communicants of Christ. Welcome to Notre Dame Parish. By next Sunday, May 10, in the year of Our Lord 1926, you will be inaugurated as new apostles of Christ. Not only will it be Mother's Day, but it will be a day you will remember as your first mystical and spiritual union with the soul of Jesus. Now I'm sure Mother Superior has already spoken to you about the special Blessed Sacrament you will be receiving that symbolizes your total oneness in Christ. Do you have any questions?"

A boy in front of me, sitting next to Roger, timidly raised his hand, and then quickly withdrew it. Father Daigle wasted no time, "Yes, young man, you had a question?"

"Ah . . . yes, Father, I did. You see, my brother told me that I should chew the Holy Wafer right up and swallow it. But Mother Superior here, well, she said we should swallow it whole. So I'm just wondering, Father, uh. . . who's . . .

"I see. My boy, I'm sure if you follow Mother Superior's advice, you'll be doing what's right. Okay? Now another reason I am here today is to ask how many of you would like to be altar servers this year?" I instantly raised my hand. But several other boys in front of me also raised theirs. Father looked at the hands in the front pew, nodded and smiled, "Good, that's good. You boys will be my new acolytes. We'll talk again next week, after the service." Then, raising his eyes just above the first pew, he looked straight at me, "I'm sorry, young lady, girls cannot be altar servers." He singled me out, and his words seemed so final. A surge of heat rushed up my neck and face. My eyes filled with tears. I could feel them trickle down my cheeks, streaking my face. "However," said Father, after seeing my reaction, "I may have a task for you." What's your name, my dear?"

"Eva. Eva Fortin, Father."

"Ah, yes, Fortin. With a fine French name like that we can certainly find something very important for you. How would you like to dress the altar for me? Setting the Holy table for the Lord's Supper is a distinction I would like for you to have. If you see me after Catechism today, we'll discuss it more."

Now, looking down at the little latch just inside the altar rail, I leaned forward and opened the gate. As I proceeded up the steps toward the altar deep inside the curvature of the apse, my boot caught the hem of my dress and I tripped, scattering the altar cloths in front of me. What is the matter with me? Pulling myself upright, my legs felt funny. I trembled. I could feel a warm trickle down my leg. Then, something gushed from the inside of my thighs. I looked down. Bright red spots dotted the amber carpet. I panicked, unable to move. As I stood there, more spots hit the rug. I scrunched my dress between my legs, prayed hard to Jesus to make this stop, and collapsed on the step, my face buried in my arms. Something was terribly wrong with me. Had I come down with a horrible disease? As I raised my head, I saw the baptismal font. That might work, I thought. Holy water might make this right, might make *me* right.

I hobbled back down the steps and started for the font. Reaching in, I cupped some water and splashed my face. Jesus please help me, I prayed. Wash away this awfulness. Make me right again. Make these damned spots disappear. Then I realized that I had nothing to soak up the water in order to clean the new spots on the carpet. Still holding my dress, I climbed back up the stairs. I grabbed one of the altar scarves from the heap, and set off once more down the steps. I threw it into the holy water and watched it sink to the bottom of the basin.

I had only one thought: to get rid of that blood. Blood. The word just slipped out. For the first time, I realized that it was blood. Coming out of me. My God! I squeezed the excess water from the scarf and returned up the altar steps to those dreadful spots. Kneeling there scrubbing at them, I thought, My God, why am I bleeding? What's wrong with me? Something must be wrong with me. People who bleed end up dying. I must be dying. My God, I must be dying! I began to cry. My tears mixed with the holy water on the carpet, and as I scrubbed harder, my fingers, pink and sore, pushed through a thin hole forming in the cloth. The drops of blood did begin to disappear. And for a brief second, I felt relieved, felt that maybe this was all a bad dream, that maybe I was really okay, not in danger after all. But I was exhausted. The scrubbing, the worry was draining me.

Sitting there, resting, I slowly pulled my sticky dress away from the inside of my thighs, and when I looked down, a bloodstained mess. My underpants stuck to my garter belt, thoroughly drenched and soaked. The nightmare had returned. The bleeding had not stopped! It was surely coming from me, and it seemed to be getting worse. How on earth was I going to get home like this? I would have to find something to stop it up, plug it up somehow. I took the soiled scarf and wedged it inside my wet panties, then I stuffed my bloody dress once more between my legs. Picking up the altar cloths one by one, I tried to distribute them over the table. Not very orderly, I thought, but it would have to do. I needed to get home and fast.

Yet I was so tired. I managed to make my way down the corridor toward the washroom. While I attempted to clean the front of my dress, I was anxious, searching the room for other rags to stuff into my panties. In the cupboard to the right above the basin I found a neat stack of washcloths and face towels. I rushed to reach for one, and the whole pile toppled, some landing at my feet, others, in the sink. As I stood in that little room, I caught my reflection in the mirror. The young girl I saw there was a stranger to me, her bangs plastered to her pale forehead, wet with perspiration. And the eyes, hollowed out, "like two burned holes in a blanket," as my mother would say, especially if I'd stayed up reading past bedtime the night before.

With the wadded rags and washcloths between my legs, I made it to the vestibule door only to stumble out of the church onto the sidewalk. I was clumsy as I turned left on to Park Street toward home. I still couldn't tell what was wrong with me. Why would I be bleeding like this? Surely I haven't caused this to happen in any way. Or had I? Was it in some way my fault? Was God punishing me for something? What had I done? My mind spun backward, tracing the day's events. Oh my God, I realized, it must be because I got caught kissing Roger Greenleaf in the girls' bathroom! My God, that's it. Maybe I'm *not* really dying! Maybe it's just God's way of punishing me for being bad. When I wake up tomorrow, it'll all be gone. This nightmare will end. "It'll all be right tomorrow," I muttered, trying to console myself.

I passed the Sacred Heart cemetery, and had about a block to go before home. Rounding the corner of Summer Street, I could see my house, two stories, brown shingles and that wrap-around porch arching to the window of my parents' bedroom. Somewhere in the distance, I heard, "Hey, Eva, where ya goin'?" as I passed Roger Greenleaf's front yard. But I had only one question on my mind: would the lights be on in my kitchen? "Nothing, thank God," I exhaled. My mother wasn't home yet. And if I'm lucky, my sister, Sara, wouldn't be home either.

Recovering the key from under the loose brick beneath the doormat, I quietly inserted it and carefully turned the lock. I pushed open the heavy door, and bearing left, placed the key on the windowsill next to the oak dining table. I switched on the light momentarily so I could see to remove my boots, but flicked it off to hide myself as I tiptoed through the kitchen. At the hallway leading to the bathroom, I peeked into the living room. I pulled back. My sister was asleep on the sofa, her rag doll draped over her chest. This will not be easy, I thought, sneaking down the hall. At the bathroom door, once again, warm blood seeped down the inside of my stockings, past my knee. Slipping into the bathroom, I closed the door as softly as I could. I placed the rubber stopper over the drain in the tub, and as it filled with cold water, I wriggled out of my blood soaked dress and peeled off my leggings. The blood stuck to my fingers; the smell, like dirty pennies. Standing there in my camisole, I looked at the soggy pile on the floor. I was about to drop the stockings onto the pile, when I heard the door behind me open slowly. Sara stood there for a moment, her mouth open wide. And then, she screamed. "Oh my God, Eva's been shot!" I grabbed her arm and hauled her into the bathroom, closing the door behind her.

"Is anyone home?" I whispered.

Sara shook her head, wiping her nose against her sweater sleeve. She started wailing, "I don't want you to die, Eva! I don't. I really don't!" We stood facing each other. I took my eight-year-old sister in my arms, her head just under my chin, her hair parted in the middle, braids trailing down her back. She quivered.

"I'm going to be all right. Really. At least I think I am. Don't worry. Please try not to worry." I said, trying to soothe her. Giving her a final squeeze, I guided her over to the toilet seat, and while she sat there, I bent over the tub to slosh and rinse my clothes. "Sara, not a word to anyone about this. Do you hear? Promise me. Please promise me. You've got to cross your heart, and hope to die."

"Oh, Eva, please don't say that word. Please, don't."

"I'm sorry, Sara, I'm sorry. I didn't mean '*die*.'" But you've got to promise me, hear? Not a word."

"I promise, but on one condition. That you tell me what's goin' on, what's happening to you?"

"Sara, I honestly don't know. But believe me, as soon as I find out, I'll let you know. Just trust me for now, okay?"

"Does Mum know? Have you asked Mum? Maybe she could tell you."

"Absolutely not, Sara. Mum does not know. And if you tell her, I'll beat you, ya' hear, so bad, you'll wish you'd never opened your trap."

"You don't have to get mad at me to get your way, Eva, not like you do with Roger Greenleaf," she said slipping off the toilet seat and making her way out. "I won't say anything, I promise." She left me kneeling at the tub, and quietly closed the door. After I finished rinsing my clothes, I drew fresh warm water into the tub and climbed in, letting my tired stained body slide deep into the pool.

About an hour later, I made my way, damp clothes in one hand, clothes rack in the other, up the hall staircase and around the banister to my bedroom. I placed my clothes on the rack next to the radiator, and settled down at my dresser. I looked up into my mirror, and this time the girl was no longer a stranger. I saw Eva, scared Eva, bad Eva. I reached down to the lefthand drawer of the vanity and pulled out my only friend.

March 27, 1930

Dear Diary,

Today has been the worst day of my life. I'm bleeding. Somewhere inside me. I don't know why. Maybe it's because I got caught in the girls' bathroom with Roger. And God's punishing me. I must be evil. But somehow it felt good. I'm really tired right now. I'll have to continue tomorrow.

P.S. I hope I'm not dying.

After slipping into my flannel nightgown, I crawled into bed. I tossed in the bedclothes, trying to get comfortable and to forget the awfulness of the day. Knees drawn up, fingers searching under the pillow, I found my rosary. Just after the Our Father, I felt a stabbing strike my stomach. Then another wave of cramps more powerful than the first. Squeezing the beads tightly in my fist, I silently screamed the Hail Mary. My stomach seized once more. Oh Jesus, let me not despair. Curling my legs up tighter under my chin, I waited, in a ball, for it all to end. But, the spasms didn't stop. Such pain, my head pounded; the blood beat in my temples. It seemed like hours that I lay there, my belly aching, churning. I felt weaker and weaker, but restless and nervous too. I couldn't calm my nerves. Somehow, I found the strength to sit up and look around the room. Except for the streak of light from the crack at the door frame, my bedroom was wrapped in darkness. I figured that I might sleep better if I closed the door tight. When I put my hand on the knob, I remember I could hear them both down in the kitchen.

My mother and grandmother were rocking and cackling. Like two hens, they scratched and squawked to the rhythm of the chairs, back and forth. Suddenly, one chair stopped. Then, my mother's voice, "Maman, I found her garter belt stained with blood on the stairs."

"The curse?" Both rocking chairs went quiet. "Jeanne. You gotta tell her now."

"I guess so, Maman. I guess it's time."

"The clean rags? She know about 'em?"

"No."

"They still in the sewing machine drawer?"

"Oui, Maman."

The following morning, I woke up to find Mémé sitting on my bed with Mum standing behind her, their faces marked with sinister grins. My grandmother was the first to speak.

"Heh, heh, heh So, ya got the curse, eh...ta "tite amie?" Then, my mother tossed my garter belt at me, threw her head back and just laughed.

"Welcome, little Eva, to the world of women."

Similes Pour Ma Tante Louise

Since she decided to let it go, her hair is white – it's beautiful.
So soft, it curls around her head like cotton on a newborn.
She was seventeen when she last looked in the mirror.
Her eyes are blue. Not a deep blue or a crystal blue
but a moody, enduring blue like a dreamy periwinkle bud.
It's a color I don't see in other places.

When I was eight years old I cheated as I dealt the Braille
playing cards. I still don't know how, but she caught me
quick like a toad catches a fly. I think it's one of the worst
things I've ever done and I did it wearing the sweater
that she made for me—rosy as my cheeks in winter.
No eyes—just knit and purl, knit and purl, over and over,
needles clicking like cricket legs in summer,
yarn coming up from the bag at her feet.

The skeins she brought home in those days were long loops
of wool. I'd stand in front of her with my arms straight out
the yarn held taut. And she would sit in her chair rocking
from side to side, keeping a rhythm as she rolled the warmth
into a ball. The tension on the strand between us just right.
And I would ask over and over again, as though I didn't
believe her, "How did you go blind, Ma Tante?"

Those were the days when it was still odd that she
could not see. Vision burrowed like a mole gone under.
But now decades have passed and her yarn is acrylic,
it comes in an easy pull skein. No time
for rolling it into balls. She's making me an afghan
and she loves it when I tell her about the green yarn –
all mossy like the stonewall out back. I'm careful
when I describe to her in detail.

By Marie Louise St. Onge

150%
from *Shutting Up Peggy Lee*

By Susan Poulin

Last night, I had this dream: it's the end of the world, and I can't decide what to wear. I know! I'm standing in the bedroom of our house. (It doesn't look like our house, but I know it's ours). Outside, the sky is dark and grey, the wind's whipping the trees, leaves everywhere, orange lightning on the horizon. I hear the screams of people as they run past our windows, their faces full of panic. A little boy's crying, clutching a teddy bear as his mother drags him along. Old men and women, teenagers, all running for their lives.

"Hurry up, Susan!" my husband calls. "We've got to get to the fallout shelter!"

"I'm trying! I'm trying!" I yell, eyes darting between my impossible pile of clothes and an empty backpack. I need a bigger bag! In desperation, I scream, "What's the weather going to be like after the apocalypse?" Then, everything goes black and I wake up.

This is what it's come to. When I was in college (and for about ten years after), my recurring dream was that, even though I'd dropped my Western Civilization class at the beginning of the semester, I find out the night before the final that the paperwork had never gone through! In order to maintain my grade point average, I somehow have to read the entire, three-inch thick book in one night to ace tomorrow's test.

I want to be prepared, you know? That's how I was raised: get the facts, brainstorm options, formulate a game plan and commit to action. We always did things 150% in my family. Team Poulin: Mom, Dad, Susan and Jane!

Like when my sister Jane and I were teenagers, the whole family decided to take up skiing. So we took lessons on Monday nights at Lost Valley, where they had night skiing, and skied every Sunday at Mount Abram. We were determined. That first season we started on the bunny slopes and ended on intermediate trails.

When we got home from skiing, we'd have a pizza party, then dialogue on a question, which is something we learned on this Parent-Teen Encounter weekend we'd gone on. "Dialoguing on a question" means that one of us would pose a question, a big question like, I don't know, "How do you feel when you think about death?" Then we would each write a letter to the family, answering the question. You couldn't just say, "Death makes me feel lonely," and leave it at that. No, you had to go a step further, so everyone could really understand what you meant. "Death makes me feel lonely, like riding the chairlift by myself at Lost Valley on a winter night with the wind chill below zero." (That kind of thing.) Then we'd read the letters out loud to each other and discuss them. Sounds kooky, I know, but really, it was a gift.

(Continued on next page)

My parents were already very active in Marriage Encounter at the time, which is a Catholic thing. It's still around, too. I visited their website. When the red and yellow logo popped up, the heart with two intersecting wedding rings and a cross overlapping, I got a little teary, in a good sort of way. We had that logo on our car. "Turn a good marriage into a great marriage." That's what it says on the Marriage Encounter website, and it works. At least it did for my Mom and Dad. There's also Engaged Encounter, Already Encountered Encounter, and the Parent-Teen Encounter Weekend, which is what we had signed up for.

When the information packet for retreat arrived, my Mom highlighted all the important stuff, and we made our list of things to bring. We were also given a homework assignment: make a family banner. Did our hearts sink? No! Team Poulin swung into action! One evening after dinner, we had a brainstorming session to come up with the design. The next week, we went out to dinner, then on to a fabric shop to buy the stuff we needed. Then we spent a weekend snacking and cutting out the pieces and putting it all together.

In the central lodge of the retreat center was a big living room with a cathedral ceiling and a railing around the perimeter, so you could look down from the second floor. When we arrived, many families had already hung their banners from the railing. We stared at the competition, amazed. I mean, a scrap of pale blue fabric with "Perkins" scrawled in magic marker? "Smith" stuck to a 12" x 12" square of brown burlap. Burlap?!

We proudly unfurled our banner: five feet by four feet. That's right, twenty square feet of turquoise felt, resplendent with brightly colored decoration. Our four initials intertwined to form two mountains with a sun rising between them. Our zodiac signs floated in the sky: Pisces, Libra, Taurus, Gemini. And below, in big, perfectly spaced letters, "POULIN." The thing was so big, it needed a dowel the size of a broomstick to hold it up.

The weekend started with a gathering of everyone in the central lodge. We noticed there were more families than banners. In fact, only about half the families had done their homework assignment. Copping out had never occurred to us as an option. But nobody was docked points. Instead, we were each given a piece of aluminum foil and told to mold it over our faces to make a mask. Then the retreat leader, Father Tom, had us crumple them up and throw our masks into the center of the room. "Time to take off our masks and get real!" he yelled. And we did!

We peeled off into our peer "rap" groups to dialogue on questions. Then we shared our dialogues with our family. We took long walks together and dialogued some more. The weekend ended with a big Mass in the central lodge. It was one of the best services I've ever attended, a real celebration, informal and inclusive, with folk music and a rousing final sermon by Father Tom. If church was always like that, who knows? I might still be a practicing Catholic.

I haven't seen that family banner in over thirty-five years, but I'm pretty sure I know where it is. When my parents were in their late '50s, I think, they had their funeral pictures taken. "Let's have our pictures done now," my Mom said, "while we still look good!" They also wrote their own obituaries and what they wanted for their service. And they put together the "death trunk." That's what they called it. A trunk filled with things they knew would mean something to Jane and me, things to make us laugh and cry. We're supposed to go through it together when they're both gone. The Poulin family banner must be in there. It's comforting to know it's waiting for us in the death trunk, a time capsule from a place that doesn't exist anymore.

History/*Histoire*

Menthe—Mémoire, vertu. Amour exalté, sagesse
Mint—Virtue, hospitality and wisdom, fidelity, protection of illness and warm feelings, eternal refreshment, wisdom

Souci—Chagrin, peine, désespoir, jalousie. Inquiétude
Marigold—Prophetic prediction

Champignon—Vie et mort. Longue vie, fertilité, mystère entre vie et mort
Mushroom—Suspicion, long life, happiness and rebirth; Immorality and eccentricity; knowledge and enlightenment

Capucine—Patriotisme
Nasturtium—Patriotism

Branche d'olivier—Paix ou victoire
Olive Branch—Peace, victory

Peuplier Blanc—Porteur d'espoir et promesse de régénérescence; attaché à l'Autre Monde, à la vie cyclique des âmes; mélancolie, souvenir des êtres disparus ...
White Poplar—Time, victory, transformation and vision. Ability to endure and conquer, to resist and to shield; association with speech,

L'if—Funéraire, militaire. Éternité, mort, immortalité, renouveau, renaissance, continuité et acceptation des cycles de vie, sérénité, tristesse terrestre passagère
Yew—Raising the dead, magic, death, rebirth

Émigration

By Doris Provencher Faucher

Chapter One, Taken from *Le Quebecois: The Virgin Forest*
Mid-April 1657

The ancient castle of the Dukes of Brittany cast its shadow over the old port of Nantes, as dinghies wended their way around and between the several river craft and ocean-sailing ships that lay at anchor in this common estuary of the Erdre and Loire rivers.

Bastien stood on the deck of the small river shallop and watched as the longboats ferried cargo from ships newly arrived with West Indian sugar, and heavy stocks of dried and salted fish from the Newfoundland banks. In the midst of this activity, sailors of the French royal navy refitted their man-of-war and replenished their supplies.

His mind wandered, as it often had these last few days. Loneliness enveloped him; he knew that he would never see his family again. Military conscription had completely changed the direction of his life, he thought ruefully.

The shallop dropped anchor, and once ashore, he walked the dock area where his attention quickly focused on the endless activity, the sounds and scents of this busy port. Horsecarts crowded the waterfront as they shuttled bales, barrels, and crates to and from the several warehouses. Dockworkers received and sorted out cargo for delivery to the merchant vessels; stevedores loaded the small transfer boats with trade goods destined for the French colonies of Canada, Acadia, and the Antilles.

Bastien noticed a man and a young adolescent engaged in earnest and animated conversation with three sailors at the end of the quay, and he saw that the two were dressed and equipped as he was, in well-worn homespun clothing, each with a canvas backpack and a blanket roll slung over his shoulder.

When the seamen cast off and the two peasants walked toward him, Bastien smiled as he recognized that they shared a strong resemblance to each other. He judged that the younger of the two must be about his brother Jehan's age.

He held out his hand to the man and introduced himself.

The stranger smiled back at him and replied: "My name is Julien and this is my son Pierre. We noticed your knapsack—Were you with the army?"

"For a while," he said as he nodded to the son. "And you?"

"No. Our friends gave these to us as going-away presents. They seemed anxious to get rid of them; they hope never to leave home again."

"Have you traveled far?" Bastien asked as a peasant woman approached them.

"Anne!" Julien called her over, and introduced her as his wife. She and Bastien nodded to each other as she moved toward her son and ran her fingers through his hair. The boy's ears flamed red; he shook his head and moved away.

Julien continued: "We left Angers at dawn yesterday and planned to be here by midday today, but we had walked part of the way when a boatman offered to carry us down the Loire, so we arrived sooner than we expected. And you?"

"I left Orléans eight days ago."

Comfortable in each other's company, they continued to wander through the bustling activity of Nantes. Julien pointed to several warehouses and said: "Those belong to the major colonial traders."

"Are you looking for work in Nouvelle-France?" Bastien asked.

"We've already signed contracts early this morning."

"Where will you go?"

"To Québec. *Sieur* Salomon needed a cooper and agreed to hire Pierre as a farm laborer and Anne as a housekeeper."

"Did you try anywhere else?"

Julien shook his head. "We were lucky enough to see him first. What are you looking for?"

"Farming in Canada."

"As far as I know," Julien volunteered, "there are two merchants looking for someone like you." He pointed to the relevant buildings. "That's where you'll find them. Good luck, *mon vieux* ..."

Bastien entered the first wooden warehouse, and found a clerk sitting behind a tall desk in a sparsely furnished front office area. The frail, elderly man appeared to be undisturbed by the commotion caused by the movement of bales and kegs in and out of storage. Bastien asked him if his employer offered any indenture contracts.

The recorder studied him from above his spectacles and replied: "Yes, Monsieur Lecoq is always looking for recruits. Do you have a letter of introduction?"

Bastien presented his pastor's written recommendation, which the clerk briefly scanned and handed back. "Very well," he said, "but before you meet with Monsieur, I should tell you that the contract is for thirty-six months and provides return passage, room, board, and wages of sixty-five livres per year. The *seigneurie* is located near the walls of Québec, the oldest and most strongly fortified settlement."

Bastien thanked him and moved toward the door. "I have one more inquiry to make, then I may be back," he explained.

The clerk seemed irritated and called: "You won't get a better offer!"

Bastien shrugged his shoulders and disregarded this harsh warning. He was no longer in the army; he now had the right to choose his own future.

Sieur Salomon returned from the warehouse, but continued to direct its workers from his desk. "What can I do for you?" he asked.

"I'm looking for indentured service in Canada. Do you have any contracts available?"

The merchant shuffled his papers. "That depends. What type of work are you looking for?"

"Farming."

"Yes, we have a few openings available, but we offer one-way passage only."

Bastien nodded. "I won't be coming back—I plan to build a farm of my own in Nouvelle-France."

Salomon studied him for a moment. "Well, you sound ambitious enough, but are you strong and healthy?"

The peasant straightened up and confidently replied: "I am."

The merchant briefly appraised him and read the letter that recommended him for employment without reservation. The pastor at Pithiviers had written that the candidate came from a good family, had traveled extensively with the cavalry, then had returned home to find his parents had died and that his younger brothers had assumed responsibility for the family farm. On the basis of having known him since baptism, the priest vouched for Bastien's honesty and his capacity for working hard and conscientiously.

Salomon handed back the letter of reference and told him: "Landowners at Trois-Rivières are always looking for farmers. If you sign a contract with me, it will be sold to another merchant when you reach Québec. Nevertheless, the agreement guarantees food and shelter during employment, provides a new pair of shoes on the day of departure, and promises to pay a willing worker like you seventy livres *tournois* for each year of service."

Bastien struggled to control his enthusiasm. "And what about tools?"

"Your employer will provide what you need as long as you work for him."

"How is Trois-Rivières different from Québec?"

Salomon's mouth curled into a smile. Such curiosity! he thought. He nested his quill in its inkwell and leaned back against the wall. "Québec is already well-developed and protected, but Trois-Rivières is a frontier trading post located four days' sail up the Saint Lawrence River from Québec, halfway to Mont Royal and Ville-Marie. The Jesuits are granting land concessions along that riverfront, but farmers must clear the virgin forest before they can sow grain and build their homes."

Bastien hesitated only briefly while he imagined himself swinging an axe and cutting down forest trees for the first time in his life. "I'd like to sign up for Trois-Rivières."

"Then you must come back at noon to sign the contract," the merchant told him dismissively as he resumed his paperwork.

The sun was halfway to its highest point when he returned to the dock area. A slight offshore breeze carried the salty scent of sea and fish, and the faint odor of tar and oak. Sounds of clashing metal and wood echoed along the docks. Sailors' voices carried clearly across the water.

Julien called him to a small grassy knoll where he and his family sat and watched the port's activity.

"Did you find what you were looking for?" he asked.

Bastien replied with a grin, "It looks like we'll be traveling together! I'm to sign the contract at noon today, and the terms are better than I expected!"

"Excellent!"

"Will your wife be joining you?" Anne asked expectantly.

Her question caught him off-guard; his lips tightened. He hesitated before he answered: "Unfortunately, I'm not married yet, but my fiancée will join me as soon as I've built a home for us."

Anne's eyes widened. "Will she sail alone, then?"

Julien frowned at his wife's curiosity, but Bastien sensed her genuine concern. "She insists on it," he replied.

"She must be an exceptional woman," Julien offered.

"Yes, she certainly is."

"Is she also from Orléans?" Anne continued in an attempt to gauge the extent of this woman's commitment. She doubted that she herself would have the courage to cross the ocean alone, without her family.

"In a way, yes. Marguerite is a *Fille du Roi* who grew up in a convent in Orléans, but was born in Artenay, a short distance from my village."

"Then she has no family of her own?" Anne asked.

He barely shook his head. "She was born to a peasant family, but she was raised by the Ursuline Sisters and came to Pithiviers as an assistant cook and housekeeper at the local manor; that's how I met her, through my brother's wife who also works there."

"Have you known her long?" the woman continued.

"Since last summer—we met shortly after I returned home from military service."

"It must have been difficult for you to leave her behind." Julien said.

"Yes, it was," his brow wrinkled in painful regret. "When I finally returned home from the war, both of my parents had died. The oldest of my four brothers had married and had a child; his family was well-established on the family farm. I helped him to restore it, but came to realize that I no longer belonged there."

"Had you volunteered for the army?" young Pierre asked eagerly.

"No, when the family corvée came due, I was barely old enough for conscription—It seemed like quite an adventure at the time."

"Then you must have been the eldest son," Julien guessed. "The farm should have been yours."

Bastien shook his head. "In better times, perhaps, but under the circumstances, I felt that my brother had earned the right to keep it, and by last winter, I knew that I could no longer be happy there. I need to develop my own land and build my own farm. My future lies across the sea."

The wind shifted; the tide had turned to ebb. One of the ships in the harbor unfurled its canvas sails; its anchor rose from the water. The new emigrants watched with fascination the increasing activity on deck and in the shrouds as the vessel slowly made its way downriver.

When church bells rang the midday Angelus, Bastien returned to Salomon's office.

"Can you read or write?" the notary asked.

"No," he replied quietly, and again found reason to regret that his grandfather had not shared this skill with his sons and grandsons.

"Then I'll read the contract to you, and answer any questions you might have."

The agreement specified that the three-year indenture would begin on the day of his embarkation, and stipulated that he would receive his new shoes at that time. It promised to provide him with a daily food allowance until then, and granted him a small advance against his first year's wages.

He accepted these terms by drawing two crossed lines at the end of the document; the notary identified these as his signature mark.

"We can always use an extra hand on the quay," Salomon offered. "The work pays ten sols per day, and you could sleep in the warehouse if you like."

Bastien's eyes brightened at this prospect. He thoughtfully fingered the five coins that would allow him to replace his tattered blanket. His food would be provided, but he would also require safe shelter, so he immediately accepted the merchant's offer.

Virtual Time Travel through Census Returns

By Denise R. Larson

When heavy, unrelenting snows hit Maine, I like to take frequent virtual trips to warm and sunny places like Greece or Hawaii by popping in a DVD or logging onto streaming Netflix. The sight of lush greenery and the sound of warm breezes through palm trees give me hope for the future—namely, Spring.

The magic of technology can transport us to exotic places for mental respite, but it also can open portals to past times. The year 2016 is the twentieth anniversary of the Franco-American Women's Institute (FAWI), but it is also the three-hundred-and-fiftieth anniversary of the first official census taken in Canada. The following year, 2017, will be the four hundredth anniversary of the arrival of the first permanent French settlers in the New World—the Hébert family. Without the brave men who founded the French trading post at Québec with Samuel de Champlain in 1608 and the intrepid pioneer women who later joined them to make it their home, there would have been no *habitants* of New France, no city of Québec, no FAWI. This is the perfect time to celebrate the triple anniversaries.

Stepping into a New World

The first family from France to arrive in Québec, the Héberts, comprised Louis Hébert, his wife, Marie Rollet, and their three children, Guillaume, Guillemette, and Anne. Louis was an apothecary in Paris who had accompanied Champlain on previous voyages, including those to Port Royal in 1605-06 and to Québec at its founding in 1608. In 1617, the Héberts sold their home near the Louvre in Paris and sailed to the new trading post, where they lived in a stone house built on Cap Diamant by the men of Québec. Louis served the post as an herbalist, growing medicinal plants as well as vegetables on his ten acres of cleared land. He also acted as aid to Champlain in procurement and civil matters. Marie provided room and board for numerous craftsmen and laborers and taught academics and household skills to her children and those of the American Indians who camped nearby.

In 1627, ten years after the Héberts arrived, there were only seventy-two people in Québec, including only five women and six girls. The population grew gradually, with more craftsmen, laborers, government clerks, and military men arriving with each ship from France. But progress at settling Québec was moving too slowly for young King Louis XIV. Immigration to Québec lagged behind expectations and the British were making inroads into New France territories. In 1663 the French king designated Québec as a royal colony and appointed a manager, an intendant, to get things moving.

Intendant Jean Talon was a meticulously organized man who wanted to find out about the land, the holdings, and the people under his supervision. He personally participated in taking the first census of the region's European inhabitants. Thanks to our virtual time machine, we can see images of the actual 1666 census at Library and Archives Canada, titled, Recensement du Canada, 1666/Census of Canada, 1666.

Let's take a virtual walk with Intendant Talon and meet the neighbors.

As we tag along on the first day of census in Québec, we learn a little about our host. Jean Talon (1625-1694) was commissioned by Louis XIV to review and organize the financial affairs of the fur-trading post and settlement at Québec, which, until 1663, had been managed—many said mismanaged—by the Company of One Hundred Associates. As Intendant of Justice, Police, and Finance, Talon had the authority to make changes, but the first thing he did was to take inventory, which included a census of all inhabitants in Québec, Montréal, and Trois-Rivières. In his door-to-door enumeration, Talon collected the name, age, and occupation of everyone residing in each domicile. In all, there were 528 families plus numerous single men who worked as laborers, craftsmen, or government workers, for a total population of 3,215. As time progressed, Talon would use the power of his office to bring to Québec a regiment of seasoned French troops to end the attacks by the Iroquois and, later, to bring hundreds of young women from France, called *filles du roi*, to marry the single men in the settlements, especially the soldiers who chose to remain in Canada.

As a sign of respect, our first stop for the census is the religious community in Québec. Bishop Laval was "named by the King first bishop (*évêsque*) of this country," according to what Talon writes in his notebook. He enters the names of the "monsieurs" in the seminary and their domestic servants, and the ages of the servants (but not that of the bishop or clergy). Saying *adieu*, we continue to the home of the Jesuits of the College of Québec. Again, Talon omits the ages of the men. But when we arrive at the home of the Ursuline Sisters, La dame de la Pelletrie (de La Peltrie), founder of the order, gives her age as 63 years old. Superior Marie Guyard de l'Incarnation is sixty-six. The ages of all the sisters, their postulants, and their boarding students are written down. The religious sisters at the hospital, our next stop, do not give their ages.

Our respects paid to the important and influential religious contingent of Québec, we move on to family residences. Talon's hand is remarkably legible, three hundred and fifty years after the act. Each page has three columns: names of members in a family, age, occupation. Family groups are divided by a horizontal line drawn across the page. Intendant Talon makes special notes about the men living alone, writing down either "not married" or "married in France."

A few houses down the road we call on Guillemette Marie Hébert, widow of Monsieur Couillard, and her son Charles Couillard, sieur des Islets. In the household there are also a domestic and three laborers. Guillemette was the daughter of Louis Hébert and Marie Rollet, who have both passed away by this time. Guillemette's granddaughter, Marguerite Nicolet and her husband, Jean-Baptiste LeGardeur, and their four children—the great-great-grandchildren of Louis and Marie—live nearby and are visited in turn, as are the other Couillard and related households.

Guillemette's niece, Françoise is at home. Françoise is the granddaughter of Louis and Marie and has several children with her husband, Guillaume Fournier, whom she married in 1651. By 1666, the Fournier household boasts five children—Louis and Marie's great-grandchildren.

Françoise's father, the Héberts' son, Guillaume, married Helene Desportes in 1634. Guillaume and Helene's only son, Joseph, died young and his only child, also named Joseph, died as a youth without descendants. But the Hébert line continues, though under different surnames, through the women of the family: their granddaughter, Françoise and their daughter, Gullemette. The other daughter of the Héberts, Anne, died in childbirth ca. 1619, and no record about the infant has been found.

Our time with Intendant Talon is limited, and he himself must hand over census taking to an assistant and tend to other matters. Modern-day genealogists are thankful for the careful records that government officials and the clergy kept during the early years of New France. Collectively, the documents are a treasure trove of history and genealogy. From them sprung a few "bibles" that trace ancestry in New France—the genealogical dictionaries by Cyprien Tanguay (*Dictionnaire généalogique des families canadiennes*) and Rene Jette (*Dictionnaire généalogique des familles du Québec*). There is also a supplement to Tanguay's work by J. Arthur Leboeuf (*Complément au Dictionnaire généalogique Tanguay*). Acadian genealogy was gathered by Stephen White in his book, *Dictionnaire généalogique des familles acadiennes*.

Another Glimpse of Our Ancestors

In *Hélène's World*, a book worth reading by anyone interested in early Québec social history, Susan McNelley weaves the life of Helene Desportes, the Héberts' daughter-in-law, into a simple but well-told story of early Québec. *Helene's World* was published by Etta Heritage Press in Lexington, Kentucky, in 2014. McNelley, who has a Master's degree in Humanities, looks from the women's viewpoint to describe the lives of the brave pioneers who left French civilization for the wilds of New France with its hazards and opportunities. Hélène Desportes is McNelley's ancestor as well as the inspiration for her work.

Books and websites can be our tickets to heritage sites and introductions to the people who lived there. *Bon voyage* to all who wish to explore *la famille Canadienne*.

Photo:
In Place Royal in Québec City, the author, Denise (Rajotte) Larson, sits at the foot of a monument to Louis XIV, who, in 1663, commissioned her ancestor Gilles Rageot to be a notary in the Royal Court in Québec.

Une femme de la terre

"Daughter of a Duke," Mama said
handing me the box with the teapot
"Pewter — the wooden top is broken
and the spout fell off when Grammie had it.
It's supposed to go
to the first daughter."

I was twenty.
Opening the box I found
"The last piece of her dowry
She escaped from France
with her father's valet and married him
The revolution had killed her father
and she was fleeing the country
She sewed jewelry
into her clothes to buy their passage."

For lifetimes this teapot
had been held in women's hands,
for decades hidden in Mama's closet,
wrapped in cloth and tissue paper
only to be stashed at the back
of *my* closet

Then in my late thirties,
I opened the box,
picked up this ancestral talisman,
four inches of pitted pewter
made in France
so long ago
I hung my earrings on it,
speaking with this ancestor
Who was she, flinging herself
into the unknown?

Daughter of a duke
or *fille du roi?*
The story changes in every generation
So "daughter of a duke"
is the story
but agents of the king and queen,
could have recruited her,
paid her dowry
to marry in New France.

Either way, in North America
she found nothing familiar
except language and religion
a comfort, perhaps.

Paired with someone
she had little time to know,
she likely married
within weeks of arrival,
set about living in the woods,
not far from the rivers
inevitably alone for long periods,
Made a garden, kept a house,
in the woods
with all that "in the woods" means.

She could drop a bear
raiding her food store with
one shot and then
preserve the meat in salt
as easily as she could calm a baby
or cook a meal.
She made friends with
the native women,
who taught her
when and where to plant crops
and forage.

Surviving it all —
déracinée, replanted,
bearing as many children
as she was 'blessed' with
when raising them
at all was victory
and every childbed
a roll of the dice,
She hung on, lasted,
sent her genes
down the centuries to me.

So if she was
a duke's daughter or
dowered by a king or queen,
as the wife of a man of New France,
what she became was
a woman of the Earth,
Une femme de la terre.

She remains here now
rooted in new land.
Pewter, an alloy, like the teapot
not silver or gold, like the story.

I have a daughter who
carries our line
and I say,
old woman of France,
you would know her as *clan.*

By Donna Hébert 10/29/13

One Night Out of Africa

Out across the Sahara into Persia, into Nepal.
I fought the sandstorms that wore my skin pale.
I loved beautiful silks, from bountiful worms.
.
played the lute on the banks of the Black Sea,
had a Goth in my bed, eloped to the cliffs
of the Caucasus, the origins of omittable sin.

Southern neighborhoods of France and Spain
I loved the olives. I bore the patina like dust.
My coverlet was fleece. Hell broke to smithereens,

I turned Protestant repented my rebellion,
Centuries in the Pyrenees, under my ribs.
I tell on my Genghis Khan roots,

travelling show of a bloodline,
I was bred for turnabout.

By Pamela Morneault Gemme

Daughter of the King

At the palace of Versailles,
noble women of France
hungered *Haute couture*.

King Louis sent men to New France
They hunted fox, ermine, sable and beaver.

The men there grew cold for want of women.
The king delivered one hundred girls.

Come by grace, come by blunder,
Girls of Gaul, Celt, nuns
with tongues of Vulgar Latin,
packed rough to sail the Atlantic.

I am descended ten generations.
The first, Constance, married a trapper
on the shores of the St Lawrence,

Their daughter toiled maple syrup
drizzled down the map
from Quebec to the Americas.
Daughter's daughters wove cotton,
spun the lathe,
served up mutton on Limoges.

I am fruit of their migration,
deluge of the forests,
My hands cupped to receive that rain.

By Pamela Morneault Gemme

Border/*La frontière*

Eucalyptus—Amour des voyages
Eucalyptus—Protecting and nurturing

Armoise—Infidélité conjugale
Mugwort (artemisia vulgaris)—Tranquillity, happiness, traveller's joy

Pervenche—Amitié de toute la vie
Periwinkle—Sweet remembrance

Sel—civilisation, compréhension du monde, ouverture, détachement
Salt—perpetuity and incorruption; represents friendship and hospitality

Poivrier—Protection, puissance virilité
Pepper—Protection, exorcism, comfort, endurance, flexibility, and stamina, fearlessness, motivation, strength

Sucre—douceur, dépendance
Sugar—Sweetness; celebrates joyous occasions and victories

Foundation Myth

On the porch, collar open, he sniffs
a pack of cigarettes, half-empty,

half-interested in pleasure despite
Prohibition. Near midnight, the sky's

still undecided, daylight heat relents,
and crickets announce an attack

they never mean to mount.
Across the road, a Packard hacks

in the drive. On its fenders idle
French boys down on whiskey runs, armed

with small, hard hands. They talk
in French fast and loud, lips illegible

to local boys who watch from a distance.
With one tender hand she grips

the back of her neck, watching
the scuffed toe of her shoe, listening

without lowering her face too low. She can
feel the moonlight blush her brow, make

her eyes two dark, delicious hollows.
Across the street behind summer vines,

he is the cigarette's orange tip, claiming
through shadow her moonlit cheek.

By Abby Paige

Hope Chest

What holds you here: the play of light
on grass dappled by frost, headstones
clutched by snow, whose familiar names
you had forgotten. You see yourself

in nails driven to the hilt, in granite
posts planted on the green, in iron taps
with hooks where buckets hang to catch
the tears the maples weep. In the police

blotter a woman reports Iraqis on her
lawn. Comical, the idea that the world
would be near here. Under the stairs,
you hear chewing and imagine mice

bedding down in your inheritance:
ox bloods, rubies, devil's eyes,
the lost marbles of ancestors, and
the Bible worn mute. You listen

as your heirlooms soften in
the hopeless chest, masticated
by time and rodents, and wonder
if you're being devoured or released.

By Abby Paige

The Undefended Border

Comment? How? *Qui?* Who? Who put this tongue in my mouth? Who says this is my tongue?

Crossing. 1898. (Pierre Wilfrid Bilodeau)

When my brothers take me through town on my last afternoon everyone wants to know

how it is not to work soil like my father. The ground here is rocks and sawdust.

My eye wanders extraordinary child yellow aproned dress

We sit on the porch *chez les Corriveau,* her tiny hand absentminded on my knee as she watches a thrush jerk here and there across the grass. She looks into my face, but

blankly as though she is tying ribbons in her head. *Ma femme, elle sera.*

Her father, poor farmer, looks at her shoes when he promises her to me.

Maman wraps a chicken for me to take and we make the usual promises, to write or come back. With the basket I board the train, peel an egg as *St-Lazare* becomes a knot

on the horizon. I never know exactly when crossing happens, only that somewhere *en route*

there turns into here. With every crossing, I become more foreign and less. I recognize the roofs of the mine and the mill, too rusted to reflect sunlight. Home now, if this is that. *Mais ici sera toujours*

Là Bas *Là Bas* *Là Bas*

Here / there / the line / denies the mix of tongues in mouths. The first words in meme's ear: The last before she left: *Faire dodo*. Do *dodo*. Sleep. She rowed off the river into

CROSSING. 1912. (JOSEPHINE CORRIVEAU BILODEAU)

Ma seour m'a dit que cet homme *this man* *this man I took* qu'il
a me choisi du berceau. *Do you take this man, the father asked, as though asking a question. Under*
the veil it looked like snow was falling, the lace obscuring his face, pious, hungry.
Then *his hands on my knees* *in the dark,*
leaves from the box elder embroidering the ceiling, this man's voice saying my name as he *takes.*
Le chemin de fer c'est un tremblement qu'ébranle la terre d'en haut ou peut-être c'est moi qui
bringuebale comme un gond malade. Le feuillage, juste en changement, un feu mourant. Je ne sais pas comment savoir quand nous avons traversé
la frontière.
Je me demande si je le sentirai. Peut-être quand on le traverse
je disparaîtrai *dispar* *être*

sky. The water drifts across / the 45th parallel, smuggling / fishy cargo. My nationality broke off, floats off   the coast of my identity.   No one speaks perfect English.   No one

Crossing. 2008. (Abigail Ellen Paige*)

* Could the names of the poet be more Anglo than those of her great-grandparents?

The list of my belongings   called a *Customs Form B4E Personal Effects Accounting Document*
                    is 5 pages long, one for each room in the house where I lived until today.
The agent initials each page without looking in or at the truck and thanks me
in English, handing back the passports, mine with its American eagle, my husband's with a crest and a crown.
                    Love is a crossing into
so I hang my hat on the night we met, when I crossed here four years ago, toward home
in a snowstorm. How did you meet him? the agent asked then; I lied, not wanting to say on-line. When I crossed in, the snow, assaulting the windshield in the cavernous dark, was
a white kind of fireworks, its downward surrender unapologetically cold. Now we cross out together, or in,
                    into—   Now
I am my language. T'as l'air d'une Quebecoise, someone tells me in French class. Sauf quand j'ouvre la bouche, I stammer and blush, my grandmother in my face if not
my mouth. My favorite French phrase these days   je ne suis pas d'ici   feels
not altogether true, but is how   I ask forgiveness   when asked for directions
                    on the streets of Montréal.

whose tongue ain't broke.   *Combien?*   How many? How many   tongues can I imperfect?

By Abby Paige

The Undefended Border

My husband wants to know why the line is always broken.
I say the poem is made of words, but the words are not
the poem. The words are the way in. The broken

lines are openings. I remember how his skin turned
gold under a streetlight the first time he took off his shirt,
and I saw his waist, small below the broadness of

his shoulders. I took hold of his shoulder blade, the narrow
rudder of a slender boat. Which is the poem? I ask,
his shoulder blade or the words: narrow, slender, boat.

~

I live beside the country of his body, the nation of his habits,
how he trims his fingernails in private, purses lips, and worries
the sleeves of shirts. My foreign tongue exasperates,

its appetites, outbursts, erotic requirements. In this body
am I immigrant or citizen? In this balkanized era, perhaps
the only optimistic gesture is an oath to stay together. We,

a federation of states, two countries, a single continent, we
invent democratic culture. That's what intimacy is. We
reasonably accommodate. Tenderly we draft our constitution.

~

The map is a story we read on the road. We take turns
driving, navigating. Between our countries, a line drawn
by compromise, its location a cartographic error

since the surveyor spent his expedition's funds on rum.
One team departed from the East, the other from the West,
and they never met.

One day I crossed three times to see him, crossing
over, crossing back, in love with the ease of it, incursion
and retreat. No map, not lost, in love with the ease of it.

~

Predators are deployed to secure the border, the same
drones that launch Hellfires over Afghanistan. It is insecure,
the border. We like its indefensible length, its lack of

definition, but we know it's natural, the instinct to patrol,
as if by stalking the clear-cut between two forests they could
keep roots from mingling. We know from being woken by

each other's nightmares side by side in a single bed
that two territories create a border by incursion. Periodically,
we change sides. The border sleeps between us.

~

There is a theater that the border runs through.
The audience watches a play performed in Stanstead
from their seats in Derby Line. When it was built, they say,

the border's exact location was unknown, as though
it had been made and hidden, or was given but needed
to be found. Where does the play reside?

Is the actor immigrant or citizen? Can a building be
a line break? An unmapped territory? What country
resides there in the dark behind the footlights?

~

We share a bed, not a country. In the dark, I don't know where
my loyalty lies. Which side of the bed, the border? With
the territory or the map? Each pleated by repeated folds and

flattenings. On the dresser one ring nests inside the other, a ripple
of promises. But the ring is not the promise. Not even the words
are the promise. The promise is a frontier, a wilderness

between. We promise each other the boundary and its
breaking. We look for a line that can't be crossed. We promise
to be indefensible in marriage. Traitors. Patriots.

By Abby Paige

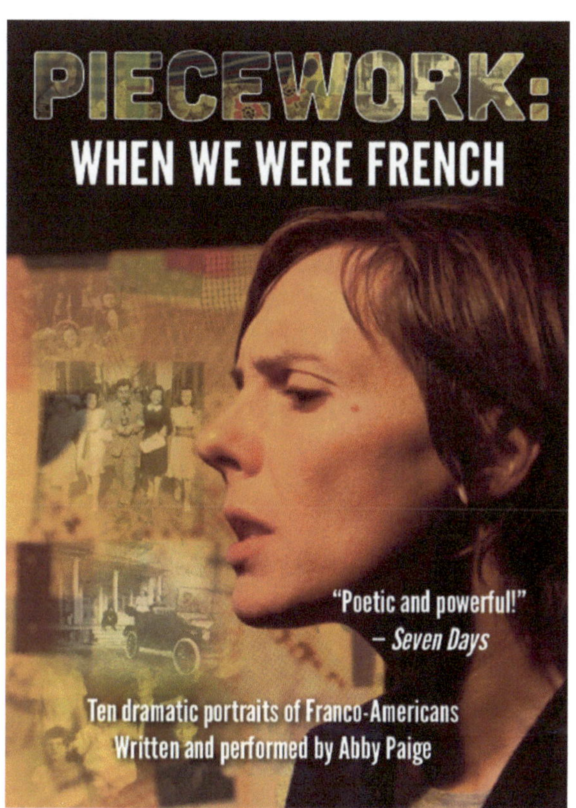

Piecework: When We Were French is the moving and hilarious one-woman show by writer and performer Abby Paige. Based on extensive research and interviews with Franco-Americans, this powerful and delightful performance explores the legacy of more than a century of French-Canadian immigration to New England.

The Red Shirt on the Line

By Amy Bouchard Morin

Photo by Rhea Côté Robbins

My mother was born in 1910 in Lille, Maine. The house where she grew up was a big house that was originally built as a hotel on the river. She told me this story many times and laughed. Now, when you think about how the St. John Valley was settled, with the settlers (sometimes whole families) coming up the river by boat, it is logical that friends or brothers would set up their homesteads across from each other and would cross the river just like we cross the road to visit or help each other. Governments can set up borders all they want, but keeping families and friends apart can be difficult to say the least. Lille is about halfway between Madawaska and Van Buren, the closest large towns on the U.S. side of the St. John River. Directly across the river in Canada the distance to Edmundston and St. Leonard, New Brunswick is the same. This was a long distance to go by horse-drawn wagon or in the winter by horse-drawn sleigh for supplies.

Now, my Uncle Henry ran a general store in Lille, which carried all the things needed for daily living from clothing to needles and thread, hardware, grain for animals, and seeds to plant, etc. The people across the river in Canada figured out in short order that rowing a boat across the river and landing it at Pépère's was a very short walk to Uncle Henry's store. There they could purchase whatever they needed and be home and back at work on their farm in no time at all. This eliminated taking a day off from working the farm. However, there was a little problem that needed to be solved.

Occasionally the border agents would check along the river for illegal crossings. Mémère knew when the agents came to Pépère's and the agents hid in the barn. So, whenever the agents were in the barn, she had a red shirt that she would wet and hang from the clothesline out the upstairs window which faced the river. The Canadians would always check the clothesline, and if there was no red shirt they knew it was safe to land. Mama said that many times when the red shirt was hung out, a boat would be halfway across and they would turn around and go home until the shirt was brought in. The agents never caught anyone crossing the border at Pépère's farm. I can't imagine that today, with our vehicles which cover the miles so quickly, this would work or be necessary, especially since 9/11 and increased border surveillance. But back in the days of horse and buggy, this way of solving a problem worked very well.

Have Guitar, Will Travel

By Josée Vachon

I've made a career in New England by singing in French. Not the plans I had coming out of college, certainly not what I expected while growing up. I've often been asked why I don't offer concerts in English, but something keeps me from going in that direction. I occasionally add a bilingual song, and I certainly converse with the audience in English, but the songs remain in French as a way to maintain their sound, their historical flavor, their cultural identity. As a songwriter, I've written a number of songs that I truly enjoy sharing on stage, yet when I try to translate them, I'm almost embarrassed of how they sound in English. Maybe this is why I prefer hearing my voice in French, the essence of my upbringing, the musicality of the language, the dialect humor that just doesn't translate but rather pulls emotions from some audience members when they realize they "got it."

I've been lucky to do what I love and make a living at it, though my parents were concerned that self-employment would bring no benefits, no steady income. I even sensed at some point they thought college had brainwashed me! A fascination with cultural identity is more philosophical than practical and I can see how they would have wondered what was the attraction. Now, as a mother of two college kids, I see the personal growth and direction they are taking and imagine how my parents could have interpreted changes in me. After the first couple of years, even I wasn't sure I'd pursue this path.

I was born in Lac-Mégantic, Québec, daughter of a Canadian Pacific railroad man, who moved us to Brownville Junction, Maine when I was just turning seven; a sleepy railroad town where Main Street actually ended in Mrs. Ouellette's driveway. The street consisted of a handful of private homes, the railroad station, a small market, the post office, the American Legion Hall and a convenience store with a few rooms above for the out-of-town workers who stayed overnight between shifts. A junction town means you finish your shift there until the next trip. If my father was "called west" on his next shift, we would see him for a day in Lac-Mégantic, but if his next three shifts were east to St. John, New Brunswick, then we could go over a week without seeing him. My mother didn't think it was going to be a permanent move, though they did buy a small house in Maine, on the condition that she would spend her entire summers back in Québec with the children. It was a great arrangement, as my younger brother and I managed to keep speaking French with that kind of environment. In Maine, we spoke daily French at home with our parents, English at school, and then three months of French in the summers with our cousins and friends. Summer daycamp (l'OTJ, Organisation des Terrains de Jeux), which I attended everyday in the summers, helped me be part of the culture, though I would also show off that I knew English by singing something at the weekly talent Fridays so I could win free chocolate milk.

Though his family is Canadian, my father was born in Moosehead, Maine because my grandfather worked there for a couple of years. At the age of two, the family moved back to Lac-Mégantic. Dad grew up speaking only French, yet at eighteen, he was drafted in the US army. He learned English quickly in those few months of basic training! As for my mother, I know moving to deep-woods Maine was a big sacrifice. She had her parents, seven siblings, and her social life in Québec. She loved fashion, music, dancing, taking walks *sur la grand rue* while window shopping and running into townspeople. Brownville was a quiet, little town, she spent her days sewing our clothes, going for walks, visiting the four French-speaking women in town, and occasionally driving an hour to shop in Bangor. It was a difficult move, but she also knew it was the right place to raise her kids if she wanted our father to be a regular part of our lives. It was a loving family upbringing, *functional* as my future bandmates would say, and unique to be raised in two cultures. Mom had to quit school by seventh grade to help raise her siblings and support the family. She often felt insecure about her lack of education and said she was "educated just enough to know I'm not." Yet, I feel that she gave us a precious gift by exposing us to our Québec heritage in such an immersed environment.

I have wonderful memories of my summers in Lac-Mégantic, as well as Christmas *réveillons* and New Year's parties in family homes in Sherbrooke; hanging out at the lake with my cousins, my uncle Simon singing around the campfire with his guitar, which I realize became a big influence for me, as we sang a variety of songs, anything from the 1930s to the 1970s. *Chansons populaires* were a mix of traditional and contemporary songs that most *québécois* would be familiar with culturally. It was the age of *les boîtes à chansons*, coffeehouse venues throughout Québec, where audiences came to hear and sing-along with the singer-songwriters. I was infatuated with everything I heard on the jukebox along with my summer friends. The music group *La Bottine Souriante*, with its infectious *québécois* foot-tapping *chansons à répondre* and fiddle tunes, was actually playing on the radio in the late '70s along with folk musicians and *chansonniers*. As I learned some of their songs on guitar, my grandmother would point out that HER father sang some of those at the turn of the century, so OUR music wasn't that new! It was a time in Québec where pride in our history, language and culture was exploding. My mother was from a family of eight, so get-togethers were always an event. Their sing-alongs could be anything from country songs by Marcel Martel and Le Soldat LeBrun, popular waltzes from French cabarets, to our arrangements of popular radio hits of the '60s and '70s like Mireille Mathieu, Joe Dassin, Georges Moustaki, and, of course, traditional songs from *La Bonne Chanson*, like my grandmother's favorite, *Partons la mer est belle*. At times, I wonder why I can hum a melody that someone might request and realize that the variety I heard growing up is ingrained in my musical memory. Does the same happen to the younger Franco-American generation who grew up hearing their relatives playing fiddle tunes or singing French songs? What melody triggers that memory? How exciting when I see it in someone's face, a smile, a tear, and oftentimes a recurring desire to find out more about their families.

"I was born in Lac-Mégantic, Québec, daughter of a Canadian Pacific railroad man, who moved us to Brownville Junction, Maine when I was just turning seven; a sleepy railroad town where Main Street actually ended in Mrs. Ouellette's driveway. The street consisted of a handful of private homes, the railroad station, a small market, the post office, the American Legion Hall and a convenience store with a few rooms above for the out-of-town workers who stayed overnight between shifts."

Maine was 33% French-Canadian descent in the '70s, but I was not aware of this fact until college. My hometown of Brownville Junction, with a population of 1,200 or so, had only a handful of people who spoke the language, though there were many French-Canadian names around: Nadeau, Ouellette, Badeau, Roussel, Hamel, Lozier, Larrabee, all families there most likely for the same reason we were, though they were already second generation. Mom's closest friend was also from the Beauce region of Québec and an immigrant to Maine like us. When I arrived, the school felt that I should repeat first grade to avoid speaking French with Tina Nadeau, a second-grade classmate whose parents spoke French. So, I got to start first grade all over again, but this time in a foreign language, learning to print even though I had just learned cursive the previous year in Québec, which was taught first in Catholic schools there. That first day of school is so vivid a memory, hearing the Charlie Brown teacher-esque voice in the animation, "*Wwa wwa wwa wwa*?" Terror, until she asked, "*Wwa, wwa, wwa, wwa,* coat*?*" a familiar word! She was probably asking me "*Veux-tu accrocher ton* coat*?*" I made the connection. Then, we were asked to count, or so I assumed, as each child began to count, row by row. When it was my turn, I had only learned to count to five in English, thanks to my dad's advanced preparation (sarcasm) ... I stopped at numeral five and everyone laughed. I remember looking at the teacher and saying in French "*J'peux compter jusqu'à 100, facilement*!", but then, that just made everyone stare.

I do remember beginning to make sense of what was being said around me by about Thanksgiving, a three-month full immersion. The teacher had asked everyone to bring a potato to school as we were going to make little turkeys out of them along with toothpicks and feathers. Of course, I totally missed this request, but the girl behind me brought an extra and gave it to me. I just stared at her, wondering what kind of gift this was... I stuck the potato in the front opening of my desk, but I was unaware that it had rolled out at some point. When the teacher asked everyone to assemble their *turkey parts*, I realized what the gift was for but panicked when I couldn't find it. My teacher put her hand on my shoulder to ask me something and I blurted out "*MY PO-TÉ-TO!!!*"—a first memory of speaking English. By the end of the Christmas holidays, I remember running down the stairs one morning, exclaiming that I had dreamt in English, then telling my friend at school that I received a *bicycle-banana* for Christmas (banana-seat bike). From then on, my memories of elementary school are normal, as things probably became less traumatic for me as I could finally communicate easily and assimilate to everyday life at school.

I think I began to feel at some point in high school that I had a special gift and should use my French positively, that being of another culture could actually be cool. French class was a breeze for me, as I already knew the vocabulary, and I was finally learning basic grammar through French I & II. It was fun to show off in that way, and then do equally well in English class. I was lucky, in that sense, that I didn't get put down for being French, compared to the many stories I've heard from Franco-American colleagues. My English teacher thought it would be interesting for the class to hear a foreign language spoken naturally, so one time he requested that I do my oral book report in French to the class. We were required to keep it at eight minutes, but when I realized I had only filled about five or so and students seemed fascinated to hear me, I quickly filled another two minutes by reciting my prayers in French with continued arm gestures and facial expressions. What I had forgotten was that we had a new student from Canada in the back of the class, and she was dying laughing at the audacity to say whatever came to mind when no one understands anyway! (Yes, I had to explain the tears of laughter from the back of the room, once the students had left.)

"Within a few months, I discovered once again that there were others who spoke French. In one of my classes, a student, Paul Morrow, saw my name on my folder and asked "*Parles-tu français?*" Surprised, I asked if he was also from Québec. "*Non, non. Van Buren.*" From where?"

My junior year of high school, I attended Dirigo Girls State, a weeklong experience for youth to learn about government, sponsored by the American Legion Auxiliary. I had brought my guitar as something personal to relax with at night, and discovered we could audition for the graduation exercises when parents came to pick us up. My roommate encouraged me to do it and I chose a French pop song I had been learning, *Sur la lune, il n'y a pas de roses*. There were girls from all over the state and after the show, I was surprised at how many came to speak to me *in French*, most of them from northern Maine. My senior year, our school was doing a talent show and I decided to repeat the same song and won the award. I think I felt safe performing something I knew no one else would know, and I appreciate the fact that despite not understanding a word, the audience and judges allowed the music to speak.

Despite my father's encouragement to apply for a civil service job at the border, I convinced my parents to send me to college. I would major in education to be a French teacher. I was accepted to our local state school, the University of Maine at Orono. Within a few months, I discovered once again that there were others who spoke French. In one of my classes, a student, Paul Morrow, saw my name on my folder and asked "*Parles-tu français?*" Surprised, I asked if he was also from Québec. "*Non, non. Van Buren.*" From where? He said there were many students on campus like us and that I should visit the Franco-American Office since the director spoke with my accent. Yvon Labbé, who I consider a mentor in developing my career path, turned out to be from the Beauce region of Québec and had also moved to Maine at an early age. I had had no plans on working that first year of college and the next thing I knew, I was typesetting a monthly newspaper called *Le FAROG Forum* (Franco-American Resource Opportunity Group) and beginning to find my identity among other students like myself.

For our office holiday get-together, a friend in my dorm, Mary-Ann Cyr, suggested I bring my guitar to the party. After sharing a few songs from family get-togethers, and some from my favorite Acadian singer at the time,

Angèle Arsenault, I was pleasantly surprised by the reactions. Before I knew it, another student, Anne-Marie Martin, and I were invited to sing on *Reflets et Lumières*, a monthly program on Maine's public television, hosted by Ludger and Steffan Duplessis on French-American life and culture. From there, the Franco-American Office staff found various opportunities for me to perform on campus as well as in the Franco-American communities and schools. One of those opportunities was the Franco-American festival in Lewiston, Maine in 1980. I was scheduled for the noon slot in the food tent. How does one prepare a one-hour show for the first time? I believe I did close to eighteen songs in that hour (the norm is maybe ten today!). I couldn't look at the audience out of fear and had no explanations for any of the songs. "Just sing and get this over with," I thought. But, the audience sang along, seemed interested, encouraging, laughing at the right spots in the humorous songs, shedding some tears on the traditional ballads. I began to relax and then a few came to speak to me after, apologizing that they didn't speak *good French* as well as me, but that it meant the world to them that a young person was singing their language. What did that mean? And why were they apologizing?

I say I've been lucky, but I am also aware that I never turned down opportunities while in and out of college. As a young, fluent performer of my culture, I was requested often as a musical *ambassadrice* for New England's Franco-Americans as part of *La Francophonie*. The early '80s were teaming with pride in hyphenated cultures: in Québec, I performed dozens of times as a Franco-American along with Franco-Ontariens, Franco-Manitobans, Acadians, etc.; as a journalist for a French college paper, I had the honor of meeting René Lévesque, prime minister of Québec, in his office along with other student journalists; when my first LP record came out in 1983, I had a release presentation in Québec City with the *Conseil de la vie française* and other organizations. Again, I know that there was strong support for me to get there from the Franco-American Office. The LP record only happened because at one of these events in Lewiston, Maine, Québec dignitaries were invited, and I performed to welcome them *chez nous*. Paradis Insurance owner, Rita Paradis, came to me after my presentation and offered me an interest-free loan to record! EAB Studios owner, Ed Boucher, was nearby and followed suit with how it could be done easily with studio musicians. Thank goodness for sales a year later, as my first car, a Datsun 310 GX (loved that car!), brought me independence and ease to get to gigs all over New England, but when it broke down, cash sales from the LP would cover repairs, until I finally got a credit card. Sometimes, older people would worry after a show, concerned that I was traveling alone as a young girl. I've always loved being on the road, and I joke around that it's in my blood to be a *voyageur* like Champlain, Cartier, and my railroad family.

Upon returning from a festival in Massachusetts, I began to feel a need to express my own words in song, to entertain to a crowd that was NOT contemporary Québec or Acadie. While driving, I began to hum something that I would have liked to hear at the festival, a type of square-dance called a Paul Jones, that could play with my double identity. Before I knew it, I had an idea for my first original song, *Entre moi* (Between Me & Myself), which seemed to truly *click* with Franco-Americans everywhere. I recorded it in 1985 and eventually recorded it live with *Chanterelle* on a Smithsonian Folkways CD.

In 1987, I was invited to host a cable TV show out of Manchester, New Hampshire, the center of New England's French communities, as some would say. *Association Canado-Américaine*, a fraternal insurance company, also provided community events, so the local cable station approached them to produce a weekly show in French. The producer, Paul Paré, chose a variety-style format, as I could provide one or two songs every show and we could have two to three guests from all over New England. My husband and I lived in Amherst, Massachusetts, and not having kids yet meant I was fairly flexible to travel there regularly. I accepted to try, as I thought it would be good exposure and experience. I also thought local cable shows last a year or two at the most (we went for eleven seasons, over five-hundred shows). We called the show *Bonjour!* so that people would know it was French when looking at the TV listings. The preparation to find French-speaking guests was shared among Paul, a couple of staff members, and myself. Some people have a knack for interviewing. I didn't realize this would be so hard until the first interview. It happened to be someone who was leaving her post and not happy about it. I naively thought I would just ask each question down the list on my notebook after she answered me, but I quickly learned the need to LISTEN! When I asked my second question, she abruptly answered "I just told you that." I'm sure I blushed, but to make it less of an embarrassing moment, I recovered by asking if she could provide more details (this could have made it worse, but somehow it worked and she went on with further explanation). Lessons learned the hard way are the best. The next interviews, I prepared with only *teaser* notes so that I could actually pay attention to the guest. It was a trying experience for me, and I don't believe I was ever a natural interviewer, but I certainly met some interesting folks and developed better listening skills. Some of the highlights of guests we had were Marcel Marceau (yes, he actually spoke; we couldn't stop him from sharing the history of mime); Céline Dion, interviewed by my co-host Carole Auger; plus over five-hundred community leaders, teachers, clergy, writers, artists, business people, and foreign French-speaking visitors. If we saw an interesting article in the paper and they had a French surname, we contacted them. Probably my favorite interview of all was with Viola Leger, the Acadian actress who played *La Sagouine*, a character written by Antonine Maillet. I found her by accident as I was performing in Fitchburg, Massachusetts at the public library auditorium one afternoon. While singing, I scanned the audience and thought I recognized her. "Impossible," I thought, "she's from New Brunswick." At intermission they announced that a special guest was here visiting her mother! She then gave a ten-minute special presentation and I jumped at the chance to invite her to *Bonjour*! A spritely, petite woman with a twinkle in the eye, she was probably the easiest and most fascinating interview for me as I discovered that I had forgotten to look at my questions and just simply had a conversation with her on camera.

The show had tremendous interest and was picked up by local cable stations throughout New England, Louisiana, Québec and New Brunswick. Maine and Rhode Island picked it up on their public television networks and we eventually reached over three million homes. I know I was tremendously lucky to be asked to host this show as it opened many doors and opportunities in the future, the first of which was an invitation from Paris, France to represent *speakerines (television hostesses)* from around the world (we were from forty-two French-speaking countries) and again a year later to perform one of my original songs, *N'oublie pas* on *Le grand échiquier*, a three-hour talk/variety show which was seen all over Europe. The show's theme that week was Francophone cultures from around the world. Some of the guests were people I had long admired: singer-poet, Gilles Vigneault, whose songs evoke the richness of Québec's heritage and culture; France's singer-songwriter, Yves Duteil, who had written a song, *La langue de chez nous*, about the French language! How many cultures actually dedicate songs to a language? The host of the show thought my song would sound great with a string quartet, so a Romanian French-speaking quartet backed me up in front of the cameras, and my thoughts while singing and trying to smile were, "I can't believe I'm here all the way from Brownville Junction, Maine." Most of the show is a blur, but my husband's family, who lived in Spain as well as Geneva, Switzerland, immediately called my husband in Massachusetts to announce they had seen me on France TV! A highlight of my career.

In 1993, one of my guests on *Bonjour!* was a fiddler from Amherst, Massachusetts, who had been recommended for her French-Canadian fiddle style. Donna Hébert was surprised to hear from me, as she had often seen my name in the local paper and thought I was a Spanish man. Of course, she wanted to come on the show, but she didn't speak French. No problem, I'd give her the translated answers ahead of time to practice and then she could let her fiddle speak French! A month later, I had a local gig in a western Massachusetts coffeehouse and worried there would be no French audiences. I called Donna and asked if she'd like to share the stage with me for the show, and, in turn, she invited guitarist Liza Constable to accompany her. Donna said she knew one song in French, if I'd let her try it. The three of us sat down and came up with a hauntingly beautiful three-part harmony to *Un Canadien errant*. We eventually went on to record it on our first CD, *French in America*. I longed to harmonize and try something new, Donna longed to find her Franco-American roots, and that night, *Chanterelle* was born. It was a surprising match as we were three such different personalities and vocal styles, but it worked and offered us a broader audience at folk festivals around the Northeast as well as Ontario, Montreal, and back to France. An all-girl band from New England, doing traditional French songs and tunes was probably a first, and we appreciated the reaction from the audiences and got to share the stage with "stars" from Québec's traditional music world. We also toured two weeks in schools and colleges with Québec stepdancer, Benoît Bourque, and I met a new friend in Vermont through the process.

Vermont Franco-American singer and activist, Martha Pellerin, strongly believed that you could be a proud Franco-American without possessing the language, and it was a great loss to all when she passed away from a terrible cancer in 1998 at the young age of thirty-six. That spring, her family and I were invited to spend a week performing in French Institute schools throughout Berlin, Germany. Honestly, the trip didn't seem like it really would happen since we barely had any follow-up communication, and as the date approached, our plane tickets still had not arrived. We finally received our tickets the day before departure along with our itinerary. Upon arriving at JFK airport we, of course, got in the wrong terminal and though we had allowed a good two hours before flying, we still found ourselves running frantically to the right place, while carrying instruments, luggage, and one-hundred spoons; yes, Martha wasn't sure we could be guaranteed the schools would provide this, so you can imagine security check.

Officer: "Spoons? May I ask why you are carrying that many?"

Us: "To teach the German kids how to play them."

Officer: "Really; may I get a demonstration?"

Me: "Of course,"

And proceeded to give him a quick display of our artistic abilities!

Oh, Martha, how I miss you. What a hilarious sight we must have been to Berlin's passersby as we got off subways, carrying guitars, mandolin, accordion and a suitcase of spoons. This was only a couple of years after the Wall had come down so the entire city was covered in construction cranes. It was difficult to find English speakers unless we went into a bank or hotel lobby, and I still don't know how we found each school on our own with only the street addresses and a subway map. Every school welcomed us and the kids participated as hoped. Martha loved sharing her culture primarily through traditional songs and stories. After our fourth song, the one-hundred spoons came out and I knew Martha had been right to bring them. But after thirty minutes of tradition, I felt we were losing their attention, and I suggested we try a blues song I do in schools in New England. It worked like magic, added another dimension to the show, and I got to hear Martha's husband, John, jam out on guitar.

I wrote *Les non non Blues* when my son was about four. The members of *Chanterelle* occasionally teased me about being too "happy" to perform the blues—that my voice wasn't made for the genre. Challenge accepted, but they would be my child's blues. It was great fun to write in just under an hour, as if the words had always been there, waiting to come out. I heard my mother in the humorous negative responses to the child asking "Can I stay up late?" "Can I watch TV all day?" "Can I keep this frog I found outside?" etc. The chorus, a plea to *Papa* to help him convince *Maman*, turned out to be a great response chorus and one of my favorites to perform in schools. The first time I tried it live in concert was at West Point Military Academy. Slightly intimidated by the auditorium filled with men in uniform, and maybe two or three female cadets, I suddenly felt like my repertoire was all wrong for the crowd, even though they were all there to hear French. "*Come on, Josée, don't let them see you doubt yourself, let them be silly along with you*." And that's just what happened. I encouraged them to do a falsetto "*OUI!*" at the last questions in the song, and four hundred men, in uniform, complied! Aah, the power of being on stage.

I've played hundreds of shows, from school assemblies to festivals, college concerts, folk and Franco-American festivals, and lots of church halls—the one place where people come out of the woodwork, a safe haven for hearing our music, sharing our stories; and these are the audiences that bring out the best humor in me. I'm always surprised at how fun it is to play WITH the audience rather than perform TO them. In the last few years, I've found myself allowing the audience to create my second set with their requests, peppering the too-often hailed nostalgic ballads with a bit of rhythmic sing-alongs to keep things entertaining. There is never an identical concert for me: the audiences vary too much and I find myself choosing whether it will be a semi-educational show about my culture, a non-Franco-American audience in which I focus on favorite poetic melodies, or else a set of toe-tapping, sing-alongs because sometimes people come to recreate what they expect from their memories. I also notice that each Franco-American community around New England has its nuances. From northern Maine to Bristol, Connecticut to Woonsocket, Rhode Island, I see and hear subtleties. New artists like Daniel Boucher from Connecticut are carrying on the language and pride through French community events and it's exciting to see *la relève*!

Renowned Acadian writer Antonine Maillet once said: "*On est pas fort, mais on est pas mort!*" (We're not very strong, but we're not dead yet!). It inspired me to write *On est toujours là* (We're still here) at the time I heard her speak in Maine. The song was meant to evoke the fact that we carry our heritage at all times, that *joie de vivre* is part of our make-up, that the next generation of Franco-Americans may have lost the language but express themselves through their music and images, even though Maillet was convinced a culture dies with its language. My children know that language to me was a large part of my life, and my oldest, upon finishing college, decided to go to Laval University for a six-week immersion in French, just to have a better handle on the gift I tried to pass on to him, like my mother did.

“L’été en Noir” (Summer in Black)

“L’été en Noir” (Summer in Black)
Gloria Goguen Sears
Colored pencil
Cranson Edition black paper
22”x 25”

My artistic process begins in natural settings. I sketch, photograph, and research subjects that inspire me to have a deeper connection with my spirituality.

I was influenced for this work by two Flemish painters working collaboratively. One, secularist, painted religious themes. The other a Jesuit, painted botanical images from the monastery garden. Together they created spiritual works framed in themes of nature.

I have combined images from nature with ancient symbols of French heritage for this work. The fleur de lis as a symbol of belonging to France. A crown symbolizes France’s evolution to the reign of King Louis. Finally, Emperor Napoleon’s golden bee that depicts immortality and the resiliency of the French people.

—**Gloria Goguen Sears**.

Nature/Seasons/*Saisons*

Angrec—Royauté
Angrec—Royalty

Frêne blanc/Frêne élevé—Solidité, immortalité
Ash Tree—Grandeur, greatness

Trèfle d'eau/Menyauthe/herbe à canards—Silence; calme repos
Buckbean, Bogbean, Menyanthes—Quiet; calm repose

Tulipe, jaune—Amour désespéré, inquiétude
Tulip, yellow—Hopeless love, declaration of love

Aigremoine—Gratitude, reconnaissance
Agrimony—Thankfulness, gratitude

Épine noire, Mère-du-bois, Pelossier ou Prunellier commun—Décision à prendre, nouvelle venue de loin, nouvel éveil. Printemps, pureté, univers, renaissance et immortalité; associé au soufre
Blackthorn—Difficulty, preparation, reward and punishment, weakness and strength, and bounty and destruction. Esoterically known as both the Mother of the Woods and the Dark Crone of the Woods and depicted in many fairy tales throughout Europe as a tree of ill omen.

Les feuilles

J'ai vu dans une feuille tombante
une vie. À un oiseau passant j'ai demandé :
« Est-ce la mienne ? »
Mais je ne parle plus le langage des oiseaux ;
c'est à peine que je m'arrête pour les écouter chanter.

Quand j'étais petite, j'ai écrit un poème.
Il y avait des arbres,
des arbres et leurs feuilles.
Ils se disaient adieu sous un ciel bleu clair d'automne.

En octobre, ma mère raclera les feuilles,
fera d'un tapis rouge, jaune et orange
une montagne pour ses petits enfants.
Elle est vieille maintenant et ça la fatigue,
mais elle aime regarder les enfants jouer.
C'est bien ça que les enfants doivent faire :
jouer.

Par Adèle Saint-Pierre

L'Eau de Pâques—an old Easter ritual

Draw spring water at Sunrise. Drink it before Sunset.

Let's resurrect the ritual as we celebrate this year.
When first rays touch the hidden spring, we'll fill our waiting jugs.
Before we dine, let's drink the health of our close kin and friends.
Some will take the water neat—others with whiskey or wine.
Joyfully raising our glasses, we'll drink to "Santé et longue vie."
Next, we'll savor the lavish feast as the rite embraces us all.
At day's end, after coffee and red velvet cake,
let's pause before saying goodbye.
Then, while the sun still lingers, we shall toast its fading light.

By Margaret S. Langford

"Field of Sunflowers"

Encaustic painting entitled "Field of Sunflowers" (20" x 24") is painted in multiple layers of tinted wax medium with imbedded plant material and sand from Maine. It exhibits the beauty and yet the hard work that goes into farming. Maine's fields are very rocky, therefore before planting, stones need to be removed resulting in many beautiful stone walls. The working barns and farmhouses also inspired work and utilitarian beauty at the same time. Sunflowers were never part of plantings, since all our fields were needed for food growing. Food that would be distributed to the needy by the city or used in the farm's dining room.

Artist Statement

Although traditional and studied in origin in oil, acrylic and encaustic, Gloria's still lifes usually have a playful and adventurous aspect to them. Along with her architectural landscapes, they are enjoyable to look at sometimes causing a search for "the story behind" the painting. Boldness is added with color, lighting and often texture to these paintings as well as her figural paintings thus creating warmth and interest. Gloria has also worked in steel, stone and wood to create sculpture. She has studied at Maine School of Art in Portland and the University of Maine in Augusta. Her works have been included in juried exhibits at the University of Southern Maine/ Lewiston-Auburn and by the Maine Arts Commission and shown at the Lewiston hospitals and gallery. Several of her large religious environmental works can be fount. at St. Philip's Church in Auburn, Maine.

—Gloria B. Limoges

Breath of a Raven

light as quicksilver
a puff of life

and on the wing
unnoticed
as fog dissolves
before the dawn

she leaves her
secret nesting place
in search of daily sustenance

snaring, carrying to her young
undeterred by weather's worst

with her wisest eye
she watches us
come and go in time

we forget her
but she remembers

her steamy mist
goes deep
into the throats
of her fledglings

after all
breath is life
first and last

betheny chambers anderson
trudy chambers price

Untitled

Stones in the briny waters,
what made you so smooth?

No cracks or ridges
like most earthly stones.

What has the ocean done to you?
You haven't any character—

no personality left.
How could you let this happen to you?

Have you been so beaten & tossed
by these monstrous waves,

like so many of the same?
No fight, no hope—

rumbled and tumbled
for many years,

you've become identical
to all of your peers.

As I pick through the millions of you,
there, now in my pocket, are the most beautiful stones.

One shaped as a heart,
another so smooth.

Who was I to be such a judge
of a beautiful stone as you?

By Nanci Breau

Winter's End

The cold, unmerciful storm is over. Though I am still mindful of the frigid sting buried deep in my soul, I thrust forward now, with every step being easier than the one before.

Within me, the icy barriers are at last slowly melting, leaving only brown, gritty dirt. But the messy sediment feeds nature's new life.

I feel my body erupting like the buds of spring. Like the buds, I am shrugging the dirt from my being, so that I can someday shine in my own beauty again.

By Nanci Breau

Solo, on the Beach

A long gull stands near the frigid waters of Popham beach. Sometimes on one leg to warm the other. Three women head towards the bird and she walks away with an air of intrusion.

She doesn't have to be alone—she chooses to. She plays at the water's edge with the waves taunting her. The relentless briny water is trying to swallow her. It doesn't matter who the champion will be, for there is no Olympic medal. She is just enjoying the day, her life. She stands fixed, only her feathers moving because of the mighty wind, for a seemingly endless period of time.

"Come briny waters, come and catch me!" she seems to be saying.

A couple approaches from around the bend, clasping a camera, ready to take a candid photograph capturing her playfulness, disturbing her peacefulness. Accosting her, she dashes into the water. The waves roar with success.

The clouds are rolling in, hiding the warmth of the sun I was so enjoying. The bird flies away, only to quickly return, as if she felt my disappointment. Landing directly in front of me, gazing at me, as if asking, "Are you also solo?"

I look at the seagull and think to myself, "Solitude is my comfort."

I lay back on my blanket, the sound of the waves are beating the shore with anger, wanting the bird back. Mother moon is calling the tide. The waves retreat.

I rest my eyes and fall asleep, alone but not lonely.

By Nanci Breau

Heavenly Bodies

At first light, the lake is still. The fog lifts slowly. The sun shines through and the beauty reveals itself. The lake reflects the charm of the land that caresses it. The trees stand tall, so proud of the reflection they see beneath them.

Meanwhile, beyond the mountains, the untamed ocean is magnificent in grandeur. The deep blue has no boundaries until it kisses the heavens. Waves roar with determination to move back the rocks that hold the savage water at bay, succeeding only after endless time to wear the sharp edges off their faces. Such a powerful rush of water to become just a slip of white foam.

The lake, on the other hand, no need to prove anything, gently pushes its waves to the shore with no more than a sigh. A loon takes flight, mirrored by the tranquil waters. It descends with such grace, wanting to be left alone for a quiet swim. Its blissful song is echoed for all of nature to hear.

The music of the open sea is the Creator's symphony. The pounding surf vibrates every bone in the human body. Then, suddenly, there is a nearly quiet stillness, while the breeze carries the sea ducks' chorus. The ducks are always in flocks, seeming to know that in these wild waters it is safer to swim in numbers. They are steadily swayed back and forth and lulled to sleep by Mother Nature.

Each breath of the lake tells of its life, sometimes with a refreshing scent, and sometimes with the odor of dead fish or of weeds ripped from their source of life.

In contrast to the lake, the ocean washes its shores twice a day and smells of brine. The water, over-salted by the Master Chef, reeks in the air. It is so prevalent one might feel as if they were seasoned and ready to be served.

Nights on the lake are truly a gift from above, warm and without enough breeze to muss a person's hair. The pesky mosquitoes dance with a right-to-bite attitude, teasing every ear with their buzzing wings. Humans always join in the dance of the mosquito with sounds of slapping hands. A full moon's glorious light shines on a canoe ride in the still of the night. The frog's mating calls are heard in stereo. Fish leap for a late night snack, leaving rings on the skin of the water. Surely, this must be a taste of heaven.

A different taste of heaven comes to the seashore in the deep night, where the fresh smell of salty air rolls in from the sea. A playful moon shines on the surf. The water now has a rich blue tone that no crayon can replicate. The sound of soft waves fills the spirit with serenity. The white foam, colored by the light of the moon, is now a fluorescent froth.

The lake and the ocean, both are surely connected to the heavens. See the moon? It has painted a road over both bodies of water as they lead to the starry paradise.

By Nanci Breau

Yellow butterfly: This photo was taken on vacation in Charleston, South Carolina on one of my many walks.

Macro Photography of Nature

by Sherri Levesque Grant

Humming Bird:
On the feeder in my backyard. This photo is zoomed 10Xs and I was only eight feet away. Look at it's tongue sticking out!

Female Cardinal: Cardinals are somewhat difficult to photograph and more so the female. She was worried about her lost baby and gave me many opportunities to photo her. She seems to be listening.

Grasshopper: Photo taken in my backyard and is a Marco. Notice the fine hairs on it's legs.

Incongruity

By Sherry Pineau Brown

It stood slowly, taking in breath. Small water bubbles formed at its flaring nostrils. Not its, *his*. This was a bull, a small bull, but the large swaying testicles defined the bull's status just the same.

A blue burst from an amateur fireworks display across the river lit up the night sky behind him. The burst sat between the joint of trees that edged the slow moving river of our lower pasture and outlined the turning metal paddles of the windmill on the near side of the bank. The windmill hasn't pumped water in years, its turning more futile than hopeful.

"After I hit him, he bounced, twice I think, across the road." The driver of the small SUV was shaken, but not as much as one would expect after having hit a two-thousand pound mass of pure muscle. "Do you think it belongs to that yellow farm?"

This was the same question I asked myself when an hour earlier a young couple knocked on the wrong front door of our hundred-year-old farmhouse to tell me that a cow was in the middle of the road. I grabbed a flashlight to search for it in the dark. It was the same question that I asked myself when, after I returned from the pointless search, I later heard the sickening smack from the SUV. If I substituted the "it" of his question with "I," it was the same question I had been asking since I moved into this place.

Do you think I belong to that yellow farm?

Our bedroom walls are not finished. They haven't been for about a month now since my husband stripped off the hideous purple-and-green-flowered wallpaper that we have slept beneath since we moved here. It has been three weeks since I spent most of the entirety of a day trying to cover the resulting horsehair plaster with joint compound. The walls sit in limbo, half of them covered with a single layer, half of them still rough with the coarse hairs. Each wall will need at least one more coat of compound. Each wall will need to be sanded. Each wall will need to be painted. My daily mantra is that I will work on the walls tomorrow.

Tomorrow has not come.

We told ourselves when we moved into this house, my husband's family farm, that we would refinish a room a year. I think I will be fifty before we finish. I am forty-one now.

We started small: the nursery, the upstairs hallway, the downstairs bathroom. The first was a priority, as a month after we moved in, I was to give birth to our first and only child; the latter, because the white seashells stenciled on cornflower blue horrified me. I wanted a rich purple. As my husband holds a deep hatred for powerful colors, we settled on a pastel lilac. The bathroom now looks like Barney the cartoon dinosaur exploded all over the walls. The stenciling, however, is gone. I put up a green shower curtain to offset the purple.

Progress.

"We have to keep at least part of the kitchen wallpapered," my husband told me. "It's tradition."

My mother-in-law taught me how to install the wallpaper by putting it up herself. I did not complain. Just as I did not complain when I found a quilted Jack-O-Lantern tablecloth on our coffee table in October, or when I came home to its replacement in November—a similar quilted piece covered in turkeys. I also did not mention the white lace doilies I found intermittently placed under photos in the dining room. I smiled at the quiet rebellion of my choice of kitchen wallpaper—a warm yellow accented with small fleur-de-lis. The fleur-de-lis, to me, is a symbol of the French, of those who came down from Quebec to work in the mills, those who my husband calls *(*in jest, *of course,* honey*)* "dirty Frenchmen."

"But you are not one of them," he tells me, "not *really*."

Even though I had two *mémères* and two *pépères* and grew up in a family full of Pineaus, Ouellettes, and Fourniers. Even though every Sunday I genuflected, Hail-Maryed, signed-the-cross, and on Christmas Eve ate *toutière* pie after Midnight Mass. Even though I tell my daughter to "close the lights" and still ask those around me to pardon my foibles when I do something backwards because I am, after all, *French*.

My husband's grandfather, I am told, wore orange every St. Patrick's Day. Orange. The color of the Protestants. The color of the English. He would never let his daughters date any of those goddamn Canucks and was probably "rolling in his grave" to know that his grandson married one of *those people*. I make it a point to wear some sort of green on St. Paddy's Day. Even though the Irish and the French fought in the mills, I tell myself it was the fight of siblings, of those who were allowed to fight with each other because they understood in a place inside themselves what it meant not to fit.

My husband and I fought over the color of the back kitchen wall, which I was thankfully allowed to paint. We decided on yellow, but my choice of a soft, warm version of the color lost to one paler.

I returned to the bathroom and switched out the green shower curtain for a dark purple one with a fleur-de-lis pattern.

Small victories.

The bull shifted its weight from one leg to another. I found nothing familiar about the creature but its gaze. Its dark chocolate coloring, the white spots along its belly, its smaller stature—I had never seen this animal before; I was sure of it. It was not one of our forty or so cows and calves that parade out to graze intermittently throughout a day. It was not one of the four heifers that I fed in the barn while my husband was away, nor was it one of the seven steers that had been sent up to the woods to another pasture. "This is not our bull." I felt a rush of relief. "This is not our bull," I repeated, this time a bit louder.

A crowd had gathered, made up of a group of intoxicated twenty-somethings returning home from a party across the river; the driver who hit the bull was forced to wait for the police and a tow truck, and my sister who lived next door in a trailer owned by my in-laws. My sister had answered my frantic call for help earlier in the evening when I told her about the couple who stopped by about the loose cow. She sent me home to take care of my daughter while she drove the road twice. *"There's no cow,"* she told me with an air of smugness. *"Those people have no idea what they are talking about."*

The bull shifted its weight from one leg to another. I found nothing familiar about the creature but its gaze. Its dark chocolate coloring, the white spots along its belly, its smaller stature – I had never seen this animal before; I was sure of it.

As we all stood staring at the bull, the youngest of the twenty-somethings asked the inevitable, "Well, whose could it be?"

I shrugged. Even though I have lived on the farm for almost five years, I barely know anyone in town. My father-in-law, Mark, a town selectman for decades, talked about each individual resident as though he knew them on an intimate level. There were the Kents and the Shores, the Veilleuxs and the Lawrences, the Richards, and of course, the Browns. My husband Xandy, who grew up on the farm, is enamored with the local old-timers. More than once, while I sat braless drinking a cup of coffee, an ancient farmer wearing Dickies and a John Deere hat knocked on our door at 6:30 a.m. to talk to Xandy about "fahm business." I keep reminding myself to put a bra on before I go downstairs, but it still rarely happens.

"Maybe it's Mert Richards' from up the road," one of the bleary-eyed partiers piped in from the back of the crowd. "I can go check if you want."

"Are you sure?" My sister added, "he lives like three miles away." My sister had lived in town for only a couple of years and had already developed a better working knowledge of the who's who of Benton, Maine, than I would ever hope to have.

"I'll go check."

We all looked back at the wounded beast. He returned the gaze.

The burst of green with accompanying thunder behind him did not cause him to even flinch.

"Should we get water for it or something? He looks like he's in shock." The "poor thing" tone of a young partier beside me caused me to brush off my embarrassment for not thinking of that sooner, and go to our barn for water and grain.

A nagging feeling of uncertainty followed close behind.

Long Meadows Farm has been in my husband's family for four generations. His great-grandfather, Charles Orman Brown (known to his friends as Orm), a machinist by trade, bought the 200-acre property during the 1930s on back taxes. By the 1940s, Orm milked Golden Guernsey cows and hired a man whose sole job it was to pump water for the herd twelve hours a day, seven days a week. Later his son Bob, a foreman at the local paper mill and a state legislator, turned to shorthorn cattle which are used for both beef and milk. Bob always said that his best day on the farm was the day that they got rid of those Guernseys. Along with working off the farm full-time, Bob built sleighs and wagons, bought and sold horses, and let the public visit the farm that his wife refused to let him live on. In the early 1970s, Bob's son Mark moved to the farm with his young wife Connie. Along with their four children, they raised chickens and beef while Mark spent his working hours in the same mill that Bob retired from. Mark spent his free summer time haying the fields that had prompted Orm to change the name from the "Colcord Farmstead" to "Long Meadows Farm." When Mark no longer made paper plates for the mill and Connie could no longer handle the hay chaff and manure, they relocated to the coast where the only critters they have to feed are Connie's cat and Mark's chocolate lab. Now Mark's son Xandy is the Farmer Brown on the property. He, like those before him, runs a "hobby farm." He spends his days behind a computer to support his farming habit—a habit that more closely resembles the strongest form of addiction.

I placed the buckets of water and grain in front of the bull, and he immediately took two steps back. My own pulse quickened as I wondered how smart it was to be advancing on a wounded animal, and a bull at that.

I retreated, slowly.

"Whose farm is this?" By this time, a State Trooper had arrived, and stood with an *I am here to assess the situation* air.

"Mine." The word felt thick on my tongue.

"Is this your property as well?" It took a moment for me to realize that he meant the bull.

"This is not our bull." I was almost screaming now.

"Any idea whose property it is?" He made a small gesture toward the bull but kept his eyes on me.

"Someone is checking with one of the farmers up the road."

The trooper, satisfied, waved over the driver of the SUV for his statement.

I stared into the bull's eyes trying to determine what I saw there. Was it fear? Was it denial? Or was it merely the realization that he did not belong here.

Three white bursts went off in the distance.

I did not grow up on a farm.

I grew up in a small, single-wide trailer with a half-acre of land. The only manure on our property was our own. The septic system had been failing for years, causing a permanent swath of grass to grow from the human sludge that seeped to the surface. Whenever our dog, a collie-mix, escaped from captivity she ran directly through the middle and tracked the smelly brown muck onto our pink shag carpeting. The closest we came to farming was when she ran next door and killed the neighbor's prize-winning hens. My mother had to go to court and pay a hefty fine for the birds which she referred to as the "most expensive damn chickens" in the state.

I have had my own dog, a Norwegian Elkhound, since she was six-weeks old. She has accompanied me everywhere—in tents in the Colorado Rockies, in questionable motel rooms across the country, on trails along the rocky coast and in the dense wilderness. People here do not know what to make of her. They call her a husky or a shepherd; some even say she must have a bit of wolf in her.

Before we moved to the farm, we worried that her hunting instincts would cause her to chase after the cattle so Xandy and I brought her for a visit to see how she would acclimate. We were right about the instincts, just not the animal choice. My in-laws owned six Rhode Island Red hens that grazed freely on the property. As we all sat on the front porch chatting and rocking, we watched agape as she chased a bird, caught it, and de-feathered it as though she was preparing it for a chicken fry. With each pendulum swing of her head feathers flew and the chicken made a sound not unlike that of a squeaky chew toy. We were finally able to loosen the bird from her grip, and it miraculously limped away. Not so miraculous, I suppose, when a day later I learned the hen had crawled off to her death. Its final resting place: the manure pit. The dog ended her trial visit that night by finding a pile of fresh green cow manure and taking a swim.

What's that old cliché about dogs and their owners?

Red dripped from the bull's nose as he shifted his weight from one side to the next. He turned to expose crimson grill marks imprinted on his chest. The thick air surrounding him smelled of sweet, wet grass tinged with the metallic scent of blood. I stepped back out of the sphere of the smell and breathed in the cool June air.

Mert Richards showed up at just about the same time that the neighboring town's fire truck rolled in. I wondered aloud why the hell we needed a fire truck; there was no fire. The truck stopped, and its helmeted passenger jumped out and began to walk the road and kick shards of plastic and glass off to the side. The driver who had remained in the truck turned the key. The engine spurted and groaned, and refused to turn over.

A white car drove slowly by me with its passenger hanging out the window, holding her cell phone at arm's length. *Smile pretty for Facebook.*

Another color burst went off in the distance.

The fire truck groaned again.

"Is this your property?" The trooper's voice brought me out of the comedy of errors. He remained in his car and looked up at Richards who stood open-mouthed, dumbfounded by the scene. Richards scratched his forehead under the ball cap that sat bill skyward on his head.

"Ayuh, I'll take responsibility for it." Richards pulled out his phone and dialed. *"We found him. He's out heah in front of Mahk Brown's farm. Do you want me to kill the bastahd?"*

"Wait, wait, wait. I thought you said this was your property. Is this your property or not?" The trooper looked up from the cruiser and tried to sound intimidating with his voice rather than his presence as his smooth face revealed his youth and inexperience.

Richards stumbled over his explanation. I pieced together that he had rented the bull to service his cows, and it had escaped. He had not seen it since Tuesday.

It was Saturday.

The bull swayed, and his hind legs drew closer together. Four days. He had been gone four days. To get to this place he would have had to pass by our entire herd of cows, some of whom were ready to be bred. And yet, he didn't stop. The herd's silence didn't let on that they even knew he was there.

"Do you think he's from that farm?" The voice came from over my left shoulder, and I saw a thin arm point towards my house. Its owner was a gaunt-looking man with only a few front teeth. I looked at my sister, who later termed the man a "Looky Lou," and told her that I should check our fence to be sure that no damage was done to it when the bull bounced. I heard myself say something about how our herd may get out.

This was not even partially true.

I needed my own escape.

With my husband out of town, the farm chores were left to me. "You shouldn't have to worry about the majority of the herd," he had told me. "They are on pasture and should be fine. I'll leave the vet number in case one gives birth early."

"When are the rest due?"

"Next week."

"Because, of course, cows never give birth early."

"Of course."

Morning and night I needed to water everything. Give hay and grain to the sheep. Hay to the heifers in the barn. Milk replacer for the two calves on the barn floor. Grain for the chickens. A scoop of food for the two feral cats. Morning and night.

The first night I "fed things" (my husband's term) as fast as I could. How could Xandy take so long doing this? From start to finish the entire process only took twenty minutes. This would be easy, as long as nothing gave birth. As long as nothing escaped.

The next morning I picked up a few of the hens. I had always been afraid of chickens, their beaks most specifically, but for some reason these did not frighten me. I picked up one squawking bird at a time and stroked her feathers until she calmed. The feathers were smooth, almost oily, and I was surprised that none of the birds tried to peck me.

That evening I spent a little longer with the sheep. My daughter loved to stay in the stall with them, petting them as they ate. I sat and watched her for a while, then talked to the calves as I fed them. "How are you guys doing this fine evening? Hungry?" One advanced on my crotch thinking I was her mother, and I put a knee up as I had been taught to avert the attempted latching. I stroked their heads as they sopped up all of their meal, which smelled like the Ovaltine my Mémère used to give us as a treat on our visits. One of the calves started to suck on the ear of the other treating her companion as a pacifier.

Somehow, I ended up spending over an hour in the barn.

The fence was, of course, untouched. I turned to walk back towards the crowd. My sister met me before I reached the bull, pleading with me to "turn around, turn around, turn around," and I looked past to see the trooper had finally exited his car and was approaching the bull.

"He's going to shoot it. Turn around," she said again. "You don't want to see this."

I instinctively did as she asked, but something within me protested. I needed to see *this*. *This* is what life on the farm meant, and I was frightened by the possibility of what my being unable to witness *this* might actually mean.

A successive burst of colors lit up the night sky behind us—white, blue, green, red, short thunder clap after short thunder clap – the finale of the display.

I turned back towards the bull, but just missed the much louder clap of thunder beside us. The trooper stood, rifle in hand, surrounded by a small puff of white smoke. Mert Richards stood beside him, his mouth yet to close.

The bull fell away from them. All four of his legs reached up into the sky, and his body twitched and convulsed. The legs kicked for what seemed like minutes, and I wondered if he would need to be shot again as this was probably the first time that this young trooper had ever fired his weapon. I questioned his accuracy. I thought of chickens running around in a frantic death dance after they lost their heads.

The convulsions stopped, and everything, for a moment, was silent.

If this were the movies the farmer and trooper would walk over and kick the bull, and the thing would jump up and charge them. I imagined their cartoon-like run into the darkness, their legs bow-legged, a blur of motion like the Road Runner's, the bull close behind jockeying his head up and down.

This was not a movie.

"Well, I guess that's it," the Looky Lou beside us said and walked back to his car. No more suffering to witness, I suppose. One by one, each of the remaining vehicles and bystanders departed. The partiers returned home to continue their party. A tow truck came for the SUV. The fire engine started and rolled back toward town. My sister continued home after our short walk to the farmhouse.

Even though it was late and my daughter would be up early, I poured a glass of wine and sat on our front porch to observe the denouement. An enormous front end loader rumbled through the darkness and stopped to position itself. Mert Richards pulled a set of chains from the bucket and wrapped one end on the loader and the other around the bull. The loader pulled back, dragged the lifeless carcass into the middle of the road, dropped its bucket, and scooped up the bull. Richards jumped in with the bull to be sure the animal was secured. Once satisfied, he leapt out and waved the machine off. It pulled into our driveway, turned, and disappeared back into black.

I finished my glass of wine, and went to bed as morning would come soon, and there were things to be fed.

The latest room to be refinished is actually the second incarnation of the space since we have lived here. After a bit of coercion, I moved my daughter from the nursery into the room my husband grew up in. I covered the nursery's walls with a dark cranberry and filled a small bookshelf with books that my husband hates. I put a two-person table, from a previous life, in the corner and set up my laptop facing the window, my back to the door. I have a perfect view of the windmill and the river, and I stop writing periodically to watch a canoe pass under the joint of trees on the far bank. I keep the door closed and root down, allowing myself a few more sentences before the opening's inevitability.

LE RUISSEAU

Au bord du ruisseau
On se penche
À la recherche du soleil égaré,
Au royaume des poissons
Où règne
La fraîcheur de la terre mouillée.

Sous les arbres encombrants
Dans sa clarté frémissante
Un étranger se mire
S'attarde
Perplexe
Nostalgique
Son automne est déjà arrivé !
En souvenir
Il se laisse bercer
Par le ruissellement des ondes câlines.
Ce refrain traverse le temps.

Autrefois...
Celui-là berçait les nuits
Au printemps de son âge
Aujourd'hui...
La même rengaine.

Sous les pluies diluviennes
Insouciant, tu t'éveilles.
Des éclats de rire montent
Jusqu'à la fenêtre.
Roule en cascades
De caillou en caillou.
File.
Va ton chemin
Verse ton eau vive
Par-delà des terres inconnues
Cours à perdre haleine
Fébrile
Réponds au vent
Tandis que sur tes rives
Des jardins de *têtes-de-violon*
Vivent leur jeunesse.

Ruisseau de mes étés
Quelque part dans la vallée
S'est perdue ta fougue primesautière
De la saison printanière.

Coule doucement la sérénité
Soupirs et murmures
À peine perceptibles
Font croire au bruissement de la pluie.
Le clapotis captivant de ton langage
Apaise.
La sagesse émane de tes eaux.
Respire
Le parfum des sous-bois
Celui des berges verdoyantes
Toi, inlassable passant.

Par Rina Boucher Soucy

Acadians/*Acadiennes*/Cajuns

Saule pleureur—tristesse, souvenir, immortalité
Les saules marquent la présence de villages d'Acadiens déportés
Weeping Willow—Mourning, forsaken
The weeping willow is the Acadian national tree.

Sarrasin—Protection et guérison; symbole de la misère des campagnes, "Le Pain des fleurs"
Buckwheat—Money, protection

Amarante—Rouge brun, amour durable
Amaranthus—Love lies bleeding, hopeless, heartless

Mouron, rouge—Rendez-vous accepté
Pimpernel, Scarlet—Assignation

Némophile—Pardon
Baby Blue Eyes (Nemophila)—Success everywhere

Chou—Gain
Cabbage—Profit

Paille—Harmonie
Corn Straw—Agreement

Paille brisée—Rupture d'un contrat
Corn Straw, Broken—Quarrel

My Journey to Writing a Book About Acadian Blankets

By Elaine Larcade-Bourque

I did not wake up one morning and decide that I would compile a book on Acadian blankets! It was many years in the making and for a long time I did not even know that my journey would lead me to this point because it was so subtle. It began when I discovered the world of Acadian brown and white cotton spinning and weaving! That was Greek to me. I had never heard of brown cotton and had seen very few blankets made with this mysterious "coton jaune" cotton! Perhaps it started before that time. As a child, I picked white cotton before it disappeared from Southwest Louisiana. As a child, I also witnessed a dramatic change in culture and traditions. My parents, both products of Acadian ancestors, had been punished for speaking French in school; therefore, they were determined that their children not be labeled "Cajun!" They spoke no French to me and my siblings, but my two living grandmothers spoke nothing but French. Even though we could not understand them, we always knew that they loved us very much! Someone once asked me when I realized that I was Cajun? I did not have to think about that question; I always knew I was Cajun.

After I was awarded an apprenticeship under Gladys LeBlanc Clark, I spent approximately ten years traveling with Mrs. Clark to festivals demonstrating Acadian spinning and weaving. During this time, I learned a little more about the tradition of Acadian blankets and realized how important this craft was to the Acadian community. It is a form of art that has disappeared because of the introduction of technology. It was not regarded as an art form at the time it was being done, but was considered a necessity for survival. Blankets were made to keep family members warm. Cotton was grown and used because funds were not available to purchase textiles or dyes. After some observation, it seems that those families that still grew the brown cotton and made their blankets into the 20th century had a stigma attached that meant you were poor. For this reason, whatever blankets still existed were soon disposed of or relegated to the back of the linen closet or the tool shed to be used as a cover for water pumps in winter, horse blankets, between the inner springs of mattresses, or burned in a bonfire with looms and spinning wheels found in attics.

It was a slow journey with many setbacks, the largest being the loss of my spouse of forty-eight years. He had encouraged me along the way; therefore, when he died, a part of me died also. I lived in a fog for several years and eventually the fog lifted, some. The fog never left my life, but it lifted enough to give me an opportunity to resume my work which I felt was so important to me and to my ancestors.

Acadia Parish—The Cormier Family

All of my work thus far had been done in Lafayette and Vermilion Parish and almost all blankets could be traced back to the LeBlanc family in some way, either by family, marriage into the LeBlanc family or neighbors and friends of the LeBlanc family.

When I started my documentation in 2013, I was excited to interview the first family in Acadian Parish, the Clesma Cormier family, a very prominent family from Mire, Louisiana. I was born in Acadian Parish in the community of Mire. Mire is located at the intersection of state highways 98 and 95. Mire was referred to as Bosco in the 1940s. According to local tradition, Bosco is from "boscoyo" or "cypress knee" which was supposedly the nickname of a humpbacked resident of the area. (Ancelet 29) This community was also called Marais Bouleur, a Cajun French expression meaning "marsh bully."

Many of the Marais Bouleur area was comprised of inhabitants who had Acadian backgrounds that can be traced to Nova Scotia or had married into the Acadian families and were considered Acadians, such as the Cormiers, Credeurs, Heberts, Melancons, Mires, Meches, Prejeans, Arceneauxs, Castilles, Trahans to name a few.

The inhabitants of this area were for the most part isolated. The region was on the edge of prairies and life on the prairies was hard. Most residents spent all their time trying to coax a meager living out of the low-lying grazing land and by growing cotton, corn, and sweet potatoes as cash crops.

The oil industry arrived in 1932. With it came money to landowners. Many of the people in Marais Bouleur were farmers. The little money they saw came once a year when they sold their crops. They immediately spent it all paying their bills and then went back into debt for another year. With successful wells on their lands, some families literally became rich overnight.

Even though it has never been incorporated, at one time, Mire had four stores. Each store was unique and different. One store had a cobbler. One of the four stores still stands today in Mire even though the ownership has been passed on to another family only recently. This General Merchandise Store was owned by Clesma Cormier, the only child of Aurelien Cormier and Cousine Agnes Credeur, as she was affectionately known to the community. Cousine Agnes was a devoted church worker, caring for the needs of the mission church until the present church was built in 1959.

The school and the church were the two important centers for much of the local activity recorded in those early years of community life. The reputation of Marais Bouleur for having good food and excellent cuisine stemmed from the many church bazaars and dinners that were held on a regular basis.

It was with great pleasure that I interviewed Cousine Agnes' granddaughters, Joyce and Dale Cormier, who had in their possession several Acadian brown cotton blankets made by their grandmother and their father's sister, Coralee Cormier, "Tante Calee." Tante Calee was also Clesma's godmother. It would be hard to tell for sure who made the blankets since both ladies did spinning and weaving and lived in the same yard. Clesma's mother always lived with him and his family. His aunt lived in a small house behind their home until she was elderly and then she also lived in the Cormier home next to the General Merchandise Store.

Clesma married Pearl Mire and they had two daughters, who were born in the 1930s. They both became school teachers in Acadian Parish and retired with thirty-some years of service. They always lived with their parents so they were able to tell me about the grandmother and aunt doing some dyeing. Joyce told me that she remembers as a child seeing her grandmother out in the back yard with a large pot of boiling water dyeing the wool from the sheep that her father kept for the family to eat. She was not allowed near the boiling pot for fear that she would be burned. Joyce tells me her mother was very protective and would tell the girls to "Go away!" Many times the boiling pot also had lye in it and the ladies would clean their cowhide chairs with the solution. This was quite common in Acadian families.

Joyce and Dale would also help Cousine Agnes care for the mission church which was located near their home and store. Cousine Agnes learned how to care for vestments, altar cloths, use of candles, arranging the catafalque (a pall-covered coffin-shaped structure used for memorial requiem masses) celebrating the mass for the dead—everything that was needed at church. She learned all this from Mrs. Galbert Prejean and probably from Mrs. Alexandre Castille. In 1928, Mrs. Galbert moved away and Cousine Agnes began taking care of the church needs in addition to sweeping, dusting, and yes, shoveling cow patties at the church entrance as well as in the cemetery. The neighbor's cows roamed about freely since the church property had no fence. She also waxed the floors, cared for the pews, ironed the altar linens and kept the vestments in order. She would rise early to arrange the church, light heaters, and clean any mess from the roaming cattle. Joyce and Dale remember having to help their grandmother do some of these unpleasant duties, sometimes reluctantly. They were happy to see the church property fenced in and cows no longer present around the church. Pearl Cormier, Joyce and Dale's mother, in turn, learned much from her mother-in-law and continued in the tradition of devoted service to the church. So did Joyce and Dale until, due to health issues, they moved away from their beloved Mire community, but cherish fond memories of growing up in a small, catholic community.

I felt that it was important to share with you some background of the area that I also grew up in until the age of twelve when my family moved to Lafayette Parish, although we have kept the family property in Mire.

I feel that my ancestors must have crossed paths with the Cormiers and the spinners and weavers must have shared some information about their art. In documenting the blankets, I have found that only in Acadia Parish was the warp done differently than most warps that I have documented in Lafayette Parish.

In trying to date the blankets that were housed in the outdoor kitchen behind the Cormier home, Joyce and I have agreed that it is hard to put an exact date but we think perhaps these blankets go back to the early 1900s or possibly the late 1800s. Joyce does not remember any brown cotton weaving done during her lifetime so this would mean possibly that Clesma's mother and Clesma's sister would have made these, or were given these as l'amour de maman by Clesma's grandmother to her daughter, Agnes. Clesma was born in 1904. The blankets were not used in the house by Joyce and Dales' mother but had been used before because the blankets had a lot of wear and tear. Edges were tattered and parts of blankets were repaired. They were treasured because instead of destroying or using the frayed, tattered blankets for outdoor uses, they were always kept in the outside kitchen in a cardboard box.

I have never encouraged a person with Acadian blankets to sell them. Many times when I have met with the owners of Acadian textiles, I tell them what a treasure they have hidden in their closet and encouraged them to hold on to their blankets and leave them for future generations in their family. I was contacted and told that the two Cormier sisters were selling their family home and had to sell much of the contents since they were moving into a smaller assisted living home. Therefore, when I met with the Cormier daughters, I knew they wanted to sell the textiles. Joyce convinced me to bring the textiles to my home and document the blankets before she sold them. The Cormier sisters have never married and have no children, so I felt really good about being a part of finding the right person to buy the blankets because I had recently met a gentleman who is collecting Acadian textiles and was looking for blankets to fill in an armoire he had just acquired. He will treasure these blankets and is so happy to add them to his collection.

I think Tante Calee (Coralie Cormier) and Agnes Credeur Cormier (Cousine Agnes) and maybe their mother would be happy to see their blankets in the hands of a collector of Acadian textiles, furnishings and Catholic artifacts from the Acadiana area!

Reference

Ancelet, Barry. "Rednecks, Roughnecks and the Bosco Stomp: The Arrival of the Oil Industry in the Marais Bouleur." *Attakapas Gazette* [The Attakapas Historical Association, Louisana] Volume XXII Number 1, SPRING 1987: 29. Print.

This is my work.

These are old Acadian Textiles I have acquired and documented.

"Film explores use of brown cotton in weavings that preserved Cajun culture"

"*Coton jaune* — Acadian Brown Cotton: A Love Story."

Such was the case of Sharon Gordon Donnan, of Los Angeles, and Suzanne Chaillot Breaux, of Lafayette, when they discovered a hand-woven Acadian blanket made from brown cotton in a Washington antique store and ended up creating a documentary on Acadian weaving titled "*Coton jaune* — Acadian Brown Cotton: A Love Story."

Donnan is a filmmaker, educator and conservator of ancient and antique textiles. Breaux is a fiber artist, weaver and costume designer specializing in Mardi Gras and theatrical costumes.

The background of the two friends played a serendipitous role in the film's creation.

Donnan spent years as a field conservator on the Peruvian north coast, excavating ancient textiles, and in Oaxaca in southern Mexico. In both places, women wove with brown cotton, Donnan said.

Breaux was raised in a Cajun household that had a loom.

She had traveled to Oaxaca to learn weaving before returning to Lafayette and entering the military.

When the two found the old Acadian blanket at the antique store, Donnan was amazed to find the use of brown cotton in Louisiana. "That's what spurred my interest," Donnan said. "I've never seen it outside of South America. Louisiana was the third place for me, and it all came together around brown cotton."

Larcade-Bourque and the filmmakers are still looking for owners of old Acadian brown cotton blankets.

—Excerpt from *The Advocate, Acadiana News*
Cheré Coen, Special to *The Advocate*
April 19, 2015

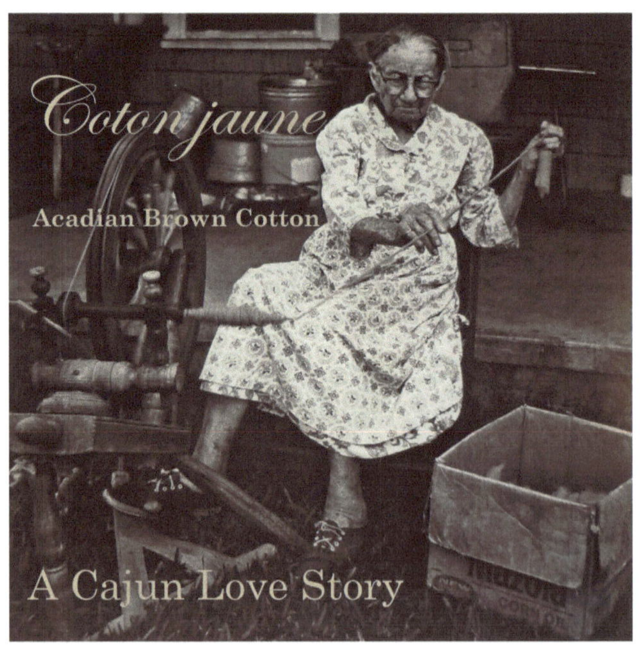

Reference material:
"L'Amour de Maman: Acadian Textile Heritage"

Louisiana State Museum, "L'Amour de Maman: Acadian Textile Heritage"
Robert S. Elliott
New Brunswick Museum
Volume 22, Fall/Automne 1985

Elliott, Robert. "Louisiana State Museum, "L'Amour de Maman: Acadian Textile Heritage"." Material Culture Review / Revue de la culture matérielle [Online], 22 (1985): n. pag. Web. 24 Jul. 2015

Acadian Archives/Archives acadiennes—Maine

The **Acadian Archives/Archives Acadiennes** at the University of Maine at Fort Kent documents, preserves, celebrates, and disseminates information about the culture, way of life, and history of the Franco-American and Acadian people of the Upper St John River Valley. A repository for manuscript materials and audiovisual documentation relevant to regional folklore, folklife, and history, the Archives serves the University community as well as individuals and organizations regionally, statewide, nationally, and internationally. Visit their website on-line for more information.

Une Oeuvre d'Amour ... A Labor of Love

By Lisa Desjardins Michaud

I have had the opportunity of getting to know Frances Dumond Levasseur better in the past three years. Although we were from the same town and her name was always familiar to me, I never really knew her.

I will always remember my first visit to her home in Old Town. I knew that she would be an excellent resource for the Franco-American Centre, and I very much wanted to add her works to the Centre's library. I was amazed to see her library filled with photos, books and files upon files of materials. I watched her knotted fingers leaf through her folders and albums all the while explaining to me what this project was and what it would consist of.

Throughout the years of our keeping in touch with one another, I have grown to highly respect and admire her; she is my mentor. She is such a wonderful, loving caring person with a captivating personality. She has shared with me her many works of restoration and preservation of our wonderful French culture and heritage. She is a tiny woman in stature but she has accomplished what many dream of accomplishing throughout their lifetime. She has touched my being, inspired me with the yearning to preserve our culture and our heritage.

Fran so graciously invited me to her home to show me her latest undertaking. She has compiled two volumes filled with *Bangor Daily News* articles of when she was a News Correspondent, titled, "La P'tite Bangor" 1971-1973. After leafing through these wonderful books, filled with articles of my hometown, I was amazed at all the hard work and dedication that Fran put into the creation of these books. I must add that she compiled these volumes all the while having failing health, battling cancer; and on top of that she is afflicted with arthritis that has severely crippled her hands. This is a person with a will, and if there was not a way, Fran would find one. Anyone who knows Fran will surely agree with me that when she wants and says she is going to do something, it gets done. As I was leaving her home, she mentioned that the work she had done, and is doing, is a labor of love. She enjoyed compiling and organizing materials so that it would be accessible for future generations. These works are priceless; generations to come will profit from these compilations, works that Fran so unselfishly dedicates much of her time to.

Frances has authored many books and founded many projects. She undertook each project with utmost dedication. Some titles of the books that she compiled are *The Madore-Laplante Genealogy*, *A Dumond Family Genealogy and Photo Album*, *A Pictorial History of the St. John Valley*, and *A Pictorial History of St. Bruno Parish*, a *Historical Calendar,* all depicting important events of the century.

She was founder of the Acadian Village along Route One in Van Buren, Maine. Also started at the time of the Acadian Village was a nonprofit organization that administers the Village's activities and business, "*l'Heritage Vivant*." She was a prime organizer of her 40th Class Reunion at Van Buren High School.

Fran is also responsible for compiling photos of Keegan, Van Buren, Cyr Plantation, Hamlin, and the Acadian Village which have been laminated. Included in these laminations are the photos of the person that the town has been named after, along with photos of that area. Again, these wonderful mats depict our heritage and our culture.

I am sure I have forgotten some of her many works, but this is just to give you an idea of the wonderful work this lady has done.

Frances has preserved Acadian History and is quick to mention that she does not want to get any recognition for this work, for it is a labor of love.

Thank you Fran, for your "labor of love."

"Acadian Village dedicates hall to first president"

"VAN BUREN – Swallows living in a birdhouse at one end of the Acadian Village's recreation hall circled incessantly Tuesday afternoon as if welcoming people to the dedication of the building in memory of Frances Dumond-Levasseur.

The Frances Levasseur Salle de Recreation is the building closest to the entrance to the village from Route One. The Salle de Recreation is one of sixteen buildings in the village and it also is a meeting hall—a place where many cultural and heritage meetings are held.

Frances Levasseur, a native of Cyr Plantation, was the Living Heritage Historical Society's first president, and the person who provided the determination and passion for the construction of the village. She was remembered Tuesday for that passion, determination and vision which brought about the only such historical village in Maine.

... The Acadian Village, constructed by the Living Heritage Historical Society, was opened for the country's bicentennial in 1976. It was selected as one of the country's best bicentennial projects.

On December 13, 1977, the village was listed in the National Register of Historic Places and is recognized as a part of the historical and cultural heritage of the country.

The sixteen buildings, which include several private homes, a school, a chapel, a store, a blacksmith shop, a barber shop and a railroad way station, resemble a thriving village of the St. John Valley in the 1800s."

Excerpt from the story published on July 04, 2001 on Page B2 in edition 1 of the *Bangor Daily News*

**Acadian Village
40th Anniversary
1976-2016**

Acadia In Northern Maine

By Anne Parent Roy

Many people in New England think of Acadia National Park as the place to spend part of their vacation. Little do they know of the wonders that they could discover if they drove 300 more miles north. They would find themselves in the middle of Acadia of the Land and Forests. Fields and fields of rolling hills and miles and miles of woodland. If they follow the map of Maine they can locate the most restful place in the whole State, Aroostook County, the Crown of Maine.

The Crown of Maine is home to the St. John River that makes the border between Maine and New Brunswick. The river can lead you to the Allagash or to Grand Falls New Brunswick.

St. John Valley, home to the St. John River, offers one of the most picturesque drives a visitor could take. The Fish River chain of lakes proves to be the ideal place to rent a cottage and relax right on the water's edge. Here is an opportunity to swim, take a boat ride, water ski or even jetski. These hidden waterways are Long Lake, Mud Lake, Square Lake, Cross Lake and Portage Lake as well as Eagle Lake and Madawaska Lake.

The area of the Acadia of the Land and Forest also abounds with many museums that allow visitors to educate themselves about the Acadians who settled the grand St. John Valley.

If the visit is at the right time of the seasons a person can take in the beauty of blooming potato fields and growing oats, barley and buckwheat fields. If the vacation happens to occur during the fall season, the experience will be even more memorable as the harvest will be in full swing.

If a scenic vacation is on your mind, then the Acadia of the Land and Forest is where you want to visit.

Bouchard Family Farms

For generations the Bouchard Family has been milling a unique, light buckwheat flour in order to prepare "Ployes" (rhymes with boys). A recipe based on the one created by the French Acadian exiles who settled in Northern Maine, Ployes are as elegant as a fine crêpe, as hearty as a breakfast pancake and as versatile as any bread. Ployes are creating their own identity. From appetizers to main course to desserts and snacks, they keep finding new ways to make meals interesting. We invite you to try a product rich in taste and history. "C'est Magnifique!" Bouchard Family Farm Ployes Mix—The first-ever original French Acadian buckwheat pancake mix farm produced in Northern Maine since 1983.

In the early 1980s potato farming had endured some extremely hard times. It was during one of these tough years when Claire Bouchard, the eldest of the five daughters, had returned from a trip to Louisiana with a French Acadian doughnut mix called beignets.

As the family sat around enjoying the doughnuts one of them asked why no one has ever made a mix for ployes. The seed was planted and soon after, the family started working on the perfect recipe for ployes. Before long the family business had moved from their kitchen into the two-car garage which was converted into a mixing and packaging facility. In 1997, a 10,000 square foot building was erected to house the entire operation. Alban Bouchard and his son Joe found a dismantled mill in Canada and took one year to piece it together in order to mill the buckwheat on site.

Today the business has been credited with saving the family farm. Twenty years ago in the Fort Kent area, there were approximately 40 potato farmers. Today there are 5. Farming as an industry has not been easy and although we have endured some stormy weather we believe that our creativity and determination have been instrumental in maintaining our way of life.

The tradition of buckwheat pancakes and ployes:

Buckwheat pancakes are a venerable old mainstay of French cookery and one finds variants of them in many parts of French North America, including the St. John Valley, the Acadian Maritimes, and Quebec.

We know that buckwheat has been cultivated in the upper St. John River Valley of Maine and New Brunswick since the late 1780s. However, for the first fifty years of settlement, farmers in the "Madawaska Settlement" (as it was then known) grew very little buckwheat. Wheat and oats were the big cereal crops until the 1830s: on average, a typical Valley farmer in the 1830s produced 111 bushels of wheat, 74 bushels of oats, and only 3 bushels of buckwheat! So Valley farmwives probably made some kind of buckwheat pancake, but what their families ate three times a day was more likely to have been wheat bread.

In the mid-1830s, however, the Valley's thriving farming community faced a crisis when wheat midge (an insect) and rust (a disease) ruined wheat crops throughout the Northeast. In response, local farmers began to substitute oats and buckwheat. By 1850, buckwheat emerged as the grain crop leader in the Valley, representing 40-45% of all grain production.

By the 1850s, visitors to the Valley commented on the delicious buckwheat pancakes which local farmwives served their families at every meal instead of wheat bread. Making buckwheat pancakes (crêpes or galettes) from buckwheat flour was a tradition which Valley farmwives inherited from their French-Canadian and Acadian ancestors. But ployes, to use the local term, were really a griddle "bread"—one served three times a day as a main dish accompaniment and for dessert. Their importance as a regular part of daily diet, and the many recipe variations which developed over succeeding generations, make ployes a truly distinctive Valley tradition.

From the 1850s until the 1950s, ployes were served in many Valley homes three times a day. Local life has changed greatly over the past fifty years, and inexpensive, ready-made breads, cereals, pasta, and cakes have largely taken the "every meal" place once held by ployes. But the ploye is still cherished as the best accompaniment for a good chicken stew, and a necessity at any meal which celebrates Valley heritage.

Bouchard Family Farm, 3 Strip Road, Fort Kent, Maine 04743

The Great Escape

He was a valiant youth, and his face, like the face of the morning,
Gladdened the earth with its light, and ripened thought into action.
She was a woman now, with the heart and hopes of a woman.

– "Evangeline," Longfellow

She was a turn-of-the-century girl, Acadian,
shapely and trim, her neckline, high and close,
bore no frills, like the sleeves snug on her wrists.

Auburn curls sprung from the cap she wore
to visit her sister in Moncton—the story for Papa.
In truth, she fled the step-mother, the fields.

No British troops had to drag her from the family
farm, deport her on their ships. Her ambition
outreached Evangeline's fated suffering.

She did not expect a Gabriel to let her pass
as she boarded the train. Always quick,
she let her wrap dangle in the aisle near his feet.

What was the season? Late fall like today,
gold sparkling on the trees they passed?
Winter, the farm under its pall, cold and white?

Whatever the weather, she smiled goodbye
to her father's cuffings once her Gabriel bent
to gather the shawl and smile at her pale ankles.

The barb was set—an arrow if you like—but
a fish hook better catches the angling nature
of this Maritime maid. The beginning of the end

for her, as they say, of Evangeline's tortured tale.
This Acadian maiden left Bouctouche alone,
only to return with her love, all in one day.

By Caroline LeBlanc

Reflexions

E-où t'étais, chère?
Y a si longtemps que j'te cherchais
Et t'étais droite-là en dessous d'mon nez
Tout c'temps-là.

J't'appréciais pas quand on vivait ensemble
C'est pas drôle.
J'connaissais même pas qui tu étais
Et....
J'étais obligée de t'écouter et t'écouter
Ecouter cette musique en français
que les vieux de 40 ans dansaient...

Mais asteur que j'suis loin de toi
Je me trouve après chercher, après chercher
Essayer de trouver le son
D'un violon
Qui me fera danser.

Ouais.
Asteur tu me fais danser
Asteur que j' t'ai trouvée
J'peux pas danser assez
J'vais mourir sans avoir assez dansé
T'es dans mes veines si forte
Tu me fais proche brailler
Tellement je t'aime
Asteur....

.....asteur que j'connais
Qui toi t'es
Et qui moi j'suis....
On s'adonne bien,
Hein,
Ma Louisiane?

Par Brenda Mounier

Tante Blanche Museum

The Madawaska Historical Society's museum is a 1970s log building named for Marguerite Blanche Thibodeau Cyr in honor of her heroic deeds during the 1797 famine. In addition to the Acadian Landing Site and the museum, two adjacent historical society buildings are part of the museum complex: a nineteenth-century schoolhouse and the Fred Albert House. Collections of artifacts (especially related to Acadian textile manufacture and domestic furnishings) are located in the buildings.

Taken from Oral Traditions - Acadian Culture in Maine, University of Maine at Fort Kent:

Another legendary figure associated with the theme of self-sacrifice is "Tante Blanche." During a 1797 famine the woman upon whom the legend is based, Marguerite-Blanche Thibodeau, performed many remarkable acts of charity. Tante Blanche was the oldest woman at Violette Brook, where she resided. Wearing snowshoes, she brought extra clothing and provisions to people suffering from hunger and cold, while the men from the community attempted to hunt for food. In this way, she is believed to have saved many lives (Albert [1920] 1985: 57). With time, Tante Blanche became renowned for her selflessness and became an object of general veneration. She was said to be able to cure the sick and the tormented, to chase out evil spirits, to find lost objects, and even to reconcile enemies (Albert 1969: 58). She is memorialized at the Madawaska Historical Society and the Tante Blanche Museum at St. David.

"Acadians Of The St. John Valley" (Part 1) is an hour-long film that discovers where these Acadians come from in old Acadie and how they made their way to the St. John Valley of Northern Maine. The film follows the plight of these refugees as they carve out a new life for themselves in a harsh landscape, making do with very little, but succeeding by carrying with them the values and skills that helped them thrive in Acadie. See how they reenact the arrival of their ancestors by canoe every year on the St. John River, find out how they have preserved their cultural artifacts, including whole buildings, and discover how they continue, to this day, to practice the traditions of their forefathers. These scenes are set against the backdrop of the beautiful St. John Valley with its forests, fields and slow flowing river.

Brenda N. Jepson
Crown of Maine Productions, Inc.
645 South Shore Road, Stockholm, Maine 04783

Acadians of the St John Valley" starring **Patricia Theriault Ezzy as Tante Blanche.** After appearing as Tante Blanche in the film, Pat discovered that she is a direct descendent of Marguerite Blanche Thibodeau, who was known at Tante Blanche. She is beloved for having saved settlers in the St John Valley during the Black Famine of 1797.

FOUILLEUSE

I.

Matchbooks wound with orphan threads,
a dented penny, yellow cats-eye,
buttons of every size, shape, and color,
kept in a tin with rusted cover:
the winter sleigh-ride.
"Your mother—Marie-Rose—was a twin, you know,"
says *ma tante* Hilda, the drapery hook.
"No, I didn't know."
"*Le jemeau* was a boy name of Patrick—*Patrice*—
but so sickly they wrap him in a burlap sack,
put him behind the kitchen stove—big coal-burning stove—
hot as blazes—winter time in Canada, you know—
the year of the Spanish flu."
"To die?"
"For *Jesus* to take, *ma 'ti-to-'une!*"

II

Four o'clock in the afternoon was prime *maman* naptime and we knew not to disturb her
In the front bedroom with cutglass doorknob so pretty to look at but burn your hand to touch.
We young ones and the two teenagers somewhere else in the house fend for ourselves
And sometimes it carries over to dinnertime but most often *maman* will wake up in time to
Scorch a few hotdogs on the fry pan and saw open a can of Campbell's pork & beans
And serve us milk if it had not gone sour and most times even if it had. *Papa* would come
Home at six o'clock sharp from the firehouse, eat something I do not know what, and turn
Around and drive to the American Legion or VFW whichever had cribbage or horseshoes
That night, drink of course, and *maman* would do something I'm not sure what, and we
Would get ourselves to bed, minus a story or kiss or sheet tucking-in. In fact, we had no
Sheets, just blankets, bare mattress, and water we could drink from the bathroom faucet
In our cupped hands.

III

Pied-a-pied, walking is knowing.
But why—*fouilleuse*—stir up things best kept buried?
Like a madness, all the names in your genealogy chart
spin around and around, buttons
in the button tin. Your hands
plough the subsoil but you plant nothing.
Snowberry—Emilie Symphorine Comeau dit LeClerc Savoie—
daughter of Marie-Esther, grand-daughter of Jean, great-grand-daughter of the original
Marie-Esther, born in exile in Groton Massachusetts in 1757.
What are you looking for?
The Village of Grand Pré was burned to the ground.
There, there is nothing.
Here, you survive.
You, daughter of Marie-Rose, *la jumelle* who was saved.
You, middle child, born in a blizzard
into immigrant Lowell, and the house of beans and franks, glass doorknobs, and
fireman's boots in the back hall.
You, scientist-poet, mother of yet another Emilie
in the long
Acadian walk home.

By Susan Rose April

AUNT NORMA PAULINE 1921 - 2003
(Another History Out Of Acadie)
By Patricia Smith Ranzoni

Silently one by one, in the infinite meadows of
heaven,
Blossomed the lovely stars, the forget-me-nots of
the angels.
— from "Evangeline"
by Henry Wadsworth Longfellow

As here in the shadows of ancient Acadia, the forest once primeval,
now paper-companied, under same stars, in the season of berry-
and rose-scent she grew up in, we pick the fruits and blossoms
of her life to press and save for the rest of ours.

How could I, a school girl memorizing lines of a poem, larger
than I was, know we lived with Acadians in Maine if no one told us?
Or that my uncle, all that he was, a mystery just as much,
would marry one as beautiful as Evangeline?

Fair was she and young, when in hope began the
long journey;...

Or that this aunt would embody the name LeBlanc (before Blanchard,
Smith, and Bennett) if no one let us know? Or what this meant?

Bowing to Longfellow for words used in reverence from this crumbling
old book of his work, an elder now, this girl wishes only to honor
another strong life and lives she left. Her family. *Elle famille.*

René Leblanc will be here anon, with his papers
and inkhorn.
Shall we not then be glad, and rejoice in the joy
of our children?

Mythical or real, the name Leblanc was chosen to carry the qualities
of venerable notary in his New France settlement of Grand Pré.

Father of twenty children was he, and more than
a hundred
Children's children rode on his knee, and heard
his great watch tick.

And how proud she was to be of this, and how she taught Clyde,
named for her father, so he could begin his search.

Four long years in the times of war had he
languished a captive,
Suffering much in an old French fort as the
friend of the English.

And how you, Clyde, Kenneth, Gerald and Jon, come from a union
just like this, people capable of loving other than their own kind.

Or finding kin in all kinds, across old hates. Even if their very cells harbor war or its urges for the rest of their forevers same as some French and English still do towards one another.
(Might Norma laugh here from her high humor? Or cry?)

Now, though warier grown, without guile or
suspicion,
Ripe in wisdom was he, but patient, and simple,
and childlike.
He was beloved by all, and most of all by the
children;

As it is told of Norma Pauline how she suffered apart from her own. How her boys mourned her and she them. A different story than Evangeline's but rending, just the same.

Soon o'er the yellow fields, in silent and mournful
procession,
Came from the neighboring hamlets and farms
the Acadian women,
Driving in ponderous wains their household
goods to the sea-shore,
Pausing and looking back to gaze once more on
their dwellings,
Ere they were shut from sight by the winding
road and the woodland.
Close at their sides their children ran, and urged
on the oxen,
While in their little hands they clasped some
fragments of playthings.

How we each come to terms the way we do when we don't understand but keep searching and trying, and trying and searching.

For he told them tales of the Loup-garou in the
forest,
And of the goblin that came in the night to
water the horses...

And how she loved hearing of her grandchildren. And how much of this do you suppose would have came down through *her* mother Alma?

....how on Christmas eve the oxen talked in the
stable,
And how the fever was cured by a spider shut up
in a nutshell,
And of the marvellous powers of four-leaved
clover and horseshoes
With whatsoever else was writ in the lore
of the village.

In the same way Jerry's candy box where he stores keepsakes from his youth is history. From the '50s more than half a century ago. Someday they will tell of a 3-cent stick of milk chocolate named *Lunch Bar*, this box once held 40 of, before their spaces, one by sweet one, got called upon for use by a schoolboy's other treasures.

For example, this layered paper bell held together with green ribbon Mrs. Trip no doubt helped him tie in second grade while his friend, Barry, worked on his creation at the desk behind. First, a gold star in the center. Then, a layer reading A MERRY CHRISTMAS, topped with TO MOTHER FROM GERALD. And how his mother has now, as he tells it, joined Barry and others from his life, on a journey to who knows where.

Maybe another dream place in the manner of her home in Skowhegan in the hands of Noi and Ken since the '80s who continue to give away shoots and roots of bleeding hearts and lilies Norma planted years ago from gardens where she would plant a tree or shrub in memory of family or friends gone on. Where they now have planted a Variegated Norway Maple for her the same because it survives well in cold and harsh conditions, staying beautiful all the while. The way they say Norma withstood her weathers, keeping, in their eyes, her class and loveliness.

Faded was she and old, when in disappointment
it ended.
Each succeeding year stole something away from
her beauty,
Leaving behind it, broader and deeper, the gloom
and the shadow.

Oh, to be in her garden again where her presence is brilliantly felt in the driveway on a starlit night where she paced for years for her boys.

Or at the Mission of San Juan Bautista in California built by the First Ones of that place she embraced all the way from the First Ones she embraced in New England. Where even as we pay tribute to her here in Maine, she is being honored out there by them, her spirit dancing again between us wherever in life she was seen and wherever she wished she could have gone, for dancing was her love.

Or back in Millinocket where Jon's heart bled closest and Pamela daughtered her last years with care. And where when we visited last year and took her my 12-day clove pickles she cried OH MY GODFRY MIGHTY! Who did you say you are? Percy and Jean? OH MY GODFRY MIGHTY! Percy and Jean and Loretta and Patricia and Linda, Ernie and Hazel and who else? Ernest and Glenroy. OH MY GODFRY MIGHTY! Ernest and Glenroy yes! and Beulah Anne and Ellen Rae who did you say you are? Asking for names again and again: Hazel, Beulah, Percy, Ernest, Loren, Harold, Richard, Maurice, Charlotte, Leo, and Kathleen and Myra the two that died. And all their kids she could name when cued and laugh and exclaim OH MY GODFRY MIGHTY! And how she and my mother gripped one another through tears for having survived those years and how very thankful we were to find her in time.

Then there appeared and spread faint streaks of
gray o'er her forehead,
Dawn of another life, that broke o'er her earthly
horizon,
As in the Eastern sky the first faint streaks of
the morning.

And now must find her in you who are of her, in whom she lives on. Mothers, are not our children each different aspects of ourselves? Do we not need all of what they have been to see ourselves lived out whole?

Children, are we not distinct portions of who our mothers have been, when together, joining her again?

But what are we mothers to do without daughters in love and in law who know what it is to be a woman? Each generation interpreting the one before, in compassion, for who knows our sorrows but another woman? And who can comfort when we cannot, but another one of us? Evangeline never knew these blessings but Norma did in Irene, Noi, Rhea and Pamela whose task it has been to listen for her female soul and know that the scarlet poinsettias she asked to be photographed with on the west coast were no less than splashes straight from a woman's bleeding heart however far back. And to understand that the afghans and quilts she hooked and stitched for you were no less than her pain transformed. May the generosity of that work warm and heal as we marvel over it, missing, knowing that in holding them, she touches us again.

Ye who believe in affection that hopes, and en-
dures, and is patient,
Ye who believe in the beauty and strength of
woman's devotion,
List to the mournful tradition still sung by the
pines of the forest...

to which she has returned.

All was ended now, the hope, and the fear, and
the sorrow,
All the aching of heart, the restless, unsatisfied
longing,
All the dull, deep pain, and constant anguish of
patience!

Home to old Acadia where she now dances free!

Still stands the forest primeval; but under the
shade of its branches
Dwells another race, with other customs and lan-
guage.
Only along the shore of the mournful and misty
Atlantic
Linger a few Acadian peasants, whose fathers
from exile
Wandered back to their native land to die in its
bosom...

as we, here, applaud one come down from them, and all of you, descending from them through her,

our Norma...
Notre Norma Pauline.

For our Blanchard-Smith cousins, descended from both an Acadian family of the Great Deportation and an English officer who participated in it.

Spirituality/*Spiritualité*

Pissenlit—Oracle, jalousie, expansion, bonne semence
Dandelion—Oracle, faithfulness, happiness, love's oracle

Pin—Pitié, éternité, avec la nuance d'éternel retour. Pont entre ciel et terre.
Pine, Black—Pity, boldness
Pine, Pitch—Philosophy
Pine, Spruce—Hope in adversity

Sainfoin—Hésitation
Sainfoin—Agitation

Salsepareille—Offre de réparation
Sarsaparilla—Love, money

Menthe poivrée—Chaleur des sentiments
Peppermint—Purification, sleep, love, healing, psychic powers, warmth and cordiality

Lilas, blanc—Amour naissant idéalisé
Lilac, White—Majesty, purity, innocence

Fraisier (fleur de)—Prévoyance. Faim de bonté.
Strawberry, flower—Goodness, perfect goodness

Pastoral

I ignored my mother that Sunday morning,
She calling me home from the pasture across the road,
To go to mass.

This meadow had beckoned me early,
Acolyte of grass, rock wall and pond,
Of the pebbled brook.
That shimmering chain to everywhere, and
Every altar,
Binding me to this joy,
I ran with the stream, lifting water in my hands,
Throwing offerings to the breeze,
And onto the tongues of cows and dragonflies there,
Onto the rocks, under my bare feet, and cow pies,
That teemed with little maggots,
White life, like the roiling of creation itself,
Before the world was flat, before earth was the center
Of universes, before the planet orbited the sun, before we sailed
So many seas, like invincible gods at the mast,
Circumnavigating, yet failing to find
The mystery of prayer at the brink,
Like at the edge of nowhere that is this place.

And to the day I said, splaying water from the stream:
"I am the maker of rainbows!"

I ignored my mother that Sunday morning,
I was gone again, no "goodbye"
And no " I'm coming, Mom," when she called,
This silence, like a shunning.
I imagined her standing on the just-swept steps,
Looking for me,
Delicate hand, untanned, raised to her brow,
The sun, the summer, too much,
Terrifying with their bids to abandon,
Like little fires licking at her heels, her church dress, her hat,
My face flickering in the flames
Of this morning of being six ,
Morning like an inhalation of a whole life's breath,
An exhalation of ecstasy, of falling, scraping knees, bleeding,
Of falling, and not caring as I ran, my eyes set on every horizon,
And there were so many of these,
Where the stream ran and almost sang, the cows lifted their eyes to blue sky,
And bowed to the grass.

By Susann Pelletier

Opening Day: Sister Beatrice Throws Out the First Pitch

Sister ascends the mound,
quiets the organist with her palms.

The catcher kneels. He needs a god-
damn miracle to rise out of this minor league limbo.

The stadium lights flicker on, they glow
in tiered rows like votive candles.

Beatrice is a Sister of Mercy but her windup looks brutal,
her leg-kick wicked. The faithful
fans murmur to see the cool white whisper
of holy underclothes.

Sister's hooded head spits forward.

The catcher's glove opens like a heart,
contracts against the fastball's whomp
and slam. His head has stopped hoping for salvation
but his heart holds on.

Organ music booms against the dome.

The leadoff hitter waits. Twenty years
since his last confession, but he crosses himself,
steps hopefully to the plate.

By Ellen LaFleche

Near me

Near me,
Bees congregate this October afternoon,
Sip hurriedly from hyssop, alyssum,
Marigold, and sunflower
Their last quaffs of this season.

Air is replete with the twin redolences
Of sweet and bitter—of those blossoms,
And of fallen apple, pine needle,
Of my last two roses,
White, now fringed with pink,
Their leaves lacework made
By tiny caterpillars I found underneath.

Near me,
Shade flits at my face, my feet,
Nudges itself into my place,
Brings its stillness and its coolness along
While sun, brilliant, calls to the upper expanse
Of grass and of garden,
All, but the moth and the bat.

There, I see how the raspberries offer a second crop,
Taste how last night's rain swelled, sweetened them.
You join me, and pick a few—
Proffer the best ones to me.
Then we walk to a wild grape arbor,
New found,
That bridges a thicket to our old apple tree.
Standing beneath,
You pull down a thick vine,
I reach up, gather clusters of grapes—
Our years of uneven harvests
In my hands.

By Susann Pelletier

Hanging Prayer Flags the Morning of the First Snow

On the empty pond, ten thousand circles interlace, rippling
a surface touched only by snow.
Above my studio door

I thread a rainbow of Tibetan prayer flags, in and out
of deck poles. Wind chills my limbs &
flags flutter

a reminder. Before their exile, this deed would have been sacrilege
to my Acadian ancestors who tacked
crucifixes

not bare of body in quiet wayside niches, over doors, each bed
in the house. The broken bulk of Christ would
hang

heavy, arms wide and nails through palms. His torso would slump
into bent legs with feet joined like upside-down
hands at prayer.

Christ's form would bear a speared side, blood painted
to accent whip lines, the stab of thorns and nails.
His human heart

pierced, the way my concentration is by a crescendo
of geese as they plow out. A water wake
unfurls

into a canopy of chevrons:
lance, flag, crucifix.

By Caroline LeBlanc

Salve Regina

The mysteries
of the Rosary
have faded
in a way
the Hail Mary
rhythms have not.

I still finger beads—
one, three, one,
ten for five decades
and more
that my mother prayed
to the Mother of Jesus.

She prayed for the Virgin
to intercede
with her son,
Jesus that is,
to help her son,
my brother that is.

These women
shared the heartbreak
of raising a son
who lost his life
to a mystery
hard to fathom.

In hymns we hailed
Mary, Queen of Heaven,
Mother of God,
the woman who gave
divinity form
after nine months

of counting her moons
without blood
of feeling her backbone
arc against
the weight of bearing
god below her ribs.

By Caroline LeBlanc

Honoring the Fifth Commandment

High in the abbey at Mont St. Michel, before the tides
came galloping in like the waters behind DeMille's chariots,
the old woman descending the stairs behind me said *"Pardon,*
j'ai besoin de tenir votre bras s'il vous plaît." I said, *"Of course"*
and gave her my arm. Beads caressed her gnarled knuckles
the silver polished by time, and her hair shone as the light
came spooling into the damp rotunda. My own mother's
rosary had been taken in the night by a robber who dared
to trespass as she slept with Hail Mary on her lips.
And when I was there, in that place of sacred battles
and wondrous nature, I thought of her,
of our private wars, and of her needing me.

Along the nave of the south wall four strong arches
like arms from above embrace La Chapelle Saint-Etienne,
the ossuary echoes an ancient moan, and the wheel
that moved the track to the cemetery floor has ground
to a halt. In the twelfth century, I'm told, the abbot
at Mont St. Michel dedicated all of this to honor his dead.
My father served during World War II, in France and all
through Europe. He delivered blood and perishables
to the front lines and he fed any man alive.
And when I was there, in that place of imprisonment
and struggle, of high tides and serenity, I thought of him,
and how I would have done anything to save him.

Out in the bay's mud flats that surround the monstrous
edifice, silt cooled my feet and the salt air stung.
I had been told that the full moon tide would arrive fast
in late afternoon. That the sea would come to St. Michel
all in a rush—an invasion that would storm the fortress.
And when I was there, in that place of past and present
swollen with the spring tide, my thoughts took me back
to what is not mine to remember, back to monks
and knights, to prisoners and guardians, to gardens
and michelettes and chanting. I did not go to mass
that day, but I know the Benedictines offer it
for the faithful and the curious.

By Marie Louise St. Onge

Soeur Louis de France, My Mother and Me

I woke this morning to snow falling outside my window
and the smell of germicide in my nose and in my head.
At 29 degrees, snow is wet and heavy, it forces
everything it touches to bend without will
or to break away from where it started.

As a young girl when I was sick, my mother would move
through the house will-less, as though on a mission directed
from above. As though with wings saving lives, inducing grandeur
where there was none. Her life and mine intertwined. We each took
our places and the air was cool.

She would pump the Red Cross bottle and the fine mist
intended to expunge my pathogen would fill the air.
With each pump she recited "mea culpa, mea culpa, mea maxima culpa."
And for the briefest moment she felt good, just as holy as a nun
sprinkling water on the bad boys at the back of the class.
But she knew it wasn't enough.

Twenty years later, I felt my discontent. It was in me,
the seed had been sown. More than anything, I wanted to retreat.
I wanted to scorn my restlessness and keep steady with expectations.
I did not want to dismantle my life.
But I knew it wasn't enough.

It isn't enough
to bend and yield to what weighs us down
nor to sanitize our existence. It isn't enough
to push to the rear the ideas that challenge us most.
We must touch and breathe and move. And sometimes
we must break away from where we started.

By Marie Louise St. Onge

The Blue Rosary

By Cléo Paradis Ouellette

At Marcel's funeral, Father Jim ended the eulogy by pointing out that Marcel had left him in charge of his vast collection of rosaries, that Marcel had over 100 rosaries which he had collected over the years and which he wanted to leave to whomever wanted one, on condition that the taker would be willing to dedicate the first decade to praying for him. We were singing in the choir for that funeral, with much fervor, I must add, as Marcel had dedicated many years as choir director for our parish.

I was surprised that Marcel had amassed such a large number of rosaries. Where did these come from? How can a bachelor without much family collect such a large number of rosaries? It really struck me.

After the funeral, after collecting my choir sheets, I made my way to the table where the rosaries had been put out on display. "They'll all be gone," I thought, as most people had already gone downstairs to the funeral lunch. But to my surprise, there were about a dozen left. "I don't really need another rosary," I said to myself. I had my own rosary from childhood and had collected several others over the years, my mother's, my sister's, and others. But, when I approached the table, one in particular attracted my attention. It was of sapphire blue beads with a bulky crucifix and medal, not really attractive as it seemed worn, clumsy, and dingy with use.

I went from one rosary to another. I knew I really didn't need another rosary, yet I could not leave that table. I looked over several of them, but my eyes kept going back to that blue one. "It's my birthstone," I reasoned. I had lost a birthstone rosary some time before, a much daintier one. I just didn't seem to shake the idea of this one. It was beckoning to me, calling my name, I felt. But why? Finally, after much hesitation, I picked it up, put it in my pocket and walked down to the luncheon.

When I returned home, I immediately set out to clean up the rosary. I put it in jewelry cleaner and gently brushed it until it shone. And did it shine! I was amazed. What a beautiful thing! It seemed to call out to me, but why? I picked it up over and over again, excited. I just couldn't shake it. What did it want to tell me? Was the person who had owned it before trying to reach me somehow? Who had owned it before Marcel collected it? What was I supposed to do?

I began to wonder about Marcel's collection. Who had left these rosaries behind? I supposed that, as people died, their children didn't want the rosaries and Marcel had just kept collecting them. How sad! What a treasure they had lost!

Years ago, the rosary was a big part of people's lives, but that seemed to be dying out. Devotion to the rosary was very strong in the years when the present older generation were quite young. Families said the rosary every day together, as a family. After supper, the dishes were hastily done and then the whole family knelt down

(Continued on next page)

and said the rosary, kneeling straight, heads bowed. No sitting on your heels, either. After the prayers were finished, then and only then, could you go out for the evening. If you went to a friend's house and they had not finished their rosary, you knelt down and finished it with them before any of you went anywhere. No one had to say anything. It was just understood.

A rosary was a treasured item. You would receive one as a first communion gift as would every other child in your class, and that rosary stayed close to you. You carried it in your pocket; you slept with it under your pillow; you clasped it tightly if you were ill or in the hospital; you twisted it around your wrist as you went into surgery; it was your anchor, your security blanket. If you lost your rosary, you soon found yourself ringing the convent doorbell to buy a new one. Ten or fifteen cents, it cost. And then, of course, you had it blessed at the next Sunday mass. It was, you felt, a lifelong friend, a lifeline. When a young person left home for Connecticut, as most young people did, Maman, or Mémère, gave him/her a rosary. When a son left for the army, she made sure his rosary went with him. Young brides even hung a rosary on the clothesline to ask for a sunny wedding day. Many a wish was cast upon that prayer bead, some answered, some not. But, you held on to your prayer and to your belief. And at your death, the rosary went down into the grave with you.

"Where has all that gone?" I wondered. In some parishes, the rosary is still said before Mass, but that, too, is becoming more rare. A few, very few, families still gather weekly to say the rosary, some for a particular intention, others for general intentions. Some follow the rosary several times a day on television with Mother Angelica. Others have a tape in their car with the rosary that goes on any time they turn on the ignition. Still others pray the rosary as they travel to other areas. Pope John Paul II had a great devotion to the rosary. He even added the Luminous Mysteries to the already established Joyful, Sorrowful, and Glorious Mysteries. Devotion to the rosary is still there, but it now seems limited to fewer and fewer people or to select groups.

Almost a hundred years ago, Our Lady of Fatima urged the three shepherd children to spread devotion to the rosary to bring about the conversion of Russia and to bring peace to the world. Devotion grew and eventually Communism in Russia fell and religious freedom was able to surface once again, somewhat. But, where are we now? Have we come full circle? In recent years, a new evil force has arisen under a religious pretense to slaughter Christians and dominate the world. Can we once again storm heaven with a renewed devotion to Mary in the rosary and reverse the oncoming peril? Is this the weapon that can turn this around, this onslaught on humanity and on civilization itself? Is this the means to bring people back to God and back into our churches? Perhaps this was a call from beyond the grave to alert us to pray. We must use this weapon, we must pray the rosary, and we must bring others to do the same.

Somehow the rosary has reduced its insistent calling out to me. I may never know the identity of the original owner of that blue rosary, but I believe that I have heard its voice and its message loud and clear. And somehow, the renewed devotion and desire to spread the word have to be enough for me.

Heal/Healing/War
Guérir/Guérison/Guerre

Ajonc—Colère
Gorse—Love and fertility, protection against evil, anger

Amarante—Immortalité, constance
Amaranth—Healing, protection, invisibility

Anémone—Persévérance
Anemone—Health, protection, healing

Angélique vraie—Inspiration, noblesse, bonheur céleste
Garden Angelica, Holy Ghost, Wild Celery—Magic and poetic inspiration, angelic healing virtues

Gentiane jaune—Douleur, souffrance
Gentian, Yellow—Ingratitude, "well-born," Intrinsic worth; integrity

Pommier (fleur de)—Amour de l'homme pour la nature
Apple blossoms—Love, healing, magic, immortality

Feuille de laurier—Sagesse et victoire
Bay Leaf—Protection, psychic powers, healing, purification, strength

Belladone—Porte malheur
Belladonna—Silence, "beautiful lady"

Achillée millefeuille—Guerre; dispute ou querelles
Achillea millefolia—War

By Way of Canada

We came to this continent from France by boat
so long ago we forgot why.
We came to these United States by way of
Canada
and on the way we lost
our children
our language
our songs
our medicine
our god
and found that we must now choose whether or not
to breed
to speak
to sing
to heal
to pray.

By Kim Chase

De Canada

On est venu de France en bateaux
il y a si longtemps qu'on oublie pourquoi.
Du Canada on est descendu aux États
et en route on a perdu
nos enfants
notre langue
nos chansons
nos remèdes
notre dieu
et puis on a trouvé qu'il fallait maintenant
qu'on choisisse, oui ou non,
de procréer
de parler
de chanter
de se guérir
de prier.

par Kim Chase

Tooth Karma

She saw them enter the restaurant together
in slow motion, her arm tucked through his
where her own fit so tidily a year ago

Stuck in the La Brea tar pits of awkwardness,
she bit down hard on a piece of shell, shattering tooth
and peace of mind

Wrenching her gaze from linked elbows,
she spat tooth and shell into her napkin,
thinking about the tripled cost—
the meal, the dentist and of course, the heartache

But fortune was kind this time
sparing the worst
The dinner was comped
and the restaurant covered the dentist

Eventually desensitized
by random sightings of the happy couple
around the neighborhood
she barely noticed when they moved away

But years passed before her tongue stopped playing
with the rebuilt tooth, and she had lost her taste for clams

By Donna Hébert

Learning Mercy, Learning Shoshanna

By Felicity Deschenes*

Mercy did not feel well at the Hanukkah celebration ... Shoshanna held her and said, "You are so special."

On page two of his book *True Love*, Thich Nhat Hanh writes that "Without understanding, love is an impossible thing." With all due respect to this great and gentle soul, I humbly propose an exception to this rule: parents' love for their children. I loved my daughter Mercy before I understood her. But understanding and loving her did eventually help me understand and then love my mother-in-law. I guess I should start at the beginning.

Dan and I had only been dating a few weeks when his mother, Shoshanna, invited us to meet her at her house and take a picnic to the lake. That morning I woke up nervous about what to wear and decided to make myself a new blouse. It wasn't quite finished when Dan arrived. He called his mother to let her know we would be about half an hour late. When we got to her house, Dan just opened the door and walked right in.

"Hi, Mom!" he said to short, thick rippled legs topped with large white cotton briefs. She backed away from the dishwasher and stood up, tugging her t-shirt down. She put her arms out in a warm greeting, ready for his hug. On top of her several chins, she had a huge smile. Her stiff dyed hair stuck out at various angles. I wondered if she thought we said we'd be an hour late.

In the two years we dated before getting married, I would find many differences between Dan's family and my family. Some might have been due to our ethnic and regional backgrounds, but in so many ways she struck me as just odd. She attracted quite a range of people. Still it evidenced both her uniqueness and generosity. Every day on her way to work, she went to the same tollbooth and, one day, even went, invited, to the toll-taker's wedding. But somehow I felt she was a little too desperate to make friends.

She called me almost daily it seemed, and sometimes called more than that. One time she called to ask how to make salmon pie. I started telling her the recipe, and she said, "I don't have anything to write with; I'm in the bathroom." As usual I asked Dan to process with me, why did she do that? Why would someone call for a recipe when she was in the bathroom? He just shrugged and said, "She calls whenever she thinks of something because she is afraid she will forget."

Fast forward to 1996, when I had another person to think and talk about with Dan—we were expecting a baby girl. Shoshanna was excited for her first grandchild, too.

When Dan told his mother I was in labor, she took a cab all the way from Framingham, Massachusetts, to the hospital in Cambridge, about twenty miles.

After twenty hours of labor, the midwife wanted the doctors to do a cesarean section. Twenty minutes later Dan held Mercy's cheek to mine.

Mercy wanted to nurse, but she couldn't really latch on. The lactation consultant's teen-aged daughter seemed to take a very good message when I called, but I didn't hear back all that day or the next. The lactation consultant found the message on the desk in her daughter's bedroom. Mercy was five days old and losing weight before we got help nursing. In retrospect, the difficulty latching on could have been our first clue development was going to be non-typical.

I loved how Mercy's big gray, then dark brown, eyes stared into mine while she nursed. When she wasn't nursing she was crying—for about five months. I felt guilty that I couldn't wait to go back to work, even to my reduced schedule. I loved her and was so fascinated with her. Still something made me realize I had held different expectations of what a baby would be like.

She was slow to roll over and never crawled. All the floors in our apartment were hardwood. We set her on one end of a blanket and her toys at the other, trying to give her an incentive to crawl. Instead, she babbled at the toys, as if she could talk them into coming to her. She didn't really move until she walked, at ten months. She wouldn't do stairs until she could walk those, too. My friend Lisa thought Mercy just wanted to be a grown-up already and skip this baby part.

She certainly sounded grown up. In her ninth month, we bought a house and moved in the weekend before Dan had to go to Memphis for a week. She sat in the middle of the kitchen floor, saying "Daddy? Daddy here?" as if we had forgotten to bring him with all our stuff. When he came home, she watched us washing the vegetables from our farm share. "Gahlic!" she correctly yelled out. We looked at each other laughing, incredulous, "How does she know that?! And where did she get that thick Boston accent?!"

** Felicity Deschenes is a pen name from the author's family tree. All names have been changed to protect privacy.*

She was a generous baby. One of my favorite pictures of her is in her high chair, offering the Clementine segment she has impaled on her right thumb. Dan loved that she enjoyed eating pickles with him. I wondered what was not to like about mashed potatoes.

Mercy did not feel well at the Hanukkah celebration around the time of her second birthday. Shoshanna held her and said, "You are so special." Apparently Mercy thought Shoshanna was talking about how Mercy felt, and Mercy replied, "Grandma, I've been special all day." It was one of the few words she ever misunderstood, but "special all day" became our slogan for her.

Later that month, her pediatrician said it was time to take away the pacifier. We had been trying to discourage the pacifier use, but often forgot to "misunderstand" her crystal clear diction around the object in her mouth. But Mercy heard and understood the doctor say it was collecting germs and could be the cause of recent ear infections. She let the pacifier go and switched to her left thumb. The dentist didn't like the thumb sucking, but he said he never heard of kids switching from pacifier to thumb, so she must really need to do it.

Eventually Mercy became a big sister to Adele, who got wherever she wanted to go as soon as she could roll. We marveled at how different children can be. Then Mercy went to the public preschool in a big school building. She came home the first day and declared, "I paid attention ALL DAY and I STILL don't know how to read." She was a wonderfully earnest little student.

From kindergarten, I got her back every day with her thumb practically glued to her palate. Why was she so stressed? Should I homeschool? I didn't really think so. Dan already understood her so much better than me. And he was worth a lot more in the job market than me.

For first and second grade she had a kind, sweet, disorganized, and unstructured teacher. She seemed not to learn any math facts and made consistent calculation errors that her teacher said not to worry about, she didn't really need to know that yet anyway. I reasoned that she also didn't need to keep practicing it wrong. I told the principal that math instruction had been a disaster and specified the teacher I wanted her to have for third grade.

In the meantime, a colleague at work suggested having Adele tested so I could make the case for a more challenging curriculum for her upcoming first-grade experience. We located an educational psychologist to do the testing.

The educational psychologist asked me questions about both Adele and Mercy, saying she wanted to test Mercy, too, since siblings are usually not so far apart. I said no. I didn't think Mercy would do so well and why put her through that. But the psychologist said she sounded verbally gifted. I scheduled them both, and as it turned out, Mercy actually went first. Whereas halfway through Adele's test, the psychologist told me a bus near us could take her to a school for the gifted (an hour away—no, thanks), she recommended further testing for Mercy given the discrepancies in her scores. I didn't know. Even though I have a doctorate in education I had given minimal attention to exceptional learning needs. I showed the results to my boss who had taught reading and special education for decades. She pronounced them "alarming."

The pediatrician gave us a referral for further testing. It turns out our quirky baby has a slightly different kind of brain. As we learned more about the more worrisome of the two diagnoses—Nonverbal Learning Disorder (NLD)—not only did her quirks seem more coherent, related, explicable, but so did those of Shoshanna.

Although she could see her school from her bedroom window, Mercy was in second grade before she would consider going there on her own. She said she was afraid she would get lost. I gained more insight into why Shoshanna might have taken a taxi twenty miles rather than drive to an unfamiliar hospital. Shoshanna used to tell the story of once pulling her car up to a stopped taxi and asking the driver if she could pay him the fare to lead her to an address. The driver didn't want to honor such a strange request but his passenger convinced him to. Similarly it had always mystified me that Shoshanna needed to come to our house first rather than just meet us at any of the kids' performances. She would drive twenty minutes extra each way to ride with us. Dan just accepted that this was easier for her. Now seeing Mercy's fear of getting lost, I thought less about how strange some of Shoshanna's decisions seemed, and began to feel more sympathetic and even impressed with her coping strategies.

NLD looks different on everyone who has it, but one can generalize a little. For example children with NLD often appear to be verbally gifted since words are their primary way for learning about the world. Mercy couldn't trust her neural system to interpret physical cues and so it's not surprising she didn't move around much as a baby. It is not uncommon to have trouble latching on when learning to nurse. As they get older their gifted verbal side helps them realize both that they are intelligent and that somehow they are not getting all the information others seem to have. This causes anxiety. Did she already know, that first day of preschool, that she might not be getting all the information? Mercy, now about to leave for college, will still occasionally suck her thumb in the privacy of home. I never asked her, but it sure looked like Shoshanna used food as stress relief.

I continue to be amazed at how well Mercy copes when her indicators are double that which is considered a "severe" degree of NLD. For five years, the school, though agreeing that she has this learning disability, would not give her any services until the worst possible age, thirteen, when the secondary anxiety began really interfering with her ability to function. I knew she could work around the learning difference, but what parent wants their child to have any difficulty? I especially wished her difficulty wasn't so "invisible."

Before we ever had her tested, she had started acting with a local children's theater, where I think she learned explicitly that facial expressions, tone of voice, and gestures carry meaning. But she can't automatically understand them the way most folks can. I am glad we told her about the test results because she has a level of self-understanding necessary for continuing to cope. One day at church, Mercy reported that a woman repeatedly moved her hand while looking at Mercy, then got up and closed the door between two rooms. Mercy realized after that the gesturing had been a request for her to do it. She was embarrassed and said, "I hate NLD!" Many people with NLD cannot interpret body language, facial expressions, or tone of voice.

Inability to interpret subtler reactions means NLD can deprive a person of feedback regarding her impression or impact on others. Still, individuals with NLD very much want relationships. If she also had such difficulty interpreting social and emotional cues, it would be no surprise that Shoshanna would get dressed for company after they arrived, or that she might have had some questionable friends. My husband always distinguished between the true friends who really cared about her and those that came to all her parties for free food or imposed their children on her for free baby-sitting. Difficulty making friends coupled with a strong desire for friendship puts people with NLD at risk of exploitative relationships.

I am not sure what the future will hold for Mercy. When her first round of test results came back, Shoshanna told Mercy that when she was a kid she had an IQ test, too, and her IQ was very low so her parents didn't expect much from her. She explained to Mercy that she worked hard and while a single mother got both bachelor's and master's degrees, rose to mid-level management, and became so expert in one of her company's computer systems that when they merged with another company, they called her out of retirement. Every now and then Mercy will refer to something Grandma told her about how you only need to learn one way to get to each place you need to go, or how important a calendar is. I think Mercy has a sense of the kind of hard work she will have to do.

When she was eleven she came in from her first successful solo bike ride. She said, "Mum bike riding is so fun! But I want you to know learning it was torture." I smiled at her. I told her I am so glad she enjoys the free feeling of riding her bike. And I told her that bike-riding is one of the hardest things for a person with NLD to learn to do, so it shows that she will be able to do anything if she wants it enough.

I know that giving children only labels for their learning differences can be controversial, and I believe that unqualified amateur diagnoses of other people's quirks might be a form of violence to them. If I am judging someone it means I am totally missing their value, their meaning in my life. But I think I can understand and work with Mercy better now because of the framework the diagnosis gives me. I think she will be able to explain her difficulties as needed when she goes out on her own. I think she will be able to ask for what she needs in order to be understood as the loving and earnest person she is. I don't think Shoshanna understood herself. She had no diagnoses, and whether she really had anything like NLD or not is hard to say, but I do know that when I looked at her with greater understanding and sympathy, as gained from learning about NLD, I appreciated her much more. Perhaps as Thich Nhat Hanh suggested, the understanding helped me love her.

In January 2006, Mercy sang for her first time at Jordan Hall, as part of the Boston Children's Chorus for their Martin Luther King Jr. Concert. At the end of the performance, against a backdrop of Adele sobbing inconsolably because we might never again see the New York singers we had hosted, I helped Shoshanna down the steep stairs of the hall while Dan got the car. Shoshanna was only sixty-one, but she had asthma and knee problems. She said, "I don't want to get old."

On the drive home and right through tooth-brushing, Adele continued sobbing. I stayed on our porch and watched Shoshanna drive away from our house, more than a little concerned about her night vision, hoping she got home safely. My mother-in-law did get home safely that night, but it would be the last time any of us saw her. She would not get old. She died, probably of asthma, home alone during a February blizzard.

I am glad Mercy and she had already had some time to talk about coping, learning and succeeding in life. I am glad I had come to a place of understanding, acceptance and love before she left. I think she realized I had.

"Beyond the Great Door" Excerpt from *COMICS*

By Lorraine Saint Pierre

In the play "Comics," the lead character has two names and is played by two actors, both of whom are onstage throughout the play. Theresa-Therese works in a mental health center where she screens clients to find out which ones are crazy and which ones are sane. It is a "screening" she does with her own thoughts, too. But Theresa-Therese has another duality that looms large in her life. Raised in a Franco-American household in Maine, she "has an American head and a French heart." The journey she takes into her split identity sets the stage for "Comics," written by Lewiston native, now living in New York City, Lorraine St. Pierre

Theresa Lachance, a thirty-two-year-old divorcée and recent graduate, has returned to the hometown of her former marriage. She works on the emergency team at the local mental health center. On call to the hospital emergency room the previous night, the scene opens at the Center, CMHS, staff meeting the following morning after she relates her assessment and disposition of the case of a patient for whom she was able to secure hospitalization.

A state of craziness is one of life's grace periods. You attain complete lucidity for a short while. It can be an extremely painful experience: some are reduced to blathering idiots, others remain in a state of frozen panic, but there are those who know what is happening. They might tell you about their experience beyond that great door. Crossing the threshold is so frightening that most never do it willingly, but are pushed through in times of stress and trauma when the absolute falseness of their lives becomes a shrieking monster. And then, once finding themselves alone, on the other side of the door looking at a world that does not care to hear about the grand illusion they are living in, much less take steps to correct it, yes, it is enough to make a person psychotic.

Most of the people who come to CMHS cannot describe the experience occurring to them. They borrow the explanations provided by the agencies, and they fit their experiences to match the mold. The spirit to live their truth is missing. Instead of a profound mystical experience they are diagnosed as undergoing an acute schizophrenic episode.

Theresa knows that spirit is lacking because of the original sin. It is situated on Canal Street, a long row of what some people see as gracious brick structures representative of the finest nineteenth century architecture. They are dungeons that have taken the souls of her people, broken their spirits, shamed them. And it continues. The whole town shares in this guilt and, try as they might, the city fathers and the members of the Chamber of Commerce cannot erase that sin.

French people are told they can rise above their seamy beginnings. Some do. They leave Chesterton and their culture. Those who remain and do not choose to rise above their "seamy" beginnings are broken, docile people; soulless, the words have been taken from them. In the three decades she has lived in Chesterton she has witnessed the French language completely disappear in all public places.

She has heard the old people talk about the acting companies that flourished in their days; there was opera, chorale music, a variety of social and artistic organizations. All dead now. A few of the city's elite sponsor artistic events, but it has nothing to do with the depressed town.

Of the many mills operating in the city at one time there is only one still functioning, and it is not doing well. The employees have been forced to buy out the owners (a Boston corporation) to keep it running. Sometimes when she is called to the hospital late at night she drives by the long row of buildings, most now occupied by small-scale factories and fly-by-night shoe shops. She wonders about the people in the last remaining mill, working with that infernal noise, the filth and the drudgery while the city sleeps. Words are powerful; they convince the people working at the Chesterton Mill that they belong there. It is what they were born and raised to do.

No one in her family has worked in the mills. It doesn't matter, it's like being black; you cannot run away from the color. As a French person, you cannot escape the mill, no matter what you do. It's the Chesterton curse.

The French are burdened with the failure of the industrial revolution. They, and the polluting mills, are something Maine could have done without. A city was built; agents scoured the Canadian countryside for workers; canals were dug for water power; Catholic churches and schools went up as fast as money could be wrested from the hands of working family members. And all for what? Within fifty years it was over. The South built more efficient mills and had cheaper labor. Chesterton never recovered from that blow. Thousands and thousands of people had been uprooted, had come with good intentions, making a commitment to a new way of life and a new country. They are bitter, humiliated people.

Theresa figures the only thing that could save Chesterton and turn it around is if the city fathers and the members of the Chamber of Commerce hosted a sacred dance and bonfire for the French people; no, not just the French, everyone in town suffers. There would be fiddles and accordions, that old '*tappage des pieds*' music with old men standing alone doing their jig, and there would be square dancing like an old time *Réveillon* with pork pies and good French beans. Then towards the end, after several days of this spiritual festival, at midnight, torches would be handed to everyone which they would touch to the bonfire and they would descend on the mills in great waves, singing all the while and shooting their torches through the multi-panelled windows. Afterward, everyone joining hands, would stand encircling the inferno, watching it burn. And, as is traditional in French homes at the new year for the father to speak to his family, the town fathers could now address their citizens with some hope for the future.

Cities, like individuals, suffer psychic wounds, but there are no shamans left to bring the people together for such a healing. Theresa's fantasy of a concerted effort remains just that. Salvation is now an individual matter. Both she and the man she committed to the state hospital have to find their own way. She cannot heal him, but she can be a sympathetic listener and ease his burden if possible.

It's no good trying to explain her reasoning to Josh about the commitment. He does not understand that two people sitting in a bleak room at one o'clock in the morning are able to speak honestly to each other about the brutality and sordidness of life. Josh is still asleep; he has not crossed the threshold and gone beyond the great door.

Once she has presented last night's case she leaves the meeting and walks upstairs to the waiting room. Josh is behind her. As she makes her way across the lobby a woman comes forward on her way downstairs. She crumples to the floor in front of her. Theresa calls to the receptionist, "I need some help, get an ambulance!"

Rachel calls out Josh's name. *Of course, he's a medical doctor!* He comes over and kneels next to the stricken woman and he begins to bully Theresa. Then she sees; he's scared. All eyes are on him, expecting more than he can possibly deliver, and he panics. After a moment, she figures that the woman is probably having an hysteric reaction.

"Let's bring her to the couch; I think she'll be alright," she tells Josh. They drag her body over, set her down and she slowly revives. Theresa leaves the building and heads for McDonald's to get a couple of coffees for herself and Paula. By the time she reaches her friend's house, Paula is already made up. The meeting has gone on too long.

"Sit here, Theresa, I'll fix your face," her friend urges her.

She sits on Paula's stool expectantly and has her face massaged with cold cream. She relaxes and makes herself comfortable, the sleepless night easing its way back into the underworld. Paula pulls a hair out of her brow.

"Ouch!"

"It's gonna look neater, more sophisticated."

Then she puts several kinds of makeup on her face; some areas are touched with screening liquid and the whole of it is topped off with powder. She looks at herself in the Hollywood-style makeup mirror, lights all around; it is a strange thing to witness. She's becoming more pronounced, a stronger character. Next comes the eye shadow.

"What color do you want?"

She points to a soft green color, Caribbean, thinking it will be a nice accent to her hazel eyes.

"Good choice."

Paula is an artist. After the color, three shades of it, comes the eye liner, widening the eyes, then mascara for the lashes. Theresa has worn makeup before, doing it in spurts. She feels stronger with it on.

Paula brushes on two peaches, one for each cheek. "Voilà, mon Chou, go out there and charm 'em. I gotta get to work."

Theresa brushes her long dark hair away from the way it normally falls to fluff it out and give it more volume.

At ten o'clock in the morning she's painted up for the proverbial battle. She drives to the house and sits on the steps for a bit before going in to bed. Fat little robins bounce around the dead lawn looking for nourishment. Two are courting, chirping and flapping their wings excitedly.

Walking into the house, she looks at the sofa on her right where she has spent every night since coming back from college and decides to go past it. She crosses the living room and opens her bedroom door. Removing her clothes, she takes each piece off and flings it to a different area of the room. Her painted face reflected in the mirror.

Waking up later, she is sick. Her head throbs, in the front of her face and the back of her skull. It hurts so much she feels nauseated and then she is sick to her stomach. She lies rocking herself gently, moaning all the while, knowing there is no physical component to this illness, but this does not comfort her because there is nothing to be done. It will have to run its course. Something is upsetting her and she will not get better until it is resolved. She is afraid of something.

Sleeping in fits, she is sick most of the day. By evening, the headache lifts and although weak, she feels better and brings a glass of milk into her bedroom along with some crackers smeared with butter and mustard.

She sits in bed looking at herself in the mirror, raising her glass to the reflection. *Here's looking at you*. Her body now free of illness is peaceful, weightless.

She puts on her nightgown and robe and goes to sit on the porch steps. The air is cold, crawling inside her robe to the satin gown beneath, chilling her, her nipples hardening against the cold satin. They are out there, millions of them, chirping away for the world to hear, little male wings furiously rubbing against each other.

It isn't that simple for the human animal, which is forced to resort to vague interpretations of symbols and signs, trying to figure out what its own soul immediately perceives and understands. Many things became known and were decided last night that she is barely aware of.

She goes back to her lighted house leaving the primitive night to the crickets. Checking the *TV Guide*, she decides to shut her mind off for the evening.

In the morning she wakes early, puts on her jogging clothes and goes out for a run, then she showers, dresses and stops at a neighborhood café for the breakfast special. It's her day at the office. The Count is there already.

Christ, that man must sleep here." Did you have a good night on duty?"

"Incredible as it may seem, I didn't have a single call. Not even Al!"

"Then why are you here? You don't have any reports."

"I don't know, I'm so used to coming in, I guess I just didn't think about it. I've got some news for you."

"What's that?"

"They've canned Jim Wilbur."

"Oohh! That's too bad. He's the best psychiatrist we've got."

"Yeah, I'm going to miss him too. I have a lot of respect for Jim. Dr. Baraka is his replacement. He's been in private practice in Chesterton for over twenty years, one of the pioneers of the field in this town. He's recovering from a serious illness and can't go back to private practice. The doctors got together and spoke to the old man about getting him some work here at the agency."

"When's he coming in?"

"Next week. This is Jim's last. I heard he found a spot at the state hospital."

She checks the schedule to see whom she will be working with this day. It's Wilbur. She's glad to have this last time with him.

The phone on Theresa's desk rings. Rachel has some attorney on the line who's talking about a client of his, locked in a closet downtown threatening to kill himself.

"Who's the lawyer?"

"It's attorney Chandler."

"Oh, Jesus!"

"Do you know him?"

"No, it's nothing." But she does know him, knows him well. They had been lovers; perhaps one of the stranger relationships she has experienced. He likes controlling others and feeling powerful. She had been suitably impressed, especially by the Harvard degree and his brilliant mind. It had not ended well between them. The more he tried to control her the more inscrutable she became. He could not stand that.

"Hello, Chandler, this is Theresa. I work at CMHC as an emergency counselor."

"Oh, it's you . . . well . . I've got a divorce client who's trying to kill himself. His wife just called me. He's locked himself in a closet and he's got a bunch of pills. "

"What's his name?"

"Philip Castonguay."

"I know him." She looks at the Count. "It's Phil; he's still drinking."

"Have you called the police?" she asks the attorney.

"Yah."

"Is there anything else I should know?"

"I expect this to be treated as a top priority. This man is ill."

"Hmm." She hangs up the phone thinking, *go soak your head, Chandler.*

"I saw him a couple of weeks ago with his wife. He had started going to A.A. meetings. I thought he was getting himself straightened out," the Count tells her.

Billy walks into the office and pulls up a chair to join them. He greets the two. She nods; the Count smiles at him.

"I saw him a month ago. It was the initial contact," Theresa replies. "He came in with his wife. It's his second. They came because of marital difficulties; his drinking. She didn't want to put up with it anymore. A good woman, she cares for Phil, but she won't stick around if he doesn't stop drinking. My feeling is he knows that. His first wife left him because of the drinking and now the same thing is happening again. He won't give up drinking and he doesn't want to lose her. Bad spot to be in."

"Who are you two talking about?" Billy wants to know.

"Phil Castonguay."

"Him again! Christ, doesn't that guy quit? I've seen him three times this week. Laura down at Detox got about five calls from him threatening to end his life. What's he done now?"

"Threatened to kill himself again," she tells him.

"I'll call Detox and A.A. to see what I can find out. What was your impression, Billy?"

"I felt he had no intention of stopping his drinking, and these suicide scares are a tactic to divert our attention from what's going on. I feel bad for his wife; she looked pretty miserable."

Billy and the Count move over to their side of the room to talk about strategy for their evening group, both men feeling good about the relationship developing among the participators. Billy is applauding the Count's wisdom; Nick, taking it all in.

Theresa calls the secretarial office and asks for Phil Castonguay's file. She then calls the several places that might have information about his current state of mind. After having gathered that knowledge she concludes her first opinion about Phil had been correct. He is now preparing the groundwork that will eventually lead to his being able to accept the terrible decision he is to make. He will not give up his drinking and his wife will leave him.

The phone rings, "Theresa, Phil Castonguay is here with two police officers," Rachel informs her.

"Give me two minutes and then send him down." She looks at the two talking men at the other desk and tells them about the call. They leave, going to another room to finish their meeting.

Phil looks wan and terribly exhausted, standing between the two officers. She points to the chairs. He will not talk. Fate, which has delivered this cruel choice is going to have its way. He has chosen to be a silent witness to its capriciousness. The officers, both agitated, fill her in to what has transpired.

She doesn't know what to do about what is going on. He's already been hospitalized within the past month at Marcotte Medical. They won't take him back. They are right; they can't help a person who won't help himself. Detox won't take him because he doesn't want to stop drinking. And he isn't psychotic so she can't send him to the state hospital. He's alone with this decision; there isn't anything she can do. She does not feel the suicide threat is serious; he's going to do it the long way, drinking himself to death.

"What's happening, Phil? It's becoming a daily occurrence that I hear your name mentioned by someone in social services. You've dropped out of A.A., you're not attending meetings anymore, you keep calling up people telling them you're in trouble, they offer help, you don't follow through. Do you want to kill yourself?"

Like a scolded boy, he keeps his head low and nods.

"I don't know what to do. You've just come out of the hospital . . ." She has said the magic word. His eyes light up. He wants out of the situation; he wants to go to bed and sleep till it all blows away. It isn't just that he has recently been a patient at Marcotte Medical; by now they know he is alcoholic and it is someone else's problem as far as the hospital is concerned.

"I'm gonna go see Dr. Wilbur and have a talk with him about it." She gets up and heads down the hall.

"Good morning, Theresa," his long slender fingers extend to receive the file she is handing him. She wants to reach over and stroke the hand, lean, elegant, patrician. It's like an intricate piece of ivory, small-veined and polished. She fills him in on the case and tells him her impressions.

"Alright, let's go take a look at him."

Once they reach her office the doctor sits at the opposite side of the room, changing the perspective. The two officers and Phil turn to him, "I understand, Mr. Castonguay, that you're feeling unable to go on, you want to kill yourself. Is that right?"

Phil nods.

"You've been in the hospital in the past month?"

He nods.

"Did they give you medication?"

"Yeah, I got a prescription for Valium. I was allowed three refills. I've got one left."

"I see from your file that you've been going to A.A. Are you still attending meetings?"

"No, I don't like going there. I'm not like those people. I'm not going back."

"It seems to me that you've got a drinking problem and there isn't anything we can do about that unless you're willing to stop drinking. It's your problem." The doctor has made his decision. He is getting up to leave.

"This man is sick; he almost killed himself!" one of the officers blurts out. "He should be hospitalized."

Wilbur stops as he passes him and says, "he's not psychotic and doesn't belong in the state hospital." He then leaves the tension-filled room. The two officers storm out after him and head for their cruiser. Phil stands slowly, never glancing back at Theresa. Fate has delivered her pronouncement.

She takes the phone off the hook after he leaves and sits quietly looking at her map. Her father had a "drinking problem." Quite a few of the uncles and cousins in her family, like her friends' families, drank too much and behaved like children. She could not recount the many times she had seen her father insensible, fallen over at the table, or on the couch, the eyes glassy, saliva coming out of his gaping mouth.

She doesn't know why people choose to drink, but she suspects it has something to do with lack of courage for many of them. They need fortification. Phil's life is hopeless; he is like a hockey puck being whacked around on an ice cold ground. Life has not delivered that sweet, warm milk to fill his belly and bring a smile to his somber face. But he is making up for it now, every night down at the Strip sucking to his heart's content.

And she is to be the witness because he wants someone to care about what is happening to him. But she turns her back to this desperate man as she did with her father. It is never easy.

She puts the phone back on the hook and records the dictation of this visit with Philip.

The rest of the day is taken up with follow-through appointments for med checks. Before leaving she stops by Jim's office to say good-bye and wish him well at his new post. She takes the long elegant hand extended to her and holds it for a few moments. "I've enjoyed working with you and getting to know you, Jim. I'm going to miss our sessions."

"It couldn't be avoided. This is the second time it's happened to me. I'll probably come back." He is not a local doctor, therefore not part of the clique; always the first to go when something comes up. He speaks about Philip Castonguay. "That was nasty business this morning. The officers didn't care for my disposition of the case."

"I called the station and spoke to one of the men explaining the situation to him, all the times we had seen him, and my appraisal of what was happening."

"But you broke confidence doing that."

"I know."

The deep blue eyes questioning her, then releasing. "It's been a pleasure working with you, Theresa. We were a good team." He smiles warmly.

"Yes, we were." She looks at the finely etched, strong face; he is a man of integrity. She leaves his office and makes her way up to the lobby. Rachel stops her, "Phone call?" She has the receiver in hand pointing at Theresa.

"I'll take it in my office." It's Chandler, upset at the treatment Philip Castonguay has received at the

(Continued on next page)

Women, War & Peace

Women, War & Peace premiered on your local PBS station and is now available on-line or on DVD. The bold five-part series challenges the conventional wisdom that war and peace is men's domain. *Women, War & Peace* spotlights the stories of women in conflict zones from Bosnia to Afghanistan and Colombia to Liberia, placing women at the center of an urgent dialogue about conflict and security, and reframing our understanding of modern warfare.—**PBS**

Notes from the Executive Producers, *Women, War & Peace*, PBS
By Abigail E. Disney, Pamela Hogan and Gini Reticker

We've been asked, how did the idea for *Women, War & Peace* start? As usual the answer is — over lunch.

In 2007, while overseeing the international current affairs series *Wide Angle* for PBS in New York City, Pam produced an interview with Iraqi-born Zainab Salbi, founder of Women for Women International. Zainab's book, *The Other Side of War*, ... In *Wide Angle*'s seven seasons on air, the war stories always seemed to focus on the men and the guns. "Who's doing the documentary about the other side of war?" she asked Zainab, certain that such a film must be in the works. "No one" was the reply. "We have to do something about that," said Pam.

At that moment, Abby and Gini were in an editing room across town working on *Pray the Devil Back to Hell*, the story of how a group of Liberian women came together to bring peace to their country after years of war. As Gini and Abby looked for archival footage to tell the women's story, they found it was surprisingly scarce ... Despite the fact that every eyewitness to the events confirmed that what the women had done was transformative, it appeared that journalists and their crews weren't interested, or the footage resulting from those days was not deemed important enough to archive.

From the onset, we knew that *Pray the Devil Back to Hell* would be one of five films in the series. The question immediately became: what other stories should we tell? ... U.N. testimony of Patrick Cammaert, a former commander of U.N. peacekeeping forces, when he observed from his own experience in multiple war zones that: "It has probably become more dangerous to be a woman than a soldier in an armed conflict." So, we decided to focus on the period in which that has happened—the last twenty years, where frontlines have disappeared and civilians have become primary targets.

To borrow a phrase from Hague prosecutor Peggy Kuo, it's our hope with this series to "shine a spotlight on women's experience in war" so the full picture can be seen.

Excerpt taken from "*Women, War, and Peace*: An Interview with Abigail Disney," Alliance for Peacebuilding:

BP: What initially sparked your interest in documentary films focusing on women, war, and peace?
Disney: I went to Liberia in 2006, just a few months after President Sirleaf was inaugurated. While there, I heard the story that *Pray the Devil Back to Hell* is based on: that women across different religious, ethnic, and educational lines effectively came together to push for an end to the long-standing civil war. I came back home obsessed with that story, saying to people that someone should make a documentary on this. Eventually my brother, who is a filmmaker, said I should make the documentary. I come from a filmmaking family, so I decided to go for it and tell the story myself.

(***Comics* continued from previous page**)

agency. "This matter isn't over. I'm going to see to it. You can't get away with treating sick people like that!"

"You're a jerk, Chandler! And you know what? You're dumb, Harvard degree or not, you're a dummy. You're so busy manipulating people, you never take stock of the real situation and you don't know what's happening."

The last case she and Jim Wilbur shared had heart failure at bottom. Phil is in the enviable position of having someone who loves him by his side, but he can't let go of past hurts so it doesn't amount to anything.

It is fitting that she and Jim shared this last case. There's nothing to be done about self-destructive people. It's their decision, they are responsible. She has made her peace with the situation and withdrawn her heart.

The Hands of War

1

In this Christmas snow, if planes get off the runway
their PA systems will crackle, “Some of our military
personnel are with us. Let’s give them a big hand....
We thank you for your service in our nation’s stand

against terror.” When I fly, I wonder if others share
my doubts, my angst about the horrors of warfare.
Does the evening news make them think a round
of cheer will dispel our soldiers’ troubles? I don’t

know soldiers who expect a hand from civilians.
True, special programs give “Families of the Fallen”
“survivor support” after a beloved’s sacrifice of life or limb,
& some count on food stamps to help feed their children.

Strapped in my too narrow seat, I sit stock-still & stare.
What would a Quaker at Meeting do if enemies were there?

2

Is an enemy near or am I a Quaker at Meeting not yet
moved to stand & speak about the last meals I ate
with my deployed husband & son? About how I savor
each crumb of memories? While they were safe at home

I read poems about Vietnam when my husband fought
as a Green Beret. The year before in DC, *Tsou Tai Tai*
taught Chinese to his group, & we treated demonstrators
at the War Moratorium on the Mall. After, I nursed “lifers”

& draftees in Okinawa while my husband & team travelled
on missions. Years later, “back in the world,” the Army’s nickel
sent him to med school, while I left our toddlers in the family’s care
& went off to Army Nurse Basic. They inoculated me against rare

diseases, but not the grief, not the terror. Vietnam loomed too large—
our hours apart, the days & nights I had nursed troops in my charge.

3

Whatever the hour, Army Nurses are charged with the health of US troops.
We fired & cleaned Colt 45s, practiced Mass Cals & debrided wounds.
Future test items, DIs signaled by pounding the podium. “Nuclear
& chemical attacks. You can survive, if you follow proper procedure.”

We watched hours of slides—Japanese maimed by the first nukes,
Americans burned & gassed. We put on & removed charcoal suits.

Troop trucks took us into deep woods for our own taste of the gas
swelled in a windowless shed. We needed no order to don our masks.

"Proper procedure will save your life," admonished our Sergeant
once again, before he led us into the fog. Too soon he barked,
"Remove your mask." Each of us gagged on gas, tears, & snot.
"Replace your mask," his hoarse bellow came like a welcome shot.

The possibility of saving troops gassed in combat felt unreal,
even if we did not die from our own battle theater ordeals.

4

Of course, I lived through my Basic Training ordeal
& travelled from Texas to Massachusetts where I filled
my arms with my sons' soft bodies. In Fort Dix's temporary
housing, roaches kept us awake. At work, I treated basic trainees—

even peace wounds psyches. My hands stroked my sons,
& I nurtured them with all the left-over vigor I had. Some
things were almost too much. Like the night our babysitter's
boyfriend stole my dead grandmother's rhinestone pins

while my sons slept in the next room. High on pot, the thieves
left a trail of Klondike Bar wrappers. It snaked from my freezer
to their stolen stash of guns. Like, the Corp's threat when I refused
a "joint" assignment four hours from my husband. It was true.

Tender enthusiasms mattered little to the Army, after all.
No surprise—common wisdom has it women's wars are small.

5

Though common wisdom has it women's wars are small,
I resigned my commission while my husband answered the call
to serve in new wars where he treated kids maimed in battle.
At home, I managed the family & gave others like me counsel.

One son had blond, the other brown hair. Both grew up
with war & chose sides—one preferred weapons,
one the medical profession—healing & wounding, front
& back on the coin of the warrior's struggle with violent forces.

At the Fort Drum gym, I've watched healthy looking men
sit to play volleyball & slide when others would run.
Their net was low, as it would be for children, as it must be
for troops who have suffered traumatic brain injuries

when bombs bounced their brains inside the caverns
of skulls, shaped so much like crucibles of cupped hands.

6

Soldiers' skulls, so like crucibles of cupped hands
bake inside Kevlar helmets worn in contested lands.
At three this morning, before their charter plane
touches down, soldiers trade Kevlar for soft caps.

It is minus nine degrees on the tarmac as the last
of the Third return from their tour in the desert—
their fourth. Bareheaded, they march into the gym
below high flying American flags & military emblems.

"You are my hero." "Welcome home," signs blare.
Adults & children wave tiny flags made of paper
in hands that do not care to stay warm under covers while
husbands & wives, father & mothers, brothers & sisters arrive.

An Army band fills our waiting-time with patriotic ditties.
Wavy white screens cycle slides of soldiers "in country."

7

In waves cycling behind white screens, my soldier is lost
& a distance farther than the missions' stands between us.
Still, we dare not cross the divide until the Command
Sergeant Major shouts his order: "DiiiSsss-Missed!"

Both phalanxes spill wave into wave onto the court.
At jump lines, I join others who have their children in tow.
Each of us searches the crowd for that beloved face
not touched—in how long? Almost before we can trace

hair or lips, photographers snap shots for papers & TV,
thrust hand-held mikes before our faces. They ask us clichéd
questions while hand in hand, we embrace each happy moment
we're given. Soon enough, our lives could be a different hell

if the sand in their boots & gloves won't go away. We know.
Christmas delays on runways? Clap your hands! It's only snow.

By Caroline LeBlanc

"Women and War"
Taken from The United States Institute of Peace

"In October 2000, the United Nations Security Council passed landmark Resolution 1325 on women, peace, and security, which linked women's experiences of conflict to the international peace and security agenda, acknowledging their peacemaking roles as well as the disproportionate impact of violent conflict on women."

I Dream of Frog

By Renee Violette

I dream Aunt Joan is pregnant, too small, I know she is not taking care of herself, she is dying. We are all dying. The news reports four nuclear bombs have been activated. We have moments. In a city. People in a building. Hard cold concrete floor. Must get food downstairs in basement quick. I am the only one who is getting things done, grabbing food. Rushing. I leave Post-it notes, directions, for people upstairs on how to contact me if they need to recover from alcoholism. Including a note for dear Ken who died last year. Loud BANG! Accident outside. I run to look out window. People rushing to accident to help. Man trapped in car. Big brown bear on sidewalk. Run back to pantry. Trying to get food into basement. We only have minutes. Frantically grabbing food and kids' toys and televisions. Man, large silent balding, filthy man, at top of stairs going slow, obstructing me. Deliberately trying to slow me down. Shove him aside. There is not enough food. Joan has the baby. I see it. I hold it. I drop it. It is small and dry.

I know it will die.

I wake up drenched in urgency, terror and desperation.

This morning I pray: God, flow through me into this project, that it may be useful to someone.

Food for today: 1 egg, 1 turkey bacon, ½ cup oatmeal, 1 cup almond milk, banana. 3-4 oz Turkey, 4 oz sweet potato (optional), 4 oz cucumber, 4 oz raw red pepper. 4 oz steak, 3 oz mushrooms and onions, 5 oz green beans, 4 oz potato. 1 oz Grapenuts, 1 cup milk, 6 oz strawberries.

It is early afternoon. I sit in my frigid car in front of a small brick coffee shop with the heat blowing on my face and call my therapist, Dr. Anna. We don't have cell phone reception in the large old farmhouse my husband David and I recently rented just north of Farmington, so I always have to drive into town. I like Dr. Anna. She is brash and direct, yet really knowledgeable. We had sessions regularly when I lived in Rockland last year, and I was relieved when she agreed to have our sessions over the phone when I moved.

She says I am wrapped up in perfectionism and it is triggering shame.

She has suggested several books on shame and I am currently a quarter of the way into *Breaking the Shame that Binds*. I find some of the psychological jargon over my head, but parts of it are interesting. I kind of just want to skip to the part where he tells me what I can do about it. Apparently that is at the end.

She tells me that I expect myself to be perfect, but perfectionism can't be a goal because it is not attainable or sustainable. She says I just need to be as good as I can be today.

I tell her about the nightmares. They are getting worse and they stay with me all through the day; sometimes, if they are vivid enough, I can feel them for two or three days. I carry them in my chest, right above the sternum. The dark heaviness of it radiates out and makes it laborious to breathe.

The first nightmare I ever remember having was when I was six years old.

My father is short and stocky. They nicknamed him "Stump" in high school. He is only 5'4 but his calves resemble the cartoon version of Popeye's forearms.

We are in Mémé and Pépé's driveway.

I am standing on the white vinyl passenger side seat in our green Volkswagen Bug.

The miss-matched yellow car door that replaced the original green one after dad had an accident is open, and I am facing my father who is standing on the pavement.

Dad is angry.

He cocks back and punches at me but I jump out of the car quick.

The punch misses my face, but as his swing whips by my head I look back and the whole fist comes off and turns into a cartoon fist.

Big, white and puffy, just like Mickey Mouse's gloves, but in a fist.

The fist has a cartoon face.

The face smiles.

It is going to get me.

I run as fast fast fast as I can down the paved walkway, up the red steps, and fling open the heavy wooden door into my grandparents' kitchen.

All of my aunts are sitting around the oval table chatting.

They don't look up.

The fist follows me into the house.

I run past the kitchen through the living room where my uncles are watching TV.

No one looks up.

I run down the narrow hall and into the bathroom and try to lock the door behind me.

I am shaking too hard.

It is coming.

Quick! Quick!

I finally get the lock to turn. I back up as far as I can, back, back against the only window in the small room.

Trembling violently.

I stare at the hollow wooden door and hold my breath.

It's happening.

The white cartoon fist slowly morphs through the door and fully forms in the bathroom with a long drawn out suction sounding POP!

It shakes itself off, focuses on me with big round cartoon googly-eyes, opens its large toothy mouth and laughs.

Dr. Anna asks me how I feel about my father.

I tell her I understand my father. He was afraid. I get that. That makes sense to me. I have used violence to control others when I was afraid. But I am ragefully resentful at those who chose to look the other way to protect their way of life. To keep things normal. Selfish bastards.

Fuck them and their stupid small worlds.

Dr. Anna listens and asks me where my frog is.

Ah, the frog.

After seeing Dr. Anna for about four weeks she asks me about my childhood family dynamics. Propped up on the flowery love seat in her log cabin home office, I ramble off the chaotic details. She leans back in her rocking chair, her slippered feet gliding over the shiny hard wood, and tilts her head.

"Hmmm … okay …" she says biting her bottom lip, "… so I want you to do an exercise."

She knows I like exercises, assignments, things I can accomplish and bring back to her in search of meaning and understanding and hopefully a clue that unlocks it all. That *A-HA!* moment that changes all of my behavior.

I know it doesn't work that way, but still I like to feel like I am *doing* something.

"Find a doll that you can connect with. One that looks like you or one that calls to you when you see it. Buy it or borrow it or whatever and take care of it. Treat it like you would treat a baby you adored. This doll is you. It's your inner child, so to speak. You are going to tell it everything you wanted to hear growing up. Bring it to the store, make sure it wears a seat belt. Make sure it gets to bed on time."

Good God, maybe not this kind of exercise, I think as I scrunch up my nose and look past her out the window at the lake.

But I nod yes anyway, and week after week she asks me if I found the doll.

"No, I haven't," I finally admit, maybe a little too forcefully.

"I went to the department store and I didn't want to "parent" any of them."

She gives me the "tell me more" look.

"You see, I've never had a doll. I've never cared about a doll. I've never wanted a doll … I don't DO dolls …."

She nods and doesn't say anything.

After a long moment I go on.

"I was thinking I could use the one my Mom gave me when I was born that I never played with. I still have it somewhere I think …"

"The look on your face tells me that you shouldn't use that doll." She interrupts. "Seriously. You look like you hate that doll. It is clear by your face that you don't like that doll at all. Your face is twisted up."

I force my face it back into its place.

"Look. It doesn't have to be a doll but it does have to be something you connect with and that you can take care of. Like … like maybe a stuffed animal."

I toss my head back and forth contemplating the idea.

"Okay, I will look."

After the session I jump in my beat-up green Subaru and drive to the local discount store. I walk in and out of the toy aisle with my arms crossed at my chest. Plastic and furry faces smile at my grimace. I think, *yeah this isn't going to work* … but just as I turn to head out I spy a small green fuzzy head sticking out from behind a bunch of stuffed bears on a stand-alone rack. I walk to the rack, lean forward and tug it out.

It is a floppy limbed, simple, big-headed frog.

Two beady black eyes and a tiny stitch of black for a smile. It is very friendly. And soft. And possibly sarcastic … I like it.

I bring it home, lift it up and announce to David that this is my inner child and I am going to nurture it. He says, "Ooookaaay …" and we laugh together.

Later that night while watching an episode of *Breaking Bad* on David's Mac, Boris, my small, black, curly-haired dog squiggles down from his perch on the back of the brown couch, sneaks the frog in his mouth from under my arm and tries to scurry into the other room.

I catch him just as he jumps off the couch, pull the frog out of his mouth, hold it in front of his face and firmly scold, "Do not eat my inner child!"

I take my inner child frog to bed.

I bring it to the dinner table.

I take it to the grocery store and it sits in the little child seat as I push around the cart.

I take it outside to lay on the striped afghan on the lawn while I read in the sun.

Sometimes I forget it when I wake up and I yell to my husband, "Can you get me my frog?!" from the couch where I sit with my coffee.

I take it to look for new shoes at the small, local shoe store on Main Street. The sales clerk greets me generously and then looks down, perplexed, at the frog I cradle. I burst out, "My therapist is making me do it!" and then throw my head back and laugh shockingly loud. She laughs too. But nervously.

I bring the frog to my next appointment with Dr. Anna and I can tell she is pleased.

"Ooh," she says, "So you found a frog? Cute. Did you get it because of the acronym?"

"Acronym?"

"Yeah, the acronym that is used in many recovery circles. FROG: Fully Relying On God."

"Nope." I smile and shake my head, "I didn't even think of that."

The hum of my idling car shifts slower and I give the accelerator a short pump to make sure it doesn't stall.

"Where is your frog?" she asks.

"I think it is on my bed," I mumble.

I have been forgetting it lately.

She suggests I take my stuffed frog to bed with me and if I wake up and feel dread or have a nightmare, talk with the frog just like I would if it were me as a little girl. Tell the stuffed frog everything is okay. Rock it back to sleep. Breathe and focus on positive thoughts and give myself the nurturing I lacked.

"Alright," I nod, glancing into the rearview mirror, "I'll do that."

I fiddle with the heat dial in my now-sweltering hot car and tell her how my previous landlord in Rockland is being ridiculously vindictive, sending mean emails and leaving long phone messages, lashing out at David and me for moving. She reassures me that I am a responsible person who has done everything correctly and that I don't have to feel guilt for requesting to break my lease.

After counseling I drive home and run upstairs to find David putting thumbtacks all through the walls and into the antique metal latch farm doors to secure his soundproofing foam for his audio voiceover job.
I feel fear. Fear this new landlord will be mad too.
As always for me, fear immediately disguises its vulnerability as anger.
Anger bubbles into rage.

Breathe …

Don't … I warn myself, standing just outside the doorway of his workroom.

But it is on my face.

"What are you doing?" I accuse and he responds curtly, "Whatever I want."

He is edgy. He hasn't had nicotine in 12 hours.

"WHAT PLANET ARE YOU FROM??!!" I scream.

"Leave me alone!" he barks back. And gets up to shut the door in my face.

"YOU ARE BREAKING THE HOUSE!" I scream louder.

"Breaking the house?!!" He yells, "No, THIS is breaking the house!"

He punches the door.

I jolt. Everything in my body jumps. A pulse of adrenaline charges in my chest, currents run up my spine and contract the muscles in my neck.

My father punches doors. And walls. And refrigerators.

My mother hangs family photos and needlepoint pictures over the large cracked sheetrock caves to cover his rage. They hang at random heights giving the impression that children decorated the pastel painted walls of our small red cape in the new development on the side of a hill.

A brown and tan needlepoint is positioned low and awkward above the light switch to my parents' bedroom. The words "Life is fragile, handle with prayer" are etched above a small bird perched on a branch surrounded by yellow flowers.

At twelve years old, when I hear hollering, I know to stay in my room out of sight. It is one of those days when the hollering is building, louder and louder and faster.

I stay quiet.

I don't move a muscle.

My body involuntarily jolts as a CRASH shakes my wall.

But then there is a quick loud hoot-like yell, a pause … and swearing.

This part isn't familiar.

Something has happened.

I wait for some quiet to pass.

I sneak out of my room and peak into the kitchen. Dad is holding a bag of ice, shaking his head and pacing back and forth by the big round antique table.

Mom is in the bathroom.

I slowly slink in and glance from her to the wall.

There is a fist-size hole in the sheetrock directly above the toilet. A four-inch glistening nail protrudes from a stud in the center of the hole. Dark red blood drips down the front porcelain toilet tank.

I look back at Mom.

She presses her lips together and gives me smilish smirk, a "see what happens" look, points at the nail and states, "Jesus put that there."

I crash down the stairs away from David who is still standing in the doorway looking as stunned as I feel. I want to smash something of his, break something, hurt him.

There is a line and he just crossed it. I need him to know he crossed it.

I want to break something he loves to punish him, make him as angry as I am, and let him know he can't fuck with me without getting hurt. But I don't see anything he values and I don't want to stick around, so I do my best. I grab his keys off the coffee table and hide them in the closet.

I run into my room and stuff two days' worth of clothing, meds, and my toothbrush in my backpack and slam the door as hard as I can on the way out.

I speed away fuming more than my old car. I slam over the potholes and think about what it would be like to move back to Portland. To just pick up and go. I glance in my rearview mirror into the backseat at my army green backpack. *At least if I leave for a few days … and don't return his calls … and then … then he will feel horrible for scaring me and he will know he crossed a line.*

But first I have to stop at McDonald's and meet with Wendy. We have an appointment for noon. Wendy is a kind, quiet woman who helped me quit drinking nine years ago. I called her last week to talk about my food issues, remembering that she had mentioned using recovery work to stop bingeing on sugar and flour. She said she would be happy to meet with me and help me with this, too.

But right now the last thing I want to do is go talk about my food issues. Especially at McDonald's.

Wendy is waiting at a yellow plastic booth with her recovery book. We are supposed to start going through the readings today but I am visibly upset and she asks me why. I tell her what just happened with David. She tells me about her marriage, about an affair, and how she used her recovery process to learn what God's will was for the marriage.

I tell her that my perception of God has changed. After spending a year in grad school reading about war and genocide, I have lost my faith in a God that has my best interest at heart. It makes it hard for me to turn things over.

She listens and nods and tells me she understands.

I feel calm around her.

David text messages me that he is sorry and wants me to come back. I don't respond, but when I leave Wendy, instead of taking a right toward Portland from the McDonald's parking lot I pause and take a left and drive home, my packed backpack jostling in the backseat.

I walk into the farmhouse mudroom and Boris greets me in his usual way, jumping up and down and doing round house flips. He looks like a Jim Henson creation, named something like a fuzzle or a muzzle. I kneel down and rub his fuzzy face saying, "Hi Boris! Hi!" until he is satisfied and prances away.

David is standing by the huge 1800s brick oven fireplace in the large living room. He tells me he is sorry, he had no right to hit the door. He is just frustrated with all of our bickering lately… and the lack of nicotine. But it is not an excuse he says, it is a reason, but it's no excuse for doing that.

To be fair I have been really nitpicky lately. I can see it in his face, I am driving him nuts and he doesn't know what to do. I have been questioning him about every little thing.

"Why did you buy 2% milk? I said 1%! I don't drink 2%! You know this but apparently you don't care!"

"Where did you put the mugs? They don't go on that shelf! Why would you put them there?"

"Why did you turn the oven on so high? It doesn't need to be that high! Didn't anyone ever teach you how to cook?"

And on and on.

I am uncomfortably aware that I am being cruel and controlling as soon as the words come out of my mouth but I can't stop them. I can't. The words have a life of their own, they are biting, vengeful and unforgiving. They are angry and they want someone to hurt. They don't care that I want to be better than this.

He walks toward me across the big pumpkin pine varnished floor with his arms open. But I don't want to hug. I shake my head no and walk away.

He stands alone and watches me go into the bathroom and shut the door.

"Adult mortality in preindustrial Quebec"

Claudine Lacroix
Direction des statistiques sociodémographiques, Institut de la statistique du Québec (précédemment employé)
Bertrand Desjardins
Département de démographie, Université de Montréal

Adult mortality in preindustrial Quebec

Introduction

French Canadian mortality has already been studied in the past by demographers. Hubert Charbonneau is one of the researchers who contributed the most to the study of this subject matter. He studied the demographic profile of the pioneers (1987) and the first Canadian-born (1975), and participated in the creation of the *Registre de la population du Québec ancien* (RPQA) database. Using the genealogies of Archange Godbout, he estimated that less than 60% of newborns reached the age of majority, or age 25, 37% reached age 50, and 5% reached age 80; about 60% of the Canadian-born who married at age 25 reached age 50 (Charbonneau 1975; Henripin 2003). **The demographer also pointed out that women suffered excess mortality during their fertile period due to childbirth complications, and that men experienced excess mortality after the age of 50.**

Methodology

The main method of analysis used consists of abridged life tables, with entries staggered according to age at first marriage and five-year age intervals. The realization of the life tables is based on the method of Louis Henry (1980). Kaplan-Meier type survival curves and log-Rank tests are used to determine whether observed differences between population groups are significant.

Women's life tables start at age 10. Although the minimum age at marriage for girls permitted by the Catholic Church was 12, six French Canadian girls in the corpus were married before reaching their twelfth birthday: one at age 10 and five at age 11. Men's life tables start at age 15 since no marriage was contracted before that age by French Canadian boys.

Results

Female excess mortality during their fertile period

At age 20, married women could expect to live 38.9 years longer and married men 42.6 years longer (Table 3). The five-year mortality quotients established for women are higher than those established for men at the exact ages of 15 to 40, or during the fertile period of women (Fig. 1). **This female excess mortality comes from the risks associated with motherhood. Indeed, many women died in childbirth or following a difficult delivery (Charbonneau 1975).** The gap between the sexes is about 33 points per thousand at exact age 15, 27 points at age 20, 28 points at ages 25 and 30, 33 points at age 35, and 22 points at age 40. At exact ages 45 to 80, five-year mortality quotients for men are slightly higher than those of women. This could be due to a selection effect for women who have reached the age of 50 and, therefore, **survived their fertile period.** In the context of the natural fertility of the time, women were having an average 9.2 children each (Charbonneau 1975; Mazan and Gagnon 2007). The women who survived their fertile period could be considered "resistant" (Mazan and Gagnon 2007).

The Kaplan-Meier survival table made for this differential mortality reveals that at age 40, when men's life expectancy catches up to that of women, 89.5% of the men in the corpus were still alive, compared to 77.8% of the women; the gap is 11.7 percentage points. The proportion of surviving men at age 40 (89.5%) is equivalent to that of the women at age 30 (89.3%). It is only at age 80 that the proportions of surviving men and women are the same (13.7% and 13.5%, respectively). In the corpus, 77% of Canadians whose marriage was celebrated at age 25 reached the age of 50, or 72% of the women and 81% of the men. The log-Rank test for this differential mortality is significant at the 1% threshold, confirming that the survival of both sexes varies significantly.

Used with permission. "Historical Studies on Mortality," special issue, *Canadian Studies in Population* 39, no. 3–4 (2012): 23–26. http://www.canpopsoc.ca/CanPopSoc/assets/File/publications/journal/2012/CSPv39n3-4p23.pdf

Motherhood

By Rhea Côté Robbins

Presentation given for "Representations of Motherhood" course at the University of Southern Maine at Lewiston/ Auburn

Subject Avoidance. Motherhood. Mamans. The cult of true womanhood. Motherhood turns into maman. The word changes to define the role. Roles.

What do I say? Such an obvious topic. As big as God really. But what words can capture the essences, not essentialisms, of the role the maman plays in the French heritage culture—who sometimes might be either gender. Depending on the reasons or circumstances, past or present—there are and nor never were ideal circumstances.

If I were to pick literatures of all types and venues, plus film, the arts in general as the mirror from which we get our mother reflections for the culture, or the words describing motherhood: STRONG and STRENGTH comes to mind with INTREPID as my latest choice.

Motherhood is a subject one thinks they automatically KNOW all there is to know on the subject from experience—having a mother, being a mother minus the official words on the event, studies, data, figures, tendencies, trends, fashion, taboos, verbiage, doctors' opinions, how-to manuals, religion/religious input/ interferences/dictates, etc.

Plus literature and all its bias/focus started me on a journey reading the research, literary criticism, and my natural predilection towards resistance of the entirely sentimental, saintly, always do-gooding mother and grandmother—maman and mémère—that really robs the woman of her full character. Give me the complex, complicated, realistic woman any day. The truth talkers.

Interpretations and their limitations. Serious hindrances result because the myth becomes the legend and the cult of true womanhood as told in the many-faceted, multiple realities in the untold of women's lives. Often, lies told in effigy.

Mocking representations of the actualities of the women's lives; their struggles glossed over. For the sake of what? Truth sacrificed to maintain the dominant culture in-denials/lies told to eradicate multiple perspectives. No problems here type of mentality. And if the women are not talking for themselves or as the French feminists say—writing the [whole] body, I question the telling. Trained as a resistive reader, literary critic, I question the gaps in the story/stories.

Good old days, *le bon vieux temps*, never existed. Compounding fallacies and fantasies solves nothing because the reality of storytelling is that the most important component is problem solving. Life asks questions and the manner in which we respond depends on the amount of freedom of voice or access to telling our own story we have. Some questions:

- In the French heritage culture how is motherhood seen or told?
- How is it valued or judged?
- Who is doing the telling? Who are they talking about or who are they talking to?
- And what is their point of view or bias?
- Who has the right or authority to talk or tell? Who does not?
- What are they saying in regard to motherhood?
- Is the motherhood story leaning more one way or the other, towards sentimentalism or reality?
- Is the woman/women full-bodied or fragmented; a caricature rather than a fully developed person?
- Is the research viable/reproducible—based on standards that actually reflect the diversity of the group—concrete, varied enough, or predetermined outcomes only proved—such as all women of the culture are "strong"?
- In regard to diversity, because not all whites are the same, when the group of women are all congregated under the "white umbrella," there is diversity among the women of Caucasian descent.
- How to formulate a definition of motherhood that constitutes multiple realities reflected or just relegated to the stereotype pie?
- Who can or cannot handle the truths about motherhood and why?
- Hold the men of the culture accountable for their part they play in creating motherhood—their silence on their sexuality, etc. Rather than their self-absolution of the responsibility of creating children. Ditto on the church's culpabilities—past and present—in the part they play touting the sainted mother and motherhood.
- France trends—of the ideal woman held up as the model—never get fat, bringing up *bébé, etc*.

- Quebec, Quiet Revolution, QCQR, happened in QC to shake off the shackles of the restraints of—*Revanche de berceaux*/revenge of the cradles, Catholic church moralities dictated, men's self-absolution in their sexuality, but what about the French heritage women of the rest of the continent? Where is our QR?
- French heritage, Franco-Americans caught in a mystic past while living completely modern lives in the current present—will the real Franco-American woman/mother please stand up?

As a result, I had to face my own truths as a mother, and after having read a few more pieces of research and literary pieces plus thinking on other representations of motherhood as subject—current authors' works and more—I came to the following conclusion: there are still taboos about certain subjects in regard to motherhood due to the already endangered species event of the fragility of the Franco-American culture/heritage that is still marked as the immigrant "other." Some of the aspects of the fragility are:

- Up against the absolute absolutes of mother France and/or French Canada.
- The event of the mother tongue—access or not to the mother "tongue"—langue.
- Orphaned as a result of the loss, or not, of the langue/mother tongue.
- Cultural child without a home.

Telling the motherhood story carries with it the dangers of telling truths unless one is freed by their own personal QR—quiet revolution. There is resistance at every turn on how to express the stories, real stories of real women's lives. Not just sainted mamans. Walls, barriers, hurdles, denials, etc., all almost insurmountable in order to just plain tell it like it is. What can I say?

Franco-American, modern women use birth control. Have abortions. Divorce. Decide not to have any children. Attempt at and sometimes fail being maman. Some carry on as others have before them, but each in her own individual way. There is no one way to be maman.

Single mothers deal, work, and achieve in the public work places. All accomplish a full-bodied experience because that is called living one's life. One could cite the stereotypes in their lives, but no one can be diluted to the ONE THING.

How can the Franco-American women's lives be characterized and marked as distinct, different, or unique? Not just a saint or battle ax. Ball buster. Overbearing, unpaid representative for the church delivering up sacrificial religious to feed the system.

Where can the truth of the actual women's live's be found? Told. Measured. Recorded. Without sanctions placed on the verbiage/words to be paid in taxes owed to whomever happens to be collecting in that era? Extortion fees paid to silence the truths. Reasons why the truths would be told:

- Certainly not for revenge, but to keep the record straight to reflect what women's lives are really like.
- Boundaries not to be redrawn to write revisionists' histories/stories.
- Stories marked to retell the male/dominant society's point of view stories in the French heritage woman's voice.
- What characteristics can be related?
- Manner of dress, décor, expressions, inclusions, exclusions, joinings, etc.
- Mothering techniques, discipline, endearments, or not, routines, etc. NOT sentimentalized/romanticized.
- Birthing techniques. Sages femmes.
- Urban/rural, both; in-between, gay, straight, bi, liberal/conservative, trans, virgin, etc.
- Choices? Are there any choices?
- Of the plethora of the women living in their communities, where is their mark?
- Not just traditional, pious piety, moral do-gooders, good two-shoes, sacrificing to the point of obliviousness.
- Rocking chair queen of all she surveys ... gets up out of the chair and does what?
- Strong-arming everyone with an iron fist ... has multiple sides to who she truly is/can be.
- Someone who takes her daily shit, pisses, bleeds once a month, spreads her legs, or sucks in return and also suckles the baby at the breast or bottle feeds. In other words, full-bodied.
- Real women of the Cult of REAL womanhood.
- Why do people work or hide behind the stereotypes?
- Or, use stereotypes as the markers of motherhood/mamans?
- Fight for the cult of truth in the true womanhood/full-bodiedness of mamans.

Anything else is not considered authentic. Give me a full-bodied character any day over the stilted, saintly sacrificial, in-denial iron lady in private/lamb in public stereotype. There can be no substitutes for the real woman.

Reference: "The Mechanization of Motherhood: Images of Maternity in Quebec Women Writers of the Quiet Revolution," Susan K. Kevra. *Ameriquests*, 4:1, 2007. Online, 2010.

In Self-published Book, Fairfield Woman Tells of Priest Who Fathered Her Son

By Amy Calder

FAIRFIELD — Judy Soucier sits in her Fairfield living room and talks tenderly about the Roman Catholic priest who fathered her child 36 years ago, but who would not commit to a lifelong relationship.

"He still was the man I loved," she says. "He still is, to this day."

Soucier, 65, wrote a book about her love affair with the priest called *Perfect: A Love Story*.

Self-published in 2008 as an autobiographical work, but with characters that have fictional names, it describes the priest's alleged, but futile, attempts to convince Soucier to abort her child and the church's alleged insistence that she go out-of-state to have the baby and then give it up for adoption. She was 28 at the time; he was 36.

Soucier now identifies the priest as the Rev. Marcel Dumoulin, who until 2004 served as pastor at the Immaculate Heart of Mary Church in Fairfield. He also served at parishes in Augusta and Winthrop. Dumoulin, 73, lives at a nursing-care facility in Lewiston, where he has Alzheimer's disease. Their son, Christian Soucier, is 36 and lives in New York City.

Catholic priests are required to be celibate; however, the Roman Catholic Diocese of Portland last week acknowledged that Dumoulin fathered Soucier's son. But the Diocese says the church would never support an abortion, as the book suggests, and would not encourage a woman to give her child up for adoption if she did not want to do that.

Soucier took Dumoulin to court in Androscoggin County on Nov. 17, 1983, seeking child support when her boy was 11. The court awarded Soucier a lump sum of $6,000, plus monthly payments until he was 18. The case was entitled "Judith Soucier vs. Marcel Dumoulin."

Soucier says she didn't at first plan to publish her story, which she initially wrote as a memoir intended for just her son, Christian Soucier.

"I wrote it because I wanted to give it to my son for Christmas in 2006," she says.

But she self-published the book and approached the *Morning Sentinel* after friends and family read the manuscript and convinced her it was a story she needed to share with the world.

"They said, 'This must be told.'"

Romance turns a corner

Soucier's book recounts her life as a teacher, friend, daughter and lover of the sea whose life takes an unexpected turn when she meets a Roman Catholic priest — Dumoulin — who in the book is called Matthew, in Lewiston, and falls in love. It forever changes her life.

The book is set mainly in Brunswick and Lewiston, where Soucier lived in the 1970s. It describes a happy romance that turns sour when she becomes pregnant.

Father Matthew takes her to a trailer at the edge of what now is a parking lot for the Marden's Surplus & Salvage store in Lewiston. There, they meet with a tall minister and the two men arrange for her to have an abortion.

Matthew then drives her to a clinic in New York City and she is prepped for the abortion, but she cannot go through with it. The book describes in detail the events that took place when Dumoulin drove her to New York for the abortion and she decided not to have the procedure, she said.

They drove home in silence. Once back in Maine, a diocesan vicar asked her to come to St. Paul's Retreat Center in Augusta. Once she arrived, the vicar urged her to leave the state, have the baby and give it up for adoption but she refused, she said. She met with him again in Portland at his request and he was unsuccessful in trying to convince her to go away, have the child and offer it for adoption. That vicar has since died.

Soucier says that afterward, another priest came to her home and said he was a messenger from the bishop, who asked that she leave the state, have the baby and give it up for adoption.

The priest allegedly offered her an envelope containing cash and said the money was separate from any travel and medical expenses, which would be paid by the church. Soucier said she did not accept it.

"He brought $3,000 and said, 'This is for you, and all arrangements and expenses will be paid,'" Soucier said.

That priest also has since died.

'Why take the back door?'

After she gave birth to her son, Soucier had minimal contact with Dumoulin; their romance ended after she became pregnant, she said.

The last time she saw him at the nursing home several months ago, his mind was merely a shell of what it once was.

"He didn't even know me," she said. "It's just very sad."

Soucier's cousin and lifelong friend, Yvette Rousseau, accompanied her on that visit.

Rousseau, 73, of Lewiston, introduced Soucier to Dumoulin many years ago and her character is featured in the book. Rousseau was a parishioner in Dumoulin's church, The Holy Family Church in Lewiston, and he was a close friend who spent time with her and her family during picnics, parties and snowmobiling trips, she said.

Rousseau, now retired after 52 years of nursing, describes herself as a devout Catholic who is disturbed by the way the church handled Soucier's pregnancy.

"I think the true message is, why doesn't the church deal with their problems the right way?" she says. "Why take the back door? Why hide it and deal with these poor little children that could have been put up for adoption or aborted? I kind of blame the church for not taking a stand. That's why the church has gotten away with so much. The Catholic Church has to take a stand on important issues."

Rousseau says her first husband reported Dumoulin's love affair with Soucier to the bishop and after that, Dumoulin stopped visiting her family for a while. She and her husband ultimately divorced and he has since died.

Rousseau says Dumoulin never acknowledged to her or anyone in her family or circle of friends that Soucier's baby was his.

"He always kind of beat around the bush about it but never actually came right out to say, 'I have a son and Judy was the mother,'" Rousseau said. "He never was honest about it. I think now, why wasn't he truthful? As close as we were, he never told us. I always felt bad about that."

Rousseau says it was as if his position as a priest was more important to him than anything else.

"He never let down his guard. The worst part was, he was trying to get rid of the child. I don't know how he could sleep at night and then preach in the pulpit. I just feel like he goofed, big time, and so did the bishop."

But despite Dumoulin's foibles, Rousseau still holds an affection for him.

"He made a mistake, he goofed, but he is human. He made a big mistake. But he's still Father Dumoulin."

She says there is no question in her mind that Soucier is telling the truth about his plans for her abortion and the church's subsequent attempts to send her away to have the baby and then give it up for adoption.

"It all took place," she says. "I've always admired her for staying strong and taking a stand. She's the strong one."

Nancy Snow is another longtime friend of Soucier who is featured as a character in the book. She saw Dumoulin and Soucier together in the early 1970s. Snow says she also admires her for carrying her baby to term and raising him, despite pressure to do otherwise.

A retired thirty-three-year teacher, Snow, 75, of Brunswick, describes Soucier as someone who loves children and is very good with older people.

"She's very kind, and if she does something, she takes on a project and she does it 110, 120 percent. She always, always went above and beyond."

Snow says she hopes big things happen with Soucier's book, which is being sold in bookstores and on the Internet.

"I thought it was wonderful and I think it would make a great movie."

'Mon Dieu. It comes back'

Father Dumoulin smiles and welcomes a guest at the nursing-care facility in Lewiston, where he shares a small room with another patient.

The retired priest appears cheerful, lounging in a recliner, wearing casual clothes and sporting a navy blue beret.

He talks easily, but does not seem to have a grasp of history. Asked when he left Immaculate Heart of Mary Church in Fairfield, he says he does not remember.

But, shown a photograph of Soucier, his face lights up immediately.

"That is good," he says. "She's good. Judy Soucier. Mon dieu. It comes back. She's so good, kind, you know. Look how beautiful that is. Oh, it's good."

He then touches the paper on which the photo is printed.

"That was the lady that was the best for me, you know?" he says. "Très bien. It's wonderful."

The neat, simply decorated room has puzzles, books, and photographs on a table.

The only clues to Dumoulin's spiritual past are a crucifix that hangs on a wall and small statues of Mary and Jesus on a bureau.

'I still try to fly'

Dumoulin's son, Christian Soucier, is an environmental consultant and marine biologist, married and living in New York City.

He declines to talk about his relationship with Dumoulin, other than to say he is not comfortable discussing it because of the priest's advanced age and medical condition.

The book, he says, is his mother's story, not his own.

"I support her 100 percent," he said. "It made her strong. What I'm most proud of is where we are today. She gave me an opportunity to go out and try to fly. I still try to fly, every day."

He says his mother worked hard all his life to provide for him and make sure he went to college — even working with pregnant and parenting teens, ironically, for the Roman Catholic Diocese of Portland. Christian Soucier ultimately earned a Ph.D. in biology with a focus on ecology evolution and behavior.

"I think that, obviously, a lot of what she experienced in our situation drove her to the career path that she took," he says. "It was the ultimate sacrifice."

When he read the book, he was horrified by the treatment his mother received, he says.

"It's true hypocrisy—there's no doubt," he says. "The hypocrisy of the church in instances like these is appalling."

He hopes the book's release provides closure for his mother, whom he never knew to have a relationship with a man while he was growing up. He says he learned why, after reading it: She long harbored a great love for Dumoulin that continues to this day.

Judy Soucier says she chose a life of celibacy after her breakup with Dumoulin.

After giving birth, she stayed home for three years to raise her son and then went back to work as a social worker for the Diocese for 11 years. She then worked for the March of Dimes for 21 years.

Judy Soucier was adopted at birth, grew up in the Catholic church in Lewiston and describes her adoptive family as loving, caring and very supportive. After her parents died, she searched for her birth-family members and found them in 2003. She moved to Fairfield to be near them in 2007.

She describes herself as a Christian but stops short of saying she is Catholic.

"I go to church, but I go to the church God built," she says, referring to nature. "I went to the Catholic church until I was pregnant with Christian. I've always believed in God. I've never lost my faith. Actually, I think I have a deeper, stronger faith than I ever did. I do know that the reason I have Christian today is, God wanted him on this earth."

Used with permission. Amy Calder, *Morning Sentinel*, January 25 2009

It Can Happen to Any Family: How Drugs Took My Daughter's Life

By Cynthia Doucette

Excerpt, Chapter One

Two hours earlier, we had left Greenville, Maine, after a weekend of snowmobiling. Halfway home, we stopped to have dinner, and before we left again, my husband, David, pulled the truck over to the service area to fill the tank. I watched him from the warmth of the cab and noticed how worn his red work hat had gotten. I made a mental note to remind him to order some new ones. His red and black plaid flannel shirt hung neatly over his jeans as he walked inside to pay the clerk. After he finished, he jumped in the truck and began rubbing his hands together to warm them up.

"Boy," he said," the weather's cold."

Even though I was eager to get home, I sat there relaxed, listening to the music on the radio. I felt sleepy as the sunshine poured inside the truck onto my face. When my cell phone rang, I was thinking how, in so many ways, our lives were good. David worked hard to keep his excavating business successful, and we were enjoying spending leisurely time together.

When I noticed my brother's number on the caller ID, I knew he wouldn't call for anything trivial, and so I clutched the cell phone to my ear as the truck sped south along the Maine Turnpike.

"Ah, it's about Candice," he said hesitantly. "Are you almost home?"

"No, we're still a couple of hours away," I answered, worried. We never knew what Candice would do next. She was our second child, 18 now, and she was clearly not making an easy transition into adult life. She had not wanted to come north with us and we had let her stay home alone for the weekend. Had that been a good decision?

Our son, Travis, was ahead of us in a separate truck with our friend, Bruce. My younger daughter Chelsey was staying with her friend, Jordyn, back in Berwick, Maine, where we lived.

"What about Candice?" I asked, thinking I was prepared for the worse.

"She got really depressed and cut herself up her arm, and I think she took some pills," he continued. "Justin and Steven are with her now at your house. They think she'll be all right."

Candice was very close to her cousins, Justin and Steven, my brother's sons, so I was glad they were with her. However, I felt anxious and helpless as we charged down the turnpike still miles from home. I was listening with all my attention.

"I got a call from her friend, Brandon. She phoned him and said she was messed up," he added. "He asked me to go check on Candice."

My brother, also named David, was in the habit of checking on her while we were gone.

I hung up and quickly exchanged words with my husband. We weren't surprised about the cutting because she had done it at least once before—the psychiatrist called it self-mutilation—but we were very concerned that it had happened again and we felt powerless being still two hours away. Then, we agreed I should call Candice. Neither David nor I knew what to expect. We never did.

A slurry, groggy voice answered the phone. I pictured her lying down while she was talking. Her depressed, sleepy tone sounded familiar.

"Hello, Candice," I said.

"WHAT!" she demanded, with a distinct attitude. She knew her Uncle David had informed me of her situation.

"Candice," I asked, ignoring her tone of voice. "Is everything all right?"

"I'm all right, Mom," she said curtly. Her voice blasted me, as cold as that day's bitter winter wind.

Her tone chilled me, and I realized it wouldn't work to try to deal with the situation before we got home. I was glad it was me and not David who was calling because he sometimes got angry when she spoke this way. He did not put up with lack of respect.

"Is Justin there with you? I want to talk with him."

Justin was in a tough situation. She was sitting beside him, and he had to be careful about what he said.

"Justin, how is she? Can you tell me what the heck is going on?" "She's okay, Aunt Cindy," he said, his reluctance to speak so strong in his voice.

"Okay, then," I said, resigned. "Let me talk to Candice again."

She came back on the phone with the same cocky attitude. "Ma, I don't want to talk about it. Bye." She hung up.

I was holding a dead phone, extremely troubled. I told David what she had said.

"What the hell is her problem now?" he complained, discouraged and fatigued. We had been there before-not with the cutting so much, but with the depression.

"I don't know," I said. "I'm angry at the way she just hung up the phone on me. I'm not calling her back to have her hang up again. David, what are we going to do?"

He kept his face to the road, staring out at the world as if to find answers.

We shared the same burden. We were sad that, in spite of all the love and support we gave our daughter, we just couldn't reach her and couldn't seem to make a difference in her life. We discussed a little about how we would deal with the situation, but we had no new thoughts to add—we were both too shaken to have any. Our child—a young woman now—clearly needed more help than we could give her and more than she was getting from others, too.

During that long ride home, David didn't talk much. He is not a man to find his answers that way. I, too, sat in silence, thinking we may need to decide to place her in the hospital, but how could we do that? I knew I just couldn't do it.

Travis was ahead of us and so he got home first. When I walked up the stairs that lead from the breezeway into the kitchen, right in front of me, near the trash can, was a huge, green garbage bag, untied. Inside there were dozens of empty beer cans. On the counter sat another empty can. The dining room chairs were pulled out away from the table, and the flower arrangement with candles in holders, normally centered in the middle, was pushed to one side.

For a moment, my loving desire to help her turned to anger, but I checked myself. Something more had to be done for Candice, and anger was not it.

"Where is Candice, Travis?" I asked, realizing immediately he hadn't known anything was wrong until he had entered our home and looked around.

"When I got here, she was leaving with her friends," he said. "I left everything the way it was for you to see what she was up to."

I learned later she had convinced Steven and Justin she was okay and said her friends would stay with her until we got home.

"Travis," I asked desperately, the feelings of the last years weighing on me, "did she seem okay to you?"

He didn't answer—he just shrugged—and walked into the office off the kitchen.

The phone rang. I rushed to the phone, thinking it might be Candice.

"Oh, hi, Chelsey," I sighed. I was happy to hear from Chelsey, but it was urgent to find Candice.

"Mom, Jordyn and I want to know if we can borrow your taibo tape?"

"Yes," I said quickly. ''Are you coming to get it?" "We'll be over in a minute."

Just as I hung up the phone, Travis yelled from the office. "Mom, come here!"

I ran into the office. He was standing in front of the computer monitor.

Candice used the computer to instant-message her friends, and before she left, she had typed an "away message" for everyone on her buddy list.

I'm sitting here alone all f,--ed up. I've cut myself and I'm bleeding. I've just snorted some Klonopin and Valium. I want to die.

"Oh my God!" I said in a voice I didn't even recognize. What am I going to do? I heard David coming into the house with all of our bags from the weekend. I ran into the kitchen as he set them down. When he looked up, he saw the look of bewilderment on my face.

"Cindy," he asked, "where's Candice? Her car's gone."

"Travis said she left with friends as he was coming in," I said anxiously. "David, I don't know what to do. What should we do?"

"Now what's the matter?"

"Go look at the computer."

He rushed into the office. I followed him and stood behind him as he read her message. He hurried to the phone and dialed her. No answer. He got angry, frustrated really.

"Where do you think she is?" he yelled.

"I don't know."

As David kept trying to call her, I paced the floor, my anxiety increasing. We called numerous times, but she wasn't picking up. The thought of her driving around after taking those drugs was very disturbing. My mind was racing. What if she veered off the road? Had an accident? She had other kids in the car. What if she hurt them? Candice was a danger to herself—and to everyone else on the road.

In the meantime, I decided to call Justin. He answered the phone right away.

"Aunt Cindy," he said, "you've got to do something about Candice.

I'm afraid for her. I've never seen her act the way she was acting tonight. She really shouldn't be alone."

Part of what he was telling me I already knew. I would have to make the decision to commit her to a hospital. My mind wandered as he talked.

"Another thing, Aunt Cindy, I think she's been trading her medication for other kids' drugs."

I was surprised. I always administered her medication to her. When needed, I gave her two Prozac once a week and Adderall once a day. True, I had not stood in front of her while she took the medication. Apparently, I could not trust her. From now on, I would have to supervise her more closely.

''Aunt Cindy," Justin continued, "I don't think you should leave her alone again on the weekend. Me and Steven weren't around this weekend when she tried to call, and I think she got lonely without anyone to talk to."

"You don't have to worry," I said firmly. "This will be the last time she'll pull this. She'll come with us, or we'll stay home."

How am I going to deal with her? I thought. I can't lock her in her room. She's 18. Am I supposed to stop living and just follow her around? That was impossible. Candice wasn't the type of kid you could control easily. She wasn't going to come with us just because we told her to. What could be done?

I called Brandon.

"Brandon, do you know where Candice is?"

"No," he said. "I haven't seen her."

"Do you know what specifically caused her to cut herself?" I asked.

"No," he said reluctantly. "When I talked to her, she was upset and told me what she was going to do."

"So you have no idea where she is?" I asked, disappointed but believing him.

"No, I don't."

I hung up. David went into the other room, alone. To kill nervous energy, I went upstairs to put away all my stuff from the weekend. I heard a car drive into the driveway. I ran to the window. It was Candice. In spite of the argument I knew we would have, I was glad she was home safely.

But just as quickly as she had pulled in, she backed out of the yard.

I ran to the top of the stairs.

"David, Candice just left the yard!"

Without a word, David shot out of the house. His truck ripped out of the driveway. He was upset. I wasn't sure what would happen if he caught up to her

---

Army Nurse Already Serving When Pearl Harbor Bombed

By Rhea Côté Robbins

Elise Pooler Lambert decided in 1941 to become an Army nurse because she knew she would become seasick on the oceans if she enlisted as a Navy nurse.

She enlisted for one year. That was before the bombing of Pearl Harbor. After Pearl Harbor, Lambert, like the other nurses, were in for the duration of World War II plus six months.

Lambert was trained in a three-year registered-nurse program at St. Elizabeth's Hospital in Boston. She graduated in 1932 at the height of the Depression.

On May 8, 1941, Lambert was sent to Tilton General Hospital at Fort Dix, New Jersey for her first assignment. Eighteen nurses arrived that day. The hospital was just being built. The nurses were housed in a bare wooden building in rooms which contained a bed, chair, and bureau. For entertainment, there was a day room with a record player and a few records.

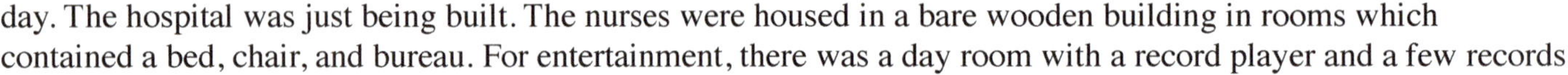

After Pearl Harbor, the Army asked for volunteers for overseas service. Lambert volunteered, and in January 1942 she was billeted in a hotel in New York City, the port of embarkation. She was given a number for herself and a shipment number for information on her destination. That was all she was given.

After the *Normandy* burned in New York Harbor, Lambert thought she was meant to be shipped out on that ship because she was sent back to Fort Dix until March.

One Sunday morning all overseas personnel were told to pack because they were to board troop trains which would take them to the port of embarkation. Lambert had time only to call her mother. On March 4, 1942, Lambert sailed from Brooklyn in a fleet of five ships with no idea where the ship was going.

The ships zigzagged on the seas to avoid detection. The troops could only guess where they were bound.

At this early state of the war the ships and troops were not ready for combat. There were no uniforms and not enough fresh water on the ships. The troops had to wash in salt water and were rationed drinking water. Fresh drinking water was taken on when the ships pulled into a secret base in Bora Bora.

The troops learned of their destination when they were required to learn about Australian currency. Lambert, the Army nurse who wanted to avoid the Navy and oceans and seasickness, had spent 41 days on the seas when the ship docked at Melbourne, Australia.

The nurses were billeted in Melbourne. They worked at Royal Melbourne Hospital and helped set up an hospital at Brisbane for American and Australian armies.

Lambert did not see casualties from the war when she was billeted at a seaside resort on the Gold Coast. She was told to enjoy the luxury while she could because the nurses eventually would get closer to the front and see more actions as well as war casualties. Meanwhile, they were outfitted with uniforms which consisted of culottes and short sleeved shirts, later changed to long slacks and long sleeved shirts because of the threat of malaria. In spite of the precautions, Lambert had malaria several times. To keep in shape, the nurses marched every day.

Lambert then received orders to move on to New Guinea. She spent her first Christmas there during the rainy season. In December 1942, Lambert was one of fifty-two nurses in a medical and surgical team who saw many casualties as the advancing army chased the Japanese out of Port Moresby, New Guinea, during the Buna Campaign.

The nurses took over a Catholic mission. They were housed in one building, and the surgery was set up in another. They slept on cots beneath mosquito nets.

At first there was no running water. The nurses were rationed a helmet full of water to clean themselves and their clothes. Showers were installed later. This was an evacuation hospital, a tent outfit, near an airstrip. A 750-bed unit grew to a 1,000-bed unit. There were air raids every night.

After almost one year at Port Moresby, Lambert moved to Dobodura which had better accommodations such as wood-framed buildings covered with heavy paper with window openings.

Lambert's mother had sent her marigold seeds. Plants grew almost overnight in the heat.

They took casualties as they came. Sometimes they worked twenty-four hours at a stretch. After the casualties left, they were given a day or two off.

Because of their living conditions, there was a lot of sharing among the nurses. They grew close, and always found a way to have fun. Lambert made many friends and kept in touch with them during the years.

Lambert was overseas until 1944 when rotations began. She then was sent to New York, and from the Separation Center, she was sent to Camp Beale, CA. She again saw casualties, and German prisoners.

Later she moved to Barnes General Hospital in Vancouver, WA where she saw more casualties who were coming back to the States to hospitals nearer their homes.

When she returned to the United States, her scrapbooks and photo albums were taken by the censors and returned later with certain parts of photos blacked out.

Once custom started during the war was a "short snorter." A short snorter was a collection of paper money gathered from as many parts of the world as a person could garner, signed by the person from whom they received the money and taped together in one long piece. Lambert's short snorter" had money from many countries.

When Lambert enlisted in the Army the chief of the nursing corps was a major, and there were seven captains in the entire Army nursing corps and a few lieutenants. Most of the nurses were second lieutenants.

Since Lambert enlisted during peacetime, she was not commissioned as an officer, but was given rank of second lieutenant when she was sent overseas. That was done so that those like her could give orders.

Lambert was commissioned into the Army when she arrived in Port Moresby and she received a $10 raise. In two years the nurses were given no promotions. When they were given promotions, the promotions did not follow the nurses when they returned to the United States.

The nurses came back as second lieutenants. The nurses who had remained stateside fared better than the nurses who had been shipped overseas. The nurses stateside were promoted to captains and majors. Lambert feels this was not right.

Lambert has attended reunions held for the fifty-two nurses with whom she served during World War II. The reunions are often held in Boston. These women have kept in touch for over fifty years.

[Elise passed away October 21, 2000. She is sadly missed.]

First published in *Bangor Daily News*, Midweek section, December 6, 1989. Used with permission

---

Elise worked diligently to gain recognition for the nurses who served during World War II:

The American Legion [Volume 133, No. 3 (September 1992)]

The Legion Remembers: "Welcome To The Jungle: In a little-known battle, 700 GIs held off the Japanese and helped save Australia"

Letter to the editor

I was a nurse in the 10th Evacuation Hospital stationed at Port Moresby, New Guinea, during the Buna-Gona campaign. I was quite perturbed to realize that the nurses were not mentioned in the articles, even though we received the Distinguished Unit Badge and the Asiatic Pacific Campaign Medal with two battle stars.

Elise Pooler Lambert
Orrington, Maine

Beyond the French and Indian War: The Impact of Wartime on the Franco-American and Native American Communities Conference, University of Maine, Franco-American Center, April 11, 1992.

"Reflections on an Era--Nurses of the 10th Evacuation Unit in New Guinea during World War II"

Panelists: Maureen Tully Lopez. **Elise Pooler Lambert**, Margaret Soule Tully, and Doris Wilms-Hale; Panel organizer: Rhea Côté Robbins, DVD Available. Contact the editor of this volume.

Hospital honors humble helper: Volunteer has traveled unique path

By Renee Ordway

BANGOR — Elise Lambert is at ease at her kitchen table in Orrington while she speaks to two strangers about a life that has taken her back and forth across the United States to Australia and New Guinea.

She eventually returned to Maine, settling here with her husband in 1949. Maine, after all, was in her blood. And if you believe that Mainers are a modest and sensible lot, well, Elise Lambert belongs here.

Such was evident Saturday morning as she recalled receiving an invitation in 1931, while living and working in Poughkeepsie, N.Y., to join President Franklin D. Roosevelt's mom for tea.

"Back in those days, ladies always wore hats. Well, I didn't have a hat," she recalled, chuckling at the memory. I said, "Well, I'm not going to buy a hat just for that."

"But one of the nuns at the hospital where I worked said I had to have something, so I got one of those little veils that some ladies wore on their heads and I wore that."

The story is just a tidbit in a life that is interesting enough to share with schoolchildren who visit the Cole Land Transportation Museum in Bangor.

But while her life has taken her down many unusual paths—she once spent forty-one days on board a ship, bathing only in salt water—it is for much simpler and humbler reasons that she was honored Sunday with the prestigious eighth annual Blessed Mother Mary Angela Service Award from the Bangor Community of Felician Sisters.

The award is presented annually to an individual or couple in recognition of outstanding service to St. Joseph Healthcare and to the community-at-large.

Lambert was a tad tickled and a bit embarrassed by the fuss.

"Sister [Mary] Norberta [the president of St. Joseph Hospital] called to tell me about it a month ago. I hemmed and hawed a bit, and finally she said, "No one has ever turned us down," Lambert recalled, raising her eyebrows just a bit at the thought.

She believes there are people around who volunteer at more organizations than she has, but acknowledges that volunteerism should not be measured by prolific service alone.

Consistency counts.

She has been a volunteer at St. Joseph Hospital for ten years and a Eucharistic minister delivering Holy Communion to homebound parishioners of St. Teresa's Church in Brewer for fifteen.

She also volunteers at the Cole museum, where she speaks to schoolchildren about her experiences as an Army nurse during World War II. She's available to go into schools to speak to history classes, though no one's ever taken her up on the offer. They should.

Lambert struggles when asked why she devotes so much of her time to volunteer work. After all, she was a practicing registered nurse for thirty-nine years. One might think she had enough of hospitals.

Her answer reflects the three things that obviously steer her life: her family, her Catholic religion and her work.

"God has been good to me," she finally says. "He blessed me with a good family and a good career. I just want to do something to pay him back for all he has done for me."

It doesn't bother her much that despite her impressive credentials as a nurse she now has to stand by as other, younger, hospital staff perform even the simplest of nursing duties.

Malpractice concerns prevent her from partaking in even the smallest medical procedures. She is, after all, a volunteer.

That's OK with her. She is still there to sit by a patient's bedside in the emergency room as they await treatment. Her warm smile and her kind face, softened by time, provide a grandmotherly type comfort to those upset or in pain.

Offering a cup of coffee to an elderly man waiting in the lobby for word of his wife's condition provides her much satisfaction.

Although she was not an emergency-room nurse, she spent a lot of time there in her role as the night supervisor at St. Joseph Hospital, where she worked from 1969 to 1975.

"Back then, you know the emergency room wasn't as busy as it was today. I remember when [the undertaker] used to bring [live] patients in the back of his hearse. I think there was only one ambulance then," she said.

So in 1986, when her husband passed away, Lambert decided to go back to the hospital as a volunteer. It had been nearly eleven years since her retirement, and she chose to volunteer in the emergency room.

"There's always something happening there," she said.

Lambert's life has put her in the middle of plenty of action, including a two-year stint as a nurse in an Army hospital in New Guinea smack in the middle of the fighting during World War II.

She got there by volunteering. At the time, she was working in New York City at a private hospital that catered primarily to rich European patients who had fled the fighting overseas.

They brought their own china and linens to the hospital, and the nurses were their caretakers. It did little to impress the young woman who thought it senseless to purchase a hat simply to wear once to a tea with the president's mother.

She found her way out through a poster of Uncle Sam that encouraged people to join the armed forces.

"Only the Navy and the Army were accepting women at that time, and since I get seasick on a rowboat, I joined the Army," she recalled, laughing at herself. "Of course, then somehow I managed to get myself on board a ship for 41 days headed for Australia."

The trip to Australia came after Dec. 7, 1941, and the Japanese bombing of Pearl Harbor. The Army was looking for volunteers to go overseas. Lambert signed up, having no idea where she was headed. She presumed she'd go to Europe. She was wrong and instead headed for the Pacific.

Aboard the ship, she was rationed one canteen of water per day and had to bathe and launder her clothes in sea water.

"You can imagine what we all did with our underwear when we got to Australia," she said.

At the time, the Japanese were at the northern border of Australia threatening to move in. Lambert was eventually moved to a tented, 1,500-bed Army hospital in New Guinea. The media called Fort Moresby the "infantryman's nightmare. The worst hellhole on earth." It was rainy season, and the threat of malaria loomed heavy over the unit.

Lambert would stay there for two years, treating wounded soldiers, eating C-rations and shedding her modesty occasionally for the chance of a shower.

She later returned to New York and joined the American Legion, where she met her husband, Daniel. The couple moved to Maine in 1949 and moved into their comfortable home on Route 15 in Orrington in 1951.

There they raised their three daughters. Lambert worked at Eastern Maine Medical Center, and in 1955 began working as a nursing supervisor at the hospital on Dow Air Force Base in Bangor. She worked there until it closed in 1968, and then started at St. Joseph.

Her commitment to St. Joseph has never wavered.

Today as a volunteer, she marvels at the changes that have revolutionized her profession.

"All of the technology. You have to be an engineer to know how to run all those machines," she said.

But despite all of the changes in the medical profession, patients and their loved ones still need a hand to hold, a cup of coffee and a friendly word.

Lambert provides that, and it is for that she was honored on Sunday.

This story was published on Nov. 25, 1996 in all editions of the *Bangor Daily News*. Used with permission.

Women's, Gender, and Sexuality Studies Program, University of Maine
"Concertation et action social: la femme Franco-Américaine," video of the Brown Bag Lunch panel: Franco-American women activists share their thoughts on how their heritage both helped and hindered their activism. Panelists include Sharon Albert (Chamber of Commerce), Sylvia Blanchard (former AFL-CIO organizer), Lou Chamberland (founder of the Women's Business Development Corporation), Catherine Charette, (Attorney), and **Elise Lambert** (World War II nurse who served in the Pacific theater of Allied Operations). Rhea Côté Robbins, Panel Organizer. Panel discussion in English. (90 min. 1994). DVD Available. Contact the editor of this volume.

Creativity/*La Créativité*

Acanthe—Amour de l'art, lien éternel
Acanthus—The arts

Avoine—Magie de la musique
Oats—The witching soul of music

Platane—Curiosité ou génie
Plane Tree—Genius

Oeillet du poète—Inspiration, finesse
Sweet William—Gallantry, a smile

Pomme de terre (fleur)—Remerciement
Potato Plant—Benevolence

Bleuet—Délicatesse, tendresse, timidité
Corn Flower (Bachelor's Buttons)—Delicacy, single blessedness, celibacy

Églantine—Poésie
Eglantine (European Sweetbrier)—Poetry, healing

Hellébore verte/Rose de carême—Interrogation, changement d'avis
Hellebore/Lenten Rose—Scandal, calumny, cure for melancholy

Cerisier (fleur de)—Bonne éducation
Cherry Blossom—Spirituality, beauty

An Interview with Florence Rose Martin

Interview By Mary Rice-Defosse, Ph.D. and Patricia Hager, Ph.D.

Make no mistake; Florence Rose Martin is an Acadian. Her license place announces it. So do her forthright manner and indomitable spirit. Above all, it is the music she carries with her. By her mother's account, she was singing at the age of two, before she could talk. A native of St. Agatha, in the St. John Valley of Maine, she inherited her love of music from family:

"I was always singing," Florence said in a recent interview in Lewiston. "My mother was always singing. We'd get up in the morning humming. Singing. I tell that to people and they don't believe me. 'You mean, as you get up you're not grouchy?' No, we sing. We hum... People in Ste. Agathe were happy people."

She recalled that after a long day's work, people would come into her grandfather's shop, a community gathering place, at suppertime. They came with guitars, fiddles, and harmonicas. They would hoist little Florence onto the counter and have her sing with her mother standing by her side. In Acadia, women in particular were "the keepers of the song" in each generation; they copied by hand favorite songs into notebooks—des *cahiers de chansons*.[1]

"We had so many songs ... like three, four, five hundred. Old French songs, and the grandmothers sang them to the daughters. The daughters sang them to the children. And we would copy them down. As a matter of fact, my father's sister had one and she gave it to me."

The two-hole, loose-leaf pages are now yellowed, a legacy from the women in her father's family, all Acadians. Florence keeps them in plastic sleeves because binders now have three holes. Her aunt, were she still living, would be one-hundred years old in January 2016.

She has another set of songs from her mother's side. After the *Grand Dérangement* when the British deported the Acadians from the rich farmlands of the Maritimes,[2] her mother's family married French-speakers in Kamouraska in the province of Quebec before settling permanently in the St. John Valley, all integrated into the Acadian society there. Some of the songs in the books date back to the 1600s.

Florence's own singing style reflects those roots, as she points out:

"This is an Acadian voice. So we sing loud. No sopranos, nothing like that. We all sang the same in St. Agatha. You've heard of Ida Roy.[3] She was born in St. Agatha. She was my mother's age. She and I sang together one time. Her daughter lived in Lewiston, and so I went to see her. And we had the same voice. We're not related but we're both from both from Ste. Agathe. Must be the water!"[4]

Florence is quick to point out differences between Acadian and Quebecois songs themselves: "In Quebec there are *chansons à répondre*. One singer sings one line and the audience or another singer repeats the same line. In Acadian, we don't do that. That's how we know if it's an Acadian song. Acadian, it's more like a story versus refrain. No answering. *Pas de chansons à répondre*. *Une chanson à répondre* would be Canadian."[5]

Florence's songbooks are a treasure trove, but they have one drawback. There are no musical notations, just lyrics.

"That's the problem. The melody got passed on by singing. Singing, singing. If you were awake you were singing, so you remembered the melodies, but they were not written down."

Some recordings have been made, as well as notation of the melodies, but not enough.

One of Florence's favorite songs is a love song. She says:

"Well, here's one, ah, it's not that old. It's only seventy years old. *Un point du ciel*. The reason that I love it is that my daughter and I sing it together. She plays a twelve-string guitar. She has a beautiful soft voice and I have a big Acadian voice, so it harmonizes."

Un coin du ciel, où on vivra tous deux, ma chérie.
Un coin du ciel où on s'aimera toute la vie.
Mon coeur t'apelle et le réclame jour et nuit.
Sois-moi fidèle. Je t'aimerai toujours, ma jolie.
(Marcel Gaston Marcel, 1952)

[A corner of heaven where we'll live together, my dear.
A corner of heaven where we'll love each other our whole lives
My heart calls you and demands to night and day.
Be faithful to me. I'll love you always, my pretty one.][6]

"This is a very, very old one. I'll just sing a verse."

Si vous voulez vivre heureuse, écoutez ma chanson.
Mariez-vous pas si jeune. Profitez du bon temps.
Quand vous serez mariée il y aura du changement.
(Anonymous)

[If you want to live a happy woman, listen to my song.
Don't get married too young. Make the most of a good time.
When you are married, things will change.]

"This song is probably 150 years old."

In addition to her French songbooks, Florence has a book of English languge songs, country "hillbilly songs."

On a quiet summer day, long ago and far away, a little girl
was kneeling by a grave.
As I stood there by her side, she was gazing at the sky.
These words I heard as to the Lord she prayed.
"Oh, Lord, please tell me, do, why you took my mom with you?
Oh, why on earth am I left all alone?
I loved her, don't you see? 'Cause she was so good to me.
She always taught me what was right from wrong."
(Hal Lone Pine [Harold Breau] "Oh Lord Please Tell Me, Do")

"Songs like that. Heard them on the radio. I used to listen to the radio and I would hear the song once and I could sit down and write it. And my mother could do the same thing."

"Most Acadian songs are sad," Florence says. She also has a whole book of war songs.

"My uncles were in the war, my grandfathers, cousins. There was always a war going on. With the Germans in 1870. Well, the English and the French. *Le Grand dérangement* and all that. Soldiers." Yet, she explains, according to Acadian historian Don Cyr, there are no true war songs about *le Grand Dérangement*, when the British deported hundreds from their lands.[7]

"I can't sing if I'm crying. Dolly Parton does, but I don't know how she does. Some songs, I can't sing; I get a couple lines and that's it. But she sings and cries at the same time. I wish I could do that. I don't know how she does it. And she's not the only one. I've noticed some other people too. I can't and my daughter either."

Florence said her daughter Daureen, who also sings but not publicly, cries easily at the sad songs.

Florence came to Lewiston just after she graduated from high school in 1956. She first worked at Kresge's, where her French contrasted with those of Quebec origin.

"Everyone there was French Canadian; 90% of people in Lewiston were French. At least 90% back then in 1956 and some of the words they used I had never heard. The nuns had never talked to us about those words. But the lady who was the floor leader where I was working, she thought the way I spoke was funny and I did not think so. And so, one time, I wanted some chocolate, to buy some chocolate. So I went to the counter and instead of saying, '*Je veux un demi-livre de chocolat*,' I said, '*Je veux un moq d'un livre*." Because that's the way we say it. It's supposed to be *moitié*, but in the St. John Valley the Acadians use "t" as a "k" or "q": *moquié*. So it came out '*moquié d'un livre*.'[8] She laughed for two days, which did not make me happy."

When she realized she was being paid the same wages as high school girls who worked just part-time, she moved on to Woolworth where she made $.70 an hour, and later a shoe shop where the wages for industrial shoe workers were $1.00 an hour. That is where she met her future husband, Richard Laliberté, and his family. It turned out that his grandmother came from Lille, Maine, the place her father had been born.

Florence continued to work in the shoe industry. They worked at Eastland Shoe in Freeport for thirteen years. With two small children at home, the daily commute became difficult. In 1972, some friends who were officers at the Cavalier Town and Country Social Club suggested the couple work there. Florence's then-husband (they have since been divorced) was treasurer, and she did anything that needed to be done: she tended bar, kept the door, and helped with the paperwork. There were live bands Thursdays through Sundays. On Fridays and Saturdays, Florence's husband played drums with the Cavaliers (originally the Royal Kingsmen). Soon her daughter Darlene, then sixteen, sang with band although she was underage; the liquor inspector gave permission because both parents were there. The bands most often played waltzes, polkas, jitterbug, and country music, including the songs of Hank Williams, Hank Snow, Kitty Wells, and Dolly Parton. People would ask Florence herself to sing old French songs. She recalls one evening going down the street to get some ice from another social club and getting talked into staying and performing a few songs at that club.

In 1973, Florence and her husband decided to found a snowshoe club.[9] The men were called the Cavaliers (*le Cavalier* in the singular in French) and the women, *Les Dames Cavalier.* Their colors were brown and pink. The club also had a drum and bugle corps that paraded with the snowshoers. Children as young as fourteen who played drums, bugle, or cymbals could join as long as their parents were members of the club.

Florence recalls travel to snowshoe conventions:

"We went To Ottawa. I sang the national anthem, the American national anthem, in Ottawa, Quebec City, and Montreal. We went to Rivière du Loup. We went to other places, little places. A city near Montreal. We used to go by bus. But at first, in '59, '60, '61, we used to go by train, the train from Lewiston to Quebec. That was fun. Then the train stopped and we used to go by buses. But this year, 2015, February 2015 was the last convention. No more. No more snowshoers. It was too expensive. Not enough people wanted to join. The buses, the hotel rooms. We had to stay Friday night, Saturday night, come back on Sunday. It was just too expensive. So this February, the last convention of all after ninety years, the last convention was in Lewiston at the Ramada. And my daughter, Darlene Rose Kritzman sang, the American National anthem and I sang the Canadian national anthem."

Florence, frequently with daughter Darlene, has performed traditional songs far and wide throughout the years. Highlights include performances for the National Council of Traditional Arts in both Augusta, Maine and Washington, DC; at the Lowell, Massachusetts Folk Festival in 1993; and at the Downeast Celtic Christmas celebration at the Center for Cultural Exchange in Portland, Maine. Florence was the only Maine resident invited to perform at Le Festival International de la Louisiane in 1993, and in 1995 she participated in the French Connection tour that traveled to Connecticut, Rhode Island, Massachusetts, several cities in Louisiana, and Quebec. In 2004, Florence and Darlene performed at the John F. Kennedy Center in Washington, DC as part of the "Homegrown Music in America Series."

There was one of Florence's songs that was particularly popular in Louisiana:

"This one is about a couple, they're married. The wife tells the husband, "I don't like it when you go to see that lady that lives next door." So they sit together, they have a drink together. So there's a lot of drinking songs. I sang this in Lafayette, Louisiana twice. 1993, 1995."

Ah, j'ai la tristesse dans ma maison.
C'est d'avoir un home qui boit sans raison.
Souvent la semaine il est toujours saoul,
Se donne pas la peine de gagner quelques sous.

Oh, tais-toi donc ma petite femme.
Tu me juges mal à propos.
Croirais-tu qu'un homme serait sans défaut.
Je suis jeune encore et j'aime le plaisir
De vider une bouteille, ça me fait réjouir.

Cela, j'en tire rien.
C'est quand tu vas voir la petite femme du voisin…

The song concludes :
Trinquons, ma petite femme. Trinquons tous les deux.
Allons à la table comme deux amoureux.
J'ai la gorge sèche, je ne peux plus chanter.
Charmante bouteille, viens donc me la mouiller.
(Anonymous)

[Ah, there's sadness in my home.
It's because my husband drinks without reason.
Often during the workweek he's always drunk
Doesn't make an effort to earn a few coins.

Oh, hush now, my little wife. You're judging me poorly on this subject.
Would you believe that a man would be without flaws?
I'm still young and I like the pleasure of emptying a bottle. It makes me happy.

Emptying a bottle, I don't care.
It's when you go off to see the neighbor man's little wife…

Let's have a toast, my little wife. Let's both toast.
Let's sit down at the table like two lovers.
My throat is dry, I can't sing any more.
Charming bottle, come wet my whistle.]

Florence continues to perform at major Acadian events where she reaffirms her connections to her roots. "This summer [2014] my daughter and I sang with Don [Cyr] at the Musée du Mont Carmel [in Lille, Maine].[10] That's where my father was baptized and made his First Communion. And my grandmother got married there twice. My grandfather got married in 1918 (and passed away from the Spanish influenza that same year) and she got remarried in 1920."

Just as the women in her family passed along their knowledge of song traditions, they also passed along crafts through the generations. Florence learned to quilt using rosettes of cloth from her grandmother.

"On my twenty-first birthday, March 15, 1959, my daughter was six weeks old and my grandmother—I was the first granddaughter, my daughter was the first great-granddaughter—came from Madawaska and spent the day with me. She showed me how to make a cushion out of satin that she had made the pattern for. She had invented it. It took one yard of taffeta and there was a piece left over after her cushion was done. With that piece of taffeta, she would make rosettes. So she showed me how to make that. They were little, little rosettes. Made of taffeta and satin. And taffeta, it fringes, so I'll tell people, 'Don't try that at home!' But this is easy. This is cotton and they're big. It's so easy!"

Between raising a family and full-time work, it took Florence twenty-seven years to make one of her grandmother's quilts. In 1982, she learned needlepoint. In 1987, she took lessons with master quilter Darlene Gauthier and has produced prize-winning, hand-stitched quilts, but those took a toll on her back. Today she sticks to quilts of large cotton rosettes. One pattern is the Acadian flag, but feeling guilty, she made sure to craft a quilt of Stars and Stripes, too.

"In 2004, the Acadians had been here four-hundred years. I made one for Moncton, New Brunswick. I made one for Annapolis Royal—it used to be Port Royal,[11] and one for the Acadian Archives in Fort Kent, and one for the library in Ste. Agathe."

Florence participated in the *Congrès Mondial Acadien* [Acadian World Congress] in the summer of 2014.[12]

"That was really great. For seventeen days. That Congrès, that part lasted for seventeen days. It was New Brunswick first—Moncton—, then Northern Maine, and then in part of Quebec that's close like Kamouraska. That's where my mother's family came from. The Acadians went up there in [the] 1770s, 1780s, and they married the French Canadians that were there. But then they came back south to find a place to live with the Acadians, so they are considered Acadian. So even if their great, great, great … [she repeats the word nine times as she counts on her fingers] grandparents came from Kamouraska, if they live in the St. John Valley, they are considered Acadians. So my mother is Acadian."

Florence notes that the people of the Valley only became Americans in 1842 when Quebec ceded the land to the United States.[13] For years, it was easy enough to cross from one side of the river to the other:

> "We only became Americans in 1842, but nobody told us that up there! The news didn't reach us 'til 1950! Across the river, in the summer, you can go barefoot without getting wet. The river gets real low sometimes. Well, you're out. Your uncle lives there, your grandmother's in Canada, your other grandmother's here. We're all related. We all have the same names. St. Basil, St. David, Madawaska, Edmonton. We all have the same last names."

Now she has a passport. She first got it because when her family traveled to the Valley in the summers, her grandchildren wanted her to take them to the dollar store in St. Basil.

Some of Florence's family still live in northern Maine. Her youngest brother, born twenty-one years after Florence, who is the eldest of eleven, owns the Long Lake Sporting Club. Her daughter Darlene is five weeks older than her uncle.

"And that happens in all the families up there. Yes, I don't know about now, but fifty years ago, sixty years ago they had an uncle or an aunt that was [younger] than them. Because the ladies there they had kids from eighteen to forty. That's twenty-two years. Like my father was the oldest of thirteen born in 1912. And his brother was born 1934. He's twenty-two years older than his brother."

"When I got married, I wanted twelve daughters. I had names for twelve girls. I didn't know anything better. I didn't know that you didn't have to have so many. And after the first one, I had such a hard time; I brought it down to five. Okay. Five is good. But then I only had two." [Darlene Rose and Daureen Ann.]

After raising a family, Florence was divorced and now enjoys her independence:

"Today, I live by myself. I eat when I want. I go to bed at seven p.m., that I like. Get up at three a.m. if I want to. So my back hurts. Go to the computer, play games. Oh, what a life! What did I do to deserve this? I tell my daughters, 'My gosh, I'm really lucky!'"

Appendix: More of Florence Martin's Songbook Lyrics

C'est la vie d'un garcon qui est la vie la plus belle
Car quand on a un peu d'argent, on peut passer notre temps à rire, à chanter, à boire à plein verre
Ne jamais penser à se marier
(Anonymous)

[It's a boy's life that is the most beautiful life
Because when we have little money, we can spend our time laughing, singing, drinking to the lees
Never thinking about getting married]

Lyrics to a traditional song about marital discord (full text)

Ah, j'ai la tristesse dans ma maison.
C'est d'avoir un homme qui boit sans raison.
Souvent la semaine il est toujours saoul,
Se donne pas la peine de gagner quelques sous.

Oh, tais-toi donc ma petite femme.
Tu me juges mal à propos.
Croirais-tu qu'un homme serait sans défaut ?
Je suis jeune encore et j'aime e plaisir
De vider une bouteille, ça me fait réjouir.

Cela, j'en tire rien.
C'est quand tu vas voir la petite femme du voisin.

Elle est belle et jolie. Je la trouve de mon goût.
Quand j'ai une petite chance, j'y vais faire un tour.

Ah, non, mon mari, comme ça, ça ne se fait pas.
Deux femmes pour un home, c'est un grand embarras.
Si tu aimes ça comme ça, continue mon mari.
Et notre voisin, je l'aime moi aussi.

Trinquons, ma petite femme. Trinquons tous les deux.
Allons à la table comme deux amoureux.
J'ai la gorge sèche, je ne peux plus chanter.
Charmante bouteille, viens donc me la mouiller.

[Ah, there's sadness in my home.
It's because my husband drinks without reason.
Often during the workweek he's always drunk
Doesn't make an effort to earn a few coins.

Oh, hush now, my little wife. You're judging me poorly on this subject.
Would you believe that a man would be without resources?
I'm still young and I like the pleasure emptying a bottle. It makes me happy.

Emptying a bottle, I don't care.
It's when you go off to see the neighbor man's little wife.

She's beautiful and pretty. I find her to my taste. When I have the chance, I take a little stroll.
Ah, no, my husband, something like that isn't done.
Two women for one man is a big shame.
If you like it like that, go ahead, my husband.
Myself, I like the neighbor man as well.

Let's have a toast, my little wife. Let's both toast.
Let's sit down at the table life two lovers.
My throat is dry, I can't sing any more.
Charming bottle, come wet my whistle.]

Lyrics to a song made famous in 1937 by Rina Ketty:
"Je n'ai qu'une maman,"
Words and music by Jacques Martel, F. Bousquet, R. Vaysse, *Étoiles de la chanson*, 1937.

Maman te voilà bien surprise
De me voir ici ce matin
Pourtant il faut que je te dise
Combien mon coeur a de chagrin
Depuis qu'un tribunal infâme
Veut qu'on vive séparément
Il vient chez nous une autre femme
Qu'on me fait appeler maman

Ecoute-moi petite mère
Je me moque bien de leurs lois
Je n'aime pas cette étrangère
Je n'ai qu'une maman c'est toi

[Mama, look how surprised you are
To see me here this morning
Nevertheless I must tell you
How much sorrow is in my heart
Ever since a notorious court
Wanted us to live apart
Into our home has come another woman
Whom they make me call Mama

Listen to me, little Mother
I don't care about their laws
I don't like this stranger
I have only one Mama, that's you]

Works Cited:

Lone Pine, Hal (Harold Breau). "Oh Lord Please Tell Me, Do." *On the Trail of the Lonesome Pine*, Bear Records, 2006.
Martel, Jacques F. Bousquet, R. Vaysse, "Je n'ai qu'une maman," *Étoiles de la chanson*, 1937.
Martel, Marcel Gaston, "Un coin du ciel." 1952.
Pelletier, Susann. *Keepers of the Song; The Franco-American Songbook Tradition*, Exhibition Catalog. Lewiston: Atrium Art Gallery, University of Southern Maine Lewiston-Auburn College, 1995. 1-5.
Rice-DeFosse, Mary and James Myall. *The Franco-Americans of Lewiston Auburn*. Charleston, SC: The History Press, 2015.

Endnotes:

1. Susann Pelletier, *Keepers of the Song; The Franco-American Songbook Tradition*, Exhibition Catalog. (Lewiston: Atrium Art Gallery, University of Southern Maine Lewiston-Auburn College, 1995), 1-5.

2. This military expulsion of the French-speaking settlers of Acadia took place during the French and Indian Wars 1755-64.

3. A legendary singer in the Acadian tradition from St. Agathe who died in 2007 at the age of eighty-five.

4. A reference to a comment made to Florence about the natives of her hometown by Lisa Ornstein, an ethnomusicologist at the Acadian Archives in Fort Kent.

5. Florence makes the distinction between Acadian and Canadian, French-Canadian, or Quebecois.

6. All translations are Mary Rice-DeFosse's.

7. Two of the most popular Acadian songs are based on Henry Wadsworth Longfellow's poem "Evangeline," first published in 1847. It is set against *le grand dérangement*, but the songs are love songs.

8. Florence wanted to buy half a pound of chocolate, but as she explains here, in the Acadian pronunciation of the word for "half" (*moitié* in standard French), the sound spelled with a "t" in standard French becomes a "k" sound spelled with a "q".

9. Snowshoeing became an organized social sport in Canada. The first snowshoe club in the United States, Le Montagnard, was founded in Lewiston 1924 by Louis-Philippe Gagné. The next year, Lewiston had enough snowshoe clubs to hold its first International Convention. See Mary Rice-DeFosse and James Myall, *The Franco-Americans of Lewiston-Auburn* (Charleston, SC: The History Press, 2015), 64-69.

10. Don Cyr is a well-known artist and an expert in Acadian history and culture from the St. John Valley.

11. Port Royal was one of the first French settlements in North America.

12. The first Acadian World Congress was held in Moncton, New Brunswick, in 1994. The second was held in 1999 in Louisiana, since that region's Cajuns are often descendants of those deported in le grand derangement. Florence describes the venues for the 2014 congress, which was held on both sides of the border between Maine and Canada.

13. The 1842 Webster-Ashburton Treaty resolved disputes about the border between Canada and the United States.

Valse du temps (Waltz of time)

Quand les fleurs montrent leurs belles couleurs
Avant qu'elles vieillissent
Quand les étoiles tombent du ciel
Sans savoir où elles se trouveront
Quand les oiseaux s'en vont en étant amoureux

Et j'essaie d'attraper le temps
Et j'essaie de me souvenir
De chaque regard, chaque son
Avant que le silence me rend sourde

Et j'ai senti mon coeur, mon âme légere
.....flottaient dans le vent
En voyant les petites feuilles
danser, tomber, se rencontrer
Pendant une valse du temps
Au clair de la lune

Par Michèle Choinière

Voici les paroles de sa chanson/composition, "Valse du temps," du CD: *Mademoiselle Voulez-Vous Danser: Franco-American Music from the New England Borderlands*, Smithsonian Folkways, 1999 et de son premier CD *Coeur Fragile*, 2003).

The Stationery Aisle

Un pays de merveilles:

Où le papier et les crayons

Deviennent des dessins ou des chansons;

Où les plumes et les autocollants

Deviennent un chef-d'oeuvre important—

Surtout sur un frigo,

Certainement pour un parent;

Où un cahier deviant un lieu

De reverie.

A wonderland:

Where paper and pencils

Become drawings and songs;

Where pens and stickers

Become an important masterpiece—

Especially on a fridge,

Certainly for a parent;

Where a notebook becomes a place

For dreaming.

By Maureen Perry

World Fiddle Day

So many tunes
Whole tunes, fragments of phrases,
Tunes I love, tunes I loathe (for no fiddler lacks an opinion)
Earworms that won't go away till I play them for an hour
And then they never go away! Hah-Hah!
Who says a tune doesn't have a sense of humor!

So many people
Old fiddlers, young—women, girls, boys, men
People who feed musicians, people who play pianos and guitars,
Who organize events so they can smile from the back row,
Whose love commits them to weekly Sunday afternoons
As a DJ at the local radio station
Or a lifetime behind a luthier's bench

So many styles
Go around the world
Scratch a culture, find a fiddler
Wherever we dance,
there is a fiddle or its kin
And the music
gets under our feet

So much feeling
The bow on the string
Opens the heart
We forget
For those brief moments of sound
That we are grounded
And not flying

So little time
Love the music
So little time
Love the dance
So little time
Love the people
So little time
Love the journey
So little time Pass it on

By Donna Hébert

La vie, c'est une danse

Moi, j'vois
la vie comme une danse.

On peut valser ou
on peut faire du ballet.

Pour nous les femmes
c'est plutôt le dernier.

Laissez-moi vous expliquer.

Imaginez.....Le ballet.

On saute en l'air
on s'pète parterre.

On se fend en quatre
des fois on est à quatre pattes.

On fait des "pas de deux."
Des fois
ce sont des vrais,
des fois
ce sont des faux
pas.

On caracole
on tourne en rond
on corcobille
on glisse
on trotte
on avance
on recule

on recule
on avance
on fait des culbutes
on se traîne
on se tord
on fait comme si on est mort
on marche en biais
sur le bout des pieds..........comme sur des pi quants.

Le ballet, c'est de l'ouvrage.
Et, quand c'est fini
tout le monde applaudit
la danse est fini...et la vie aussi.

Et oui...pour nous autres les femmes, la vie c'est un grand "balai"....
et, souvent, c'est un grand "mop" aussi.

Par Brenda Mounier

Voltige à la Vertige

Il faut vite l'attraper
car il va passer
comme un clin d'oeil.

Si tu l'as pas bien vu,
si tu l'as pas bien connu
Comment le décrire?
Comment le dire?

E-où le placer?
E-où l'encadrer?
Peut-être l'encager
derrière des barres hor i zon tales?

On est chanceux
s'il revient
sur ces pas.

LA,
on peut
le mettre
là où on veut....
dans un cadre de cahier,
sur un bout de papier.

Faut pas lâcher,
faut courir après
et l'attraper
dans le filet
de...
de lignes de papier
et vite le coincer
vite avant de l'oublier....ces pensées
ces idées,
ce papillon .....d'inspiration.

Par Brenda Mounier

Women's Ways of Publishing

As I Live and Dream

By Gertrude M. Coté

Excerpt—Introduction

Because I must have been a cause of despair to my teachers and surely was a trial to my parents as one of those "must-know-why" youngsters, and because I feel that turnabout is fair play, I will begin by telling you why I have embarked on this presumptuous adventure of trying to write a book.

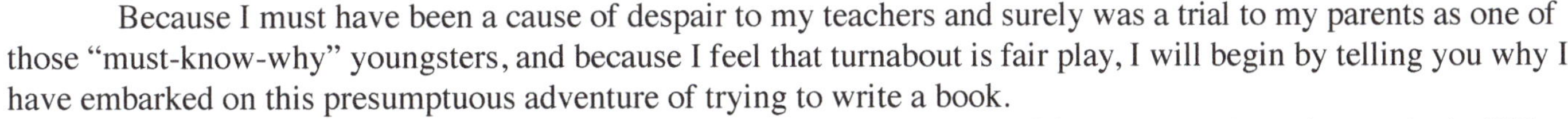

For almost every letter and article I have written in the past ten or fifteen years, I have been asked: "Why don't you write a book?"

When I try to explain that writing a letter and turning author are two very different tasks, I am lectured and called lazy. "How do you know you can't write, have you ever tried?" My sister cuts ads asking for new writers and dares me to argue with her; my husband throws up his hands and vows I am wasting God-given talent. They almost have me believing, at least have me wondering, if maybe—well, I suppose I could try. I have nothing to lose but a few illusions ... Since I haven't enough imagination to create characters, then action for the characters, I will have to write about folks that are. As I know very little of other people's activities, their irks and quirks, it leave me but on field of action—"Us Cotes," with a dip here and there in the past to "Us Metiviers." And I believe I shall call my ramblings "As I Live and Dream," because that is exactly what it will be.

***As I Live and Dream*, A Dirigo Edition, Manchester, Maine Copyright 1953**
Printed on paper made by Oxford Paper Company of Rumford, Maine

---

Marcella Bélanger Violette Scrapbooks, 1920-2005

This collection housed at the Acadian Archives at the University of Maine at Fort Kent consists of twenty-five scrapbooks of documents relating to Marcella Bélanger Violette's lifetime of public service. The scrapbooks, comprised of more than 3,000 pages, cover the time period from 1920 through 2004. A wide range of topics are included in the collection, with key areas being the town of Van Buren, the St. John Valley, Franco-Americans, the Acadians, Bilingualism, Education, Politics, St. Bruno's Church in Van Buren, the Good Shepard Sisters, the Allagash Wilderness Waterway and the Violette family. Each volume is filled with photos, newspaper articles, letters, cards, telegrams, postcards, brochures, and other items Marcella carefully selected for inclusion. Researchers studying any of the main topics areas and the general public simply browsing will benefit from this unique resource (see the Collection Guide for a more detailed description of each scrapbook). These scrapbooks were collected and created by Marcella and archivally preserved by her daughter-in-law, Holly Ramsdell Violette.

Marcella Bélanger (Violette) was born and raised in Van Buren, Maine. She married Elmer Violette and became the mother of five children (Dennis, Marc, Paul, Louise, and Tom). She highly valued education, receiving her B.A from The College of New Rochelle and an M.A. in French and English from Boston University. In 1953 she earned her Ph.D. from L'Université Saint Louis Maillet, Edmundston, New Brunswick. Marcella was the first St. John Valley woman to receive a doctoral degree. Her dissertation entitled "French Influence in the St. John Valley" would become part of her life's work to celebrate and promote her Franco-American and Acadian heritage. In addition to her advocacy of the culture and language of the St. John Valley, she was a teacher and lecturer on family life and the role of women in society.

...more Women's Ways of Publishing

Journal writing...

Aunt Clara's Notebook, circa 1905, age 13-14

By/par Clara Picher, June 21, 1891—February 25, 1964
She lived all her life at 88-94 Water Street, Waterville, Maine

About the journal

The journal was written on a lined copybook, using an ink pen. It was written in beautiful handwriting. Over time the pages have yellowed. The front and back covers are missing, and the first and last pages are torn.

Discovery of the journal

The journal was discovered along with family photo albums around 2012, by Colleen Cruise. She brought it to the attention of her cousin, Annette Picher Houston, and they attempted to translate it. They sought help also from Bunnie Picher, who keeps the family genealogical records.

Help was also given by Rhea Côté Robbins and Danielle Gaillard-Picher with songs which they helped find on the internet.

Our arrangement

The journal was translated page by page as written. A copy was made of Clara's writing in French (mostly), and then the English translation follows immediately. When she wrote lyrics to songs, Clara did not use conventional poetic form of line-by-line. Often she ignored punctuation.—Annette Picher Houston

Clara's Index

Clara included an index on the last page of the journal, although it is incomplete.
The journal is not arranged by category; however, there are inclusions about:
—Family history
—Town happenings
—Prayers
—Poems and songs
—Recipes
—Love charms

Clara describing herself:

A L'age de 13 ans et 5 mois je mesurais 5 pieds 4 pouces. Tour de ceinture 34 pouces. Tour de buste 33 pouces. Tour de hanche 36 pouces. Tour de jambe 14 1/2 pouces. La longueur du pieds 9 1/2 pouces. Grosseur du poignet 6 1/2 pouces. Longueur du bras 28 1/2 pouces. J'avais les yeux gris. Tour de cuise 24 pouces. Et, Clara Picher - 31 Mai 1902 -l'age de: 10 ans, 11 mois, 2 jours (First Communion date).

At the age of 13 years and 5 months I measured 5 feet 4 inches. Around my waist (I measured) 34 inches. Around the bust 33 inches. Around the hips 36 inches. Around the leg 14 1/2 inches. The length of my foot is 9 1/2 inches. Size of my fist is 6 1/2 inches. The length of my arm is 28 1/2 inches. I have grey eyes. Around my thigh is 24 inches. Clara Picher, May 31, 1902, 10 years, 11 months, 2 days on her First Communion Day.

Page 14

La jubilé des femmes a duré une semaine commencent le 18 Octobre 1904, a sept heures et demi de soir et la messe était cinq heures et demi et huit heures les chemin de croix a trois heures et le sermon a sept heuree demi la mission a été prêché par le Rev. Père LaLande de Montreal et elle s'est terminé le dimanche le 23rd Octobre les femmes ont recut la benediction papale et les objects de piété ont aussi été bénie et plusieures femmes et filles ont été reçu du scapulaire bleu et noire.

The Jubilee of women lasted one week beginning October 18, 1904, at seven thirty in the evening and Mass was at five o'clock and at eight. The Stations of the Cross was at three o'clock and the sermon at seven thirty. The mission was preached by the Rev. Father LaLande of Montreal and finished on Sunday the 23rd October. The women received a papal blessing and devotional objects were also blessed and many women and girls received blue and black scapulars.

Crime
C'est dans la nuit du 2 de Novembre 1902 vers deux heures, qu'Eduard Dostie essaya de tuer sa femme mais il n'a pas réussi.

It was in the night of 2 November 1902 about two o'clock, Edward Dostie tried to kill his wife, but he did not succeed.

Page 22
Recettes
Balayé les tapis
Mettre de sel sur les tapis et les balayer les tapis viennent bien clair.
Put salt on the carpets and sweep them and the carpets will come clean.

Recipes, continued
Another cure for headache is to walk backwards. (In English)

PAGE 27
Language de mouchoir
Le passer sur la bouche, "Je desire faire votre connaissance."
Le passer sur les yeux, "Vous m'affliger."
Le tenir par le milieu, "Vous êtes trop pressé."
Le laisser tomber, "Soyons amis."
Le tourner dans la main, "Je vous hais."
Le passer sur la joue gauche, "Je vous aime."
Le tourner dans la main gauche, "J'en aime un autre."
Le filier, (sic), "Je voudrais vous parler."
Le jeter sur l'épaule, "Puisez moi."
Le passez sur le front gueulel, "Qu'un vous voit."
Le passer sur l'oil droit, "Vous êtes changé."
Le laisser reposer sur les yeux ,"Vous êtes cruel."
Le placer dans sa poche, "Assez pour le présent."

Language of the Handkerchief
Passing it over your mouth, I want to get to know you.
Passing it over your eyes, you bother me.
Holding it by the middle, you are rushing me.
Letting it fall, let's be friends.
Twisting it in your hands, I hate you.
Passing it over the left cheek, I love you.
Turning it in the left hand, I love another.
Folding it, I want to talk to you.
Throwing it over the shoulder, draw me [to you]
Passing it over the front jaw, someone sees you.
Passing it over the right eye, you are different.
Letting it rest over your eyes, you are cruel.
Putting it in your pocket, enough for now.

Picture is of Clara and Bella in front of the Picher Store, prior to the addition. They called this portion the "Candy Store" and the girls worked there. Scene is 94 Water Street, opposite Gold Street, looking North. Clara Picher began to work in the Gédéon Picher Store on the 31st of July, 1905, at the age of 14 years, 2 months and 2 days.

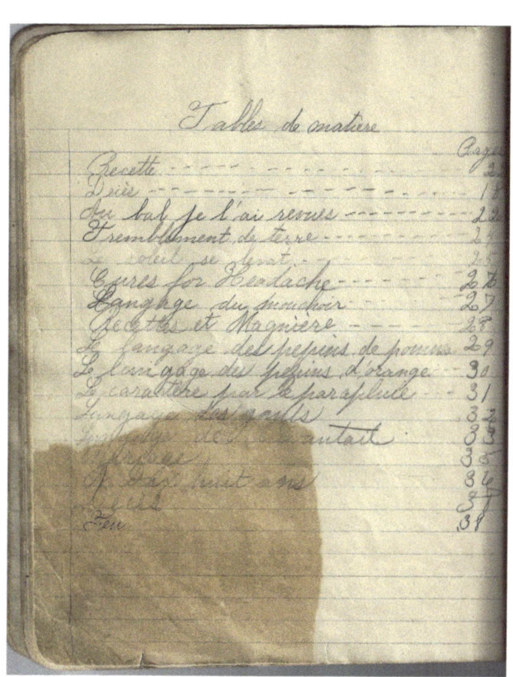

Tables de matiere

...and more Women's Ways of Publishing Letter writing...

Excerpts from letters written to Alma R. from her friend Theresa. Letters transcribed by Alma's grand-nephew, Steve.

A teenager, Theresa _____, in Waterville corresponded with her friend Alma R. Theresa's family had lived in Vassalboro, but moved to Waterville by 1915. Alma, in 1915, was in high school at Brewster Free Academy in Wolfeboro, New Hampshire Misspellings have been left as in the original.

Waterville, Maine
Sept. 12, 1915

Dear Alma: —

... Wednesday, Thursday, & Friday I was camping at Snow Pond (Waterville Me.) with 8 others including chaperone. We are starting an older girls' camp fire here although little "it" is going to belong. I am very axious for it to start for I always wanted to be one. I go to Junior High tomorrow which is realy the 9th grade, only they have put in the eighth grade system here so it will be called eighth grade even if it is the last year. you understand? well, I must close now. I wish you would write more often you used to.

Lovingly
Theresa

Waterville Me
Oct. 10, 1915

Dear Bob: —[aka Alma R.]

Excuse pencil but I cant find the ink. I have decided not to join the campfire [i.e., Campfire Girls club] after all because the croud that are going to belong are all younger girls & live in the South part of the city which is the French section so nearly all of my friends (& meself!) have changed our minds about joining this one. I am sorry in a way for I think The Camp Fire Girls is a great organization. But I am going to be very busy this winter & would not have time for the work, which is another reason for my change of mind.

Everly
Theresa.

"The Franco-American community of Waterville , Maine has been largely ignored until very recently. This, of course, was partially due to the fact that they were not predominant in the upper echelons of local politics, business, and industry before the 1950s because of discrimination and economic insecurity. Within their own ethnic community there were remarkable number of leaders in privately owned, small, ethnic businesses and in the professions. ... In the extended Franco-American family, connections and ties among relatives from 1890 to 1940 were viewed as being stronger during the first and second generation Franco-Americans. In the interviews with Franco-Americans, respect for parents, for siblings, for the institution of marriage, for the authority of the father, and for the raising of children were all highly regarded attributes among the French. The language of French, the religion and the culture were all perpetrated and enforced through the family and the church. ... The Franco-Americans of Waterville who were employed at the Lockwood Cotton Hill are a small sample of a larger group of French textile workers that by 1900 comprised one third of all the textile workers of New England. Prior to the Maine child labor laws of 1907 and 1909, many of these textile workers in Waterville were under the age of sixteen, often as young as nine. ... When dealing with the Lockwood's labor force in the early years, the role of child labor and child labor laws must be considered. Prior to 1907, the minimum age for children to work in the industry was twelve, but there are many indications ... from oral accounts that people often changed the ages on birth certificates in order that children may work in the cotton mill. ... Franco-Americans have come under consistent criticism not only from the Yankee population but from other ethnic groups for depriving their children of education. They did not abuse child labor as much as previously thought. The 1905 *Report of the Immigration Commission* indicated that while French-Canadian children contributed one third to the family income, Irish children contributed forty-five percent."

Excerpt: Bernier, Margaret, "Labor study of the Franco-American Community of Waterville, Maine from 1890 to 1940" (1981). Colby College. Senior Scholar Papers. Paper 25.

Publish as Film: "Down by The River's Edge"

By Susan Gagnon

A fourth-generation Franco-American, Susan Gagnon is a descendant of hard-working papermakers and textile workers who immigrated from Quebec, Prince Edward Island, and New Brunswick, Canada, to the "petit village" of Chisholm, at the south end of Jay, Maine seeking work in the developing Otis Paper Mill.

In 1998, after the birth of her first grandchild Adeline, Gagnon found there were rare accounts of the silenced voices of the early French-Canadian immigrants.

Gagnon researched documents, articles and photographs for over fifteen years compiling her own collection. When hearing of the closing of the Otis Mill in 2009, Gagnon borrowed camera equipment from Mt. Blue Community Access TV in Farmington and began filming the Otis Paper Mill and heartfelt stories from over twenty retired paper makers. The historic mill closed in June 2009.

Down by The River's Edge was a collaboration with Mt. Blue Community Access TV in Farmington. The documentary sheds light on the immigration of men who left their homeland searching for a better life for their families and details the struggles and triumphs they faced as the first Roman Catholic immigrant settlers in the "petit village" of Chisholm, wedged between the foothills and the powerful Androscoggin River. Sometimes leaving their families behind for years, they left Quebec and the Maritime Provinces of Canada, and across the Atlantic from Italy, Czechoslovakia, and Ireland seeking and finding employment in the developing paper industry in the 1890s through the 1920s, until earning enough money to bring their families to the region.

Stories record their cultural and language barriers as they strived to adapt to their new lives in their foothills of Maine, and they wove the fabric of the community of Chisholm and the trinity of the community: the Otis Mill, the Androscoggin River, and the St. Rose of Lima Church where these new immigrants practiced their devout Roman Catholic faith and built the brick and mortar of their new community.

The film also details the untold accounts of how French-Canadians in the 1850s walked down from Quebec, Canada, to Farmington, Maine, to work as seasonal farm laborers, returning back to Quebec after the harvest season and repeatedly coming back to the region until they had enough money to bring their entire family to Farmington. Several decades later their descendants moved to Chisholm to work in the paper mill.

Gagnon narrates a collage of images from her childhood living in a three-decker tenement building, a stone's throw away from the Otis Mill where all the men in her family worked. Historic images and stories are shared by papermakers who were deeply affected by the 2009 closing of Otis Mill.

Gagnon filmed, wrote the screenplay and produced the documentary, *Down by The River's Edge,* which took four years to complete. Mt. Blue Community Access TV Station Director, J.P. Fortier was editor of the film and Geoff Cyr was assistant editor.

Down by The River's Edge, Gagnon's first film, was screened at Jay in April 2013. Also screened at Biddeford, Maine; Gold Leaf sponsored a screening at the University of Maine at Farmington. With additional screenings at the University of Southern Maine At Lewiston-Auburn College; the Franco-American Center at the University of Maine; the Railroad Square Cinema in Waterville, Maine; the Farmington Historical Society; the Livermore Falls History Night in 2014; the 2014 Emerge Film Festival in Lewiston, Maine; and at the 2014 World Acadian Congress in Edmundston, New Brunswick, Canada. The film placed 2nd in the Documentary Category at the 2014 Alliance for Community Media Northeast Film Festival.

Publish as song
"A Place Called Beautiful"

Also sending this song—Martha Pellerin's words to her husband John Drury in the two weeks before she died. She was near death and kept asking John to help her to the door. She said the relatives were there to take her to a place called beautiful and she'd be there for him when it was his turn. And not to be afraid. I wrote them down and it took two years to put it together as a song. Then in 2003, I recorded it—voice and piano—with La Bottine pianist Denis Frechette at his studio in Joliette. It's the only thing I've composed on the piano and the harmonic progression is interesting. Then he died in 2008. Heartbreaking. So it became the last track on my "In Full Bloom/En pleine floraison" CD in 2009. The song is called "A Place Called Beautiful."—**Donna Hébert**

Martha Pellerin Drury
1961-1998
"A Place Called Beautiful"

The room is full of ghosts

My mother, aunts, and more

They're standing all around the bed

It's time for me to go

won't you help me to the door?

Please don't worry, darlings

I've seen it in a dream

And even though I have no map,

I'll find it just the same

My Mother's voice will lead me on

To where I have to go

I'm not afraid,

So take my hand,

And bless me, for I know

I'm going to a place called Beautiful

They're waiting for me there

It's time for me to put it down

This earthly burden that I bear

Leaving you behind, my loves,

I leave the best of friends

Don't fear for me—I'm not afraid

When it's your turn I'll be there too

I am not lost—my spirit lives

I'll find you once again

Fine Art Photographer—Linda Griffith Artist's Statement

An internationally exhibited fine art photographer, Linda Griffith expresses in her work a sophisticated grasp of the medium's temporal underpinnings, as well as of subconscious compositional elements. A Fulbright scholar in theatre and award-winning playwright, Linda has coupled her Bachelor of Fine Arts degree in Directing to her Master's Degree in Social Work and psychotherapeutic expertise to enrich her lifelong work in photography every step of the way. Drama's premise of conflict, opposed by a Rankian homage to fear of inertia and the problem death presents to human consciousness, is evident throughout her career. Her images are noted for an existential edge that transforms street and landscape captures, equally, into rare, visual experiences. As critic Daniel Sean Kaye put it "...beautiful, dramatic, haunting work."

In 1999, a jury of New York museum directors and curators honored Griffith as "... one of the most talented emerging artists at the turn of the century and the millennium" for her violent image entitled "Not Everything Is Forgivable," typical of her bold execution of photographic images in that period that "reported" on psychic states in documentarian style while simultaneously relying on extensive manipulation. While masterful in producing graphical statements reflecting painstaking adjustments that trade on the medium's unique power to depict and comment on the human condition (e.g., "Dialogue with Government"), Griffith is now equally celebrated for minimally edited landscapes that inexplicably grip the viewer in near-hypnotic states of engagement.

When asked what it is about "The Secret Life of Light" (a portfolio of 75 remote Arctic landscapes five years in the making) and the emerging portfolio of Sonoran Desert images entitled "Spirit Walk," that imbues seemingly innocuous landscapes with such a startling, gripping quality, she explains:

My work is about time, and time is clearly about vibration. Whether or not we consciously perceive the sound emanating from a photograph or the light emanating from a concerto, both exist in all experiences of art. I try to bring a particular vibratory state of responsiveness into my handling of the camera, its direction, focus, and the rhythmic repetition of exposures—entering the energy field of the subject.

Like the rock on a riverbank that can report to the sensitive mind of a Native American details from centuries of activity that the rock has witnessed in that place, a photograph contains a vibrational imprint of the history passing through the lens from landscape to viewer on light and sound waves. While for most photographers, interaction with these waves is a subconscious process, great photographers like Henri Cartier-Bresson, for example, have composed, I believe, with a mindful self-eradicating transparency. They bring line, tonality and shape into the frame because they hear the songs of those elements in concert with not only a focal point, but within the whole of the living moment on which the shutter is opening as an extension of the photographer's own vibrational, egoless dance within the energy of the scene.

I constantly seek to entrain myself with the vibration of what I'm seeing, hoping to become personally invisible in service to the light and sounds channeling through the lens. This is something psychotherapists do all the time when "getting on the same wavelength" with clients, the process having been first identified by Virginia Satir and developed by Grinder and Bandler, authorities in the practice of hypnotic induction. When I am successfully "in synch" with the landscape, I'm able to bring to the viewer an image that is actually alive on the wall and radiating in present time subconscious information from that place.

While considered by some to be "woo woo," entrainment is fairly well understood scientifically. Karl Pribram, in the late 1970s, was among the earliest neurobiological researchers to grasp the visual entrainment phenomenon which he described using the metaphor of a hologram projected onto the surface of the brain by stimulus passing through the central nervous system. Entrainment is a prerequisite to empathy and, as an artist, I experience this phenomenon within a spiritual paradigm, especially when in the presence of terrain as profoundly communicative as the Arctic.

I've been told this portfolio is mesmerizing and that is evidence to me that, in fact, the vibrational entrainment state in which it was created is presently manifesting in the viewer, opening a channel through which the subject of the image is speaking beyond the constraints of gallery time and space. This is, quintessentially, the unique power of photography over every other medium. It's why one of the earliest consumer applications involved families commissioning photographs of their dead. The Native American disdain for photographs is similarly based on the belief that they contain the stolen spirit. Consider our own rush to the shoebox full of snapshots at the time of a loved one's death: it is to feel the life still held in those images.

As a child I spent hours "entering into" snapshots carefully preserved in my mother's photo album, and it's from that marrow-deep understanding of vibration out of which I now create. Specifically, "The Secret Life of Light" is a portfolio that uses these principles in concert with the tenants of ecopsychology to entrain the viewer to the healing vibrational state of the subject landscape. **(Continued on next two pages)**

The Visitation #2600
10.5x17 on 12x18

September 6, 2008 from atop Cleary Summit, 20 miles north of Fairbanks. I had arrived early and stood alone from about 10:00 p.m., hoping the aurora would rise. About 11:00 p.m., I heard a car with no headlights pull up about 30 feet from where I was standing with my tripod. I heard someone get out. I said hello but no answer came. So we both just stood there in silence and total darkness. At 12:01 a.m. I heard the stranger gasp along with me as I took this photo of what was before us. I felt paralyzed. The sky went dark. I heard a car door close, an engine start, headlights then shot into the woods, found the road and vanished.

We Cannot Pretend #6321
10.5 x 17 on 12 x 18
© 2014 Linda Griffith

Dalton Range #8405
10.5 x 17 on 12 x 18
© 2014 Linda Griffith

In the Playtime of Light #9343
10 x 17 on 12 x 18
© 2014 Linda Griffith

Griffith's work has drawn the attention of respected museums, including the Center for Maine Contemporary Art which featured two images from "The Secret Life of Light" in the museum's 2010 Biennial Exhibition. Similarly, The Noyes Museum, Philadelphia Sketch Club, and Woodmere Museum have all exhibited her work. Katherine Ware as the Curator of Photographs at the Philadelphia Museum of Art in 2003 chose Griffith as the recipient of the Shaun Miller Memorial Award for her simple but, again, disturbingly evocative image entitled "Homestead," in retrospect, a clear foreshadowing of the increasingly haunting "The Secret Life of Light" and "Spirit Walk."

It would appear that in the last decade and a half, Griffith's talent has fulfilled the millennial promise expressed by some of the most respected authorities on fine art photography: "complex," "disturbing," "transformative," and "unprecedented" are among descriptors frequently applied to her artistic vision of supraconscious imagery consistently expressed in prints that speak with startling intimacy.

Chasing Molly—Irene Bedard

By Colin W. Sargent
***Portland Monthly Magazine*, Summerguide 2010**

The actress who voiced *Pocahontas* is out to rescue Native Americana from Hollywood's cliches by putting the story of Maine's iconic, silent-film star, who danced for royalty and took Paris by fire, up on the silver screen.

The voice of Disney's *Pocahontas* is seductive and smooth as she speaks on the telephone–*exactly* the impression actress Irene Bedard doesn't want to convey, because even our politically-correct-obsessed 21st century dismisses Native Americans by over-romanticizing them.

Bedard, who bears an uncanny resemblance to Indian Island's princess Molly Spotted Elk (born Mary Alice Nelson), dreams of producing a movie about the raven-haired beauty.

The 1920s Penobscot actress, dancer, musician, poet, and nightclub siren performed in Broadway venues, danced for European royalty, and lived the life of a glamorous ex-pat in Paris until forced to flee during World War II. It's a story full of irony and wistfulness that Bedard first became aware of over a decade ago when she read the actress's biography, *Molly Spotted Elk: A Penobscot in Paris*, by Bunny McBride, a Pulitzer Prize-nominated writer who spends summers in Bar Harbor researching and working with the Abbe Museum. The book vividly recounts the story of Maine's Penobscot Nation and its famous daughter.

But can a film project about a gorgeous Native American starlet–"*the first*," Bedard points out, who unabashedly shimmered on screen–avoid stereotypes?

Bedard knows about these dangers too well. She's got Maine roots (her mother was an Inupiat Eskimo and her father a French Canadian/Cree from Skowhegan), and she, too, has struggled as an actress to find the courage to rise above exploitation, even from well-meaning production companies.

"It's so funny," says Bedard, 43, of the Disney role that made *her* a household voice to little girls across the globe. "Pocahontas was only eleven and a half when she met John Smith, and twelve when she threw herself over him to save him."

So why did a politically aware woman of twenty-seven agree to play the part?

"Growing up, I *loved* Disney on Sunday nights. You'd see the castle and Tinkerbell going across the screen. I knew being part of something like that could be something your grandchildren will see."

Disney or not, it was still an emotional decision. She grew up hearing the word "Pocahontas" used pejoratively. "To me, the one thing that stuck in my mind was having been called 'Pocahontas' in a derogatory way." (As in, 'Nice parallel parking, Pocahontas.')

Besides, this serious actress had already experienced the indignation of having her character role neatly wrapped in a pretty little package in the Disney live-action film *Squanto: A Warrior's Tale*.

"My first line in the movie is, 'Was there good hunting, Squanto?' A stereotypical line. *He'd just come back from the ocean* and had been gone for weeks on a hunt. Men don't survive from this! There was this huge relief and celebration, and the very first thing she says is, 'Squanto, was there good hunting?' I fought the battle, and I lost the battle to a certain point. What I did was, knowing it was a Disney movie, I ran up to him and said the *same words* in a *different* way."

Bedard's intentional change of tone–from innocent and earnest to suggestive and coquettish–made her point, and then it went straight to the cutting-room floor. Her dialogue was edited to a single word: "Squanto!"

"But I accomplished my goal in sort of a sideways way. I learned I not only had to stand up for the personal directives of my character but also the cultural perspectives of my character. The best way was not to say, 'No, this doesn't work.' It was, 'Let me show you, let me teach you, here's an alternative.'"

On the set of *Lakota Woman*, knowing Bedard was wrestling with the guilt and wonder of taking on the *Pocahontas* gig, "the famous Native American actress Tantoo Cardinal saw me thinking about it and said, 'Irene, I know you. You're strong and a native woman. I know you will fight every battle that needs to be fought. You are the right person for this job. *Take it*.'

"It was another 'manifest destiny' part. I'd just done *Squanto*, one of the manifest destiny characters, and now it's *Pocahontas*–a manifest destiny character written into a history by the victors … [portraying Indians as those] who helped and pushed along the prevailing society. I went down and met with [Disney]."

Which brings us, after many ambitious roles and hunts for edgy, modern parts for Native American actresses, to Bedard's dream of chasing Molly Spotted Elk and her legend to make a movie that will make a difference, that will not require "compromised truth."

"I have started Bundle of Arrows production company. Our first projects are a couple of contemporary projects with full native cast and crew, but Molly Spotted Elk is something I've had in mind for so long. I'd like to work with a French production entity or director so we can shoot in Paris. Her story is epic in scale, so I need a director who can do it."

Because Molly Spotted Elk was a gifted poet and what the Penobscots call "one of the hard ones" (that is, endowed with spiritual powers), Bedard envisions mystical interior monologue to accompany Molly's deep story arc.

"She's coming from this small place and going to New York City and trying to fit into the prevalent society and realizing she's not going to be able to take what's truly at her heart–her cultural beauty–with her, because there was no place for it to shine."

Molly's search for cultural acceptance eventually draws her to Paris, where–like Josephine Baker–she found appreciation for her caramel skin and unusual cultural heritage. "[It was] go to Paris, go to what's close to your heart, you know, *make this trek across the ocean* to be this really exotic human being who doesn't speak their language, yet [in daring to do this] she finds a way to become herself with her particular artistic beauty and really grow and become a beautiful, shining thing."

Molly was happy in France, where she met and eventually married French political journalist Jean Archambaud. They had a daughter, Jean. When World War II hit France, Molly and her daughter had to flee across the Pyrenees without her husband (a known anti-Nazi activist), who was directing the Red Cross Relief efforts near Bordeaux. Molly never saw or heard from him again.

It was a turning point in Molly's life. "She went through a real dark period and was institutionalized for a time. Then she went to New York, but her soul was damaged … I think going back to Indian Island in Maine and discovering her poetry and dance and basket weaving and the creativity–I think that idea, of walking in beauty, was her triumph in life. She learned how to find beauty on her own terms."

Asked which scenes she's itching to shoot first, Bedard says immediately, "I think of her being in the chorus line in vaudeville, where there's this line of women and they move at the same time, wear the same clothes, and yet there's something *so different*, so out-of-this-world, about her.

"When she fought to say, 'Hey, I want to perform traditional dances,' they put her in a short outfit with a feather on her head. It was such a stereotype in the shape of sexual dismissal and spiritually where she wasn't coming from."

As for how Bedard will avoid caricature within the Molly project, she's going to visit Maine extensively to better understand Molly's haunts here.

"Oh, yes. Definitely. My father actually was from Skowhegan, so I have family in Maine that I visit; in fact, I'll be there this summer."

Because she understands the importance of getting things right, Bedard is willing to take her time with this project.

"I'm just one woman, doing the work I can do. I don't speak for all Native Americans because no one can. I try my best to be honest and truthful … My whole concept is to bring us into contemporary society. We've done the historical stories; now it's time to be romantic, comedic, and contemporary, and a lot of Molly's life [resonates with this]."

What might Molly tell Bedard, her fellow actor, from across the years once filming begins? "She'd tell me that loving her daughter, and the love she had for her husband, was the most important work of her life. The love of her people. For her, it's all about finding your true heart through love and beauty."

Used with permission by author/editor.

Creativity as a treatment model

Ousted from her order, 'Sister Lucy' found her own way to support needy Mainers

Lucy Poulin founded the H.O.M.E. Cooperative in Orland in 1970.
Gabor Degre, Photographer, Bangor Daily News

By Meg Haskell, Bangor Daily News

ORLAND, Maine—The H.O.M.E. craft cooperative and shelter community has occupied its prominent hilltop campus just north of Bucksport on Route One since it was founded in 1970. It's easy to drive right past without stopping, despite the battered letter board sign at the corner of Schoolhouse Road inviting a visit to the craft shop, open from 8 a.m. to 4 p.m., seven days per week, all year round.

But the H.O.M.E. campus—the apt acronym stands for the more proletariat Homeworkers Organized for More Employment—is way more than a crafts outlet. It's more like a medieval village.

The twenty-three-acre site includes crafting workshops for leather, pottery, weaving, stained glass, quilting and woodworking, to be sure. There also is short-term shelter housing for about fifteen indigent men, women and families and low-cost permanent housing for a few older adults who have nowhere else to live because of mild developmental disabilities or other conditions. There's a busy sawmill and shingle mill, an auto repair shop, a bustling soup kitchen, a food pantry, a licensed day care center and an administrative office.

Together, the campus employs a total of about 40 workers, some from outside the H.O.M.E. village and some from within, including shelter clients. There's a small chapel, too, where nondenominational services are held each Sunday and where Alcoholics Anonymous holds a regular Monday meeting.

"Basically, there are three reasons people come to us," said Lucy Poulin, the former Carmelite nun who founded the grass-roots organization 46 years ago and, at seventy-five, still serves as its director. "They need a place to live, they want to make the world a better place, or they want to take the Gospels seriously."

For Poulin—still fondly called "Sister Lucy" by those who have known her longest—taking the Gospels seriously includes honoring the literal intention of the Second Commandment.

"If you truly love your neighbor as yourself," she said, "you don't put them in a shelter at night and throw them out on the street in the morning. Everything you have, you want for them as well."

For her, that means providing not only a bed and meal but a community with relationships, responsibilities, meaningful work, security and a future.

"Social isolation crushes people," Poulin said. "Community makes them whole."

A hands-on ministry

Poulin grew up poor on a farm in Fairfield Center, one of eleven children raised by her widowed mother. Taking on many of the chores and projects of farm life from a young age, she developed a strong work ethic and a deep sense of each person's contributions to the family's well-being.

At twenty-six, she joined a small community of Carmelite sisters based in New Hampshire. A few years later, eager to return to her home state, she was reassigned to a Carmelite community in Bucksport and found herself working closely with local families struggling to make ends meet.

In 1970, Poulin established the H.O.M.E. crafts cooperative as a way for local women to market quilts, knitwear and other handcrafted items, purchasing the twenty-three-acre hilltop site for its visibility and the presence of the simple building that would become the crafts store. Almost immediately, she recognized a larger mission to serve the poor of the area with housing, food, medical care and a material sense of community. It would take years for H.O.M.E. to shed its early, miscast reputation as a commune or a cult, she said, but the work there has always been directly grounded in the Works of Mercy laid out unambiguously in the Bible: Feed the hungry, clothe the naked, shelter the homeless.

Poulin's hands-on approach to working with the poor set her at odds with the more prayerful Carmelites, she said, and led to her expulsion from the order shortly after H.O.M.E. was founded.

"The priest told me I had 'an incorrect spirit of poverty,'" she recalled. "I wasn't contemplative enough; I was out here helping people instead. It was very difficult at the time, but I got over it."

In retrospect, she sees that the experience refined her faith and helped align the gritty work of her hands with the loftier meditations of her heart. "It deepened me. Now, I am more prayerful, more devoted to Scripture. I try to practice the presence of God in every minute."

Supporting Maine's neediest

Over the ensuing decades, guided by the motto "to serve first those who suffer most," Poulin has cobbled together a sprawling, loose-jointed, shoestring organization that has served thousands of Maine's neediest residents.

Beyond its high-visibility hilltop site in Orland, H.O.M.E. is active in a number of other Maine communities, including nearby Bucksport and Ellsworth, where it provides short-term shelter and transitional housing for about 30 adults and families. It has built clusters of affordable homes in communities such as Sedgwick and Dedham, using a model that allows low-income families to purchase their homes while the organization retains ownership of the land, which is managed for timber production for the sawmill and shingle mill in Orland.

Secluded Mandala Farm on Toddy Pond in Orland, where Poulin lives with her adopted son, Jimmy, who is affected by fetal alcohol syndrome, is home to five other permanent residents and a menagerie of livestock and pets, as well as providing thirteen family-friendly shelter beds with an average occupancy of three to six months.

The farm was envisioned as a peaceful haven for Poulin and other core workers, a place to regroup from the stresses of the H.O.M.E. campus.

"We wanted a place to be quiet, to retreat to after our workdays in Orland," Poulin said. "But then, of course, we began to take our work home anyway."

Mandala Farm is technically owned by St. Francis Community, a separate nonprofit Poulin established in 1975 when H.O.M.E. was growing rapidly. The organization also is affiliated with Emmaus International, a nonreligious movement that combats poverty and exclusion.

Now, although the two organizations have different missions, they are deeply integrated. For example, the Emmaus shelter in Ellsworth is owned by St. Francis Community but administered by H.O.M.E. Funding to renovate the former post office was provided in part by Emmaus International.

Supporting H.O.M.E.

Though the H.O.M.E. enterprise is far-flung and unwieldy, supporters agree it serves an essential function in the communities it serves. Hancock County Sheriff Scott Kane said his office refers people to the shelter services and soup kitchen regularly and occasionally even delivers clients who have no transportation.

And although the mix of transient shelter clients sometimes causes predictable problems, often related to substance abuse, "I don't expect we respond to their sites more than to anywhere else," he said. "They've been very helpful in meeting the needs around here. I tip my hat to them for what they do."

Kane did note that in 1999, H.O.M.E. was the site of a dramatic shoot-out when officers responded to tips that a suspect featured on the television show "America's Most Wanted" was staying at the Orland shelter. The tips turned out to be accurate, and convicted sex offender Richard Burdick of Massachusetts was captured there.

At the Orland town office, Ed Rankin, chairman of the Board of Selectmen, said, "They do a lot and help a lot of people."

Although H.O.M.E.'s tax-exempt status affects town revenues, that impact is more than offset by the benefits of not having to provide municipal solutions to homelessness and hunger.

"We have no problem with them," he said.

Although it draws state and federal funding for some services, H.O.M.E. relies heavily on donations from private foundations, churches and individuals, including some former clients. In addition, church groups and college students from across the Northeast regularly spend weeklong work sessions tending to backlogged maintenance and other projects.

"It may not be very dramatic or very elegant, but it has been a huge support to that whole area," the Rev. Susie Craig, a retired Congregationalist minister who now lives in Wiscasset, said.

In 1987, Craig was a seminary student in Greenwich, Connecticut, when she first watched a video about H.O.M.E. and its mission in rural Maine. Over the past thirty years, she said, support for the organization has spread through areas of Connecticut, resulting in reliable donations of money, volunteer labor and more. Youth groups visit each spring to give of their time and energy, an experience Craig called "life-changing" for young people confronting the face of rural poverty.

(Continued on next page)

Immigration as Creativity

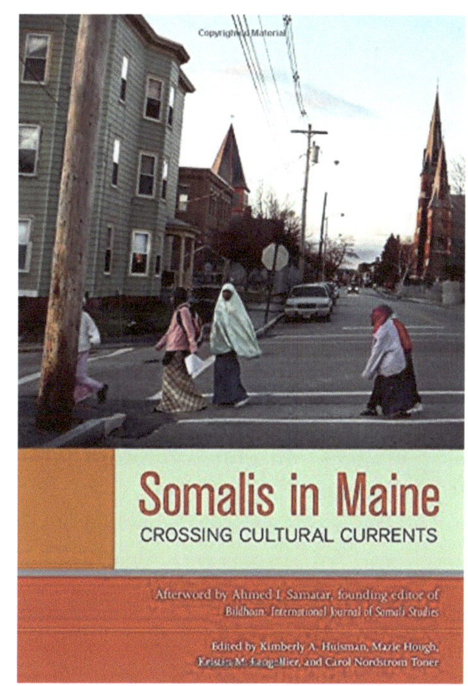

Somalis in Maine: Crossing Cultural Currents

Editors: Mazie Hough, Kimberly A. Huisman, Kristin M. Langellier, Carol Nordstrom Toner
Afterword by: Ahmed I. Samatar

Lewiston, a mill town of about thirty-six thousand people, is the second-largest city in Maine. It is also home to some three thousand Somali refugees. After initially being resettled in larger cities elsewhere, Somalis began to arrive in Lewiston by the dozens, then the hundreds, after hearing stories of Maine's attractions through family networks. Today, cross-cultural interactions are reshaping the identities of Somalis—and adding new chapters to the immigrant history of Maine.

Somalis in Maine offers a kaleidoscope of voices that situate the story of Somalis' migration to Lewiston within a larger cultural narrative. Combining academic analysis with refugees' personal stories, this anthology includes reflections on leaving Somalia, the experiences of Somali youth in U.S. schools, the reasons for Somali secondary migration to Lewiston, the employment of many Lewiston Somalis at Maine icon L. L. Bean, and community dialogues with white Mainers. Somalis in Maine seeks to counter stereotypes of refugees as being socially dependent and unable to assimilate, to convey the richness and diversity of Somali culture, and to contribute to a greater understanding of the intertwined futures of Somalis and Americans.

"*Somalis in Maine: Crossing Cultural Currents* enhances our understanding of recent immigration in the United States by exploring the experiences of East African Muslim refugees in Maine. Through a combination of scholarly essays and first-hand accounts by Somali community members, this work sheds light on pre-migration experiences in Somalia, regional migrations in Africa, migration to and re-migration in the United States, and settlement and community formation in Lewiston, Maine. Somalis in Maine illustrates well the challenges that Somali immigrants have faced in all of these aspects of the migration experience. This work also considers the tensions Somalis have faced within their own community as they have sought to adapt to life in U.S. society. Like the French-Canadian immigrants who preceded them to Lewiston, Somalis appear to be actively negotiating the terms of their entry into U.S. society, thus challenging contemporary notions of the process of assimilation."
—Mark Paul Richard, State University of New York at Plattsburgh; author of *Loyal but French: The Negotiation of Identity by French-Canadian Descendants in the United States*

French Somaliland (French: Côte française des Somalis, literally "French Coast of Somalis" Somali: Dhulka Faransiiska ee Soomaaliya) was a French colony in the Horn of Africa. It existed between 1883 and 1967.

(Continued from previous page)

Poulin, who has created a small management team to learn the ropes of running H.O.M.E. as she approaches retirement, acknowledges poverty, hunger and homelessness continue to plague Hancock County, despite a lifetime's dedication to combating them. She doesn't know what the future holds for the complex organization she has created, only that the need for compassionate, non-judgmental, non-bureaucratic intervention never ends.

"I don't think about things too much," she said. "This is day-by-day work for me. I get up early every morning. I read the New Testament. I say the Rosary, which helps me focus on truth, reality, simplicity and what really matters. I feed the birds. I find it very helpful."

This story was published on April 02, 2016 in all editions of the *Bangor Daily News*. Used with permission.

Book tells of Somali experience in Maine

By Abigail Curtis, *Bangor Daily News*

BELFAST, Maine—When thousands of Somali refugees began settling in Lewiston in 2002, the city was not prepared — with the mayor at one point writing a now-infamous open letter to the newcomers asking them to stop coming.

The resulting culture clashes between Lewiston and the Somali community at times made national headlines.

Kim Huisman, a University of Maine Sociology professor who now lives in Belfast, at that time was working with Bosnian Muslim refugees in Burlington, Vermont. When she was hired to teach at the University of Maine, she knew she wanted to work with the Somali community in a collaborative way.

The resulting project by Huisman, other faculty and staff members and Somali students has resulted in the book, *Somalis in Maine: Crossing Cultural Currents*, which is published by North Atlantic Books and distributed by Random House.

The book contains personal stories, ethnography and essays about the interactions between Somali refugees and Americans in Lewiston.

The editors, including Huisman, hope the book will provide a good alternative to those other headlines, which have over the years focused more on negative images and events.

"When the economy's not doing well, refugees and immigrants tend to be scapegoats," Huisman said recently. "The book tends to be a counter-narrative to that."

Some of the chapters are by Somali refugees who became University of Maine students, including Nasra Mohamed, who wrote about her 2009 return to the refugee camps in Dadaab, Kenya, where she had spent ten years of her childhood.

"These people chose Dadaab not because it is their dream place to live but because it is better than what is happening in Mogadishu," she wrote. "They left their homes and joined their fellow Somalis to live in huts made of sticks and mud covered with plastic. What many once thought was a temporary relocation has become their permanent home ... The camp is like a prison, one that I remember clearly. Somali refugees all have one dream, one way out: to resettle in a peaceful country."

Some of that resettlement began in the United States after the United Nations High Commission for Refugees in 1999 encouraged the country to take in about 12,000 minority Bantu Somalis.

One of the nation's thirty-four resettlement cities is Portland, where about 4,000 Somalis have settled.

Lewiston is not one of those resettlement communities, and when Somalis began telling their relatives about the affordable housing and good schools in that safe city, municipal leaders were not prepared.

"Lewiston did not see this coming," Huisman said.

When then-Mayor Laurier T. Raymond wrote the 2002 letter to the Somalis, it was a turning point, the sociologist said.

There were rallies of support for the refugees and rallies against them, including a small demonstration by a white supremacist group in January 2003 and a much-larger counter-demonstration.

And there also was the Somali Narrative Project, which began at the University in 2004 with three Somali students who were eager to read about the history of their home country.

The group started reading about the history of colonialism in Somalia, a war-torn country in the Horn of Africa.

The experience of learning more was powerful.

"It was really enriching, and just great," Huisman said.

As the project grew, the group began a reader's theater presentation around the state to provide people with a glimpse of the background and history of the refugees.

Somalis in Maine includes pieces by Huisman, Mazie Hough, the Associate Director of the Women's and Gender Studies Program, Kristin Langellier retired professor of Communication and Journalism, and Carol Nordstrom Toner, Director of the Maine Studies Program all at the University of Maine.

This story was published on July 07, 2011 in all editions of the *Bangor Daily News*. Used with permission.

My Mother's Walls

By Lanette Landry Petrie, 1942-2015

An excerpt

In the past, the Franco-American Center of the University of Maine sponsored an art exhibit in Portland, Maine called "Migrant Within." I had the opportunity to be present when the planning was taking place. I wondered what Franco-American art would look like. Would I recognize it as being Franco-American? What would set it apart from other art? I have had very little exposure to art such as in a studio exhibition. Art was considered an elitist thing. People with money had works of art and visited galleries, not working-class folks. Even libraries were foreign places to me. In my family, if you were caught reading when you didn't have to, you were seen as anti-social or angry with someone. Our social and behavioral skills were highly developed as children, but scholastically we were expected to do the best we could but not expected to excel. There was no aspiration to further our education after high school. This "Migrant Within" experience set me off on a mental search for the art in my life. I thought first about "what is art?" I decided that art, in my life, is that which one appreciates enough to hang on their walls or display for everyone's enjoyment, so I looked around the walls of my mother's house to see what we appreciated enough to hang or display. The following is a picture story of Franco-American art on my mother's walls. (This excerpt does not include the pictures.)

This house was purchased in 1942 by Eugene and Joan (Pelletier) Landry. It is on Bullen Street in Bradley, Maine and is situated next door to Joan's mother and father. On the south side of the Pelletier home was the home of Lena (Guay) Pelletier's sister, Albertine Smith, and across the street from Mémère's house is the Guay family farm homestead. In this environment, the Landry family raised their ten children. I was second-born and two weeks old when we moved to this house. This house has had several changes over the years to its present condition. As the family grew, bedrooms were added and the traditional porch added to the front of the house. It was originally covered with brown brick like gravel siding, then Masonite, and finally in 1994 with vinyl. It has a rock cellar where mama kept all the canning jars and the furnace in later years. As a child, I remember the house being heated with a big, black cookstove that had been converted from wood to oil in the kitchen and an end-heater in the living room in the winter. I still can see my brothers sitting on the lip of the kitchen stove getting dressed and the girls hiding behind the front room stove. I also can hear the baby birds chirping and hitting against the metal cover on the chimney that was used in the summer to plug the hole. My father was very proud of the acre of land that he owned. He would tell us that we had an acre of land to play on, so we had no need to leave the yard. Consequently, the yard was always full of kids. We lived on a dead-end street so even the street was user friendly. We played hop scotch, jump rope, and marbles, sailed boats from one end of the culvert to the other, and rode bikes. Life was very simple then. ...

... As I had been living with this project for weeks it took on a life of its own. Those of my siblings who know about it have been very supportive and anxious to see the final product. As I sat in various groupings and asked about how they felt in mama's house, with these walls, the following comments were made:

It's a chronicle of our family, particularly for my brother who lives away.

Sex is a problem in your mother's bedroom, says one brother-in-law, because of all the holy pictures; but it never was for your father-in-law mama said.

Every spring cleaning and having to wash all those pictures.

It makes us proud.

I get a kick out of the goofy glasses and hairdos.

I can't take a good picture and hate seeing me on the wall.

Neat to see the graduations.

I sometimes wonder if the pictures are the only thing holding up the house.

I liked moving from one wall to the next.

Lanette describes the artifacts on the walls of her mother's house. Family photos, spoon collections, religious items and more. Many who read her book, agree with her about the description of what constitutes art for many Franco-Americans in their homes.

Contributors to the anthology—Listed by first name, alphabetically.

Abby Paige is a Franco-American writer and performer who was born and raised in northern Vermont. A descendant of early settlers to both New France and New England, she is grateful that the generosity of America's native peoples has made it possible for her family to inhabit the territory north of Boston and south of Québec City since the early seventeenth century. Abby began performing stand-up and sketch comedy as an undergraduate and went on to become a featured writer and performer with the award-winning San Francisco comedy collective, Killing My Lobster. In Vermont she has written and performed for television, film, radio, and the stage, including her own solo show, *Piecework: When We Were French*, which explores the legacy of Québécois immigration to northern New England. The show was commissioned for the 2009 Champlain Quadricentennial in Burlington and subsequently toured throughout New England; it is now available on DVD. Her poetry and essays have appeared in Canada and the U.S. in publications including *The Los Angeles Review of Books*, *The* Montreal Review of Books, Bitch Magazine, *Room Magazine*, Hunger Mountain Review, and Arc Poetry Magazine. Abby received her BA from Vassar College and her MFA from the Bennington Writing Seminars, and she is a former Fulbright scholar. She immigrated to Canada in 2008 and currently lives in New Brunswick.

Abigail E. Disney is an executive producer of *Women, War & Peace*, producer of the film *Pray the Devil Back to Hell* and writer on *Peace Unveiled*, the third film in the series about Afghanistan. Her longtime passion for women's issues and peace building led her to producing films. She has executive produced films that address various social issues, including *Family Affair, Playground, Sun Come Up* (Academy Award® Nominee 2011, Best Documentary Short) and *Return*, and is involved in several more films in various stages of development and production. [The family name, originally d'Isigny ("from Isigny"), is of Norman French derivation, coming from the town of Isigny-sur-Mer. The Disneys, among others, descended from Normans who settled in England around the 11th century.—Wikipedia]

Adèle Saint-Pierre is a native of Jay, Maine. She lives and works in New York City.

Alberte T. Gastonguay, (1906-1978) was born to Albert T. Gastonguay and Rebecca Gastonguay. She married Joseph S. Sasserville in 1934 who died two years after they married. They had one son, Albert, who worked for the CIA. Alberte became interested in writing upon reading the writings of "Liane" aka Camille Lessard who wrote a regular column for *Le Messager* in Lewiston, Maine. In 1933, she wrote her one and only book, *La jeune Franco-Américaine*.

Angela Hebert born in Biddeford, Maine, was fortunate enough to grow up in and around a farmhouse bought by her great-great pépère, Belonie Tanguay, a lumberjack, who eventually had his own lumbering camp. He then retired from that job, and sold raspberries door-to-door, keeping the extended family generally fed. She grew up in a bilingual town and home, but doesn't quite have the language. Many of her students, though, whom she teaches at a city community college in New Jersey, are bilingual. She lives in Long Beach, NY with her husband Don and their two cats, Hank and Gina.

Ann Marie Staples, née Cardin, was born in Rochester, New Hampshire where she still lives with her husband and pets. She continues to worship in same parish in which she was baptized and regrets the slow disappearance of her French-Canadian culture in the region. She is the Academic Coordinator for the World Language Department in nearby Dover High School and experiences flashbacks while teaching French to English speakers with French names. Her thoughts manifest in standard French, *Joual*, and English. She produces brief personal essays to ground the spurts of old memories and document the richness of growing up Franglo-American in the 1950s and '60s.

Amy Bouchard Morin retired in 2001 from the Canadian-American Center at the University of Maine. She was the first non-faculty member of the University to take part in an exchange with the University of Angers in France. Amy was also an editor of the *Nos Histoires de l'Île* anthology written from research and interviews with people who grew up on French Island in Old Town, Maine. She now presents the story of French Island to students in Old Town schools and classes at the University of Maine with Lisa Michaud from the Franco-American Center.

Ann G. Forcier is a writer/therapist who lives in western Massachusetts. Her current work-in-progress is a fiction-memoir about some of the women in her ancestral tree. The women hail from Paris, Brittany and other ancien regime provinces in France, and from Acadia, Québec, and New England. Her blog is at Wordpress.

Anne Marie Prudhomme lives in New York and is of Franco-American descent. She was raised in New England in North Reading, Massachusetts. Anne Marie is interested in the American working class experience, particularly as it relates to ethnicity and the literary canon. Anne Marie has experience teaching English at the high school level. She received an A.A. from Borough of Manhattan Community College, CUNY, and received both a B.A. and an M.A. in English, from Brooklyn

College, CUNY. Her M.A. thesis is entitled: "On the Road and Out of Peyton Place: The Franco American Working Class New England Voice of Jean-Louis Kerouac and Marie-Grace De Repentigny Metalious." Her research was selected for presentation at the *Wolfe Institute Pizer Graduate Research Colloquium*. An outline of this talk was published on-line in *moé pi toé: Promoting Franco-American Women's Voices*.

Anne Parent Roy was born in Hamlin Plantation, Maine. Her father was a farmer and her mom a housewife and mother to three children. Roy grew up in Hamlin went to the St. Joseph Parish school and graduated from the eighth grade. Roy then attended Sacred Heart High School in Van Buren followed by college at the State Teacher's College in Fort Kent. Roy became a teacher in 1964 and taught at Loring Air Force Base near Limestone, Maine for twenty-four years and eight years in Limestone, Maine until she retired in 2002. Roy became the President of L'Heritage Vivant —Living Heritage Historical Society in 1982. The Society owns and operates The Acadian Village—Village Acadien in Van Buren. Roy oversees the maintenance and the operation of the Acadian Village. Roy is also a member of the Maine Acadian Heritage Council, Le Club Français de la Valle St. Jean, The Daughters of Isabella, The American Legion Ladies Auxiliary and also served for five years on the World Acadian Congress 2014/ Le Congress Mondial Acadien 2014. Roy has one daughter, three step-children and eight grandchildren.

Annette Picher Houston was born and grew up in Waterville, Maine; attended Colby College majoring in Art; became an art teacher after being married, living in Germany for three years with her husband Ken, who was in the Air Force, and two of their three children were born in Germany. She taught art in the Waterville and Fairfield, Maine schools for twenty-five years before moving to Newport, Maine as a Gifted and Talented Program Consultant in 1989. She moved to West Lebanon, New Hampshire, in 2010, where she continues to teach art to senior citizens, paints and creates art quilts, and enjoys being a member of the International Women's Club and the Northern Light Quilting Guild.

Annette Sampon-Nicolas Jean-Pierre Sampont came to the United States in 1847 from the village of Sampont, in the Belgian province of Luxembourg. Accompanied by his wife and eight children, they settled in Wisconsin. As time passed and several of his children moved out West, some families dropped the "T" from their name.

During the Second World War, my father, Victor J. Sampon, (10/22/1923-9/21/2011), descendant of Jean-Pierre Sampon, met my mother, Anne-Marie Jardon (8/8/1926-11/14/2006), in Belgium.

They married, and I, Annette Elisabeth Louise Marie Henriette Bernadette Sampon, was born in Belgium (12/19/1949). Several years later, with my brothers, we moved to Wisconsin. My first language is French, culturally I am French, and also a proud naturalized American citizen.

In August 1986, I married Alain Nicolas, a Frenchman from Bethoncourt, France, also a naturalized American citizen. Our children, Claire and Julien, first generation Americans, born in Virginia, are bilingual and proud of their Belgian-French-American heritage.

My parents were French teachers at Wayland Academy in Wisconsin. I have been teaching French and Francophone literature and culture at Hollins University in Roanoke, Virginia since 1985.

I am proud to be a French heritage woman.

Annie Proulx is the author of eight books, including the novel *The Shipping News* and the story collection *Close Range*. Her many honors include a Pulitzer Prize, a National Book Award, the Irish Times International Fiction Prize, and a PEN/Faulkner award. Her story "Brokeback Mountain," which originally appeared in *The New Yorker*, was made into an Academy Award-winning film. Her most recent novel is *Barkskins*. She lives in Seattle.

Barbara Ouellette Ouellette was born in Old Town, Maine to Maurice Jules Ouellette, and Meledore Marie Brillant Ouellette. I grew up on Treat and Webster Island, better known as French Island. I was the middle child of five children; two sisters, and two brothers. As almost everyone who lived on French Island, I was raised Catholic, and attended parochial school from kindergarten to grade eight. I married at the young age of twenty to Jean Paul Ouellette. Fortunately, he was brought up in a Franco family, and has the same ideals, and morals that I was brought up with. I have one son who lives and works in Portland, Maine.

I am the first in my family to graduate from college with a four-year degree. For my family, graduating from high school was the best education, and you did not need to go further. Both my parents finished eighth grade and did not go to high school. I was fortunate to be employed at the University of Maine for forty-two years, and to be able to work on obtaining my college education. This education was both formal and informal. Working in an academic setting afforded many benefits beyond earning a salary, having medical and vacation leave. I started my career at the University as a Secretary, and am retiring from the same University with the title of Assistant Dean in the Honors College. I was supported both by my family and colleagues, which allowed me to pursue my education, and offered many opportunities to advance myself in my career. I attribute my success in my education and career to the values and hard work ethic that both my parents exhibited at home.

Betheny Chambers Anderson was born and grew up in Caribou, Maine, graduated from Caribou High School and the University of Maine at Orono. In addition to potato farming, she taught visual arts in grades K-6, was a vocational school instructor and Adult Arts educator. Her Aroostook County Calendar is in its 36th edition. She is the author and illustrator of the children's book, *Fiddleheads and Freda, A Story About Maine*. She is the mother of two sons and three grandchildren. In retirement, she enjoys serving on the local school board, fishing with her husband and creating coloring books for all ages.

Betty-Ann Khoury-Burns is the author of the story that is set in 1920s small town Maine, titled "Fall" is based on true events that depict twelve-year-old Eva's passage from girlhood innocence into womanhood, an emergence complicated by fear of her body's changes and guilt for her desire, products of her culture and religious upbringing.

I am a semi-retired psychotherapist living in Maine, who continues to be intrigued by how the two domains of literature and psychology inform one another. In 1993, I explored one aspect of this relationship in my doctoral dissertation, "Summoning the Cohorts: Multiple Personality Response in the Life and Work of Virginia Woolf."

I'm currently working on my memoirs, from which "Fall" is excerpted. Autobiographical fiction, this novel explores Anna's journey (Eva's daughter) through the deaths of her mother, father, brother, and finally her husband, the last causing her to lose her emotional center.

Brenda Mounier Cette Louisianaise, née dans le petit village de Ville Platte et élevée dans une famille de cinq filles, dont les parents ne parlaient pas anglais, Brenda Mounier est fière de sa langue et sa culture Cadjine. Sa carrière faite dans l'enseignement, Brenda a travaillé avec des "élèves" de 9 à 89 ans à travers une période de 34 ans.

Après avoir réalisé deux vidéos pédagogiques (une, en anglais, une, en français) sur l'histoire des Acadiens, fait pour enfants, et par enfants, son rôle dans la cause Cadjine en Louisiane comprend aussi actrice dans le Théâtre Cadien, animatrice pour le Festival International de Louisiane, et récipiendaire à plusieurs reprises du Prix de Poésie offert par le CODOFIL et publié dans Feu Follet à l'Université de Louisiane à Lafayette. Elle n'est inspirée à écrire qu'en français, la langue de sa petite enfance et de son expression la plus intime.

Actuellement retraitée depuis 2006, Brenda Mounier continue à partager sa passion pour sa langue et la culture. Dans un effort pour sauvegarder et, d'un sens, reclamer la langue qui leur ont été volé dans le mi-vingtième siècle, elle s'occupe à enseigner des classes d'alphabétisation pour adultes parlant le français Cadjin, en utilisant exclusivement de la littérature écrite par autres Cadjins.

Brenda lâcher la patate? Jamais !

Bridget Robbins was raised in northern and central Maine. She is an avid reader, amateur insect enthusiast, hiker and cross-country skier and loves to doodle in her spare time. Bridget is the artist who created the cover art.

Camille Lessard Bissonnette, (1883-1970) is the author of *Canuck*, emigrated from Quebec to Lewiston with her family in 1904 at the age of twenty. Although she left that city a few years later and subsequently resided in various parts of Canada and the United States—she died at Long Beach, California—she never forgot her experiences working in a textile mill in Lewiston for four years before finding employment as a feature writer for *Le Messager*, the local French-language newspaper. Her novel, which appeared in 1936, is set in Lowell, Massachusetts, in 1900, but she drew heavily upon her experiences in Lewiston. A well-structured story that grips the modern reader with insight into the women's immigrant experience. *Canuck* is probably the most important novel in French, now translated.

Caroline LeBlanc, former Army Nurse and civilian nurse psychotherapist, has had her poetry and essays published in the US and abroad. In 2010, Oiseau Press published Smokey Ink and a Touch of Honeysuckle, her chapbook about life as an Army wife, and the descendant of 17th century Acadian/French Canadian settlers in North America. She regularly contributes interviews and book reviews to Poetry Matters, a blog staffed by Spalding University alumni. As Writer in Residence at the American Military Family Museum, she wrote the script for the museum's traveling museum exhibit; co-produced and created the script for Telling Albuquerque and 4 Voices stage performances; facilitated Standing Down, a NM Humanities Council book discussion group for veterans and family members; and hosted the Women Veterans Writing Salon in Albuquerque. Before leaving the Fort Drum, NY area in 2012, she offered Writing For Your Life programs to wounded warriors and military family members. In 2011, Spalding University awarded her a Master's of Fine Arts in Creative Writing. Included in this volume, "The Great Escape," by Caroline LeBlanc won Second Place, NMPS Convention Contest, 2014. Also, "Hanging Prayer Flags the Morning of the First Snow" by Caroline LeBlanc won First Prize, North Country Writer's Conference, 2011. Her visual art has been in numerous group shows in New York and New Mexico. She is a founding member of the Albuquerque-based Apronistas Collective of women artists who regularly mount community art shows highlighting women's rights and ecological issues. Since 1969, she has been an Army wife, and she has been an Army mother since 1995.

Carolyna Saint Germain, M.A., is the author of *Stewards for the Earth* (Balboa Press). Although she holds a Master's Degree in French Literature, she attests that the natural world has been, and is her primary teacher and mentor. She officiates and teaches ceremonies that she calls *Blessingways*. For the last forty-five years, she has participated in ceremonies and performed *Blessingways* with Native American elders, and spiritual leaders from all over the world experiencing mindful awareness and conscious connection with nature, our Mother Earth. She is a spiritual ecologist teaching the art of *Blessingways*. She currently lives with her husband, children and grandchildren in the Pacific Northwest.

Cathy Plourde is a writer and publisher, founder and director of Add Verb Productions for fifteen years. The scripts and program materials for *You the Man* and *The Thin Line* have been published with their Australian translations, and *Out & Allied vols. 1 & 2* continue to help communities be better allies for LGBTQI youth. She's co-edited with Catriona McHardy an anthology about survivors of sexual violence who have found a full life, called *Making Out Like a Virgin: sex, desire & intimacy after sexual trauma*. She enjoys adventuring around the world with her wife.

Cecile Poulin is a native Mainer who grew up in the mill city of Lewiston. Her enchantment with words began with her papa's stories of loups garoux and le bonhomme sept heure. Her MFA comes from the University of Southern Maine's Stonecoast Creative Writing program. But her writing evolves from her strong Franco heritage and pride. *Je me souviens …*

Celeste Roberge was born in Biddeford, Maine where her parents immigrated from Québec following World War II. She attended parochial schools for ten years, and she studied at l'Université de Sherbrooke, Québec as an exchange student in the early 1970s. She was involved with the Franco-American Center at the University of Maine during the early 1970s. She has been a Professor of Sculpture at the University of Florida for twenty years. She maintains a studio in South Portland, Maine. More of her work can be seen at her website.

Chris Cunningham is fourth-generation French Canadian, and proud of her ancestral roots that began in Québec in 1670. She lives on the West Coast and has been writing nonfiction freelance for more than fifteen years, primarily for newspapers and magazines. Her family thanks Joe Manning for his research on Lewis Hine which has introduced many families to Lewis Hines' photos and their own ancestors' labor histories.

Claire Bouffard Chase was the mother of **Kim Chase**. Her "nom de fille" was Marie Eva Claire Bouffard.

Clara Picher At the age of thirteen years and five months I measured 5 feet 4 inches. Around my waist (I measured) 34 inches. Around the bust 33 inches. Around the hips 36 inches. Around the leg 14 1/2 inches. The length of my foot is 9 1/2 inches. Size of my fist is 6 1/2 inches. The length of my arm is 28 1/2 inches. I have grey eyes. Around my thigh is 24 inches. Clara Picher, May 31, 1902, 10 years, 11 months, 2 days on her First Communion Day. Clara at eighteen took over the family store and the family and ran both all her life.

Cléo Paradis Ouellette was born in 1936 in Frenchville, Maine, of Franco-American parents. Her home language was French. She received her early education at Dewey school and at Wisdom High School. During these formative years, children were punished for speaking French in school. In high school, they were told by teachers from city areas that they would never amount to anything since they spoke neither French nor English. This made Cléo decide that she would learn to speak and teach French and English "just to show them." She majored in those subjects and received her bachelor's degree at St. Joseph's College in Windham, Maine. She later received her Master's Degree in Education from the University of Maine at Orono.

In 1960, Cléo married a local accountant, Jean Paul Ouellette. They had six children and raised a young orphaned cousin. Cléo taught French and English for over thirty-three years, twenty-nine at her alma mater, Wisdom High School, and two at the University of Maine at Fort Kent. During this time, she made two trips to France, one to accompany students and one to study at l'Université de Dijon for a summer.

Cléo has received several major awards: Meritorious Service—Maine Education Association; Wall of Fame for Work, Women, and Community; Franco-American Hall of Fame in Augusta; Acadian Achievement Award, among others. Her mémoires of childhood experiences, *Le Bord d'en Avant*, was published in Normand Beaupré's *Voix Francophones de Chez Nous* in 2009.

Although retired for the last nineteen years, she keeps very busy volunteering for school, school board for twelve years, civic, community, cultural—Maine Acadian Heritage Council and church activities—religion teacher and aide, lector, choir, etc. at Ste. Luce Catholic Church. In 2011, she founded a French preschool for three to five year-olds which is still thriving. She continues to live in Frenchville with her husband of fifty-five years.

Cori Modisette As the oldest child and only daughter of my Irish mother and French-English father, followed by four brothers, growing up in the '60s and '70s in New England might have been oppressive for a young, headstrong girl. However, my Air Force officer father recognized early on that I was an independent thinker, an agile and competitive challenger, and a voracious reader. I was the child he brought to the public library every week, encouraged to choose any fiction or non-fiction text that might be of interest. My parents enrolled me in a parochial school from 5th through 7th grades, moving me into a public high school when advised by the principal/parish priest that a broader education base might better serve me. Rather than feel intimidated by authority, my father taught me the fine art of respectful disagreement, and showed me the value of always getting the facts straight before questioning a decision. I'm sure that later on, as a teenager, my resistance to the house and school rules were a constant source of consternation. To his credit, his faith in me never faltered.

As an adult, I traveled all over the world with my father —with our huge family of brothers, sisters-in-law, my sons and daughter, my nieces and nephews, and most often, the two of us. We shared many interests, often separating for an afternoon to explore our individual preferences. Mine were art museums, parks, and all manner of boutiques —his included cathedrals, formal gardens and military history. We agreed on all varieties of musical and theatrical performing arts, fine and not-so-fine dining, the local zoos, casinos, breathtaking scenery, and chatting up anyone who would listen.

As a television meteorologist for thirty- plus years, it was awesome to have the weather dedicated to me on the 6:00 news every year on my birthday. I know the names of all the clouds, how to multiply or divide any recipe, the pleasure of being able to replicate a delicious restaurant dish, repair a flat tire, sink a hook shot, win a little in Blackjack, and how to let my own kids know how smart and important they are. To this day, my father's influence guides me through troubled waters. I'll never forget him.

I wrote this sonnet for his funeral, and I'm so proud of the meter, the rhythm, the rhyme, the imagery and the tribute to the greatest man I will ever know—my DAD.

Cynthia Doucette, a former Mrs. Maine International, 2008, Cindy has worked tirelessly since her daughter's death, including appearances on Fox News and she has written a book entitled, *It Can Happen to Any Family*. Cindy worked with Steve Marois at Reality Productions and hosted a show that aired in Maine. The show was called, "It Can Happen To Any Family." Cindy and her husband David have been married for thirty-seven years. They have three children: Travis, Candice and Chelsey. She is a self-employed cosmetologist for thirty-six years and assists her husband with their family excavating and logging business.

Darlene Rose is a singer and songwriter who plays 12-string guitar. When she was eighteen, she wrote and recorded a country song called "Don't Throw Stones" which helped her win the award for New Artist of the Year in the State of Maine in 1978. Darlene harmonizes with her mom, Florence Rose Martin, and accompanies her on guitar. Together they performed at the 2014 Acadian World Congress some of the original French Acadian songs Florence has collected and preserved since she was young. Darlene sang and played professionally for several years before starting a family and continues to sing and play at the church she attends.

Dawn Gagnon writes for the *Bangor Daily News*. She is originally from the St. John Valley in Northern Maine.

Denis Ledoux has been exploring Franco-America since he was an adolescent. Having done extensive genealogy, he learned he shares with many others a common ancestor: Jean Côté who arrived in Canada in 1634. Most recently he has been at work on a collection of two novellas and one short story which he calls "French Boys." "French Boys" will be available in the fall of 2016. Denis has also worked with memoir writers for decades. He leads The Memoir Network through which he coaches, edits and ghostwrites memoirs into existence. He lives in Lisbon Falls, Maine.

He shares on-line an excerpt from his book *We Were Not Spoiled / A Franco-American Memoir*, an account of Lucille Ledoux's first thirty years. Lucille Verreault Ledoux raised six children. Widowed before her youngest daughters were out of the house, she considered having finished raising them alone as a special accomplishment. Lucille passed away on May 5, 2015, surrounded by 10 members of her family. She is missed.

Denise (Rajotte) Larson is a freelance writer and editor with a special interest in the history of the American Northeast and Francadian (French-Canadian Acadian American) genealogy. She is the author of *Companions of Champlain: Founding Families of Québec, 1608-1635* published in 2008 and of numerous articles on history and genealogy published in *Le Forum*, *Echoes*, and on-line at *Genealogical Pointers* and other websites. She grew up in a Francadian family and parish in Connecticut, worked overseas for the Foreign Service and in the United States as a journalist, and has returned to her roots in Maine with her husband, a retired U.S. Marine.

Donna Hébert started as both a writer and a musician, wedging the door open with songs, poetry and lowly press releases. She's flung it open wide with her first novel, *The Blue Dress*, and *The Fiddler's Eye*, her first collection of poetry and song lyrics. Donna's essays and poetry have been published by the Franco-American Women's Institute, 'ezine, *moé pi toé* and *Strings Magazine*. Her fiddling blog is available on-line. Cited by Massachusetts Governor Deval Patrick for "outstanding artistic achievement," Donna is a Massachusetts Artist's Fellow in the Folk Arts. She has two original songs on Smithsonian anthologies and has tutored eight fiddle apprentices through the National Endowment's Master-Apprenticeship program in the Folk Arts. She also teaches fiddle and performance at Smith, Amherst and Mt. Holyoke Colleges. A singer and fiddler in Celtic group Mist Covered Mountains, Donna also directs yearly children's performances at Old Songs and Philadelphia Folk Festivals. She and Franco-American singer Josée Vachon are performing again in the northeast and Donna also tours with fiddler Jane Rothfield in Panache.

Doris Belisle-Bonneau of Auburn serves on the Board of Directors for the Franco American Collection at the University of Southern Maine's Lewiston-Auburn College, represents Franco American interests on the L/A Advisory Committee and co-chairs the Academic Affairs Committee. Since 2003, she has volunteered at d'Youville Pavilion in Lewiston with a focus on serving the French speaking residents. She co-created and developed the Maine French Heritage Language Program under the auspices of the Franco Center and the University of Maine at Augusta. The program provides an after-school culture and language program for students from kindergarten to grade 6. In addition, she served 2 terms as trustee to the Maine Community Colleges and is presently trustee to the Auburn Public Library.

Doris Provencher Faucher, 1934-1915, held a Master's degree in Education. Based on ten years of research, her series of historical novels depicts the French ethnic experience in North America, beginning with Bastien's and Marguerite's arrival and settlement in New France in the mid-17th century. She and her husband live in southern Maine. The oldest of their four children was born during their yearlong stay in France.
Her first novel, *Le Québécois: The Virgin Forest*, related the challenges they faced in establishing their family in the Canadian wilderness. It was followed by *The Rapids*, highlighting life among the first Canadian-born generation. *Imperial Conflict* extends the saga of Bastien and Marguerite's family through the historical evolution of Nouvelle France from 1715 through 1756. *Imperial Conquest,* is the fourth and final book of the Québécois series.

Elaine Larcade-Bourque is an Acadian brown/white cotton spinner and weaver. All of my crafts have developed out of my first love, gardening. In my garden, I grow brown/white cotton for spinning and weaving, gourds that I use to make baskets and Santa Claus ornaments, and Jobs Tear seeds and old roses, from which I make rosaries.

As a young child, I lived in Acadia Parish, near Bosco, often referred to as the "Marais Bouleur" area. My family moved to Lafayette Parish when I was a teenager. I have lived in the small community of Milton near the Vermilion River, since 1959 when I married Russell Bourque. When Milton High School became an elementary-middle school in 1966, I was hired as the secretary and worked at Milton school for 31 years. My three children came to school with me until they entered high school.

After my children were grown, I attempted to do some spinning and weaving on my own. In 1989, I was awarded an apprenticeship under Mrs. Gladys LeBlanc-Clark by the Louisiana Division of the Arts. For 1 year I was able to visit with Mrs. Clark and watch and learn from her. Many people say spinning is a skill and I agree, but when I would watch Mrs. Clark spin I would think, surely this is an art! After much practice it may become an art!
Mrs. Clark and I traveled together for approximately 10 years, demonstrating at Louisiana Folklife Festivals the art of Acadian spinning and weaving.

Although three of my great-grandmothers (all descendants of the Acadians who were thrown out of Nova Scotia) spun and wove both cotton and wool many years ago, the tradition of Acadian weaving had almost disappeared when I was growing up. As a child, I do not remember seeing anyone spin or weave. My father was a farmer and did grow the white cotton which I would help harvest in late summer, but I did not see any brown cotton growing in our area .

There are several spinners and weavers in our area today, but very few, if any, are growing the brown cotton, *coton jaune*, as the Acadians referred to it. The brown cotton is short staple and very time consuming to gin, but I enjoy working with brown cotton because it is such a pretty, natural color and gets prettier with age. Since we have no cotton gins in our area, I grow only enough brown cotton to gin by hand and demonstrate at festivals.

I try to have woven samples that are representative of the materials and patterns that were used by the Acadian spinners and weavers of the South Louisiana area. I know that when the Acadians were thrown out of Nova Scotia and came to Louisiana they brought their weaving skills with them. They never grew brown cotton in Nova Scotia but probably found it still growing in the Southwest Louisiana area by the Indians and slaves who were friendly towards the Acadians. The Acadians used the brown cotton to make their blankets and their clothing.

Today, Acadian textiles are looked upon by textile collectors as a "one of a kind" work of art and labor of love. Because we may lose this tradition that was so important and necessary to the Southwest Louisiana area, I hope to continue and preserve the tradition of Acadian brown and white cotton spinning and weaving as long as I can.

Elise Pooler Lambert, 1911-2000, decided in 1941 to become an Army nurse because she knew she would become seasick on the oceans if she enlisted as a Navy nurse. Lambert was trained in a three-year registered-nurse program at St. Elizabeth's Hospital in Boston. She graduated in 1932 at the height of the Depression. Lambert was overseas until 1944 when rotations began. She then was sent to New York, and from the Separation Center, she was sent to Camp Beale, CA. Stateside, she was a practicing registered nurse for thirty-nine years. Lambert made it her lifelong work to address the situation of recognition for the World War II women and their service to the war effort.

Elizabeth Bragdon Fuller lives in Aroostook County, Maine with her husband and six rescue cats. She knits daily and has not yet attempted to make her mother's doughnut recipe.

Ellen LaFlèche has published three chapbooks of poetry: *Workers' Rites* (Providence Athenaeum, 2011); *Ovarian* (Dallas Poets Community Press, 2011) and *Beatrice* (Tiger's Eye Press, 2015). She won the Ruth Stone Poetry Prize, the Philbrick Poetry Prize, the Joe Gouviea Outermost Poetry Prize, the New Millennium Poetry Prize (tied with Jim Glenn Thatcher) and honorable mention in the Robinson Jeffers Tor House Poetry Prize for her poem about her husband's death from ALS. She is assistant judge of the North Street Book Prize.

Emily Cote is studying Secondary Education at the University of Maine at Farmington. Her mother is a British citizen and her father is of Franco-American descent, giving her unique insights into different culture and family practices. Her Franco-American heritage remains close to her, as she grew up in the house in which generations of her French family lived in Waterville, Maine. She appreciates the little things she has learned about both sides of her family, the good and the bad.

Florence Rose Martin is a proud French Acadian who is helping to keep the traditions of her culture alive through preserving the traditional music she grew up with. Florence was born March 15, 1938 in Ste.-Agathe, Maine in the heart of the St. John Valley. The people of St.-Agathe are primarily of French Acadian descent. Florence was the eldest of eleven children born to O'Neil Elphege Martin and Albertine Marie Chasse. Florence was educated at the local convent school, Notre-Dame de la Sagesse (the Daughters of Wisdom order of nuns) in Ste.-Agathe. During her years in school she learned how to read and write English, but she could not speak the language, as French was the primary language in both home and school. Upon graduation, she was invited by her aunt to move to Lewiston, where she ran a Franco-American social club and where she continued to be involved in traditional Franco-American music, as well as "hillbilly" music. Florence recalls that even as a young child, she would write down the songs that were sung to her and that were common around her home. In 1990, she made a two-notebook set of these handwritten songs (over 130 songs), "I know over 600 songs," that she donated to the Ste.-Agathe Historical Society. French Canadian Music was featured at the Library of Congress in The American Folklife Center's annual concert series, "Homegrown 2004: The Music of America," May 18, 2004 with Florence Martin singing.

Frances A. Levasseur, 1930-2000, a native of Cyr Plantation, Maine, was the Living Heritage Historical Society's first president, and the person who provided the determination and passion for the construction of the Acadian Village, Van Buren, Maine. The sixteen buildings, which include several private homes, a school, a chapel, a store, a blacksmith shop, a barber shop and a railroad way station, resemble a thriving village of the St. John Valley in the 1800s. On December 13, 1977, the village was listed in the National Register of Historic Places and is recognized as a part of the historical and cultural heritage of the country. It was Levasseur's dream that the village not only be a historical site, but also a learning center for the education of the young people of the area.

Felicity Deschenes is a pen name from the author's family tree. All names have been changed to protect privacy.

Georgette B. Bérubé (1927 - 2005) from Lewiston served in both the Maine House and Senate from 1971 to 2000, Mme. Bérubé had more state legislative service than any other woman in Maine's history. In 1982, she was a candidate for Governor of Maine. For many years she hosted a French radio show in central Maine and served on the Finance Council of the Catholic Diocese of Maine. Mme. Bérubé was proud of her French heritage and her many contributions to her community and to her State made a difference in the lives of all of her constituents. We join her family and the citizens of this State in celebrating the life and accomplishments of this exceptional woman and we acknowledge the innumerable contributions that she made to the Franco-American community. She wrote *Thank You, Georgette* about her foray into politics.

Géraldine Pelletier Chassé, (1923-2015), was a charter member of the Acadian Cultural Committee and the Maine Acadian Heritage Council. In addition, she founded the Madawaska Historical Society and was instrumental in starting 6 other historical societies in the St. John Valley. She also created the Genealogy Research Center at the Madawaska Public Library and the Acadian Cultural Exchange of northern Maine. In 1970 Geraldine began publication of the Madawaska Historical Society Newsletter and has also published extensively on local Acadian history and folklore. She was a primary organizer of the Annual Acadian Festival, serves on the advisory board of the Acadian Archives and was a member of the St. John Valley Tourist Bureau. Geraldine was the first recipient of the Acadian Achievement Award and was selected as Madawaska's Citizen of the Month by the Greater Madawaska Chamber of Commerce.

Gertrude Metivier Côté, (1909-1977) was born in Canada. Mother of nine children, when she wrote her book *As I Live and Dream*, about her Canadian childhood and life in Rumford, Maine. She wrote all of her life starting as a letter writer at age twelve and a correspondent for several Maine newspapers. As she wrote the book, she also learned to type—so states the newspaper interview. After her book was published, she was invited to submit a copy for the Maine Author Collection of the Maine State Library. She conducted a week-long radio interview tour of Maine upon publication of her book. Her husband took a week of vacation to cover for her in her absence.

Gloria Goguen Sears has been creating art for most of her life. Her first publication was in the fifth grade when she won the Best Dental Drawing competition with "From the Dentist Office" and was published in the American Dental Association Magazine. Her current works are interpretations of nature and whimsy in colored pencil. Born to an Acadian father, Jean Bernard of New Brunswick and an Irish/English mother, Joan Amelia of Newfoundland. She is a first-generation Franco American living and creating in the Boston, Massachusetts area.

Gloria B. Limoges My parents, Louis and Yvette (Martineau) Brochu, were from Québec Province; they came to Lewiston, Maine with their respective families in search of work at a time when the family farms in Canada could no longer support them. Both my parents became naturalized citizens and eventually worked as superintendent and matron of the Lewiston City (Poor) Farm. Our home was part of a four-story brick building where someone requesting help from the city would be given shelter. I am one of four siblings. (Louise Gervais of Lewiston, Maine; Thomas Brochu from Boca Raton, FL; and Carmen Goecke from Coeur D'Alene, ID). I married another Franco-American, Dr. Robert D. Limoges, whose family settled in Fitchburg, MA. I have two children (Bradford Limoges from Colorado (with two children) and Suzanne Crellin from California (with two children).

Ida Bourgoin Roy, 1921-2007, famed folk singer of the St. John Valley, was born to Patrick Bourgoin and Alvine Marquis in Stockholm, Maine, on April 17, 1921. In 1929 the family moved to a farm on Flat Mountain in St. Agatha. There, Ida resided until she married on November 10, 1941 at the age of twenty, to Rosaire Roy, Sr. She and her new husband took residence in Little Black Lake where they bought a farm. There they raised their family.

Irene Bedard (born July 22, 1967) is a Native American actress, who has played many Native American characters in a variety of films, most notably Pocahontas in the 1995 film *Pocahontas*. She was born in Anchorage, Alaska to an Inupiat Esikmo mother and a father of French Canadian/Cree descent.

Jacquie Giasson Fuller grew up in Lewiston, Maine, a member of a large French family in which "franglais" was the language of choice. She loved the powerful rumblings of the Androscoggin River as it drove the machinery that kept her ancestors employed. She loved her father's bar, and is grateful for a messy childhood within the walls of her four-story tenement, and the walls of poverty which held her community together. She has written many short stories and articles based in her hometown of Lewiston, Maine. After thirty-five years of living away, shes delighted to have recently returned home.

Jan Hitchcock's family of origin refer to "and a little French" in their background, but informal genealogical research suggests this would have to have been a quite distant relation. Her poem and experience of French culture are based instead on twenty-four years teaching at the University of Southern Maine's Lewiston-Auburn College, especially the privilege she had during those early years of knowing Madeleine Giguère. Coincidentally, in 1997, the year she wrote the first version of "The Archiving" for Madeleine, Jan's experience of French culture expanded further, through her marriage into a first-generation Maine French-Canadian family.

Janet Shideler, Ph.D. is Professor of French at Siena College. She received her BA in French from Trinity College of the University of Toronto, her MA in French from McGill University, and her Ph.D. in French from the University of Massachusetts Amherst. Summer work while she was a student brought her in touch with Franco-Americans. That chance encounter, combined with her own experiences as an immigrant and the daughter of an immigrant, encouraged her to study Franco-American women in particular. Almost two decades have passed since she published *Camille Lessard-Bissonnette: The Quiet Evolution of French-Canadian Immigrants in New* England in 1998, but she remains committed to teaching about the community that changed her personal and professional life and about the author whose example of strength, courage and wisdom inspires her still.

Jeanne Douillard is an independent scholar specializing in the story of the French in New England. Her interest has led her to craft a most compelling story, which she now wants to share with the larger community. She has put together a talk accompanied by a PowerPoint presentation in which she tells the complex story of her people in the Americas. A native of Springfield, Massachusetts, she received a BA in Biology in 1972. Further studies led to a certificate in Medical Technology at the former Springfield Hospital in Springfield, Massachusetts, in 1974. Over the years, she has worked as a teacher, manager, financial analyst, potter, and business owner. In the 1970s she was a college instructor and Dean of Students. In her latest employment, she worked for the Franklin County Chamber of Commerce as director of the Visitor's Center in Greenfield, Massachusetts, until it closed in 2010. Since then she has spent her time in research and writing. She is currently involved in several writing projects for *The Republican* in Springfield, Massachusetts.

Jeri Theriault has three chapbooks—*In the Museum of Surrender* (Encircle Publications, 2013), *Catholic* (Pudding House, 2002) and *Corn Dance* (Nightshade Press, 1994); her poems have been published in journals (*Paterson Literary Review, Beloit Poetry Journal, Rattle, The Atlanta Review*) and anthologies (*Orpheus and Company, Contemporary Poems on Greek Mythology, French Connections: An Anthology of Poetry by Franco-Americans,* and *The Return of Kral Majales, Prague's International Literary Renaissance 1990-2010).* A Fulbright recipient (1998-99) and Pushcart Prize nominee (2006), Jeri holds an MFA from Vermont College of Fine Arts. She lives in Portland, Maine where she teaches in the English Department at Waynflete School.

Josée Vachon Born in Québec and raised in Maine, Josée has been sharing her Franco-American upbringing for over twenty-five years through traditional and contemporary folksongs from Québec and Acadia and through her own compositions.

Though she often entertained at family gatherings, she began singing publicly with the support of the Franco-American Center at the University of Maine, where she discovered others who shared her rich heritage. After receiving her BA in Romance Languages in 1984, she continued to perform, quickly gaining recognition as a new Franco-American voice through early performances at state festivals in Maine and at schools and parish soirées.

In 1999 she received the National Culture through the Arts Award from NYSAFLT, (New York State Association of Foreign Language Teachers), and was inducted into the French-Canadian Hall of Fame Class of 2007 for the American-French Genealogical Society.

Judith Rose Lacadie Hill I was born in 1954 and spent the first eighteen years of my life on French Island along with many cousins, aunts, and uncles. French Island is an island on the Penobscot River, nestled between the city of Old Town and the town of Milford, Maine, and has been the home to French-Canadians and their descendants since the 1850s. As kids, we tirelessly played games in the streets, meanwhile, relatives kept close eye. It didn't matter if we were playing hide and seek, tin-can alley, or "Red Rover, Red Rover," familiar faces observed from their porches, oftentimes well after dark. Relatives were like second parents who looked after us from their front roadside seats, and would scold us when they thought we were doing something dangerous. The small French community existing on the island was also a very social group; we were always visiting each other and family gatherings were frequent. Sundays were special, as everyone dressed up nicely and gathered for church. After graduating from Old Town High School I went on to graduate from Massachusetts College of Art (Bachelor of Fine Arts, Textiles) and the University of Maine (Master of Science in Human Development, Textiles).

My father, Harold Lacadie, grew up on French Island along with his aunts, uncles, grandparents and cousins, all of whom were descendants of French Canadians who migrated to Maine between 1870 and 1910 in search of jobs. After many lengthy trips to Canada, my father was able to trace his lineage back to the 1600s. He discovered he was a descendent of Marie de Beauregard, one of the King's Daughters. Before he died in 2013 he had official documents made for his daughters and granddaughters verifying we were all one of the King's Daughters. In 1992 a group of French Island natives, including my father, came together and wrote the book *Nos Histoires de l'Île*, a documentation of the first known settlement as well as the memories and experiences of the people who lived there.

The dam on the Penobscot River, just one-half mile south of French Island, was breached in 2012 as part of the River Restoration Project, allowing anadromous fish to migrate upriver to spawn. The water receded and the shores surrounding French Island became a physical documentation of the legal dumping of garbage into the Penobscot River in the early to mid-1900s. Broken dishes, bottles, pottery, rusted metal objects, and 100-year-old artifacts from the logging industry littered the shores. A collection of this glass is encased in one of my submitted pieces of work, a wire basket sculpture called *French Island*. *French Island* is a reflection of my life growing up in a French community and the domestic lives of the women who helped raise me.

Judy Dow is an Abenaki educator. She teaches science, history and math through art residency programs throughout the Northeast. Currently she has been working with Gedakina and their "We are all related" program sharing children's literature with students in an effort to introduce them to Native authors and their stories. Judy continues daily to teach and connect basketry and beading as a way to learn core curriculum. These skills often get over-looked, where the bigger picture is lost or not even seen in a world of departmentalization. Judy's work has been on exhibit throughout the US and Canada including displays at the National Museum of the American Indians in Washington DC, McCord Museum and Botanical Garden in Montreal, the University of Vermont and New Hampshire, and eight of her baskets made from recycled materials were part of a three year tour with Honor the Earth Impacted Nations, visiting New York City, Minneapolis, Santa Fe, Portland, Chicago and more.

Juliana L'Heureux is a native of Baltimore Maryland, Juliana L'Heureux is a registered nurse who worked in community health for 20 years, in Maine. Writing about Franco-Americans became an avocation when the Portland newspaper was seeking a columnist to replace their French-language writer, after she went to work at the American embassy, in Paris, France. Her reporting about Franco-Americans began with stories about her husband's family's traditions. Soon after beginning the column *Les Franco-Américains*, the scope of the topics she covered expanded to include nearly all French cultural, historic, religious, and linguistic subjects that contributed to the four-hundred-plus years of the Franco-American experience in Maine and New England. In addition to covering the news about Franco-Americans, her writings include essays and blogs. She and her husband Richard live in Topsham, Maine.

Kim Chase is a second-generation bilingual Franco-American Vermonter. She has published essay, short stories, poetry and articles and is currently working on a book, whose working title is "By Way of Canada," about French-Canadians and Franco-Americans in Vermont. She has taught French, English and English Language Learners for the past thirty years, on every level from preschool to adult learner. She currently teaches French at Hunt Middle School in Burlington, Vermont. **Claire Bouffard Chase** was her mother. Her "nom de fille" was Marie Eva Claire Bouffard.

Kristin M. Langellier, Ph.D., Southern Illinois University is a Midwest Franco-American who moved to Maine in 1980. She recently retired as Professor in the Department of Communication and Journalism at the University of Maine where she taught courses in communication studies and participates in Franco American Studies and Women's and Gender Studies. Her research interests focus on how we make experiences into stories as tellers and listeners, including Franco American family storytelling. She has numerous article-length publications and two books: *Storytelling in Daily Life: Performing Narrative* (2004), co-authored with Eric E. Peterson; and *Somalis in Maine: Crossing Cultural Currents,* co-authored with Kimberly Huisman, et al.

Lanette Landry Petrie 1942-2015, was born on September 10, 1942 to Franco-American parents, Eugene and Joan (Pelletier) Landry in Bradley, Maine. She is second born of ten children, was married September 2, 1962 to Richard Petrie and has two daughters and a grown granddaughter. She retired as a secretary from the University of Maine in 1999.

Laurie Meunier Graves is a fifth generation Franco-American who was born in Waterville, Maine. For seven years, she and her husband, Clif Graves, published a literary magazine called *Wolf Moon Journal*, where she wrote essays and reviews. She currently has a blog called *Notes from the Hinterland*, in which she writes about food, family, community, nature, and the environment.

Linda Cote Dube I started doing genealogy since 1976, and never stopped. I have amassed a huge collection of information from newspapers, books, town records, obituary cards, etc. I have collected names A-to-Z of the people prevalent in the St. John Valley and Canada.

Linda Griffith, M.S.W., D.C.S.W., is a ninth-generation descendant of Jean Etienne Benezet and Judith de la Meganelle, parents of the celebrated Philadelphian "Quaker Saint," Anthony Benezet (named for his Catholic ancestor, Saint Anthony Benezet the Bridge Builder, a child who miraculously initiated the construction of the Pont d'Avignon in 1177 by hoisting a block of stone weighing a ton into place on the bank of the River Rhone.) Sharing not only the Philadelphia birthplace of her outspoken Uncle Anthony (who championed animal rights, founded the first school for black children and the first college for women), Linda shares his determination to seek justice for the disadvantaged, having taken Bucks County, Pennsylvania, into federal court in 1987 over its cover-up of extensive abuse and neglect of nursing home residents in the county's care.

A Bachelor of Fine Arts graduate (Lake Erie College, 1972), she is the founder of the Wilma Theatre in Philadelphia and an award-winning fine photographer who was declared in 1999 by a jury of New York museum and gallery curators to be "One of the most talented emerging artists at the turn of the century and the millennium." Her work is represented online at her website where "The Secret Life of Light" collection of seventy-five images created during a lone spiritual journey to the Arctic Ocean can be found.

"I am soooo French. It explains both the trouble and achievements I've enjoyed in my life, a passion for creating from the heart, celebrating this earth and speaking out with love for the most vulnerable among us. The mantle of French heritage is a gift I cherish beyond all measure and by which I've navigated through more than one tight turn in my road."

Lisa Cote Day is an Exclusive Wedding and Family Portrait Photographer in Belgrade, Maine. Her passion for photography comes from understanding there is nothing more important than family and celebrating milestones in people's lives, as well as remembering our ancestors and the struggles they endured.

Lisa Desjardins Michaud I am originally from the beautiful St. John Valley, a small town in Northern Maine called Van Buren. I was born there and lived there until the age of thirty. Born to French-speaking parents, in a French-speaking community. I spoke mostly French until the age of five when I started school. We associated ourselves with being Acadian, when in fact we're a mixture of Québécois as well as Acadian. My family lines of Desjardins, Berube are from Québec and then I have the Acadian side of Soucy and Thibodeau. But, for some reason we were content in associating ourselves with Acadian side, that is who we were. I lived in this small close-knit community for thirty years, married, had a child, and later divorced. I began working at the University of Maine in Orono in January of 1996. There was an opening at the Franco-American Center, I applied and was hired in September of 1996 as the secretary. In 1998, I was promoted to Communications Coordinator/Managing Editor of *Le Forum.* I have been assembling the Centre's bilingual cultural quarterly journal since I began working at the Centre. My role in editing the *Le Forum* is about encouraging writers to share their work, their voice, their creativeness with others. My motivations in compiling the issues of *Le Forum* are all these gifted and talented contributors who allow their voices and experiences to be shared. *Le Forum* can be viewed on-line.

Lorraine Saint Pierre, formerly of Lewiston, Maine, received an MFA in creative writing from Sarah Lawrence College, Bronxville, NY. She has been Artist in Residence, University of Maine, Orono, ME,
Colonist, (twice,) at The Farm, An Art Colony For Women, Poughkeepsie, NY. Ms. Saint Pierre works as a seeress, spiritual counselor in private practice, professional name—LuhrenLoup.

A partial list of her work includes novels, *COMICS; 53; Alice in the World; Converting Hull 1042*; memoir, *Manhattan Seeress*; poetry, *Chapbook, The Arcanum;* and acting, theatrical one-act film, *Waste & Void*; *In The Cards*, documentary about her life and work; *The Spirit of John Lennon*: filmed ritual with artist Gianni Motti at Metro Pictures Art Gallery. You can visit her website where she posts weekly journal, essays, poetry, horoscopes.

Louise Tanguay-Ricker was born in Verdun, Québec. She has been living in the United States for over thirty-five years and considers herself first-generation Franco-American. She has many years of experience working in grants and development for major universities and teaching French to young children, using music and storytelling as her principal approach. She currently works at Bowdoin College, and is a frequent participant and performer in various Franco-American gatherings and salons. She comes from a family of musicians and artists and has a passion for singing traditional French songs. She currently lives in Readfield, Maine with her husband Greg, their two daughters Anne-Marie and Madeleine, their dog Frodo and cat Willow.

Lucia M. Cormier (11/20/1909 – 1/26/1993) was born in Rumford, Maine and graduated from College of Saint Elizabeth in New Jersey. A fluent French speaker, Cormier returned to Rumford and eventually headed the modern language department at her high school alma mater. In 1940 she completed her education with an M.A. from Columbia University. She never married and had no children. She became active in politics only in 1945 at the age of thirty-four by attending a local Democratic Party meeting. Within a year, she ran for and won a seat in the Maine House of Representatives. Cormier, a Democrat from Rumford, served in the Maine House of Representatives from 1947 to 1950 and 1953 to 1960. In 1960, Cormier left the Legislature and became the Democratic nominee for United States Senate. Her opponent was incumbent Republican Margaret Chase Smith. On September 5, 1960, Cormier and Smith appeared on the cover of *Time* magazine. The Cormier-Chase Smith election was the first all-woman election for Senate in United States history. Cormier lost in the general election after receiving only 38.4% of the vote. Democratic President John F. Kennedy appointed Cormier to the position of collector of customs for Maine and New Hampshire. She maintained that position until her retirement in 1974. Cormier died in Daytona Beach, Florida in January 1993.

Lucie Therrien Recording and video/DVD artist, composer/songwriter, author/poet, historian, teacher and film maker, and native of Newport, Vermont, was educated in French schools in the Province of Québec, and has toured over five continents.

Her appearances include foreign consulates, government agencies, Parliament conventions, conferences, TV-5 International, PBS-TV and Radio, the "Good Day Show!" in Boston, CBC-TV/Radio-Canada, other radio stations, universities, schools, festivals, nationally and internationally. She has published 15 recordings, four videos/DVDs, two research projects, a songbook and a book/CD Set. All are distributed or co-published by various companies across the USA and beyond.

Therrien holds a B.A. degree in Piano Performance and a M.A. in Music History. She has been the recipient of two New Hampshire Council of the Arts Fellowship Finalist Awards in 1991 & 1995, and four Traditional Arts Awards between 1999 and 2005. In 1993, she received both a nomination to the National Folk Heritage Fellowship of the National Endowment of the Arts, and the New Hampshire Governor's Arts Awards. In 1997, Therrien merited an award for her third video from the Council on the Arts, and was included in the publication *The International Who's Who in International Music*.

She has participated in cultural exchanges in Québec, France, Martinique, North Africa, Vietnam, and Cuba, meriting a 2004 appointment to the American and Canadian French Cultural Exchange Commission of the New Hampshire Government. Lucie is included on a CD compilation of Franco-American artists on the Folkways Records label and was a presenter for the Franco-American section of the Smithsonian Institution Washington D.C. festival, July 4th, 1999. Her life and media activity is archived at the State Library in Concord, New Hampshire. Being a nationally certified music teacher, she maintains a music studio called "Studio Do-Ré-Mi," in Portsmouth.

Sister Lucy Poulin is the founder and driving force behind H.O.M.E. (Homeworkers Organized for More Employment), a co-op in Orland, Maine. Born in Fairfield, Maine, Lucy joined a Carmelite order in 1957. One of her assignments while she belonged to the convent was to help local women find markets for their handiwork. H.O.M.E. evolved from this project and led to her leaving the convent to become the group's full-time director in the mid-70s.

Lynn Plourde is the author of twenty-nine children's books, including *Pigs in the Mud in the Middle of the Rud, Wild Child, The Dump Man's Treasures, Margaret Chase Smith: A Woman for President, Lost Trail: Nine Days Alone in the Wilderness* (Donn Fendler's story), *You're Wearing THAT to School?!* and *Merry Moosey Christmas*. She does numerous author visits to schools, teaching young authors how to become better writers. Lynn previously worked as a speech-language therapist in Maine public schools; that career also led to her first publications, ten educational books for teachers, including the *Classroom Listening and Speaking* series.

Lynn is proud of her one hundred percent Franco-American heritage, including the Plourde, Ambrose, Jacques, and Clukey sides of her family. She was born in Dexter, Maine, and grew up in Skowhegan, Maine, where her Mémère and Pépère Plourde lived across the street from her and where there were many multi-generation, rumpus-room gatherings filled with singing, stories, and food—lots of food! Lynn used to "elder-sit" her great-grandmother, Grammy Jacques, when her grandparents went out dancing. Grammy Jacques only spoke French, other than a few phrases, such as, "Open dee light." The Pépère in this story is based on Lynn's father, Leon Plourde Jr. He told countless stories of the family homestead in North Caribou, Maine, where he lived until he was five years-old when he moved to Skowhegan and learned to speak English when he went to school with the nuns as his teachers. Lynn's mother, Charlene Ambrose Plourde, grew up in a home where her parents only spoke French when they didn't want their children to know what they were talking about. So unfortunately, Lynn did not grow up in a French-speaking family.

Lynn currently lives in Winthrop, Maine, with her husband Paul Knowles, where she enjoys reading, walks, yoga, snowshoeing, and kayaking. You can learn more about Lynn and her books on her website.

Madeleine Dinora Giguère (1925-2004), the only child of Dr. Eustache and Dinora (Cailler) Giguère, was an internationally recognized sociologist, known locally and regionally as "la marraine" (the godmother) of Franco-Americans. Ms. Giguère had a long and distinguished academic career, specializing in ethnic and women's issues.

After her local education at Jordan School and Lewiston High School, she went on to obtain higher degrees at the Ursulines' College of New Rochelle, Fordham University, and Columbia University. Professor Giguère taught at St. Joseph's College and Boston College before accepting a position at the University of Southern Maine (previously known as Gorham State College) in 1967. She served there for more than two decades, establishing Franco-American Studies as a legitimate and important part of her curriculum.

The author and editor of numerous groundbreaking publications about Franco-Americans, she was an internationally recognized authority on the analysis of the U.S. Census since 1970. Professor Giguère was instrumental in having ethnic heritage questions included in these fundamental national surveys, and because of her meticulous examination of this data, the Franco-Americans' quiet presence in Maine and throughout New England was documented and made more visible.

She was a much sought-after lecturer on her demographic findings about this four-century-old branch of the French Republic. Upon her retirement in 1990, she was instrumental in establishing the Franco-American Heritage Collection at Lewiston-Auburn College. She served for seven years as volunteer director of this archive of local and regional history of immigrants from Québec and Acadia, and contributed her substantial private collection to its holdings. The Reading Room at the Franco-American Collection is named in her honor.

Marcella Bélanger Violette was born and raised in Van Buren, Maine. She married Elmer Violette and became the mother of five children (Dennis, Marc, Paul, Louise, and Tom). She highly valued education receiving her B.A. from The College of New Rochelle and an M.A. in French and English from Boston University. In 1953 she earned her Ph.D. from L'Université Saint Louis Maillet, Edmundston, New Brunswick. Marcella was the first St. John Valley woman to receive a doctoral degree. Her dissertation entitled "French Influence in the St. John Valley" would become part of her life's work to celebrate and promote her Franco-American and Acadian heritage. In addition to her advocacy of the culture and language of the St. John Valley, she was a teacher and lecturer on family life and the role of women in society.

Margaret Bernier is the author of "Labor study of the Franco-American community of Waterville, Maine from 1890 to 1940," Colby College, Waterville, Maine. (1981). *Senior Scholar Papers*. Paper 25. This paper is dedicated to Felexine Bolduc Bernier her daughter, Fernande, and her son Albert. In her introduction she writes, "The traditional view held about the Franco-Americans, who for the most part of the late nineteenth and early twentieth centuries were blue collar workers, is one of a docile hard-working group who "lacked" the desire to improve their careers and their financial and social status. The "blame" for their status of blue collar workers, for the absence of French men [and women] in the upper stratus of local industries and for their "reluctance" to assume Yankee roles in politics etc. has been placed on their supposed "inherent traits" such as their docile nature, their lack of interest in the education of their children, and their low self-esteem that forced them to accept the menial positions offered by the textile industry the railroads and other mills. This view is absolutely wrong."

Margaret Chase Smith was born in Skowhegan, Maine, on December 14, 1897. Margaret's maternal grandfather, born Lambert Morin in 1843 at St. Georges, Québec, Canada, came to Skowhegan as a child ... At some point, Lambert Morin changed his name to John L. Murray. For much of his life he recognized it was difficult to be a French-Canadian Catholic in Maine. Margaret's paternal grandfather George Chase married Caroline Morin (Murray) in Our Lady of Lourdes Catholic Church, October 25, 1896. Therefore, Margaret is of French-Canadian heritage from her mother's side.

Margaret's entry into politics came through the career of Clyde Smith, the man she married in 1930. Clyde was elected to the United States House of Representatives in 1936; Margaret served as his secretary. When Clyde died in 1940, Margaret succeeded her husband. After four terms in the House, she won election to the United States Senate in 1948. In so doing, she became the first woman elected to both houses of Congress.

Senator Smith came to national attention on June 1, 1950, when she became the first member of the Senate to denounce the tactics used by colleague Joseph McCarthy in his anticommunist crusade. Following her "Declaration of Conscience" speech, some pundits speculated that she might be the vice-presidential candidate on the 1952 Republican ticket. The opportunity, however, never materialized. In 1964, Senator Smith pursued her own political ambitions, running in several Republican presidential primaries. She took her candidacy all the way to the Republican National Convention in San Francisco, where she became the first woman to have her name placed in nomination for the presidency by either of the two major parties. In the final balloting, Smith refused to withdraw and so wound up coming in second to the Republican nominee, Senator Barry Goldwater.

After four terms in the Senate and thirty-two years in Congress, Senator Smith lost re-election in 1972. She retired to her home in Skowhegan and began planning for the establishment of a library. The Margaret Chase Smith Library opened in 1982 and for the next dozen years, she presided over the facility, meeting with admirers, former constituents, politicians, policymakers, researchers, and school children. Margaret Chase Smith died at her home on Memorial Day, May 29, 1995.

Margaret Sullivan Langford, Ph.D. Professor Emerita of French, Keene State College (Retired 2012)

When I married Robert F. (known as "Steve") Langford in 1970, I entered a new world filled with extended Franco-American family members, their friends, and friends of their friends. I already knew Steve and his cousin Bob Fournier, the New Hampshire Foreign Language Consultant. Gradually, I began to live in two worlds, which intersected at times, and not at others. In one I was an Irish-American professor of French. Raised in the Midwest and Far West, I'd come from California to teach in the East. In the other, I was Steve's wife and Bob's cousin now fascinated by everything Franco-American.

My new Franco-American world was full of surprises. When least expected, I would either find myself witnessing something I'd only read about or would learn something entirely new. When we were first married, ma tante Pearl invited us to her 80th birthday party. Steve presented me formally in French. Ma tante smiled approvingly as she and I conversed in French also. After the fact, Steve told me that Pearl, the family matriarch, had approved of our marriage. I felt transported back to the 1700s. Then, as we were celebrating our first Easter with Steve's relatives, I found myself taking part in a very ancient ritual that the poem *Eau de Pâques* describes. On another occasion, I heard my mother-in-law using an expression that I'd read in a 19th century novel. Madelaine didn't know Flaubert's *Madame Bovary*. Nevertheless, at a funeral, I heard her swearing very genteelly, just as Emma would have in such circumstances. "Sac-à-papier," said Madelaine. And last of all, I mustn't forget Ida's contribution. Ma tante had been a mill-worker, as had her mother before her. When I interviewed Ida, she explained a feature of mill life that books and experts had told me nothing about. When her mother, a spinner, fell ill, teenager Ida took over the job until she recovered. That was a blessing. The family could not afford to lose the paycheck.

Non-Contestant, *Ida,* and *L'Eau de Pâques* all bear witness to other "phenomena" I observed in my late husband's world. For my in-laws and friends, they weren't—and aren't—"phenomena" just a part of life. I'm continuing to express my appreciation of that life—through poetry.

Marguerite-Blanch Thibodeau Cyr (1738-1810), was a healer, midwife, and pioneer, was part of the migration from the French settlements of Acadia to Madawaska Territory on the south side of the St. John River Valley in the State of Maine. Marguerite was an Acadian heroine who saved her village in Northern Maine's Aroostook County, from starvation, in 1797, during a winter famine and brutal snow storm.

Marian desCognets was born and raised in Williamstown, Massachusetts. She received a Bachelor of Arts in History from North Adams State College in North Adams, Massachusetts. She then studied Canadian History and received her Master of Arts from the University of Maine in Orono. After completing the Teachers for Secondary Schools Program at the University of Southern Maine in Gorham, desCognets taught at New Mexico Military Institute until her retirement. She lives in Roswell, New Mexico.

Marie Louise St. Onge is the Executive Director of Kennebunk Land Trust. A published author, her work has appeared in numerous literary magazines across the country. She was the Executive Editor of *Ad Hoc Monadnock, A Literary Anthology*; and a contributor to *French Class*, *French Canadian American Writings on Identity, Culture, and Place*. She has served on non-profit boards, held corporate positions in the high tech field, and worked in the areas of women's health services and advocacy. Marie Louise enjoys "playing" in various art mediums, and currently makes her home on the coast of Maine.

Martha Pellerin Drury was born in Barre, Vermont of first-generation American of a French-Canadian family; she turned her heritage into a lifelong project. But with her passion and charisma, Martha made it all Vermonters' ancestry. She grew up in a house full of music. When she saw her cultural traditions slowly disappearing into mainstream American culture—even within the Franco-American community—she became an active proponent of collecting and performing the music of her childhood and connecting newer generations of Franco-Americans to their cultural heritage. She was most visible to the public as founder and member of Jeter le Pont (Bridging the Gap). With Dana Whittle and Claude Methé, Jeter championed traditional French–Canadian folk music, bringing Martha's heritage to Vermonters, many of whom shared the heritage and others who loved it. Martha was the program developer for ActFANE (Action for Franco-Americans in the Northeast) and the proprietor of Franglais Enterprises, which sought to promote understanding of Franco-American and French-Canadian culture through traditional arts.

Mary Ellms is an academic advisor and first-year seminar instructor at The University of Maine. She is of Québecois descent and has lived in Central Maine her entire life. She received an M.A. in Communication and a B.F.A. in Creative Writing from two Maine universities. Her recent writing has discussed presentations of surveillance and privacy on television and film, and she is interested in further researching representations of class, race, and gender in mass culture. She recently married her fiancé, a man of Sicilian descent.

Mary Rice-DeFosse, Ph.D., Yale University, Professor of French and Francophone Studies. She also teaches in the programs in Women and Gender Studies, African American Studies and American Cultural Studies. She did her doctoral work at Yale University and at the École Normale Supérieure in Paris. She specializes in French literature of the nineteenth century, revolution, and social change and has published on George Sand, Flora Tristan, Marie d'Agoult, Charles Nodier and Gustave Flaubert. She was a co-editor for the nineteenth-century for A Feminist *Encyclopedia of French Literature* and co-edited a special volume of *Women in French Studies, Écriture Courante*, with Cathy Yandell. She is a past President of Women in French, an international professional organization, allied to the Modern Language Association, which supports research on women writers of French expression and serves on the editorial board of Women in French Studies. She is currently researching the writing of the poet Louise Colet.

Professor Rice-DeFosse also specializes in the history, literature and culture of the local French-speakers and their descendants. She recently completed a documentary, *Les Soeurs Grises/The Grey Nuns: Elles sont venues, elles ont servi/They Came, They Served*, which features oral history interviews with local community members by Bates students and interns. This research on the interactions between the Sisters of Charity and the community they served was funded by the Harward Center of Bates College. The video documentary is a central part of a permanent exhibit of the same title at the Franco-American Heritage Center in Lewiston, a collaborative effort of Professor Rice-DeFosse, Annette Bourque of St. Mary's Health Systems, and Rita Dubé of the Center and made possible by a major grant from the Maine Humanities Council.

Maureen Perry Born and raised in Lewiston, Perry serves as a librarian for the University of Southern Maine. She also serves on the Board of Directors for The University of Southern Maine's Franco-American Collection. She loves sharing poetry at Open Mics, in print, or online.

Melissa MacCrae writes, knits, crochets and teaches at her home in Brewer, Maine.

Michele Choiniere is an award-winning Smithsonian Folkways recording artist, with a radiant, compelling voice. Her music and artistry capture a delicate sensibility, overlaying a raw authenticity. Her concerts transport audiences to another time of wistful cafe-cabaret culture, with riveting rhythmic melodies or a wistful lament, which stay with you long after the concert has ended.

Born into a musical Franco-American family in northern Vermont, Michele began performing traditional Franco-American music at an early age with her father Fabio, an accomplished harmonica player. In 1995, she began writing and composing her own songs and has performed for audiences throughout New England, Québec and France. Her lyrics and music focus on nature, romance and social issues connected to being Franco-American.

She has been featured on TV-5 International's "Visions d'Amérique," which was broadcast to Francophone nations worldwide, as well as on Vermont Public Television's "Rural Delivery" and "Profile." She has recorded an archival family collection of Franco-American music with her father and is featured on the Smithsonian Folkways CD *Mademoiselle Voulez-Vous Danser: Franco-American music from the New England Borderlands* released in 1999. In 2003, Michele self-released her debut solo album, Coeur Fragile, following up with her 2010 release of *La Violette* to critical acclaim. Among other accolades, Michele has appeared in concert at the American Folk Festival (Bangor, Maine), the Lowell Folk Festival (Massachusetts), the Great Lakes Folk Festival (East Lansing, Michigan) and the Tadoussac Folk Festival (Québec). She is a recognized "master artist," having been awarded the prestigious and competitive Governor's Heritage Award in 2007. She is a member of the Vermont Arts Council's American Masterpieces program, as well as a juried Arts Council performer and teaching Artist.

Michele's performances blend traditional Franco-American and Québec folk songs, original compositions, jazz standards, and an occasional French classic.

Nanci Breau was born and raised in Lewiston, Maine. After graduating from high school in 1968, she worked for 10 years at her mother's business, Madeleine's Beauty Salon in downtown Lewiston. In order to raise three children, she became a full-time mother. When her youngest entered school, she started working for Lewiston Public Schools as a Special Education Technician. Twenty-seven years later, she is now retiring and looking forward to more time to roller skate, write, kayak, care for her grandchildren, and become a Literacy Volunteer for new Mainers.

Nicole Ouellette, a Fort Kent native, now runs her two businesses in Bar Harbor: Breaking Even Communications (an internet marketing firm) and Anchorspace (a shared office/coworkingspace). A short dog enthusiast, she lives in Bar Harbor with her basset mix Brandy. She loves young adult novels, blogging, and avocados. She's also a proud Francophone.

Norman Beaupré was born in southern Maine and educated bilingually, French and English. He graduated with a B.A. from St. Francis College, Maine in 1967 and earned both a Master's Degree in 1968 and a Ph.D. in 1974 from Brown University. He joined the faculty of St. Francis College, now the University of New England, in 1969, and taught there for 30 years until he retired as Professor Emeritus in 2000. He taught French literature and world literature in translation, French Impressionism and developed a course on Transcultural Health Care.

He often traveled to Paris and took two sabbaticals there. He went to Brazil on a Fulbright grant, took a leave of absence to study Spanish and the traditional healing—*curanderism*—in Mexico in 1997 and traveled to several other places in the world such as Belgium, Croatia, Spain and Portugal. He's a published author having written nineteen books, so far. He writes both in French and in English. His latest novel, *The Fallen Divina—Maria Callas,* will be published soon. His one-woman play, a long dramatic monologue, was produced in Paris in early October 2008 at the Théâtre des Déchargeurs followed by two more performances one in Dijon and the other in Angers.

He has received several awards among which are being named to the Franco-American Hall of Fame by the Maine State Legislature in 2007 and awarded the medal of the Order of Arts and Literature from the French Ministry of Arts and Communications in June 2008. He shares online his work titled "Heritage of a Full Life, Full Heart: Evangéline Thibodeau Beaupré" and "Laura's Hair." His work appears on the anthology website.

Pamela Morneault Gemme was working on commercial jingles up until she began publishing poetry. Pamela lives in Boston, Massachusetts. Recent or forthcoming publications include *Protest Poems. Org., Contemporary American Voices, The Fib Review, J Journal, Eclipse Literary Journal.*

Patricia Smith Ranzoni Mixed-blood Yankee, traces her paternal Canadian-American line to Huguenot Willetts of the Gaspé. She started life among French neighbors on the Dodlin in Enfield whose Saturday orange cakes offered to a young passerby pushing a carriage her mother never forgot. She grew up in Bucksport where her woodsman father brought them after World War II for work at the paper mill with many Franco schoolmates and considers herself privileged to have had the esteemed Joel Morneault for band and chorus, from whom she learned the importance of saying "thank you." She and her husband started married life as UM students renting in Old Town from the Dupuis – Collinses who treated them like family. With the advent of the internet she tracked her genealogy through earliest Maine and Maritime Canada to identify French-rooted words and ways of her people, having become a grateful student and ally of Franco-American presences and an initiator of cross-cultural poetry exchanges. She is Poet Laureate of Bucksport, Maine

Paula Currie-Raymond has been working in education for thirty years. She currently holds a Master's degree in Special Education with a concentration in Behavior Modification from the University of Maine at Orono and earned a bachelor's degree in Business from Thomas College. She is also certified in Math and English. At this time, Ms. Raymond holds a position as an educator for the Mid-Maine Regional Adult Community Education (MMRACE) Department where she teaches a variety of subjects to Adult Education students and Credit Recovery students. Ms. Raymond is an active member of the South End Neighborhood Association, a group dedicated to the revitalization of an historical community in Waterville, Maine. Paula Currie-Raymond is a native of Waterville and was born and raised in the South End of town commonly known as "Down the Plains." She currently resides with her husband in Oakland, Maine.

Patricia M. Hager is an Instructor of Writing, Coordinator of the Writing Center, and founder of the Multicultural Center at University of Southern Maine's Lewiston-Auburn College. Her writing has been published in newspapers, magazines and academic journals. She is passionate about discovering the past and present nuances of Lewiston's rich cultural landscape.

Rachel Breckinridge I am a twenty-year old female who lives in the United States, New England. I attend Maine College of Art as an Illustration major. I have taken French classes at the Franco-American Centre, my local high school, and at the Language Exchange in Maine. My family has a French Canadian background, making French the second spoken language among our extended family.

Renee Violette is a Franco-American first-generation college graduate who was born and raised in a small paper mill town in Maine. As an emerging writer she uses her insight gained from over ten years of personal recovery work and her education to shed light on family dynamics and social experiences. Renee holds a Master of Arts Degree in Interdisciplinary Studies from the University of Maine. She currently resides anywhere she feels like.

Rhea Côté Robbins was brought up bilingually in a Franco-American neighborhood in Waterville known as the South End. She currently lives in South Brewer. Côté Robbins is the author of creative nonfiction, memoirs titled, *'down the Plains,'* and *Wednesday's Child*, winner of the Maine Writers and Publishers Alliance Chapbook Award. She is editor of *Canuck and Other Stories*, an anthology of translations of early 20th century Franco-American women writers who wrote about their immigration experience. She is the founder and director of the Franco-American Women's Institute, FAWI, which disseminates information about the contributions of the French heritage women's lives. FAWI is celebrating its 20th Anniversary in 2016. She is currently editing a book collection of one-hundred plus French heritage women's submitted works to celebrate FAWI's 20th Anniversary, titled, *Heliotrope—French Heritage Women Create!* This book project was crowdfunded by the Franco-American community and its many supporters. Côté Robbins' writing and research has appeared in many publications. She is currently working on research in expanding the definition of the French heritage women and their "hidden contributions."

Rina Boucher Soucy Born in Baker-Brook, New Brunswick, Canada, Rina Boucher Soucy began her education in a one-room parochial schoolhouse, went to college and pursued a career teaching secondary French and History in New Brunswick and Maine along the Canadian-American border in the Upper St. John Valley. The picturesque region and her terrestrial roots contributed to enrich her soul. Such influence touches her writings, giving the writing its peculiar voice. Her poetry celebrates the cycle of the seasons and the people living on both sides of the St John River, their activities and their feelings: people divided by a river frontier but united by roots so deeply interwoven.

Some of her poems appeared in *RAFALE*, a literary supplement to *Le Forum* and in *Revue Rivière*, a bilingual multidisciplinary Journal of Arts and Ideas published by the University of Maine at Fort Kent. In 2011, she published a first book of poetry *Sérénade saisonnière* chosen as one of the six finalists for Le prix France-Acadie.

Sadie E. Kendall, Kendall Farms, creator of Kendall Farms Crème Fraîche

It was 1978. I was at the doorstep of law school when I made my first pot of cheese. Song of my soul! So I followed my heart and studied dairy science instead of law.

Fresh out of California Polytechnic Institute, San Luis Obispo, in 1981 I established Kendall Cheese Company. Initially, crème fraîche was a secondary product, but, by 1987, it had taken control of my business and my life. (little wonder, my grandmother's name was "Cloutier" and her roots, Normandy).

Kendall Cheese Company became Kendall Farms, producer of one product only, Kendall Farms Crème Fraîche.

In the' 80s, it wasn't easy to find a cream producer willing to take the extra care and time required for our cream. After several false starts, a perfect match was made. We found a producer small enough to be willing to take the extra time. Then came the careful selection of starters, with a proper mix to bring out the beauty of that cream. Finally, it was right, perfect. We have been supplying the finest shops and chefs in California ever since.

Sally Bellerose My writing has always involved themes of lesbian identity, sexuality, illness, and class. Whether I'm writing about my parents, my own parenting, growing up in the '60s, nursing, love, friendship, whatever, the basic themes don't seem to change. The more I write the more interested I become in the messy, confusing, and complicated relationships of anger, humor, and transcendence.

My awards include a Fellowship from The National Endowment for the Arts, The Barbara Deming Prize, and The Rick DeMarinis Award. My work appears in *a call to nursing*, *Crab Orchard Review, The Sun, Naugatuck River Review, Cutthroat, Per Contra,* and dozens of other publications. My novel *The Girls Club* won the Bywater Prize and was published by Bywater Books in 2011.

Sharon Gordon Donnan, of Los Angeles, and **Suzanne Chaillot Breaux,** of Lafayette, "*Coton jaune* — Acadian Brown Cotton: A Love Story." Donnan is a filmmaker, educator and conservator of ancient and antique textiles. Breaux is a fiber artist, weaver and costume designer specializing in Mardi Gras and theatrical costumes.

Sherri Levesque Grant Was born in 1957, in Willimantic, Connecticut . and lives in Bangor, Maine. I am the mother of three and grandmother of six. My father was born in Richmond, Vermont (Albert Benoit Levesque). His father was born in Canada (1881) and entered into the US at St. Albans Vermont in 1912 with his family at the age of thirty-one. Both grandparents and great-grandparents were also born in Québec, QC.

I was not exposed to my French heritage as my grandparents had passed before I was born, my immediate family lived in Connecticut, and my father was estranged from his five siblings (except one brother). But I do have the inherent pride of the French. This is something I feel deep inside of me. It's not something I was taught as I remember my father did not speak of his family or heritage. The only time I heard him speak the French language was when he and his brother were together and it was only brief conversations in French, as were the visits with my uncle.

I have always enjoyed gardening, sewing, cooking, and doing crafts. Photography intrigued me for many years, but I never pursued the art until the age of digital photography. (This allowed me to make many mistakes which could be easily corrected!) My passion is macro photography of nature. This allows my subject to be viewed close up with all the details of the unique features of the subject. Many times I capture "other" facets that are in the picture that may not be noticeable with the naked eye, i.e. a spider web, a droplet of water, a mosquito on a frog, or hair on the legs of a fly. Part of the satisfaction of my photography is those types of things that show up unexpectedly in my photos. Plus, getting close to my subject can be challenging, which, when I get the perfect shot, e.g., is very satisfying!

Sherry Pineau Brown was born in Waterville, Maine, the daughter of an Ouellette and a Pineau. She spent childhood summers raking wild Maine blueberries and collegiate summers working shift-work at the defunct Otis Mill in Jay, Maine. Sherry attended the University of Maine at Orono for undergraduate studies, and the University of Denver for her graduate degree. She has taught at both Thomas College and Kennebec Valley Community College, and currently teaches English at Waterville Senior High School. She has been published in the *Maine Review* and is the recipient of an Honorable Mention for Short Fiction in the 2008 Maine Literary Awards. She currently lives on a farm in Benton, Maine with her husband and daughter.

Susan Rose April lives in Maryland, and has a MFA in Writing from Vermont College, a MS in the Physical Sciences from the University of Chicago, and a BS in Environmental Science from the University of Massachusetts at Lowell. After over 25 years as a consulting scientist for federal agencies such as the Department of Energy and the EPA, she now focuses on creative writing. She is inspired by her early days growing up in a French Canadian-American family in Lowell and Dracut, Massachusetts. With Acadian heritage on her father's side, she has been tracing the exile and return pathways of her Acadian family lines who were deported to Massachusetts and Maryland. Her poetry has been published in a number of journals and was featured in *French Class: French Canadian-American Writings on Identity, Culture, and Place* (Loom Press, 1999). Her nature essays have appeared in *Bird Watching Digest*. She is working on a novel, "Pal," about a girl lost in the Canadian wilderness who is saved by a dog.

Susan Gagnon is a fourth-generation Franco-American, she is a descendant of hard working papermakers and textile workers who immigrated from Québec, Prince Edward Island and New Brunswick, Canada to the petit village of Chisholm, Maine at the south end of Jay, Maine seeking work in the developing Otis Paper Mill. She created the film, *Down by The River's Edge* in collaboration with Mt. Blue Community Access TV in Farmington, Maine. Gagnon, a member of the Franco-American Women's Institute, worked as a Medical Receptionist for twenty years supporting her four children as a single mother; was Assistant Project Director of Foothills Art's Continental Harmony in 1999; and past Contributing Writer for Harris Publications. She was employed as Community Health Advocate at the Healthy Community Coalition, raising $8,000 for a new playground in Chisholm; Coordinator for the Community Health Visioning Conference in 2002; and awarded The Grange Community Citizen Award by North Jay Grange for her work as a Community Health Advocate in 2003. She is past member of

Jay Historical Society and prior owner of Cobweb Corner Collectibles. Gagnon was an active member of the University of Maine at Farmington's Diversity Committee and a panelist on "Immigrant Refugees to Maine," and for Seniors Plus on "Celebrating Franco-American Traditions," in 2001. In 2005 she presented her original essay, "Into Light and Voice" at the Nordica Celebration of Women in the Arts at Nordica Auditorium. Gagnon enjoys scrapbooking, flea markets and spending time with her four children and nine grandchildren. Gagnon lives in the western mountains of Maine.

Susan T. Landry was cofounder and managing editor of the print literary magazine *Lifeboat: A Journal of Memoir,* in the early 2000s, and founder and editor of the online literary journal, *Run to the Roundhouse, Nellie*, 2012 -2015. She has had short-form memoir and poetry published in several journals, including *mgversion2>datura*, *Brevity*, *Word Riot*, *Pindeldyboz, Maine Coast Review*, *Mr. Beller's Neighborhood,* and *Little Star.* She grew up in Massachusetts, spent twenty-five years in NYC, and now lives in Maine.

Susan Poulin Selected by *Portland Monthly Magazine* as one of the "Ten Most Intriguing People in Maine," writer/performer Susan Poulin has been creating and touring her original theatrical productions since 1992. She was a featured performer in *The Mirth of Venus* and *The Mirth Canal* at the Institute of Contemporary Art in Boston, The Maine Festival, the Minneapolis Fringe Theater Festival and Portland, Maine's Cassandra Project. Her work has been supported by the New Hampshire State Council on the Arts, the Maine Arts Commission and the Maine Humanities Council. Susan is also a popular keynote speaker and has brought her humor and insight to presentations for a wide variety of organizations. As her alter-ego, Ida, Susan writes the popular Maine humor blog and podcast, *Just Ask Ida,* and is the author of *Finding Your Inner Moose: Ida LeClair's Guide to Living the Good Life* published by Islandport Press. Her second book *The Sweet Life: Ida LeClair's Guide to Love and Marriage*, was published in May, 2016. Her newest project is "The View From He'ah," a talk show hosted by Ida and produced by PPMtv. Please visit Susan's website online.

Susann Pelletier, a Lewiston, Maine native, began writing poems when she was eleven years old. Her work gives voice to her deep connections to family and place in Franco-America, as well as her vision of social justice and dignity at home and beyond our borders. Her articles and poems have been published here and abroad in anthologies, literary journals, chapbooks, and political and environmental magazines. Susann has worked as a journalist, editorial consultant, market gardener, college instructor, and co-editor of a progressive monthly. She finds great pleasure sharing with young people her love of poetry and offering creative writing workshops. A pacifist, Susann is committed to non-violent social change and has been an activist since her teens in the late 1960's. Susann is a board member and volunteer for Maine People's Alliance, and currently serves on the Androscoggin Valley Housing and Worker Justice Committee, Campaign Vote! Media Team, and the Racial Justice Strategy Committee. This year, Maine People's Alliance has taken a lead role among Maine organizations in bringing racial justice issues to the forefront of all of its work, and offering trainings to other groups. A long-time advocate of local and sustainable organic food systems, Susann and her family participate in a Maine-products food cooperative, community-supported agriculture (CSA), and also grow and preserve their own organic vegetables, fruit and herbs.

Sylvie Charron, a native of France, holds an M.A. from the Sorbonne and a Ph.D. from the University of Wisconsin. She was Professor of French at the University of Maine at Farmington for 25 years and chaired the International Studies Program for several years. She is a strong proponent of study abroad and of nurturing bilateral exchanges with universities abroad. She connected her students with their local French roots, and exposed them to Franco-American, Québecois and Acadian cultures and literatures. She strongly believes in the value of early second language acquisition, served on numerous K-16 commissions for the State of Maine and led numerous workshops for practicing language teachers.

She has a long standing interest in literary voices calling for social change and expressing the human condition at the margins of society. In recent years, she focused on regional and immigrant francophone literature. She translated several books into English. After years of study of George Sand, a nineteenth century socialist and feminist, she translated *The Marquise and Pauline* by George Sand. Another book, *Grapes of Despair* by Tahar Ben Jelloun focuses on North African immigrants in France and *Canuck* by Camille Lessard-Bissonnette depicts the life of Franco Americans in the factories of Lewiston at the turn of the 20th century. In a recent article for the Canadian literary magazine *Liaisons* (2014), she celebrates the rich local patois in works by Grégoire Chabot and Normand Beaupré.

As a service to the community, she translated historical road panels on routes 201, 16 and 27 in Maine and numerous *Museum in the Streets* panels in Maine and France. She also organized three ethnic music festivals at Head of Falls in Waterville, Maine, to celebrate local cultures.

Trudy Chambers Price was born in Island Falls and grew up in Caribou, Maine, where she picked many potatoes. She graduated from Caribou High School and the University of Maine at Orono. She has been an elementary school teacher, dairy farmer, Book Service Director at Maine Writers & Publishers Alliance, bookstore manager, worked at Islandport Press in sales and marketing. In retirement, she enjoys reading, writing, quilting, rug hooking, jigsaw puzzles and living in rural Freedom. She and her husband have two sons and three grandchildren. She is the author of *The Cows Are Out! Two Decades on a Maine Dairy Farm.*

Acknowledgement of previously published submissions:

Bellerose, Sally. "Beau Pere." *Rock and Sling*. Rock and Sling Press. Eds. Susan Cowger and Kris Chritensen. Volume 3 Issue 2. Fall 2006. Print. Used by permission of the author.

Bellerose, Sally. "Bikini." *A Gallery of Readers*, edited by Carol Edelstein and Robert Barber, Gallery of Readers Press, Northampton MA, 2009. Print. Used by permission of the author.

Bellerose, Sally."Bikini." *Wisdom of Our Mothers*, edited by Eric Bowen, Familia Books, Bellingham, WA. 2010. Print. Used by permission of the author.

LeBlanc, Caroline. "The Hands of War." *Levure littéraire*. Ed. Sherri Dratfield. France, Numéro 10. http://levurelitteraire.com/caroline-leblanc/, 2014. Used by permission of the author.

LeBlanc, Caroline. "Salve Regina." *Santa Fe Literary Review*. Ed. Sudasi Clement. Sante Fe Community College, Sante Fe, NM, 2013. Print. Used by permission of the author.

Paige, Abby. "Foundation Myth." *Saranac Review*. SUNY College at Plattsburgh, Plattsburgh, NY. Issue 6, 2010. Print. Used by permission of the author.

Paige, Abby. "Hope Chest." *The WRUV Reader: A Vermont Writers' Anthology*. Ed. Chris Evans. University of Vermont Student Media. 2012. Print. Used by permission of the author.

Paige, Abby. "The Undefended Border" (I). *Rhino Poetry Forum*. 2011. Print. (Winner, 2011 Founders' Prize) Used by permission of the author.

Paige, Abby. "The Undefended Border" (II). *Room Magazine*. Issue 36.4, 2013. Print. Used by permission of the author.

www.ingramcontent.com/pod-product-compliance
Lightning Source LLC
Chambersburg PA
CBHW041125100726
47911CB00002B/41
* 9 7 8 0 9 6 6 8 5 3 6 5 0 *